HIDDEN
IN PLAIN
SIGHT

Tim Smith

TrineDay

Hidden in Plain Sight: How the House Select Committee on Assassinations Played Games with the Evidence in the Execution of President John F. Kennedy
Copyright © 2023 Timothy Smith

Published by:
Trine Day LLC
PO Box 577
Walterville, OR 97489
1-800-556-2012
www.TrineDay.com
TrineDay@icloud.com

Library of Congress Control Number: 2023940568

Smith, Timothy.
–1st ed.
p. cm.

Epub (ISBN-13) 978-1-63424-435-0
Trade Paperback (ISBN-13) 978-1-63424-434-3
1. Assassination. 2. Kennedy, John F. 1917-1963 Assassination. 3. Report of the President's Commission on the Assassination of President John F. Kennedy (United States. Warren Commission). 4. Presidents Assassination United States . 5. True crime literature. I. Smith, Timothy. II. Title

First Edition
10 9 8 7 6 5 4 3 2 1

Printed in the USA
Distribution to the Trade by:
Independent Publishers Group (IPG)
814 North Franklin Street
Chicago, Illinois 60610
312.337.0747
www.ipgbook.com

Dedicated to Gary Kling and Mike Mellinger, who passed away a few years ago, but whose friendship will live on forever. They made reading and learning fun and were as well-read as any two people I have ever met. They are missed every day, but their memories drive me forward on days when I don't feel like going that direction.

And to Mortimer Adler and Charles Van Doren, whose influence over me in the great western canon of books, taught me how to read both carefully and for better understanding. Their skills and tools I learned from them, are still in use every time I pick up a book, no matter if I am reading Dante, Shakespeare, Woodsworth, The Old Testament, or a document from the National Archives. They taught me how to be a better reader. Period. Their book, *How To Read A Book*, is a must read for everyone. They also have passed on, but not away.

Contents

PREFACE

*H*idden In Plain Sight is a work that is almost twenty-five years in the making. It grew out of a previous attempt, which ended up at almost 125 pages in length. I soon realized it was way too short of what I hoped would be a thorough analysis of my stated goal. That goal was to construct a guide of the fifty-two witnesses that testified publicly before the House Select Committee on Assassinations. So, in 2021 I decided to resurrect that project from the dusty ruins of my computer and see if I could breathe both life and exegetical analysis into the data.

The project, I soon discovered, was highly technical, examining a myriad of analysis techniques: neutron activation, photographic, ballistics, acoustical, film, physics, ear and eye witness testimony, forensic pathology, x-ray, foreign travels, Secret Service, FBI, and CIA scrutiny.

This meant I had to do a lot of research and contact the best in each field that I was grappling with. It also meant I had to be up-to-date with the research and be somewhat conversant with the Warren Commission, The Rockefeller Commission, The Clark Panel, The House Select Committee on Assassinations (HSCA), The JFK Records Act, The Assassination Records and Review Board ARRB), and the release of a myriad of documents as a result, especially the ARRB. I leaned and stood on the shoulders of many that have gone before me, some now gone and some still with us,

I also knew that if I only analyzed the testimonies of the fifty-two witnesses that appeared before the HSCA, I would have a document that stopped in December of 1978. That was not exactly going to be a show-stopper. I needed to analyze what they said and compare it with what was said before they gave testimony, but then I also needed to bring the evidence up to date. In other words, I needed to know what was said afterwards and what has been discovered later on down the road by independent inquiry. I tried to bring the evidence into the year 2022. Any oversights or mishaps along the way, I take full responsibility. You realize fairly quickly that the evidence in the JFK case can be overwhelming, to say the least.

I have no doubt that some will think I was too hard on some and not hard enough on others. I can only say, please read what I write slowly and carefully and attempt to see the nuance of what I am trying to convey. I do believe the *evidence* indicates a conspiracy to kill President Kennedy and I hope I demonstrate that in this book. You will see that a lot of the so-called evidence of the lone gunman theory falls flat on its face, like Goliath of old. One thing I discovered in the process, when you and I listen very carefully to what Warren Commission sycophants are saying, is that most of the time I heard sophistry, demagoguery, *ipse dixit* argumentation (it is so, because I say so), or vague generalizations, like "you just can't accept that someone insignificant can murder someone who is significant." To be honest, that line of reasoning is something I have never entertained. I try to look at the evidence and be as honest as I can about the data.

I have chosen to document everything in the text, via internal documentation. This will save the reader from turning back and forth throughout the book. I purposely do not have an index at the end of the book, because I think the best way to read the book is chronologically and see how it builds, but also to see the structure of the witnesses and how that plays a part in the mindset of the HSCA. Professor Blakey told me in 1998 that he attempted to construct a series of witnesses that would lend itself to a scientific approach to the evidence. You will have to decide if what he did was successful.

I invite you to read and hopefully learn more about the case that will satisfy your hunger for truth. The world changed as a result of November 22, 1963 and I think the execution of John F. Kennedy contributed largely to that alteration.

Enjoy!

JOHN BOWDEN CONNALLY

SEPTEMBER 6, 1978

On September 6, 1978, Governor John B. Connally, along with his wife Nellie, gave testimony before the House Select Committee on Assassinations (subsequently simply referred to as the HSCA) in Washington D.C.

G overnor John Connally was the first of 52 witnesses to appear before the House Select Committee on Assassinations, along with his wife Nellie. When I interviewed Professor G. Robert Blakey, in the late 90's in his office on the campus of the University of Notre Dame, he told me the 52 witnesses they called to testify were the way in which the HSCA presented their findings and evidence to the American Public. I will now use this as a guide to not only present the evidence of the HSCA, but to update that evidence to the present day. A lot has happened since 1978: The Assassinations Record Review Board has released c. two and a half million pages of documents, since the JFK Records Act following the Oliver Stone movie, *JFK;*, and I will also share important discoveries by independent researchers as well.

Connally was the governor of Texas in 1963. He was one of 9 people who appeared before the Warren Commission (John Connally, Nellie Connally, Dr. Humes, Marina Oswald, Thomas Kelley, James Rowley, James Malley, Earl Ruby, and Jack Revill) who would also appear before the House Select Committee on Assassinations. For the most part, Governor Connally repeated his testimony he had given before the Warren Commission fourteen years earlier. There is a treasure trove of information, however, to glean from the testimony of Governor Connally and his wife. Some are obvious, while others are not.

Warren Commission disciple David Belin once argued that the murder of J.D. Tippit was the Rosetta Stone of the JFK assassination, when in fact, Governor Connally of Texas is quite possibly where we should focus our eyes when watching the Zapruder film. We need to recalibrate our vision, and not just on the moving Z-film, but study as much as we can within each individual frame, measuring and looking for anomalies to see if there is anything we can view that previously went unnoticed. We all need to be better noticers.

If you want the evidence to be on your side, you will have to first look and dig through as many original sources as you can find. I will quote extensively from the original testimonies of all 52 witnesses, documenting internally within the text, as they testified before the House Select Committee on Assassinations (HSCA). I will refer to Warren Commission testimony when necessary as well. We need fresh eyes when we look at the evidence and must do so without falling prey to the lullaby effect. We think we know the evidence so well that we stop asking questions, therefore not discovering anything fresh or new. That kind of a presuppositional position that ceases to ask questions, however, does not do the case any good. We also need to read things that push back against what we believe, to see if our views can withstand scrutiny, otherwise, we are just agreeing with ourselves, which is not honest research. At the end of the day, you still have to observe as many original sources as you can. You need to watch all of the films, look at all of the photographs, interview witnesses, which has become increasingly more difficult since mortality visits everyone eventually. Ask as many questions as you can and especially be aware of any updating of the evidence, as there have been some substantial discoveries in the past twenty years, especially since the revelations through the Assassination

Records and Review Board, as well as individual researchers. You can find all kinds of information defending just about any theory imaginable, but you have to enlist Rene Descartes at some point and engage in a method of doubt. Sometimes critical researchers think they need to defend everything, which is a mistake. There are some things you will have to concede, but not to worry, there is still an embarrassment of riches to choose from to prove there was a conspiracy to kill John Kennedy. In the end, Vincent Salandria was right, however, it is a False Mystery. It was painfully obvious early on that a conspiracy had taken place. But we still need to put everything to as much rigor as possible and see what path it takes us down and what is left standing. Keep in mind, and it may be obvious, but *the assassination only happened one way*. That one way is what we are trying to ascertain, lo, these many years later.

Our eyes are always on President Kennedy when watching the Zapruder film and for good reason: he was the President of the United States. If we look, however, c. 25 inches in front of JFK and observe Governor Connally, we will begin to notice certain things. The problem: if you ignore the Texas governor, you will miss things that unfold during the Z-film and will be unable to connect dots that are vitally important to explain the evidence accurately. We simply don't tend to see Connally in the Z-film, because we are always looking at President Kennedy. This chapter will endeavor to disclose why we should take a closer look at Connally.

Governor Connally is the focal point of a massive controversy in this case and has been since the day it happened. The Warren Commission, in April of 1964, prepared the Single Bullet Hypothesis, that stated CE-399 hit the two men somewhere close to Z-189 (House Select Committee on Assassinations) and Z-210 (Warren Commission), and after this the last shot made a distinctively red explosion in Z-313. What's more, and this is usually not a path many go down, because for everything to fall into place, this entire scenario is completely predicated on Oswald and his capacity to accomplish the shooting task.

From the onset there were three different shooting sequence scenarios: The *Warren Commission* designated two possibilities, as it was not dogmatic about the initial sequence of shots, saying the first shot hit both JFK and Governor Connally from the rear. The second shot missed everything and the third shot hit JFK in the head at Zapruder frame 313 from

5

the rear. They also entertained the possibility that the first shot missed, the second shot struck JFK and Governor Connally from the rear and the third shot hit JFK in the head at frame 313, also from the rear.

The FBI said the sequence was as follows: the first shot hit JFK from the rear, the second shot hit Governor Connally from the rear, and the third shot hit JFK in the head at frame 313, again from the rear.

The CIA had their own shot sequence as well, saying the first shot hit JFK in the throat from the front, the second shot hit Governor Connally from the rear, and the third shot hit JFK from the front, striking him in the head at frame 313.

All of this is moot if Oswald cannot do the required shooting. A few researchers have noticed things about Oswald that would limit his ability to perform what the Warren Commission said he in fact did that day. I will mention four that have been observed by researchers over the years, which bears repeating here. Oswald's abilities break down in the area of four categories, though we could list more: **Firstly**, if he had been the lone assassin, his *mechanical ineptness and lack of aptitude*, which got him fired from Jaggers-Chiles-Stovall, not to mention his inability to drive a car at age 24, seem to contradict his ability to execute his mission that day. Oswald is certainly not the ideal person to be shooting at a moving target, going downhill and traveling from right to left, given his perfunctory mechanical skills.

Secondly, you then add his *visual observation difficulties*, which according to CE-3134, in a study done by the Mayo Clinic, in Rochester, Minnesota for the Warren Commission, indicated Oswald could not perceive the full field of a word, which led to what they called language blindness. He would look at the word independence and see inpendanc, abanded for abandoned, or opion instead of opinion. If he couldn't see the full field of a word a few inches away, how could he possibly see the full field of a target some 265 feet away, as the car is descending down Elm street? The gun shot high and to the right from 15 yards away when fired (and this is after the FBI had placed it in a vice grip), which would be another problem, since the limousine was moving from right to left (the opposite of what the vice grip results indicated) at the time of the head shot at Z-313.

Thirdly, he had not fired a gun for 1,661 days, or 4 years, 6 months and 16 days, from May 6, 1959 (while in the Marines where he scored a 191at the qualifying range, with an M-1 rifle, a much superior weapon to the Mannlicher-Carcano. Had he scored a 189 he would have been sent home as unfit for combat or duty, being said to have "maggie's drawers") to November 22, 1963, which, as Dean Andrews stated in his Warren Commission testimony, highly mitigated against Oswald performing the feat, because it takes *continuing practice* (11 H 330) to maintain a skill level high enough to do what the assassin(s) did that day. Listen to the exchange between Wesley Liebeler, of the Warren Commission and Dean Andrews:

> **Mr. Liebeler:** "Do you remember telling the FBI that you wouldn't be able to recognize him again if you saw him?"
>
> **Mr. Andrews:** "Probably did. Been a long time. There's three people I am going to find: One of them is the real guy that killed the President; the Mexican; and Clay Bertrand."
>
> **Mr. Liebeler:** "Do you mean to suggest by that statement that you have considerable doubt in your mind that Oswald killed the President?"
>
> **Mr. Andrews:** "I know good and well he did not. With that weapon, he couldn't have been capable of making three controlled shots in that short time."
>
> **Mr. Liebeler:** "You are basing your opinion on reports that you have received over news media as to how many shots were fired in what period of time; is that correct?"
>
> **Mr. Andrews:** "I am basing my opinion on five years as an ordnanceman in the Navy. You can lean into those things, and with throwing the bolts – if I couldn't do it myself, 8 hours a day, doing this for a living, constantly on the range, I know this civilian couldn't do it. He might have been a sharp marksman at one time, but if you don't lean into that rifle and don't squeeze and control consistently, your brain can tell you how to do it, but you don't have the capability."
>
> **Mr. Liebeler:** "You have used a pronoun in this last series of statements, the pronoun "it." You are making certain assumptions as to what actually happened, or you have a certain notion in your mind as to what happened based on material you read in the newspaper?"
>
> **Mr. Andrews:** "It doesn't make any difference. What you have to do is lean into a weapon, and, to fire three shots controlled with accuracy, this boy couldn't do it. Forget the President."

7

Mr. Liebeler: "You base that judgment on the fact that, in your own experience, it is difficult to do that sort of thing?"

Mr. Andrews: "You have to stay with it. You just don't pick up a rifle or a pistol or whatever weapon you are using and stay proficient with it. You have to know what you are doing. You have to be a conniver. This boy could have connived the deal, but I think he is a patsy. Somebody else pulled the trigger."

Mr. Liebeler: "However, as we have indicated, it is your opinion. You don't have any evidence other than what you have already told us about your surmise and opinions about the rifle on which to base that statement; is that correct? If you do, I want to know what it is."

Mr. Andrews: "If I did, I would give it to you. It's just taking the 5 years and thinking about it a bit. I have fired as much as 40,000 rounds of ammo a day for 7 days a week. You get pretty good with it as long as you keep firing. Then I have gone back after 2 weeks. I used to be able to take a shotgun, go on a skeet, and pop 100 out of 100. After 2 weeks, I could only pop 60 of them. I would have to start shooting again, same way with the rifle and machineguns. Every other person I knew, same thing happened to them. You just have to stay at it." (11 H 330)

Andrew's testimony is both telling and obdurate against the Oswald scenario stated by the Warren Commission. Speaking from Andrew's experience, there was little doubt that Oswald, or anyone else for that matter that didn't practice consistently, would not have been able to perform the feat on November 22, 1963.

Oswald scored a 212 in December of 1956 with no wind, where he rehearsed a great deal prior to qualifying, and with an M-1 rifle, using a fixed target. Strangely, this ought to have assigned him the level of a sharpshooter, the second most elevated of the three classes, yet on his card that day he was given an mm rating, which is that of a marksman, the least of the three classifications (Rankings: marksman, sharpshooter and the highest being expert). So, which one is the mistake, the score or the ranking? An odd error. Keep in mind, to say Oswald scored the second most elevated score when there are just three classifications, additionally implies he scored the second lowest.

The score of 191 was considerably lower than his initial score of 212, meaning his score and accuracy got progressively worse over a three-year period.

To support Andrews testimony, Lt. Col. Folsom stated in his Warren Commission testimony, responding to the statement by Mr. John Ely, that Oswald *"was not a particularly outstanding shot,"* which Col. Folsom reacted to by saying, *"No, no, he was not."* (8 H 311) Not long before this short conversation we have a considerably telling exchange between Ely and Colonel Folsom:

> **Mr. Ely:** "Is it possible, Colonel, to tell anything from this scorebook, assuming for the moment that it was accurately maintained, concerning the marksmanship of Lee Harvey Oswald?"
>
> **Colonel Folsom:** "Well, yes. But very generally. For instance, at 200 yards slow fire on Tuesday, at 200 yards slow fire, offhand position–"
>
> **Mr. Ely:** *"You are referring, are you not, to the page designated 22 in Oswald's scorebook?"*
>
> **Colonel Folsom:** *"Right--well, 22 as opposed to 23. He got out in the three ring, which is not good. They should be able to keep them-- all 10 shots within the four ring."*
>
> **Mr. Ely:** "And even if his weapon needed a great deal of adjustment in terms of elevation or windage, he still would have a closer group than that if he were a good shot?"
>
> **Colonel Folsom:** *"Yes. As a matter of fact, at 200 yards, people should get a score of between 48 and 50 in the offhand position."*
>
> **Mr. Ely:** "And what was his score?"
>
> **Colonel Folsom:** *"Well, total shown on page 22 would be he got a score of 34 out of a possible 50 on Tuesday, as shown on page 22 of his record book. On Wednesday, he got a score of 38, improved four points. Do you want to compute these?"*
>
> **Mr. Ely:** *I don't see any point in doing this page by page."* (8 H 311)

Of course not, and Col. Folsom would only answer one more question before he was dismissed:

> **Mr. Ely:** In other words, he had a good day the day he fired for qualification?
>
> **Colonel Folsom:** I would say so.

To continue would implicate Oswald's incompetence even further, and a greater amount would have made Oswald look even more inferior, hence the redirection to change the subject. Oswald got 34 and 38 out of 50, when Folsom said he should have gotten between 48 to 50, not to mention how many he got outside the four-ring. Please do not lose focus that this is with vastly superior conditions and a much better rifle. This assertion by Folsom is critical, in light of the fact that the Warren Commission needs to portray Oswald as a world expert rifleman, or at the very least a darn good shot.

Furthermore, **fourthly**, the rifle he supposedly used on the day of the assassination was complete junk. FBI fingerprint expert Sebastian Latona went over that rifle with high intensity magnification and couldn't find a smudge anywhere on the rifle, because as he said, in an exchange with Hale Boggs about weapons fingerprints:

> **Representative Boggs:** *"May I ask another question in this connection. A weapon of this type, in your examination do you find a lot of other prints on it as well? You do not?"*
>
> **Mr. Latona:** *"No. First of all the weapon itself is a cheap one as you can see. It is one that----"*
>
> **Representative Boggs:** *"Is what?"*
>
> **Mr. Latona:** *"A cheap old weapon. The wood is to the point where it won't take a good print to begin with hardly. The metal isn't of the best, and not readily susceptible to a latent print."* (4 H 29)

It is a *"cheap old weapon."* So, Oswald, who lacks normal mechanical aptitude, has perceptual challenges, had not discharged a firearm in four and a half years, was utilizing a cheap old weapon, was a fairly poor shot, not to mention how he would have sighted the gun in after assembling it at his arrival at the TSBD, (the Warren Commission accepted that he got the weapon to the TSBD in two pieces, wood and metal), would not have been the person of choice to be a sniper on that day.

As we begin our journey through the 3.07 acres of land called Dealey Plaza, looking for clues to figure out what happened on that day, remember the famous quote attributed to Sherlock Holmes, *"when you have eliminated the impossible, whatever is left, however improbable, has to be the truth."* We need to go back to the beginning and apply Occam's Razor, i.e., the easiest explanation is most often the correct one. Things are sometimes complicated, to be sure, but more often than not, if we just apply common sense, we can save ourselves a lot of unnecessary sweat and toil. The amount of time wasted on minutia has hurt the case tremendously, as Vincent Salandria has argued, not to mention our own self-destruction from time-to-time, as we have often met the enemy and they are us. It is as Salandria said early on as a critic of the official version, it is *A False Mystery*. Often when we go back to the beginning, we find our earlier perceptions are the most accurate. The researchers have been their own worst nightmares. Having said that, there is still a hefty amount of evidence that needs to be addressed.

So, let us start. We can argue as to the veracity of the FBI's timing that it would require 2.3 seconds to work the bolt on the Carcano, which having had one and also having worked the bolt on several occasions, I confirm that seems to be an accurate take on the timing necessary to work the bolt. All of this is likely irrelevant, since I take the position that Oswald probably never ordered or fired the rifle in evidence, CE-139 (the Carcano rifle). So ultimately, the point is moot.

The speed of the film running through Zapruder's camera seems pretty solid as well, running at a constant speed of 18.3 fps. The HSCA Report may help with the speed of the film going through the Bell and Howell camera:

> "the 18.3 frame per second rate of the Zapruder film was an average of the 18.0 to 18.5 frame per second rate determined in 1964 by the FBI under laboratory conditions in which the camera was set and run in the manner that Zapruder said he had operated it at the time of the assassination. Given the 18.0 to 18.5 frames per second average running speed of the film, a differential of four frames is a differential of less than a quarter of a second. For this reason, an absolute correlation between events in the recording and the observable reactions on the film was not expected. If there were no observable correlation between the tape and film, however, substantial questions concerning the authenticity of the tape could be raised." (HSCA Report 84).

There are implications in Connally's testimony that help us figure out where the governor was positioned in relationship to President Kennedy (which is vitally important to help us understand the location, timing and sequence of shots fired), what he would have heard and when his wounds (*five*) would have occurred, the head shot(*s*) to JFK and what that means in relationship to Connally's wounds (again, vitally important). Also, what you see on the Zapruder film (often called the Z-film throughout this book) when looking at Governor Connally and what that has to say about the shot sequence and their angles, the mystery of his Stetson hat, and what his doctors thought about his wounds, and finally what all of this says about the infamous single bullet theory is a lot to unpack, but it all needs to be addressed with precision. Connally's testimony helps us do just that and figure out the all-important questions and hopefully some of their answers.

When Governor and Mrs. Connally testified before the Warren Commission and their interrogator Arlen Specter, whose background was *military intelligence,* gets past the material concerning why Kennedy came to Texas and other sundry issues, such as fund raising and the motorcade course, the Connally's rapidly find themselves on Elm street and the conversation gets more serious.

So, let's delve into the material, which can be confusing, as we try to sort it all out. Allow us to start by examining where Governor Connally was situated in the vehicle and his relationship to JFK. There has been a lot of examination throughout the years concerning the relationship of Governor Connally to President Kennedy in the limousine during the shooting sequence of the two occupants. Connally was sitting c. 25 inches in front of President Kennedy in a jump seat, not a full seat. What bullet(s) hit whom and when? Were they ever struck by the same bullet or were they separate bullets? Do their reactions in the limousine help us with any of this?

Connally's own testimony, before the Warren Commission and the HSCA, in addition to different perceptions, is important. He professed to have heard the sound of the rifle and realized it was a rifle shot. He had served in World War II and was an experienced hunter, so it isn't surprising he would have offered this remark. He professed to have heard the sound and afterward the bullet that hit him. The speed of sound travels at 1,125 feet each second or 375 yards, so it would have been unimaginable, hence impossible, for Connally to have heard the sound of the rifle before feeling the shot hitting him. The bullet would have hit him before the echoes of the sound waves resounded in his ears, since the projectile was traveling c. 2,200 feet each second. Put another way, basic arithmetic would have the bullet traveling at c. 114 feet for each frame of the Zapruder film, or every eighteenth of a second. In other words, one snap of your finger and each shooting sequence is over. The governor is wrong about his perceptions, but it is an inaccuracy I think we all can live with. He was the governor of Texas, not a professor of physics.

A number of researchers have noticed JFK reacting as early as Z-206/207, as his head abruptly shifts to the right in Z-207. JFK then disappears behind the Stemmons freeway sign and his elbows go upward as he reappears in Z-223, which is less than one second (17 Z-frames) later. It would be difficult to blink in that amount of time.

Ten-year-old Rosemary Willis, seen wearing a white-hooded coat and a red skirt, also seems to be reacting at Z-206. She comes to a stop c. Z-206/207 and by Z-216 is looking toward the Grassy Knoll, though she is reacting much earlier c. Z-190. This would demand that the gun was fired before the reaction time of Rosemary Willis in Z-190, as the bullet traveled faster than the sound would reach Rosemary's ears. These are approximations, obviously.

Connally, affirming before the HSCA, said he was turning to his right to see President Kennedy, however, he was unable to see him (I HSCA 53). That implies Kennedy was sitting far enough to Connally's left (looking from the rear of the limousine) that turning to the right to see him was to no avail. Since the bullet was traveling 12 degrees from right to left, it is not difficult to see the silliness of the single bullet hypothesis, even at this point. Kennedy was too far to Connally's left, again looking from the rear of the limo, for a shot to strike Kennedy in his back and exit his throat and then enter and go into John Connally. The hole in Kennedy's neck was 3mm and straight out, which the right to left 12-degree angle would appear to discredit and not be in a straight line from that angle, *if fired from the Texas School Book Depository*. Also, this is without referencing that the bullet, as per the House Select Committee on Assassinations forensics/medical panel said, that when it left Kennedy's throat was rising at 11 degrees, which would have been too high to have struck John Connally, had he been sitting in its path, which he wasn't. See this for exactly what it is. If the back wound is ascending at 11 degrees, (which the HSCA Forensic Pathology panel all consented to, notwithstanding eight of the nine pathologists trusted in the Single Bullet Hypothesis.) I have this on record on a VHS recording where this was agreed upon by Dr. Cyril Wecht and Dr. Michael Baden, who was the head of the Forensics Pathology Panel for the HSCA, when

13

they were at COPA in 1995 in Washington, D.C. Then the bullet would need to arrive somewhere below the level plain of entrance to be rising once it struck JFK. That dispenses with both the Texas School Book Depository and Lee Harvey Oswald, or any other individual doing the shooting from behind and above, most notably from the sixth floor SE window in the Texas School book Depository.

It is also intriguing that Connally did not remember getting hit on his wrist or in his leg, which may suggest he had already been struck in his back and chest and had gone into shock. If CE-399 (the so-called magic bullet) did as we have been told, Connally would be somewhat contorted, possibly going into shock, not to mention unadulterated agony as he is seen appearing on the west side of the Stemmons Freeway sign, looking from the south side of Elm street. However, he appears, at that point, and for another 3/4 of a second (c. 13-14 Zapruder frames), to be unharmed.

When Kennedy is next seen, his elbows fan outward and his clenched hands are going upwards towards his throat, yet he never grabs it, obviously, as his fists are closed and tightened.

Somewhere between Z-225-227 (or a little earlier), as is evident from the bullet holes in Kennedy's suit coat and dress shirt, he was shot in the back. It is offensive to express that the wound was at the base of the neck, despite Gerald Ford confessing to moving the wound for clarity in 1997. Clarity for whom? If the wound is below the neck, it is in his back, or above his back would place the wound in his neck. This is basic anatomy. Members of the HSCA forensic pathology panel concluded that the back wound traveled upwards at an angle of c. eleven degrees, which lines up perfectly with JFK's throat wound, likewise ascending at c. 11 degrees as it left his throat.

Kennedy was in a seat elevated and higher than the jump seat that the Texas Governor was sitting in at the time the bullets began to arrive inside the limousine (*the back seat could not be raised up or let down when the bubble top was off*). In fact, here is what Governor Connally said about that topic before the Warren Commission:

> **Mr. Specter:** What was the relative height of the jump seats, Governor, with respect to the seat of the President and Mrs. Kennedy immediately to your rear?
>
> **Governor Connally:** They were somewhat lower. The back seat of that particular Lincoln limousine, which is a specially designed

and built automobile, as you know, for the President of the United States, has an adjustable back seat. It can be lowered or raised. I would say *the back seat was approximately 6 inches higher than the jump seats on which Mrs. Connally and I sat.* (4 H 131)

A shot going upwards in JFK would not hit Governor Connally. The throat wound is the exit wound to the back entrance wound. It was 3 mm in size and circular. Take a look at the lower part of the throat wound intently in Fox-1, the post-mortem autopsy photograph, and you can see what seems, by all accounts, to be a semi-circle (if you look at the upper part of the throat wound you will also see a semi-circle), which I would contend is the shot leaving JFK's throat from the back injury, both of which are rising at c. 11 degrees. It is an ideal in-shoot, out-shoot trajectory.

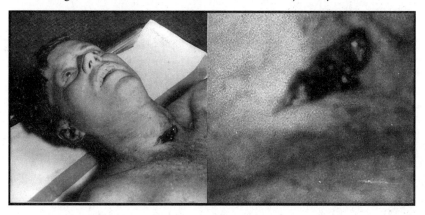

Fox -1

If a bullet strikes Kennedy in the back and exits upward and straight, as the 3 mm wound suggests, it either hits the chrome on the top of the front window of the limousine or sails over that window and goes halfway down the city of Dallas. *It is possible that the upward direction may have occurred because of the bullet slightly catching one of the cervical vertebrae,* as stated in one of the Death Certificates (there are actually 3 death certificates for JFK), by Admiral Burkley. It doesn't make any difference where the shooter is set, a shot that entered JFK's back, rose and left a small, circular (not oblique) hole, did not strike Governor Connally. Connally is attempting to find JFK in the back seat, after the President had been hit. Connally's physicians said his response would have been without delay, given the obliteration to Connally's right 5th

15

rib. Subsequently, the magic bullet is a façade, as countless pieces of evidence are in this case. There are simply an excessive number of pieces of evidence that are phony or suspect. Sorting it all out is not easy. One of the things we have to do when it comes to the evidence in this case is knowing when to discard data and when not to discard. Once you eliminate the magic bullet, it changes everything, as the elimination of other pieces of evidence will do the same; as we will see as we progress through the data. I'm not arguing that the Zapruder film has been forged or that Billy Lovelady is really Oswald on the front step of the TSBD. Having said that, there are pieces of evidence that do need to end up in an evidence dumpster: NAA evidence prior to Eric Randich, Z-312 seemingly showing forward movement, and an acoustics update thanks to Don Thomas, etc.

Though Kennedy seems to be hit by the time we see him in Z-225, Connally does not appear to have been struck at this point. Connally is beginning to turn to his right in an attempt to see the President but is unable to view him. And then very quickly, as he was endeavoring to look over his shoulder and to his left, he said he was hit in the back with what felt like being punched by a fist.

But if the Warren Commission is right about Kennedy being hit at Z-210, then according to the 2.3 seconds required to work the bolt on the Carcano, Connally would not have been hit until 43 frames later (2.3 seconds) at Z-255, which is way too late, as Connally is reacting by Z-237/238, hence the need for the single-bullet theory explanation. If JFK was hit at Z-210, then Connally would have been hit no later than Z-211, longer than it would have taken for the governor to react to having c. 10 cm of his right 5th rib annihilated, as suggested by his doctors, especially by Dr. Shaw.

The single-bullet theory says that a bullet struck JFK in his back and then went from Kennedy's throat into Connally's back, and then traversed into the top part of Connally's wrist, because according to the Warren Commission, Connally had the top of his wrist lying against his chest.

Z-230 establishes that Connally's wrist (before he responds to being hit a little less than half a second later) is gripping his Stetson hat higher than the position of the exit damage from his chest, (to prove this look at Z-230, and then compare it with a picture of Connally's suit jacket in Robert Groden's, *The Killing of the President* and the two do not line up at all), which he would not have been able to do if he had been shot through the wrist. Keep in mind, John Connally did not realize he had even been shot in the wrist until two days after he awoke in Parkland Hospital. Take a look at frame Z-230 and see what you think.

Why is no one reacting, especially the Secret Service inside the presidential limousine? Unlike Roy Kellerman, who is motionless, only Secret Service agent Clint Hill moves when he hears gunfire. The driver of the limousine, William Greer, turns around twice to observe the president during the shooting. Why twice? He had to know JFK and/or Governor Connally was hit and that he should exit Dealey Plaza, as soon as possible. William Greer was a late comer as a Secret Service driver. Secret Service agent Thomas Shipman, JFK's regular SS driver, died suddenly at age 51 of a heart attack at Camp David. He is the only person, ever to die at camp David. Had it not been for this unexpected death, Greer would not have been the driver on November 22, 1963. Vince Palamara once asked Greer's son in a telephone exchange as to what his dad thought of JFK. His response was: "well, we were Methodist and JFK was a Catholic."

Kellerman turns to his left before the fatal headshot in Z-313 and then turns back around, making no attempt to do anything at all. He is completely ineffectual. Why doesn't Greer step on the gas and take off the moment he hears gunfire? Against Secret Service protocol? I highly doubt he would have been written up for stepping on the gas and possibly saving the president's life. We know Kellerman radioed that they had been hit, but it seems too little, too late.

It appears that Connally was struck c. Z-237-238, as evidenced by his right shoulder and his right side slumping. His Stetson hat is no longer visible. It seems that his cheeks are puffy, his hair is now disheveled, and he is frowning or contorting to some extent.

Warren Commission disciples have purported that Connally was so aligned in comparison to Kennedy that a projectile fired from the 6th floor window, could journey from right to left at a twelve degree angle, enter the base of JFK's *neck*, navigate the body, exit in the front of the throat, and then proceed on a twelve-degree left to right direction and do all of the destruction to Governor Connally. The idiocy of this has become offensive, despite what Warren Commission sycophants say or how they say it. Sketches and diagrams are worthless in light of

17

watching the Zapruder film. It is amazing how many people think they are convincing just by their sound, cadence, or volume of their voices. I teach logic and you would flunk bringing that silliness into my classroom. *Ipse dixit* arguments may work raising your children, but not examining evidence in a homicide. In other words, when you do the work, you don't have to do the dance.

Why not shoot Kennedy as the limousine was coming down Houston street, as many have suggested? It appears to border on the ludicrous that Oswald would say to himself, *"You know, I think I'll pass on the straight on shot as he is coming down Houston street directly at me, lest I be accused of taking the easy shot. I would rather wait until the vehicle makes a 121-degree left-hand turn, where it will at that point begin to move away from me, continue downhill, moving right to left, vanish behind an oak tree momentarily and afterward when it initially appears, and dare I say immediately, I will fire a shot within an eighteenth of a second of its reappearance, just to show the world how incredible I am."* Beyond ridiculous.

Connally was hurt worse than we may have thought. He was shot in his upper back near his right arm pit, as the bullet went through Connally's chest, moving along his right 5th rib, destroying ten centimeters, where it then exited underneath his right nipple, moving downward.

As Connally acknowledged, he and JFK were hit by independent shots, thus shooters plural, hence a conspiracy. It is a story he rehashed frequently and stayed with all through his life. He never wavered.

Nellie Connally attempted to reach for her husband in an attempt to help or shelter him. Connally then utters, "They're going to kill us all" in what some have thought was an utterance suggesting a conspiracy in the midst of the shooting itself. Connally heard a shot and seemed to be aware he and JFK had been hit by separate bullets. It is pushing the limits of credulity to take those words literally. It seems to me it is simply a general statement meaning the forces behind this have now descended upon us. Period.

At that point, time seemed to freeze, where nothing occurs from c. Z-237 until Z-313, 76 frames, or 4.2 seconds. It is becoming increasingly clear in the limousine that something is horribly wrong.

Nellie seemed to know before Jackie, as she looks befuddled for some time. The driver William Greer didn't know how to get to the hospital, but he eventually caught up with Jesse Curry and followed him there.

In Z-313, the President is hit in the right temporal region of his skull from a point tangentially. The acoustics evidence seems to indicate it was about 12 feet west of the corner of the stockade fence, from the grassy knoll. At this point, JFK does moves back 2.18 inches and if you remove Z-312 as a shot from the rear (more on this in chapter seven), the only other option is a shot from the right front, using the logic of Occam's razor and Sherlock Holmes.

Connally appeared before the HSCA and seemed to have the same remembrance that he had fourteen years earlier when he testified before the Warren Commission. He was articulate and clear about what happened that day. He was as reliable before the HSCA as he was before the Warren Commission. Governor Connally talks precisely to this speed of sound contention mentioned earlier, though admittedly this is small in the bigger picture of things:

> **Mr. Sawyer**: "I suppose, too, that--I have just been thinking since I heard your testimony and I am sure you have thought about it, many, many more times, and without either being a medical expert or a ballistic expert, I presume it is reasonable to assume that with a Mannlicher/Carcano traveling at least twice the speed of sound, the projectile must be 2,200 feet per second, or more, I assume, that the bullet would reach you before the sound would reach you, and with that kind of an impact on your nervous system, whether conscious or not, you probably wouldn't have registered the sound, if there was one, of the bullet that hit you?"

> **Mr. Connally**: "I think that is precisely what happened, Congressman, no question about it. That is why I don't think there is any way the first bullet hit me. I heard that sound. And I had not been hit, I heard the first rifle shot, and I did not hear, was not conscious of the shot that hit me, and obviously the bullet reached me before the sound did. So the shock of the hit that I took, I was just totally unconscious of the sound, yet by the third shot, when Mrs. Connally pulled me down in her lap, I was awake, my eyes were open, I heard the shot fired, I heard it hit, and I saw the results, very clearly and you know--you have a lot of expert testimony, and I am delighted with the work of this committee, because hopefully we can clear up some of the speculation and the questions that have been asked over the years, but let me assure you that we may be wrong in what we say, we may be wrong in our impression, we may be wrong when asked pre-

cise questions about time, whether it is 2 seconds or 10 seconds under those circumstances I can't say with certainty the precise second that things happen, but the things that we do remember, and the things that we are testifying to here today, Congressman, are as indelibly etched in our minds as anything could ever be, and I will merely ask you to give yourselves the test, ask any adult person, over the age of 30, in this country, or over the age of 35 we will say, where they were when they first heard the news of the assassination. They can tell you where they were, what they were doing, and who they were with. I have not asked one human being in the world, not anywhere in the world, that hasn't been able to tell me where they were, what they were doing, and who they were with at the time they first heard the news.

The only point I am making is that there are certain impacts on human consciousness, on the human mind, that are indelibly etched there, and these things are engraved in our minds, beyond any doubt.

I can't, I am not going to argue with a ballistic expert or acoustics expert about the precise time or the frame of the Zapruder films, I can't tell you precisely whether it is frame 231 or 234, when the first evidence shows that I am reacting to the shot, but what we are saying to you, the things that we say to you with certain definiteness, it is because we are absolutely sure, at least in our own minds, that that is what happened and that is what we remember." (I HSCA 55-56)

The fragments found in Kennedy's skull seem to support non-jacketed ammunition. Dr. David Mantik has often stated that jacketed rounds are highly unlikely to leave fragments when entering a human skull. Z-313 was lethal, but there was another head shot to JFK c. Z 326—328, that drove JFK's head forward 4.8 inches and exited out the right side of his head, and then struck the Governor in the wrist and thigh and drove him forward (more clarification on this later) onto the floor of the limousine.

Watch JFK's head intently when viewing the Zapruder film. After he is hit at Z-313, his body goes motionless as he is driven against the back seat, but then, in less than one second (c. 7/10's of a second), his head goes forward, further and quicker than in any other place in the Zapruder film, as he is hit again. John Connally transitions from glancing upward c. Z-312, but then 7/10's of a second later, he is face down in front of the jump seats on the floor. He didn't realize he had even been shot in the wrist, an injury that severed the radius bone and then deposited a fragment in his left femur. Five wounds. Three to JFK (one to his back and two to the head from two different directions) and two to Connally (one to his back and then the second from the bullet that first struck JFK in the back of his head c. Z-327/328 and then proceeded to strike Governor Connally in his wrist and left femur). Most people heard three shots. This is most likely due to shot three and four coming right on top of each other, only 7/10's of a second apart, and could have easily sounded like one shot, especially in the confusion and because the people there were not listening for gunshots or to view an execution, but to watch a presidential motorcade.

The first shot: JFK's first bullet wound went into his back and exited his throat. It may have hit the chrome of the windshield or exited above the windshield and went beyond the triple underpass. It is possible that it hit the front of the underpass and a fragment then grazed Tague. We simply do not know.

The second shot: Connally was shot in the back and that bullet exited his chest. Because of the damage to his right fifth rib, it likely explains the fragments in front of his jump seat, which weren't discovered until they were found in the White House garage later that evening. There are different possibilities; however, this appears as feasible as any to me.

The third shot: Kennedy was struck at Z-313 in the right temporal region of his skull and that bullet exited through the rear of his head. This bullet was fatal to the president. Given the accuracy of shots, these seem to have been professionals using rifles that day, mechanics who knew precisely how to operate the equipment and they did not miss. I reiterate, there were no misses that day.

The fourth shot: JFK was struck a third time, the second head wound, c. Z-326 – 328, which broke up as it left Kennedy, or when it wounded Connally, possibly explaining the fragments that hit the windshield of the limousine. No shots went through the windshield, though many have claimed this over the years. The windshield was not bulletproof, however, as JFK limousine expert Pamela McElwain Brown shared with me in an email, dated July 16, 2022: "Nothing on ss100x on 11.22.63 was bulletproof. The windshield was a stock LCC windshield."

21

Allow us to get back to John Connally's back wound, which is absolutely critical, because the advocates of the single bullet hypothesis consistently prefer to uphold that his back wound was elliptical, elongated and about 3.0 cm in length. This elongated back wound hypothesis has been upheld and proliferated by Warren Commission safeguards like Dr. John Lattimer, Dr. Michael Baden, and Gerald Posner. One problem: it is wrong. Dr. Shaw depicted it as "a wound of 1.5 cm." The elongated wound theory is based on the grounds that the injury was evidently one of entry from a sideways, tumbling position, or tangentially, as the medical world likes to portray it. Assuming this would have occurred, the injury ought to be the length of the projectile, which was 3.0 cm, however it wasn't. It was an entry wound of 1.5 cm (the same size as JFK's back of the head wound). As Milicent Cranor stated in her wonderful article, *Big Lie about a Small Wound in Connally's Back*: "Why do supporters of the SBT say the wound was 3 centimeters long, when, in fact, it was only half as long? Why was the 1.5 centimeter wound a problem? Defenders of the theory say that if the Carcano bullet had struck sideways (as opposed to nose-on), it would have created a wound the same size as its length (3 centimeters), and such a long wound would be proof the bullet had been tumbling. If it had been tumbling, this presumably would be proof it had struck something else on its way to Connally's back. The something else in this case: John F. Kennedy."

It is fascinating that the hole in regard to Governor Connally's jacket, in the back, is 1.5 cm and the hole in the back of his shirt is 1.5 cm, as expressed by Robert Frazier before the Warren Commission (5 H 64). This by itself would appear to alleviate the likelihood that the back injury of Connally was 3.0 cm. Dr. Shaw, who operated on Connally, said the original back wound was 1.5 cm, or five-eighths of an inch (4 H 104). It became 3.0 cm after Dr. Shaw carefully enlarged it and after he did so, the wound then looked elliptical when amplifying the incision to roughly 3 cm, as he expressed in his Warren Commission testimony:

> Mr. Specter: Will you continue now and further describe the treatment which you performed?
>
> Dr. Shaw: Attention was next turned to the wound of entrance. The skin surrounding *the wound was removed in an elliptical fashion, enlarging the incision to approximately 3cm.* (6 H 88)

Read the accompanying exchange:

> Mr. Specter: Is the size and dimension of the hole accurate on scale, or would you care to make any adjustment or modification in that characterization by picture?
>
> Dr. Shaw: As the wound entry is marked on this figure, I would say that the scale is larger than the actual wound or the actual depicting of the wound should be. As I described it, it was approximately *a centimeter and a half in length.*
>
> Mr. Specter: Would you draw, Dr. Shaw, right above the shoulder as best you can recollect, what that wound of entry appeared at the time you first observed it? Would you put your initials right beside that?
>
> (*The witness, Dr. Shaw, complied with the request of Mr. Specter.*)
> (6 H 86)

As I reread Dr. Shaw's testimony before the Warren Commission, this consistently irritated me. The official version and the Warren Commission followers were continually bringing this up. The exit wound in JFK's throat is circular and seems, by all accounts, to be leaving in a straight line when observed by Dr. Perry's first observation at Parkland Hospital, though he thought it was an entrance wound. *The entrance wound in Connally's back was elliptical, however, only after Dr. Shaw, by his own admission, had cleaned it up during surgery.* On the off chance that the bullet departed Kennedy's throat, both circular and straight, then how is it possible that it would tumble off to the right during the transfer from JFK to JBC, which would have taken c. 10/1,000th of a second. Ridiculous. Is there any hard proof of anybody portraying his back wound as elliptical, before Dr. Shaw so portrayed it, after he cleaned up the wound and dressed it? Not that I am aware. The scar on Connally's back was 2.9 cm, or one and one-eighth inches, not 5 cm, or 2 inches, as Dr. Michael Baden manufactured it on page 19 in his book, *Unnatural Death: Confessions of a Medical Examiner.*

The following table is taken from Milicent Cranor's (who always does very fine work on the case, especially with the medical evidence), *Trajectory of a Lie, Part III, Big Lie About a Small Wound in Connally's Back* that should make the point even clearer:

TABLE. Connally's Back Wound – the Hole Story

ITEM	SIZE (Centimeters)	SIZE (Inches)	REFERENCE
Entrance into JFK's Scalp and Skull	1.5	5/8	Autopsy Report, p.4 (WR 541)
Connally's Jacket (back)	1.5	5/8	FBI 5 WCH 64
Connally's Shirt (back)	1.5	5/8	FBI 5 WCH 64
Connally's Back Wound (original size)	1.5	5/8	Robert Shaw MD 4 WCH 104, 107; 6 WCH 85, 86
Wound after Enlargement	3	1 ¼	Robert Shaw MD 6 WCH 88
Connally's Back Wound (original size) FALSE	3	1 ¼	John Lattimer MD *Medical Times* 1974; 102 November:33-56; *Kennedy and Lincoln*, Harcourt Brace Jovanovich, 1980, pp264-269 Gus Russo *Live by the Sword: The Secret War Against Castro and the Death of JFK* Bancroft Press, 1998, p.297 Dale Myers "Secrets of a Homicide" Website www.jfkfiles.com/jfk/html/concl2.htm
Scar	2.9	1 1/8	Michael Baden MD 7 HSCA 143
Scar FALSE	5	2	Michael Baden MD *Unnatural Death: Confessions of a Medical Examiner*, Random House 1989, p.20

Another sign that the wound might not have been from tumbling or that it was elliptical was that Dr. Shaw said the damage to the Governor's fifth rib was a "tunneling wound," (VII HSCA 149) which destroyed 10 cm of his right fifth rib. Dr. Shaw said the rib, not his back, may have been struck tangentially. He likewise said the bullet certainly "hit the actual rib, by the slick manner by which it stripped the rib out without harming the muscles that lay on one or the other side of it." (4 H 116)

A quick note about another item that consistently comes up by Warren Commission defenders is the alleged lapel flip at Zapruder frame 224. Gerald Posner made a lot of this in his 1993 book, *Case Closed*. However, even Dr. Michael Baden in a debate with Dr. Cyril Wecht at New York University in 1993, excused the lapel flapping as a pointless furor, taking note that there was a cross breeze that day that was sufficiently able to have effectively knocked Jackie's hat off twice during the motorcade, once not long before the vehicle turned onto Elm Street.

Governor Connally had 5 wounds, a back wound, chest wound (not to mention 4 inches of his right fifth rib being blown to bits), top wrist wound, bottom wrist wound and a left femur wound (despite the fact that no bullet was found there, only a small fragment that he carried with him until the day he died).

His chest wound, moving laterally and downward into his right shoulder, annihilating one rib and exiting from his chest, may have ricocheted and damaged the chrome in the vehicle, which we know something did, or went over the windshield and was never found, as stated earlier. The two fragments they found in the car later that evening, might have come from Connally's wrist, or from his chest wound, as also referenced earlier. After he received his chest wound, he is pictured holding his Stetson hat, which would have been inconceivable if the chest bullet did any additional damage, because the Governor was likewise wounded on the top of his right wrist, with the bullet shattering bone and nerve structures on the distal end of the radius. More later on as to why I don't think this bullet which exited his chest is responsible for the wrist or thigh wounds.

There was a lot of fragmenting going on, some of which might be effectively explained by damage to the limousine and fragments on the floorboard, not to mention the wound in his femur, which was a fragment and not a whole bullet. Indeed, the fragment was 1mm in size,

imbedded in the femur, with little tissue damage. What isn't easily clarified is the whole bullet found at Parkland, not a fragment 1 mm in size
(which is what they should have found on the stretcher, not a whole
bullet, since a whole bullet was never discovered in Connally during
surgery) said to have come from Connally. Strangely, they never found
an entire bullet in Connally, or anyone for that matter, which is what
you would expect if the last person the bullet struck was Connally.

Remember the magic bullet as demonstrated to the general public,
was missing slightly more than one grain of metal. A grain is the smallest unit of measurement as far as weight. One grain is the equivalent of
one-four hundred and thirty-seventh of an ounce. Yet, metal was recovered from all three of Connally's wounds, whether those pieces, given
up to officers of the Texas Department of Public Safety and never seen
again, were fragments or flakes. They most certainly added up to more
than 1/437th of an ounce.

When you look at a clear copy of the Zapruder film frames, there is
something that is very striking. When you contrast Z-326 with Z-335,
there is a gigantic distinction in the size of JFK's head wound. Something
has occurred. JFK is driven in reverse 2.18 inches in Z-312-313. He is
then driven forward, however, c. 4.8 inches between Z-328-330. That is
a lot farther than the distance when he endures the deadly head shot in
Z-313. All in all, something has driven JFK forward, as expressed earlier,
further and quicker (c. Z-328) than at the fatal headshot in Z-312-313.

Let's summarize: JFK is hit tangentially on the right side of his skull
in Z-313, driven backwards, causing a massive hole in the rear of his
head (medical personnel at both Parkland and Bethesda attest to this),
then 7/10 of a second later c. Z-328, he is hit again from behind and
that bullet goes through the already made hole in the back of his head,
exiting out the right side of his already damaged skull, making that
wound a lot bigger as a result, which explains the huge difference in the
size of his temporal wound from Z-328-335. Look at the photographs
below and the difference is stunning. It also explains Connally's wrist
wound, which could not have occurred at Z-237-238, because he is still
holding his Stetson hat, which he would not have been able to do if his
radius bone had been hit.

Again, something hit JFK with enough force to drive him forward
further and quicker at Z-328 than at any other point in the Zapruder

film. Interestingly, at this point in the film, Connally is lined up perfectly to receive the wrist wound after JFK has been hit in the head a second time (you need to watch the film in close-up to see this. It is clear, however, when you do, as was exhibited at Wecht 2013 by Mr. Keith Fitzgerald working in concert with Dr. Josiah Thompson) within 7/10 of a second after Z-313. When Connally is hit the second time, he rolls over like a rag doll. If you look carefully, you can see the blood on Connally's back, but also the blood on Connally's wrist/white shirt and that blood on his wrist is seen for the first time at this point of the Z-film c. Z-328-335.

Governor Connally testified before the Warren Commission, that he was mindful of the chest wound, but he had no idea at the time he had been injured in the wrist or thigh (4 H 135).

The joined testimony of the Governor and his wife seemingly destroys the possibility of the Single Bullet Theory. It is a simple progression: 1st shot hit JFK as he is seen clutching toward his throat, which was seen by Mrs. Connally. The 2nd shot hit the Governor as he and his wife so affirmed. The 3rd shot hit JFK in the head (Z-313), as the two of them testified. As far as the 4th shot, compare Z-326 and Z-337 and something has transpired. The wound has enlarged sizably. This doesn't clarify everything, except it explains the distinction in the size of the head wound on JFK (between Z-326 and Z-337) and it does explain Connally's wrist wound and why he rolls over so rapidly at this exact moment. I would recommend that if you doubt these findings, realize they are nothing new, as I will explain toward the end of this chapter.

What is new, is the visual demonstration of this at Wecht 2103, when Mr. Keith Fitzgerald, who gave a video presentation after Josiah Thompson had completed his part of the talk, so clearly exhibits. As I watched the presentation, and with clear precision, what I have expressed in the previously mentioned pages was confirmed in the Fitzgerald presentation. Investigate and see what you think. I was convinced this was a genuine possibility years prior, when I read the HSCA report and volume five of the hearings and volume six with the photographic evidence, but I was unable to verify anything because of a lack of available evidence with the Z-film. But Z-327 kept coming up during the HSCA and I was always suspicious and now, the acoustics evidence also seems to justify a shot c. Z-326-328. It has now become a fait accompli in my mind.

What Mr. Fitzgerald and Dr. Thompson did, to their credit, was bring it to the table for everyone to view, up close and personal, which is what I had suspected since the mid 1980's. As researchers, we shouldn't care who discovered it, only that it supports what a lot of us have been saying for years, that there was a conspiracy to kill President Kennedy. It no longer abides alone on the last day testimony near the end of Volume 5 of the House Select Committee Hearings. Now everyone can see it for what it is, a shot 7/10's of a second after the fatal head shot of Z-313, at c. Z-328. It is the fourth and final shot that struck both JFK and Governor Connally.

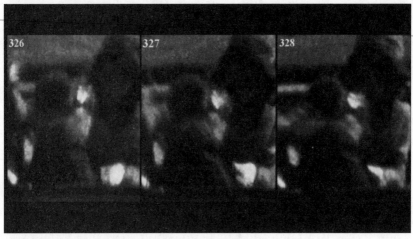

Z-326-328

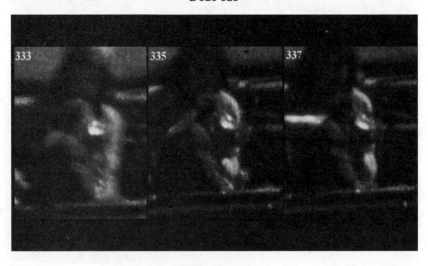

Z-333, 335, 337

The following quotations from the HSCA suggests they were at least considering this as a possibility:

> G. Robert Blakey in summarizing the scientific evidence, states on the last day the committee met, that *"based upon the proposition that the fourth and final shot fired at the limousine struck President Kennedy at Zapruder frame 312. If Zapruder frame 312 actually reflects the time of the third shot rather than the fourth, the timing of the first, second and fourth shots would then correspond respectively with Zapruder frames 182, 212, and 327. The possibility that the fourth shot occurred at Zapruder Frame 327 would require a finding, in light of the neutron activation analysis, the ballistics tests and the medical testimony, that both the third and the fourth shots hit President Kennedy in the head."* (V HSCA 693)

> The possibility of a bullet striking President Kennedy at Z-327 rears its head again in more closing comments by Blakey, *"To look further at the question of the direction from which the wound-inflicting bullets came, the committee had available to it--again this afternoon--its engineering analysis and consultant for the head-shot trajectory. The purpose of Mr. Canning's testimony was to determine if any conclusions of the committee's expert consultant might have been changed by the refinement of the acoustical data. He would have addressed this afternoon the question, Could the fourth shot have occurred at Zapruder frame 327 and have come, as it must have in light of the other evidence, from the depository? His conclusion, based on rough figures, is that it is highly unlikely that a bullet fired from the depository could have struck the President as number four at frame 327."* (V HSCA 695)

> *"... Dr. Michael Baden, Chairman of the Committee's Forensic Pathology Panel, acknowledged there was a possibility, although highly remote, that the head wound depicted in Zapruder Frame 312 could have been caused by a shot from the grassy knoll, and that the medical evidence of it had been destroyed by a shot from the rear a fraction of a second later."* G Robert Blakey, (HSCA Public Hearings December 29, 1978)

> *"The significance of this, the Committee reasoned, was the realization that it could mean that the President's fatal head wound was caused by the shooter from the grassy knoll, not Oswald."* (HSCA Report)

> *"For that bullet to have destroyed the medical evidence of the President being hit at Zapruder Frame 312 (from a shot fired from the*

29

grassy knoll), it would had to have struck (the rear of the President's head) at Zapruder Frames 328-329 (by a shot fired from the TSBD)... " (HSCA Report)

"The Committee believed that the fourth impulse pattern probably represented that fatal head shot to the President that hit at Zapruder frame 312. Nevertheless, the possibility of frame 312 representing the shot fired from the grassy knoll, with the fourth shot consequently occurring at frame 328, was also considered. The problem with this possibility is that it appeared to be inconsistent with other scientific evidence that established that all the shots that struck the President and the Governor came from the Texas School Book depository." (HSCA Report 85)

"Dr. Baden acknowledged this extraordinarily remote possibility in discussions with the Committee staff...

He was prepared to respond to questions concerning this theoretical possibility during the December 29, 1978 hearing, but because of the time spent on the acoustical evidence during that hearing, Dr. Baden's scheduled appearance before the committee was canceled." (HSCA Report)

"I looked at the film very carefully to see if I could relate the position of Governor Connally's right arm to the movement when the missile struck the President's head, presumably the third missile... " Dr. Charles Gregory, (4 H 128)

"I think it is possible that a fragment from that particular missile may have escaped and struck the Governor's right arm." Dr. Charles Gregory, (4 H 128)

"... The (HSCA) Forensic Pathology Panel cannot rule out the possibility, if confined only to the surgical evidence, that the wound to Governor Connally's wrist was caused by a large fragment of the bullet which struck the President's head.

Assuming the head shot (at Frame 313) was the grassy knoll shot, Zapruder made significant panning errors after both the third (312-313) and fourth (328-329) shots." (HSCA Report)

And finally, if you read Volume VI of the HSCA, Photographic Evidence Report, you will see they address the issue of Z-327 on **pages 58-62**. They conclude that, *"frame 327 does not take in the alleged sniper's window. For this reason, it is highly unlikely that the head wounds were in-*

flicted by firing a bullet from the southeast window that impacted at the time of Zapruder frame 327."

They only allow for the possibility of a head shot coming from the southeast corner window, even though they admit earlier, on page 59 of the possibility that JFK was struck in the head at Z-312-313 and Z-327. They suggest very strongly a bullet striking Kennedy 7/10's of a second after the previous shot, so their shot sequence is: 1st shot (c. Z-189), then 1.6 seconds later a second shot (c. Z-236-238), then 4.2 seconds later the third shot (Z-313) and finally 0.7 seconds later (Z-326-328), the final and fourth shot. There was enough evidence that the HSCA at least entertained this possibility, though eventually rejected it, as they already had the next to the last shot fired from the Grassy Knoll missing, hence the fourth shot came at Z-312-313 and was the fatal head shot, for the HSCA.

I read about this when I first obtained a copy of volume VI of the HSCA volumes and pondered it as much as I could and as much as I had documentation to support the notion of a shot at Z-327-328. I was puzzled as to why it kept coming up in the HSCA volumes. In the mid-eighties, when I finally found a copy of the HSCA volumes, I discussed this with a couple of my friends who were interested in the case. Not having a copy of the Zapruder film and having only seen it once or twice in March of 1975, we could not make much of it. The measurements were available in Josiah Thompson's, *Six Seconds in Dallas* on page 91, but I did not have a copy of his book at the time, so was unaware of those measurements. I lived in a small town and the local library was not well-stocked in JFK assassination literature. Now seeing it up close and personal and able to make measurements, there seems to be vindication for a shot c. Z-327-328. The acoustics seem to support this today, as the recent work by Donald Thomas verifies (more on the acoustics later)

2

Danell Brill "Nellie" Connally

September 6, 1978

On September 6, 1978, Nellie Connally testified before the HSCA, along with her husband Governor John B. Connally in Washington D.C.

"You can't say Dallas doesn't love you, Mr. President."
– Nellie Connally

Actually, you can say that, simply by watching the Zapruder film. To paraphrase Ralph Yarborough, who was two cars behind the presidential limousine, he stated in *The Men Who Killed Kennedy* series that he saw rousing and smiling faces along the motorcade route, but when he looked up at the open windows in the buildings, he never saw a smile, but instead scowling and angry faces.

Mrs. Connally testified with her husband before the House Select Committee on Assassinations, just as she did before the Warren Commission in 1964. She spent some time referring to how they got everything organized and ready for the President and the First Lady. She was assuming the role of state mother, hoping everything would be conducted properly. And then, of course, she refers to her now famous remark to the President as they turned onto Houston Street, approaching the Texas School Book Depository, "You can't say Dallas doesn't love you." Moments later, shots were fired.

She seems to speak forthrightly and with confidence, especially when it came to what she said about the second shot that hit the Governor:

> Mr. Cornwell: "So you agree that your recollection is it was the second shot that hit the Governor?"
>
> Mrs. Connally: "***I know it was the second shot that hit the Governor.***" (I HSCA 44)

To quote, "I heard three shots, I had three reactions, three separate reactions. The first shot, then I looked and saw the President, the second shot, John, and third, all this matter all over us" (I HSCA 44).

The exchange with Mr. Dodd is as significant:

> Mr. Dodd: "Thank you, Mr. Chairman. Governor and Mrs. Connally, to repeat what my colleagues have said, we do appreciate your being here this morning, particularly in recounting what must have been one of the most agonizing if not the most agonizing moments of your lives. I would like to just go back over, if I could, those seconds at the time that the shots rang out. Let me try and repeat what I understood to be your testimony, you correct me if I am wrong anywhere in terms of my understanding of the sequence of events as they occurred. First, you, Mrs. Connally, because there is a bit of a difference as I heard both of your responses. You heard a shot, what appeared or sounded like a shot, a sharp noise, to you? You turned to your left or your right?"
>
> Mrs. Connally: "My right."
>
> Mr. Dodd: "You turned to your right. As you turned around and saw the President, you saw him clutching his throat?"
>
> Mrs. Connally: "I saw him reach up to his throat."
>
> Mr. Dodd: "Both hands were on his throat?"
>
> Mrs. Connally: "Yes, sir."
>
> Mr. Dodd: "Did you see any blood at all?"
>
> Mrs. Connally: "No."
>
> Mr. Dodd: "Then did you turn back or did you hear the second shot?"
>
> Mrs. Connally: "See, I don't know, I don't know."

33

Mr. Dodd: "You don't know which you did first?"

Mrs. Connally: "What do you mean? "

Mr. Dodd: "Well, you saw him clutch."

Mrs. Connally: *"I looked back and I guess I just stayed looking back until I heard the second shot."*

Mr. Dodd: *"So, you are still looking at the President and it is your recollection that you then heard what sounded like a second shot?"*

Mrs. Connally: *"Yes."*

Mr. Dodd: *"Is that correct?"*

Mrs. Connally: *"Yes. What was a second shot."*

Mr. Dodd: *"At that point your husband, Governor Connally, slumped over in your direction?"*

Mrs. Connally: *"No, he lunged forward and then just kind of collapsed."* (Most likely the shot at Z-327/328, as I have been referring)

Mr. Dodd: *"And, then collapsed."*

Mrs. Connally: "But not just straight up."

Mr. Dodd: "And then you heard a third shot or what appeared to be a third shot?"

Mrs. Connally: "After I pulled him down."

Mr. Dodd: "You did hear—"

Mrs. Connally: "I did hear a third shot."

Mr. Dodd: "At that point you then noticed the material?"

Mrs. Connally: "All over."

Mr. Dodd: "The blood and so forth?"

Mrs. Connally: "Yes."

Mr. Dodd: "When you turned and saw the President holding his throat, as I understood your testimony, the President didn't utter any sound or any word at all, to your recollection?"

Mrs. Connally: "Nothing." (I HSCA 52-53)

The HSCA endeavored to make Mrs. Connally guess and appear confused about whether she was looking at the President or her husband, when the second shot was fired. At the point when this came up with the previously mentioned exchange with Mr. Dodd, she said she thinks she was looking at the President when her husband was hit with the second round of gunfire. She said the President responded to the first gunshot by appearing to grasp at his throat, while the governor appeared to show no response at all.

It is interesting to see how Governor Connally squares with the Zapruder film, as stated by Mrs. Connally. Watch him in the Zapruder film. As you anticipate Z-313, the JFK head shot, observe Connally. He recoils forward about *7/10's of a second after Z-313*, and the only conceivable rationale is that he was shot somewhere near Z-327/328, as stated in chapter one. Keep in mind, he had no idea he had been shot in the wrist or the leg, until Sunday afternoon, the 24th, when he awoke from the trauma. Jackie remains motionless and holding JFK for several frames.

She testified to hearing Mrs. Kennedy say, after the third shot, "I have his brains in my hand." Mrs. Connally had stated the same thing before the Warren Commission (4 H 148). The Commission was willing to print this account, but when Mrs. Kennedy testified behind closed doors, she told what she saw *without being asked*, the [*references to wounds were deleted*]. The Warren Commission refused to print them in the volume containing her testimony. Here is what she said, thanks to the Freedom of Information Act, that the Warren Commission refused to print: *"I was trying to hold his hair on. From the front there was nothing -- I suppose there must have been. But from the back you could see, you know, you were trying to hold his hair on, and his skull on. .... I could see a piece of his skull sort of wedge-shaped, like that, and I remember that it was flesh colored with little ridges at the top."* Admittedly disturbing, but necessary concerning the wounds of her husband.

Connally went from looking upward in Z-312 to being face down on the floor at c. Z-330, a second later. There are very few things, I would suggest, you can do that quickly, in one second. Connally was not responding in any reasoned manner. He was going into shock. This is due to the development of his second wound, at c. Z-327-328. This was brought up in the testimony of Dr. Robert Shaw before the Warren Commission.

It cannot be overemphasized that when Mrs. Connally discussed the shots, she mentioned over and over, that she realized the President was hit with the first shot, as she saw him respond by reaching up toward his throat. Her husband had not been hit at this point. Then she heard the second shot and saw her husband's response, which was after the first shot and the President's reaction. Then the third shot (Z-313) was heard and its effects felt. If Mrs. Connally is right about the first shot and the President's response, combined with her view about the Governor responding to the second shot, then this by itself invalidates the Single Bullet Theory, and requires a second shooter, likewise requiring a conspiracy.

When Mr. Devine started questioning Mrs. Connally, he said he wasn't sure that she testified before the Warren Commission; both she and her husband did and you would figure he had done a at least a modicum of homework to read her testimony before the Warren Commission and be prepared. I suspect he knew he planned to question her. This is all about being informed, not necessarily trying to trip her up and deceive her in any way. It's tied in with taking your mandate seriously when scrutinizing an observer who was in the limousine with the President of the United States when he was killed. When the Grassy Knoll is addressed, there doesn't appear to be a lot of room given to its possibility as a position for an assassin (which is odd, since the HSCA will later claim someone did shoot from behind the picket fence on the grassy knoll, suggesting the probability of a conspiracy) as the following brief back and forth would indicate:

Mr. Devine: "I would take it then by negative implication that you heard no shots coming from your right front?"

Mr. Connally: "No, sir, I did not."

Mr. Devine: "In the area that has often been described as the grassy knoll?"

Mr. Connally: "No, sir. And I don't believe any came from there."

Mrs. Connally: We responded to all these shots, so if something came from the front we certainly would have responded to it, a noise from the front, I would think." (I HSCA 47)

Mrs. Connally was to some degree uncooperative as the years progressed. When Governor Connally died in June of 1993, she could have permitted the remaining metal to be removed; it would possibly have been 'case solved'. If that metal was taken from his chest, wrist, and thigh, and some did remain, it would no doubt have added up to considerably more than the two grains missing from CE-399. Again, a grain is defined as the smallest unit of weight, and 437.5 grains equal one ounce, as referenced beforehand in her husband's testimony. That implies that CE-399 was only missing 2/437.5 of an ounce. That is somewhere in the weight of a piece of dust. There are 7000 grains to a pound, so CE-399 was missing 1/3500 of a pound. Infinitesimal.

When Mrs. Connally and her husband testify, you get the impression they are recounting the story precisely as they remembered it. They thought all the shots came from the Texas School Book Depository. Sadly, they were not believed by either the Warren Commission or the House Select Committee on Assassinations when it came to the shot sequence.

03

ROBERT GRODEN

SEPTEMBER 6, 1978

O n September 6, 1978, Robert Groden gave testimony before the HSCA in Washington D.C.

G. Robert Blakey, chief counsel of the House Select Committee, stated in his introduction before Robert Groden testified, that he was in "a unique position to present to the committee the state of the knowledge of the critical community prior to the work of the committee and to articulate for it and the American people the crucial issues raised by the critical community, particularly as they were rooted in the photos available of the assassination" (I HSCA 61).

This is exactly what Robert Groden did. A lot of research has been done since 1978, but at that time what Robert brought up were some of the most pertinent issues within the research community. They are somewhat different today, with such things as the controversy over the alteration of the Zapruder film, and locating the original Nix and Muchmore films, along with neutron activation analysis, acoustical evidence, more discoveries within the Zapruder film, Oswald and the CIA, the role of military intelligence, ballistics, ARRB discoveries, etc.

Nix Film

Muchmore Film

The Zapruder film was at the National Archives very early on and people could view it with an appointment. Some early researchers like Vincent Salandria and Josiah Thompson went there and viewed a very grainy copy, but they did view it. As a point of record, the original Zapruder film is presently in cold storage at the National Archives.

On Thursday, March 6, 1975, The Zapruder film appeared and was shown for the first time on live TV on "Goodnight America", introduced on NBC and hosted by Geraldo Rivera. Rivera took a big risk and had to assume all liability if Time-Life decided to sue. ABC would be held accountable for nothing. It would all be on Rivera's shoulders. That big risk paid off and eventually led to the formation of the House Select Committee on Assassinations.

Photographic analyst Robert Groden and civil rights activist and comedian Dick Gregory carried a bootleg copy of the film to the program studio, talked about their different views of conspiracy with the host Geraldo Rivera, and then after many chidings by Rivera concerning the dramatic nature within the Zapruder film, it was shown.

I met Dick Gregory at COPA 98 in Dallas. What I most remember about him was how warm and kind he was to everyone, taking time to talk with all those who approached him. He is missed.

When the film was finally shown, it was haunting to see the President's head snap backwards, which seemingly destroyed the previous Warren Commission investigation that had happened twelve years earlier. We had been told that the president had been shot from behind, but now it was up close and personal; and it was obvious he was shot from the front as well. I can remember watching this broadcast with a few of my friends. We were aware of what the government had said about the president's head going forward and that a shot came from the rear. We sat there in stunned silence. I looked over to one of my friends and asked, "what did you just see?" We all, obviously, thought the same thing. What the %#@*&^#$%!!! We talked for hours into the night and wondered what kind of turn the case would now take. I then said, "Groden obviously knew about this before the program. How long do you think he was aware of it?" It was dark outside and creepy inside. Little did I know the path I would take as a result of that night. My friends lost interest and hardly stayed up with the case at all after that night. They simply got on with their lives. I sensed they were somewhat discouraged. I became more curious.

In fact, the Zapruder film had already been shown by Groden at Georgetown University and at a few other venues and conferences to a limited audience, but this time millions saw it.

Life sold it back to the Zapruder family for the amount of $1, basically to save face since they were coming under severe criticism for not showing it or making it available to be shown, especially after it appeared on "Goodnight America". There was a lot of negotiation on what to do with it, as it almost went to the National Archives or the Library of Congress. The purchase of the film seemed to be for the express purpose of not making the film available, but that may be too simplistic. Time-Life has been criticized for not showing the film, but they didn't have the ability to do so, as they were a printed news organization, not a broadcast media outlet. Their silence about not letting the film be shown on a reputable news broadcast was both discouraging and depressing.

They also seemed to be trying to honor Abraham Zapruder and not let it get exploited. They made some mistakes and, in the end, *Life* didn't recoup their investment, partially because of Groden showing the film on "Good Morning America" and the release of the film *JFK*. They ended up giving it back to the Zapruder family, as it had become a huge headache.

Dan Rather of CBS saw the Zapruder film and went on TV to report that the shot that struck the President in his head drove him forward. He was referring to Z-313, of course, which was the exact opposite of what actually happened. His head does go forward c. Z-327-328, but he would not have been able to see that by watching a copy of the film in 1963.

I don't know how many times Dan Rather has seen the 26.55 seconds of film. He claims seeing the limo make the left turn onto Elm Street, which he didn't, because Zapruder was rewinding his camera at that point and not shooting film. The limousine was already coming down Elm St. when Zapruder began filming. Rather expressed, "The movies show President Kennedy's open, black (it was actually midnight blue) limousine, make a left turn, off Houston street on to Elm Street…" A left-hand turn onto Elm street is not shown anywhere on the film, though Zapruder did think he had filmed that sequence, but actually did not. I assume he was describing the geography from Houston street to Elm street, as he was narrating his experience.

The opening seven seconds of his film show several motorcycles leading in advance of the limo, and then there is a gap of a couple seconds, and afterward the limousine appears after it has already turned and is starting to travel down Elm street. I can see how someone, only seeing the film a few times and concentrating on other things they saw in the film, could make this mistake. To me or anyone to focus on something like this is also a mistake and simply a red herring.

Richard Trask said that CBS blundered in not securing the film. At one point they did offer Time-Life $100,000 for one showing of the film – but were turned down. (Richard Trask, *Pictures of the Pain*, pp. 90-91)

By November 25, 1963, Time-Life's Richard Stolley again reached out to amateur photographer Abraham Zapruder, this time with the purpose to buy the rights to the Zapruder film. It was Patsy Swank, not Stolley, however, that first learned, on behalf of *Life*, of the existence of the Zapruder film.

Richard Stolley, who was negotiating for Time-Life, reached out to Zapruder for the express purpose of purchasing rights to the film. Zapruder didn't seem to be interested in any sort of discussions with anyone except Stolley. Their meetings covered the span of several hours, but Zapruder was a savvy business man and he knew exactly what he was doing. Zapruder's shrewdness would ultimately make millions of dollars for the Zapruder family and their heirs.

Stolley realized the amount he was authorized to spend, as the publisher of *Life*, C. D. Jackson, who was in Chicago at the time, had apparently given Stolley strict orders on what he could offer. Stolley and Time-Life were eventually successful, but the question is: Why did Time-Life want the Zapruder film at all? Their motive seemed to be the purchase of print rights, which they used and made sure it didn't fall into the hands of someone who would exploit it, which is what Zapruder was afraid of the most.

They did publish some grainy black and white frames in a weekly issue of *Life* and later printed some color frames in a Memorial issue. Keep in mind, a few government agencies (FBI and Secret Service) already had copies of the Zapruder film before Stolley and Zapruder had finished their negotiations. *Life* would eventually publish 28 regular-size frames, two larger frames, and one much larger frame. That, however, was it.

Zapruder agreed to sell his original and three first-generation copies of the film, and all rights, "whether domestic, foreign, newsreel, television, motion picture, or otherwise of the film." Zapruder, or his heirs, were to receive a total of $150,000, with the first $25,000 paid immediately, and five supplementary payments, each due on January 3 of years

1964-1968. Interestingly, Zapruder was also to be given a 50% royalty agreement once Time-Life had regained its $150,000 investment. Their first $25,000 bought them the rights to use "frames" of the movie, which they have done in varying degrees from November of 1963 to date. The other $125,000 bought the film rights.

Richard Trask wrote, "Time, Inc., also agreed to '…present said film to the public in a manner consonant with good taste and dignity.'" (Richard Trask, *Pictures of the Pain*, pp. 90-92) It is obvious that in a relatively short amount of time, Zapruder had thoroughly thought through all of the financial ramifications of what he wanted.

Time-Life never authorized a media outlet to show the film. When the film was shown on Goodnight America", it demonstrated to the American public and made us all aware of the distortion, seeing the horrifying image of the backward head-snap, advanced upon us all by the Warren Commission, and also the House Select Committee on Assassinations years later. That second investigation, which took place in the late 1970's, is what this book is about. This will no doubt never happen again and most likely was, to quote the title of Gaeton Fonzi's book about the inner workings of the HSCA, *The Last Investigation*.

Credit Robert Groden for showing the Zapruder film to the world that evening on "Goodnight America" in 1975; it is absolutely one of the pivotal moments in the history of the Kennedy assassination, along with the film *JFK* in 1991, and eventually the Assassination Records and Review Board in the late nineties. Groden, ABC, Geraldo Rivera et al, could have been sued by Time-Life for copyright infringement, but somehow escaped that legal riddle. We would eventually see superior copies of the Zapruder film later on and all were the result of what happened that night on "Goodnight America".

Those 26.55 seconds of film is the story of the assassination. When we get back to our initial impressions of the film, what we see is actually what occurred. History has time and again taken us back to our first impressions and accurately so. It seems to have been hidden in plain sight.

T.S. Eliot has a wonderful quatrain in his **Four Quartets**:

> We shall not cease from exploration
> And the end of all our exploring
> Will be to arrive where we started
> And know the place for the first time

Often, when we go back to early days of the Kennedy case, what we saw has come to be exactly what happened. We have too often gotten buried in the minutiae of the evidence and lost sight what Vincent Salandria warned us about. He had been right all along – it is a False Mystery.

There has been a lot of speculation in recent years as to whether the Z-film has been altered. (Listen to episode 103 of *Midnight Writer News* where Robert Groden is interviewed by S. T. Patrick about the so-called Z-film alteration and it is Groden at his best. His knowledge of photography and especially the Z-film is quite impressive) The odd thing for me has always been that if the film was altered, and it always seems to be suggested by people who obviously believe in a conspiracy, then why did the people trying to halt that belief do such a terrible job. The one place and the most obvious place that seems to show a shot from the front, hence conspiracy, is the one place where they forgot to alter the film? Ridiculous, I know.

Besides, and what I am saying here is nothing new, if you alter the Z-film, wouldn't you also have to alter the Nix and Muchmore films, as they show the same fatal headshot to JFK as the Z-film does, but from the opposite side of Elm street. Zapruder is facing south, while Nix and Muchmore are facing north. They all correspond with each other, which seems to confirm the film's legitimacy.

The original Nix film is missing, which led to the book written by Orville Nix's granddaughter, Gayle Nix Jackson entitled, *The Missing JFK Assassination Film: The Mystery Surrounding the Orville Nix Home Movie of November 22, 1963*. Orville Nix apparently showed his film to the FBI, then to *LIFE*, and sold it to UPI for $5,000 on December 6, 1963. No one has seen the original Nix film since it was loaned to the HSCA in the late 70's, except for the person that presently possesses it. Groden says the HSCA did return the film to UPI. (There is an excellent historical chronology of the Nix film in Ms. Jackson's aforementioned book by Chris Scally that narrates the entire history of the film).

Marie Muchmore was an employee of Justin McCarty Dress Manufacturer in Dallas located at 707 Young Street, four blocks south of the Texas School Book Depository. On November 22, 1963, Muchmore was in Dealey Plaza with five co-workers, including Wilma Bond, who had a camera and took still photos, while watching the presidential motorcade. Muchmore stood near the northwest corner of Main Street and Houston Street with her 8 mm Keystone movie camera and awaited the president's arrival.

The Muchmore film consists of seven sequences: six before the assassination, and one during the shooting. Muchmore began filming the presidential motorcade with her movie camera from her initial location near the northwest corner of Main and Houston Streets as the motorcade turned onto Houston Street into Dealey Plaza.

She then turned and walked with Wilma Bond several yards northwestward to again film the President's limousine as it went down Elm Street. Her film then captured the fatal shot to the President's head looking north as does the Nix film; and sees the limousine from c. 138 feet away. The film ends seconds later as Secret Service agent Clint Hill, attempting to protect President Kennedy, runs and quickly climbs on board the accelerating limousine.

Mrs. Muchmore stated that after the car turned on Elm Street from Houston Street, she heard a loud noise which, at first, she thought was a firecracker, but then with the crowd of people running in all directions and hearing two further noises sounding like gunfire, she began to run to find a place to hide. The film now belongs to the Associated Press Television News, which restored it in 2002.

The following issues were the topics that were brought up by the committee, along with some elaboration by Groden: the number, timing, and directions of the shots; the photographic evidence that touches upon the Warren Commission's conclusion that Oswald fired at the President from the Texas School Book Depository; the photographic evidence that bears upon the Warren Commission's conclusion that there were no other gunmen in Dealey Plaza other than Lee Harvey Oswald; what issues had been presented to the committee's scientific panels that had been raised by the various photographs depicting the crowd in Dealey Plaza at the time of the assassination and shortly thereafter; what types of questions related to conspiracy were raised by the photographic evidence; the photographic evidence that gave rise to the possibility of an alibi defense for Lee Harvey Oswald; the backyard photographs; other photographs pertaining to the Kennedy assassination that have had their authenticity questioned; and finally a series of clarification questions about issues raised by Mr. Goldsmith and other members of the committee. That is a lot to think about and digest and we will unpack and seek clarification about all of it.

Mr. Goldsmith begins the questioning:

> Mr. Goldsmith: "Mr. Groden, would you please state your name and occupation for the record?"
>
> Mr. Groden: "Robert Groden, photo-optics technician." (I HSCA 62)

He then proceeds to the number, timing, and direction of the shots, as put forth by the Warren Commission. In responding to the number and timing for the shots, Groden says that "the first frame where he reappears from behind the road sign is Zapruder frame number 225. The headshot occurs at 313. The difference between the two frames would give the time-span of which the Warren Commission claimed it happened, which would be, indeed, 5.6 seconds" (I HSCA 64).

Groden's math is simply wrong. There is not a doubt in my mind that Bob Groden knows this and simply misspoke.

While I am sure Groden knows it was Z-210, he said Z-225, which he has just stated to the committee was the frame where JFK first appears from behind the Stemmons Freeway sign. In this sequence, 88 Zapruder frames, or 4.8 seconds, are recorded between Z-225 and Z-313, so that will not fit the official timeclock in this incorrect sequence. If you start at Z-313 and multiply 5.6 seconds by 18.3 frames per second, (this would be 102 Z-frames) which is the running time of the Zapruder film, you then arrive back at Z-210. Then, if you go from the Warren Commission's Z-210 to its Z-313, it is 5.6 seconds. Groden certainly knows this.

The President emerges from behind the Stemmons Freeway sign in Z-223, with his left elbow appearing, indicating he was hit before Z-225, and most likely before Z-223, but exactly how much earlier we do not know.

Groden then stated that if the first or the third shot had missed, then the amount of time for the assassination could be as long as 7.9 seconds (I HSCA 63). Josiah Thompson, in his book, *Last Second in Dallas*, suggests 8.3 seconds, which I tend to lean in that direction more and more. Again, working back from Z-326 (the last shot in the sequence of shots) and that 8.3 x 18.3 would put the first muzzle blast around Z-175. 7.9 seconds would put the first shot somewhere around Z-182. The time duration also has to take into account the 2.3 seconds the FBI determined was necessary to work the bolt on the rifle. The 2.3 figure is the FBI time span to work the bolt, without aiming. With a Mannlicher-Carcano, it is difficult to work the bolt without substantial effort on your shoulder, so you work the bolt, then return the weapon to its position, and then sight it in through an inferior, cheap scope. Howard Donahue, for CBS, in 1967, did get off three shots in 4.8 seconds, and hit the target. The 18.3 fps time speed of Zapruder's Bell and Howell camera may not be exact gospel, though based on the averages of the camera running between 18.0 fps and 18.5 fps, the 18.3 fps is probably accurate, as I stated earlier in chapter one. That being said, however, Donahue did practice with the bolt before firing, did not score three hits until his third try and did not, and I repeat, did not, use CE-139 (the Carcano found on the sixth floor of the TSBD). Another difference: Donahue was an expert shot. Oswald was not.

There is a possibility that a shot was fired before Z-190, because at that moment Phil Willis' daughter unexpectedly stopped and looked back over her right shoulder. The problem is that if this is true, and we don't know for sure if it is, then that bullet may have missed, which troubles me, because whoever was shooting that day wasn't missing. They were professionals and deadly accurate.

Consider the following: If the proposed running of Zapruder's camera was at 18.3 frames per second (the HSCA seemed to confirm this) and the Carcano rifle required 2.3 seconds to recycle without aiming, then that would be simply 18.3 x 2.3, or 42.09 Zapruder frames, and that is just to fire and work the bolt, without re-aiming. Assuming there is a shot at Z-190, then that means there cannot be another until Z-230.09, so this may be why the official version needs the first shot to hit both men. The problem is that there is no indication that the bullet broke Connally's right fifth rib and radius bone, before embedding itself in his left femur at Z-190. He would have to wait another 48 frames later to react, or else you have two assassins. Keep in mind that once the rifle is fired, the damage is done in the speed it takes to snap your finger. The bullet would be traveling c. 114 feet for every Zapruder frame, or c. 114 feet for every 1/18 of a second.

The conventional understanding of the wounding of Governor Connally is presented next. The rationale is as follows: "If the President were hit between 210 and 224, it was requiring a minimum firing time of 2.3 seconds, which is 43 frames (2.3 seconds). That is, if the President were hit, let's say, at frame 210, a separate bullet could not have hit Governor Connally until 253. Also, if the President were not hit until 224, we would have to add 43 frames (2.3 seconds) to that to locate where Governor Connally would be hit (which would have been Z-267). However, the Governor shows a very marked reaction by frame 237 to 238, which is only 1.6 seconds away, too soon for another shot to have been fired, according to the FBI, but certainly soon enough for a second shooter. Governor Connally's right shoulder buckles sharply, his cheeks will puff out and his hair will become immediately disheveled. All in one frame [*1/18 of a second*]" (I HSCA 66-67).

Perceptions differ. Responses aren't always instantaneous, but the governor's physical responses seemed to have immediate reactions, which is what Connally's surgeon affirmed would have taken place regarding Connally's wounds. Since we can suggest that Governor Connally was hit just before Z-237-238, his physicians, in reviewing the Z-film, estimated Z-234-236, remarking that an injury that broke bones would create a prompt response.

Whatever one may insist about the Zapruder film, the responses that JFK has on the film appear to demonstrate, at least on a superficial level, that the head shot came from the right front side and struck JFK in the right temporal area of his skull. As was expressed in chapter 1, there is the point in the Zapruder film where he pitches forward (Z-327-328) and even further than in Z-313, though this isn't as pronounced as other reactions on the Z-film, which may have something to do with the pressure vessel of the cranial cavity already being ruptured as a result of Z-313. The acknowledgment of a head shot to JFK at c. Z-327-328 would create about 8.3 seconds for the duration of the shooting. The evidence appears to support this proposition, which answers some of the confusion about the shot sequence, especially in connection with the acoustics evidence.

The throat shot is not demonstrable or seen as an entrance wound when viewing the Zapruder film. One could contend that the throat shot entered small in the back and exited bigger, hence the frontal grasp, which I know is not what we would expect. Or, the first response was where the shot hit in the throat, and the best evidence of this is that the Parkland doctors saw the wound before the tracheotomy. The issue, however, and I emphasize that the back wound is rising at 11 degrees, as is the throat wound, so the bullet could have left his throat and gone half-way down the streets of Dallas, never to be seen again. If the throat wound is one of entrance, both it and the back would be falling at 11 degrees and would have lodged in the back seat of the limo to be easily found, which it, of course, wasn't. Having said all of this, I do not state these findings via divine fiat. I know about the evidence of a frontal shot to JFK's throat and how some of my colleagues would argue for the possibility of the initial shot impacting JFK's throat. We have to try to connect this, however, with his back wound, which I am not able to do.

Groden points out that when the Warren Commission published their volumes of hearings and exhibits, they reversed key frames that would make the backward motion of the President not as apparent, which is true. In volume eighteen of the Warren exhibits they published the frames in the following order, keeping in mind that Z-313 is the point of impact on the President's head: Z-313, 315, 314, and 316. This almost indicates frontal, not backward movement. Those who believe the assassination was a conspiracy, feel this was not an accidental printing error. As stated earlier, J. Edgar Hoover said it was a printing error, but that is nonsense, as you are able to see part of the earlier frame in each later one. In 313, you see part of 312; in 314, you see part of 315; in 315, you see the halo of 313; in 316 you see part of 314. This unique, or one-time-only Z-frame blunder reminds us of the only recorded epileptic seizure on a Presidential motorcade route, which just happened to be in Dealey Plaza just before JFK arrives, or the only time anyone opened an umbrella (let alone in sunny, 68 degree weather) in the 1,037 days of JFK's presidency was done at the precise moment he was being assassinated (*See chapter 41 for more on Umbrella Man*). A pattern begins to emerge.

By the way, it was almost by accident that Zapruder filmed anything that day. His camera was at home and he was urged to make the fourteen-mile drive home to get it. When he returned, crowds were gathering to watch the motorcade.

The epileptic seizure is worth a comment or two. Amateur photographer Charles Bronson (not the actor, obviously), standing with his wife

49

on top of the concrete abutment on the south west corner of Main and Houston Streets, viewed this epileptic episode further north on Houston and records it on motion picture film: "Approximately 6 minutes before President Kennedy arrived in the Dealey Plaza area there was a commotion diagonally across from the School Book Depository Building on Houston Street. An ambulance, with its lights flashing, arrived on the scene, and they evidently loaded someone in it that needed hospitalization. I thought I would capture that little bit of excitement as I aimed my movie camera, so I moved my movie camera in that direction and shot [92] frames as I recall." (Richard Trask, *Pictures of the Pain; Photography and the Assassination of President Kennedy*, p. 281- *noting that Bronson had just recently purchased the camera at a pawn shop on Elm Street.*)

The epileptic incident probably transpired c. 12:15, but that event would seem to have utilized more time. The epileptic man, whose name was Jerry Belknap, suffered the seizure. An ambulance call went out c. 12:19, but it would have taken some time to get through the sizeable traffic flow, park the ambulance, secure and load Belknap into the ambulance, and then set out for Parkland hospital.

Bronson estimates this occurred c. 12:24 (if you subtract 6 minutes from 12:30) and this harmonizes with James Altgen's observations, as he saw the ambulance lights and sirens go under the triple underpass as the President's motorcade was turning right from Harwood onto Main Street.

Belknap could have suffered his seizure in the 12:15-12:17 range, as there were pedestrians giving him comfort, but if you add the ambulance event, it would make it c. 12:24. There is no way to know whether this could have been a diversion of some sort. We will never know, but this event is at least moderately suspicious. The spot of the epileptic seizure may be even more suspicious, as it was where the Pilot car carrying **Dep. Chief George L. Lumpkin** and **Lt. Col. George L. Whitmeyer** U.S. Army Reserve, East Texas Section Commander, both connected with **military intelligence**, stopped briefly around that time, most likely to communicate with James Powell (**military intelligence**), who was standing on that corner and took a picture of the 6th floor SE window in the TSBD.

Aubrey Rike expressed that here were several ambulance calls to that actual area of the epileptic seizure in days preceding the assassination. The ambulance that showed up and left c.12:24 makes for an intriguing

curiosity, since Belknap left the hospital, never entering it, only to return days after the fact to make right his account. (*some of this information due to the author's conversations with Mr. Rike, 1995.*)

Another problem occurred with the October 2, 1964 issue of Life
magazine, or the case of 3 *Life* (*Life*, October 2, 1964) magazines. I
have all three issues and this shenanigan was beyond ridiculous. *Life*
magazine published its story of Oswald's lone-assassin conviction by
the Warren Commission on February 21, 1964, before any real investigation was done. The October 2, 1964 issue had its plates broken two
times, meaning there were three different editions of the same magazine, and differing Zapruder frames carried the same caption, making
some of them unashamedly misleading. This would have been a very
expensive publishing process. The Zapruder frames depicted in at least
two of the issues misled the general public egregiously.

In the first edition, frame 323 was included, representing an image
just about one-half second after the head impact at Z-313, but showing
the president's head almost touching the rear seat of the limousine. The
caption indicated that the particular photo showed the president's head
snapping.

In another edition, Z-313, clearly of greater interest but not as damaging to the official version as Z-323, then replaced Z-323, and the caption was changed to suggest that the head was exploding forward, which
of course it wasn't and they knew it wasn't, since they had purchased the
Z-film 11 months earlier.

As noted, to break the plates and re-tool an issue carries with it an
excessive cost (I believe stated by some to be in the neighborhood of
$150,000, which, oddly, is what Time-Life paid for the Zapruder film in
1963) and it was done twice.

If *Life* magazine allowed the movie version of events to be seen, it
would have greatly compromised the official version and made *Life*
magazine look like a co-conspirator. It would have exposed the charade.
They did print frames of the Zapruder film out of order. In fact, they asserted that JFK turned completely around in the direction of the person
who killed him in the December 1963 issue, despite the fact that upper management of *Life* magazine had viewed the film often and knew
better. They switched frames and wrote untrue captions, when indeed
they knew the truth. It has been known from the inception of the event

that they exerted a huge effort to keep the lid on the truth of the assassination, as they would never allow it to surface from Pandora's box. Time-Life seems to be culpable, but then again, so is almost all of the mainstream media. (*See Appendix #4 for more research done by John Kelin on this matter, reprinted with permission by the author*).

Oddly, all of the editions of *Life* make a hero out of Howard Brennan, overlooking his perjury before the Warren Commission. Brennan's claim to fame wouldn't lessen as late as 2007, when Vincent Bugliosi, trotted him out on stage once more, only to embarrass himself by using him as a star that he never was. Even G. Robert Blakey told me in 1998 that he would have never used Brennan as a witness before the HSCA and thought he was shameful to the case. His testimony is beyond offensive. (**Please see Appendix #1 and *The Curious Case of Howard Brennan***)

The Zapruder film was shown at the Garrison trial to a few people, but it was anything but a good copy. When an inferior copy was shown, after twelve years, it led to the United States Congress addressing the faults of the Warren Commission on live TV, via PBS. They at times excoriated the Warren Commission, yet oddly came to the same conclusion concerning Oswald. They said there was a *probable* conspiracy, saying in fact there had been a shot from the grassy knoll, but guess what, it missed everything. Their coverup was only gaining steam.

The subject then turned to the photographic evidence that touched upon the Warren Commission's conclusion that Oswald fired at the President from the Texas School Book Depository.

Groden said there were no photographs that he was aware of that showed Oswald in the SE corner 6th floor window, or that anyone had seen him on the sixth floor during the assassination. He then addressed the Dillard photograph, taken within seconds of the assassination, as well as "the final photograph, the one on the right, on the bottom, was a very similar photograph taken by an *Army intelligence* man by the name of *Powell*, who was standing diagonally across the corners of Houston and Elm looking up. He took this photograph somewhere between 30 seconds and several minutes after the assassination. I am not clear as to the actual time." (I HSCA 105)

Now let's see how Groden develops these photos and what the research community knows about them. Three pieces of photographic evidence that may tell us something about what happened on that fateful day: a still photograph taken from the *Hughes* film, the photograph taken by *Dillard*, and finally a photograph taken by a man named *Powell* was put into evidence.

The **Hughes** film is discussed first. Groden suggests the appearance of movement in the SE window, and the window next to it. The Hughes film is significant, but independent film experts need to give their take. It is not clear whether it shows physical movement or apparent movement due to artifacts of blowing the film up to that degree, however having said that, in an email exchange with Martin Shackleford, he stated that there seems to be movement in those windows in the film, but it is such a tiny part of the frame that any movement could simply be an artifact (*email exchange on September 19, 2020*).

The **Dillard** photograph came under question as to whether it showed anything in the SE corner window. There has been some speculation of someone finding an image in the photo. There is someone in the west end window in the Dillard photo, at least that is what I see when I look at it. This photograph was taken after Robert Jackson, who said he looked up and saw a rifle protruding out of the window; but didn't have any film loaded in his camera at the time, so Dillard quickly took a picture of the window.

The **Robert Powell**, (who has connections with **military intelligence**), photograph comes up next, which supposedly shows a whitish shape in the window, that Groden said could be enhanced to bring out the image. It does show what looks a bit like an elbow, but that is it.

The attention then turns to the photographic evidence that bears upon the Warren Commission's conclusion that there were no other gunmen in Dealey Plaza other than Lee Harvey Oswald. Groden then turns to Altgens #6, (James "Ike" Altgens was the only professional photographer on foot in the Plaza that day and was a field reporter for the Associated Press) which supposedly shows a man on a fire escape in the background, possibly in distress, but hard to be dogmatic. Just to the left and below is a window to a broom closet, which has given rise to the belief that a possible shooter may have been there. The problem is that he would have been in view of a roomful of women. As far as the Dal-Tex building is concerned, it would have to be from an upper floor. One researcher had a physicist do the math on the angle from the aforementioned position. Remember, JFK's car is almost invisible because it is lower; going down the hill and the higher car behind it has six men elevated, four on the running boards and two up on the seat. It also has a windshield that has to be cleared. The physicist stated that a shot from the Dal-Tex building would only clear the Secret Service car by seven inches.

Groden then posits the possibility that the individual (who has come to be known as Black Dog man) seen behind the retaining wall in Willis #5 is the same individual (though you really only see the image, not the guy) seen for eighteen frames (1 second) in Z-413. Martin Shackleford, who has done an enormous amount of research on the photographic evidence in the case, says the image is of one of the men standing on the steps (*See the entire article "R.I.P. : Black Dog Man" with illustrations in Appendix #3 of this book, reprinted with permission by the author*). I know from being in the Plaza, that Zapruder would have been able to pretty much touch the person (I am speaking hyperbolically, but not extremely so). Zapruder was 52 feet from the corner of the stockade fence from where he was positioned. JFK was 93 feet away from the corner of the stockade fence at the time of the head shot in Z-313. The pyracantha bushes are a couple of feet from his position, and the shooter, between Zapruder and the bushes, would have been very close. Having said that, read Appendix #3, and you will see what is really happening.

* * *

As far as the famous **Moorman** photograph is concerned, the guy in Z-413 seems to be visible in the Moorman photo. People who want to see things in the Moorman photo have done so. It was a Polaroid camera, something you would use for non-professional events like confirmation ceremonies or baptisms, and not to be confused with the kind of camera(s) transported by an Altgens or Bob Jackson or some other professional photographer. Moorman took two other photos earlier, which showed the Sexton Building (which housed the Texas School Book Depository and was owned by D. H. Byrd) in the background. One of these is in Richard Trask's excellent book, *Pictures of the Pain*, and shows the motorcycle cop descending Elm Street.

There is an artifact (or person) in the Moorman photo around twelve feet west of the corner of the stockade fence, if you are looking from the south side of Elm street, that can't be explained by shrubbery, a tree,

The Mary Moorman photograph

a pole or some other sort of non-human artifact, on the grounds that there wasn't a tree, pole, or any sort of non-human artifact there on that day, or today for that matter. Every time I have been to Dealey Plaza, I have stood at that precise spot behind the stockade fence and there is nothing there. I have looked at a lot of photos of the stockade fence not long after the assassination and into the 90's and there isn't anything there, yet there is something there in the Moorman photograph. Josiah Thompson addresses this and goes in depth in what he thinks it means and that the acoustic evidence seems to place an assassin at that spot, in his most recent book, *Last Second in Dallas*.

Josiah Thompson had S. M. Holland stand in that spot soon after the assassination and took a photo, to compare it with what appears to be a person in the Moorman photograph and he came up with what looks to be a similar shape and appearance, to what we see in the Moorman picture. I think there was somebody there and if there is, it may very well be the only picture we have of a shooter that day, however grainy, because of the sort of camera that was utilized.

Mr. Goldsmith asks about what issues introduced to the committee's scientific panels had been raised by the different photos portraying the crowd in Dealey Plaza at the hour of the assassination and shortly

Mary Moorman

thereafter. He additionally asked Groden concerning the kinds of inquiries identified with conspiracy that were raised by the photographic
evidence. Two people are referenced. They are *Umbrella Man* and *Joseph Milteer*.

Umbrella man is an individual who acted quite strangely on the day
of the assassination. "As the President's car went by, the man we call the
umbrella man opened his umbrella and raised it as the President went
by, pumped it in the air and turned it in a clockwise manner. This is very
evident in the Zapruder film" (I HSCA 114). He then simply sat down,
looked both ways, and walked away eventually departing the Plaza. The
1999 Rickerby photograph discovery may shed some light on this, but
at this point of the committee's tenure, Louis Steven Witt had not yet
been revealed to the general public (***more on this in chapter 41***).

The next individual Groden named was Joseph Milteer. He was a right-wing fanatic, who had his conversation taped by William Somerset, an undercover informant for the FBI and the Miami police. The discussion mentions a high-powered rifle, an office building, and how a patsy would be set up to take the fall. Milteer reportedly called Somerset from Dallas on November 22nd. He then called him again from Jacksonville, Florida, which was tape recorded on the 23rd, where Milteer remarked that he wasn't guessing and that things went according to plan.

Another photograph by Altgens (known as Altgens #5) shows a man on the East Side of Houston Street that looks a lot like Joseph Milteer standing in front of the County Records Building.

Joseph Milteer?

The Photographic Panel for the HSCA determined that it wasn't Milteer due to the wrong height, though there was one dissenter on that panel. There are a variety of heights given for Milteer over the years, from 5'4" to 5'10". The so-called balding of Milteer in Altgens #5 could be because he really was balding. When Don Adams, a rookie FBI agent, was allowed to ask Milteer questions, he was given five by his superiors to ask him after the assassination took place and ordered that nothing else be asked. Odd. Adams was never told about the taped conversation that Milteer had with Somerset; also extremely odd. Someone is controlling the narrative. Don Adams knew Milteer personally and immediately identified him in Altgens #5. Regardless of what you think of Milteer, he was precise about what he said was going to happen: rifle, office building, and a patsy that was set up. Sure, he was a crackpot racist, but for whatever reason, he seemingly knew what was going to happen on November 22, 1963.

Groden insists Milteer was there to see the execution, but if you put someone in the spot where Milteer is shown (I have stood on that spot and you would not have been able to see JFK's limo at the time of the head shot), he could not have seen the final shot sequence. If it was Milteer, he was there to experience the assassination, not observe it. Remember, Altgens is snapping and running and moving about rather quickly. He can get from Houston to where he took Altgens #6, the photo of Billy Lovelady in the doorway of the TSBD. (Unfortunately, Billy Nolan Lovelady would die of a heart attack in Colorado at the age of 41. His wife said they were required to move five times, because people kept violating their home in order to steal the shirt her husband was wearing as he stood in the doorway of the TSBD on November 22,1963). Creepy.

Altgens can cover ground a lot quicker than a limousine traveling c. 11-12 mph, because he is cutting off the intervening space diagonally, but only by being near the corner of Main and Houston and going diagonally to the spot where he took #6. (*There is an amazing replica of Dealey Plaza you can view on the internet, which shows the cars and people moving about during the motorcade route. It's called Motorcade 63. It is very well done.*) If he is in the mid-block area, he simply won't get there, because it shortens the limousines travel time, and he has to deal with the reflecting pools. I agree with Groden on this one. Research done by some respectable researchers indicate with a high probability that it is in fact, Milteer. If you read Don Adams book, *From an Office Building with a High-powered Rifle*, the story becomes even more clear.

The famous tramps or hobos come into question next. Groden raised the possibility that there are resemblances between the three tramps and the following people: Frank Sturgis and E. Howard Hunt, of Watergate fame; he also mentions Fred Lee Crissman. I don't see that myself and never have. They could have been involved on a peripheral level, as their attire and look is not traditional hobo garb. Some feel they were involved at least tangentially. To what extent they were tramps is still being debated and probably always will be, but these guys that traveled from one destination to another destination are clearly not in high administrative positions. Though as the movie *JFK* postulates, their shoes are fairly new and they appear to be clean shaven, again not a typical hobo look. They may have been given a few dollars and then told to be in the railroad yard and run and make a disturbance (they could have been told it was a protest, who knows) when the car went by. They would draw attention away from the shooter(s), if seen. Their arrest records were released in the early nineties. (Gedney, Abrams and Doyle are their names)

Jim Garrison, on January 31, 1968, made an appearance on the Tonight Show, hosted by Johnny Carson. It was during this program that Garrison attempted to play up the hobo angle and tried to show the tramp or hobo photographs and stated that other arrests had been made besides Oswald. Garrison stated the men just vanished; however, that is not precisely accurate. They were kept on vagrancy charges for three or four days and then released.

The photographic evidence that gives rise to an alibi defense for Lee Harvey Oswald was next on the docket. Again, Groden raises the issue of Lovelady in the doorway of the Texas School Book Depository in Altgens #6. There are a lot of assumptions made from Altgens #6, but when all of the related photos and films are studied, there is no doubt it is Lovelady in the doorway. Lovelady, as shown in the Altgens photograph, is wearing an almost identical shirt to the one Lee Harvey Oswald was arrested in, or at least the camera suggests such. He would later appear for a photograph wearing a red and white striped shirt. Wesley Frazier and others were nearby and they identified the guy as Lovelady. Marguerite Oswald was shown the photo and said, "that's my son," but she was identifying the man to the left of Lovelady, as you look at the photo. He is wearing a hat and is next to a woman holding a child, whom Marguerite told the Warren Commission was Marina and the baby. I am without speech.

The famous backyard photographs finally come up, and they stir up as much controversy today as they did in 1978. Lee Harvey Oswald was shown the backyard photographs on the 23rd of November. They were found on the 22nd. The problems that continue and still persist, however, are the size ratio, the shadow discrepancies, the famous crop line seen in CE 133-A, and the chin and neck differential. The HSCA photographic panel deemed they were authentic. People who advocate the official position have always said they were genuine, while conspiratorial theorists have been somewhat divided on the issue. Some have claimed they were authentic (such as Hal Verb), while some have inferred fakery of some sort. Marina told me, in one of three phone conversations I had with her in the nineties, that she took the pictures, but that she only remembered taking two of them. She also was somewhat confused as to where her husband was precisely standing. One was found among the possessions of George DeMohrenschildt. Oswald's mother supposedly flushed one down the toilet. I would think it would be very difficult to flush an 8 x 10 photograph down the toilet, but okay. One was sent to *The Militant*, whose staff recalled receiving it, then apparently got rid of it, afraid it was some kind of an effort to set them up for something. I think and have always thought the photos are authentic, but with only one of the three negatives available, some kind of meddling can't be completely ruled out, but unlikely. At least two witnesses reported seeing an enlarged backyard photo prior to the assassination at their Dallas photo shop. Ultimately, I agree with Marina. I think they are legitimate and as for the crop line on the chin, it is only in one of them, when in fact, shouldn't it be in all three?

As I said, the crop line is certainly visible on 133-A, but only 133-A. The photographic panel found nothing sinister about the crop line and gave rational explanations for it. This probably wouldn't be an issue if it weren't for the chin that seems so apparently out of sync with other pictures of Oswald, whose chin seems more pointed, and with a cleft.

There is a photo of Oswald, however, just as he is getting into a DPD elevator, which gives him the same chin as the backyard photos. It is dubious to draw conclusions about almost anything when all you have is one still photograph to observe.

Groden then brings up the point about rifle discrepancy and the possible differences, which is always interesting. As far as the Mauser/Carcano discrepancy is concerned, some people, like Anthony Summers, simply think it was an identification mistake. Roger Craig, however, stated that from a very close angle (c. 6 inches) he saw 7.65 Mauser stamped on the side of the rifle. Seymour Weitzman signed an affidavit declaring it to be a Mauser. Weitzman knew guns and at one time owned his own gun shop in Texas.

The rifle found on the 6th floor of the Texas School Book Depository is not the same length as the one ordered from Klein's Sporting Goods, which was 4 inches shorter in length (the one he ordered from Kleins was 36 inches long, but the one he received was 40.2 inches long) than the one found on the 6th floor. Since Oswald's P.O. Box has his name and his name only on that box, meaning that only Lee H Oswald can receive mail there, it begs the question as to how Alek Hidell could have received the rifle at that box (since the order form was made out to Alek Hidell). Stewart Galanor prints the postal regulations for 1963 in his book *Cover Up* and they specifically state that anyone other than Lee H Oswald, would not have been able to receive mail there. So how did Oswald get the rifle from the post office? It is a question that needs an answer.

Another point that recently was brought out in the very fine Oliver Stone documentary written by Jim DiEugenio, *JFK: Destiny Betrayed*, showed photographs of CE-139 being taken out of the TSBD by Carl Day and you can clearly see the sling mount embedded into the side of the stock on the rifle. In the backyard photographs, Oswald is seen holding the same rifle, apparently, but the sling mount is fastened to the bottom of the stock and barrel and not on the side of the stock. This presents a problem for the official version.

The rifle ordering riddle is bizarre. From the website Harvey and Lee, John Armstrong points out a story you simply cannot make up, in an article he wrote entitled: *Oswald Did NOT Purchase a Rifle from Kleins*

John Armstrong states the following:

> **MAIL ORDER RIFLE.** According to the Warren Commission Lee HARVEY Oswald left his job at Jaggers-Chiles-Stovall during the morning of March 12, walked 11 blocks to the downtown post office, purchased a postal money order, and then mailed his order for the rifle to Klein's Sporting Goods in Chicago before returning to work. But the letter was postmarked 10:30 am, and company time records show that Oswald never left his job. He worked continuously from 8:00 am through 12:15 pm on 9 different printing jobs.

61

The Warren Commission never pointed out that the envelope, time stamped 10:30 am, was not mailed from the downtown post office where the money order was purchased. It was stamped and mailed in "zone 12," which was several miles west of the downtown post office and across the Trinity River. In order for this letter to have reached Chicago the following day, it would have to have been picked up by a mail carrier sometime after 10:30 am, delivered to the Industrial Station post office in zone 7, and then sorted and bagged into an airmail pouch. And the airmail pouch would have to have been delivered by another mail carrier to Love field and then placed aboard an aircraft prior to its 12 o'clock noon departure.

If we are to believe the Warren Commission, then we believe that Oswald skipped work for an undetermined period of time on the morning of March 12, walked 11 blocks to the post office, purchased a postal money order, traveled several miles across the Trinity River in order to mail the letter, and then returned to his job unnoticed. And then, if we believe the Warren Commission, this letter was picked up by a mail carrier sometime after 10:30 am in zone 12, delivered to the post office in zone 7, sorted and placed into an airmail pouch, transported to the Love Field Airport, and loaded aboard the last flight to Chicago before the plane departed at noon. This money order was allegedly received by Klein's Sporting Goods in Chicago the following morning, was included with over a thousand other mail orders from around the country, and then deposited into Klein's bank account. If this sounds a little far-fetched, believe me, it gets better.

All US Postal Money orders have unique serial numbers. In the fall of 1962, Oswald purchased numerous money orders from the same downtown post office and mailed them to Washington, DC in order to repay a loan from the government for his travel expenses incurred when he returned to the USA from Russia. These money orders were purchased in numerical sequence beginning in November 1962. These serial numbers show that some 1200 money orders per week were purchased at the downtown post office in Dallas. At this rate we see that Oswald's alleged purchase of a money order on March 12, 1963 should have been numbered 2,202,011,935. But the serial number of the money order published in the Warren Volumes was more than 118,000 numbers higher. At the rate of 1200 money orders per week, this money order should have been purchased in late 1964 or early 1965. In other words, this money order could easily have been pulled from a stack of fresh, unsold money orders by a postal official in Dallas, sometime after the assassination, and then given to the FBI. A close look at the details surrounding the "finding" of the money order the day after the assassination strongly suggests that this is what happened.

His pistol is even more bizarre. Oswald supposedly sent $10 (which was only a third of the cost, when 50% was needed to secure the purchase) when he requested the pistol and then asked to pay for the rest when it came to the post office, c.o.d. Is he serious? Unheard of in that day or any other day of which I am aware. Who was going to pay for the remainder of the bill? Harry Holmes? It doesn't make any sense.

Wesley Frazier was a resident close to the Paine home where Oswald's wife was living and became aware of hiring needs at the Book Depository. This is how Oswald came to learn of the vacancy which he ultimately filled, thanks to the ubiquitous Ruth Paine, who always seems to be everywhere at just the right time. Frazier later drove Oswald home to the Paine residence on weekends, and always took Oswald back to work on Monday. The only exception to that pattern was on November 21, 1963, a Thursday, when Frazier drove Oswald to Irving, Texas to the home of Ruth Paine where his wife, Marina, was living.

Disciples of the official version (Chris Matthews used to love to bring this up) have always complained that Oswald didn't start working at the TSBD until mid-October, when the plans for the motorcade in Dallas didn't occur until later, so he obviously wasn't being put into place, but this is simply false. Plans were made as early as June of that year. They were originally going to have JFK come to Texas in late August to coincide with LBJ's birthday, but it didn't work out. The motorcade was well in place before Oswald was hired at the TSBD.

On the evening of the 22nd, Frazier was picked up by the police as he was found at the bedside of his ailing father. He was taken home, had his .303 Enfield rifle and ammunition seized, and was then taken to Dallas Police headquarters, where he was interrogated and put on a polygraph machine.

His subsequent Warren Commission testimony was more exculpatory than it was damaging to Lee Oswald, as both Frazier and his sister, Linnie Mae Randle, testified that the package Oswald was carrying on the morning of November 22nd, and they are the only two who saw it, was not longer than 27 or 28 inches, and the 40.2-inch Mannlicher Carcano rifle, when broken down, still required 34 inches of space, plus room taken up by the wrapping paper. Keep in mind, Frazier used to sell curtain rods professionally, so his perceptions might be more dependable than somebody who never sold them.

Did Oswald enter the Book Depository with a small paper bag, which contained a rifle, the Mannlicher-Carcano, broken down. This would require a quick assembling of the rifle on an upper floor of the building and could easily have raised suspicions had someone caught him. We are assuming that Oswald put the two pieces of the rifle together. What would he have used? When Oswald was in the Soviet Union, and something needed to be fixed, like his radio, he would have someone that he knew repair it for him, as Ernst Titovets stated in a documentary called, *Lee Harvey Oswald Behind The Iron Curtain*. As stated in chapter one, he was mechanically inept. Was it brought by Oswald simply for a prop to be found later that day, making Oswald look culpable. If so, Oswald unwittingly brought evidence against himself without realizing it. With all of this being said, I am not convinced Oswald brought curtain rods to the TSBD on the morning of the assassination. We tend to push back against the possibility that Oswald brought the Carcano to work that morning, but I'm not so sure.

If he did, then how does the Warren Commission or the HSCA explain how he would have sighted in the rifle? Accuracy could be realized under those conditions when using a world-class sniper weapon, otherwise a gun made in 1891 and not sighted in has little value in a situation like the one on November 22, 1963.

The gun itself is complete junk. A number of Warren Commission witnesses said so, but eventually they brought in an Army *"expert"* to prove that it was a high-class weapon. Embarrassing.

The facts say otherwise. The guns that were the batch-lot from which C2766 came were sold by the pound to a Canadian firm which then cannibalized the pieces, taking a usable stock and putting it with a surviving barrel and trigger assembly, as if it was a rifle version of Mr. Potato Head, and then wholesaling them out at $3 each, to be sold retail at $12.95.

The page that A. Hidell ordered the weapon from contained several other rifles for sale. Almost all of them were touted as being very good rifles, except the $12.95 Mannlicher Carcano, and all of them cost more than the Mannlicher, too.

The FBI could not get the gun to shoot straight, having to attach shims under the telescopic sight and locking the weapon tightly in a bench vice. The gun fired high and to the right of its target at a distance of only fifteen yards. At the distance of sixty yards, it would have missed by several feet, and the car was going down from right to left while the gun fired high and to the right. Problematic.

Problems remain about the ammunition, as the FBI never could figure out where Oswald got ammunition for the Carcano. Thousands of man hours in gun shops proved futile over a fifty-mile radius. They found nothing.

Hidell did purchase the rifle, but he needed bullets, obviously, and there is zero evidence of him having any. Bullets were not sold with the rifle, and the clip necessary to hold six bullets (aside from the one in the chamber) did not come with the rifle. We are lacking an origin story, unfortunately.

Of the three conveniently discovered cartridges on the sixth floor, one was found to possess a badly dented rim, making the cartridge that held a useable bullet highly suspicious. It also doesn't help that Capt. Fritz picked up the shells and then tossed them back down on to the floor, totally contaminating the crime scene. He was recorded doing this by Tom Alyea and we still have the video.

Texas School Book Depository mail wrapper Troy Eugene West arrived at work on November 22, as was his custom, usually about ten minutes early in order to get the coffee brewing. He would later testify that he did not see Lee Oswald that morning; "I had been seeing him every morning, you know. He would come to work. Excepting the morning, I didn't see him that morning at all." (Deposition of Troy Eugene West, 6 H 358)

West would also testify he never saw Oswald around the paper or tape machines, and that Lee Oswald was never seen to wrap mail, nor did he have any idea about Oswald borrowing any paper or tape. Never. It must be recalled that the tape came from the machine wet, which means it had to be applied on the spot. We are asked to believe that Lee Oswald took Texas School Book Depository paper and wet tape and subsequently smuggled it to Ruth Paine's garage, only to make a paper sack to hold a rifle. Ridiculousness is gaining a lot of momentum here.

Almost as bad and ridiculous is the story of Depository employee Bonnie Ray Williams, which has him eating his chicken lunch and soda

65

on the 6th floor, near the SE corner window just minutes before the president is shot, while the sniper waits hidden behind boxes hoping Williams consumes his lunch in time to run to the window and fire off the needed shots at JFK. Williams told the Warren Commission that he ate lunch on the sixth floor from around noon until 12:15, perhaps even until 12:20, and that he saw no one else on the floor. This was, at the most, just ten or fifteen minutes before the President's motorcade passed in front of the Depository. Neither of these scenarios seem to fit.

Remember, Buell Wesley Frazier described the bag he saw on the back seat of his automobile and depicted it constantly as a grocery sack: "…It is right as you get out of the grocery store, just more or less out of a package—you have seen some of these brown paper sacks you can obtain from any, most of the stores, some varieties—but it was a package just roughly about two feet long." (2 H 226)

Frazier describes the bag he saw as a grocery-type bag and makes no reference to the kind of paper used in his place of employment. It would have been quite easy for him to reference the paper at the TSBD in the shipping and wrapping room. If it was TSBD paper, you would think he would have mentioned it, but he never did.

Frazier is a simple man telling an honest story. I have never bought into the fact that Frazier is sinister in any way. He comes across as a decent man to me. His recent book on his connection to Lee Harvey Oswald needs to be read by everyone, as it fills in gaps we were unaware of until the publication of his book. It is entitled, *Steering the Truth: My Eternal Connection to JFK and Lee Harvey Oswald*. I will let you read it to discover a heretofore mentioned factoid that is both creepy and revelatory. I believe him.

Frazier's statement that Lee Oswald carried the bag cupped in his palm and tucked under his armpit has always intrigued me. We know it is impossible for the rifle to be carried that way given its length. The only two people who could have observed Oswald as he cupped the package were Frazier and Oswald.

I highly doubt he was cupping the rifle because of the early morning drizzle. I make no pretense at being a weapons expert, but I used to own a Mannlicher-Carcano. Remember, Oswald purportedly buried the Mannlicher-Carcano in the wet earth following the Walker attempt (April 10, 1963) and did not retrieve it for a few days.

And now he's concerned that it will get a little wet? Based on the size of, and care provided for the mysterious package, it may not have been a rifle. It may have been curtain rods, as Oswald said. We have to at least entertain that possibility. Or, we have to also entertain the possibility, as I said earlier, that it was the Carcano and Oswald was simply following orders and taking it to the sixth floor as a prop. I go back and forth on this issue. As you read this, pause and ask yourself, what is your gut saying he brought to work that day. More and more I lean toward the rifle, but not in any dogmatic fashion.

There is no proof Oswald ever fired CE-139 and certainly no proof he was a frequent visitor at the local rifle range. The shot fired at General Edwin Walker, U.S. Army, was attributed to Oswald, but the bullet found was initially described as a *lead-jacketed* 30.06, not a copper-jacketed 6.5 mm bullet.

I will always hold to the resolve that Oswald *could not*, not did not, shoot at President Kennedy that day. Those shots are possible if someone is an expert with a rifle of high quality, but Oswald does not fit into that mold. Joe Rogan, on his podcast recently stated that the shot was quite easy and I agree, if, and only if, you are Joe Rogan with a modern day rifle, but not Lee Oswald with a piece of Italian war surplus junk. The Mannlicher-Carcano was invented to fire volleys of bullets into a crowd hoping to hit someone. It is cheap mail-order junk. Nothing more.

The next topic to raise its head deals with photographs pertaining to the Kennedy assassination that have had their authenticity questioned. The three issues that serve as a nexus are: the apparent different sightings of Oswald at different places and at different times, when he can be accounted for at a definite spot, the discrepancies between the autopsy photographs and the witness testimony from the Parkland personnel, and the seemingly different heights of Lee Harvey Oswald.

> Mr. Goldsmith: "Is it fair to say that these photographs all pertain to what has become known as the second Oswald theory?"
>
> Mr. Groden: "I would say that it reflects on one of the second Oswald theories, there being basically two. That is, the idea of the switched identity or an imposter Oswald, in that case, and the other issue would relate to various incidents around Dallas, Oklahoma, Mexico, various portions of the United States, which would tend to show a Lee Harvey Oswald when the Lee Harvey

Oswald as we know him would appear to have been at another point of doing something else at the same specific time." (I HSCA 133—134)

John Armstrong has been under fire for some time due to his highly developed dual Oswald theory. This is nothing new, as Richard Popkin was making similar claims in 1966 with his book, *The Second Oswald,* though not to the degree that Armstrong does. Armstrong has raised the bar and developed his case to new heights. He may have taken it too far, but he also may be onto something, as there are certain anomalies that have to be dealt with. Someone seems to be impersonating and framing Lee Harvey Oswald. It seems as if his resumé is constantly being updated. There are just too many legitimate sightings, but there are also a number of totally bogus ones. What is important to realize is that the sightings seem to occur in isolation: a market, a barber shop, a rifle range not well attended, a hotel parking lot, a furniture shop, at a gunsmith, a car dealership. There is no sighting of Oswald where he rants to hundreds or even dozens of people. These sightings seem to be well choreographed. There are two things that the planners and plotters did not take into account: that Oswald could not drive and Abraham Zapruder would show up with a camera on November 22, 1963. The fake sightings seem to involve Oswald driving in every case and we know Lee Harvey Oswald couldn't drive, even at age 24.

The differences between the autopsy photographs and the Parkland witnesses are next for discussion. The autopsy photos may have been taken at various points during the autopsy, though Dr. Humes claims they were all taken at the beginning of the autopsy, yet you never see the traditional Y-incision in any of the photos, so at least the ones we have seen indicate they were taken at the opening of the postmortem examination. There are many we haven't seen or, I am sure, never will.

The back of the head photos are the only dubious autopsy photos, as far as I'm concerned. In 3-D, there is a rectangular patch on those photos, but you don't see any strands of hair when viewed in stereo, just a black matté of sorts. Robert Groden noticed this when he was doing stereoscopic viewing of the HSCA materials, when he served as a consultant. Just get a stereo viewer, (you'll need a pair of 3-D glasses or what are also called hand-held Lorgnette 3D stereo print viewers) and look at the back of the head using two color photos and then using two black and white photos, if you can secure them. As I did recently, stereo viewing can be a valuable tool for studying the photographic evidence. The two photos cannot be exact, but have to be slightly different, as far as angle is concerned, for this to work. I have also viewed the head wound in the Zapruder film in 3-D. You really need to do this.

As I interpret Fox-8 (see below), which if you have a clear copy and mine are taken from very good second-generation negatives, it is easy to see JFK's neck and the slight folding of the skin on his neck. Once you see that, it is pretty easy to orient. The skin has been reflected back off from the skull and the massive defect in the right rear of JFK's head is there quite clearly. There are also two circular holes in the right temporal region of his skull, *suggesting* the entrance wound seen in Z-313 and possibly the departure of a bullet fired at Z-327/328. The government has never released any of the autopsy photos and if it wasn't for James Fox via Mark Crouch via Walt Brown, who have supplied researchers with very good second-generation prints, we might not have the few that we do.

Fox-8

As far as the height discrepancies concerning Lee Harvey Oswald, not only does his height change, but he has different eye colors. This is seen in Oswald's two vastly different passport applications.

The rest of the session was taken up with a series of miscellaneous questions from different members of the committee. Mr. Devine noted that he thought Governor Connally actually faces President Kennedy when he turns to his right, when he attempts to get a look at JFK once the shots commence firing. Connally, however, never turns all the way around. This is an impression from a flat image. Study frame pairs with a stereo viewer, and it will be clear. Even if Connally does turn to his right and looks at JFK, it is not until Z-286, well after they have both been hit. Again, stereoscopic viewing may dispel this as an illusion. Connally rises up, gets a look before Nellie pulls him down, and before he rockets forward after Z-313, at Z-328.

Mr. Fauntroy asks if a camera would pick up smoke emitted from a Mannlicher-Carcano rifle. Groden refers him to the 1967 film that showed smoke being emitted from a Carcano rifle shot from the Texas School Book Depository. Rifles did emit smoke. Remember that photos of the 1966 University of Texas shootings show smoke clouds from the rifle on the tower. In this case, the cameras don't lie.

As far as there being smoke in the Moorman photograph, it depends on whom you ask. Some see it, some don't. There may be smoke in the photograph, but certainly not in the Weigman frame. I don't see it, and I would sincerely like someone who does see it to show it to me.

Mr. Ford then asks about Jackie, and what she was doing on the trunk of the car immediately after the shooting. There has been speculation that she picked up a chunk of JFK's brain or skull. We know she did, because she handed it to a medical person at Parkland, though she has no memory of climbing out on the trunk of the limousine.

Robert Groden has contributed greatly to the photographic evidence department and was responsible for showing the Zapruder film to the general public in March of 1975, which eventually led to the House Select Committee on Assassinations.

I have shared a few meals with Robert over the years, had some wonderful conversations and found him to be incredibly kind and warm in those exchanges and always willing to share details of what he knows about the case.

His contributions to the Kennedy case are both legendary and critically important. Robert lives in the Dallas area, at least the last I knew, and seems to know everyone in the case and has stories to tell that go into the night and early the next morning.

He still is fighting the good fight almost every weekend in Dealey Plaza.

IDA DOX
SEPTEMBER 7, 1978

On September 7, 1978, Ida Dox gave testimony before the HSCA in Washington D.C.

Ida Dox was born on July 8, 1927 in Honduras, Central America and came to the United States in 1947. She received her Bachelor of Fine Arts from Newcomb College of Tulane University in New Orleans in 1950. She obtained her Master of Science degree from Johns Hopkins University in 1954 and her Doctorate of Philosophy from the University of Maryland in 1990.

She was a medical illustrator at Georgetown University Medical Center in Washington D.C. from1954-1969. She was chosen to be the medical illustrator for the Select Commission on Assassinations of John F. Kennedy and Martin Luther King, Junior of the United States House of Representatives in Washington D.C. from 1978-1979. She had been a medical illustrator and author, in Bethesda, Maryland since 1969.

At the time of the public hearings, she was a medical illustrator for the Department of Medical-Dental Communication at the Georgetown University Schools of Medicine and Dentistry. She was also an author of many textbooks on illustrated medical dictionaries, one of which I purchased off of Amazon.

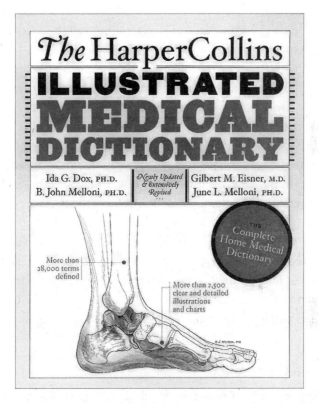

She died on October 18, 2013 at the age of 86. Dox was her maiden name, but her married name was Ida Melloni, as she married John Melloni in 1954.

The House Committee on Assassinations contacted the Georgetown Medical School, which in turn recommended Ida Dox as a medical illustrator. She appeared before the Committee to testify in public session. She had been working with the medical panel for some time and was asked to explain her role, working with the autopsy photographs and x-rays, which would demonstrate the location and severity of the bullet wounds.

Blakey impugned and disregarded the Parkland doctors by juxtaposing the comments of two of their doctors, Dr. McClelland, who said that JFK had "a massive head and brain injury from a gunshot wound of the left temple," (an obvious misspeak and red herring by Blakey, when McClelland understandably meant right temple) to the dissimilar description of Parkland's *neuro-surgeon* Kemp Clark, who is said to have "observed a large gaping hole in the rear of the President's head." Blakey further undermines the weight of their evidence by stating that "they only worked on the President for a short time, and they were trying to save him, which was not a possibility either way." (I HSCA 142)

I talked with Robert McClelland on the phone on two different occasions and he confirmed to me what I just stated that it was, in fact, a misspeak and that yes, it was on the right side of JFK's skull in the temporal area.

Ida Dox had an opportunity to garner some integrity by testifying that she did enhance the wound in JFK's cowlick area, or rather superimposed a wound where there wasn't one, in Fox–3. She couldn't because the person who told her to do it was there in attendance: her boss, Dr. Michael Baden. More about that in due course.

Andrew Purdy, who handled much of the medical aspect of the questioning, was called upon to question Ms. Dox. He began by asking her to expand on how it was determined what to illustrate for the Select Committee. A seemingly fair question. She said, "the committee, the medical panel, *and myself*... decided that the photographs taken at autopsy should be copied to illustrate the position of the wounds. The photographs that were selected were the ones that best showed the injuries." (I HSCA 146)

You have to wonder why they would ask Ms. Dox, an artist, to help decide which wounds to draw and illustrate. She's a medical illustrator, not a medical doctor. She draws the human anatomy, but certainly doesn't cut or treat wounds in a doctor's office or hospital.

"The photographs taken at autopsy should be copied to illustrate the position of the wounds." (I HSCA 146) This all seems like an unnecessary step. The autopsy photos would have done a much better job at this and removed a lot of interpretive speculation. If you recall, Harold Rydberg made illustrations of the wounds in JFK by Dr. Humes explaining what he wanted in the sketch, without even looking at the autopsy photos as they went along. This is grossly irresponsible. Humes lied to Rydberg, who argued both strenuously and vociferously against the entire process years later. Dox at least looked at the autopsy photos and proceeded to copy and trace them for the committee; but was told to place a wound in President Kennedy's cowlick area by using a picture from a pathology book that Dr. Baden had helped write years earlier after the closing of the Clark Panel. Dox, unlike Rydberg, would never argue in that same vein, unfortunately.

The Warren Commission never wanted to put the autopsy photos into evidence and neither did the HSCA, because to do so would mean you would have to print and include them in your report. In other words, put them into evidence.

I'm not sure what the HSCA thought would happen by putting the illustrations of Ida Dox into evidence. The Dox drawings are the least graphic of the autopsy photos that we know about, but they still don't hide what little of graphic nature they show. The Warren Commission could get away with it, because nobody was going to see the photographs, and that was a fault that remained in place for years. When the HSCA chose drawings, instead of the actual photos, they were mostly identical to a couple of the autopsy photos in their detail, though things were left out and cleaned up a bit. Nothing had changed fourteen years after the Warren Commission, as neither the Commission nor the House Select Committee on Assassinations, to their shame, put the autopsy photographs into evidence. The difference is the HSCA could no longer get away with it, since the autopsy photos would soon be in the public forum. This was inevitable.

Dox told how she made the illustrations and never hinted that they differed in any way from the actual photographs. I am sure at some point, that someone told Ida Dox exactly what to do with reference to the red spot in Fox-3, the back of the head autopsy photograph.

In fact, some of the records obtained from the National Archives do everything, except come right out and say just that. Does this make Ida culpable? Probably. I am sure she was just doing what she was told and may have been told it would illustrate what the medical panel was trying to explain. She is less culpable than Baden, to be sure.

If Mr. Purdy and other members of Congress would have had copies of the autopsy photos in front of them and side-by-side with the Dox illustrations of the same photos, it would have been eerily obvious to them. Nobody on the HSCA wanted Fox-3 and the Dox drawing of Fox-3 even remotely close to each other. The comparison would have been embarrassing for the committee, especially the forensic pathology panel. Why?

Because the photos and the drawings by Ms. Dox would easily demonstrate the differences between the two. The differences would have been recognized immediately, particularly with reference to the wound in the cowlick, not discernable in the photograph, but manifestly obvious in the drawing.

> Mr. Purdy: "Ms. Dox, prior to today, did you have the opportunity to review the enlargements of your drawings to ensure that they are accurate?"
>
> Ms. Dox: "Yes, I did. I looked at them very, very carefully and they are my drawings except that they are **photographically enhanced**. They haven't been altered in any way" (I HSCA 148)

I can think of one! Her answer concerning accuracy was that she compared them to make sure that they were in fact her drawings and if they had been rehabilitated in any way. She had to know this wasn't true, because she says that they were photographically enhanced. Is she referring to the cowlick area in Fox-3. We don't know exactly, but this would have been the time to say she had in fact done just that! The documents I received from the National Archives indicate she did enhance at least the back of the head photograph. Mr. Purdy should have pressed the point and asked her to clarify.

The Warren Commission and The House Select Committee on Assassinations both deceived the American public when it came to being forthright about the autopsy photos and the medical evidence in general. It is an embarrassment to read and attempt to work through the subterfuge, duplicity and fraud.

The HSCA agreed not to use the actual photos in an act of sensitivity, but to use *identical* sketches made by a medical illustrator. I am not sure how this would have put the Kennedy family in a state of ease. The President's image had already been displayed in death and on television, three years earlier, which is extremely graphic in live action. Whether it was a photograph or a rendering by a medical illustrator, it is much ado about nothing. Again, the American public had already seen the clear nature, leaving nothing to the imagination, of the Zapruder film on national television in March of 1975. How would this have shocked them?

But the real problem is that the autopsy photo that Dox copied of the back of the head, and the resulting sketch she made are ages apart. Ida Dox deceptively depicted the rear head entrance wound, so finally, while the inquiring public was finally allowed to see the actual wounds fifteen years after the event, they were deceptively illustrated once again. Who knows what she was thinking, as I am sure she did whatever Dr. Baden told her.

The decision not to use the original photographs was probably made by the Committee members. An arrangement was reached that they would publish the drawings, but only those deemed essential. The Dox drawing of the head wound was withheld from publication and it was not in the hundreds of pages of her file I received from the National Archives, or in the HSCA volumes. It was shown, however, on the 1988 NOVA documentary on the Kennedy assassination.

She also responded to Purdy's question by stating that "the photographs that were selected were the ones that best showed the injuries" (I HSCA 146). Ms. Dox said she copied four photographs: the back of the head (Fox-3), the upper back (Fox-5), the side of the head (Fox-4) [*never shown during public testimony*], and the front of the neck (Fox-1). Key photos were clearly withheld, some say on grounds of taste. They were examined by the forensics panel and other experts, but not displayed or published. The top of the head photo (Fox-6 & 7) was not chosen. As stated, the side of the head photo drawn by Ms. Dox was not shown during public testimony either. She was asked to draw the head wound photo (Fox-4), but when they saw it, they decided not to publish it. The autopsy photograph, upon which it was based, had already been seen by the committee before they re-looked at it, so I cannot imagine what they expected to see.

The back of the head photo (Fox-3) was shown during the public testimony of Ms. Dox. The only problem is that the alleged entrance wound in the cowlick area is much more visible in her drawing, than on the original Fox-3 photograph. Conversely, her drawing of the back wound (Fox-5) omits the possibility of an entrance wound that has been alleged by some critics, not to mention that his back was cleaned up quite a bit. Whether there are other possibilities concerning Fox-5, it should have at least been drawn. It also places the back wound much too high. The autopsy face sheet, as did his suit coat and shirt, as did Dr. Humes, places the back wound in the upper right posterior thorax at about the level of the third thoracic vertebra, which would be approximately five and three-eighths inches below the crest of the shoulder. The Dox wound appears much too high.

When Mr. Purdy asked how she copied the photographs, Ms. Dox stated that she did it by "placing a piece of tracing paper directly on the photograph, then all the details were very carefully traced…so that no detail could be overlooked or omitted or altered in any way" (I HSCA 147). As noted, the upper entry head wound was altered. Period. Perjury, most likely, but I really believe it is more being afraid to disagree with Dr. Baden when he told her what he wanted. Hard to tell. Things were omitted, especially on the back wound (Fox-5), where obvious detail is missing, and also on the back of the head wound (Fox-3), where the alleged cowlick area wound is much clearer and pronounced in her drawings than in the autopsy photographs themselves, because, as I stated earlier, there isn't a bullet wound in the cowlick area! Isn't this, again, much ado about nothing? This could have been avoided, knowing that the drawings are no substitute for the photos. The original photos should have been available to researchers and the public alike, at least as soon as the Warren Commission closed up shop, but legally they haven't been released to this day.

Purdy goes on to say that Ms. Dox made other drawings to illustrate the conclusions of the forensic pathology panel. We are not exactly sure what these other drawings are, only to assume they are in the Committee's files, or ones that show the brain and the one that shows the semi-skeletal structure of JFK and his head, demonstrating the path of the bullet.

The release of the Assassination Records Review Board medical materials did not tell us any more on this particular subject. I don't recall this issue even being addressed, in reference to Ms. Dox. The truth is, in relationship to Ms. Dox, the ARRB made no difference at all. I'm frankly amazed that nobody at the ARRB asked the obvious question: Why are the Dox drawings and the photographs from which they are exactly made, so different? Sadly, Ms. Dox was not questioned by the ARRB, and she could have been since she didn't pass away until 2013.

In her next to the last question, Ms. Dox says that a frame of "film taken during the motorcade was photographed and the outline of the President's head was used so that the ... head of the President ... in the position that the medical panel decided was necessary" (I HSCA 147-148). They were probably doing what they thought was adequate, but left themselves open to immense criticism, just as their predecessor, the Warren Commission did.

Ms. Dox worked for the Committee, under the direction of Professor Blakey. In that capacity, she was assigned to assist the Committee by preparing drawings from the autopsy photos for possible publication. She was working under Blakey's direction and Dr. Baden, or perhaps Andrew Purdy's, since he guided most of the medical aspects of the case. Ultimately, Dr. Baden made the call on what Ms. Dox drew and, in some cases, how to draw it. As you listen and read the testimony of Ida Dox, you can only reflect about what should have been asked.

I contacted Ms. Dox in October of 1999. I had two conversations with her on the telephone. It all started with a question I had regarding HSCA Exhibit F-302, which was a drawing of President Kennedy's brain, that was put into evidence during the testimony of Dr. Humes. What followed was both puzzling and frustrating. I will go into detail about what Ms. Dox said about the sketching of JFK's brain, parts of her testimony that she now denies ever saying, enhancement of the wounds that she drew for the Committee (which has to do with some correspondence between her and Dr. Baden that I requested and received from The National Archives and published in this chapter), and other sundry matters, some of which I have already briefly mentioned.

I prepared for my conversations with Ms. Dox by reading every document I received from the National Archives concerning her. There was a sense of discovery, but more so of clarification. I'm not one who looks for a demon under every shingle, nor is it my purpose to attempt to discredit someone who appears on the surface to be a nice lady who was just following orders and instructions. There were some things that did seem a bit odd, however, and other things that I still don't understand as I write this. The following information is based on those two telephone conversations I had with Ms. Dox.

In the first conversation I had with here on October 14, 1999, I asked her the following questions:

Question #1: How many photographs were you shown?

When I asked Mrs. Dox this question on the phone she quickly replied, "I can't remember." This is intriguing. If she had been shown 75 photos, okay, she can't recall, but she testified before the HSCA that it was four, at least that is how many she drew. She doesn't seem to be guessing before the HSCA during her public testimony. I don't care how many zillion wounds she has illustrated, as one of the first humans on the planet to see those autopsy photos of JFK, you would think she could remember the number. Maybe not perfectly, but certainly not "I don't remember." Even an estimate would have been nice.

Questions #2: Were you ever shown a photograph of the brain?

She emphatically stated, "no!" This first surfaced for me when I noticed HSCA exhibit F-302 in David Lifton's book, "*Best Evidence.*" During Dr. Humes testimony, exhibit F-302 is introduced, with no data whatsoever. It is said to be a drawing of the brain. There are two kinds of representations in Lifton's book. In the cases of the actual line drawings, they are represented in full, the throat wound cropped so as not to show the face. The brain drawing, however, is in mid-text, so that may be why it is different from the others. It also has no signature on it. The other Dox drawings are reproduced in full and have a signature in the lower corner. It may have been a simple matter of a tracing of a tracing, or some sort, so it could be reproduced in text, without going to the photo section, which is different paper.

The only available rendering of the brain, however, absent the photographs, is the drawing/tracing created by Ida Dox, and I have already noted my criticisms of her efforts. In her brain illustration, the left cerebral hemisphere is intact, while the right cerebral hemisphere resembles a swirling pattern, with some disruption, but seemingly no real loss of brain tissue.

The two lobes of the cerebellum are intact and unremarkable. That flies in the face of the doctors from Parkland, who testified to seeing cerebellum extruding from the large wound in the back of the head, and here, we are presented with no cerebellum damage and no large wound in the back of the head.

The problem with the brain is extremely difficult to grasp to coincide with the official version. I now defer to the subsequent named documentaries mentioned in the following paragraphs of this section. The night of the autopsy it supposedly weighed 1500 grams, when the average adult male's brain is closer to c.1330 grams. This is compounded by the fact that several individuals testified that c. half of it was missing when removed from JFK on the night of the autopsy. It was seen by Clint Hill, who was staring into the back of President Kennedy's head on a speedy, several mile ride to Parkland hospital and said there was nothing he could see inside of his skull. He said this as recently as 2021 in the documentary, "*JFK Unsolved: The Real Conspiracies.*"

FBI agent Francis O'Neill said there was a massive wound in the back of JFK's head and that at least half of his brain was missing when he saw it being removed at the autopsy. Mortician Tom Robinson also claimed there was a massive hole in the back of JFK's head. Dr. Mantik did measurements of the brain from the x-rays taken the night of the autopsy, when he visited the National Archives and his conclusions were that one-third of JFK's brain was missing. This is what is seen from the x-rays of JFK, but the Dox drawings show a much more intact brain, disrupted, but not missing one-third of its mass.

As stated on the documentary *JFK: Destiny Betrayed*, ARRB medical consultant, Robert Kirschner said that when he saw alleged pictures of JFK's brain, that it looked like a brain that was very-well fixed, because it was all grey, with no pink at all and looked like it had been fixed in formulin for about 2-3 weeks. Problem: JFK's brain was examined 2-3 days after he was killed.

The logic: JFK's brain could not have been this disrupted by a single shot to the back of the head by Lee Harvey Oswald or anyone else. So, you replace JFK's brain, what was left of it, with a phony brain that isn't as disrupted to retain the official version. The autopsy was performed at Bethesda Naval Hospital, which was a teaching hospital, and to quote Dr. Michael Chesser, "there would not have been a shortage of brains there to retrieve to support the lone assassin theory." Disturbing.

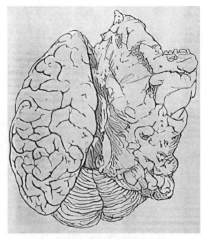

HSCA Exhibit F-302

Question #3: Were the wounds enhanced for the sake of clarity?

Her response, "No, of course not." This is interesting. At Wecht 2003, I asked Dr. Baden about this and was told that Dox was given other gunshot wounds to draw in order to enhance the visibility. You have to look for something even resembling a wound in the Fox-3 photograph. It looks more like a blood droplet, but not a bullet wound.

He told me that Dox had been given other photos (see later in the text for the documents), of other individuals with wounds, in order that she would be able to highlight JFK's wound, so people wouldn't miss where the actual head wound was. Other researchers have talked with Dr. Baden about this and received similar responses.

What follows after this paragraph is a copy of the Dox drawing of Fox-3 and the actual Fox-3 autopsy photo and then a few pages of documents I received from the National Archives, both of which were sent to Ida Dox by the HSCA, including *"you can do much better," Ida*, from Michael Baden. How can you do "much better" than the autopsy photos you are directly looking at and tracing; or, is "much better" referring to placing a bullet wound where there isn't one in the cowlick area? Ida Dox lied to me on the phone when she said she wasn't given any pictures to use to enhance what wasn't there. Here are some of the documents I got from the Archives, after I requested every document they had concerning Ida Dox. Unlike the Ida Dox drawing, the actual wound is not visible in Fox-3, and no other photographs show it either.

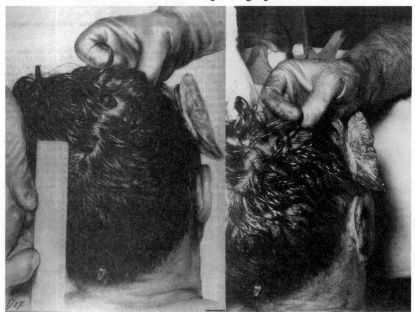

    Dox drawing of Fox-3   Actual Fox-3 autopsy photograph

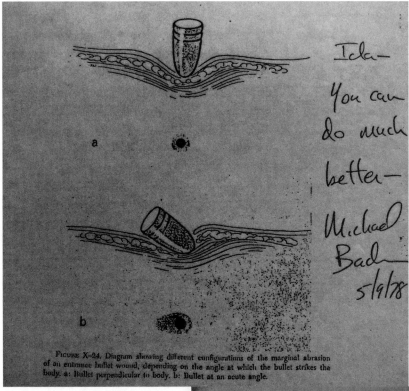

Ida—
You can
do much
better—
Michael
Baden
5/9/78

FIGURE X-24. Diagram showing different configurations of the marginal abrasion of an entrance bullet wound, depending on the angle at which the bullet strikes the body. a: Bullet perpendicular to body. b: Bullet at an acute angle.

Ida—"You can do much better"—
Michael Baden.

Bullet wound to the head from the pathology book written by Baden, et al.

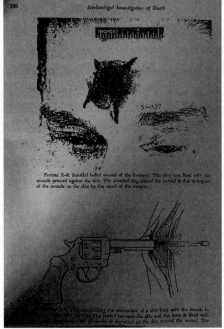

The Forensic Pathology Panel of the House Select Committee was so thoroughly caught up in their findings, that the upper artifact, the red spot, and what they said was the actual entry wound, led to their failure on how badly they had been duped.

This is critical to the ongoing investigation and needs to be considered again. Originally, the HSCA worked from medical illustrations, done by medical illustrator Ida Dox. Unfortunately, Ms. Dox, who was allowed to commit perjury before the House Select Committee, altered the wound that some have identified as simply a red spot or droplet.

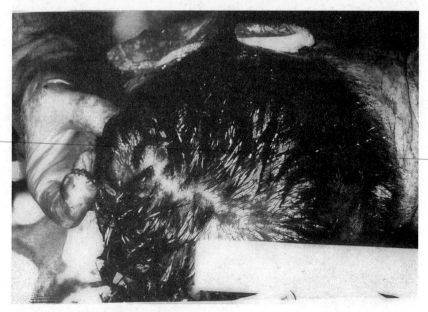

Fox-3

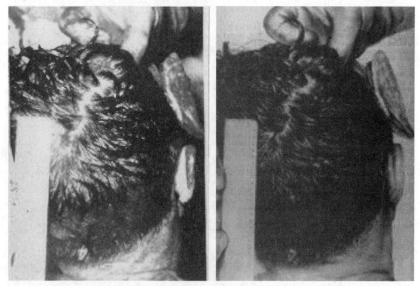

Fox-3 Fox-3 Dox Drawing

KENNEDY

006436

OUTSIDE CONTACT REPORT

DATE 3/20/78 TIME 10:41

I. Identifying Information:

Name *Michael Baden* Telephone 212/mu 4 – 1600

Address *N. Y. Med. Examiner Office*

Type of Contact: X Telephone
                    — Person

II. Summary of Contact:

Called to remind Dr. Baden that he
agreed to obtain various photographs of
typical bullet wounds in people and clothing —
as well as x-rays, for our medical report.
Said 5x7 photos would be fine,
detailing entrance and exit wounds of back,
head skull leveling and clothing.
(Re: Connally x-ray — new x-rays far
more helpful than enhancing old, poor x-ray.
If we can't do new ones, then we should
reconsider doing enhancement of old ones.)
Also asked him to prepare x-rays of
entrance + exit wounds of skulls.
Asked him to try to finish photos + x-rays in 2 weeks.

III. Recommended Follow-up (if any):

Signature: *Andy Purdy*

Purdy asking for photos of typical bullet wounds. Keep in mind, this is in the Dox materials sent to me from the National Archives.

Any assessment of the photographs shows nothing even slightly comparable to what Dox drew. I often have copies of the autopsy picture known as Fox-3 and also of the Dox illustration of that same autopsy picture at my public talks. When some of the audience comes up front to look at them, it usually produces some kind of audible gasp. They look and look; but can never find a bullet wound in Fox-3, because it isn't there.

Flanagan to Baden, asking for photos of typical in-shoot wounds. Why?

They then gravitate to the Dox drawing and immediately see the scam. Then I put them closer together, side-by-side and then they seem to get either angry or annoyed.

Now they can see up close and personal that something sinister was going on with the medical evidence. The alteration becomes obvious.

Ida Dox was given the autopsy photographs and was requested to make sketches for the HSCA, a procedure in itself that calls into question the sanity of the people doing it, as if a drawing of gore is not almost as unpleasant as a photo of gore.

The reader is invited, strongly urged, to view the Fox-3 autopsy photo and then view the same cowlick area in the Dox (Fox-3) drawings that I have placed in this book. You will be surprised if you have never done this before.

What is cited as an artifact, and not by any means proof of an entry wound in the Fox photograph, becomes a glaring bullet hole thanks to Ida Dox, who was given additional photos as stated, showing bullet wounds of other people and not of John Kennedy, so that she could highlight and forge the JFK sketches. There is no doubt in my mind that the reason for moving the back of the head wound four inches higher is to explain the massive wound in JFK's right temporal area of his skull. If you move the wound up, then you have a seemingly perfect inshoot-outshoot scenario. If not, you have to explain how a bullet traveling downward from sixty feet in the air and behind can emerge on the upper right side of Kennedy's temporal bone. Possible, but highly improbable.

The explanation I can assert is what I have already said in chapter one concerning Governor Connally, that a second head shot at c. Z-327, 7/10ths of a second after Z-313, explains this precisely, and if so, then there was no need to invent a head wound in the cowlick area, as Z-327 explains it perfectly. What is disheartening is that chapter one on Governor Connelly documents that the HSCA was suggesting a shot c. Z-327, but then the Committee wasn't renewed (as it was a Select, not a Standing committee) and the data became inactive.

That alone brings into question the honesty of the entire HSCA investigation, and the charge against Dox is not a pointless one. The question then becomes two-fold: first, why, (excepting the necessity to maintain the lone-assassin fiction) was the wound altered in order to make it obvious to any John Q citizen viewing the Dox drawing and Fox-3 autopsy photo, when trained pathologists could not and did not identify it from the photograph which Dox claimed she copied exactly?

Secondly, whose decision was it to alter the wound and whose decision was it not to make the obvious comparison between the actual photo and the altered drawing during the HSCA hearings? Baden seems to be candidate number 1.

A little background on Baden and the Clark Panel is probably appropriate at this point. In the late 1960's the public was screaming for a reinvestigation. David Slawson at the Department of Justice wrote a memo to Ramsey Clark explaining that if they don't do something the conspiracy fringe will get Congress to reopen the whole thing. This is also happening at the same time as the Garrison investigation, which scared the intelligence community, so they needed to calm the storms in Louisiana. Slawson suggests an investigation limited to the medical evidence and so the Clark panel is born. The Clark Panel relocates all the wounds, four inches higher on the head and four inches lower on the back. Why? If left where they were in the autopsy report, then Oswald couldn't have done it. The plan succeeds and the public is quieted. Meanwhile, the prominent pathologists, having been thrown together to make up the Clark Panel, then decide to write a pathology book. Ramsey Clark writes its foreword. A young, inexperienced pathologist named Michael Baden, is asked to contribute to the book as well. It's not much; but associating his name with theirs launches his career. Michael Baden, along with Russell Fisher, (who served on the Clark Panel) and Charles Petty, John Coe and George Loquvam (all of whom will serve with Baden on the HSCA forensic pathology panel), later contribute to a book entitled, *Forensic pathology: A Handbook for Pathologists.*

Ten years later, Baden is asked to head the HSCA's medical panel. He insists he not serve on it alone, so there is no question of impropriety; so he fills it up with friends, save a lone critic named Dr. Cyril Wecht. Before they would ever meet, Baden went in to examine the autopsy materials. He then sat down and wrote a memo which echoes every point made in the Clark Panel report. He moved the wounds up on JFK's skull and down on JFK's back, to exactly the same points the Clark Panel had chosen.

At the first meeting of the medical panel (Baden is the only panelist to have seen the autopsy materials at this point, though Wecht had gotten permission to see them in the early seventies), he presents them with his findings and calls for a vote to see if another meeting of the panel is necessary. Wecht says yes. The record does not reflect how the others voted but plans for the other panelists to see the materials were not initiated for several weeks.

This brings us back to Dox and Baden. Dox is permitted to see the photos and to make a set of drawings, which she denied to me on the telephone (though this is exactly what she stated in her public testimony in September of 1978). She then leaves them for Baden to approve. Baden sees the drawings and calls Andy Purdy, who writes a memo to himself that says, "get a photo of a typical wound of entry." (In another memo dated 4/24/78, Purdy states that he needs to remind Baden to get wound comparison photos and X-rays). The next document in the record is a photocopy of a page out of the pathology book Baden and the Clark Panelists wrote. At the top of the photo of a tiny bullet wound to the head, Baden wrote, "Ida you can do much better." Again, and as I stated earlier, I am not sure how you can do better than the original autopsy photos. So, *better*? In what sense. Location? The wound itself? Quite baffling, if not disturbing.

On October 28, 1999, I called Ida Dox for the second time. She had hung up on me at the end our first conversation. This time the conversation lasted a bit longer and was much more detailed. The following questions were asked Ida Dox at this time:

Question #1: Did you see color or black and white photographs?

She quickly said, "Color." The color photos certainly show the wounds better, but apparently not as good as the Dox tracing. You would also think that black and white would be better to trace from. The fact that a lay observer can tell in a second that the tracings are accurate, except for the wounds, should raise questions immediately. The aforementioned data, along with the Baden and Purdy memos speak volumes to this point.

Question #2: I asked her again about how many photographs she saw.

This time she got defensive. I simply reminded her that my previous notes stated that she could not recall, but that she had stated in her testimony that she had drawn four. I was seeking clarification – and thought perhaps there was a possibility she had been shown others. I was very polite and was genuinely not trying to trick her or confront her in any way. She was silent and so I proceeded.

Question #3: I asked her if security was tight while viewing the autopsy photographs in the National Archives.

She indicated that security was very tight. I was reminded that RFK was in a panic that such stuff would go public. It was difficult enough that the Dox drawings went public, but something had to. Her public testimony suggests she had worked from some kind of originals while being watched at the Archives. This led me to the next obvious question.

Question #4: Did she have a set of autopsy photographs made, so as not to take up the Archive's employees' time?

At this point she got very defensive, especially when I read her public testimony where she says this is exactly what had transpired. I was lucky the conversation went any further at all, as she was not happy. I was not accusing her of anything, still only seeking clarification. Her testimony, again, indicates she was given knock-off copies to use outside the Archives, as she added detail like Humes' gloves, so as not to keep the Archives busy.

Question #5: I then asked her again if she had drawn F-302, which is JFK's brain?

She simply said, "I can't remember." I don't care if it has been twenty years plus, you can't tell me that you wouldn't remember drawing a picture of the brain, which just happens to be that of the President of the United States! The absurdity of this is beyond belief. Exhibit F-302 does come up during Dr. Baden's testimony. He uses the drawing of the brain, which he says that Ida Dox drew, to show the intact nature of the cerebellum, thus attempting to prove that Dr. Humes et al, could not possibly be correct in locating the entrance wound to the rear of JFK's head in the area of the external occipital protuberance. It wasn't until Dr. Humes' testimony that F-302 was formally entered into evidence.

During the session at the end of each testimony, when everyone is given five minutes to ask questions if they want to, Mr. Fithian asks about the possibility of metal fragments being in the brain. In Baden's testimony he displayed F-302, and says that in the right, front area side of the brain there was an oblong, blue discoloration, but that it was not a metal object. He stated that the Forensic Pathology Panel determined that it was blood vessels that had been sheered away. Baden went on to explain that there were many pictures taken of the brain, and that some had toothpicks in the damaged part for identification purposes by the doctors at the autopsy.

It still, however, doesn't explain why Ms. Dox told me that she never saw any photographs of JFK's brain, let alone draw them for the committee. Dr. Baden said there were several pictures of the brain, and that Ms. Dox drew at least one for the committee to illustrate for the Forensic Pathology Panel that the cerebellum was not injured because of the rear entrance head shot to President Kennedy (I HSCA 304).

Question #6: Did the photographs of JFK's neck wound show the face as well?

She told me that the pictures did show his face and that there had been some talk of blurring the face. The tracings, however, do not show the face of the President. That was all she addressed with this question.

Question #7: I again asked her if she was shown other photographs of wounds in order to enhance the ones on her tracings/drawings?

She got very defensive and refused to talk any further. In fact, she said, "I don't think I want to talk about this any further." I again tried to assure her that I was not attempting to confront her, only clarify what I had discovered from other researchers and documents from the National Archives. This didn't seem to quell her anger, but she suggested I contact Professor Blakey, which I did. The data from the first conversation has already dealt with this question in full, but nonetheless, I thought I would give her another chance to verify what I had documentation for from the National Archives. I still refuse to believe you would forget doing something like this, especially in reference to the President of the United States. I don't care how much time has passed, certain events in our lives are indelibly engrained in our psyche. This event would have to at least be up for a possible nomination.

Question #8: I asked if there were any other medical illustrators besides her?

She told me that she was the only one. In fact, she also worked for the Committee on the tracings/drawings concerning Dr. Martin Luther King, Jr. She received $16,000.00, not counting $125.00 per day, plus expenses for services rendered. This also included appearing as an expert during the public hearings. She was not required to write any reports, only that her medical illustrations would appear in the Committee's final report. She spent 125 and one-half days consulting and providing services. The final tally, financially speaking, would be: $31,625, plus expenses. That's not bad money for 125 days' worth of work, especially in 1978.

Question #9: I asked her how long it took to make the illustrations?

She was kind enough to explain that it took a long time, months as far as the entire process, and that it was very tedious work.

There were some things that were missed in her public testimony, that was gone over with her in her practice questions beforehand, which I still have copies of from the National Archives. She was supposed to mention that she was to duplicate the autopsy photographs which show the key wound areas, reconstructions of wound areas with internal structures, and illustrate what happens to soft tissue and bones when they are struck by bullets. Most of these can be seen in Volume I of the HSCA Hearings when Dr. Baden is testifying.

She also stated in her practice questions that blood on the skin and blood on the gloved hands were removed, as well as background details. She stated in her public testimony that she worked very closely with the medical panel, especially Dr. Michael Baden. Based on the previously mentioned discoveries from the Archives, her statement was only the tip of the iceberg.

All in all, I found Ida Dox to be somewhat reticent to talk about the issues that I brought up to her. She was kind and cordial, but obviously on edge during the two conversations. She was most irritated by the question of enhancing any of the wounds, but I was never aggressive or combative, only attempting to clarify what I had discovered. I was told by one researcher, in reference to my questioning her about whether she drew the brain, that it is hard to believe that something called the Dox drawing and entered into evidence (or at least referred to constantly) during the hearings, that were nationally televised, could now be credibly disclaimed as not being her work. He told me to think about what I was suggesting. I never suggested she didn't draw F-302 (the brain), only wondered why she didn't sign off on it, when she did on every other illustration. I also was puzzled as to why she would deny something like this; I wasn't implying something sinister, but her responses certainly did.

I was also told that I was probably running into a simple failure of memory, after two decades. I was cautioned not to go down this path and get involved in a hypothesis alleging major forgery of evidence, when all I had was a simple error of memory.

I really did appreciate the words of caution and took them seriously. I generally respect my colleagues in this field and take their words thoughtfully. I wasn't implying forgery of evidence, or even questioning whether she had drawn the illustration of F-302; again, only seeking clarification of the data I had before me. It made me question the integrity of Dr. Baden, more than that of Ida Dox. She was merely following orders and protocol; the others, well, I'll leave that up to each individual researcher to decide.

A Final Comment: The thirteen questions they asked Ms. Dox is nothing but procedural, chain of evidence testimony and makes no statement about that which was under scrutiny, except that it is frightfully dishonest, and certainly Ida Dox had to know it when she was testifying.

The first question that needed to be asked was: *Why were so-called exact drawings or tracings necessary to be used in place of the actual photographs?*

There is absolutely no rational answer to this question. It does not seem like it was done out of respect for the President or the President's family, because the drawings are just as graphic as the original photographs in some areas.

Certain background material had been removed from the tracings. In the drawing which shows the circular bone extending from the right-front scalp, the inference from the drawing would be that the photo would have been taken with the President's body posed, sitting up.

In actuality, the body was lying on its left side. In the photo, one of the pathologists looms up from Kennedy's side as the pathologist is standing and Kennedy is on his side on the examining table.

If there can be one reason attributed to the use of drawings, it was to certify what the House Select Medical Panel wanted. I have written elsewhere that a number of researchers have noted the difference between the photographs, particularly the back of the head photo, with its absence of any visible wound, to the Dox drawing, which clearly showed an obvious entry wound in the cowlick.

The difference has to be placed in time perspective. As Dox noted in her testimony, she was under observation all the time while she was working at the National Archives with the originals of the photos. Yet she could have access to copies of those photos, to complete the tracings of the doctors' hands, or rulers, in HSCA rooms.

In 1978, those photographs had never been seen by the general public, and an individual could only get into the National Archives to view them, if you were a medical doctor.

Thus, the first time the wounds were truly seen in some manner other than the Zapruder film or the absurd Rydberg drawings, contrived for the Warren Commission, were the Dox drawings.

And therein lies the reason for the drawings. With the Fox photographs in my possession, and other researches too for some time and prints available in quantity, it was clear that the back of the head photo and the back of the head drawing were very different.

From here, it was now a matter of forcing Commander Humes to change his testimony to reflect that the cowlick entry was the correct site, and not the original autopsy finding, located four inches lower. Humes refused to change his findings when he testified before the Medical Panel, but he sold out altogether when he was on television in front of the HSCA itself. Flannagan, Purdy, and Baden were all part of a collusion to cover up the medical evidence in this case, especially the wound in the back of JFK's head, which they moved upward four inches. The documents strongly suggest this

Humes moved both wounds—the head and the back—approximately ten centimeters or four inches. Reprehensible.

05

DR. LOWELL LEVINE

SEPTEMBER 7, 1978

On September 7, 1978, Dr. Lowell Levine testified before the HSCA in Washington, D.C.

D r. Lowell Levine received his DDS degree from the New York University College of Dentistry in 1963. As Mr. Blakey stated in his narration, "Dr. Levine has been in charge of identification of a large number of mass disasters, both in the United States and abroad" (I HSCA 148). He was summoned to verify whether the autopsy X-rays were actually of President Kennedy.

There has always been speculation about the autopsy X-rays and photographs. Experts on both sides seemingly state with the same amount of confidence and certitude that the X-rays are either authentic or inauthentic. Certainly, it would behoove all of us to go directly to the individual who took them the night of the autopsy, Jerrol Custer. His reflections and reactions to the controversy are candid and important.

In recent years, Dr. David Mantik has viewed the originals at the National Archives, and has posited tampering and alteration of localized portions of the lateral X-ray. He interviewed John Ebersole, M.D. on December 2, 1992, who was the Navy medical officer in charge of radiology during the autopsy of JFK, though the actual X-rays were taken by Jerrol Custer, who was an enlisted medical technician. You can read the transcript of Mantik's phone interview with John Ebersole on his website, *The Mantik View*, which I highly recommend. When Dr. Mantik brought up the mysterious 6.5mm fragment on the AP X-ray, Dr. Ebersole shut down the conversation immediately. The two would never talk again. Ebersole died shortly thereafter.

All Levine was expected to do was to verify whether the X-rays were of JFK. For that purpose, a dental comparison was sufficient. Alteration is another issue, and not within the expertise of Levine's field of study. I certainly think they are JFK's X-rays, but tampering is a whole separate issue. There have been all kinds of claims regarding the X-rays, some very far-fetched, but the questions Dr. Mantik raises about the x-rays being tampered with are both serious and germane to the Kennedy case.

> Mr. Purdy: "Do X-rays exist showing the teeth and jaws of President Kennedy taken prior to the autopsy X-ray?"
>
> Dr. Levine: "Yes sir, they do."
>
> Mr. Purdy: "Where are they?"
>
> Dr. Levine: "There were 22 such films in the custody of the National Archives." (I HSCA 149)

He testified there was "absolutely no question" that the X-rays in evidence were of the skull of the late President (I HSCA 152). His report stated, "It is further my opinion that the unique and individual dental and hard tissue characteristics which may be interpreted from Autopsy films 1, 2, 3 could not be simulated." (I HSCA 173)

The dental X-rays of President Kennedy, even while alive, were padlocked inside the National Archives; close in geographical proximity are the X-rays used for dental comparison and appraisal, which were taken at Bethesda Naval Hospital.

When Levine compares a couple of fillings that are seen in the autopsy X-rays of JFK, one that is W-shaped and another that is kidney-shaped, with pre-assassination dental X-rays, the evidence seems irrefutable. No one, at least to my knowledge, has ever seriously advanced the theory that the autopsy X-ray is someone other than President Kennedy.

Again, Dr. Mantik, who suggests localized tampering, comments on the possible use of double overlays to mask the severity of the rear portion.

The following is a summary of statements Dr. Mantik has made concerning the x-rays: the x-ray really shows the area where the plate is fixed. This might be an oversimplification, but it is where it all begins. When you put a plate under the left side of JFK's head (his left side, no wound), the X-ray shows a solid mass in the rear. Had they put the plate under the right side, a different story. Some believe that the frontal X-ray is far more revealing than originally thought. As most people look at it, they immediately conclude massive damage to the face, not shown in the autopsy photographs. The massive hole is there, as are radiating fractures. The X-ray plate was put under the back of JFK's head, so that may be showing the huge hole in the rear and the accompanying radiating fractures that are visible in the lateral X-ray.

Dr. Mantik has been troubled, however, for some time concerning the 6.5 mm metallic object on President John F. Kennedy's anterior-posterior (AP) skull X-ray. It was not seen during the autopsy on November 22, 1963, but first appeared in 1968 with the release of the Clark Panel Report. Since there is scant, if any, evidence that links Oswald to the 6.5 mm Carcano rifle (CE-139) and since any commonality of bullets in the area of neutron activation analysis (more on this later) has been refuted by metallurgist Eric Randich, the mysterious 6.5 mm fragment that appears on the AP x-ray is not just suspicious, but criminal, not to mention a little too convenient. It is hard to believe no one noticed this the night of the autopsy or mentioned it in the autopsy report. Unless it wasn't there on the night of the autopsy.

Look at the lateral X-ray on the next page. There are radiating fractures that begin exactly where Humes, et al, said. There are also radiating fractures where the HSCA said. To me, however, the lateral X-ray, showing the skullcap displaced, suggests that those upper fractures are where the bullet left, in the upper back of the head (as so many witnesses said). The frontal X-ray shows crossing fractures, which is literally an

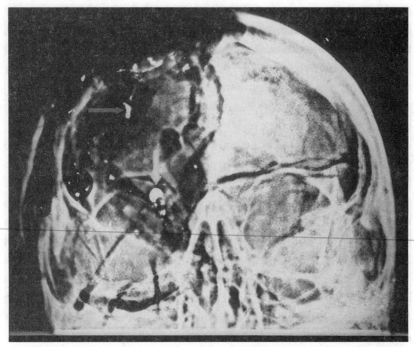

Anterior-posterior (AP) skull X-ray of JFK with the 6.5 mm metallic object

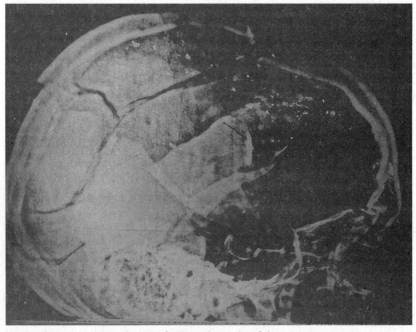

Lateral x-ray of JFK on the night of the autopsy

impossibility. If a rock hits the front window of your car, the result will be a sort of spider web fracturing and radiating outward. Then a second rock hits that same car window twelve inches away. Another hole, and more spiderwebbing, but the webs will stop where they intersect, and cannot radiate through each other. But JFK's X-rays do, which is at the least peculiar, if not dubious.

The lateral x-ray also shows the top of JFK's skull peppered with tiny metallic fragments, the larger ones in the rear and the smaller ones in the front of his skull, indicating a shot from the front, because the larger fragments would make their way to the rear of the skull due to their weight and size, while the smaller fragments would not go as far for the opposite reason, small and they don't weigh as much.

Dr. Levine was simply brought in to verify the authenticity of the X-rays. Let us be clear. He did that, but that still doesn't address possible tampering. He was subsequently used by Gerald Posner to attempt to verify the remains of Dr. Josef Mengele. He has been used to verify the skeletal remains of victims of airplane crashes. He is highly esteemed and anyone who deals with the medical evidence has to address the findings of Dr. Levine.

As an aside that may or not be relevant, Dr. Levine was a consultant to Dr. Michael Baden when he was the New York Chief Medical Examiner in New York City.

06

CALVIN MCCAMY
SEPTEMBER 7, 12, 14, 15 1978

On September 7, 12, 14, and 15 of 1978, Mr. Calvin McCamy testified before the HSCA in Washington, D.C.

Calvin McCamy received a BS degree in chemical engineering and an MS degree in physics from the University of Minnesota. Mr. McCamy is a fellow of the Optical Society of America, the Society of Motion Picture and Television Engineers and the Society of Photographic Scientists and Engineers (I HSCA 148). McCamy was asked to testify on behalf of the authenticity of the autopsy photographs.

McCamy verified that what he examined hadn't been physically altered. That is a very limited finding, and doesn't address whether the pho-

100

tographs (color transparencies, not negatives) were the originals or not, as the latter finding would be beyond the scope of what he was doing.

As I mentioned in another chapter, with the help of Martin Shackleford and other people I consulted, I have been able to view the front (neck wound), back and top of the head photo stereoscopically, and see no indication of oddities. I say this, not because I have a particular area of expertise in this field, but I have learned from others who are far more competent than I in the arena of photography. They have been quite helpful, especially Martin.

To alter photos is not easily performed and difficult to alter photos so well, that a stereo view wouldn't show an anomaly, but not impossible, especially in the digital age. But these photos, you will recall, were examined stereoscopically more than twenty years ago, when it would have been much more difficult to convincingly alter them. It is easier to alter a photo in two dimensions than it is to alter a stereo pair in three dimensions. It is also difficult to alter a negative, because of its extremely small size. It would be akin to altering something that is microscopically small. You could also apply this logic to the alleged *altering* of the Zapruder film.

The back of the head autopsy photograph was altered to conceal the wound in the occipital region of the skull. To look at what I am discussing, you can get a variety of stereo viewers, the cheapest and easiest is a little handheld lorgnette-type viewer, which can be very helpful.

Martin Shackleford was, again, extremely helpful in guiding me along and helping me understand what stereo viewing was all about. He sent me copies of stereo viewing of the following photographs: the back of the head (By using a color back of the head image, and a black and white of the head image, each at a slightly different angle. He created the first back of the head stereo view. Two copies of the same photograph don't create a stereo view. Each has to be taken from a slightly different angle, just as each eye sees things from a slightly different angle); an anaglyph stereo view of the top of the head photos; a stereo pair of the back photos. Stereo views recreate what the eye would see if it were there. Thus, each view has to be slightly different. Normally a stereo pair is photographed with the view portions about three inches apart. Two copies of the same photo just produce a stereo view of a flat image, with no depth.

To see if it was possible to detect any evidence of faking, Mr. McCamy spent about twenty days examining the autopsy photographs to interpret them and concluded that he "found no disturbing of the surface of the film. We found nothing taken away from the film or added to the film, no evidence of any cutting or pasting or construction of a montage, in short, found no evidence whatsoever of any such faking" (I HSCA 176-177).

Remember, Dr. Humes said in his ARRB deposition in 1996, that all of the photographs were taken at the beginning of the autopsy, excluding Fox-8 (which shows the scalp reflected). The 10 Fox photographs demonstrate damage in some areas that is not remotely apparent in the other autopsy photographs. There is the lemon-sized flap visible in the photo of the back of the head (Fox-3), which shows skull bone, and it is blown forward and outward. This is not even visible in the stare of death neck wound (Fox -1, 2), the back wound (Fox-5), or the Groden right superior profile (G-1), which shows (as does the stare of death photo), a rather matted tissue configuration in that area. Harry Livingstone begins to dilate on this in the photo section of *High Treason II*, which may be worth looking at and reading.

Through the years, the critics have painstakingly questioned the authenticity of the autopsy photographs. It is hard to believe that the back of the head photo was not altered, as the photo seems to have two focal points, and the hair on the upper back of the head is wet and looks real, while the hair on the lower back of the head appears dry to me and the work of an artist who was good with charcoal pencils. When I asked my wife to look at it stereoscopically, and she has worked in the salon business for over 25 years, both as an employee and as an owner, her response was immediate, "where is the hair?" Indeed. Where is it? What you don't see in Fox-3 are any strands of hair in the right lower occipital region, but instead a flat, matted area, where the expected exit wound from Z-313 should be. And clearly, no matter how you explain it, there is not a hint or a suggestion of the entry in the rear described at the autopsy, 2.5 cm to the right of midline and slightly above the external occipital protuberance. This is not objecting about what the Parkland witnesses saw, as most conspiratorial theorists are usually ventilating about, but about what the Bethesda autopsy personnel viewed. Now, as has been said before, you cannot have it both ways, and while it has always been said, Humes, et al, were incompetent or worse, if that is true, then why should we believe the wound described above? The only answer I can give is that virtually anyone could have found the same wound, although they might not be familiar with the external occipital protuberance and simply called it the bump on the back of the head. This is clearly not the HSCA's wound, which is up in the cowlick area.

Also, when you look at Fox-3 stereoscopically the area where everyone said was a blown-out hole, is flatter, almost 2-D compared to the rest, which manifestly looks 3-D. It appears to be dry, when everything around it looks wet. Why?

McCamy states, "In this case, we must remember we are looking at professional photographs taken at short range, not distant photographs, so there is very little difficulty in identifying the person and the things seen" (I HSCA 179).

Yet, it doesn't. On one stare of death, you can see the words Bethesda, or U. S. Naval Hospital identifying marks in the photo. Without some kind of an identification plate, they are just photographs of a random corpse.

There is a famous picture, taken on the morning of the twenty-second of November, in Ft. Worth. President Kennedy is speaking at the microphone. He clearly has just had a haircut and does not create the impression of having long hair. Yet, look at the hair in the left lateral and the top of the head photos. It is far more than in the aforementioned morning speech photograph in Ft. Worth, or at least seemingly.

All of this is pure speculation, admittedly, but the greater point is that a split-second photograph of anyone can be interpreted a hundred different ways. When all the dust settles, the only photograph I think that may have been altered is the back of the head photograph, Fox-3. When you have over 40 trained, medical personnel at both Parkland and Bethesda all saying they saw a huge defect in the occipital-parietal of JFK's skull and then you look at Fox-3 and there is no gaping hole, what evidence are we to believe?

When McCamy is about to comment on each of the four autopsy photographs he viewed in stereo, Andy Purdy censors him immediately. When witnesses are cut off, it is normally because they are about to start talking about issues not on the preconceived script, that was gone over not just with McCamy, but with all of the witnesses, before they testified. I have no idea why Andy Purdy did this, except at the very least it is rude. If you bring an expert in to testify, then you should have the courtesy to let them speak. It would have been awkward for Purdy, had McCamy said, as many have, "this back of the head photo, could be anybody." We do, however, have McCamy's comments through documents received from the National Archives. He said "there was one pair showing the back of the head. The parallax was very clearly demonstrable. When this pair of photographs was viewed stereoscopically, the millimeter scale held by the head [sic] of one member of the autopsy team appears to be about 100 mm in front of the back of the head. On a photograph showing the back of the neck area, the parallax is clearly demonstrable. The right-eye view was more of the right side of the neck and parts of the body seen beyond the neck. On these views, the gloved hands of the members of the autopsy team appear to protrude from the picture and the millimeter scale seems to be somewhat impressed into the skin and flesh. This is not so apparent in the single pictures; but is quite apparent in the stereoscopic view. In a pair of views of the front, showing the neck wound and the face, the parallax is clearly demonstrable, more of the pupil of the left eye is visible, across the end of the nose, in the stereoscopic right-eye view. In the two views of the excavated skull, the parallax is very demonstrable. The stereoscopic shows considerable depth between the outer part of the skull and the lower depths of the excavation."

On September 12, 1978, the testimony of Calvin McCamy began for the second time before the committee. He would testify on four different days, the 7th, 12th, 14th and 15th of September. As Blakey stated, he was "here today to testify on part of the trajectory analysis that utilizes the Zapruder film. He will also discuss the photogrammetric technique that was used to locate precisely the position of the limousine at the time the shots that struck the President and Governor Connally were fired." (II HSCA 141)

Blakey's narration is somewhat hypocritical, especially when compared to Dr. Wecht's testimony. McCamy made statements, that, when Dr. Wecht made similar ones, he was shut down and not allowed to analyze the Zapruder film. McCamy, however, is allowed to pontificate without restraint. They said the Zapruder film was one-dimensional and that you couldn't draw any data from it to analyze, but oddly, McCamy is allowed to and no one dares object to what he is saying.

Apparently the Zapruder film has gained further dimensions, or McCamy has gained extra-dimensional perceptions, perhaps even metaphysical insights into the world of film analysis.

Mr. Goldsmith: "Mr. McCamy, for what purposes were the photographic panel and contractors asked to review the Zapruder film at its most recent conference?"

Mr. McCamy: "Our first purpose was to ascertain from the photographic evidence, if possible, the first signs that the President or Governor Connally were in distress. The second objective was to ascertain from the photographic evidence, if possible [*but not allowed by Wecht*] whether or not the President and the Governor were in positions in the limousine that would be consistent with the single-bullet theory."

Mr. Goldsmith: "How many panel members actually participated in the review of the Zapruder film, Mr. McCamy?"

Mr. McCamy: "There were about twenty people altogether. The films were viewed many times in many sessions. They were not all present at all times. When we voted on specific issues, about 15 people voted."

Mr. Goldsmith: "*And did you view any particular version of the Zapruder film?*"

Mr. McCamy: "*Yes; we had a copy, a direct copy, of the Zapruder film. We also had special films that were prepared by Mr. Groden. These were rotoscoped, which means that they were slightly enlarged and stabilized.*" (II H 142)

In 1978, there was not a controversy about there being more than one version of the Zapruder film. Film alteration was never an issue at this time, as far as I can remember. The quality of the copy could be addressed, especially since they were not going to be using the original, and not inquiring about the version that was being utilized. The book, *Twenty-Six Seconds*, by Alexandra Zapruder was one of many sources that cleared up the notion as to whether the Zapruder film had been altered. It wasn't, as far I was able to ascertain. Her book was a pleasant surprise to read concerning this particular point.

Mr. Goldsmith: "*Would you state at this time, Mr. McCamy, what the panel's conclusion was about when President Kennedy first showed a reaction to some severe external stimulus?*"

Mr. McCamy: "*Yes. The panel generally tended to agree that there was some sign of distress before frame 207. We took a vote on that, and the vote was 12 to 5 that there was photographic evidence of some distress by that time.*"

Mr. Goldsmith: "Would you indicate at this point whether frame 207 is before or after the President goes behind the sign? By 'sign' I am referring to the sign that obstructed Abraham Zapruder's line of sight."

Mr. McCamy: "The President's head is partially obscured by the sign at that time, so this is just as he was going behind the sign."

Mr. Goldsmith: "And what was the panel's conclusion about when Governor Connally first appeared to be showing a reaction to some severe external stimulus?

Mr. McCamy: "The vote was 11 to 3 that there was some sign of distress by frame 226, which is just immediately after he comes out from behind the sign."

Mr. Goldsmith: "Finally, would you indicate now what the panel's opinion was about whether the relative alignment of the two men in the vehicle was consistent with the single bullet theory?"

Mr. McCamy: "Yes. The positions of the men were examined on these films just prior to the time that the limousine went behind the sign, and it was agreed 15 to 1 that the men were in positions that were consistent with the single bullet theory." (II H 143)

Cyril Wecht was not permitted to give any estimations about the Zapruder film, because he was not an expert in photography, but McCamy was allowed free rein about whatever he wanted to without any push back at all. The official version was given priority, specifically to its most ardent disciples.

Here's a quote from McCamy that clarifies the extent of this study. As he describes the Zapruder film: "He now goes behind the sign, and only a fraction of a second later we see his hands moving upward. He has a **gasping expression**. His hands are in the classic position of a person who has been startled.

He now begins to raise his arms into what I would call a defensive position. He may be clutching at the throat wound. He maintains this attitude, tuning again sharply to his wife, who clearly recognizes the situation by now. He moves toward his wife. His wife notices Connally. The President is now moving toward his wife, turning his head toward her, leaning forward, and leaning to the left. His head is quite a ways down, as you can see. His wife apparently inspects the wound or the damage to his clothing at least. That is the head shot." (II HSCA 144-145)

This is beyond silly, yet it comes off as something cloaked as a panel full of professionals and specialists. Gasping expression isn't very helpful, since McCamy is supposed to be interpreting the autopsy photographs. JFK's hands are balled-up in tight fists, which was exactly how they were when he was removed from the coffin at Bethesda.

As far as President Kennedy's head being considerably forward, it is no more than three inches lower, in Z-312, than it was at Z-205, before he went behind the Stemmons Freeway sign. He does move slightly forward, though less than an inch, *as does everyone in the car*, because the driver is either slowing down or tapping the break, but then JFK goes back and to the left after being shot in the right temporal region of his skull in Z-313.

View Z-312 and see what you discover. His head does not appear to be down in any disproportionate manner. As a result, you now have an entire team of photo professionals that don't seem to be using their proficiency at all.

One final comment concerning Fox-3: Let me say this stronger than I did earlier in this chapter. I challenge anyone to look at this autopsy photo stereoscopically; it is embarrassingly obvious that the right rear doesn't look anything like the rest of the photo. Everything else in the photo is clear and distinct, but not the right rear portion, which has no distinct hair strands that are visible. It is a muddled mess. Someone has tampered with it, pure and simple. Even if you only look at the color version of Fox-3, non-stereoscopically, that portion of JFK's head does not look like the rest of the photograph.

The remainder of McCamy's testimony is as follows:

> Mr. Goldsmith: "Mr. McCamy, referring to these exhibits, would you explain the results of the panel's visual inspection of the chin area in these photographs?"
>
> Mr. McCamy: "Yes; there had been an allegation that on a photograph of Oswald, there was a line directly across his chin, and this has been cited as evidence that the upper part of the head had been added onto another chin. So, we looked very carefully at all of the original materials [*that nobody else had*] to see if there were any tell-tale line across here. What we found was that on second

and third and more generation prints, or prints that were published in books, there was a tendency to build up more and more contrast here so that this looks more and more like a line. That line is nowhere near as pronounced on the original materials."

He was saying that the line in question was imaginary. Another line was studied, "and there is indeed a very fine line that comes from the ear, comes down here, and over into here.

Now that fine line is actually too fine to be a photographic image." (II HSCA 398—399)

A Dallas Police photo is introduced. Some lines are just because book copies of photos are often lousy copies; but when there is an actual line, it isn't really part of the photo. "That very fine line is in fact the edge of the water spot. When the film was processed, a drop of water remained there. When the water dried, it deposited a very fine line of minerals, and that is apparent on this picture. I have seen exactly these same water spots on the area of his shirt and on the butt of the rifle, so we know that these water spots exist all over." (II HSCA 400)

Conclusion: it seems that every variance is justified by bringing in experts to vouch for them. All kinds of experts testify in court. So, in a lot of instances, they are meaningless.

> Mr. McCamy: "This photograph is quite remarkable. This was taken by the Dallas police. It shows that it isn't the picture that has a line across the chin. *It is the man that has a line across the chin.* He actually has an indentation right here, and that does show up in these photographs, right in the center and right here. There is a crease there, so that is a natural thing we find, but I think that it is also important to note here the exact shape of the chin. It is quite flat across here and rounds down in this way. So that if that chin were illuminated from directly above, the light would fall down to here, to about that point, where it would seem to cut off quite straight. So, this photograph gives us a good reason why the chin seems to be so flat at the bottom." (II HSCA 402)

The backyard photographs have produced more heat than light over the years. If the line through the chin in 133-A is actually there, then why not in 133-B and 133-C? It is suspicious that in one of the backyard photos Oswald has a ring on his left hand and in another one he has a ring on his right hand. Odd. The backyard photos are important, however, for a reason already stated, because they show the sling mount attached to the bottom of the barrel and stock and not imbedded into the side of the stock as when Carl Day is bringing CE-139 out of the TSBD. This is massively incriminating, suggesting there were two rifles, or two Carcanos.

Then there was the issue of the shadows to deal with.

> Mr. Goldsmith: "Mr. McCamy, how did the panel address the question of the shadows in the backyard pictures?"
>
> Mr. McCamy: "This was addressed by a vanishing point analysis
>
> Mr. Goldsmith: "What do you mean by 'vanishing point analysis.'?"
>
> Mr. McCamy: "*The sun is very distant*, so far away that we can consider it to be at infinity, and as a result, if we draw a line from an object to the shadow of the object, and we do this in a number of places in a scene, all of those lines are parallel lines." (II HSCA 409)

The question then moves from shadows to different head composites.

> Mr. Goldsmith: "Mr. McCamy, another allegation that has been made is that the heads in these photographs are identical, thereby, suggesting that one head has been used for three different composites.

How did the panel tackle this issue?"

> Mr. McCamy: "The panel simply looked at these three pictures and found it quite puzzling that anyone would say that they are the same. He has a different look on his face on each of these pictures. Here he is rather smiling. More of his eyes were shown in this picture than in the others. In this one, he is frowning. The lower part of his lip is puffed out. And in this picture, he has a rather gentle smile on his faces. They are so different that it is just apparent from the photographs." (II HSCA 415)

07

Dr. Michael Baden
September 7, 1978

On September 7, 1978, Dr. Michael Baden testified before the HSCA in Washington, D.C.

C hief Counsel, G. Robert Blakey, introduced Dr. Michael Baden. He "received his M.D. degree from New York University School of Medicine in 1959 and completed his residency in pathology at Bellevue Hospital in 1964. He is, of course, the chairman of the committee's panel reviewing the autopsy" (I HSCA 179-180).

He was born in 1934 in New York City. He has also been involved in the inquiries into the deaths of, among others, John Belushi, Medgar Evers, David Carradine, and Czar Nicholas II and his family. Dr. Baden testified with precision and eloquence. His testimony was technical, yet Baden was able to explain difficult issues with plain language and examples.

Though I disagree with many of his interpretations, *most* of the facts he presents to the committee are seemingly not in dispute. He also has to be interpreted for what it was. He couldn't just come out and say Humes, et al, were fully incompetent, though at times does so indirectly. He does mention that the Forensic Pathology Panel interrogated Dr. Humes, Dr. Boswell, Dr. Finck, and the radiologist, Dr. Ebersole. It does seem odd that the only member of the nine person panel who was left out when doing that questioning of Dr. Humes was the lone dissenter, Dr. Cyril Wecht (more about whom in due course).

> Mr. Klein: "Despite the absence of the brain and the fact that the panel doctors were not present at the autopsy, were the panel members able to reach conclusions with respect to the cause of death, the number of wounds, the location of the wounds, and the path of the bullets through the body?

> Dr. Baden: "Yes, sir."

> Mr. Klein: "Are you testifying today as a representative of the entire panel of forensic pathologists?"

> Dr. Baden: "Yes, I am."

> Mr. Klein: "Did any members of the panel disagree with the conclusions reached by the panel?"

> Dr. Baden: "The essential conclusions were unanimously agreed to by eight of the panel members. One panel member, Dr. Wecht, did dissent in some important aspects of the conclusions."

> Mr. Klein: "Doctor, since Dr. Wecht will be testifying before the committee today, I will ask you from this point on to confine your testimony to the conclusions reached by the other members of the panel."

> Dr. Baden: "Yes."

> Mr. Klein: "What was the cause of death of President John F. Kennedy?"

> Dr. Baden: "President Kennedy died as a result of two gunshot wounds of the head, brain, back and neck areas of the body." (I HSCA 185)

> Mr. Klein: "What does this particular drawing portray?"

> Dr. Baden: "This particular drawing shows the back of the president and the head where I am pointing to, and a perforation of the skin of the **right upper back** with, a centimeter ruler alongside."

> Mr. Klein: "Doctor, does this diagram fairly and accurately represent the location of the wound in the President's right upper back?"

> Dr. Baden: "Yes, it does." (I HSCA 186-187)

This seems a little odd, since Dr. Baden has never seen the President's body. The only thing he saw were photographs and the drawings made from those autopsy pictures. It seems a little arrogant to speak with such certitude that his wound location can be as precise as he states here. This appears to be way above his pay grade.

> Dr. Baden: "The panel was able to conclude after examining the photographs and the details of the perforation in the right upper back, that this perforation was a gunshot **wound of entrance** and is characterized uniquely by an abrasion collar, a roughening of the edges around the entrance perforation, which is more apparent in the photographs than the blowup, but which clearly depicts the perforation as an **entrance gunshot wound**." (I HSCA 189)

> Dr. Baden: "….when a bullet exits the body through the skin, proceeding from inside the body to the outsides, it does not cause, usually, except under special circumstances, this same type of rubbing effect on the edges of the skin [*abrasion collar*].

"In this other diagram that Miss Dox has prepared is an example of a bullet entering the skin at an angle. When the bullet enters at an angle, the skin is stretched prior to perforation unequally so that one part of the abrasion collar is wider than another part and this produces a perforation that is asymmetric and indicates directionality; thus the abrasion collar establishes not only that it is an entrance would but also the direction that the bullet is traveling.

"When a bullet enters head-on at a 90-degree angle, the abrasion collar surrounding is equal, uniformly equal. When it enters at an angle, part of the abrasion collar is wider than the other part and this assists in establishing direction of the bullet track."

> Mr. Klein: "And the panel found an abrasion collar on the wound of the President's back of the kind you have shown us in these drawings?"

> Dr. Baden: "Yes, sir. This represents a diagram, a blowup of the actual entrance perforation of the skin showing an abrasion collar. The abrasion collar is wider toward 3 o'clock than toward 9 o'clock which would indicate a directionality from right to left and toward the middle part of the body, which was the impression of the doctors on reviewing the photographs initially at the Archives." (I HSCA 192)

Attempting to lift out the salient points in Dr. Baden's testimony will be difficult. This is the aim of this entire work, but so much of what he said is both relevant and germane, that filtering through the material is not easy. I should like to begin, however, with the fact that Dr. Baden said the abrasion collar on the back wound was wider at 3:00, than at 9:00, suggesting a right to left direction. Remember, Governor Connally was sitting far enough outboard of President Kennedy that he couldn't see him when he turned to his right as the shots rang out. A right to left trajectory would make sense if someone was firing from the SE corner of the sixth floor window of the Texas School book Depository, but not in concert with the Single Bullet Theory. As was stated in the chapter on Governor Connally, the answer could be found that Connally's back wound became elliptical, but only after Dr. Shaw, by his own admission, had cleaned it up during surgery (6 H 88).

What Dr. Baden didn't say regarding the back wound, is something that both he and Dr. Wecht have since said, that the back wound was traveling upward at eleven degrees. *The eleven degrees upward was new in 1978* and shatters the Single Bullet Theory. Bullet wounds can go anywhere, once inside the body, because of deflecting off bones. Baden is saying the bullet entered, and rose, which could be a simple way of matching the holes: a back wound to the throat exit v. the ridiculous neck-to-neck explanation of Dr. Humes.

It was the photographic panel who actually used the eleven-degree comment of trajectory. The pathology panel did not say that the back wound was lower than or level with the throat wound, and they did not ascribe any degree of angle to it. Dr. Baden (COPA 1995) and Dr. Wecht (Crossfire, September 1993) have since used the eleven degrees and rising when they comment on the back wound, which if the back wound is rising has to be below the throat wound. Baden said that the Forensic pathology panel "concluded that there is a fracture of the transverse process of the first vertebra which could have been caused by the bullet striking it directly or by the force of the cavity created by the bullet passing near to it" (I HSCA 305). Given that the death certificate places the back-wound entry at the level of the third thoracic vertebra, the rising back wound, however so slight, does not suggest a shooter from behind and sixty feet in the air, coming from the TSBD.

The back wound seems to be the point of entry and that it is most probable that it did transit and exit the throat. The evidence shows that the back wound is lower, even if only slightly, than the throat wound. Since Kennedy is sitting nearly upright in the Zapruder film, that when the bullet exited his throat, from which it would have been traveling slightly upward, it may have gone to parts unknown in the city of Dallas. It may be the bullet, though I highly doubt it, found in two pieces in the front seat, having dinged the windshield and chrome strip. It just may have exited the limousine entirely, never to be recovered or seen again.

The problem, as Stewart Galanor points out in his wonderful book *Cover-Up*, is the holes get smaller from back to front, the opposite of what would be expected: jacket (15mm), shirt (10mm), back (7mm), to the throat (5mm). We do have to remember that a clothing hole involves weak fibers and can easily be bigger than the projectile. The back/neck hole was only measured by Humes, so is of little value, and the 5mm was an estimate. Since exit wounds are usually larger than entrance wounds, this would be somewhat strange, but certainly not impossible.

> Mr. Klein: "Using the blowup, would you tell us what the panel learned from the photograph?"
>
> Dr. Baden: "The panel learned from the photograph that a tracheostomy incision, an incision to aid the dying President in breathing, had been made on the front of the neck at the hospital and is a typical type of tracheostomy incision; *and the panel also noted a semicircular defect at the lower margin of the tracheostomy which required further evaluation.*" (1 HSCA 217)

Dr. Baden also mentions that the tracheostomy was "*a typical type*" (I HSCA 217). He may have been referring to the incision being typical, not the evident tearing that followed, perhaps while the body was being moved, with JFK's head falling backwards and causing the tear that we see in Fox-1 and Fox-2. Dr. Perry, who performed the tracheostomy, said it was a slit in the throat of about an inch in width, and then remarked that the wound he saw in the Fox-1 and Fox-2 autopsy photos was the job of a butcher, but not him.

Baden then mentions the slit-like tear in the left upper portion of the shirt, just beneath the left shirt collar. There are some that posit these slits and nicks were made with a scalpel as the president's clothes were being quickly removed at Parkland. Lab tests on the shirt revealed no copper present, and there quite likely would have been if a Carcano bullet had gone through it. There also doesn't seem to be any fiber striations on the magic bullet. The official explanation is the nicks were caused by the exiting bullet. The only other alternative is that it was caused by the scalpel, as his tie was cut off at Parkland. *They noted the fibers pushed out forward, as one would expect with an exiting bullet, again suggesting the hole in JFK's neck was an exit wound.* The only purpose of such an inquiry into what happened would be to determine that either the nicks and slits were not caused by a bullet; or were the result of a bullet exiting. The results are either caused by a bullet or a scalpel. It seems to be clear that the bullet was exiting.

Baden then shows a Dox drawing that shows various bullet trajectory possibilities, depending on the position of the President at the time the missile struck. One of the paths illustrates the back wound traveling upward, which is what the Forensic Pathology panel determined. Maybe this was done to show options, as the evidence wasn't strong enough to narrow it down. Recall, they moved the back of the head wound quite a bit and did not account for the Humes placement. Also, the lateral X-ray shows radiating fractures down low, where Humes put the entrance wound; there are also fractures higher up, and what appears to be a table of skull, pushed up and back. These contradictions need to be explained. The problem is enhanced by the fact that the metallic dust fragments shown on the lateral x-ray are from the higher wound, not from the Humes wound. Two shots to the head? One front, one back? It is certainly an interesting hypothesis: the rear shot at Z-312 (through the research of **David Wimp**, we can now demonstrate that the movement at Z-312 is minimal, 0.95 inches, which is also the forward movement between frames Z-310 and Z-312) The head going forward, more than 0.95 inches, is an allusion based on what are called photographic smears, because Zapruder moved his 8 mm camera. Z-312/313 is a frontal shot tangentially, while Z-328 is the shot from the rear. This would certainly explain the high and low wound on the lateral x-ray. The high head wound at Z-328 and the low wound at Z-312/313 makes the most sense to me. This distinction reveals so much about the case, without which certain aspects just aren't explainable very well. Z-312 supposedly drove JFK forward just a couple of inches, but we now know this is a photographic illusion. The most recent evidence, that the

HSCA at least marginally considered in their Report and in volume V of the hearings, is that the rear head shot takes place less than a second (7/10) after Z-313 at c. Z-328 and the latter shot explains Connally's wrist wound and the fragment in his left femur. The frontal wound was a fragmenting round and would have damaged the part of the limousine it hit with its shards, had that occurred. Z-313 was the kill shot.

Baden says the wound in the back of JFK was placed too high, by about two inches (I would say 4 inches, or c. 10 cm), and the head wound was too low in the Rydberg drawings done for the Warren Commission. Rydberg placed the back wound too high. (and protested loudly later on) Again, I don't think it is an either or, because David Wimp's discovery of the illusory movement of JFK's head going forward at Z-312 and Keith Fitzgerald's discovery, or at least clarification of JFK's head actually going forward at Z-328, explains things quite nicely. Baden believes the wound was in the cowlick area.

Baden then refers to JFK's back wound, when all too many Warren Commission defenders, called it a neck wound. He has literally relocated it anatomically. What is crucial here, and this goes back to the point of locating the entry aspect of the abrasion collar in the back wound at 3:00, and not at 9:00. If that bullet that was going from right to left and struck a person where it struck JFK in the back and was fired from sixty to seventy feet above (the sixth floor of the Texas School Book Depository is sixty feet, plus the decline of Elm Street), where would the bullet then go? The doubtful answer is the front of the throat, unless you remind yourself that bullets can do strange things, and that Baden was willing to make the angle eleven degrees upward, where Humes had it eleven degrees downward. How do you profess to be a doctor, a pathologist, and a head of United States Navy laboratories, and view the body of an assassinated president on the day of the killing and be wrong on the fatal wound by four inches? It is unthinkable. 4mm would be outrageous, but this is almost 100mm. Let's put 4 inches in perspective and I've made this point before, though I believe this illustration has its origin with Dr. Gary Aguilar. It is the difference in a football being on its own ten-yard line (the EOP) or on its opponents ten-yard line (the cowlick area).

If you raise that shot another four inches, it takes off the top of Bill Greer's head. Rydberg was nothing more than a Warren Commission lackey. He drew what Humes told him to draw, anatomically farcical as those illustrations are, but Ida Dox is not any better at the end of the day. Rydberg never saw the photos of the president, but Ms. Dox did. Dr. Humes had to have seen the drawings by Rydberg and signed off on them. Sad and irresponsible.

Though Rydberg never saw the autopsy photos, House Select Committee on Assassinations Chairman Louis Stokes did and addressed Dr. Michael Baden. Stokes told Baden that the Committee, or at least certain members, had viewed the actual autopsy photographs, which are sealed in the National Archives.

"The committee feels it would be in extremely poor taste for this committee to submit those photographs to public view. It also, in our opinion, would be an invasion of the privacy of the President's family. It is for that reason that these photographs will remain sealed and will not be displayed during the course of these hearings." (I HSCA 180)

If it would be obtuse to put the autopsy photos on public display, then what was the reason to submit the autopsy drawings, traced and drawn, for public consumption?

There are some variations; and Dox certainly betrayed us about the location of the head wound. The Zapruder film had already been seen on national television. It's not like we had no idea what the results would be when autopsy pictures were taken. The Zapruder film is everywhere to see on YouTube in all of its ghoulish delight, but the autopsy pictures are off limits? It seems a little inconsistent.

Again, as stated in chapter 4, the three illustrations made by Ida Dox of the autopsy pictures shown were the stare of death (Fox-1), only going to the President's chin; the wound in the right upper back (Fox-5), but not showing a wound in the cowlick area; and a depiction of the back of the head (Fox-3), showing the cowlick wound, some tissue in the hairline, and a fold of skull evident on the right side of President Kennedy's head. She drew another of the autopsy photos of the side of the head that was not shown during the HSCA public hearings.

Dr. Baden estimated "that well more than 100,000 medico-legal autopsies have been performed or supervised by the panel members collectively in the course of their official capacities." (I HSCA 185)

Baden then states that the President's clothing "was examined by me and by each of the panel members at the Archives where the clothing is kept, *preserved, and guarded*." (I HSCA 196)

This seems professionally silly. It sounds very respectful; but appears more like a smoke screen. The clothing was positioned on a mannequin and Baden stated, "The jacket and the clothing had been torn at Parkland Hospital by the examining physicians in the course of providing emergency care to the President."

> Mr. Klein: "And with respect to the wounds to the President's back, what did the panel learn from that clothing?"
>
> Dr. Baden: "In the jacket and underlying shirt there is a perforation of the fabric *that corresponds directly with the location of the perforation of the skin of the upper right back* that, the panel concluded, was an entrance gunshot perforation that entered the back of the President. This is correspondingly seen in the shirt beneath." (I HSCA 196)

The late Sen. Arlen Specter and Warren Commission junior counsel, as late as 2003, stood at a lectern in Pittsburgh, Pennsylvania at the Wecht Symposium and asserted that the wound was in the President's neck. Baden testifies, however, that the wound was exactly where it was shown both in the clothing and on the Fox-5 autopsy photo, well down from the neck and located in his back. You can't have it both ways.

> Dr. Baden: "The X-rays show, first, that there is no missile present in the body at the time the X-rays were taken. This X-ray, No. 9, was taken before the autopsy, this one, No. 8, during the autopsy. Further, there is evidence of injury to the right of the neck with air and gas shadows, in the right side of the neck and *an irregularity of one of the spines, a portion of one spine of the President; that is, the first thoracic vertebra* which is, also apparent on the blowup and which the panel, and in consultation with the radiology experts, concluded represents a *fracture-type injury to that vertebra*." (I HSCA 199)

No one has responded to Dr. Baden's claim that President Kennedy sustained a *"fracture-type injury"* to that vertebra, which might have been serious in terms of post-surgery recovery, let alone explain CE-399's upward direction as it exited from JFK's throat.

The Warren Commission always stated that had the President received this wound alone, he would have survived and had a routine recuperation. I'm not exactly sure how they knew this, however, with any degree of certitude.

Secondly, the President's personal physician, Admiral Burkley, stated that his reading of the x-rays indicated that the damage was at the level of the *third thoracic vertebrae.* I would personally side with Dr. Burkely, because Baden testified that the back wound was a perfect correspondence to the holes in the coat and shirt when fastened to a mannequin at the level of the first thoracic vertebrae. The problem is that those three holes, however, do not line up with the *first thoracic vertebrae,* as Baden affirmed. Some people observe agreement and conformity with Dr. Burkley's prior analysis of the X-rays. I agree.

Dr. Baden then exhibited what has been called the stare of death autopsy photograph, or Fox–1. It is cropped, so as not to show JFK's face, just the jagged wound in his throat.

> Mr. Klein: "Using the blowup, would you tell us what the panel learned from the photograph?"
>
> Dr. Baden: "The panel learned from the photograph that a tracheostomy, incision, an incision to aid the dying President in breathing, had been made on the front of the neck at the hospital and is a **typical** type of tracheostomy incision; **and the panel also noted a semicircular defect at the lower margin of the tracheostomy which required further evaluation.**" (I HSCA 217)

Humes claimed he could not locate the margins of a wound in the throat of JFK and apparently learned later that the placement of the tracheostomy had been through that bullet wound. I've looked at those photos dozens of times and you can certainly see the boundaries of a wound. In fact, if you look closely, you can see a semi-circle at both the top edge and on the bottom edge of the incision and if closed up would approximate a circle, i.e., a bullet hole.

As mentioned earlier, Baden then described the slit as a typical type of tracheostomy incision. Dr. Perry told Bob Groden, when looking at Fox-1, that he didn't make that incision. As stated earlier, he insisted he never would have made that kind of an opening and, in fact, it was grotesque and not his work. The following question needed to be asked: how wide was the endotracheal tube that was placed into the incision? This seems to be both relevant and important.

> Mr. Klein: "Doctor, directing your attention to the clothing already received as exhibits, would you tell us what the pan-

el learned from that clothing with respect to the wound of the President's neck?"

Dr. Baden: "Yes, sir. On examining the clothing of the President, there is present in the upper left portion of the shirt, just beneath the left shirt collar, a slit-like tear. This slit-like tear corresponds directly with the area of perforation in the anterior neck seen on the photographs taken prior to the autopsy and is characteristic of a bullet *perforation of exit in which the perforation is not necessarily as round as the entrance perforation.*

The entrance on the back is a spherical perforation, normal for an entrance wound. The perforation in the front of the shirt, slit-like, is typical for an exit puncture of a bullet, based on the margins of the wound seen in both Fox-1 and Fox-2.

There is also associated with this tear in the shirt fabric a tear or nick of the tie the President was wearing, which corresponds to that same area of the body when the tie is made into a knot as he was wearing at the time of the shooting." (I HSCA 217)

According to the chemical analysis of the shirt and tie, neither contained any trace of copper, which is the principal component of the copper-jacketed bullet.

The only people who saw the wound described it as a round puncture, which they associated with a wound of entry. Without observing the wound, how can someone possibly ascertain its characteristics?

Technical difficulties abound at this point. If the bullet actually created the slit and tie damage, which is at variance with the testimony of Dr. Carrico, who placed the wound "above the level of JFK's collar." According to the magic bullet, at least some of the material from JFK's clothing would have then been pushed forward into Governor Connally's back. This seems to be vitally important and often overlooked, but it shouldn't be.

In Dr. Shaw's testimony, however, he never mentions any fabric in Governor Connally's back wound that had made the journey from JFK's skin or clothing, when he describes his procedure when cleaning it up and ascertaining the damage. In case of point, no such fabric or other foreign substances were ever noted during the treatment of the Governor's wound, which you think would have been mentioned when Dr. Shaw treated his back wound. There are **six materials** in view here: JFK's coat, shirt and tie and Connally's coat, dress shirt and undershirt. There was no trace at all of any fabric of JFK's in any of the three holes of Governor Connally, mentioned above. Why not? I think we know the answer.

This is just one more factor to the incongruity of CE 399, the magic bullet. When first encountered, it was not comprised of any fiber striations, blood, or tissue and this bullet had passed through JFK's coat, shirt, (entrance) shirt (exit), tie, Connally coat, dress shirt, undershirt (entrance) undershirt (exit) dress shirt, coat, coat at wrist, shirt at wrist (entrance), shirt at wrist (exit), coat at wrist, trousers—**fifteen different sets of clothing fibers** and didn't have any blood, tissue, or fiber striations at all? This seems to be ridiculous.

That was beyond magical, bordering on the supernatural. This bullet will happily oblige any request you put forth, as Dr. Wecht has said many times.

On the other hand:

> Mr. Klein: "Doctor, on the basis of the foregoing evidence, photos and X-rays taken at the autopsy, interviews of the surgeons who attended the President at Parkland Hospital, and the autopsy report, did the panel unanimously conclude that a bullet entered the upper right back of the President and exited from the front of his neck?"
>
> Dr. Baden: "Every member of the panel so concluded." (I HSCA 217, 230, and passim)

The Warren Commission spoke about a wound to the rear of the President's *neck*, but the neck is in the middle of the body, not the right side. Ergo, Baden's locating of the JFK back wound on the upper right of his back meant that every member of the medical panel was calling the Warren Commission a liar, masquerading the obvious to the House Select Committee on Assassinations medical panel?

In response, an Ida Dox drawing was displayed, representing the bullet's path from JFK's back to his neck. The wound can have multiple explanations, "depending on the position of the President at the time the missile struck," Baden said.

> Baden continues: "We cannot on the basis of the autopsy findings alone, in this instance, determine from whence the bullet came." (I HSCA 231)

True, but we know what JFK's position was, based on photographs and the Zapruder film.

Baden then shows "a drawing made for the Warren Commission depicting the same track from the back to the front neck area we have been expressing."

> Mr. Klein: "Doctor, does that drawing made for the Warren Commission fairly and accurately represent the location of the entry and the exit wound and the path of the bullet?"
>
> Dr. Baden: "Not precisely. The exit perforation in the neck *is approximately in the proper area,* but *the entrance wound in the back is higher than the medical panel concluded from examining the documents, the photographs as to the point of entrance. We place the entrance perforation a bit lower—almost two inches lower than depicted in the Warren Commission exhibit."* (I HSCA 233)

Compare the autopsy photo and Rydberg drawings, and you will see that the back wounds are over four inches apart. But if Baden is right that Rydberg's drawing is wrong by two inches, wouldn't the autopsy photo also be incorrect by two inches? As long as the autopsy photo is not altered, it will never be incorrect.

A Dox drawing of Fox-3 was shown to Baden, in which the entrance wound has been greatly embellished, and the Select Committee of the House of Representatives had to know it was. According to Baden, the entrance wound was in the cowlick area, despite knowing that it wasn't. [*A four-inch difference from Humes' placement*]. Then Baden asserted that "the detail in the photograph is much better than that in the blowup," which is completely and utterly false.

Baden depicted the wound in the cowlick area as "a typical gunshot wound of entrance" and that it corresponded in many of its features very closely with the gunshot wound of entrance in the right upper back, especially as to the appearance of the abrasion collar and as to its size.

"The Panel further concluded that the lower area under question is clearly extraneous dried brain tissue on top of scalp hair." (I HSCA 238)

Of course it did, because Baden had Ida Dox superimpose a wound she got from a pathology book and was told to place it in the cowlick area. It looked like a typical gunshot wound of entrance, because it was! The only problem is that it was a gunshot entrance wound from a pathology book that Dr. Baden had participated in after the Clark panel closed up shop.

At best it is a dried blood droplet. He knew what he was saying was completely false, but since the Clark Panel moved the wound up four inches, without ever examining President Kennedy's body, he wasn't about to let his old colleagues down who helped launch his career.

The lateral head X-rays were then shown:

Mr. Klein: "What did the panel learn from those X-rays?"

Dr. Baden: "The panel learned from these X-rays that there was extensive fracturing of the bones of the skull of the President as manifested by these various lines and irregularities, that there was displacement of some bony fragments as a result of this explosive type injury to the skull as seen on the X-ray, and that there are many small white areas in the X-ray film that are metallic fragments resulting from a bullet having passed through the skull and fragmenting to a small degree."

Mr. Klein: "Are those X-rays consistent with a bullet having entered the President's head high on top of the head and passed through?"

Dr. Baden: "Yes, sir. This is clearly demonstrated in these X-rays, and as comparison, the X-ray on the extreme left is an X-ray taken of President Kennedy during life showing the normal appearance of the skull with the various skull bones in their normal appearance and illustrates the extensive damage of the skull present at the time of the autopsy.

"The panel concluded, and all of the radiologist consultants with whom the panel spoke and met with, all concluded that without question there is an entrance bullet hole on the upper portion of the skull at the area I am pointing to where the bone itself has been displaced, and that this corresponds precisely with the point in the cowlick area on the overlying skin has the appearance of an entrance would, that the track of the bullet then proceeded from back to front and toward the right causing extensive damage to the head." (I HSCA 241—242)

The radiologist who needed to be contacted and conferred with was Dr. John Ebersole, who had been the radiologist on the night of the autopsy. He lived until 1993 and could have been consulted, but the HSCA chose not to have him testify during public testimony. That was a mistake. The X-rays he was responsible for show two fractures: one where Humes indicated (to the right and slightly above the external occipital protuberance) and Baden's proposed entrance, four inches higher. Again, I am more convinced that the discrepancy here is solved by recognizing that JFK is shot in the head c. Z-312/313 (tangential frontal shot) and then 7/10 of a second later c. Z-327/328 (rear shot in the back of JFK's head).

I wonder if Humes would have acquiesced to a four-inch mistake, if Ebersole had been present?

Keep in mind, the Baden entry wound in the cowlick did not exist as a wound in the autopsy report. That is because it never happened. The dishevelment in the top of JFK's skull was the result of a shot from the front (Z-313), while the Humes' wound is the result of a shot from the rear (Z-327/328).

> Mr. Klein: "Are these X-rays consistent with a bullet having passed through the President's head?"
>
> Dr. Baden: "Yes; there is extensive damage to the right side of the skull area, shown more clearly in the enhancement of the X-ray, and there are extensive fracture lines radiating from the point of entrance marked by this *relatively large metal fragment* and the X-ray lines extending from it. This corresponds precisely to the point of entrance beneath the cowlick area and shows the extensive loss of bone at that area." (I HSCA 244-245)

The inside-of-the-skull photo (not one of the Dox drawings, as Baden has the photo placed in front of him) is then displayed.

> Mr. Klein: "Doctor, do you recognize that photograph and that blowup?"
>
> Dr. Baden: "Yes; this is a detail of one of the autopsy photographs, in fact the only photograph that shows any internal structures of the President at the time of autopsy [*he was never shown the brain, or lack of brain photos, based on this statement*] as opposed to all of the other photographs which are of the outside of the body. This photograph shows the bullet exit area on the right side of the head and is seen in better detail and sharper on the photograph than in the blowup. The photograph shows the front right part of the skull of the President and the semicircular defect that I am pointing to corresponds with the black dot present on the previous exhibit. This is a portion of a gunshot wound of exit as determined by the panel because of the beveling of the outer

layer of bone visible in the photographs, which is also described in the autopsy report. Beveling refers to the breaking away of bone in a concave pattern as when a BB goes through plate glass causing a concavity in the glass in the direction in which the BB is proceeding.

This also happens when a bullet enters and exits skull bone and other bones. It is the conclusion of the panel that *this is unquestionably an exit perforation.*" (I HSCA 247—248)

I am not persuaded with the visibility of the beveling on the autopsy photos. Also, how do the bone fragments fit so neatly when a bone fragment that was found the next day [*the Harper fragment*] is not yet addressed?

> Mr. Klein: "Doctor, do you recognize that blowup?"
>
> Dr. Baden: "Yes, sir, this is a blowup of one of the X-rays, one of the 14 X-rays kept at the Archives, showing 3 fragments of bone received by Dr. Humes and Dr. Boswell in the autopsy room while they were performing the autopsy on the President, that had been retrieved from the limousine in which the President had been riding. The doctors looked at the bone fragments, took X-rays of the bone fragments, inserted this particular bone fragment against this semicircle and concluded that they matched and fitted together. On this larger triangular fragment there is at one edge metal fragments seen on the X-ray that the panel concluded, and the autopsy physicians concluded, were part of the exit perforation through the bone and that there is beveling on this bony fragment of the outer aspect of the bone. In addition, a portion of a suture line is also present on one edge of this fragment.

A suture line refers to the point at which two bones join. This suture line assisted the panel in precisely identifying from where the fragment derived. The panel concluded that this was part of the gunshot wound of exit on the right side of the head of the President." (I HSCA 249-250)

Was any testing ever done to establish what kind of metal was present? It doesn't seem like it.

> Mr. Klein: "Doctor, directing your attention to the autopsy reports which have already been received as exhibits, in what ways was the autopsy report consistent with the other evidence available with respect to the wound to the President's head?

Dr. Baden: "The autopsy reports did indicate that the gunshot wound of the head of the President came from behind, proceeded in a forward direction, and exited the right side of the skull. This is consistent with the finds of the panel."

Mr. Klein: "In what ways was the autopsy report not consistent with the other evidence available to the panel?"

Dr. Baden: "The location and placement of the gunshot wound of entrance was *significantly different on examination by the panel members than the autopsy pathologists had indicated. The panel members unanimously placed the gunshot wound of entrance in the back of the head approximately 4 inches above the point indicated in the autopsy report prepared by Dr. Humes and Boswell.*"

Mr. Klein: "So the panel concluded that the autopsy report placed the wound in the back of the head 4 inches too low?"

Dr. Baden: "That is correct; as recorded in the original autopsy." (I HSCA 250)

The back wound placement was inaccurate because it revolved around the Warren Commission's need to have it located above the throat wound, so it would look like a normal "in and out" wound. They needed this to cement the single-bullet theory.

How on earth do you make a four-inch mistake during an autopsy of the President of the United States, while he is obviously in a sedentary position lying supine on a table directly in front of you, with his head just a couple of inches away? Baden should have been less confident, since he wasn't working with the body of the president, only x-rays and photos, with some of those photos in desperate need of interpretation.

Precision was demanded, especially because it was the most shocking murder of the 20th century. How would the HSCA medical panel explain that there was a four-inch discrepancy had this gone to trial? Not easily.

Baden was called to testify; he lied and knew he was lying. But there are no rules of perjury here, so there was nothing to worry about. It also didn't hurt that he was the head of the medical panel for the HSCA and as a result would be more apt to get away with things and not be questioned. Remember, Dr. Humes also testified before this same committee. Did he so bungle the autopsy at Bethesda hospital, that when asked about the head wound, would he have dared to say the unspeakable, "Are you referring to the first head wound (Z-312/313), or the second (Z-327/328)?"

As asserted in the movie *JFK*, "We are through the looking glass, people."

Baden would later present the results of the head shot and use Z-312 as a point of reference, and state that the direction of the bullet was downward. But there is no bullet striking JFK from the rear at frame 312 as we have already addressed, and the "so-called" forward head movement of JFK in Z-312 is the result of a photographic smear because Zapruder jerked the film. Any forward movement due to a bullet striking JFK in the back of the head at Z-312 is simply false, which also eliminates any kind of neuromuscular reaction or jet effect taking place used as an explanation. It can finally be thrown into the dumpster of non-evidence

> Mr. Klein: "Do you recognize that drawing, Doctor?"
>
> Dr. Baden: "Yes, sir, this is the drawing prepared for the Warren Commission attempting to illustrate the gunshot wound that entered the back of the President's head."
>
> Mr. Klein: "Does that drawing fairly and accurately represent the location of the wounds and the path of the bullet in the President's head?"
>
> Dr. Baden: "Not in the area of the location of the entrance perforation, but it does illustrate the general concept that it is a gunshot wound from the back proceeding to the front. That the panel agrees with."

However, the panel places the entrance perforation 4 inches higher in the back of the head than the illustration for the Commission shows.

> Mr. Klein: "Doctor, you have testified that the President was hit by two bullets, one of which entered his upper right back, and the other entered high on the back of his head. Did the panel reach any conclusions as to whether each of these wounds would have been fatal in and of itself?"
>
> Dr. Baden: "Yes, the panel did conclude, without question, that the gunshot wound that struck the head of the President in and of itself would be fatal. The panel could not unanimously agree

as to whether or not the gunshot wound through the back and neck would necessarily be fatal because of the failure to examine the bullet track at the time of the autopsy—dissect the track. As a result, **we do not know whether there was injury to the spine of the President** or to major blood vessels. If the spine or blood vessels were injured, that bullet also could have been fatal, but we are unable to conclusively agree on that question." (I HSCA 254—256)

Baden had previously maintained a fracture-type wound to the vertebrae, using only the x-rays. He now testifies there was no injury to the spine, where earlier he said there was. There was damage, and he had already attested to it. Which is it?

The wounds to the governor are then addressed, and the testimonies of Connally's doctors is in the record. Baden is asked to appraise the X-rays of Connally:

> Mr. Klein: "And was there any indication that the bullet was still in the Governor, or did the X-ray show the bullet had passed through?"
>
> Dr. Baden: "There was no evidence of any missile or bullet present on the X-rays taken of the Governor at the time of admission to Parkland Hospital." (I HSCA 285)

Connally was operated on by Parkland's thoracic surgeon for his back and chest wound, and then by a different operating team who repaired the damage to the wrist and the thigh. The thoracic surgeon told the media that the surgery was now going to be concluded and they were going to get the bullet out, when according to the Single Bullet Theory, that bullet had already fallen out of the governor and embedded itself under the padding on a gurney and was now on its way back to Washington D.C. via Air Force One. So, which is it? Were they going to retrieve the bullet or was the bullet on its way back to Washington D.C.? Again, you can't have it both ways.

There was metal revealed on the X-ray of Connally's femur, and based on the reports of his operation, it was not removed, but was embedded in his femur until the day he died. It wasn't a bullet, obviously, only a fragment. Baden stated that the medical panel members had spoken with Dr. Shaw, but Dr. Gregory had already passed away.

That was lucky for Dr. Gregory, as Baden stated that he changed his reports, and that modification, helped in the discovery of the magic bullet theory:

"Dr. Gregory did have occasion to modify his reports. Initially, during the course of surgery, he thought that the wound on the under-surface of the wrist, the hand aspect of the wrist, might be an entrance wound, but in his final reports after full evaluation Dr. Gregory and subsequently all of the surgeons and all of the panel pathologists do agree that the bullet entered on the thumb side top or dorsal aspect of the forearm and exited the undersurface of the wrist." (I HSCA 287)

I find it simply unimaginable that a surgeon would arrive at a medical decision during the occurrence of an operation and then later change it. He was making explanations on the damaged wrist at the time of the surgery, not looking at X-rays fifteen years later. A huge difference.

We have to always remember that careers, pensions, promotions and status are all on the line. People were threatened, as in the case of Dr. Humes threatening Dr. Perry. Whoever was behind this was playing for keeps.

> Mr. Klein: "And was there any indication that the bullet was still in the Governor, or did the X-ray show the bullet had passed through?"
>
> Dr. Baden: "There was no evidence of any missile or bullet present on the X-rays taken of the Governor at the time of admission to Parkland Hospital." (I HSCA 285)

Clearly, there were traces of metal in all of the governors' damaged regions, embedded in the femur or in the wrist, which would certainly be confirmation of a bullet. There is only discussion of the bullet. In discussing the wrist X-ray of the Governor, Baden will comment on the fragments:

> "There are fractures of one bone, the radius bone, just before it enlarges to articulate or meet with the wrist bones, and there are present in the photographs, the X-rays, **multiple metal fragments**, evidence of a bullet having passed through causing the fractures and losing **a small amount of metal substance**." (I HSCA 289-290)

If these merged fragments of Governor Connally, in addition to what was in the chest, plus that which was embedded in the femur, amounts to more than $1/437^{th}$ of an ounce, then they did not come from anyone's magic bullet, since that was the amount of loss to the bullet, as the Warren Commission had so stated. Dr. Baden is aware of this, as he testified and comprehending that he came close to saying the wrong thing, immediately corrected his statement:

> Dr. Baden: "Subsequent X-rays of the wrist in the process of heal-ing after surgery does reveal that *the __largest__ of the metal fragments although still a very __small__ fragment* seen in the preoperative blow-up of the X-ray, was removed at the time of surgery. This was sub-sequently given to the Archives for preservation." (I HSCA 290)

Baden goes from large to small rather quickly in his testimony. The fragment was given to the Archives for preservation. He probably meant the X-ray showing the fragment, but that's not what he said.

In reference to the thigh wound received by the Governor, there is more linguistic nonsense: "The panel learned that there was no bullet nor significant portion of bullet present in the thigh; this was also con-firmed by the fact that the surgeons *did explore the wound* in the thigh surgically and found no bullet." (I HSCA 293)

> Dr. Baden: "This is the lower thigh bone in the blowup. This is the knee area and the left thigh of Governor Connally. The blow-up on your left is a side view showing a small piece of white irreg-ularity with an arrow which is on the original X-rays, put there by the treating physicians in Parkland Hospital and interpreted by some physicians initially and in testimony to the Warren Com-mission as being metal from a bullet within the thigh bone itself.
>
> "The direct frontal view shows the thigh from the front rather than from the side. The [view] shows *the same metal fragment* which in the interpretation of the medical panel members, the panel's consultant radiologists and Dr. Reynolds, who reported on the X-rays at Parkland Hospital, is not in the bone but is im-mediately beneath the skin on the inside of the thigh. What was interpreted by some doctors as being within the bone is really an artifact, that is, a marking produced by dirt or a scratch, et cetera, and does not represent an injury to the bone." (I HSCA 294)

This seems extremely muddled and imprecise to me.

> Dr. Baden: "We concluded that the bullet did enter the skin of the thigh, but that it was a spent bullet and it did not penetrate

more than a half inch or so into the skin, and that in fact the bullet was not present in the thigh when treatment was provided to Governor Connally in the operating room."

Mr. Klein: "Doctor, did the panel reach any conclusion as to what happened to the bullet which had entered the thigh?"

Dr. Baden: "Yes, the panel concluded after reviewing all of the medical evidence *and other evidence and circumstances* as to how the Governor was treated, that the bullet had *partially entered, the thigh and then had dropped out.*" (I HSCA 294)

No medical doctor or personnel testified that the bullet "*had partially entered the thigh.*"

The bullet dropped out! Is he serious? How is this even allowed in the record. The bullet was not thrown at Governor Connally, but entered his femur, assumably with enough force, even at the point of the single bullet nonsense, to stay in and not fall out. Not only did it fall out, but when did this happen? Wouldn't it had to have fallen out before the doctors began to operate? They wouldn't have noticed a missing bullet. Bullets don't enter skin and then just fall back out. When a bullet breaks skin and lodges in whatever area it is entering, hemorrhaging occurs and tissue encases itself around the bullet. This rant could go on for days, but you get the point, absurdity beyond any ability to believe. And no comment or objection by anyone!

Mr. Klein proceeds:

Mr. Klein: "Has the panel reached a conclusion as to whether these wounds were all caused by one bullet?"

Dr. Baden: "Yes, sir. The panel did conclude that these wounds were caused by one bullet." (I HSCA 296)

Baden should have at least said that it was *possible* that one bullet caused all of the damage, but saying that it did *definitively* is simply above his ability to know. Connally shows two reactions (Z-237/238 and Z-327/328) to wounding in the Zapruder film. He is proudly definitive that one bullet did it. I wouldn't be so sure and neither should he.

Connally's surgeons didn't think all the damage could have been caused by one bullet, because of the multiple fragments said to be in the wrist. The nurse in the operating room was handing pieces of metal to a Texas Ranger, (never to be seen again) and if the pieces of metal she handed over weighed more than $1/437^{th}$ of an ounce, the magic bullet is simply a façade.

Baden doesn't take long to affirm and declare with great passion the magic bullet theory.

> Mr. Klein: "Doctor, you have also testified that the panel unanimously concluded that a bullet entered the President's upper right back and exited from the front of his neck. Did the panel reach a conclusion as to whether the same bullet which entered the President's upper right back could have then exited from the front of his neck and struck Governor Connally and caused the wounds that he received?"

> Dr. Baden: "Yes; the panel concluded, based on the enlarged nature of the entrance perforation in the Governor's back, that the bullet was wobbling when it struck him and had to have struck something before striking the Governor; that this entrance perforation of the Governor's back could have resulted from a missile that had come through the neck of the President on the basis of the autopsy findings alone; that in taking other evidence into consideration, such as the position of the President and the position of the Governor in the car, the findings are entirely consistent with a single bullet exit exiting the front of the President's neck and reentering the back of the Governor." (I HSCA 296—297)

Kennedy, who was sitting closely behind Governor Connally, had a wound in his throat that the people (doctors) who saw it said it was a circular, typical *entry* wound. So the wound in Kennedy was circular, yet within two feet between the president and the governor the bullet that made a circular opening began to wobble within a micro-second, for no apparent reason. It then supposedly made a wound in Connally that resembled that which is oblique or tilted. But why did it begin to wobble? Remember, I don't think the Connally back wound was oblong or oblique at the point of entry. This was done by Dr. Shaw as he was cleaning the wound during Connally's operation, as explored in chapter one concerning Governor Connally. So, the evidence seems to suggest that the bullet wasn't wobbling after all.

The reasoning descends rapidly:

> Mr. Klein: "Doctor, did the panel reach a conclusion as to whether this **bullet** [CE-399] is consistent with having entered Presi-

dent Kennedy's upper right back, exited through the front of his neck, and entered Governor Connally and caused the wounds that the Governor received?"

Dr. Baden: "Yes, the panel did conclude, all but one, Dr. Wecht, who will testify later, that this bullet is in fact consistent with having caused all of the wounds described that in fact, this bullet is significantly flattened at one end and is not in a virgin state."

Mr. Klein: "Doctor, you have testified that the panel collectively performed or were responsible for over 100,000 autopsies. You have also testified that the panel members read the autopsy report and spoke with the doctors who performed the autopsy on President Kennedy. Did the panel members reach any conclusions with respect to the procedures used during the course of the autopsy on President Kennedy?"

Dr. Baden: "Yes, Mr. Klein, they did, but just as an additional evidence for the panel, on why we felt that the bullet went through the President and the Governor, was the information that we were able to accumulate that indicates clearly there is no other bullet than this bullet and the bullet fragments that passed through the head of the President that was found, there is no evidence of other bullet injury to any other occupants of the car *or in the car itself*, which was part of the information we considered when we concluded in constructing the bullet trajectory." Baden then answered the originally stated question: "The panel did conclude that there were a number of deficiencies in the manner in which the autopsy of the President was done." (I HSCA 298)

To posit Oswald as the lone assassin, [*the "knoll shot" missed … according to the HSCA*], they [*the HSCA*] were forced to accept the magic bullet theory just like their predecessors the Warren Commission. What if CE- 399 had not been surreptitiously found on or near a gurney at Parkland Hospital? A scenario that is a total and absolute fiction. What kind of questions would we be asking today? Hard to tell, but we would be wondering about a lot of things like the shot sequence of both men and the various accompanying wounds.

The Warren Commission and the HSCA argument is as ridiculous and nonsensical, as is the conclusion that Oswald fired three shots just because there were three cartridge casings found. What if Oswald had pocketed the casings and dumped them somewhere between the bus and the taxi? No one did any canvasing that I know about and probably wouldn't have if my suggested scenario had taken place. Would this mean there was no assassination that took place that day?

The Warren Commission and the HSCA had to fit too many wounds into too few bullets, so they both did exactly the same thing and reached the same conclusion, except the ridiculously missed shot at Z-312/313, which was postulated by the HSCA. And even though Baden, speaking on behalf of the medical panel, *though he was highly critical of Dr. Humes, et al*, came up with the identical conclusion. It seems as if the fix was in.

Baden was critical of the Bethesda autopsy, but you need to read what the panel reported on:

> "...the panel will document its full critical analysis from the improper assumption of jurisdiction [*not Humes' fault*] of the dead body and deficiencies in the qualifications of the pathologists who did the autopsy, to the failure of the prosecutors to contact the doctors who treated the President at Parkland Hospital and failure to inspect the clothing, to the inadequate documentation of injuries, lack of proper preservation of evidence, and incompleteness of the autopsy." (I HSCA 298)

Baden essentially says that Humes, Boswell and Finck were incompetent, however their autopsy got the conclusion right. Whoever it was that wanted no autopsy got exactly what they yearned for, unqualified people, a lack of jurisdiction, and insufficient materials available. Not to mention a **military presence** in the autopsy room that at least partially guided the procedure. Does that prove a plot? You piece the puzzle together and see where it leads.

The second-round of questions from Congressman Preyer, essentially says that doctors, unlike medical examiners, don't really know the difference between entrance and exit wounds, but agreed that Kennedy's throat wound could have been misidentified for an exit wound because it exited through skin held firmly in place by the shirt and tie.

> Dr. Baden: "An exit perforation through firm skin is smaller than through lax skin." (I HSCA 300)

I'm not a medical doctor or a surgeon, but I can suggest that an exit wound is usually much bigger where it comes out, because that bullet is pushing an enormous amount of human tissue in front of it.

Baden makes an assertion that flies in the face of many of the Parkland doctors, regarding the positioning of the head wound:

> "...photographs of the brain were examined by the panel members and do show the injury to the brain itself is on the top portion of the brain. The bottom portion or undersurface of the brain, which would have had to have been injured if the bullet perforated in the lower area as indicated in the autopsy report, was intact. If a bullet entered in this lower area, the cerebellum portion of the brain would have had to be injured and it was not injured." (I HSCA 301)

Baden never saw photos of President Kennedy's brain. The Parkland doctors stated that brain tissue, cerebrum and cerebellum, were present on the gurney on which the President was lying supine. Both brain portions are differently colored. What motive would the Parkland doctors have for lying?

Humes testified to a large amount of damage to the cerebral peduncles, which are suction-cup like objects that sit at the bottom of the brain, just above the roof of the mouth. How could they have been damaged if the only bullet that did any damage to JFK's head entered at the top of his head, pushed forward, downward, and to the right and exited on the right side of the skull, doing minimal damage to the upper part of the right cerebrum?

It is one thing to reject Humes' entry wounds. His neck entry was placed very conveniently, so as not to raise any controversy. His head wound justified itself with a shot from above and behind and as a result was accepted for fifteen years. In stating that he visually observed damage to the cerebral peduncles, only to learn that based on X-rays and Dox drawings he was wrong, is a weird and peculiar twist. Humes had the brain in his hands. He made observations in his effort to remove the brain. (2 H 356 and *passim*).

Can anyone help with the problem of fakery, because it is a massive problem? At least it is to me and I have never understood it. It is an issue that simply isn't addressed very much. I have always tried to shun the fakery issue, because if most or all of the evidence has been faked, then what is there to discuss? Baden's entire argument is made on doubtful photos (especially Fox-3) and doubtful X-rays (the lateral X-ray, AP X-ray), and this is in the face of a dozen or more well-qualified medical individuals who saw things completely differently from what Dr. Baden is testifying to before the House Committee on Assassinations.

Baden then rejects Dr. Robert Shaw and his testimony before the Warren Commission, who operated on Governor Connally; saying that Shaw stated before the Commission that the single bullet theory was unsound, but that he did this because of "what was told to him by Governor Connally and Mrs. Connally at the time he treated the Governor in Parkland Hospital; his basis is what they heard, what they observed, what they perceived….He does not make that determination on the basis of the medical, surgical, or pathological findings." (I HSCA 302)

Shaw's comment was simply that, CE-399 could not have done all the damage, because of the amount of metal fragments described in Governor Connally's wrist. I doubt if he heard this from Governor and Mrs. Connally.

The testimony of Dr. Michael Baden resumed c. 1:30 p.m. after a morning recess at 11:45 a.m.

Baden continued to maintain his firmness on the "higher, by 4 inches" head entry wound, by pointing out metal in that area, which would coincide with an entry wound. It's not very visible on the X-ray and the entry wound is unquestionably not visible on the autopsy photo. The blood droplet itself, not a wound, is barely distinguishable.

We should all remember that Jerrol Custer indicated he had been asked to come back for additional X-rays, after Kennedy's body was long gone, and that a 6.5mm piece of metal was attached to the head that he was X-raying. I interviewed Custer in the early nineties and he told me this account. This is the metal fragment that Dr. Mantik sees on the X-ray that he is highly suspicious of and for good reason.

Baden was questioned whether the lower entry to the back of JFK's head could be a wound, and he emphatically denied it. The enhanced X-rays show fracture lines radiating from that point. You can't get away from two shots to JFK's head at Z-312/313 and Z-327/328. It explains so many things and answers so many questions.

Baden bemoaned that the brain was not available for examination; but noted that the Dox drawing of it "shows how the brain looked when it was examined **and before it was misplaced or lost.**" (1 HSCA 304)

But it wasn't lost, at least not really. The brain we see in the X-rays is not the same brain that was drawn by Ida Dox. The brain we see in the

X-rays is damaged with c. one-third of it missing, while the Dox drawing shows a disrupted brain, but not with the kind of loss that we see on the X-ray. Ergo, there were two brains. Disturbing? That is precisely the point.

Is Baden kidding? It doesn't seem like it. Misplaced? Could it still be in the Archives somewhere? Or, lost? This is ridiculous. It is beyond the pale of being sensible that you would lose the brain of an assassinated President of the United States, at least not on purpose. Yet, they did.

The brain was destroyed, but the question is, why? The exact details are not known, but misplaced or lost is just dishonest, and Dr. Baden knew it. The destroyed brain would not have indicated one bullet from behind, because one bullet would not have caused that much damage.

Baden disagreed with the Rockefeller Commission that there were fragments of a bullet left behind by the bullet that struck JFK in the back and exited his throat. He said it was similar to the Connally bone fragment; this is an artifact "due to a piece of dirt present on the X-ray cassette or that it was produced during the X-ray developing process which occurs not uncommonly as can be seen on other of the President's X-rays." (1 HSCA 305)

Notice that there is always dirt or artifacts where possible evidence would be at odds with the official version. Baden was asked if the bullet that struck a piece of Kennedy's spine or vertebra would still leave "the neat, clean exit wound in the throat?"

> Dr. Baden: "Yes, sir. Usually, when a bullet strikes something of substance it will begin to wobble, but as a bullet wobbles, there are times when it will be aligned in a straight-on directional course. As I am demonstrating by using this wooden pointer there are times when, even if it is wobbling as it is moving, it will be in a straight on position." (I HSCA 305)

As for Dr. Humes:

> "As a result of that move [*of the body from Texas*] many things happened. In all fairness, Dr. Humes is here and will speak later. Some people assume authority and upon authors authority is thrust as happened to Dr. Humes. He was later to become president of the American Society of Clinical Pathologists. A well experienced hospital pathologist in the scheme of things, he had not been exposed to many gunshot wounds and had not

performed autopsies in deaths due to shooting previously; neither had the other autopsy pathologists present. So, they were required to do an autopsy that by experience and by the way our society is structured in the United States, is reserved for forensic pathologists and coroner's pathologists. As a result of that, certain things didn't happen." (I HSCA 311)

Baden then gives us a list: documentation, photos, measurements, talking with the attending physician. Also, the clothing as it "gives information as to distance, as to whether the bullet is wobbling, et cetera. The clothing was not examined." (I HSCA 311)

"I wish to point out and emphasize that the doctors performed the autopsy in Bethesda in a *military situation*, with *a lot of superior officers* who were *not forensic pathologists* present…" (I HSCA 312)

Is Dr. Baden implying that the attendance of higher-ranking officers, by their presence of rank caused problems? Hard to say. There seems to be an undercurrent to what Baden is saying without actually saying it. He will, however, never admit it.

Baden went on to expound that an entry would make a "hole, like that seen on the back of the President's jacket, but an exit wound would produce a slit-like wound, as seen on the President's shirt, *with no fabric missing, as was the case in the back wound*." (I HSCA 315)

Is he saying a bullet going in makes a hole in the clothing, but a bullet going out only makes a slit. That is certainly a new way of looking at it.

Baden was slightly ambiguous when asked about the head motion going backwards in the Zapruder film; and pointed out that the medical panel had done more than 100,000 autopsies, and the first murder they ever witnessed was that committed by Jack Ruby, followed by their screening of the Zapruder film:

"Apart from those two instances, and an occasional wartime film clip, it is unique to see a person's reaction to a gunshot wound. We cannot say with all our experiences with gunshot wounds, what movement a head should have when struck, a live head, a live breathing head with blood going through, with the skin alive and the bones alive. How such a real head would react to a gunshot wound is beyond the limits of scientific study and recorded in the annals of medical literature, nor in the experience of the panel members. We cannot say with any degree of medical certainty precisely how we would expect the President's head to move when shot." (I HSCA 316)

This seems to be an evasive non-answer. He is suggesting that the blood is flowing through skin and bones, and as a result the laws of physics are not active. There is a lot of footage of people lined up in front of a mass grave and some military person walking behind them, puts a bullet in each head as he passes. Every one of those pitches forward into the pit. No one fell backward, upon the executioner. To paraphrase Baden, they also had blood going through their bodies, and subsequently out of, the skin and bones. The laws of physics, like the law of gravity, cannot be repealed in order to guarantee the survival of a lone-assassin myth perpetrated upon an unsuspicious public by deceitful individuals, for reasons not known.

Baden responded to Representative McKinney that a large percentage of the head bullet had been retrieved from the car.

"A great proportion of it, a large proportion of it." (I HSCA 316)

The two fragments found in the car weighed a total of 66 grains, or 40.86% of a 161 grain bullet.

Congressman Sawyer said that the Zapruder film shows a pause between the wounding of the President and Governor Connally, which is true. Dr. Baden gave a medical sleight-of-hand response, saying that people don't always know when they have been wounded. That is not what the surgeons said who operated on Governor Connally. They, in fact, said the governor would have responded rather abruptly due to where he was hit.

Mr. Sawyer: "Do you observe, too, in that film though, while the President was visibly reacting and the Governor was at least not, to my ability to observe, showing any reaction as yet, he was still holding in his right hand his hat and that that wrist was supposedly shattered by that bullet. Does that disturb you at all?

Dr. Baden: "I think disturb is probably an accurate phrase. Yes, it causes me concern. However, the problem is clearly—

Mr. Sawyer: "Aside from concern, how can a man be still holding the hat when his wrist is shattered?"

Dr. Baden: "Although it appears incongruent, clearly we of the panel have all had experience in which persons have been seriously injured and have not known they were injured for a few minutes. In evaluating all the evidence, there is no question that Govern Connally did, in fact, hold his hat after he was shot and after the bullet passed through his wrist—this would be the case even if one did not accept the 'single bullet theory.'

He did hold that hat after the wrist was injured and he didn't know the wrist was injured."

Mr. Sawyer: "*The wrist should have known it, you would think.*"

Dr. Baden: "The wrist knew. The bone was broken." (I HSCA 321)

I don't think that Connally was wounded in the wrist as early as a lot of people do. I think the wrist and femur wounds are a result of the head shot that passed through President Kennedy c. Z-327. You have to see the Zapruder film to understand this and that was never more forceful and vivid, as stated earlier, than at Wecht 2013, when **Keith Fitzgerald** illustrated this with his showing of the Zapruder film, up close and personal. You can view what I am talking about by going to YouTube and begin watching at the 45:00 mark to see the footage I have been talking about: https://video.search.yahoo.com/yhs/search?fr=yhs-trp-001&ei=UTF-8&hsimp=yhs-001&hspart=trp&p=you+tube+josiah+thompson&type=Y143_F163_201897_102620#id=1&vid=d954ad72c37585c3e7c263cee-0a563aa&action=click

Now for the silliest of all:

Mr. Sawyer: "And now, when you combine that with what I thought was a very persuasive and impressive testimony of both Governor Connally and Mrs. Connally, adding that to it, you still feel that does not militate against your single bullet theory?"

Dr. Baden: "The experience of all of us in forensic pathology and of many in criminal justice, is that, unfortunately, as much as I am impressed with Governor Connally's testimony and his ability to recall and his ability to survive what happened to him, as a forensic pathologist, I have learned not to rely on eyewitnesses or on persons who were present or who were injured in the course of a homicide, particularly when this comes in contact with autopsy findings." (I HSCA 321)

It did seem refreshing that someone asked the right question, finally. Baden's indication that "the wrist knew," is tantamount to saying, the wrist knew, but the cable to the brain was blocked somehow causing a pause in reaction time. Again, this is only important if you think Connally was shot much earlier than I do; as, I maintain that Connally received his wrist and leg wounds c. Z-327/328.

All Dr. Michael Baden is doing is deliberately confusing the comittee, for the sake of keeping alive the single-bullet theory, which would then perpetuate the lone assassin theory.

08

Dr. James J. Humes
September 7, 1978

On September 7, 1978, Dr. James J. Humes testified before the HSCA in Washington, D.C.

What follows is what Jim DiEugenio calls the Three Faces of Dr. Humes. The autopsy on President John F. Kennedy is certainly one of the most controversial aspects, if not the most controversial aspect, of the JFK assassination. It has spawned the most bizarre theories, some of which are beyond ridiculous, others are outright obscene, yet some researchers' conclusions are probably closer to reality than the actual autopsy protocol. What I propose to do is to take a look at the record of Commander Dr. James Joseph Humes, the lead autopsy doctor on the evening of November 22, 1963. We will cover his testimony before the Warren Commission, House Select Committee on Assassinations, and the Assassination Records and Review Board.

The Warren Commission: the back-of-the-head wound is low

Dr. Humes testified before the Warren Commission in 1964, the House Select Committee on Assassinations in 1978, and the Assassination Records Review Board in 1996. These three different interrogations deserve examination. Many questions have loomed – and still remain – as to what *really* happened during the evening of November 22, 1963. Humes was the head autopsy doctor that night. To quote Al Smith, "Let's take a look at the record." Our decisions about believing him will rest largely on his testimony, correlated with other data we have assimilated over the years.

On March 16, 1964, Dr. Humes appeared before the Warren Commission with Arlen Specter, the Commission's designated medical attorney, handling most of the inquiry. Commander Humes stated that "the body was received at 25 minutes before 8 and the autopsy began at approximately 8:00 p.m. on that evening" (2 H 349).

The time of 8:00 pm and all times that are associated with it, beginning around 5:55 pm, when the plane landed at Andrews Air Force base, has led rise to the body alteration theory, directed by David Lifton. He has accumulated quite a few followers over the years, so I thought the following short piece will give another way of looking at this problem.

The following is an interesting piece written by researcher Walt Brown, entitled *Body Alteration?: It's all about Gravity.*

> David Lifton, in his book *Best Evidence*, argues that the body was altered, either in route, meaning body snatchers took it out of the coffin between the touchdown of Air Force One and the beginning of the autopsy at Bethesda, suggesting that someone hijacked the body and then took it to some black ops site to reconfigure the body promptly, which is beyond the stroke of silliness. You just simply could not have done what Lifton is saying was done that quickly. Dr. Cyril Wecht said it would have been highly unlikely to perform this kind of a feat on a human corpse that quickly. No one would have been able to. You just cannot overhaul and alter a body that abruptly. Photographs are obviously a different story, especially if you have years to deal and work with them. Despite what McCamy might say, no matter what you say about the back of the head photo, if that is all you have, there is no way to say whom that individual is. The stare of death does look like JFK, but would we say that if we didn't know it was him.

I'm not saying it isn't him, only that we should be careful not to rush to judgment.

Body alteration? I think not. JFK's body was not embezzled by some covert team of intelligence agents. It went from Parkland hospital to Air Force 1 and then on to Bethesda.

There was no autopsy before the autopsy. For all these years, we've decried Humes, and rightly so, as inept, yet he was able to work miracles in a few minutes when nobody was looking? I hardly think so.

At 7 pm on 11/22, nobody really knew what alterations would have been necessary to make the body look like lone-assassin, (Oswald only) results. The kind of reconstruction work that would have been required would have taken many hours, according to Dr. Cyril Wecht.

So, what did happen? The key is gravity. Lifton's story is based on cherry-picked perceptions; one individual testified that the body arrived at 4:30 pm EST, but it only left Dallas at 3:48 EST, 42 minutes earlier. One observer saw the coffin opened, with JFK dressed in a suit (nope). Another saw JFK's neck wound sutured when the coffin was open (nope). Floyd Riebe, photo assistant to John T. Stringer (a civilian), claimed he took over 100 photos that have never been seen. But his claim also was that he used the same camera that Stringer used, which required dual strobe lights for flashes, and the insertion and removal of photo-paper cassettes for each photo. 100 photos would have taken an immense amount of time, and it seems likely that Stringer would have realized something was wrong with 100 flashes that he did not cause. (Riebe retracted this to the ARRB). One observer saw a whole bullet fall out of JFK's head, and no whole bullet could have survived any head shot. (nope)

The entire Lifton premise is based on the Sibert-O'Neill statement, essentially hearsay, that there had been surgery to the head, namely in the top of the skull. Considering how poorly Sibert-O'Neill spelled the names of those present for their report, it seems a reasonable argument that they were not quoting Humes exactly. If Humes had said, "This looks like surgical damage," would he have meant a severe wound or that surgery had been performed. Sibert-O'Neill never followed up what they thought they heard. The other anomalies revolved around a shipping coffin and/or body bag.

The photos that show the coffin being onloaded at Love Field demand attention. The coffin weighed 800 lbs. and the contents weighed 172 lbs. The crew of JFK aides trying to get that coffin up the portable stairs had a horrible time because of the weight and the need to go one stair at a time. You can even see people on the sides of the stairs trying to help.

When they got to the top, the coffin would not go into the plane because of the handles on the sides, so S/As Hill and Kellerman broke them off. Gerald Blaine, in his Secret Service Memoir, said the handles broke when the coffin was rammed into the opening, but that's ridiculous because it was impossible to push the coffin forward in any way that would have generated enough speed to allow the handles to break off. Once the handles were broken off, the coffin was slid into place in the rear compartment, where JBK [Jackie Kennedy] and the "Irish Mafia" remained after the swearing in of LBJ. The coffin was guarded; the body was not stolen, and it was *not* moved in order for someone to do cosmetology in the belly of the plane.

At 5:55 EST, the plane landed at Andrews. RFK ran through the plane to be with Jackie, who, along with the Irish Mafia, were still in proximity to the coffin. It was then slid to the door and onto the lift platform put alongside the plane. Gravity was now in place. The coffin was (of course) lowered much more easily than it had been raised. When the lift halted, the coffin was still 4.5 to 5 feet off the ground; it only had to be lowered to get it into the Navy ambulance, but it took a serious crew, with the Military District of Washington (MDW) casket team assisting JFK's aides. Off to Bethesda, with SS, JBK, and RFK in the ambulance.

A unique situation arose at the morgue loading dock, and this is critical to understanding what happened. Bethesda served as a hospital for VIPs in government, and navy personnel. For those that died at Bethesda and needed an autopsy, the Bethesda facilities were used. From there, the deceased were removed, either in body bags or shipping coffins, to appropriate mortuaries. But there is no record of deceased individuals at any time ever arriving at Bethesda in a burial coffin to be autopsied. It just makes absolutely no sense.

If there was a chance arrival, it challenged the layout, because the Bethesda morgue loading dock is much higher than the level of the platform in the ambulance. With a body bag or shipping coffin arrival (and not a VIP), the body bag or the coffin could be, with help, lifted up and onto the morgue platform.

But not in JFK's case. The medical folks added to the problem by having a gurney atop the platform, so JFK's handle-free coffin would have had to be elevated almost seven feet to get it on top of the gurney.

The only way it could have been done, without handles, would have been to stand it on its end and hope it didn't topple. But the men in the MDW casket team were fanatics about their work, and they were not going to risk JFK's remains tumbling to the base of the coffin, or worse still, the coffin falling and popping open.

At that point, and with that challenge in mind, I believe JFK's remains were quietly removed and put in either a body bag or a shipping coffin, uploaded onto the morgue ramp and taken inside. The empty coffin, no longer a challenge to the remains of the President, was then raised up and taken in, empty. It was all about gravity.

Early in the questioning, Dr. Humes mentions that the autopsy photos were not all taken at the same time, but "were made as the need became apparent to make such" (2 H 349). It goes without saying that it would be challenging if not impossible to take pictures of the body at the same time you take photos of the interior of the skull cavity, even though the latter group of exposures have vanished without a trace.

This point will come up again during his ARRB deposition. The photos made before the proceedings began were, as Humes stated, "the face of the President, the massive head-wound and the large defect associated with it." He mentions 15-20 shots being made before these proceedings finished. This number seems low, especially when there was litigation in 1993 to have 257 photos and x-rays released. Part of that bizarre numerical inconsistency is due to the fact that some of the so-called Fox poses involved four exposures, multiplying Humes' 15-20 estimate to 60-80, but still coming up short. Add to that the bizarre fact that three full sets of X-rays were taken, as they were determined to X-ray until they found something, and the number grows again.

The point is that Humes indicated the autopsy photos were not all taken at once, but throughout the procedure as the need arose. Specter asked Dr. Humes to dilate on the neck wound, which really means the back wound, which was five and three-eighths inches down from the top of the shirt and coat collars. It has been argued that JFK's coat was bunched, but although that could explain some discrepancy in the coat, it would not explain the shirt.

There never was or ever will be a neck wound in the back. This needs to be settled once and for all. Whether you agree with Admiral Burkley's assertion on the death certificate, or just look at the autopsy pictures, President Kennedy was shot in the back, not the neck. This is important for the sake of accuracy: the Gerald Ford revelation, as stated earlier in this book, about changing the language in the Warren Report from "back" to "back of neck," which he confessed to doing "for the sake of clarity in 1997," was in fact, a key element in salvaging the Single Bullet Theory, which is the foundational point for the government's case against Oswald, and also for there being only one shooter firing that fateful day. Specter then asked if it would have helped to have the photos and x-rays, to which Humes responded that it might be helpful. Specter follows this up with a rather memorable observation: "Is taking photos and x-rays routine or something out of the ordinary?" (2 H 350). Having Harold Rydberg execute medical illustrations for the Commission volumes because the autopsy photographs weren't available, was both unnecessary and absurd. Humes relied on deceitful drawings in testifying before the Commission and he and fellow pathologist Thornton Boswell described those drawings for Rydberg, instead of using the actual photographs, which he did not see until November 1, 1966. That is two and a half years after the fact. Recall: the third pathologist, Pierre Finck, did not appear until the brain had been removed, later in the autopsy.

Simply compare the Rydberg drawings with the actual stills of the Zapruder film and you might conclude they are from two different crimes. The Rydberg drawing of JFK's head is not in the slightest bit in the same position as Zapruder frame 312, when compared with each other. Keep in mind that, early in the history of this case, the only way you could compare frame 312 with the Rydberg drawings was to actually own a set of the 26 volumes of hearings and exhibits (and the frames only went up to Zapruder frame 334 in the Warren Commission volumes).

This is the death of the President of the United States. It should surprise no one that Rydberg, upon seeing the photos after he made the drawings, immediately impugned the accuracy of his own drawings. Dox, at best, admitted to having help with her tracings by having the autopsy photos supplied to her. Humes went on to describe the posterior wounds. The back wound was 7 x 4 mm; it had a long axis roughly parallel to the long axis of the vertical column. The back-of-the-head wound was 2.5 cm to the right of midline and slightly above the external occipital protuber-ance. There was also a wound of exit, which created a huge defect over the right side of the skull, leaving fractures and fragments. Its greatest diame-ter was 13 cm. Humes stated that, after they reflected the scalp, they found a corresponding defect on both tables of the skull. After Humes described the head wound, Specter asked him if he was referring to the wound on the lower part of the neck. Specter, throughout his interrogation of the doctors, is always trying to divert, deflect, or ask them hypotheticals that are irrelevant to the evidence at hand. Does he have an agenda? Yes. If you doubt that assertion, then I ask you to please go back and read his ques-tioning of any of the medical personnel.

Humes went on to say that portions of JFK's skull came apart when they reflected the scalp. This has led some to believe that the President's head cracked like an eggshell, when it exploded due to the force of the missile entry. Humes said they received three portions of skull late in the evening or early morning hours of the 23rd. There is no tangible ev-idence as to the provenance of the skull pieces, or who delivered them. Remember, the Harper fragment did not arrive until the next day.

They were roughly put together to account for the portion of the de-fect that Humes thought was the exit wound. It still left one-fourth of the defect unaccounted for. Again, fragments of scalp fell to the table as it was reflected.

Humes then mentioned their attempt to locate non-movable points of reference. He mentions the mastoid process and the acromion pro-cess. Basically, the measurements are movable if the torso can swivel. When Humes measured the back wound at 14 cm below the mastoid process, he is measuring the back in terms of the ear. Was the body straight? Arched back? Arched forward? These factors would make a significant difference in determining the actual distance. The head wound, however, is 2.5 cm to the right of midline and slightly above the external occipital protuberance, which is fixed and not movable. An attempt to "take probes and have them satisfactorily fall through [a] definite path" proved unsuccessful. (2 H 361) Robert Knudsen, White House photographer (*HSCA Agency File Number 014028*), when in-terviewed by Andrew Purdy, stated he saw "at least two probes going through the body of President Kennedy; there may have been as many as three." This will come up again during Humes' ARRB encounter. Another possibility, if they didn't use probes, is that the back wound was not penetrable, because the doctors never bothered to rotate the musculature of JFK, which could have loosened things up enough for them to correctly probe the wound. James Jenkins, in his recent publication, insists that the lungs were not penetrated.

Dr. Humes said he didn't talk with Dr. Perry at Parkland until the next day, November 23rd. I find it hard to believe that anyone, including Dr. George Burkley, who was the only medical person to have been at both Parkland and Bethesda, wouldn't have said something to the pathologists, especially if he saw the throat wound before the tracheotomy was performed, an assumption many have claimed, but not proven. There has been a lot of controversy about whether Dr. Humes made the customary Y-incision or some alternative, perhaps a U-incision. Humes stated to the Warren Commission, as well as putting it in the autopsy report, that he made the customary Y-incision, perhaps because someone did not want JFK's adrenal glands examined. This will also come up during his ARRB discussion, where he repeats his claim that he made the Y-incision. Humes said he saw JFK's clothing for the first time the day before his WC testimony. This implies many things; the most obvious being negligence on Humes' part, assisted by the Secret Service. He addressed this issue again during his ARRB questioning.

Humes stated that the missile traversed JFK's neck from interior to exterior, due to an analysis of the fibers on the front side of the shirt. This also correlates with the left anterior tie defect. This depends on what is the cause of the cut shirt and tie nick. This could be the result of a scalpel cut when his clothing was removed; Harold Weisberg argued this in a letter to the *Washington Post* of January 11, 1992.

Humes went on to say that the wound in the anterior portion of the neck was physically lower than the posterior wound in the back. This has to be the party line for the Single Bullet Theory to survive. A mere look at the autopsy photo showing the back wound (Fox-5) warrants this as dubious. Again, as stated earlier, at the COPA conference in 1995, investigator Andy Purdy and both Dr. Cyril Wecht and Dr. Michael Baden agreed to this, that the back wound entered at a slightly upward angle, 11 degrees, based on the abrasion collar around the entry wound. What the Forensic Pathology Panel did, in conjunction with the work of astrophysicist Thomas Canning, was have JFK leaning sufficiently forward so that a level of upward track through the body itself became a downward path. (VII HSCA 87, 100) Therefore JFK was leaning sharply forward, while behind the Stemmons Freeway sign. And he does this for precisely .9 seconds. But since JFK was sitting nearly upright in the car, the photographic panel for the HSCA concluded that the back wound was even with or lower than the throat wound. But in a very odd reference, the photographic panel said it would leave the final figures up to Thomas Canning. (See footnote in VI HSCA 33)

Humes stated that he didn't feel the X-rays would assist the Commission materially in specifying the nature of the wounds. This may make more sense when we get to his testimony before the ARRB. It seems an odd sort of reasoning for a medical doctor to say the X-rays wouldn't help or assist the Commission in determining the nature of JFK's wounds. Another point of controversy in recent years was in respect to what Dr. Humes actually burned in his fireplace the weekend of the assassination. He stated before the Warren Commission that the draft of the autopsy report was "burned in the fireplace of my recreation room" (2 H 373). There was a question as to whether he burned an autopsy draft or his autopsy notes – a significant difference. This will get cleared up when we get to his ARRB testimony. Dr. Humes concluded his testimony by declaring that CE-399 could not have inflicted the wound to Governor Connally's wrist or left thigh, due to the fragments that were discarded while the jacket of the bullet remained intact. He implied that one bullet could have caused both wrist and thigh wounds, but not CE-399. He also suggested that one bullet could have penetrated President Kennedy and also Governor Connally, but not have caused any further damage. This is a key point that is very much underplayed.

House Select Committee on Assassinations: the-back- of-the-head wound rises four inches

On September 7, 1978, Commander Humes, appearing before the HSCA, was asked a scant 44 questions by Gary Cornwell. This should not pose much of a surprise, since the Warren Commission asked all three autopsy doctors a total of only 304 questions (Humes was asked 215; Boswell and Finck essentially nodded their heads to what Humes had already replied to Specter). With little exaggeration, it could be stated that the testimony of Commander Humes could be the entire autopsy statement. To say, "Humes, Boswell, and Finck," only means they were all in the same room together at the same time, which Specter allowed them to be while testifying, though you would think the opposite should have been done to avoid collusion. Specter asked Boswell if he agreed with Humes, which turned him into a bobblehead of agreement. Specter questioned Finck more than he did Boswell. This was odd, because a lot of cutting had been done before Finck entered the morgue. What is disturbing is that at least 92 other witnesses were asked more questions than the three pathologists combined. Thoroughness was not the aim of the Commission. But for the HSCA, the third question that Mr. Cornwell asked already makes you think Dr. Humes is being excused for his incompetence. Cornwell asked: "You had received special education and training in the field of pathology; is that correct?" Humes: "That is correct, yes, sir" (I HSCA 324).

Humes then states the autopsy began "about 7:30 pm in the evening and after some preliminary examinations, about 8 or 8:15" (I HSCA 324). He said they noticed almost immediately the two wounds, one in the head and one in the back of the neck. Humes is rather liberal, as was Specter before him, with the use of "back of the neck," since the photos, drawings, and clothing all show the wound in the upper back. Humes, responding to a question by Mr. Cornwell, said the autopsy ended around midnight, even though he said 11 pm to the Warren Commission.

The questioning then turned to the subject of Dr. Humes being interviewed by the Forensic Pathology Panel in the Archives. When Mr. Cornwell said the panel disagreed with Dr. Humes about the location of the head wound, Humes – on the PBS videotaping of the proceedings – was visibly shaken. He attempted to jot down some notes, while at the same time steadying his hand to do so. He told the panel that the small droplet, which looks like a piece of tissue paper one applies to a cut while shaving, in the lower portion of Fox-3 (F-48 according to the HSCA exhibits) was a "wound of entry and that that was the only wound of entry" (I HSCA 325). Cornwell then proceeded to an observation by Dr. Petty about the supposed defect in the cowlick area (in looking closely at this, the supposed wound appears to be somewhat below JFK's cowlick area, which was higher on his head). Yet, the alleged defect is much more apparent in the Ida Dox drawings than in the Fox-3 autopsy photograph, as was stated earlier in chapter four. This is because, as we know, Dox was given pictures of gunshot wounds, which she then superimposed in that area of the skull, highly exaggerating what was really there. Documents revealing this kind of alteration by Dox, urged on by Baden, were declassified years later, making it even more offensive. In fact, with Dr. Baden present, Dr. Randy Robertson and myself presented these findings separately, without knowing what the other was going to present, at Cyril Wecht's Duquesne Conference in 2003.

Both the back of the head photograph and the Dox drawing are easily obtainable on the internet. Compare and prepare to be bedazzled. Humes replied to Petty, when interviewed by the forensic panel in the National Archives:

> I don't know what that is. No. 1, I can assure you that as we reflected the scalp to get to this point, there was no defect corresponding to this in the skull at any point. I don't know what that is. It could be to me clotted blood. I don't, I just don't know what it is, but it **certainly** was not any wound of entrance. (I HSCA 326)

Humes then stated to Cornwell that he only had short notice to prepare and hoped they could straighten things out. Humes saw the wound on the night of the autopsy. He knew the HSCA location of the wound was too high. There are certainly valid reservations that the image in the cowlick area is even a wound at all, as we have already stated. To look at both of the back of the head photos, as inventoried in HSCA Vol. VII (*medical and firearms evidence*) and seen in stereo viewing will help with the orientation. And guess what, in fact, it does. We now have two back of the head photos, thanks to Robert Groden.

Cornwell continued verbal probing about the head wound: "If… you have a more well-considered or a different opinion or whether your opinion is still the same, as to where the point of entry is?" Humes then made a rather weird characterization as to his appearance before the pathology panel: "Yes, I think I do have a different opinion. No. 1, it was a casual kind of discussion that we were having with the panel members, as I recall it" (I HSCA 327). Humes then digressed about the photographs, saying that he first saw them on November 1, 1966, and again on January 27, 1967, when the three autopsy doctors (he indicated Finck wasn't there when talking to the ARRB) went to the Archives to categorize and summarize their findings. Finck was not present for the

November 1966 look-see; he was brought back to DC from Viet Nam for the 1967 event.

Humes then stunned everyone when he said that the alleged cowlick area wound would fit as being above and to the right of the external occipital protuberance, and:

> ...is clearly in the location of where we said *approximately* where it was...therefore, I believe that is the wound of entry... By the same token, the object in the lower portion, which I apparently and I believe now erroneously previously identified...is far below the external occipital protuberance and would not fit with the original autopsy findings (I HSCA 327).

Dr. Humes seemed unaware of Baden's hidden agenda. Michael Baden was determined to have the HSCA panel agree with the Ramsey Clark Panel of 1968. In that brief medical affair, Dr. Russell Fisher and his three cohorts made five corrections to the original autopsy description. (more:https://www.historymatters.com/essays/jfkmed/How-5Investigations/How5InvestigationsGotItWrong_3.htm)

What is amazing about that act of medical alchemy is that Fisher did it all, without exhuming the body or consulting with the original pathologists, which is probably why Humes appeared surprised before the HSCA. One of the things Fisher did was to raise the rear skull wound 4 inches upward. Yet Cornwell probed no further. Is there any wonder that some critics have suggested the photos may have been tampered with, if the doctor who performed the autopsy can't remember where the wound of entrance is located on the head of the President of the United States while looking directly at them? This will be even more evident during his ARRB testimony in regard to the X-rays. Mr. Cornwell then asked Humes to step to the easel to locate the wound of entrance on the lateral X-ray of the skull. It is obvious when you watch his testimony on video that Dr. Humes was very reluctant to address the easel. Humes agreed with Dr. Baden on the location of the wound to the skull at the point of a fracture line that juts out a bit. He concludes this tête-à-tête by saying they were presently engaged in semantics about the location of the wound of entrance to the head. After all that has preceded, with Humes admitting he was wrong about the head wound entrance, changing from slightly above the external occipital protuberance to the area of the cowlick, he then revealed something that is equally shocking.

Mr. Cornwell: "The testimony today indicated that the panel places that (*head wound entrance*) at approximately 10 centimeters [*c. 4 inches*] above the external occipital protuberance. Would that discrepancy be explainable?"

Dr. Humes: "Well, I have a little trouble with that; 10 centimeters is a significant—4 inches" (I HSCA 329).

Cornwell did not ask Humes to expand on the dilemma. The question is: What does Dr. James J. Humes believe about the wound of entrance to the head? He seemed to agree with the forensic panel and then turns right around and states that 4 inches is significant, though he has a little trouble with that. So do a lot of other people. This issue will be revisited during his ARRB testimony.

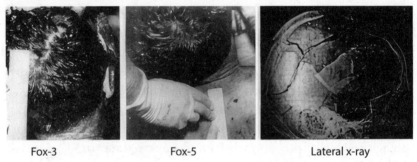

Fox-3   Fox-5   Lateral x-ray

When Humes and Boswell were behind closed doors talking with the medical panel, they were both quite vociferous that the entrance wound in the back of the head was below the external occipital protuberance. When the cowlick wound is then pointed out to him he says, "No, no. That is no wound."

Humes stated that he stayed with the morticians to help prepare the President's body until about 5:00 a.m. He began to write the autopsy report about 11:00 pm the next evening. He finished about 3 or 4 o'clock the following morning, Sunday the 24th. Cornwell asked Humes: "was the distance between the wound and the external occipital protuberance noted on those notes?" Humes replied: "…not…in any greater detail than appears in the final report" (I HSCA 330). He thought the photographs and X-rays would suffice to accurately locate this wound. He will share that same notion with the ARRB. Is it Humes' contention that this would be better than the body itself, which he had? How does this explain the ruler in the Fox-3 autopsy photograph? Was someone not measuring? This seems to have been the most opportune time to measure the exact location of the wound. He then continued about the autopsy notes, saying the original notes had the President's blood on them and he didn't want them to fall into potentially untrustworthy hands after the fact. He will give a more detailed account before the ARRB. Didn't military procedure bind him to turn the notes over to his commanding officer, after he adapted the information from them into his report? He wouldn't have been allowed to take them out of the building. What he took out and what his affidavit specifies are "draft notes." In other words, a rough outline of notes for an autopsy report. He then wrote a more coherent draft the next day and burned the "draft notes" in his home fireplace. Given the circumstances under which they were written, they may have gotten blood on them, perhaps from the original notes, or from Humes' gloves or clothing, that is if he wrote draft notes before changing out of his autopsy garb. Or, it was the original notes that he burned and he did not want to admit that.

Humes closed his testimony by restating he had no reason to change his opinion that only one bullet struck President Kennedy in the back of the head, without ever being asked. He doesn't seem as sure, however, as to *where* that bullet struck. Cornwell closed the questioning and no one else raised one question to Dr. Humes. Odd, that the one man who may have the most vital information about the condition of the late President's body isn't probed more aggressively? You get the feeling the Committee is somewhat embarrassed for Dr. Humes, given his somewhat waffling testimony. They shouldn't have been.

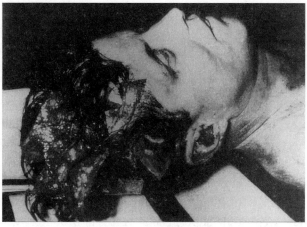

Groden Superior Right Profile (G-1)

Assassination Records Review Board: the back-of-the-head wound disappears

On February 13, 1996, the Assassination Records Review Board questioned Dr. Humes for almost 7 hours. The examination was conducted by Jeremy Gunn, General Counsel of the ARRB. Early in the questioning, Gunn asked Humes about JFK's adrenal glands. Humes seems irritated – as he does throughout the deposition – and said about his conversation with Dr. Burkley, "…the nature of that conversation I don't think I should discuss with you people" (ARRB 29). I have never understood why Humes was so annoyed about JFK's adrenal glands being discussed. The Parkland doctors spoke without hesitation of what they often called his "adrenal insufficiency." Why he would feel so bound to what was by then a non-secret befuddles me. The Kennedys no doubt didn't want JFK's Addison's Disease exposed, but in 1996, it seems foolish to try and avoid it as some kind of taboo subject.

Humes repeated that he called Dr. Perry the next morning about 8 or 9 o'clock – which gives us a time frame – and only then learned about the wound in JFK's throat. The most recent information on this is that Dr. Perry did talk with Bethesda before the sun rose the next morning and as a result Dr. Perry didn't get much sleep the night of November 22nd. Before the Warren Commission, he claimed that he "had to take one of my children to a religious function that morning, but then I returned and made some phone calls and got hold of the people in Dallas, which was unavailable to us during the course of the examination." Is he serious? He tried, but couldn't get in touch with any of the Parkland doctors, specifically Dr. Perry. So, let's see if I get this right: the FBI could compile a complete dossier on Lee Harvey Oswald within hours of the assassination, but no one could seem to find the most important doctor in the world on that night, the one who had obliterated that anterior neck wound with his tracheotomy. Recent data would suggest otherwise. Humes admitted to not knowing about standard autopsy protocol for gunshot wounds and autopsy of the neck. He stated early in this testimony that he had experience with gunshot wounds at Tripler Hospital in Hawaii and possibly in San Diego. In this part of his testimony, Dr. Humes still refers to the back wound as the back of the neck, which is amazing after the Clark Panel and the HSCA. He repeats there were some superficial attempts at probing, but the effort was aborted. He doesn't deny probing, perhaps because of what Robert Knudsen told the HSCA, but only says it wasn't effective. He also mentions he should have requested JFK's clothing. He also remembers giving Dr. Burkley JFK's brain in a pail after his interment. He said that Robert Kennedy, being the spokesperson for the family, wanted to inter it with the body. He stated he gave it to Dr. Burkley about ten days after the autopsy, after JFK had been interred. So, what was the point?

Another oddity is that Dr. Humes claimed to have never even seen the autopsy manual produced by the Departments of the Army, Navy, and Air Force, dated July 1960. If this seems like topic hopping, it is because the ARRB did this periodically. Humes admitted the possibility of phone calls during the autopsy, but that he was not directly involved. There are witnesses who report calls between Parkland and Bethesda the evening of the autopsy. Humes said one of the biggest problems that night was the people in the autopsy room. He says he should have thrown them all out. He approximates 15-20 people were in the room that night. In the recent work by Jim Jenkins, *At the Cold Shoulder of History*, the number is suggested as 30 or 31. Humes appeared frustrated, however, as to who was actually in the autopsy room.

One of the reasons Humes had no idea who assistants like Jerrol Custer, John Stringer, and Paul O'Connor were, is that he didn't do autopsies. At this stage of his career, he was really an administrator. He initially said that Admiral Calvin Galloway wasn't there, but then says he may have been, but played no role whatsoever. Yet Galloway was the commander at Bethesda Medical Center. He can't recall Admiral Edward Kenney being there either, though he may have stuck his head in the door at some point. Kenney was the Surgeon General of the United States Navy, the highest medical officer in the corps. He says if General Philip Wehle was in there, he was unaware of it. This certainly doesn't seem to line up with the Sibert-O'Neill report, which stated the presence of both Galloway and Wehle. When asked why he didn't weigh the brain, thymus, or thyroid, Humes repeated, "I don't know." He went on to say that he didn't understand why Dr. Burkley verified and signed the autopsy report. He didn't recall him doing this.

Dr. Humes stated that all of the photos, excluding Fox-8, were taken before the head was cleaned. Fox-8 was taken, obviously, after the brain was removed, near the end of the autopsy. As a sidebar, he thought most of the X-rays were taken before the photographs. He also remarked they had all of the X-rays developed during the autopsy. As he stated to the Warren Commission, the skull fell apart when he reflected the scalp. When discussing the removal of the brain, he never mentions Paul O'Connor, though he is listed in the Sibert-O'Neill report. Humes stated that Dr. Boswell may have helped him remove the brain; he wasn't sure. He felt the brain was disrupted by the "force of the blow rather than by the particular passage of any missile..." (ARRB 103). He said the lacerations were in the mid-brain posteriorly. Keep in mind, when Humes testified before the Warren Commission, he said, "at the time of the post-mortem examination, we noted that clearly visible in the large skull defect and exuding from it was lacerated brain tissue which, on close inspection, proved to represent the major portion of the right cerebral hemisphere." In other words, one of the two hemispheres was almost completely missing. Oddly, that same brain, when weighed at the supplementary examination, was assessed to weigh more than a normal human brain.

On page 111 of his ARRB deposition, Dr. Humes said he spent 30-45 minutes examining the cranium after the brain was removed. How could you not remember exactly where the point of entry was in the rear of the head?

He said they didn't actually record the autopsy, because that procedure was relatively new and they had just begun doing that; but it had started recently and you would think that especially with the autopsy of the President of the United States you would want to record the proceedings for posterity – unless there were external forces that felt otherwise. Humes said: "I don't think any real thought was given to it, to tell the truth" (ARRB 118). Apparently, a lot of things weren't given much thought that night.

When the burning of his notes came up for discussion, he gave rationale as to why he did it. He remembered going to Greenfield Village, home of the Henry Ford museum, and seeing the chair Lincoln was sitting in when he was shot. He said the tour guide pointed out a drop of Lincoln's blood on the back of the chair. He thought that was macabre and didn't want anyone to ever get these documents, hence the burning of the notes. What follows is some quibbling as to whether he burned his autopsy notes or a draft of the report, Humes replied, "It was handwritten notes and the first draft that was burned" (ARRB 134). Later, Humes goes further: "Everything that I personally prepared until I got to the status of the handwritten document that later was transcribed was destroyed" (ARRB 134). He only wanted to hand Dr. Burkley a completed version … everything else was burned. He added that he may have burned a draft of the report due to spelling errors. "I don't know. I can't recall. I absolutely can't recall" (ARRB 138). So much for a good memory – an absolute pre-requisite for an individual whose work might well include courtroom testimony. When questioned about non-movable points for measurement, Humes got annoyed, he asked if he did anything wrong, and said that he didn't want to get into a debate. When asked about Burkley placing the back wound at about the level of the third thoracic vertebra, Humes said he didn't know if that was correct, since he didn't measure from which vertebra it was. He went on to say, "I think that's much lower than it actually was" (ARRB 141-142).

Mr. Gunn then proceeded to have Dr. Humes comment on the Fox autopsy photographs. He begins with Fox-4, which is the left profile. The only comments by Humes are in regard to any incisions being made before the photo was taken. Humes denied this, with the exception of having to make a coronal incision to remove the brain.

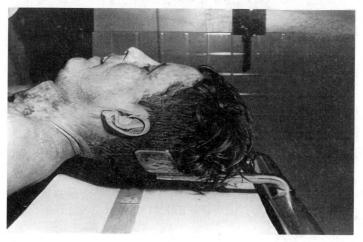

Fox - 4

The second photo was the right superior profile, sometimes referred to as G-1 (Groden-1). When asked about the triangular shaped object above the right ear – what the late Harry Livingstone referred to as the "devil ear"—Humes replied, "That's a flap of skin turned back" (ARRB 158). What Livingstone referred to as "bat wing configuration sutures," Humes dismissed as a "piece of skull" (ARRB 159). The other sharp line that creates another V, Humes again said it's another piece of skull. On the top of JFK's head, there is matter that is extruding; Humes notes "that's scalp reflected that way" (ARRB 160).

The next photos were Fox-6 and Fox-7. The matter on the top of the head Humes says is simply scalp folded back. In reference to the object over where the right ear would be, Humes says it is a piece of bone.

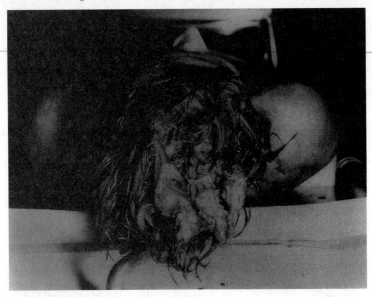

Fox - 7

The fourth photos Humes looked at was Fox-5, which is the back-wound photo. Humes stated there may have been some slight cleaning in this photograph. When asked about the ruler, he said they may have been trying to record visually the size of the wound. Gunn then asked about the two marks, one at approximately the second-centimeter line and the other at the six-centimeter line. Humes said the one lower in the back may represent a drop of blood; when questioned directly about it, Humes then said, "I have no idea" (ARRB 167). He did not think there were two wounds of entry in the picture. Gunn then digressed about the head wound and missing bone and Humes responded, "It was just a hole. Not a significant missing bone" (ibid, 171). During this same exchange, Humes says something that is significant. When Gunn asked him if there was any missing bone in the rear of the skull, Humes said, "There basically wasn't any... not a significant missing bone."

The reader should understand a key issue at this point. According to the record, the Harper fragment was discovered the day *after* the assassination. It was given over to some medical experts in Dallas, photos were made, and then it transferred to the FBI. The Bureau flew it to Washington where it was given to Admiral Burkley. After that, it disappeared. Which means that Humes never saw it. It is certainly an important piece of evidence that represents a rather significant area of space, according to David Mantik, on the rear of Kennedy's skull. (See the photos presented by Dr. Mantik in *Murder In Dealey Plaza*, pp. 226-227) Could Humes really not have been aware of any of this? And if so, why did Jeremy Gunn not bring it up in the questioning at this point?

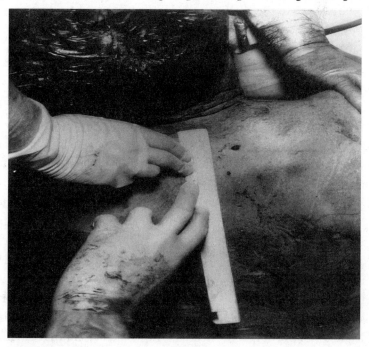

Fox - 5

The discussion then went to Fox-1 and Fox-2, usually referred to as the "stare of death picture" in the photographic record. This showed Kennedy from the front, thus including the tracheotomy. Humes suggested there might be an *exit* wound in the inferior portion of the wound that was obliterated by that tracheotomy. (ibid, 175)

Humes then proceeded on to Fox-3, the back-of-the-head photograph. When Dr. Humes was in closed session with the HSCA forensic panel, he picked the **lower point**, the little white droplet, as the entrance wound. And this is what the three autopsy doctors said was the entry point of the rear skull wound on the night of the autopsy. Then before the HSCA in public session, he chose the **higher point** *(though he said he had trouble with the placement of the HSCA)*, near the cowlick area, as the point of entrance. Now, before the ARRB, **he can't pick either**, while looking at the photograph. (ARRB 180-83) He was simply unable to identify the entrance wound in the back of the head. He then went on to say he isn't aware of where the HSCA forensic panel placed the wound. He commented that it is possible the scalp is being pulled forward in Fox-3. He added that he cannot place the entry wound in the high mark, close to the cowlick area. He also doesn't have the "foggiest idea" of what the marking is toward the bottom (white droplet), near the hairline (ARRB 180). He says he has problems identifying the entry wound in the photos (maybe because the photo of Fox-3 had been altered in the right occipital region and confused Humes), but didn't on the night of the autopsy. He also says he can't see **ANY** wound in the upper area in the black and white copy of Fox-3. The flap above the ear was possibly dura, according to Humes. Despite what any of us might think, and for whatever it is worth, and no matter what anyone thinks of the photos, the doctors at Parkland Hospital, the morticians, Mrs. Kennedy, and Clint Hill and almost all of the medical personnel place a wound in the back of the head. And although Humes was befuddled by the photos as presented to him by Gunn, the lead pathologist did revert back to his original work for the lower location of the skull wound in his 1992 interviews for the *Journal of the American Medical Association.* And with Gunn, as we shall see, Humes seemed to defer to that earlier opinion.

Humes waffled once again, when asked about a reflected scalp photo of the posterior portion of the head. He now said he cannot recall it specifically. He can't seem to identify Fox-8, the mystery autopsy photo, as either posterior, frontal, or parietal. He says the scalp is reflected downward in Fox-8. Humes seemed to imply that the large gaping hole is an exit wound, though you get the impression he thought he was looking at the temporal-parietal area of the head, not the occipital region. Humes also seemed troubled about not seeing a photo of the interior of the thorax. He regretted not having a photo of the posterior cranial fossa, where the defect was. On page 203 of the deposition, Humes stated that the right side of the brain, the cerebrum, appears to be intact. He says, "That's not right, because it was not" (ARRB). He then realizes he was looking at the photo of the brain backwards. In his confusion, he suggested the left cerebrum was disrupted due to the explosion of the bullet striking the skull and the brain bouncing off the interior of the head. The discussion turned to the X-rays, with the anterior-posterior X-ray discussed initially. He said the large gap in the top right quadrant was the result of being removed by the path of the missile. The second x-ray, lateral, was then probed for any details Dr. Humes might be able to add to the record. He noticed fracture lines in the top of the parietal bone as well as into the occipital bone. He thought there were fragments towards the vertex in this picture. He also said he had previously seen fragments corresponding to a small occipital wound in the x-ray, but now doesn't see it (ARRB 222).

Again, this is a key evidentiary point that Gunn seemed to understand and was prepared for. In the autopsy report in the Warren Report, Humes described a line of particles in Kennedy's skull that went from the low wound in the posterior up to a line of particles up higher. Gunn expressed it like this:

> Jeremy Gunn: "Do you recall having seen an X-ray previously that had fragments corresponding to a small occipital wound?"
>
> Dr. Humes: "Well I reported that I did, so I must have. But I don't see them now."

In other words, the way this lower wound connected to the particle lines in the upper skull was now gone. Did someone make them disappear? In other words, was the X ray altered? Or as some people think: Did that lower to upper trail simply never exist? If it did not, then did the trail of fragments in the upper skull forensically reveal a shot from the front? At any trial of Oswald this, like the Harper fragment, would have been a significant issue for the defense. And it would pose a serious problem for the prosecution.

Humes also said he didn't understand the big, non-opaque area that takes up half the skull. He didn't remember seeing this the night of the autopsy. He was then asked, rather awkwardly, about the existence of a photo or X-ray of a probe inserted into the posterior thorax. Humes responded, "No, absolutely not" (ARRB 224). Yet, in his Warren Commission testimony, he talked about superficially attempting to insert a probe. He also mentioned taking X-rays of extremities in case a missile might have lodged there, but no serious pieces of metal were ever found.

The interview concluded with Humes stating how confused he has been and how even more confused he was before the HSCA. The final page of the deposition, in a letter from Dr. Humes to Mr. Jeremy Gunn said:

> I experienced great difficulty in interpreting the location of the wound of entrance in the posterior scalp from the photograph. This may be because of the angle from which it was taken, or the position of the head, etc. It is obvious that the location of the external occipital protuberance cannot be ascertained from the photograph. I most firmly believe that the location of the wound was exactly where I measured it to be in relation to the external occipital protuberance and so recorded it in the autopsy report. After all that was my direct observation in the morgue and I believe it to be far more reliable than attempting to interpret what I believe to be a photograph which is subject to various interpretations. (ARRB 248).

Did Humes suffer from intellectual agnosia? He didn't seem to remember the location of the alleged entrance wound into the back of the head of the President of the United States. From his different testimonies over the years, he couldn't seem to recall a number of things. Dr. Humes seemed to want all of this to just go away, but as long as doubts, inconsistencies and subterfuge exist, hopefully there will be enough interest around to keep poring over the record, trying to figure out what really happened. Dr. Humes passed away in May of 1999. I think we can agree that at a trial of Lee Harvey Oswald, the defense would have looked forward to cross-examining Dr. Humes. That questioning would not have resembled the superficial examination given to Humes by Arlen Specter for the Warren Commission.

Addendum: from James Jenkins' book, *At the Cold Shoulder of History:* Earlier, it was noted that Humes was uncertain about Galloway and others; more to the point, he had no idea who James Jenkins or Paul O'Connor were. Jenkins stated for the record that he had never assisted in an autopsy performed by Humes, whom he characterized as "... more of an administrator." So, the autopsy of the murdered president was conducted by a man who knew none of the corpsmen involved. The second pathologist, Boswell, was a moonlighting lab pathologist, and the final addition to the lineup was supposed to be the guy to keep them informed by reviewing their work, an Army Lt. Colonel. The radiologist was not a pathology radiologist but a radiation oncologist. When Humes asked for an outside forensic pathologist to join them, the request was denied. Dr. Milton Halpern, the medical examiner in New York City, expected to be called in to oversee the autopsy. He was surprised when he was not contacted. We, however, are not.

09

Dr. Cyril Wecht

September 7, 1978

On Sept. 7, 1978, Dr. Cyril Wecht gave testimony before the HSCA in Washington, D.C.

As one of the Forensic Pathology panel members, former Allegheny County, Pennsylvania, coroner and former President of the American Academy of Forensic Sciences, Dr. Cyril Wecht, M.D., J.D. vociferously dissented that all shots came from the rear. He asserted that the single bullet theory was medically impossible and that the evidence did not rule out the possibility of a shot being fired from the right front and striking the president in the head. The eight other panel members, however, disagreed and the House Select Committee properly accepted their findings as representing the consensus of medical expertise. (I HSCA 332-373)

Wecht was the dissenting member of the medical panel. He was the only member of the panel to dissent. Dr. Wecht was extremely critical in 1978 and still is until this present day. He has never relented in fighting the good fight for the cause of truth, which he is still doing in his nineties.

> Mr. Purdy: "Dr. Wecht, what are the major conclusions of the forensic pathology panel with which you are in disagreement?"
>
> Dr. Wecht: "The major disagreement is the single-bullet theory which I deem to be the very essence of the Warren Commission report's conclusions and all the other corroborating panels and groups since that time.
>
> It is the sine qua non of the Warren Commission report's conclusions vis-à-vis a sole assassin, as Dr. Wecht often says. Without the single-bullet theory, there has to be more than one assassin, whether it is Oswald or anybody else.
>
> I am in disagreement with various other conclusions of the panel. I am most unhappy and have been extremely dismayed by their failure to insist upon the performance of appropriate experiments, which I believe could have been undertaken with a reasonable degree of expenditure of time, energy, and money to once and for all show whether a bullet, a 6.5 millimeter, copper-jacketed, lead-core piece of military-type ammunition could indeed strike a rib and a radius in a human being and emerge in the condition which Commission exhibit 399 is today.
>
> I am extremely unhappy about the fact that a greater and more intensive effort was not made to locate the missing pieces of very important medical evidence in this case, which I pointed out back in the summer of 1972. Not that I was the first to learn of this, but amazingly, nobody had made that public disclosure prior to that time. I have raised some questions concerning the head wound and the possibility, albeit remote, of a second shot fired in synchronized fashion from the right side or the lower right rear, synchronized with the head shot that struck the President in the back of the head." (I HSCA 332—333)

Wecht exercised visuals, including CE-399, pointing out its pristine look, except for a dent taken out of its nose portion that was used for spectrographic analysis and a slight extrusion at its base. Bullets fired into cotton wadding, by the Warren Commission, had more of the lead core extruding at the base, as well as a bullet fired into the carcass of a goat, that broke one rib, and appeared flattened and compressed. And remember, these are Warren Commission exhibits he is using (see

HSCA exhibit F-294), not Dr. Wecht's own experiments. He mentions Dr. John Nichols, a colleague, who performed similar tests using his own money. Technological advances since 1964 could make these experiments fully realized. "Why our panel of distinguished experts with all our expertise and this staff representing a very prominent committee, which, in turn, represents the House of Representatives of the United States Congress, why such tests could not be performed is beyond me. I feel constrained to say that they were not performed because people knew full well what the results would be." (I HSCA 337)

Dr. Wecht 's next statement is one that, if you have followed his JFK talks, has been uttered on several different occasions and numerous times at different conferences throughout the years. Dr. Baden has commented that these kind of bullet appearances are not scarce or uncommon. Wecht contended that,

> I have repeatedly, limited to the context of forensic pathology, numerous times implored, beseeched, urged, in writing, orally, privately, collectively, my colleagues; to come up with one bullet that has done this. I am not talking about 50 percent of the time plus one, 5 percent or 1 percent—just one bullet that has done this..... I stand here today and I wonder where that bullet is? Maybe it will be presented by the next member of the majority who has conveniently been sandwiched on the other side of me sometime tomorrow. (I HSCA 337)

Dr. Wecht asserts that Kennedy and Connally were not struck by the same bullet for the following reasons: trajectories, their placement in the limousine, and their times to being shot.

The question of Connally still gripping his hat arises:

> Mr. Purdy: "Dr. Wecht, in your opinion, could Governor Connally have incurred the damage to his wrist which is described in the medical reports and still be holding the hat as shown in this photograph?"

> Dr. Wecht: "No; absolutely not. In [HSCA Exhibit F-245], which is a blowup of Zapruder frame 230, we are told under the single bullet theory that Governor John Connally, for a period of approximately one and a half seconds, has already been shot through the right chest with the right lung pierced and collapsed, through the right wrist, and the distal end of the radius comminuted and the radial nerve partially severed."

"I heard some vague reference to a nerve in the prior testimony, but I didn't hear the follow-through discussion that I was waiting for about nerve damage. There was nerve damage, yes, to the radial nerve. And the thumb which holds this large Texas white Stetson that is required for it to be in apposition with the index or index and middle fingers to hold that hat is innervated by the radial nerve. Note in Frame-245 that the hat is still being held and Governor Connally is not reacting. This is again a very alert individual, under a very special circumstance and I do not believe or accept for one moment the story that we must believe under the single bullet theory that this gentleman, at this point, one and a half seconds previously, has already been shot through his chest, through his chest, through his wrist, and into his left thigh."

Mr. Purdy: "Dr. Wecht, is it your opinion based on this exhibit, JFK exhibit F-245, that Governor Connally is not yet injured in any way?"

Dr. Wecht: "Yes; that is my opinion."

Mr. Purdy: "Dr. Wecht, is it possible that he had been injured prior to this frame but has not yet manifested a reaction?

Dr. Wecht: "No; I do not believe so, not given the nature and extents of his wounds, the multiplicity and the areas damaged, I do not believe that." (I HSCA 342—343)

Purdy then asks Wecht about his stating that JFK and Governor Connally do not line up in a horizontal trajectory and then Dr. Wecht comes back with a response that I am sure caused shockwaves within the room, or at least it should have:

Dr. Wecht: "... *The panel, to the best of my recollection, was in unanimous agreement that there was a <u>slight upward trajectory [of]</u> the bullet through John F. Kennedy, that is to say, that the bullet wound of entrance on the President's back, lined up with the bullet wound of exit in the front of the President's neck drawing a straight line, showed that vertically <u>the bullet had moved slightly upward, slightly, but upward</u>."*
"That is extremely important for two reasons. One, under the single bullet theory – with Oswald as the sole assassin, or anybody else, in the sixth-floor window, southeast corner of the Tex-

as School Book Depository Building, you have the bullet coming down at a downward angle of around 20-25 degrees, something like that, maybe a little less. It had originally been postulated, I think, by the autopsy team, and the initial investigators, at considerably more [of a steep downward angle]. How in the world can a bullet be fired from the sixth-floor window, strike the President in the back, and yet have a slightly upward direction?

There was nothing there to cause it to change its course. And then with the slightly upward direction, outside the President's neck, that bullet then embarked upon a rollercoaster ride with a major dip, because it then proceeded, under the single bullet theory, through Governor John Connally at a 25-degree angle of declination.

To my knowledge, there has never been any disagreement among the proponents and defenders of the Warren Commission report or the critics, about the angle of declination in John Connally – maybe a degree or two. We have that bullet going through the Governor at about 25 degrees downward. How does a bullet that is moving slightly upward in the President proceed then to move downward 25 degrees in John Connally. This is what I cannot understand...The vertical and horizontal trajectory of this bullet, 399, under the single bullet theory is absolutely unfathomable, indefensible, and incredible." (I HSCA 344)

As stated in Dr. Baden's testimony, but it needs repeating, **this is monumentally huge!** If that bullet is rising via the back wound, then the single bullet theory is defunct. That bullet cannot be rising at 11 degrees and exit his throat upward at 11 degrees and then go into John Connally's back. It also cannot be fired from the SE corner of the sixth floor of the TSBD. This should put the single bullet theory to rest forever. Wecht went on to insist that the medical panel had minimized the nature and seriousness of this [*Connally's comminuted/fragmented wrist wound*] fracture. From a man with the mass of Governor Connally, and with the size of his radius bone shattered and fragmented, not just cracked, a bullet would not emerge in near virginal condition.

"In that relationship I also want to point out that I heard testimony here today, as I heard discussed previously by our panel that we don't really know if the right fifth rib was damaged; if so, and how much; and whether it was struck directly, or perhaps the fracture might have been caused by implosion, or whatever. **I don't know where this speculation comes from.** I know indeed

what the operating surgeon on Friday, November 22, 1963 at
Parkland Hospital said about what he found when he explored
Governor John Connally's chest. He found 5 inches of that bone
literally pulverized." (I HSCA 345)

Wecht said that the throat wound was erroneously said to be an entrance wound by the doctors at Parkland hospital, because it was not
distorted by hitting any objects in-between that would cause disfigure-
ment. As a result, the bullet would not have swayed or wobbled.

Mr. Cornwell then literally dropped a bullet on the table (*I am sure,
however, it was not CE 399*) and asked Dr. Wecht if he would expect the
bullet to be deformed in any way. Wecht said No, of course. This was
just silly. It was showmanship and nothing else. Was Cornwell attempting to compare a bullet dropped from a few inches to a bullet travelling
c. 2,200 feet per second and striking two large bones in six-foot four
Texan Governor John Connally with this little circus stunt. Embarrassing. There then followed, what I call antics in semantics, and what led
to a lengthy debate over the intersection of two x/y axes. It went something like this: what would the necessary speed of CE 399 need to be to
fragment Connally's wrist/radius bone? And what speed is needed to
cause harm not observable on CE 399? It seems to me that Cornwell is
trying to prove that here is some mysterious intersecting point, at some
unknown and cryptic unspoken rate, given that the bullet slowed down
in its channel through Kennedy and then through Connally's chest, fast
enough to fragment the wrist, but not fast enough to cause it to deform
in breaking the wrist. This is an old canard used by Gerald Posner on
the program *Crossfire* when he debated Dr. Wecht in the early nineties.

Congressman Dodd used his time to characterize Wecht's expertise
was in forensic pathology, but not in photographic analysis, as an attempt
to cheapen Dr. Wecht's authority with his observations of the Zapruder
film, even though others were able to do this, like Dr. Calvin McCamy,
without ever being confronted with the same amount of credulity.

Wecht insisted it was necessary for the House Committee to go to
any length necessary to find out where the President's brain was, for a
proper pathological study.

Committee Counsel Robert Blakey stated that this had been done,
which did include depositions from "all of the people associated with
the reburial of the President's body. ... As I indicated earlier this morn-

ing, a Kennedy family spokesman did indicate that Robert Kennedy expressed concerns that these materials could conceivably be placed on public display many years from now and he wanted to prevent that. I would infer from that that the most likely result is that the President's brother destroyed the documents". (I HSCA 368)

The remainder of Dr. Wecht's testimony was an assault to discredit him and render his testimony moot. It makes the HSCA look cheap and petty, because Dr. Wecht was the only person they did this with, at least to this extent. It was a double standard of how they questioned Dr. Wecht and everyone else. Dr. McCamy, was allowed to speak authoritatively about subjects he was not well-versed in – or had any kind of expertise stated in their bona fides. If you were a sycophant of the Warren Commission, then you were allowed all kinds of latitude, but if you suggested the possibility of a conspiracy, then you were attacked in ways that other witnesses were not.

Dr. Wecht was courteous in his closing remarks, making statements that were quite good and should be taken seriously. He was firm when it came to the medical evidence, even though nobody seemed to follow what he was trying to explain. His closing remarks should be required reading for all who do research on the Kennedy assassination. One researcher called it the Gettysburg Address of the Kennedy Assassination. I would agree. (I HSCA 371—373)

Cyril Wecht testified to *four shots* striking the two people who were shot in the limousine. One was the head shot, which we have all viewed more times than needed.

He insisted that the medical panel found that the Kennedy back-bullet was rising in trajectory, 11 degrees to be exact, and could easily have gone out over the top of the car, as I have postulated in chapter one. He was adamant that CE 399 did not cause Connally's wrist damage, which I have attempted to buttress throughout this book. The Kennedy back-bullet doesn't seem to have done Connally's wrist damage either, as it was rising when leaving JFK's throat. CE-399 didn't generate a comminuted *fracture* in Governor Connally's wrist because it is not distorted, which agrees with my assertion, and others, that the bullet that caused the wrist damage in Connally most likely arrived at Z-327. (Josiah Thompson expands on this better than anyone in his most recent book, *Last Second in Dallas*).

Vincent Bugliosi has been very critical of the critical research community. Bugliosi seemed to always ask, "Where did the bullet go when it left JFK's throat?" It could have gone over the top of the windshield once it exited Kennedy's neck, but very difficult to say with any certitude. Yet, Bugliosi suggests that the research community's lack of precision suggests that we have no idea, and because of this, the bullet going into Connally's right shoulder, which is a fantasy at best, was somehow preserved. This kind of arguing from Bugliosi is what Socrates despised from the Sophists, as he said, "they made the worse appear the better reason." I never feel I need all of the answers to any given subject, because for the Kennedy assassination, especially, spoliation of evidence and early bungling has forever hindered us from having all of the answers. We have a lot, but not all, and that is okay, because we don't need to have all of the answers to prove our case.

The reason people twist words is because they are the ones who don't have the answers or don't want the truth to emerge, so they must attempt to discredit or argue ad hominem, because in a lot of instances, that is all they have. But I think the overall reason is they had and still have an agenda.

In a conversation I had with Dr. Wecht at COPA 1998 in Dallas, I asked if I could put forth a couple of JFK assassination questions. Wecht, ever gracious, agreed. I asked what his main emphasis was that he was attempting to articulate when he testified before the HSCA.

He said, "I needed to present to them what I thought were the two most significant pieces of forensic evidence, the (1) *rising angle of the one bullet,* and the (2) *total lack of deformity on CE-399,* regarding the comminuted fracture of a thick bone." And he did so with precision.

They may not have realized the inference, because the House Select Committee did not want to hear about it, I assure you. It was an opportunity for him to bash them had he chosen to, but he didn't.

The next witness, Dr. Charles Petty was there to bracket Wecht's dissent, as Wecht himself suggested, between Dr. Baden and his.

In the end it seems far more of the questions were intended to discredit, or worse, demonize him, instead of giving his ideas a fair hearing. The HSCA medical finding that the bullet hitting Kennedy in the back and exiting the neck, however, and was traveling upward was and is **critical**.

10

DR. CHARLES PETTY –
SEPTEMBER 8, 1978

On Sept. 8, 1978, Dr. Charles S. Petty gave testimony before the HSCA in Washington, D.C.

D r. Charles Petty received an M.D. degree, cum laude, from Harvard Medical School in 1950 and completed his residency in pathology in 1955 at the New England Deaconess Hospital in Boston, MA. The American Board of Pathology certifies him in the areas of pathology anatomy, clinical pathology, and forensic pathology. He is a fellow of the American Academy of Forensic Science, the American Association of Pathologists, and the American Society of Clinical Pathologists and the College of American Pathologists.

Dr. Petty begins with a clear disassociation that he has ever had any interest in the Kennedy assassination. He seems to take great pride in not having any prior interest or contact with the evidence used for interpreting the status of the case. He was one of eight that was considered the majority, with Dr. Wecht being the lone dissenter.

Dr. Petty's testimony may have been devoted to debunking the objections to the single bullet theory by Dr. Cyril Wecht, who was sandwiched between Dr. Humes and Dr. Petty. As I said in the previous chapter, Dr. Wecht mentions this in his testimony. It is interesting to note that Dr. Wecht is mentioned 10 times during the mere 10 questions that were asked of Dr. Petty. Professor Blakey was doing everything to reinforce the Single Bullet Theory. Some feel that Dr. Wecht was being pushed out of the loop in the later portion of the forensic pathology panel's term. It is also possible he was grouped categorically and anyone who followed Dr. Wecht would have been an advocate of the magic bullet theory, as Wecht was the lone dissenter on the medical panel. Dr. Petty was only asked a few questions, but in the course of his answers, he made statements that are controversial to this day.

To maintain the single bullet theory, the bullet would have to go upward, as the entrance was lower than the exit. On the other hand, with the car going down an incline, and Kennedy leaning forward, the idea is that the bullet went downward relative to Dealey Plaza, and upward relative to the upright plane of JFK's body. As we have already seen, The Forensic Pathology Panel concluded that the back wound entered at a slightly upward angle based on the abrasion collar around the entry wound. Both Dr. Wecht and Dr. Baden have stated 11 degrees upward publicly, though no degree is stated in the Forensic Pathology Panel's conclusion (of course not). The Forensic Pathology Panel, in conjunction with the work of Thomas Canning (who conducted trajectory analysis), had JFK leaning sufficiently forward that a level of upward track through the body itself became a downward path, which is simply refuted with your eyes. Why this silliness continues to get perpetrated is beyond me. Look at the Z-film for yourself and the Willis photos. JFK was not leaning forward, however, when struck in the back; he was simply sitting upright.

Dr. Petty states: "Yes, sir. I believe that they were struck by the same bullet and I have so previously stated in the preliminary report of the panel… I think it is necessary at this point to sum up, in a sense, the flight of the bullet and its effect on those it struck. *The bullet that struck the late President in the upper right back area and then went on to penetrate the soft structures of the neck and to exit in the front of the neck was, as has been indicated already, traveling in a somewhat upward direction anatomically speaking.*

175

... But the President was not upright at the time he was shot, he was certainly not in the anatomic position, and this explains, I believe, the objection that Dr. Wecht had and his argument that he could not understand how the bullet pursued a downward track from where it was discharged, then an upward track in the President and then a downward track into Mr. Connally." (1 HSCA 376—377)

Dr. Petty does not know the exact position that JFK was in when he was assumingly shot when behind the Stemmons Freeway sign. JFK was behind the Stemmons Freeway sign for 0.9 seconds. When he emerges on the west side of the sign, JFK had already been shot. Dr. Petty would have to view the Willis slides and there is no indication that he had done so. Phil Willis claimed in his Warren Commission testimony that one of his photos was taken at the moment he heard the first shot.

In the Willis photograph, JFK is sitting upright and back against the seat. Petty would have to prove that JFK was leaning forward, but there is no evidence that this happened, when we look at both the Zapruder film and the Willis photograph. JFK does drift forward, but only after he is shot and just before the head shot.

The Willis slide shows President Kennedy sitting flush against the back of the seat of the presidential limousine. The limousine was 21 feet long, but only 12 feet of passenger space. That means whoever is shooting into that moving limo was going to have to be deadly accurate. They were.

Dr. Petty is voicing loudly for reasons unknown to me, but I have my suspicions. Science, unfortunately, isn't always honest. Maybe all who have studied this case see exactly what is going on, as we have seen it a hundred times before.

Dr. Petty went on to answer Mr. Preyer about what the bullet did after it entered President Kennedy's back. He said it "did not go through the spinal column" (I HSCA 377). There seem to be two schools of thought on this. Dr. John K. Lattimer in his book *Kennedy and Lincoln—Medical and Ballistic Comparisons of Their Assassinations*, shows one of JFK's X-rays that indicate a nick in the spinal column, hence the possible reason for the bullet rising at 11 degrees, as stated earlier, when it leaves JFK's throat. But it was rising at 11 degrees when it entered his back, so while I myself have intimated an 11-degree rise due to nicking the spinal column, this can only explain the 11-degree departure from JFK's throat, not the 11-degree entrance into JFK's back.

Others seem to interpret the X-rays as originally showing bullet fragments, then bone fragments that apparently are found to be artifacts similar to those on other X-rays the night of the autopsy. Still others have thought that the bullet hit no bone and that if there was damage to a bone, it likely resulted from pressure effects of the passing bullet. In other words, secondary damage.

Dr. Petty said, "one cannot determine by looking at a flat two-dimensional view of one side of the limousine and the contained individuals precisely what relationship they had one to another" (I HSCA 377). This is important in determining the occupants' relationship, not only on a horizontal plane, but a vertical one as well. This is vital when discussing the single bullet theory. The more fundamental reason for not being able to determine their relationship is that we do not know for sure, to a certainty, when President Kennedy was first hit from the rear, at least not precisely. This seems to be the crux of the problem. There was a time, as stated earlier, albeit for only 0.9 seconds, when they were obscured because of the Stemmons Freeway sign. Before that, it is very hard to make sense of absolute positions. They are not, however, flat. Stereo viewing is easy to do, and someone who knows how to properly feed the data into a computer can get accurate three-dimensional information, which can be studied from any angle. I have looked at their positions in the car stereoscopically and based on what I saw, the single bullet theory is not unlikely, it is impossible. We also have more than one film and photo to work from for various points.

Dr. Petty went on to say that there "is no evidence that that bullet actually penetrated the rib" (I HSCA 377). Governor Connally's rib, however, was badly shattered, not merely slapped. It turned a human rib into a bunch of match heads. This seems a little odd if the bullet merely slapped against it as Petty suggests. I know of no other doctor who has ever postulated this theory. The only other possibility is that this may have been secondary pressure damage with no actual contact, but highly doubtful.

"The X-rays fail to show any evidence of particles of metal in the chest" (I HSCA 378). This may well be true. There were metal traces on his clothes. What is known is that metal was left in Governor Connally. That was never in doubt. The surgeons report indicated they had fixed the chest wound and were getting ready to go back to the other wounds and remove *the bullet* in Connally's thigh. This would have been difficult, as stated earlier, given the fact that CE-399 was half-way back to Washington, D.C., aboard Air Force One at this time.

When Mr. Preyer asked Dr. Petty if "it was accurate to say that the bullet went through the wrist bone," Dr. Petty replied: "I don't believe it did" (I HSCA 380). This seems very odd, because when you look at the X-ray, the bone was literally sliced in half on an angle. This X-ray has been published (see Josiah Thompson's, *Six Seconds in Dallas pp. 148, 152*) and seems to demonstrate that Petty is wrong.

In respect to frangible bullets, Dr. Petty stated that they are produced in .22 caliber loads and not in larger weapons. Again, apparently, Dr. Petty can be a ballistics expert, but Dr. Wecht cannot. Hand loading makes a variety of variations possible. He is strictly talking about what is available off the shelf, which is a mistake. It has also been suggested that full metal jacketed Carcano bullets can be turned into frangible-type bullets by scratching their noses. He went on to say that if Kennedy had been hit on the right side of the head, then the left side of his brain would show such evidence. According to Petty, "There are no such fragments" (I HSCA 379). The head X-ray of President Kennedy, however, would support a frangible bullet, as there was a halo-like spray (a snowstorm of fragments) of 40-50 fragments throughout the remaining cortex area. There was a trail of dustlike fragments in the X-ray. This would account for a portion of a bullet. Where is the rest? The question is if the magic bullet could do all it did and come out undamaged, how did the same type of bullet go all to pieces?

Finally, Dr. Petty states that "there is no evidence whatsoever that the President was shot either from the side or from the front" (I HSCA 380). Roy Kellerman said he was right next to the surgeon and the entrance wound was in front of the right ear (in the sideburn area). To me, this seems to be proof of a frontal/side entrance wound; whether or not someone believes it is another matter. Just look at Fox-8 with the scalp reflected and you will see what could be two bullet holes in the temporal region on JFK's right side. Kellerman's observation would agree with the same spot where an impact is shown on the Zapruder film. The Groden right superior profile autopsy photograph also seems to contradict Dr. Petty. The testimony Petty gave, however, would support a rear-entrance wound.

This testimony is obviously going in the lone-assassin Warren Commission route. The evidence, however, does not seem to support his points or conclusion.

From then on, Petty simply becomes a typical Warren Commission sycophant. (I have both audio and video of Dr. Petty's testimony. It is hard to sit through, as you feel at times, though his testimony is brief, that you're simply listening to a parrot).

Chief Counsel Robert Blakey then described and became his own personal envoy for the single-bullet theory, although his information was mistaken and he certainly had to recognize it.

Blakey then attempts to go over the tests from Edgewood Arsenal:

> "In part, as a result of these tests, the Commission concluded: One, that Governor Connally's wounds were caused by one bullet and that the bullet that traversed the President's neck probably then proceeded to inflict all of the wounds to Governor Connally.
>
> Two, that a bullet fired from the Mannlicher-Carcano rifle at a distance of approximately 270 feet would cause a wound similar to the wound discovered in the President's head." (I HSCA 382)

This just simply is false, so let us listen to the testimony of Dr. Alfred Olivier as he testified before the Warren Commission:

> *"We were aiming, as described in the autopsy report if I remember correctly the point two centimeters to the right of the external occipital protuberance and slightly above it. We placed a mark on the skull at that point, according to the autopsy the bullet emerged through the superorbital process, ..."* (5 H 88—89)

Blakey is obfuscating and I'm being nice. He stated that Olivier's tests supported that a bullet struck JFK high on the top of his head and then appeared on the right temporal parietal region of his skull. If Olivier is working from the autopsy's original aiming point, the low entry wound around the EOP, it had to have then exited above the President's eye. There is only one problem with this: there isn't a scintilla of evidence that it happened that way. I guess Dr. Olivier was perusing an autopsy report I have never seen.

Sadly, the House Select Committee's forensic/medical panel never did authenticate the tests done at Edgewood Arsenal. If you have read

179

the Warren volumes, then you get a sense that the same worn path is being walked down once again. Sure, it is no longer Arlen Specter, but now we have similar incarnations of the same dishonest approach to truth. The Sophists are running the show. In other words, nothing has changed. You can see the end of the tunnel, even at this point, and it isn't any more enjoyable to observe here than it was during the Warren Commission hearings.

11

LARRY STURDIVAN –
SEPTEMBER 8, 1978

On September 8, 1978, Larry Sturdivan testified before the HSCA in Washington, D.C.

M r. Larry Sturdivan followed the testimony of Dr. Petty. He is
stated to be a physical scientist, Aberdeen Proving Ground
Vulnerability Laboratory, Aberdeen, Maryland. Sturdivan's
expertise consists of a B.S. in physics from Oklahoma State University
and an M.S. in statistics from the University of Delaware.

Keep in mind as you begin to read this chapter that Chief Counsel
Blakey wanted a scientific aura to the public witnesses. You be the judge
on how that worked or didn't work out at the arrival of truth. In the end,
I think it backfired and the HSCA did not get a conspiracy of the science,
because it was simply regurgitated Warren Commission results under the
guise of science. It was sad to read, sadder to watch on video, and pathetic
to read in their final report. (The HSCA did admit a probable conspiracy
because of a shot from the knoll, but, lo, it missed, not to mention there
didn't seem to be any connection between that shooter and Lee Harvey

Oswald. They agreed with the Warren Commission that there were three shots and that Lee Oswald fired all of the shots into the limousine.)

The questioning begins with:

> Mr. Mathews: "Are you considered an expert in the wound ballistics field?"
>
> Mr. Sturdivan: "I would think so; yes."
>
> Mr. Mathews: *"How many additional experts would you say are presently in the United States or the world, for that matter?"*
>
> Mr. Sturdivan: *"Well, outside of a handful of experts within our own laboratories, there are probably very few, even in the free world. Some people do experiments, research and various aspects of like blunt trauma from automobile accidents and things like this, but as far as the whole wound ballistics field, there are very few experts."* (I HSCA 385)

This seems to be somewhat exaggerative, to say the least. The entire world? Is he including the Soviet bloc, France, Italy, Germany? But it makes Sturdivan look good in padding his own *bona fides*. If you listen carefully, he seems to be regurgitating the Warren Commission right from the start.

This is apparent, as he launches into data concerning the Mannlicher-Carcano rifle. When you think of how low grade of a rifle the Carcano was and is, not to mention that it is the only rifle on the ordering page from Klein's Sporting Goods that isn't touted as being a good weapon of choice. Almost every other rifle has something good said about it, but not the Carcano. It is also the least expensive rifle on the advertisement page financially speaking, so I guess you get what you pay for, if Oswald in fact ever ordered the rifle and if he did, he certainly never picked it up from his P. O. Box at the Post Office. It gets worse.

> Mr. Matthews: "Will you say that the Mannlicher-Carcano 6.5 millimeter bullet, is a stable bullet?"
>
> Mr. Sturdivan: "It is a very stable bullet, perhaps one of the most stable bullets that we have ever done experimentation with." (1 HSCA 386)

This isn't remotely close to being the truth. There is no such thing as a Mannlicher-Carcano bullet. They do not exist and never have existed anywhere. The 6.5 millimeter bullets are produced by companies that manufacture cartridges, but not produced by a company called Mannlicher-Carcano. There is no such thing as a Mannlicher-Carcano bullet or a Mannlicher-Carcano company that produces Mannlicher- Carcano bullets. I think you get the point. This might be nitpicking, but Mr. Sturdivan chose the high road earlier by indicating he was a world class ballistics expert. God helps us.

This kind of beginning seems to put a question mark on Sturdivan's authority and believability. One of the many issues that Sturdivan has been denounced for by the critical research community, and justifiably so, is his positioning of JFK's body in the limo for the single bullet theory to work. On page 155 of his book, *The JFK Myths*, he repeats the worn-out position that JFK was leaning forward enough for the rising bullet to actually descend out of Kennedy's throat, even though the back wound and the throat wound are both rising at 11 degrees. Look at the Zapruder film in still frame, Z-189 and Z-225 and at no point before (Z-189) or after the Stemmons Freeway sign (Z-225) where he already shows signs of being hit by a bullet, is he sitting in any position, except upright. Can we please put this nonsense to rest? Look for yourself. The evidence just isn't there, as JFK was not leaning forward and people who spout off about it know better. Believe whatever you want to, but at least be honest with the evidence.

The back wound is lower than the throat wound and the HSCA knew this. JFK was not leaning forward and they knew that to, so what we have here is an attempt to obfuscate the reality of November 22, 1963. The fact that you have letters after your name doesn't prove accuracy or truthfulness, obviously. At the end of the day, to quote Burt Lancaster in the movie *Elmer Gantry*, the scientists were simply *tramps in a silk shirt*. They looked the part but didn't

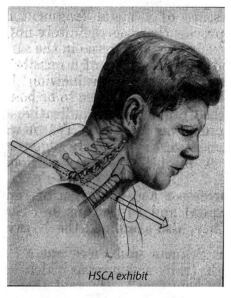

HSCA exhibit

183

speak honestly about the evidence. The Sophists strike once again. Or, to quote Shakespeare, and also stated in the movie *JFK*, "they may smile and smile, and be a villain". This is subterfuge from start to finish.

Z-189

Z-225

Sturdivan then claims that both an M-14 and an M-16 can go through gelatin blocks, but not as easily as a Mannlicher-Carcano, even though both the M-14 and the M-16 have a higher muzzle velocity. This is nothing new. We have heard all of this prior to the HSCA.

Sturdivan agrees with Dr. Wecht about reenactments of the assassination for scientific purposes, of course. Dr. Cyril Wecht testified that such a re-creation not being done was *the* principal deficiency of the HSCA.

Sturdivan did imply that certain factors would have to be thought through before engaging in such an experiment, because replication could be difficult. It is safe to say that had this taken place, it would have destroyed anything the Warren Commission could make any assertion concerning the single bullet theory (I HSCA 399ff).

Sturdivan then, in typical Warren Commission retroactive fashion, *denied the prospect of any kind of normal kind of bullet* having come into the scenario with respect to the President's head wound:

> Mr. Mathews: "… The committee has received some evidence to the effect that the second shot that hit President Kennedy entered through the rear of the skull and out the right front.
>
> "As you can see from the exhibits, the President's head seemed to have exploded. This explosion has led many people to conclude that the President may have been shot with an exploding bullet or a frangible bullet. By studying these exhibits, could you comment on whether that theory is a possibility?"
>
> Mr. Sturdivan: "**Literally, an exploding bullet would be a bullet which would have some high explosive incorporated within the structure of the bullet that would be detonated on impact on bone or soft tissue. Such bullets do exist.**
>
> "A frangible bullet is one that is made to deform very rapidly and, in fact, most of them are made of some sort of matrix with metallic powder inside that matrix. And essentially, I think that you could probably not tell the difference between the skull that had been hit with an exploding bullet, one that had been hit with a frangible bullet or one that had been hit with a hollow point or soft-nose hunting bullet or a hard jacketed military bullet that had deformed massively on the skull at impact.
>
> "In fact, all of those situations would look, in a film like this which was taken at ordinary speeds, to be very similar." (I HSCA 400—401)

Why would anyone use a variety of ammunition, when the inferior bullets used in the Mannlicher-Carcano yield the same results and are more stable? This statement makes no sense. We are simply getting more nonsensical babble at this point and that is sad, because I am sure Mr. Sturdivan could have added something interesting to the record, but he chose to simply become a disciple of the official version, a version that would only slightly change with the HSCA; but keep the same basic results.

Mr. Sturdivan has to keep in mind, as we all do, that the assassination only happened one way. Throw all of the hypotheticals out the window and let's just deal with reality, without any preconceived biases or notions. Blakey wanted science, but all he seemed to be getting was a thin veneer, with a lot of subterfuge underneath.

> Mr. Mathews: "Mr. Sturdivan, taking a look at JFK exhibit F-53, which is an X-ray of President Kennedy's skull, can you give us your opinion as to whether the President may have been hit with an exploding bullet?"
>
> Mr. Sturdivan: "Well, this adds considerable amount of evidence to the pictures that were not conclusive. In this enhanced X-ray of the skull, the scattering of the fragments throughout the wound tract are characteristic of a deforming bullet. This bullet could either be a jacketed bullet that had deformed on impact or a soft nosed or hollow point bullet that was fully jacket and, therefore, not losing all of its mass.
>
> It is not characteristic of an exploding bullet or frangible bullet because in either of those cases, the fragments would have been much more numerous and much smaller. A very small fragment has very high drag in tissue and consequently, none of those would have penetrated very far.
>
> In those cases, you would definitely have seen a cloud of metallic fragments very near the entrance wound. So, this case is typical of a deforming jacketed bullet leaving fragments along its path as it goes.
>
> *Incidentally, those fragments that are left by the bullet are also very small and do not move very far from their initial, from the place where they departed the bullet.*
>
> Consequently, they tend to be clustered very closely around the track of the bullet." (I HSCA 401)

You cannot have it both ways, unless you are testifying as a Warren Commission wolf in sheep's clothing. Sturdivan testified that small fragments would have not have invaded very far. There is a problem, however, as some fragments did penetrate throughout the track of the missile, with the large fragments traveling further into the skull than the smaller ones, which is what you would expect, indicating a shot from the front when looking at the AP X-ray taken of JFK on the night of the autopsy. Sturdivan continued, "this case is typical of a deforming jacketed bullet leaving fragments along its path as it goes." If the exit wound of that bullet was in the right temporal region of JFK's skull, as indicated by the autopsy, with the famous flap of scalp, how would the HSCA ballistics expert explain the two large fragments found behind the right eye of JFK which places them ahead of the exit? This would be an impossibility, unless I beat the drum one more time: a shot from the front at Z-313 and a shot from the rear at Z-327/328.

What follows is beyond hypocritical and offensive. When Dr. Wecht disapproved of the findings of the pathology panel, he was asked if he could claim any expertise in wound ballistics, and he conceded that he could not. Sturdivan, who is the ballistics expert, is immediately confronted with questions of forensic pathology, without being asked whether he could perform a function other than wound ballistics. He simply proceeded to do so and was allowed to without objection. There was an agenda that I hope you are discerning. The hypocrisy is offensive on every level. How many human skull X-rays had he reviewed previously and where are his *bona fides* to justify such action? That question was never asked and for good reason.

It is clear to me there was only one direction this investigation was going to traverse and the goal it was going to reach. It was the discovery of a dictabelt recording that destroyed predetermined propositions that were in sync with the Warren Commission and the lone assassin nonsense.

The quality of the Mannlicher-Carcano is then addressed and Mr. Sturdivan does show some minor hesitancy and concern about the rifle, which the research community has been uttering for quite some time.

Mr. Fauntroy: "Will the gentleman yield? *As you prepare to show the movie, it is my understanding that you used the Mannlicher-Carcano rifle that was found on the sixth floor of the Texas School Book Depository Building or was this another rifle?"*

187

Mr. Sturdivan: *"Well, sir, we had two rifles. Both of them were used fairly extensively, but we did not want to over-use the Oswald rifle because of the wear and the change of the characteristics. So I cannot state for a certainty which of these were shot with which rifle. But, some of them were shot with the Oswald rifle and some with the other rifle."* (I HSCA 402—403)

Keep in mind that on November 22, 1963 (the day of the Kennedy assassination), Sturdivan agreed to take a job involving wound ballistics from the Aberdeen Proving Ground, where he monitored ballistic tests conducted at the Biophysics Laboratory of Edgewood Arsenal during the Warren Commission's investigation. In 1978, as a senior researcher, he became the ***Army's contact*** (**military intelligence**) with the House Select Committee on Assassinations (HSCA) when they reinvestigated the Kennedy case. When he was asked questions by Mr. Mathews he was responding to film footage of tests done for the Warren Commission being shown to the HSCA. Notice what he says in his exchange with Mr. Mathews about the departing bullet in those tests. (*I have italicized and boldened the relevant part*)

Mr. Mathews. "The bullet is gone now; is that correct?"

Mr. Sturdivan. "Pieces of the bullet have exited the skull. It is hard to tell whether they have actually gone out of the frame or whether they may be incorporated into that white mass which is mostly bone with a little bit of gelatin tissue simulant in it.

As you can see, the radial velocity has already begun to fracture the skull extensively along and across suture lines.

As you can see, each of the two skulls that we have observed so far have moved in the direction of the bullet. In other words, both of them have been given some momentum in the direction that the bullet was going. This third one also shows momentum in the direction that the bullet was going, showing that the head of the President would probably go with the bullet.

This is amplified, however, in these skulls because they are not tied to a human body. They are free to move from the table.

Also, you will see that as ***the skull goes forward***, [*away from the rifle*] some of the material of the skull and the contents were blown out toward us. Consequently, ***the opposing momentum carries the skull away from us***, rotates it away from us so that we can actually see the bottom part of the skull in this shot. In fact, ***all 10 of the***

skulls that we shot did essentially the same thing. They gained a little bit of momentum consistent with one or a little better foot-per-second velocity that would have been imparted by the bullet and they also lost material toward us, that is, toward its right and, therefore, rotated toward its left." (I HSCA 403-404)

The HSCA assume that these tests prove that CE 399 nicked a rib in Governor Connally, but fail to disclose that in doing so, Connally's rib was turned into shards for a distance of five inches, or c. 10 cm. Initially, Mr. Sturdivan stated that the bullet was traveling with a muzzle velocity of 2,000-2,200 feet per second, slowing to perhaps 1,800 feet per second before hitting the victim. A long discussion arises, involving a change in the speed to 2,700 to 2,800 feet per second, which is quite an upgrade. (I HSCA 406ff)

Bullets don't gain speed when they travel through air or through human bodies for that matter, but they will slow down. I say that, of course, without expertise in ballistics, but as a professor of Logic at the college level, I have the ability to follow the line of an argument quite well. CE- 399, the magic bullet, could have done the damage assigned to it. I guess the same could be said for a spear. It could have done such damage, under equally miraculous circumstances, but, a more vague answer to an absolutely specific inquiry could not have been imagined, at least by me. CE-399 is alleged to have shattered a rib and the right distal radius, one of the denser bones in the human body. Therefore, it could not have emerged in its present-day condition after striking that much bone and doing that much damage.

The President moving backward [*though very little, according to Sturdivan*] is simple to see:

> "The President's motion is a neuromuscular reaction. Nerves are stimulated by other nerves, by electricity, by chemical means, or they can also be stimulated by mechanical means, and we have all had the experiences with that when you bang your crazy bone, you get a stimulus of the nerves, a motion sometimes, sometimes a partial paralysis for a little while. This is mechanical stimulation of the nerves." (I HSCA 415)

This is an attempt to resurrect the neuromuscular reaction or the jet-effect as explanations for the initial forward movement and then the backward head snap of JFK at Z-313, ad infinitum, ad nausea. Why doesn't the same physical experience apply to John Connally when his wrist nerve was destroyed, yet he held onto his Stetson hat for quite some time? The movement seen in the Zapruder film at frame 313 is written off to a neuromuscular reaction, not bullet force. Yet, a neuromuscular reaction does necessitate a brain to transfer electrical energy to create that reaction. The head, it is stated, would not move because of the bullet. Really? Okay. Believe what you will, but we have to keep reminding ourselves that there is no discernable forward movement of JFK's head at Z-312, (as David Wimp discovered) but there is a shot that strikes JFK at Z-313 in the right temporal region tangentially and then a head shot from the rear at Z-327/328.

It thus becomes a serious proposition to explain how a bullet strikes, which destroyed one-third of JFK's brain, and could still allow that brain to do what was suggested. Besides, in chapter one concerning the testimony of Governor Connally, strong rationale is given against why a neuromuscular reaction or the jet-effect is pure fiction, because Kennedy is **not** struck in the rear by a bullet in Z-312, as stated in the previous paragraph, so no explanation works, right or wrong. It is an illusion due to a photographic swipe because Zapruder moved the camera. Knowing this changes everything when it comes to the shot sequence in this case.

The witness is clear that the bullet exiting the front of President Kennedy's throat would have had some wobble or yaw, (which is odd since we have already been told that a bullet fired from a Mannlicher-Carcano is very stable, more so than an M-14 or an M-16. Make up your mind Mr. Sturdivan) but no explanation is requested or given as to how the exit wound from the President could have been such a neat, small round wound that it could have been confused for an entry wound; nor is it stated how such a yaw could have provided that neat exit and then entered Governor Connally's back sideways, which I don't think it did as explained in chapter one.

From the Warren Commission *experts* (think military, as Arlen Specter had a **military intelligence** background as well), to this HSCA *expert*, (also *military*) it becomes tiring to hear how high the quality of the Mannlicher Carcano and its ammunition was.

The experts are unanimous: ballistics experts dissented. Sebastian Latona, the FBI fingerprint expert, considered the Mannlicher-Carcano glorified junk.

Sturdivan's vocal intonation, (and I know because I own all of the HSCA testimony on audio and about one-third on video) gives the distinct impression that the witness was almost bragging that the tests did not have to involve human cadavers, which, by definition, are already dead, but instead used anesthetized goats, which by definition were living animals prior to the experiments conducted in this testimony.

The reader would probably be surprised how many animals are killed in varying government experiments. Knowing of the LSD tests done in the 1950s and beyond, we can only wonder how many human victims could be counted.

12

MONTY C. LUTZ – DONALD E. CHAMPAGNE –
JOHN S. BATES, JR. – ANDREW M. NEWQUIST
SEPTEMBER 8, 1978

On September 8, 1978, Monty Lutz, Donald Champagne, John Bates, Andrew Newquist, and George Wilson testified before the HSCA in Washington, D.C.

The following four men (five if you include George Wilson) testified together on the same day, hence, I have linkedthese four witnessess testified together on the same day since they bore witness about the same basic questions: *Mr. Monty Lutz* from the Regional Crime Laboratory, Wisconsin State; *Mr. Donald Champagne* from the Florida Department of Criminal Law Enforcement Crime Laboratory in Tallahassee, Fla.; *Mr. John S. Bates, Jr.*, New York State Police Scientific Laboratory, Albany, N.Y.; and *Mr. Andrew Martin Newquist*, from the Iowa Department of Public Safety Bureau of Criminal Investigation, Des Moines, Iowa. *George R. Wilson*; through his assistance, the facilities at the Metropolitan Police Department Firearms Laboratory in the District of Columbia were secured. His expertise in the area of firearms identification greatly assisted the panel's conduct of its inquiry.

Chief Counsel Robert Blakey introduced the matters to be addressed:

> Chairman Stokes: "The committee will come to order. This Chair recognizes Professor Blakey."
>
> Mr. Blakey: "Thank you, Mr. Chairman. Mr. Chairman, the testimony now to be taken concerns forensic firearms identification—the science of identifying fired bullets and cartridge cases with particular firearms. But first, some background information will be helpful. Soon after the assassination, Dallas police suspected the shots originated at the Texas School Book Depository. At 1:13 p.m. central standard time Deputy Sheriff Luke Mooney discovered three used cartridge cases lying on the floor near the southeast corner window of the sixth story. The cartridge cases were later. [*11 hours later*] turned over to the FBI" [*they had no jurisdiction*]. (I HSCA 442)

It is not a significant concern whether the standard time of 1:12 is rendered to 1:13. What is a serious concern is the juxtaposition of events: allegedly, witnesses pointed out the window immediately, *yet it took **forty-three minutes** <u>for anybody</u> **to get to that window**.* That seems to strain the forensic imagination well beyond the breaking point. It is also unacceptable.

The cartridges went to the FBI and were never seen again by the Dallas Police, where the murder of President John F. Kennedy is still an open homicide. Dallas officials are quick to note that they have no evidence with which to prosecute anyone.

Chief Counsel Blakey commented,

> "At 1:22 p.m. Deputy Sheriff Eugene Boone and Deputy Constable Seymour Weitzman discovered a bolt-action rifle equipped with a telescopic sight. It was also on the floor of the sixth story of the book depository, near the northwest corner. Weitzman, though neither he nor Boone actually handled the weapon, described it as a 7.65 German Mauser, although it was subsequently determined to be a 6.5 millimeter Mannlicher-Carcano Italian military rifle. It contained one round a full copper-jacketed military-type bullet manufactured by Western Cartridge Co." (I HSCA 442)

The weapon did contain one bullet when discovered, but that doesn't tell us anything about other bullets fired from the weapon that day. There is no proof at all that any bullets were fired from the rifle that day. No one has ever made that claim. No one smelled the barrel. There has never been any proof that Oswald purchased a clip for the rifle. The one remaining bullet that was chambered is not a problem, but the clip should have been ejected from the rifle when that took place. But, when the rifle was discovered, the clip was still attached to the rifle.

Mr. Sturdivan's testimony about the capabilities of a "Mannli-cher-Carcano bullet", (there is no such thing) is now reversed by Professor Blakey. That bullet is now identified as being made by Western Cartridge, which is an Italian firm now non-operational, though it had made the Mannlicher-Carcano rifle. For some bizarre reason, the United States government bought four million of these bullets, which is odd since they did not possess any weapons that would hold such cartridges. The U.S. government was purchasing and delivering weaponry with cartridges to places where provoking revolution and installing despots supposedly to bring about democracy was being incited and provoked, but not issued for any United States weapons.

Blakey then stated, "In addition, a bullet that had been recovered in an attempted assault on Gen. Edwin A. Walker on April 10, 1963, would become the subject of evidentiary significance in the assassination… The FBI was unable, however, to link the bullet fired at General Walker with the rifle, though it said the badly mutilated bullet showed the characteristics of a round that had been fired by a Mannlicher-Carcano. [*The police initially identified it as a .30-06* **steel-jacketed** *bullet; There was no proof of identity. Firing at General Walker would only demonstrate that Oswald loathed right-wingers and would not hesitate to shoot at one. It does not follow that he would shoot at both right and left-wingers.*] (I HSCA 442-443)

> Mr. McDonald: "And when you conducted firearms tests of this weapon, was there a representative of the National Archives present at all times?"
>
> Mr. Lutz: "Yes, sir." (I HSCA 446)

This is silly; of course there would be a National Archives representative there. Are there people who think otherwise? With critical evidence being used, a watchdog would be ever-present. It wouldn't happen any other way.

Mr. McDonald: "Mr. Lutz, could a 6.5 millimeter Mannli-cher-Carcano rifle be easily mistaken for a German Mauser, and before you answer the question, if we could have marked for identification JFK exhibit F-96. If you would utilize the chart in explaining your answer."

Mr. Lutz: "In regard to that question, there are considerable similarities between the 6.5 millimeter Mannlicher-Carcano ri-fle in conjunction with numerous rifles of several countries and several sources of origin. The similarities with the 7.65 German Mauser are quite a few. The similarities that would be noted be-tween the Carcano and the 7.65 German Mauser are depicted in this particular photograph that I have here. The photograph that I have put together represents several rifles that have the general class characteristics or the overall silhouette design for this par-ticular rifle.

The features that could possibly be confused with the Man-nlicher-Carcano rifle and an Argentine Mauser would be the Mannlicher-type magazine protruding from the bottom of the receiver area. The feature that is common on all bolt action ri-fles, the operating handle or the bolt handle protruding from the right side, on all of these rifles." (I HSCA 446)

The witness produced photographic evidence of the similarities be-tween the Italian Mannlicher-Carcano and one or more modifications of the German Mauser rifle. The Warren Commission didn't do this, as I have always said, but they certainly should have.

The first question put to the firearms panel, was a requested portray-al of the weapon, Warren Commission CE-139, the Mannlicher-Carca-no rifle. Mr. Lutz, spoke for the panel and stated:

"The characteristics of this rifle is that it is a six-shot repeating ri-fle. It is clip-fed with the capacity of a six round in-line clip being capable of being loaded and inserted into the top of the maga-zine, in the magazine area. It is a bolt-action rifle, and is of Italian manufacture and 6.5 millimeter Mannlicher-Carcano caliber." (I HSCA 446)

The weapon has the ability of firing seven rounds, not just six. One live round can be in the chamber, with six additional rounds in the clip. Secondly, the closing part of the statement, however, is elusive and should have been expanded upon. What isn't mentioned may be more important. When was the gun produced? (1891-1941) Where was it constructed? What kind of reputation did it have, especially among firearms connoisseurs? As stated earlier, the Mannlicher-Carcano was the cheapest rifle on a page that had other rifles being displayed or advertised by Klein's Sporting Goods in Chicago. Several of the other rifles have positive recommendations made by the National Rifle Association. The Mannlicher-Carcano appears, but with only the price listed and that is it. Period. There are prices given both with a scope or without a scope.

The next testimony will argue that the Italian Mannlicher-Carcano and German Mauser comparisons are many. We know they were the primary weapons of armies that lost, both Italy and Germany. But these experts had the understanding to bring photos that demonstrated the possible similarities, unlike the Warren Commission in 1964.

> Mr. McDonald: "To a casual observer would it be easy to mistake a Carcano for a Mauser?"
>
> Mr. Lutz: "Yes, sir; I believe it would." (I HSCA 447)

To whom? What about trained police officers, especially those who used to own a gun shop and sold rifles and handguns for a living? To John Q Citizen? To someone who has minimal knowledge of the two rifles, can one Carcano look like a Mauser, and yet actually be different? A gun expert can tell you about those differences.

Lutz continues...

> Mr. McDonald: *"Would you in your opinion classify it as an accurate scope?"*
>
> Mr. Lutz: *"The accuracy is fairly undependable, as far as once getting the rifle sighted in and it is very cheaply made, the scope itself has a crosshair reticle that is subject to movement or being capable of being dislodged from dropping, from impact, or a very sharp recoil. So the accuracy would be somewhat questionable for this particular type of a scope."* (I HSCA 449)

This is an admission that the scope was viewed as of having little value. It was plastic garbage. What should have been asked, but wasn't, was how could the gun have been sighted in with any manner of accuracy, having allegedly been assembled in the building, though how we have

LUTZ, CHAMPAGNE, BATES JR., NEWQUIST – SEPTEMBER 8, 1978

no idea. Rifles have to be sighted in to have any manner of accuracy, especially old ones that originated in 1891 with their production stopping in 1941. Keep that in mind throughout the rest of this chapter.

> Mr. McDonald: "What kind of scope is it?"
>
> Mr. Lutz: "This is a four-power Ordinance Optics telescopic sight with a crosshair reticle."

Lutz went on to describe that the mounting of the scope was placed on the only part on the gun where it could be mounted, as the Carcano weapon was not meant to have a telescopic sight.

> Mr. McDonald: "Well, with the scope on [CE] 139, could it be possibly classified as a left-handed scope?"
>
> Mr. Lutz: "Definitely not. There is no such thing as a left-handed scope." (I HSCA 449)

Continuing forward, another expert, Donald Champagne, testified to the dent in one of the three spent cartridges, and stated that in their tests of the Mannlicher-Carcano, it was noticed that during the ejection from the chamber, one of the test-fired cartridges had an indentation in it. (I HSCA 454) We aren't told how bad the dent was, especially when compared to the actual dented shell found on the sixth floor of the TSBD. The identical witness testified to comparable, or similar markings on the cartridge cases to those that were test fired from CE-139. The similarities may be there, but they would not be able to tell, nor could modern technology thirty years later, when the markings were made.

The final expert to testify, Andrew M. Newquist, stated that the two larger bullet fragments found in the limousine were fired from CE 139, the rifle found in the Texas School Book Depository (this will come under scrutiny, *and will be proven incorrect,* during Neutron Activation Analysis testimony and improved upon with recent discoveries in the past ten years or so; so let's not rush to judgment).

Mr. McDonald asked, "Were you able to reach a conclusion as to what rifle fired CE-573, the Walker bullet?"

> Mr. Newquist: "No, we were not, due to the distortion of CE-573 [Walker bullet] and lacking a significant correspondence of individual characteristics with the test, no conclusion could be reached." (1HSCA 472)

They were not asked if the bullet was lead or copper jacketed. They should have, because the reports I have read over the years all say lead-jacketed bullet in reference to the Walker shooting, eliminating it from ammunition supposedly used from the alleged Oswald rifle, CE-139.

There is no evidence, only hypothesis concerning the events of April 10, 1963, that Oswald had ever fired the gun at General Walker; there is also no proof, except from the words of a VERY cooperative, yet scared spouse, that he ever practiced with the weapon.

Mr. McDonald then asks Mr. Bates about comparing their test firings with the FBI's test fires:

> Mr. McDonald: "And you are saying in your test fires, your comparison with the FBI test fires, you could not say that those bullets came from CE-139?"
>
> Mr. Bates: "That is correct."
>
> Mr. McDonald: "Would you have expected that result considering the number of times that CE-139 has been fired over the years?"
>
> Mr. Bates: "Yes, we would have."
>
> Mr. McDonald: "Would you explain?"
>
> Mr. Bates: "Our inability to identify our panel tests with each other and the failure to identify the panel tests with the FBI tests is believed by us to be due by one or a combination of several factors. No. 1, repeated test firing of CE-139 over the years causing extensive changes in the individual rifling characteristics within the barrel of the weapon. No. 2, natural variations caused by the high velocity of the 6.5 bullet resulting in extreme heat and friction during the passage of the bullet through the bore of the weapon.

And No. 3, deterioration of the rifling surfaces over an extended period of time due to the absence of proper cleaning, maintenance and/or protective lubrication." (I HSCA 464)

The contention is that the evidence could be seen as inconclusive because the weapon was fired too many times after November 22, 1963, for comparison purposes, doesn't mesh when I have asked firearms experts about the same inquiry. They said that would have nothing to do with it.

Newquist adds:

> "No, we were not, due to the distortion of CE-573 [*Walker bullet*] and lacking a significant correspondence of individual characteristics with the test, no conclusion could be reached." (I HSCA 472)

The witness was never asked if it was a copper-jacketed bullet. He should have been.

Monty Lutz would return and describe how the magazine operated and how the clip worked to a variety of other congressmen asking questions. He said that Dallas police Lieutenant Carl Day found the clip in the weapon when it was discovered, but added that their tests showed that the clip did not automatically eject when the concluding round was chambered:

> "However, **in many cases**, and in this particular case, where we functioned the rifle, fed cartridges through it, we found this clip to stay in the rifle after the last round had been stripped and fed into the chamber. Because the lips or the edges of the clip many times will open up, they will spring against the walls on the inside of the box magazine and it will hang up in that area, and even though it is supposed to drop out, many times it will hang up in that area." (I HSCA 482)

As Donald Champagne would say later,

> "Yes. Without the clip the weapon would not function properly. The cartridges would lie loose in the magazine." (I HSCA 483)

This is formidable information. If the rifle was that unreliable and dysfunctional, why would someone use it, instead of a superior weapon that was far less likely to cause problems for the mechanic doing the shooting. You are shooting at the President of the United States; you would never take that kind of a risk.

If the shooter practiced with the weapon beforehand, you would think they would have been aware of the clip dysfunction, suggesting that Oswald or anyone else would not have used the Carcano in such a tense, important situation. It raises the possibility that the shooter did not know about the problem, which seems highly unlikely, if they are about to attempt to assassinate the President of the United States.

Go to a gun shop and talk with anyone there who has experience with firearms. Tell them that someone has a Mannlicher-Carcano, but hasn't fired it in over four years, with no practice, and see if they think that this individual would be a better shot than he was four and a half years earlier, using a much better weapon in a superior setting.

A tedious question, but with a very easy answer: Not a chance.

> Mr. Edgar: "And you indicated earlier—I believe, one of the panel members did—that it would be possible for an average marksman to shoot fairly accurately with the rifle without using the scope; is that not correct?"
>
> Mr. Lutz: "Yes, sir, that would be."
>
> Mr. Edgar: "Can you describe further why that is so? Why wouldn't you use the scope in every occasion, if it is connected to the rifle?"
>
> Mr. Lutz: "This scope, I will apply the principle to it. We are dealing with a four-power or a magnification of 4. The field of view is 18, meaning an 18-foot circle at 100 yards. So it is a 4 x 18 scope, a relatively small circle to locate your target in when you are firing and recovering from the recoil in successive shots. So to align your target to get a sighting position, by placing the stock into the shoulder, the head has to be adjusted or moved slightly to the left to align the way that the scope is mounted on the left-hand side and get into position to fire.
>
> The scope itself is also designed so that the crosshair, the reticles, do not remain in the exact center position. When you adjust windage or elevation those crosshairs move, so that you are not looking dead center in the object itself.
>
> A more natural and easier form or position to fire is to put the rifle against the shoulder, the cheek on the stock, and look right down the center, straight ahead from where you are now positioned, and align **the iron sights, the fixed iron sights that are presently on the rifle.**" [*This is Chief Counsel Blakey's ace in the hole.*]
>
> ...
>
> Mr. Edgar: "Are you indicating that in rapid-fire use of that rifle it would probably be easier to use the rifle without using the scope?"
>
> Mr. Lutz: "For me it would be considerably easier, yes."

Mr. Edgar: "Considering the physical layout of Dealey Plaza, would the shots at the President have been more feasible without a scope *for a person of less than marksman proficiency,* in other words, for someone not as proficient as a police sharpshooter?"

Mr. Lutz: "I believe that it would. The ability to grasp the rifle and put it into the shoulder and recover after each firing is considerably easier using just the iron sights." (1HSCA 483-484) [*Then why have a scope mounted, since the rifle was not built to have a scope mounted?*]

The point here seems to be that if you fire the rifle, work the bolt, and then realign the scope, too much time has now occurred, especially according to the 5.6 seconds of the FBI/Warren Commission to complete the assassination. In other words, the scope is designed so that the crosshair, the reticles, do not remain in the precise center position. When you fine-tune for windage or altitude, those crosshairs also move, so that you are not looking dead center at the objective itself.

After the bolt has been worked and a cartridge recycled, to readjust the weapon to the proper firing position, and then re-acquire the target. You obviously want to succeed on the first, because once that takes place, working the bolt and realigning the scope takes too much time to execute.

It did have the appearance of a sniper's weapon because of the scope mounted, but it was most assuredly not one.

A more comfortable position to fire from is to put the rifle against the shoulder and look down the center, straight ahead from where you are now positioned, and align the iron sights, the *fixed* iron sights that are presently on the rifle. The gun would be acceptable, using the iron sights, for an average marksman. Even without the sighting-in question, it presupposes that the average marksman, which Lee Oswald was not, had practiced regularly. Nobody asked about someone performing these feats with very little experience, especially in the last four and a half years of his life. They did not ask, because they could not ask.

Mr. Edgar: "Considering the physical layout of Dealey Plaza, would the shots at the President have been more feasible without a scope for a person of less than marksman proficiency, in other words, for someone not as proficient as a police sharpshooter?"

Mr. Lutz: "I believe that it would. The ability to grasp the rifle and put it into the shoulder and recover after each firing is considerably easier using just the iron sights."

Mr. Edgar: "Does any member of the panel have any differing points or related points that they would like to make in relationship to the questions that we have asked revolving around the rifle?"

Mr. Bates: "No."

Mr. Newquist: "No."

Mr. Wilson: "No, sir." (I HSCA 484-485)

The gun has now experienced a resurrection, as its reliability is seen after the shoddiness of the scope is slighted, the gun becomes an excellent weapon, using the iron sights. A rebirth has occurred.

It was not a weapon designed for iron sights use or a scope. It was a weapon of mass warfare, where the shooter fired into a crowded formation and hoped to hit something.

Given the successes in World War II by the Italian Army, and it was the Italian rifle of choice at that time, I would suggest the loss of a war is a greater testament to a weapon's quality than the testimony of a handful of patriotic, government foils who for some reason can't and won't say it was junk.

Both Lutz and Bates did testify that some weapons, in fact, do discharge smoke when fired, including the Mannlicher-Carcano, which was an answer to the following question:

Mr. Edgar: "When the assassination occurred many people in Dealey said they saw puffs of smoke coming from the direction of the grassy knoll. Do rifles or handguns emit smoke that is discernible to the human eye?"

Mr. Lutz: "Yes, sir; they do." (I HSCA 485)

There were many witnesses who claimed to see smoke coming from the direction of the grassy knoll, but not one witness made that claim about the Texas School Book Depository.

Mr. Fithian: "Thank you, Mr. Chairman. I wonder if the panel, any one of all of you, would comment on what has been one of the widely written about and discussed features of the actual shooting. As I understand it, the distance from the window where Oswald was supposed to have been located to the President was 165 feet. With that weapon which you now have inspected and test fired, how difficult a shot is it with the scope or without the scope, sort of from left to right?"

Mr. Lutz: "The answer I would give, I believe, would be that it would not appear to be a difficult shot with either device with reasonable training or a reasonable capability of a firer that was familiar with that firearm.

The iron sights would have provided a better capability because of the problems of sighting through the other device, through the telescopic sight, but I feel that it could have very easily been accomplished from that distance with that rifle."

Mr. Fithian: "And with the car moving at the estimated speed?"

Mr. Lutz: "From the data I have about the movement of the vehicle and the speeds involved, I still feel that it would not have been a difficult target at that distance."

Mr. Fithian: "Is there any other member of the panel who believes that it would be somehow an exceptional feat to have hit the target from that range?"

Mr. Bates: "I don't believe so, no."

Mr. Champagne: "No, sir." (I HSCA 488)

The successful shots into the limousine were not difficult, unless Lee Oswald is doing the shooting with CE-139, which was war surplus junk, though claimed to be the alleged murder rifle.

The accuracy required on November 22, 1963, according to the firearms panel, made the shots easily achievable, but they never explain that if it is so easily accomplished, then why did the experts in 1963 and 1964 fail to reproduce the shots during their recreations of the event, and there is not a word of evidence that these experts testifying before the HSCA ever attempted to duplicate the shots they are so easily advocating for, especially with CE-139.

A topic, not discussed in great detail, was the trigger mechanism of the Mannlicher-Carcano, which is a two-stage trigger mechanism.

Mr. Edgar: "... Is the two-stage trigger unusual for a military weapon? Second, does a two-stage trigger affect the accuracy of a weapon?"

Mr. Lutz: "The answer to the first question is that the two-stage trigger is not uncommon in a military firearm or especially rifles.

They are designed with a two-stage trigger, that two-stage trigger being defined as a mechanism or a type of firing system that allows for some slack or a distance of travel for that trigger before it engages into the sear mechanism and then pressure being applied and allowing the rifle or firearm to fire.

So, military rifles are designed with a two-stage trigger. The only ones that I have encountered that did not have the two-stage capability were those that had been worked over for marksmanship shooting, that two-stage feature being intentionally eliminated. As issued, the military rifle many times has that two-stage capability." (I HSCA 489—490)

An odd exchange then occurs and is ignored:

Mr. Edgar: "When *we* were demonstrating the action of it [*CE-139, the rifle*] we discovered that you could fairly quickly use the bolt action of that particular rifle. Would it be safe to say, in other words, that this bolt action would not prohibit Lee Harvey Oswald from firing the shots in the required time limit that has been estimated were the time between the first and the last shot?"

Mr. Champagne: "No, sir." (I HSCA 490)

Is that 5.6 seconds, or the more accurate time of 8.3 seconds, given the latest research by David Wimp and Keith Fitzgerald? For years 5.6 seconds was readily accepted by almost everyone as a fait accompli. We know the answer, but we also know better than 5.6 seconds.

Having made such a statement, Mr. Champagne states that because the weapon had been fired c. 100 times, since it was located in the Depository building, "that it would significantly alter the markings and the identifications." (I HSCA 492) That means a ballistic match was no longer possible because of 100 rounds being fired.

13

VINCENT P. GUINN –
SEPTEMBER 8, 1978

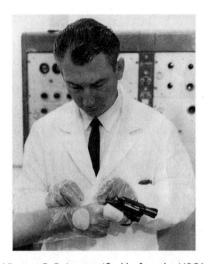

On Sept.8, 1978, Dr. Vincent P. Guinn testified before the HSCA in Washington, D.C.

D r. Guinn was a chemistry professor at the University of California at Irvine at the time of his testimony. He was also head of the activation analysis program of the general atomic division of General Dynamics Corporation.

Guinn's testimony has been controversial over the years and has become the magical sleight of hand of the ballistics evidence. It has been ascertained in the last fifteen years that *batch lots* of bullets can be quite diverse, resulting in this scientific discovery: A number of criminal convictions based on relational connections of ammunition lead to reversals in prison convictions.

Guinn was a government disciple. He was not a complete sellout, but merely someone who was going to tow the party line. Guinn was loyal to science, but also very protective of it.

According to Chief Counsel Blakey, the FBI had conducted "emission spectography" on the assassination bullets, along with neutron-activation analysis, however, both proved *inconclusive*. Blakey also stated that the results of those FBI tests were not revealed until the 1970s. In reality, however, the fragments that the FBI tested were ruined and extinguished in the testing process, so Guinn was there to explain and describe the process.

Guinn commented that the Western Cartridge Company made four batches of bullets that were appropriate for the 6.5 Mannlicher-Carcano rifle that was the subject of inquiry, though there was no justification stated as to why such ammunition would be manufactured when American weapons did not use it.

Each of the four batches, numbered 6,000, 6,001, 6,002, and 6,003 for documentation purposes, was produced in 1954, with one million shells in each batch. "... and reportedly those are the only lots they ever produced, and we had boxes from each of those lots." (I HSCA 494)

Why did the Western Cartridge Company decide in 1954, to make some Mannlicher-Carcano ammunition? It seems absurd. There would not have remotely been a need for it. Of course not. There should have been questions as to why that ammunition was being produced.

Everyone in the research community has always maintained that President Kennedy was killed and Governor Connally wounded with the nine-year-old ammunition cited. But no metal was removed from either man that would prove convincingly that it was 1954 ammunition. The 1954 revelation might explain why so many people, including Clint Hill, said in his Warren Commission testimony that the two shots he heard sounded differently. Could it have been as early as 1891 ammunition? There was one large and two small fragments taken from Governor Connally in 1963. This was a new and interesting revelation in 1978, but why was it not publicized in 1963 or 1964?

What were the size of those fragments? Based on how much was missing from CE-399, were those fragments weighed to see if it put the weight over the normal weight of CE-399, hence, another reason to discount the single bullet theory.

And now after almost sixty years, there is not a piece of evidence that Lee Oswald ever acquired any bullets for CE-139, the rifle found on the sixth floor of the School Book Depository building.

So, with regard to neutron activation analysis, let us examine the current status of the science. This subject isn't that hard to grasp, however, it is simply no longer applicable. The FBI quit utilizing neutron activation analysis, after it reasoned that ballistics lead analysis of that kind was not sound science. For quite a long time, Warren Commission advocates, such as HSCA director, G. Robert Blakey, beat their chests that NAA (neutron activation analysis) was the lynchpin that connected Oswald (or more accurately the bullets fired that day) and CE-139, thus proclaiming him guilty of executing Kennedy, because he supposedly ordered the rifle in question.

The NAA was now being titled with another type of terminology, comparative bullet lead analysis (CBLA). In the mid 2000's there were new advancements in the field. The field had been under investigation for some time and after two papers were published in peer review journals, everything changed. Cliff Spiegelman, William Tobin, William D. James, Simon J. Sheather, Stuart Wexler and D. Max Roundhill published an article in 2007 in *The Annals of Applied Statistics*, vol. 1 no. 2 (2007), pp. 287-301, entitled, "Chemical and Forensic Analysis of JFK Assassination Bullet Lots: Is a Second Shooter Possible?" A year earlier in 2006, Erik Randich and Patrick M. Grant had published an article in the *Journal of Forensic Sciences* designated, "Proper Assessment of the JFK Assassination Bullet Lead Evidence from Metallurgical and Statistical Perspectives," vol. 51 no. 4 (July 2006), pp. 717-728.

The lone laboratory in the country that did this sort of analysis was run by the FBI. There was mounting incredulity about NAA/CBLA, because on September 1, 2005 the FBI shut down their only NAA/CBLA research facility and forbade FBI specialists from giving evidence about NAA/CBLA. It was ending as a result of the untrustworthiness of the process. It was being considered "junk science," as Dr. Gary Aguilar likes to call it. What's more, presently, so does Professor Blakey, who was its most ardent defender.

This breakthrough bombshell destroyed and invalidated any NAA/CBLA evidence used to support the single bullet theory. Why? The samples that Dr. Guinn tested were: **CE-399** (the magic bullet), **CE-842** (fragment from Connally's wrist), **CE-840** (3 fragments from the rear floor of the limousine), **CE-843** (fragment from JFK's head) and **CE-567** (fragment from the front car seat). Guinn's conclusion: the six fragments came from just two bullets. CE-842 can be matched to CE-399, because both have high concentrations of Sb (antimony). CE-840 and CE-567, and the four fragments found in the car, can be matched to CE-843, because all five have relatively low concentrations of Sb. (I HSCA 504)

Guinn claimed that the concentration and amount of antimony was consistent within each aforementioned bullet. (I HSCA 505) The HSCA depended and leaned heavily upon Guinn to ratify their single bullet theory that they so politely inherited from the Warren Commission. (HSCA Report 45)

Spiegelman et al, pointed out that "random matches to assassination fragments of bullets from the same box are not as rare as Dr. Guinn, who was not a metallurgist, testified. Most importantly, our studies and analyses of individual bullet compositions, bullet lead source compositions and compositional mixtures in packaged retail boxes show that Dr, Guinn's statement about the uniqueness of individual bullets from the brand of bullets believed to be used in the assassination are seriously flawed." (Spiegelman et al, 289) The authors bought boxes from two separate lots of Mannlicher-Carcano bullets and expressed in their article that they "then analyzed 10 bullets from each box. The measurement approach was similar to that used by Dr. Guinn except that we used more appropriate standards, a known quality control procedure, and analyzed physical samples having a known geometry. *One of the bullets analyzed matched an assassination fragment.* We also found that many bullets in the same box have matching antimony and silver levels; this discovery is contrary to Dr. Guinn's testimony that based on these two elements virtually every bullet of this type is unique." (Spiegelman et al, 290)

As Jim DiEugenio points out in his article entitled, *Death of the NAA Verdict,* that there had been some criticism from the research community by Wallace Milam and Art Snyder, but they both unfortunately suffered from a fatal flaw, as did Dr. Guinn. None of them was a metallurgist. Erik Randich is a metallurgist. Jim goes on to say that Randich discovered that the lead alloy for MC ammunition, far from being exclusive, was the same as Remington would use. So, one of Guinn's stakes, the particular identifiability of MC ammunition, has now collapsed.

No bullet contains unadulterated lead, but they have an assortment of amounts of copper, tin, arsenic and antimony in differing levels. The process for bullets without copper or steel jackets incorporates an additional measure of antimony, including up to five percent of the alloy, which solidifies the lead adequately to permit the bullets to work without a jacket.

Guinn noticed the variable proportions of antimony in the JFK bullet fragments, and erroneously accepted that this inconstancy was a characteristic of that brand of bullet. Truth be told, it is an element in a lot of jacketed bullets. He additionally guaranteed that the antimony inside an individual bullet is distributed equally. This turned out not to be valid for the Western Cartridge Company bullets, in which antimony is generally concentrated around crystals of lead.

The present research shows that degrees of antimony in bullet fragments have no essential connection to the number of bullets from which those fragments originated. Fragments which contain comparative levels of antimony could emerge from one bullet; but could also come from several bullets. Fragments which contain varying levels of antimony could emerge from several projectiles; but could also come from various areas within one bullet. So, neutron activation analysis can't be utilized to decide the origin of bullet fragments. The technique is no longer, at this point utilized by the FBI for this purpose.

There is now no reason to believe that the bullet fragments retrieved from Governor Connally's wrist have any connection with CE-399, the magic bullet. The lack of damage to the base of CE-399 makes it highly unlikely that the fragments of lead came from that bullet, which appears to have been entered into evidence fraudulently at a later date. In other words, there is no provenance for CE0-399, no chain of custody. If Governor Connally's wrist wound was not caused by the bullet that struck Kennedy in his back, then the single-bullet theory is false, and more than one gunman must have been involved in the assassination. Nor is there any reason to suppose that the two large fragments of copper-jacketed bullets retrieved from the presidential limousine, CE-567 and CE-840, have any connection with the shot or shots to President Kennedy's head. The presence of dozens of tiny particles of bullet lead in JFK's skull suggests very strongly that a non-jacketed bullet had been used. Such a bullet could not have been associated with any of the shells found in the TSBD. Again, the implication is that more than one gunman was involved.

Keep in mind that Grant and Randich, in their aforementioned paper stated that, "the extant evidence is consistent with any number of between two and five rounds fired in Dealey Plaza during the shooting." As Josiah Thompson, in his recent work, *Last Second in Dallas*, on page 192 states, "the fragments tested from Kennedy's head could no longer be linked to a larger fragment from Oswald's rifle. The "phantom bullet" from the knoll was no longer a phantom." This evidence completely undermines Guinn's linkage of all the fragments to two bullets projected from CE-139, or any other rifle for that matter. Interestingly, this also applied to the Walker bullet as well. There is no justification that would link that bullet to CE-139 either, especially since it was noted to be a 30.06, lead-jacketed bullet at the time of the shooting.

What is odd, is that this is exactly what the Warren Commission had stated about their NAA results (they initially did spectrographic analysis by removing some of the tip of CE-399, easily seen on any photograph of the bullet – and then proceeded to do NAA tests) when they tested those same fragments in 1964 – inconclusive. The results of antimony ranged from 636 ppm to 1125 ppm. This was a massively wide range, allowing for a wide difference and this led the FBI to declare all NAA tests to be inadequate. The damn was beginning to show leakage.

Chief Counsel Blakey then decided to do more NAA testing, even though the Warren Commission had already done so with inconclusive results. And in a complete reversal, now the HSCA is saying that two bullets and only two bullets entered the limousine and collided with President Kennedy and Governor Connally. They also stated that it was determined that all of the bullet lead trace metal analysis was shown to have come from the Western Cartridge Company's Mannlicher-Carcano manufacture, connecting the bullets and its fragments to the rifle found on the sixth floor of the TSBD. They declared also that fragments from Governor Connally's wrist were identified with CE-399 that had also gone through Kennedy. Ergo, the single bullet theory has been rubber stamped and vindication was justified. But the leak mentioned earlier was gaining volume and now producing a torrent river.

Warren Commission sycophants like Gerald Posner, Larry Sturdivan, and Ken Rahn were beyond gleeful.

Blakey's NAA lynchpin, however, no longer had much grip; and like so many other pieces of evidence (like the ridiculous forward-head-movement myth at Z-312) *isn't actually there.* Now, the silly single-bullet theory has been refuted multiple times already in these chapters; and now, neutron activation analysis has come to be seen for what it really is – junk science – or, fake evidence and worthy of being tossed into the trash bin of delusion. The dam was now producing a flood of problems for the Lone-Commie-Loser crowd.

14

WILLIAM K. HARTMAN
SEPTEMBER 11, 1978

On Sept. 11, 1978, Dr. William Hartman testified before the HSCA in Washington, D.C.

William K. Hartman had a Ph.D. in astronomy from the University of Arizona. He had been assistant professor at the University Arizona Lunar and Planetary Laboratory, associate and senior scientist at the IIT Research Institute. He served as photo analyst for the Air Force University of Colorado study of UFO's and served as photo analyst and co-investigator on the Mariner 9 mission to photograph Mars.

Mr. Hartman was called back the same day to contradict the acoustic analysis by saying the jiggles did not overlie with the shot progression as proposed by Dr. Barger earlier in the day.

Chairman Stokes commented before William Hartman's testimony that Mr. Justice Holmes used to say that the first requirement of a good theory was that it fit the facts. Technically, this thesis would exonerate

Oswald. JFK was killed by someone who could shoot with precision. Oswald couldn't. (II HSCA 1)

Stokes went on to say that,

> "since all of the evidence in the Kennedy investigation is not in, it is not yet possible to fit any theory to the facts. A final resolution of the questions that may be raised by today's evidence must, therefore, await the conclusion of our hearings and the submission of our final report in December." (II HSCA 1)

Chief Counsel Robert Blakey seems to be guiding the committee in the prescribed direction and to the port in which he wants to dock. "Put succinctly: resolving the question of the number of those who participated in the assassination itself—a lone assassin or more than one gunman, that is a conspiracy, may well hinge on the number of shots fired, the interval between them, and the direction from which they were fired." (II HSCA 2)

The previous day's witnesses, the firearms panel, could have provided a wealth of data with respect to the shot intervals, but the correct questions were never asked. This could have been both probative and revealing. It wasn't.

Blakey then brought up the value of eyewitness testimony, then quickly reversed paths by stating that eyewitness testimony was widely diverse. Blakey spoke of observers who believed there were from two to six shots, and the time was between five and six seconds.

This is technically an incorrect calculation of the data, but over-all not terribly disconcerting. The shots and timing did have wider variances, but on the average, Blakey was fairly accurate. Emmett Hudson, Dealey Plaza grounds keeper, spikes the data by claiming the assassination took c. *two minutes*. He is visible in some photos and films standing on the steps going up to the grassy knoll. Elizabeth Loftus, a professor of Psychology at the University of California, Irvine, wrote the famous book on the unreliability of eyewitness testimony, entitled, *Eyewitness Testimony*. Everyone should read this book.

If the Weigman film truly shows smoke emitting and lingering, then the smoke would appear between four and seven seconds after Z-313, and that frame appears between 5.6 and **8.3** seconds after the first shot is fired (Josiah Thompson argues for this latter figure in his most recent book, *Last Second in Dallas*).

Blakey then reveals some new evidence, a sound recording that had not yet been analyzed, and a jiggle-effect view of the Zapruder film that has brought fresh science into the inquiry. This was all new in 1978.

Dr. William Hartmann was chosen to testify with respect to the jiggle effect. His resumé included authoring a planetary textbook, as well as co-authoring a book about the planet Mars.

Hartmann expressed that he had been present for some reenactment

"on August 20 when the committee did some test firing with the rifle *similar* to the one believed to have been used, and I found, first of all, that this was a very loud noise, louder than I had suspected, and in fact I attempted to take some pictures simultaneously with the gunfire and found that in three out of three cases my pictures were blurred when they were taken with gunfire and not when they were taken at other times.

In fact, I think my pictures were probably more blurred, showed a larger startled reaction than Mr. Zapruder's." (II HSCA 5)

Hartmann tended to embellish the sound of the Mannlicher replica rifle, and his reaction while filming. It's odd that he didn't appreciate why the Carcano was so loud during the reenactment. The re-enactment of August 20th was a blocked-off occurrence. The November 22nd motorcade and eventual assassination was observed by hundreds of people and vehicles and thousands upon thousands of decibels of shouting and motor vehicle noise, both automobile and motorcycle. Those myriad of decibels, now gone, would make the Carcano sound louder, as it would any rifle, which may also cause greater jiggling while filming.

Mr. Cornwell: "Dr. Hartmann, can you tell us, from the analysis that you just described, precisely when the shots were fired?

Hartmann answered with photographic gibberish, but not a response to the inquiry. From there his analysis is truly sui generis, to say the least, as he lives in the arena of the jiggle, and certainly not of the film. He conjectures that we know there was a wound at 313, and the jiggle is ongoing from 313 to 319, that "The shot was probably fired at 310." (II HSCA 15)

But if Oswald's alleged rifle is fired at Z-310, the bullet would have traveled 485 feet by Z-313, or 220 feet further than it needed to, given that the bullet would have traveled on the average of 114 feet per Zapruder frame, or 1/18 of a second.

> Mr. Cornwell: "And would it be accurate to state that the second largest area of blur of jiggle, apart from the one which occurred shortly after the head shot, would be in the earlier portion of the film?"

> Mr. Hartmann: "That is correct."

> Mr. Cornwell: "What frame is that associated with?"

> Mr. Hartmann: "About frames 190 to 200 there is a strong blur reaction initiated. So having concluded that this is, in fact, that the blur sequence around 313 to 319 is in fact a response to the gunshots, I would think that the logical inference would be that the blur sequence, the blur episode, running typically from 190 to 200 is also a response to a possible gunshot. And we know that the President emerged from behind the sign somewhat later, some frames later, showing in fact a reaction to such a wound. So this could very well be the blur or startle reaction to the gunshot that caused the back wound to the President."

> Mr. Cornwell: "And what, if any, corroboration is provided by this analysis to the Warren Commission's conclusion that the President and the Governor may have been shot in the vicinity of frame 210."

> Mr. Hartmann: "Yes, they picked 210. I would say that to pick 210 in the face of this current evidence [*it's not evidence, it's opinion*], to pick 210 as the time for that first shot, which is the Warren Commission's conclusion, would not be warranted from this evidence, because the blur before frame 210, from 190 to 200, is clearly much larger than any blur after frame 210. In fact, there is really very little evidence for a blur in the appropriate amount of time after frame 210."

Furthermore, there is some photo evidence that tends to support the thought of a shot in the time frame shortly before 190. For example, there is the Phillip Willis photograph which shows Mr. Zapruder in the background and the motorcade passing in between. Because the motorcade is in between, it is quite possibly quite easy, to determine exactly which Zapruder frame that corresponds to, because you can tell which part of the motorcade is passing between Zapruder and Willis.

215

And Willis said that he took that photograph as a reaction. He pressed the shutter as a reaction to what he perceived as the first shot, at least a shot."

Well, as it turns out, that frame is 202. So that means that Mr. Willis is telling us that he pressed the shutter as part of his reaction to a shot, and he was reacting at frame 202, while here we see that Mr. Zapruder is in the middle of his reaction at frame 202. So that is very nice consistent evidence that something happened, say, at 190, or shortly before 190." (II HSCA 14—15)

This is very erudite, but ultimately complete nonsense. Who would we expect to react first, the individual shot or the person holding the camera. It would presumably be the person being shot, since the bullet would be traveling faster than the speed of sound, which is 1,125 feet, or 375 yards per second.

President Kennedy does not manifest any visible reaction to being shot until Z-225, but his left elbow can be seen spreading out *as he appears* from behind the Stemmons Freeway sign in Z-223. It will continue its rising in Z-224 and be seen completely by Z-225. Because of the 0.9 seconds JFK was behind the Stemmons Freeway sign, we can only guesstimate about times with any precision.

There seems to be some proof for a shot just prior to Z-190, because of Phil Willis' daughter suddenly stopping and looking back over her right shoulder, which shot missed. This has always troubled me. The people shooting that day were professionals and we are supposed to believe they didn't miss that day, except c. Z-190. This is highly unlikely. If the Zapruder camera was running at 18.3 frames per second, which the HSCA tested that it was an average, and if the Mannlicher-Carcano rifle took 2.3 seconds to recycle without aiming, the arithmetic is quite easy to compute. 18.3 x 2.3, or 42.09 Zapruder frames, would mean that if there was a shot c. 190, another shot cannot occur until Z-232, necessitating that the first shot has to hit both men, but there is nothing to indicate that Connally is hit that early and then waits another 48 Zapruder frames (c. Z-237/238) to react, after breaking two bones. Or, you have two assassins.

Please don't miss the importance of this. If the lone assassin theory is accurate, and if the alleged assassin, Oswald, is the only one shooting, then every shot fired has to wait 42 frames of the Zapruder film before any subsequent shot can occur. This alone eliminates forever the lone assassin and the single bullet theory. It is amazing what simple arithmetic can accomplish.

Human reaction time can vary from very prompt, as Connally's doctors characterized his response to having his right fifth rib shattered to having taken place rather quickly, due to the trauma he sustained by his injuries. A camera will jiggle very quickly, but it does take a certain amount of time. If it is only ½ of a second, that is nine Zapruder frames. You can see from this that every Zapruder frame is crucial in the analysis of the crime and critical when analyzing the data of the assassination.

Chief Counsel Robert Blakey deferred further questioning of Dr. Hartman until the completion of the analysis of the acoustic tape that was discovered. He stated:

> "The committee then forwarded the tape it had obtained from Mary Ferrell to B. B. & N. [*Bolt, Beranek, and Newman is the acoustic firm that worked on the sounds of shots at Kent State and the 18-minute Watergate gap*], but no audible sounds could be discerned in the analysis." (II HSCA 16)

What can be concluded from Hartmann's testimony?

Not as much as we would have liked, with the possible exception that it proves the HSCA at least tried to do something decisive. Credit for that.

We needed a full understanding of the jiggle analysis, because there is no scientific guarantee that it was a reaction to a shot, to multiple shots, or to motorcycle backfires, or other noises in the plaza that day.

How do you precisely figure out when the trigger of the rifle was pulled in regard to making the holder of the camera jiggle? Therein lies the problem.

The prevailing idea has always been that President Kennedy and Governor Connally reacted when they were hit, but their reactions do not remotely match up to any exact jiggles.

The President is clearly hit at Z-223, or more accurate to say that is when it became physically visible that he had been wounded. Connally does not react for more than a half second after Z-223; and does not reveal any of JFK's responses in Z-223-225 until Z-234-Z-238.

Could Zapruder, who needed Marilyn Sitzman, one of his employees, to steady him on that pedestal, have jiggled the camera in a reaction to his need to remain fixed on his subject as he swiveled a few degrees in the process of filming? Certainly possible. Is it possible that Sitzman jiggled and that caused Zapruder to jiggle as well? Sitzman's appearance was quite happenstance, as she initially went to the bank on her lunch hour to open up an account. When she got there, the bank was closed, so she strolled over to the plaza and saw Zapruder, who asked her to stay and help steady him due to his bouts with vertigo. For the record, Marilyn Sitzman was no friend of John Kennedy.

After a recess, Dr. Hartman's testimony resumed, when Dr. Green (more about in due course) was finished. Hartmann was recalled to seemingly contradict the acoustic analysis by essentially saying that the jiggles did not overlap with the shot sequence as postulated by Dr. Barger earlier in the day.

Congressman Fithian once again demonstrated the age-old legal principle that you never ask a question that you do not know the answer to:

> Mr. Fithian: "Dr. Hartmann, I really don't have very many questions and I don't think it will take long.

Are the jiggle analysis techniques used by yourself and your associates for your presentation here today common interpretation techniques? In other words, what I am asking is: Have they been used to help interpret photos and films other than those from Dealey Plaza?"

> Mr. Hartmann: "I think the correct answer is no. In fact, I would like to emphasize that unlike much of the scientific data that you are getting such as on the acoustic work or the neutron activation analysis, this kind of technique *does not have some scientific tradition* of routine measurements, you do the measurements this way, this way, this way, and you get such and such an answer."
>
> Here we are much more in a situation of making a common-sense hypothesis at the beginning, meaning, based on our common experience (that a person is likely to react and the best information which I mentioned in my testimony indicates that people do react to that sort of thing and we tried to measure the film to see if there was a reaction, looked at each step as we went along and got the results I showed you."
>
> Mr. Fithian: "To the best of your knowledge, did the Warren Commission employ this technique?"
>
> Mr. Hartmann: "I believe they did not. I think that the frame 210 that they identified was identified solely on criteria of some

FBI agents estimating when a wound occurred and also that they constrained their shot times by this tree which grew in front of the window. *They tended not to want to call for a shot when the President was behind this tree."* (II HSCA 130-131)

There were serious variables left unasked and unanswered. Would jiggles decrease in concentration with the added shots? The first explosion might cause a jiggle, but would the second, third, and fourth cause identical jiggles or would they lessen as the photographer became familiarized to the blasts?

Zapruder suffered from vertigo, and though the pedestal was only four feet high, Zapruder was concerned enough for his safety that he asked Marilyn Sitzman to steady him and lessen his vertigo anxieties.

Given the elements of vertigo and Sitzman, it is possible there would have been a jiggle or two in the film, simply from Zapruder's nerves or Sitzman nudging him slightly in providing him assistance, as alluded to earlier. I am not submitting or declaring it happened that way, but merely suggesting a possibility and a speculation."

Hartmann did expound on some of the weaknesses of his own position:

"I think I was the only one in the group who stood on Zapruder's pedestal. That is not far from where the others were in the sequence of shots as was just indicated. But I stood on Zapruder's pedestal during that whole first sequence and the shots from the depository, this is my framework, I am looking out at the street. I had the sensation of a very large sound filling the street area up the street toward the depository but the shots from the knoll were extremely loud in this ear and left my right ear ringing and my left ear not ringing.

"So I had a very strong sensation from that shot, so I would have expected the witness to be more definite that there was something to the right if there had been a shot fired there." (II HSCA 131)

Hartmann's analysis, "the shots from the knoll were extremely loud" is grounded that in the reconstruction, a Mannlicher-Carcano was fired from that location, the knoll. There is no indication whatsoever that CE-139 was used on the knoll, or a Carcano of any kind; and it would be easy to suggest it would be the last likely weapon used there. So,

Hartmann's perception does not prevent the shot(s) from a less-noisy weapon.

Zapruder was definite about something and that something was not ever asked about. At the end of his testimony before the Warren Commission, he stated, "You know there was indication there were two…" and he was told, by Warren Commission staff counsel Wesley Liebeler, "Your films were extremely helpful to the work of the Commission, Mr. Zapruder." (7 H 576)

Hartman did reference a shot, or blur at c. Z-331-332, which would correspond with the latest and most recent findings of Keith Fitzgerald, Don Thomas and a study by Richard Mullen, in concert with Dr. James Barger: the final shot to the back of JFK's head at Z-327/328.

15

DR. JAMES E. BARGER
SEPTEMBER 11, 1978 &
DECEMBER 29, 1978 (REDUX)

On Sept.r 11, 1978, Dr. James E. Barger testified before the HSCA in Washington, D.C.

James Barger appeared twice before the Committee, with September 11 being his first appearance. He testified again on the last day of testimony, December 29, 1978.

Gary Cornwell begins the questioning by asking him about the time when the committee brought a tape recording and the Dictabelt of the Dallas Police Department's recordings of transmissions on November 22, 1963.

> Mr. Cornwell: "At that point in time, what did the committee ask you to try to do with that tape recording?"
>
> Dr. Barger: "Mr. Cornwell, there was a series of questions that were asked in increasing order of difficulty.
>
> "The first question and the least difficult potentially to answer was, simply, was the motorcycle with the stuck transmitter likely

to have been in Dealey Plaza. If so, was the sound of shots recorded thereon or detectable thereon. And if that turned out to be the
case, how many shots. If that could be determined, what was the
time sequence between them, and if that could be determined,
from what locations were the shots fired. And if by chance that
also could be determined, what weapons fired the shots?" (II
HSCA 18)

Barger did a wonderful job using layman's terms to explain technical scientific processes. His findings were controversial then as they are
now, but less so, mostly due to the work of Don Thomas. The process
used to isolate sounds is somewhat contentious even today. He was
thorough when he explained things and seemed to understand a bigger
picture than what he was called to testify about. He was as serious as Dr.
Guinn was, however, about the science.

Barger and his colleagues were able to isolate a segment of time, c.
five and a half minutes, when it was determined that the motorcycle microphone was stuck open. Barger then transformed it from sound into
graphic images, not unlike a polygraph print out, which extended c. 234
linear feet. (II HSCA 27)

Barger then isolated that segment and cross-matched the time signatures on the two known police radio frequencies, and arrived at a
cautious, conjectural time of 12:30:47, which Barger felt was too far
along from a time standpoint, to represent the *first pulse* which could
be deduced as a shot. He added that he later found out that the two
different radio channel clocks are only synchronized once per year, on
January 1; 325 days before the assassination, and as a result there was
a one-minute discrepancy in regards to synchronization. As a result,
Barger determined that his original 12:30:47 time appraisal had the potential of embellishment, and as a result, the pulse that was noted on the
234 linear-foot spread sheet contained "shots fired" data. (II HSCA 42)

Barger stated that the impulse pattern found in the five-minute time
range (an approximation) was not repeated anywhere in the 234 linear
feet, so he was assured there were no other similar impulses, and that
the five-and-a half-minute range is the only place where gunshot impulses were located.

As Barger was going through his checklist of requirements to demonstrate gunshots, Cornwell injects a break question: "At this point then

you had devised six screening tests, any one of which I take it might have been sufficient to rule out these impulses as being gunshots, and they in fact passed all six tests, is that correct?

Dr. Barger: "Quite so." (II HSCA 46-47)

At this juncture, Dr. Barger thought that an acoustical reconstruction would be of worth.

Mr. Cornwell: "In other words, you suggested to the committee they go back to Dealey Plaza and fire a rifle there so you could record it and see exactly what it looked like in that urban environment?"

Dr. Barger: "That is correct." (II HSCA 47)

Barger thought another opinion was in order, which demonstrates his integrity. The committee was in concert with this suggestion and engaged the services of Mark Weiss and Ernest Aschkenasy of Queens College.

Barger warned there would be difficulties faced with an acoustical reconstruction in the urban environment of Dealey Plaza, and there was a myriad of them: they could certainly not assume that if there was a second gun, it would have been a Mannlicher-Carcano, but they did, in fact, use a Mannlicher-Carcano for the grassy knoll impulse. There was no justification for this, but a hundred or so reasons could be given as to why it wouldn't have been used. I am not sure why they assumed a Carcano was used and not some other rifle. They would not have known for certain what kind of ammunition would have been used, of course, especially if they didn't know exactly what kind of a rifle was being used; the exact positioning of the motorcycle is at least somewhat questionable, but Don Thomas does seem to narrow down that dilemma. The point of this is that all of these variables would have been very difficult to ascertain.

Later findings have been contested by those who do not want to believe in any kind of conspiracy, but the scientists involved in all of this have earned our reverence for their expertise.

Barger explained where the positions of the microphones were, and the character of the different test selections, and then went into how he gauged or tabulated the results. It was an extremely complicated journey through the land of mathematics and physics. It is not for the faint of heart.

Gary Cornwell appeared to have a better than average knowledge of Barger's testimony, and was able to ask intuitive questions as a result. It was nice to see someone prepared as Cornwell was.

Barger then explained how false alarms could make his findings suspect, and how those findings searched painstakingly for false alarms, indicating the noise of the motorcycle itself could cause a problem. You would have to take into account the motorcycle slowing down and speeding up and evaluate those patterns in concert with the shot impulses and be able to distinguish between the two. Pinpointing the motorcycle, using films and photographs can be easily done, however. You can determine the turn it took from Houston to Elm and that wide 121 degree turn from the aforementioned streets. The motorcycle would slow down, coast for a bit, and then accelerate when it was comfortably out of the turn.

> Mr. Cornwell: Dr. Barger, does that conclude your description of the analysis that you performed?"
>
> Dr. Barger: "Yes, it does."
>
> Mr. Cornwell: "Let me then ask you in sum, is it fair and accurate to state that after all of the analysis there is evidence of four shots on the Dallas Police Department tape, and that the acoustical sounds that may represent those shots are spaced as follows: between the first and second, approximately 1.6 seconds, between the second and third, approximately 5.9 seconds, and between the third and fourth approximately 0.5 of a second?"
>
> Dr. Barger: "Yes, that is a possible conclusion." (II HSCA 69)

After a recess of a little over an hour, an extensive cross-examination was embarked on by Indiana representative Fithian, followed by the speed round of five-minute opportunities by each of the other congressional colleagues.

Dr. Barger attested to four shots based on the re-creation. There were only two sites re-created, the sixth-floor window and the grassy knoll. Other sites could have been put to the test, such as the Dal-Tex building, the County Records Building, the southwest corner of the Depository building, different places along the knoll, as well as other positionings.

Was this sufficient? Probably not, but it was a start and a whole lot better than the Warren Commission ever produced.

Barger's examination is based on the time of 18.3 frames per second of the Zapruder film, a time not challenged, but as stated earlier in the book, the HSCA did tests and came up with c.18.3 fps, which seems to be fairly accurate. We would need Zapruder's camera, but that was never going to see Dealey Plaza again or be used for any kind of experimentation.

The first Barger scenario does not seem to work at all.

The second scenario: if the first shot is c. Z-174-175, then the second shot c. Z-204, then the third shot c. Z-313, and finally the fourth shot c. Z-322, a different narrative emerges.

Shot #1, at Z 174-175, could line up to what some call Kennedy's flinch as well as to the daughter of Phil Willis reacting and turning. There are less problems with this scenario, but difficulties still exist. There doesn't seem to be a wound exacted with this shot, which is problematic, because these were serious shooters, professionals, that I seriously doubt missed their target that day. Shot #2, at Z-204 seems too early for the back wound to JFK and also doesn't address the back and chest wounds to Connally. Shot #3 Z-313 is a constant, without any variation. Shot #4 Z-322, is the point in the Z-film where Connally is shot out of his wife's clutch, which is perceptible on the film, but none of the parties ever testified to it. It would account for Connally's wrist and thigh wounds, however, as I stated in chapter one concerning John Connally.

The second hypothesis has more legitimacy than the first, but remains deficient, as I would put the final shot closer to Z-327-328.

Regardless of the possible hypotheses available, one central fact is clear from the data: One person fired three shots from the rear and one person fired one shot from the right front.

The Committee reconvened at 1:30 p.m., with Congressman Fithian leading the cross-examination, which was prefaced with the statement,

> "And as you must be aware, this poses as very serious evidence for us in that it does not corroborate some other evidence that we have," there seems to clearly be an agenda on the part of Fithian to diminish the findings of four shots, inasmuch as the absurd proposition of three shots only rested primarily on the number of cartridges found.

"And I want to go back now, so that I am clear and others in the room are clear, as to just what it was that you set out to ascertain by the tests that you ran in Dallas when you went back and sort of re-created the shot pattern.

"What was it that you were specifically trying to do?" (II HSCA 69-70)

Barger explained how the 36 microphones were spaced, why there were 36, and the necessity to ascertain the margin of error. Barger is worth reading, so we can understand how a scientist analytically approaches an issue, as opposed to predisposed disciples of the Warren Commission. It got inane at times, unfortunately:

Congressman Floyd Fithian:

"Now to the layman, it would seem that if you are going to re-create a test, that you might have wanted to use instead of the most modern microphone equipment, you might have wanted to use, as nearly as you could find, microphones and transmitters identical to those which you believed to have been on the original motorcycle. And I would like some explanation as to why you chose not to use the motorcycle microphone, which you have indicated at one point in your testimony you had indeed used, from the Massachusetts police. Evidently that kind of a microphone or transmitter is available.

Why then did you use a more sophisticated system of microphones?"

Dr. Barger: "A more sophisticated system?"

Mr. Fithian: "Yes, more sophisticated than obviously was on the stuck transmitter.'"

Dr. Barger: "Why did we use the more sophisticated?"

Mr. Fithian: "Why did you?"

Dr. Barger: "There are two reasons. In the first place, as I showed, the radio distorts and limits the amplitude of loud sounds. Each radio does that in detail in a different way. We weren't seeking to look at the wave form of each sound echo, only the time at which it occurred. The radio does not distort the time at which it occurs, nor does the more sophisticated equipment that we used.

"The more sophisticated equipment that we used is known to be reliable and not to fail in times of stress in the middle of a sensitive test. Old motorcycle radios from those earlier days are known not to be very reliable, nor are they found in the quantities we required. Therefore, we selected a system that would give us the equivalent data but more reliably." (II HSCA 71-72)

Fithian seems to try and discredit the research, but we are already used to this being done to anyone who is at variance with the official version. At other times he and Dr. Barger, who answers Mr. Fithian with precision, seem to be in sync, and Barger is able to give answers that satisfy Fithian. At times there appears to be bad blood between these two individuals. You can't always tell if Fithian dislikes the scientists or the conclusions they arrive at, or what he perceives they are going to say.

Dr. Barger to Congressman Fithian: will you let me get away with that? Shall I proceed? Very well." (II HSCA 66)

It is an unusual give-and-take. Fithian was prepared and did his homework, thank goodness. He asked smart questions and also demanded clarifications for a lot of the jargon that was used.

Perhaps it was an adversarial proceeding to bring so much expert jargon into the arena where the conclusion that four shots were fired would be lost. Hard to say.

> Mr. Fithian: "While they are doing that [preparing exhibits], let me ask you sort of the central question.
>
> Is it your conclusion that you proved that there were four shots?"
>
> Dr. Barger: "No."
>
> Mr. Fithian: "With regard to the groupings of shots what do you prove then?"
>
> Dr. Barger: "As regards the grouping of the shots, we demonstrated with high confidence that if there are four shots, we demonstrated the times at which they occurred, and the intervals between them were described by Mr. Cornwell, 1.6 seconds, was it 5.9, and 0.5"
>
> Mr. Fithian: "Would you repeat that again, please?"
>
> Dr. Barger: "Yes."
>
> Mr. Fithian: "The distance, the time frame between the first and the second shot is what?"
>
> Dr. Barger: "1.6 seconds."

Mr. Fithian: "And between the second *and what you perceived to be a possible third shot*?"

Dr. Barger: "5.9."

Mr. Fithian. "And between *the possible third and possible fourth shot*?"

Dr. Barger: "0.5."

Mr. Fithian: "0.5?"

Dr. Barger: "0.5, one-half second."

Mr. Fithian: "One-half second. So, what you are saying, Doctor, is that if there were four shots fired, they came at those intervals."

Dr. Barger: "Yes." (II HSCA 74—75)

Fithian then suggests some hypothesizing, and that was where I mentally left the room and whether perfectly correct or skewed, the data should not be dragged through the mud of potential speculation. It should rise or fall on its own merit.

Fithian raised questions concerning Governor Connally's testimony that he heard an added shot, heard it hit the President with a clear and distinct sound, and he then clapped his hand to imitate the sound. Then:

Mr. Fithian: "Now, as I interpret what the Governor said, after he had been hit, and Mrs. Connally had pulled him down into her lap, he was still conscious, and he heard what sounded like a shot, and then heard what sounded like the bullet striking the President's head. Now, No. 1, if in fact the speed of the bullet is supersonic, you could not hear it in that sequence; am I correct?"

Dr. Barger: "That is correct."

Mr. Fithian: "In other words, he would have had to have heard the bullet striking the skull first, and then the muzzle blast would come at some fraction of time after that?"

Dr. Barger: "That is correct." (II HSCA 82)

This becomes a problem in logic: if there is a four-shot assassination scenario, then Governor Connally might have heard the shot at Z-304, and then heard the bullet that impacted the President's skull a fraction of a second ahead of the sound of the shot which produced it. And, just as Connally believed until his dying day that he did not hear the shot that hit him, when in fact he didn't hear the shot that killed the President. Just a thought.

Yet that possibility does not arise in the exchange:

Fithian maintained his goal by using word play to terminate the knoll shot:

> "I want to return to that troublesome shot from the grassy knoll, the third one that comes just ahead of the obvious head shot." (II HSCA 84)

The grassy knoll shot has always been a source of trouble and controversy. Fithian seems to be suggesting in ipse dixit fashion that the head shot did not originate from the grassy knoll.

It is almost pathetic to watch, or listen, to Fithian do everything possible to eradicate the grassy knoll shot from the calculation. I guess the official version is going to be defended no matter what.

Fithian even introduces a phrase unknown to the previous investigative group:

> Mr. Fithian: "I would ask staff counsel Cornwell whether or not we have additional information on the chain of custody." (II HSCA 89)

> Mr. Fithian: "Mr. Barger, I certainly want to thank you for your answers and your insight and I would appreciate your final collective judgment as to whether *there are three or four impulses on that tape that could represent gunshots?*"

> Dr. Barger: "We have endeavored, Mr. Fithian, to make as powerful a detection test as we could devise and to lower the acceptance threshold of those matches that passed the threshold so that all likely correct detections would emerge. In so doing, we found that the process had sufficient noise in it that some of the detections that passed our threshold are false alarms.

> "We believe that the chances are very high that we have in fact located the motorcycle, and, of course, that was done by matching sounds of gunfire. Therefore, to believe the probability that there were at least two shots is very high because it would take at least two to establish that pattern on the chart. You can't draw a straight line through one point.

> "The indication is that there are probably somewhere between three, maybe six additional false alarms that we cannot

on our own information correctly identify as false alarms. Therefore, we think each of the detections that we have made is about
equally likely to be a false alarm.

"As there is only one detection remaining for the third
shot—I don't remember what color it was, but it was the knoll
shot, it is about equally likely that it is a false alarm. There it is
about equally likely that there were three shots. However, there
is an equal likelihood that there were four, and if there were, we
have determined the time at which they occurred and, we also
believe, the location from which they came." (II HSCA 90)

In summary and in review of Dr. Barger, (he will appear a second
time at the end of December and at that point I will go over his clarifications and update the evidence in the light of the research by Don Thomas) the HSCA hired Bolt, Beranek and Newman (BBN) of Cambridge,
Massachusetts, a firm specializing in scientific analysis to examine the
Dallas Police tape dictabelt. BBN had pioneered the analysis of sound
recordings to determine the timing and direction of gunfire through its
study of a tape recording of the 1970 Kent State shooting. (II HSCA 17)

Dr. Barger was BBN's chief scientist. He conducted a series of tests
and determined the reel-to-reel tape was an exact duplicate of the original dictabelt. He then converted the tape recording to digitized wave-
forms, similar to the peaks and valleys of an electrocardiogram. Barger
then filtered out such noise as the repeated firings of a motorcycle engine. He then selected six sequences of impulses that might possibly
represent gunshots. He finally established that all six impulse sequences
occurred during the time of the assassination at different intervals. (the
central dispatcher's office recorded the precise time that every message
they received came in). The HSCA would eventually admit to four of
the six impulses. (VIII HSCA 1-185)

Barger's initial analysis established a distinct possibility that the tape
contained the sounds of gunshots. Now it became necessary to record
the sounds of gunfire in Dealey Plaza in order to compare them with
the impulses on the tape. Therefore, in August of 1978, BBN recorded the sounds of shots fired from the sixth-floor window of the Texas
School Book Depository building and from the grassy knoll. Barger discovered that four of the impulses on the Dallas Police tape matched the
recorded sounds of gunfire in the reconstruction. Because the matches
were not exact, Barger eventually concluded that the probability that

the four possible shots found by the correlation detector include at least two correct detections is high, about 96%. The probability that there are three correct detections is lower, about 75%. The probability that all four are correct is only about 29%. The combined probability that there are three correct detections, and that the third (knoll) shot is among them is about 47%. (VIII HSCA 47-48)

Remember, it was Barger who testified about the most striking new development in the HSCA's investigation. As a result of the efforts of a group of Dallas researchers, the Committee learned of the existence of a tape recording of Dallas Police radio transmissions, and the researcher's analysis that it contained the sound of the shots.

The Committee now had audio evidence that a shot came from the front, but medical evidence that shots came from the rear. The Committee was going to conclude that the President was shot by Oswald, but that another shooter had fired and missed. The Committee may have been wrong to rely on its acoustics conclusion so heavily, as dissenting expert opinion was bound to come – and soon.

The serious blow to the acoustical evidence came in a 1982 report by the National Academy of Sciences. A panel of distinguished scientists concluded that the Committee's studies do not demonstrate there was a grassy knoll shot. At the core of the finding lay, not some abstruse scientist's deduction, but the curiosity of a rock drummer in Ohio: Steve Barber.

Barber came to the controversy by way of a girlie magazine. In the summer of 1979 *Gallery* offered its readers, besides the nudes, a record of the section of the police dictabelt that included the noises said to be gunshots. He played it again and again and detected something the experts had missed. What had been thought to be unintelligible crosstalk, conversation coming in from another radio channel, Barber's ear identified as the voice of Sheriff Bill Decker in one of the lead cars of the motorcade. The Sheriff's voice occurs at the same point on the recording as the sound impulses that the Committee's experts said were gunshots. What he is saying is "Move all men available out of my department back into the railroad yards there … to try to determine just what and where it happened down there. And hold everything secure until the homicide and other investigators can get there." Clearly Decker did not issue his orders till *after* the shooting, so Barber's discovery triggered an onslaught on the acoustics evidence. Because of the timing, the Academy of Sciences was to conclude, the sounds on the recording had to be something other than gunshots; static perhaps, but not gunshots.

Barger is unrepentant, in spite of the Academy's decision. He said he used an entirely different method of identifying the time at which the recording was made. His method involved noting what time the police dispatcher said it was. Barger's method was much more straightforward, and much less subject to error by some extraneous artifact than was the Academy's method. His method was more robust.

While Sheriff Decker's orders obviously came a minute or so after the shooting, Dr. Barger insists that this could have been caused in several ways. The Dictabelt needle could have jumped back, as sometimes occurred with that old-fashioned system, or the illusion of crosstalk may have been caused during copying of the original police recording.

Dr. Barger stands by his original findings. The number of detections he made in the tests, and the speed of the detections – the odds that could happen by chance are about one in twenty, Barger said. Barger will appear again at the end of this book in redux fashion and will update what was said here and bring it into the year 2022. Hopefully the acoustics evidence will become even more clear in Dr. Barger's redux.

16

PAUL MCCAGHREN
SEPTEMBER 11, 1978

On Sept. 11, 1978, Paul McCaghren gave testimony before the HSCA in Washington, D.C.

Paul McCaghren was the former lieutenant of burglary and theft of the Dallas Police Department in 1963. His role would prove to be the foundation stone in their investigation, ultimately leading to the conclusion of conspiracy. He was later part of a special team assigned to investigate the shooting of Oswald in the basement of Dallas City Hall.

The story of Paul McCaghren starts with a man named Jack Moriority, investigator for the HSCA, who surfaces quite a bit when taking a look at HSCA archives and records. His sleuthing capabilities paid off in great dividends.

He journeyed to Dallas and talked with Morris Brumley, who was a retired detective. Paul McCaghren had started a private investigation firm which had hired Brumley. During the sixties Charles Batchelor had replaced Jesse Curry, who had retired in 1966 and had put Paul Mc-

Caghren in charge of materials that he found outside of his office space in a file cabinet locked with a bolt and which was supposedly connected with the Kennedy assassination. He apparently retrieved the materials from the cabinet and put them in the attic of his home. McCaghren held on to the materials for nine years until he gave them over to the HSCA, by giving them to Jack Moriority. Prior to this occurring, McCaghren was advised to "take charge of the material. Make sure that no unauthorized person came in contact with the material." (II HSCA 109)

Brumley sat in with McCaghren, as Moriority interviewed him. Moriority was given an envelope with the dictabelt tapes of channel one and two, which documented the dialogues of the police, the day of the assassination. He also turned over the transcripts of both of those two channels. Moriority was acute and knew there were serious ramifications to what had been handed over to him. Not only were there original documents and tapes that McCaghren provided the HSCA, but also a crucial November 22, 1963 dispatch tape along with the dictabelts that recorded the communication and transmission from the motorcycle with the open mike.

Moriority handed them over to Professor Blakey who redirected them to Dr. James Barger and B.B.N. for analysis. To supplement the analysis of the tape, B.B.N. experts also went to Dallas to conduct an acoustical reenactment based on the "live firing in Dealey Plaza." (II HSCA 111)

Keep in mind, McCaghren had these materials for nine years, before he turned them over. He swore before the committee that no one, not even himself, tampered with anything that was removed from the locked filing cabinet.

This additional item forced the committee to alter its original presumption that a sole assassin fired all the shots from the rear. The evidence was this Dallas police tape of the gunshots. This was huge and eventually forced the committee to draw its second main conclusion:

"Scientific acoustical evidence establishes a high probability that two gunmen fired at President John F. Kennedy." (HSCA Report 65)

17

DAVID GREEN
SEPTEMBER 11, 1978

On September 11, 1978, Dr. David Green testified before the HSCA Washington, D.C.

D r. David Green, Professor of psychophysics and chairman of the department of psychology and social relations at Harvard University testified next concerning psychoacoustics. (II HSCA 111) Dr. Green's testimony is an attempt at data collection, by linking the findings of Bolt, Beranek, & Newman with the audio discernments of 178 individuals who indicated they heard shots on November 22, 1963.

He went to Dealey Plaza with assistants at the same time the acoustical analysis tests were being performed by Dr. Barger. They positioned themselves in different locales to compare the sound and blasts that they heard and then attempted to correlate them with the volleys gathered from the witnesses after the assassination. It is an attempt to have science interact with human observations, with all of its fragilities. How you could possibly isolate the positions where one person would hear

235

the shots better than another person? It seems like too many variables to be very precise.

Dr. Green stated that after the first sequence of shots, totaling 17 in number, they were in 94 percent agreement with their responses. He said, however, that "when you are situated immediately at the Texas School Book Depository, which was our general location for the second sequence of shots, two things are rather confusing ... you directly localize the source in whatever direction you were facing ... the sound sweeps down the building and the apparent source of the sound is rather large." (II HSCA 119). He said that he and his assistants were in about 90 percent agreement.

When it came to the shots from the grassy knoll, with the exception of McFadden, they all scored 100 percent. His conclusion was that it was a very easy place to localize sound. When this kind of expertise is placed alongside the witnesses who were there on November 22, 1963, the percentages are drastically different. Of 178 people who were questioned, 46 said that the Texas School Book Depository was the origin of the shots. Twenty stated they thought the knoll is where the shots originated. About 44 percent said they didn't know the location of the shots. Only four witnesses gave dual locations, according to Dr. Green.

Two observations seem obvious: The experts, who know what to listen for, are markedly more accurate than the witnesses who were there for the day to simply watch a motorcade and catch a glimpse of the president.

Secondly, the dual location statistic seems amazingly low. The difference between the two parties don't seem to contradict each other as much as they show the wide gulf between the actual event and a staged production.

Green brought a number of ear witnesses with him. Human acoustics are far less dependent on precision of understanding than might seem apparent.

The study of the 178 witnesses is an interesting exercise. I secured the study from the National Archives and while it may not sound like an interesting read, it was actually quite engaging to peruse the different responses of the witnesses in the Plaza. An exact science; albeit, anything but. There is, however, truth with a small t, that can be ascertained from the research that was done.

18

THOMAS CANNING –
SEPTEMBER 12, 1978

On Sept. 12, 1978, Thomas Canning testified before the HSCA in Washington, D.C.

Thomas Canning was an engineer with NASA's Space Project Division. He had degrees in mechanical engineering and aeronautics from Stanford University. Canning constructed a scale model to illustrate "the final product from information by the committee from its various panels." (II HSCA 154)

Canning was not asked if he had ever been employed by the Reily Coffee Company, which is where a lot of people worked who ended up at NASA.

The Forensic Pathology Panel had already determined that the fatal head shot came from above and behind the president, but it was unable to determine, from the available medical evidence, whether the bullet that entered Kennedy's back had been fired from above, below, or on a level plane. The House Select Committee, therefore, decided to have an expert conduct a trajectory analysis to pinpoint the origin of the shots.

Enter Thomas Canning. He presented a model of trajectory that is quite familiar to the research community. And completely wrong.

When it comes to the wounds, Canning displayed Kennedy's head wound as being "determined by the forensic pathology panel to be 9 centimeters above the external occipital protuberance which is a little pointed structure at the base of the skull.

That inshoot wound was shown, and it is dimensioned in the right-hand figure, the frontal view, as being 1.8 centimeters to the right of the mid-plane of the skull.

The outshoot wound was shown to be 5 ½ centimeters to the right [*of what?*] and to lie on what is called the coronal suture.

The outshoot wound is 11 centimeters forward of the inshoot wound. If one draws a line straight forward through the outshoot wound in the right lateral projection, it turns out to be very close to 90 degrees relative to the external facial axis as determined from a study of the relative tissue thicknesses, of American males. (II HSCA 159—160)

Why do we have forensic pathologists perform autopsies? According to the HSCA, Humes never did establish with any precision a wound of entrance or exit; he was wrong by 10 centimeters with his head wound entrance according to the HSCA forensic pathology panel; and cited no anatomically specific exit location.

That indicates that this data was not obtained from the President's body, but from photos and X-rays; so again, what is the point of doing autopsies when you could always just refer to the X-rays and autopsy photos?

As stated, the bullet did not journey far through the President's head, as the outshoot was cited as being c. 4 inches in front of the inshoot. How two pencil point-sized fragments wound up behind the eye remains somewhat cryptic, and a greater dilemma is produced when it is ruminated that the bullet – or fragments – are to have exited at a virtual 90 degrees from the entrance, yet the fragments that are believed to have come from the head shot wound up in a place certainly NOT 90 degrees to the right of the inshoot wound.

It begins to substantiate an apprehension I've had for some time: the two limousine fragments are responsible for the damage to Connally's wrist. His chest wound bullet did not do that damage. You know what I am going to allude to once again: Z-313 frontal shot, followed quickly with a head shot from the rear at Z-327/328, with this final shot causing the damage to Connally's wrist and leaving a fragment in his left femur.

Canning suggests that if his assessment of President Kennedy's head, in Z-312, was inaccurate by one inch, it could badly bias all determinations of trajectories. At least he is honest.

A few pages later, the following interchange between Counsel Goldsmith and Congressman Floyd Fithian takes place:

> Congressman Fithian: "I was informed [by whom?] the distance [muzzle to JFK, at time of head shot] would be about 250 feet; is that correct?"
>
> Mr. Goldsmith: "That is correct, Mr. Congressman. At the time of the head shot the distance between the limousine [irrelevant: the limousine was not shot] and the book depository building is *about 250 feet*. [Hardly precise: 265 feet and several inches] At the time of the back neck shot [no longer "upper back"] it was approximately 170 feet or 150 feet...." (Discussion held during the House Select Committee testimony of Tom Canning, II HSCA 196)

"*About?*"

"Approximately?"

Not exactly mathematically precise!

There is no way to even profess to consider a trajectory, as opposed to a hypothetical projection, based on anything less than categorically precise numbers. The head shot was said to be 265 feet 9 inches away; "about 250 feet" is an error of 15 feet plus, or 5.6%, *hardly within the realm of what is known as "scientific error."*

The "upper back" shot, in an attempt to revert it to its correct location, was only guessed at in the Warren Commission reconstruction, was denounced as dishonest by the surveyors (Brenneman and West) who did it and were then asked to sign off on measurements that they did in no way discover and then later protested vociferously.

The fact that the House Select Committee is guessing, like the Warren Commission, while attempting to maintain a strong tradition, albeit an erroneous and deceitful tradition.

As the movie *JFK* asks, "and they sold this lemon to the American public?" The only rescuing usefulness of the technologically superior House Select Committee on Assassinations was that they postulated a high probability of a fourth shot, from the grassy knoll, *guaranteeing a conspiracy.*

Canning also supported the magic bullet by avoiding Wecht and the consensus of the medical panel with the 11 degree upward rise of JFK's back wound:

> "...if he [Connally] had avoided the bullet which exited the President's neck, we have a problem of finding where did that bullet go?" (II HSCA 198)

The only rational argument ever suggested for the magic bullet is, that it left Kennedy and had to go *somewhere*. Not exactly *Aristotelian logic at its best. This kind of statement is usually followed up in my Logic class with a very sarcastic, duh!*

Perhaps it did go somewhere, but that is hardly the point. *Where* did it go and from whence did it come are the two major questions.

The medical panel determined that the Kennedy back-to-neck bullet was rising in its trajectory, and it is certainly not rising in this model trajectory by Thomas Canning, so he is not only at variance with Dr. Wecht, but also with the entire forensic pathology panel.

So where did it go? Possibly somewhere on the far side of the Triple Underpass, never to be seen again.

There is a sort of logical deduction that claims if you cannot conclude where the bullet could have gone, then it had to have hit the Governor of Texas. These kind of if/or postulations are very dangerous in Logic. It is often done to stymie your opponent and force them to choose from only two options. Usually a bad idea in philosophy.

Canning would also testify, and render worthless the totality of his efforts, that the "error circle" – the area that had to be allowed for the margin of scientific miscalculation, could have conceivably permitted a shot from the Dal-Tex Building, or, the County Records Building. (II HSCA 199)

The committee divorced itself from any reliability by depending upon the analysis of their NASA expert, for determining the trajectory of the bullets that struck President Kennedy and Governor Connally. Canning used the location of the wounds on the two men, the position of the limousine, the alignment of the occupants of the vehicle, and other information to arrive at his calculations.

Those calculations demonstrated that both the "single bullet" and the fatal head shot could have been fired from the sixth-floor southeast corner window of the Book Depository building (HSCA Report 48).

In permitting Canning to perform his trajectory analysis, the committee ignored the advice of its own Pathology Panel. The panel cautioned that there is no reliable method of determining the missile trajectory, particularly if precision within the range of a few degrees is required. This was illustrated by Canning's rejection of the objective medical evidence. Instead of using the true location of the entrance wound in Kennedy's back (approximately five inches below the crest of the shoulder), *Canning arbitrarily raised it three inches in order to arrive at a trajectory consistent with the sixth-floor window.* He also computed the angle of the wound as twenty-one degrees downward. This was nothing less than a blatant distortion of the medical evidence, which proved that the bullet entered the president's back at a "slightly upward" (c. 11 degrees) angle.

Despite similar distortions of other parts of the objective medical data, Canning's trajectory analysis resulted in margins of error, by his own admission, that would have permitted the assassins to have fired from such diverse locations as the fourth, fifth, sixth, and seventh floors, and the roof of the Depository, as well as from the two upper floors of the neighboring Dal-Tex building. The total number of sniper locations that would fit Canning's analysis is seventy! Clearly, such lack of precision, as well as the manipulation of the objective medical data, opposes any serious inferences to be drawn from his trajectory analysis. (VII HSCA 168-169; VI HSCA 43-56)

From various sources Canning determined where the President's car was on Elm Street at Z-312. To establish the head orientation, Canning worked from Z-312. This meant that his basic starting datum was Zapruder's camera. If he could fix the position of the camera, the distance to Kennedy's head, and how his wound-determined straight line related to the straight line of sight from Zapruder, he could plot the backward course of the bullet - i.e., its trajectory.

In theory the method was fine. He could trace his bullet source without ever having to say or know anything about true north, the angle of Elm Street and the car, or the angle of Oswald's shot relative to the midline of the car. But in practice the method was complicated; it could not escape the simple eyeballing estimates Canning abjured in oral testimony, and it was based on certain assumptions that Canning never spelled out or gave reason for believing.

The complications arose with the obvious fact that Kennedy was not showing an exact, erect profile to the camera. His head was rotated and tilted away from Zapruder. And it was nodded forward. Canning told the committee that he addressed this problem by constructing a model of Kennedy's head and torso and taking a series of what he called "calibration photographs," a system that freed him from more eyeball estimates.

The system seems to have consisted of putting the mannequin in various different positions, photographing them, and comparing them to one another and to Z-312.

If the comparison was done with more than a ruler, protractor, and eyeball, we are never told. In oral testimony, when the committee was shown the model photograph said to duplicate Kennedy in Z-312, Senator Dodd of Connecticut noted that it didn't look nearly so tilted as Z-312. Canning replied,

> "I can assure you the images play games with you." (II HSCA 193)

After further questioning he conceded that the interpretation of these features is a major source of potential error. Before his testimony was done, Canning conceded that there was enough potential error in his method for his radius of possible gun sources to extend not just beyond the Texas School Book Depository to the Dal-Tex building across the street, but beyond the Dal-Tex to the Records building. (II HSCA 193 - 199)

To make the final estimate of the degree of forward movement of Kennedy's head, the HSCA trajectory team found the model photo they judged was the best Z-312 replica. It shows the mannequin tilted toward a descending plumb bob. The essence of the reference system is shown by that vertical line delineated by the plumb, as stated in oral testimony.

It is not sufficient to argue that Z-312 was enough for their purposes. Canning himself told the committee that it was a difficult frame to work with. It might have been easier if he had worked with all of it, that is, if he had used the car, which was done for the back shot.

Given the immense amount of time the report says was spent measuring and re-measuring, it seems it would have been possible to do a parallel tracking of the trajectory by fixing Kennedy's head relative to the midline of the car and measuring the angle backward from the known position of the car.

In 1964, to accommodate what the Warren Commission believed about the inshoot-outshoot, the Commission simply decreed a forward head tilt of 59 degrees. This is not meant to imply that Canning did not say what he honestly believed. He pointed out to the committee the discomforting news that the trajectory of the head shot bullet did not fit with the windshield damage that the committee would maintain was caused by "the bullet" after it exited from the skull.

Consider this single vulnerability in the HSCA trajectory analysis: It depends entirely on the assumption that Zapruder held his camera perfectly vertical. The HSCA's own much ridiculed "jiggles" analysis (aimed at trying to identify when Zapruder jumped or was startled because he heard the shots) cites many times when the camera jittered in his hand. Still the HSCA used a straight-to-the-earth plumb line attributing a no-tilt attitude to the camera. A skeptical viewer looking at Z-312 might ask why, when the limousine is still to Zapruder's left, and it is going down a 3-degree slope, the front of the car appears to be slightly higher than the back. Is it possible Zapruder has his camera tilted slightly to the right?

What is most telling is the letter that Mr. Canning wrote to Professor Blakey tallying his apprehensions on how the HSCA compartmentalized, which was, to him, disturbing and bothersome:

January 5, 1978
Professor Robert Blakely [sic]
Chief Counsel,
House Select Committee on Assassinations
U.S. House of Representatives
House Office Bldg.

Annex No. 2
Washington D.C. 20515

Dear Professor Blakely: [sic]

When I was asked to participate in analysis of the physical evidence regarding the assassination of John Kennedy, I welcomed the opportunity to help set the record straight. I did not anticipate that study of the photographic record of itself would reveal major discrepancies in the Warren Commission findings. Such has turned out to be the case.

I have not set out to write this note to comment on results; my report does that. What I do wish to convey is my judgement of how the parts of the overall investigation which I could observe were conducted. The compartmentalization which you either fostered or permitted to develop in the technical investigations made it nearly impossible to do good work in reasonable time and at reasonable cost.

The staff lawyers clearly were working in the tradition of adversaries; this would be acceptable if the adversary were ignorance or deception. The adversaries I perceive were the staff lawyers themselves. Each seemed to "protect" his own assigned group at the expense of getting to the heart of the matter by encouraging – or even demanding cooperation with the other participants. The most frustrating problem for me was to get quantitative data – and even consistent descriptions – from the forensic pathologists.

Of somewhat less importance in gaining overall acceptance of what I consider to be a quite impressive improvement in understanding, was the manner in which the results of the investigation were conveyed in hearings. I don't propose to alter the trial-like atmosphere, but when long-winded engineers and Congressmen are allowed to waste literally hours on utter trivia, I do object.

I needn't remind you of the importance of managing time when many expensive people are participating and particularly when millions are watching. To allow staff and witnesses to overrun their planned allotments to the detriment of the whole planned presentation indicates that either the plan or its execution has been weak.

Clearly the participation of the Congressmen in subsequent questioning, though necessary, uses time somewhat inefficiently; even here enough experience must have accumulated to anticipate the problem and lead you and Chairman Stokes to deal with it.

Much of this rather negative reaction to the hearings themselves stems from my being strongly persuaded to rush through a difficult analysis at the last minute, abandon my regular pursuits for two days, try to boil down forty-five minutes of testimony to thirty, and then listen and watch while two hours' of excellent testimony is allowed to dribble out over most of a day.

Permit me to end my not altogether complimentary letter by saying that it was for the most part an interesting and enjoyable experience. On balance, the entire effort would be justified solely by the strong indication of conspiracy at the Plaza. I particularly enjoyed working with Jane Downey and Mickey Goldsmith. Their help in piercing some of the partitions and their remarkably quick, intelligent response to my needs was exemplary. They also proved to be good critics in helping me make my results clear.

Sincerely,

Thomas N. Canning

No comment necessary.

19

Marina Oswald Porter –
September 13, 14 1978

On Sept. 13, 1978, Marina Oswald Porter testified before the HSCA in Washington, D.C.

A s Ruth Paine was asked the most questions of those who appeared before the Warren Commission, so Marina Oswald achieved that dubious distinction before the House Select Committee on Assassinations. It is important to cover, if for no other reason than she was married to the alleged assassin. Marina's testimony has morphed over the years; but is always both interesting and challenging to peruse.

Mr. Stokes asked that everyone remain seated when Marina Oswald entered the room for the proceedings. The same was done for former President Gerald Ford.

Was there any real concern that someone was going to try to assassinate Marina? And why would sitting down not allow that to happen, if someone really wanted to. This seems much ado about nothing and leaning on the side of ridiculous.

Blakey then began his narration that would become the norm in these proceedings, in which I have them all in a notebook that I purchased years ago. You almost get the impression that his narrations were an act of foreshadowing of what he KNEW the witnesses would say, or at least what questions would be asked. In case of point, this is exactly what happened. The witnesses would go over their questions ahead of time before they testified. There were not many surprises with this kind of choreography. Blakey soon began with "After Lee Harvey Oswald was arrested in connection with the assassination of President Kennedy and then shot to death by Jack Ruby, Mrs. Oswald testified a total of four times before the Warren Commission. All of her testimony was in closed session." (II HSCA 206)

To say that Marina gave testimony four times is technically true, but it was over the span of 9 different days: February 2-6, June 11. July 24, September 6, 1964.

All of her testimony was in closed session, which was the choice of the Warren Commission and one they would regret, because it simply displayed a sense of secrecy. Mark Lane was the only witness to appear in public session. This was known from the very beginning, so I'm not sure to whom Blakey is talking.

Marina initially discussed her move to Minsk, where she would first meet Lee Oswald, to live with her aunt and uncle. She lived with "Ilya and Valentina Prusakova." (II HSCA 207)

It may be straining at a gnat to swallow a camel, but to be more precise you never would have said, Ilya and Valentina Prusakova in 1964. The reason for this is because the two particular names would be Ilya Prusakov (male gender) and Valentina Prusakova (female gender). The family name would have been stated and preserved in the male gender.

> Mr. McDonald: "And where was he employed?"
>
> Mrs. Porter: "He was working for the MVD in the city of Minsk."
>
> Mr. McDonald: "And what is that, the MVD?"
>
> Mrs. Porter: "It is the Ministry of Internal Affairs."
>
> Mr. McDonald: "And what did he do at the MVD?"
>
> Mrs. Porter: "I do not know what he exactly did, except I know he has a profession as an engineer."
>
> Mr. McDonald: "Did he ever discuss his job with you?"

247

Mrs. Porter: "No."

Mr. McDonald: "Did he ever discuss his job at home?"

Mrs. Porter: "No." ...

Mr. McDonald: "Did you ever study English in the Soviet Union?"

Mrs. Porter: "Me? No."

The following is in regard to her initial meeting at the dance with Lee Oswald:

Mr. McDonald: "Did he tell you he was an American?"

Mrs. Porter: "No, not at that—not during the dancing, no."

Mr. McDonald: "At this time you were speaking in Russian together?"

Mrs. Porter: "Yes. He spoke with accent so I assumed he was maybe from another state, which is customary in Russia. People from other states do speak with accents because they do not speak Russian. They speak different languages."

Mr. McDonald: "So when you say another state, you mean another Russian state?"

Mrs. Porter: "Yes, like Estonia, Lithuania, something like that."

Mr. McDonald: "Did you suspect at all that he was an American?"

Mrs. Porter: "No, not at all." (II HSCA 207-208)

Marina has stated many times through the years that she thought Oswald was from the Baltic region of the old Soviet Union, which would include Estonia, Latvia, and Lithuania. She never identified Oswald, nor did she suspect that he was an American in the earliest days of their meeting.

So, who taught Oswald Russian, and who taught him Russian without an American inflection? How much Russian could he speak? He was good enough that he at least fooled Marina. There is no recording of Oswald ever speaking Russian when he was here in the United States. It is a very difficult language to learn and even more difficult to write, so how did Lee Oswald master the Russian language, when the Mayo Clinic came to the conclusion that he suffered from language blindness? (see CE-3134) This occurs when the individual cannot see the full field of a word and ends up crunching, or compacting, a word, which then becomes shortened. One example would be taking the word opinion and spelling it as opion.

Knowing this about Oswald suggests serious limitations, not only in language, but also with his ability to shoot from a distance of 265 feet from 60 feet in the air, at a car moving from right to left, especially when the alleged Carcano, when tested, shot high and to the right when fired. Yet, when it comes to the Russian language, he is almost flawless, but not so with his English proficiencies.

> Mr. McDonald: "**When do you recall him first expressing opinions against the United States?**"
>
> Mrs. Porter: "**A few months after the marriage when I found out that he is wishing to return to his homeland. Then he started complaining about the bad weather in Russia and how eager he will be to go back.**"
>
> Mr. McDonald: "Can you recall Oswald expressing at this time, soon after your marriage but prior to the return, prior to your return to the United States, do you recall him expressing any views about the United States or its political system, either pro or con, for or against"—
>
> Mrs. Porter: "No."
>
> Mr. McDonald: "And specifically regarding John Kennedy?"
>
> Mrs. Porter: **What I learned about John Kennedy it was only through Lee practically, and he always spoke very complimentary about the President. He was very happy when John Kennedy was elected.**" [*she did not meet Lee Harvey Oswald until more than four months after the November, presidential election of 1960.*]
>
> Mr. McDonald: "And you are saying, while you were still in the Soviet Union, he was very complimentary about John Kennedy?"
>
> Mrs. Porter: "Yes, it seemed like he was talking about how young and attractive the President of the United States is."
>
> Mr. McDonald: "Can you recall during this time when he ever expressed any contrary views about Kennedy?"
>
> Mrs. Porter: "Never." (II HSCA 209—210)

Oswald seemed to be in a perpetual state of agitation and always discontented. He was abusive toward Marina on several occasions, especially after they came to America. He had trouble keeping employment, so where did he get his money? More than one researcher has done the math and the numbers don't seem to add up. Doug Horne has pointed out, after checking Oswald's pay from the Marines, that he did not get paid a dime from them the last quarter he was enlisted. There also don't seem to be many accounts of Lee Oswald demonstrating much emotion, except when getting mad at Marina. He didn't seem to enjoy his jobs and was always getting reprimanded or fired. He seemed to go out of his way to let everyone know he was a Communist, or at least had leftist leanings. What is odd is that his bosses were extremely right wing and the last people on earth who would want to listen to his "red" propaganda. The only exception to this is his job at the TSBD, because while working there he never brought up his stay in the Soviet Union, spoke any Russian, didn't read *The Worker* or *The Militant*, or call anyone by 'comrade'. He quietly did his work and as a result, there wasn't any complaint as to his work performance. Why? He needed to keep this job, as probably communicated to him by his handler.

Apparently, Marina did not want to come to the United States:

> Mr. McDonald: "Is that true, that you did not have any idea that he had been in touch with the American Embassy?
>
> Mrs. Porter: "No, that was the condition of me accepting his proposal, because I asked him before marriage if you ever be able or will come back to United States, and he said no, so I assumed that he will be living in Soviet Union all the time."
>
> Mr. McDonald: "At that time what was your attitude toward the United States?"
>
> Mrs. Porter: "Well, I did not know that much about United States, but I was curious to find out about. I did not have any hostility toward United States." (II HSCA 211)

Later in her testimony she will claim that she hated the United States. Which Marina are we getting there – and which one are we getting today?

> Mr. Preyer: "Did he ever mention to you that he had contact with the KGB, the Soviet intelligence agency?"
>
> Mrs. Porter: "No."
>
> Mr. Preyer: "In your deposition, one of the depositions you gave the committee, I believe you stated that you both assumed that

the KGB was observing you. What is the basis for that conclusion?"

Mrs. Porter: "Well, from Russian newspaper you assume that they don't print exactly what is going on in United States, and I mean act like they maybe mistrust them, so it wasn't surprising for them to keep eye on a foreigner." ...

Mr. Preyer: "Did you and Lee think that our apartment was bugged?"

Mrs. Porter: "Yes, we did."

Mr. Preyer: "Why did you expect the bug in your apartment?"

Mrs. Porter: "Well, because like I do not even know if bug will take any electricity, but our electric needle would be running while you turn all electrical appliances off. It would still be moving. So, we did not know what the reason for that was, except we assumed we had been watched.

Another assumption is that this is quite customary in Soviet Union to keep eye on somebody." (II HSCA 215)

Mr. Preyer: "Did Lee have a rifle, a gun, a rifle, while he was living in Minsk?"

Mrs. Porter: "Yes, he did."

Mr. Preyer: "Did he hunt with it? If so, how often did he go hunting?"

Mrs. Porter: "Not during our marriage he didn't, but he did belong to hunting club, and he said that he did previous to our marriage." (II HSCA 216)

It was prohibited for Russians to own rifles and November 22, 1963 in Dallas may indicate why. In Russia you hunt with a shotgun, but never with a rifle. Russians are usually suspicious about what lurks beyond what they can see, so a rifle would give someone a distinct advantage over you and that was not about to happen in the old Soviet Union.

Marina was not an expert on guns or rifles of any kind, nor did she have any interest. To her they were all the same. This comes mostly out of disinterest. One rifle or gun was the same as another to her.

After Gary Powers and his U-2 spy plane was shot down, Oswald did purchase a shotgun and joined the Hunting Club. Yuri Nosenko

251

claimed that Oswald could not hit a rabbit from a few feet away. This suggests volumes that have either already been stated or implied. Before Lee Oswald ever encountered Marina, he began the process of returning to the United States, most likely because of the downing of the U-2 spy plane and after the trial of Gary Powers. Did Oswald fear some kind of repercussion? Hard to say; but knowing that he once worked very closely to the U-2 spy planes in Atsugi, Japan, it isn't a bad hunch.

> Mr. Preyer: "You mentioned earlier that after you were married, you and Lee thought the apartment was bugged. Did you think that your mail or Lee's mail was being opened?"

> Mrs. Porter: "We assumed that it was. Letters are censored that come from foreign countries."

Mail was habitually opened – and we know the CIA had intercepted several pieces of Oswald's mail, including some of his mother's as well.

> Mr. Preyer: "*Did you feel that you and Lee were being watched, that is, did you see any strange men outside of your apartment who appeared to be loitering near your apartment?*"

> Mrs. Porter: "*I don't remember right now.*"

Marina has discriminating agnosia throughout her entire testimony. Anything we might guess as to why, is just that, a guess. She could have been so young and so used to it living in Russia, that maybe things that happened were natural and she didn't think it was important. Hard to say.

> Mr. Preyer: "Specifically did he ever talk about President Kennedy?"

> Mrs. Porter: "Whatever he said about President Kennedy, it was only good, always." …

> Mr. Preyer: "From Lee's conversation, did you think he wanted to become a citizen of the Soviet Union at this time?"

> Mrs. Porter: "Once Lee, I believe he applied for, he sent a letter to university in Moscow, and he was very, very disappointed when he was refused to become a student of this university, and I think that maybe was a changing point about him staying or leaving definitely Soviet Union. He was very disappointed. I do assume that he might have stayed longer, or maybe forever, if he was granted permission to become a student." (II HSCA 216—217, *passim*)

Marina met Lee in March 1961, although she was obviously unaware at that time that Oswald was making plans to return to the United Sates by February, 1962. This is all predicated that the testimony of Marina Oswald Porter is accurate.

> Mr. Preyer: "Did you ever suspect that Lee might be a spy of some sort for either the KGB or for the U.S. CIA?"
>
> Mrs. Porter: "Well, it crossed my mind sometime, I am sorry to admit that."
>
> Mr. Preyer: "I am sorry?"
>
> Mrs. Porter: "It did cross my mind sometime during out life in Russia; yes, because he will be writing with those papers and writing something in English, and I don't know. Maybe he was making reports to somebody and didn't want me to know."
>
> Mr. Preyer: "When it crossed your mind, did you think he was a spy for the United States or for the Soviet Union?"
>
> Mrs. Porter: "For United States."
>
> Mr. Preyer: "And you based that on the fact that he often was writing notes in English which you did not understand?"
>
> Mrs. Porter: "Yes."

I have no reservation in thinking that if Marina had ruminated for one second about the possibility that Lee Oswald was a spy for the United States, she would have departed and never looked back.

Mr. Preyer then brought up Lee Oswald listening to the radio with his friend Pavel Golovachev, though Marina was unsure if Pavel was there or not, but his wife, "you know, me being a woman, what do you know about politics, you know. So I really do not recall what the comments were." (II HSCA 219)

> Mr. Preyer: "When you arrived in New York from the Soviet Union, did Lee bring his rifle with him?"
>
> Mrs. Porter: "I don't remember. I don't' think it can go through the customs with the rifle."
>
> Mr. Preyer: "You did go through the customs in New York?"
>
> Mrs. Porter: "Yes." (II HSCA 220)

Oleg Nechiporenko states in his book, *Passport to Assassination*, the story of Oswald trading in his weapon while still in the Soviet Union.

Rifles, but not shotguns, were illegal at that time in Russia and the penalty was quite unsympathetic.

The Oswalds eventually went through U.S. Customs in Hoboken, New Jersey,

> Mr. McDonald: "Mrs. Porter, did you and your husband have any Cuban friends in Minsk?"
>
> Mrs. Porter: "Not friends, but I think Lee met some Cuban students that were going to university in Minsk."
>
> Mr. McDonald: "Do you recall their names?"
>
> Mrs. Porter: "I do believe he mentioned some names, but I do not recall them at all."
>
> Mr. McDonald: "And how well did you know them?"
>
> Mrs. Porter: "I did not know them at all."...
>
> Mr. McDonald: "At this time did he speak of Cuba? Did Lee speak of Cuba in favorable terms? Did he talk about Cuba at all?"
>
> Mrs. Porter: "Yes."
>
> Mr. McDonald: "What did he say?"
>
> Mrs. Porter: "He did like Fidel Castro, and at the time so did I, because he was presented to Russian public as a very good fellow. So at the time all Soviets, I mean all young people were curious about new government in Cuba, and how they will do it, and so he was very appealing at that time."
>
> Mr. McDonald: "What did Lee say about Fidel?"
>
> Mrs. Porter: "He said that he did like him as a leader very well."
> (II HSCA 221-222)

Marina comes across as being confused about Lee's contact with the FBI when they got back to the United States, specifically in Fort Worth:

> Mr. McDonald: "When Lee first got to Fort Worth, you first went there when you went back to Texas, was he contacted by the FBI?"
>
> Mrs. Porter: "That is what he told me, that the gentleman who wanted to talk to him, came along, was FBI agent. That is what he told me."
>
> Mr. McDonald: "When did he tell you about this?"

Mrs. Porter: "After living with Robert for a while we moved in our home and Lee on the job and one afternoon some gentleman came knocking on the door."

Mr. McDonald: "This is Robert Oswald, his brother?"

Mrs. Porter: "Yes."

Mr. McDonald: "You are saying living with Robert?"

Mrs. Porter: "Oh, yes and Lee went outside and talk with this man, and when he come back, he told me that it was the FBI who were bugging him, asking questions about the Soviet Union, things like that."

Mr. McDonald: "What was Lee's reaction? How did he appear to you when he came back in?"

Mrs. Porter: "Well, he was very knot up—quite angry about it. He told me that it would be very difficult for him to find a job or keep a job if they keep bugging him." (II HSCA 225)

This takes a second to sort out, but her story seems to be fictitious. FBI S/As John Fain and Tom Carter contacted Oswald when he first arrived in Fort Worth. At a future date they invited him to have a talk with them inside their car. He later showed up at their FBI office. First, she says it happened after they had moved out of his brother's house, while Lee was at work. The story then morphs into the incident taking place at his brother Robert's house, while Lee was there. I couldn't begin to guess which version is true.

Mr. McDonald: "Up to this time, and we are only talking up to this time in Fort Worth, on your early arrival, had you ever heard Lee ever mention in discussion or did you ever overhear him talking with anyone about assassination as a political act?"

Mrs. Porter: "No."

Mr. McDonald: "Did you ever hear him talk at all about assassination up to this point?"

Mrs. Porter: "No." (II HSCA 228)

Again, Marina is not a ballistics expert. No surprise here.

Mr. McDonald: "When do you first recall seeing Lee with a rifle in the United States?"

Mrs. Porter: "I cannot pinpoint exact month, you know, date of any kind."

Mr. McDonald: "Where did you first see it?"

Mrs. Porter: "I do not remember where or when, but I can say that Lee did have a rifle during life in the United States."

Mr. McDonald: "Do you know whether it was the same rifle that he had in the Soviet Union?"

Mrs. Porter: "Well, logically, it cannot be, because you cannot go through the customs without declaring the rifle. I would not really know."

Mr. McDonald: "Mr. Chairman, let the record reflect that Mrs. Porter was unable to identify Lee Harvey Oswald's rifle, which was marked CE-139 before the Warren Commission. She was unable to identify it in 1964 when she testified before the Warren Commission, and consequently we will not show it to her today since such a showing would serve no useful purpose."

Mrs. Porter: "Thank you."

Mr. McDonald: "When you first saw the rifle in the United States, did you ask him what it was for?"

Mrs. Porter: "*I don't remember what I asked him about. I know I wasn't pleased with having a rifle in the house.*"

Mr. McDonald: "What did he say about it?"

Mrs. Porter: "Well, in a matter of, that's it's a manly thing to like or something like that. Most men do like to hunt or do like to play with the rifle."

Mr. McDonald: "Do you recall seeing him taking it out frequently from wherever he kept it, either to handle it or clean it, to look at it, do whatever?"

Mrs. Porter: "Yes, I did see him cleaning the rifle. That is true."

Mr. McDonald: "How often?"

Mrs. Porter: "Maybe once a week."

Mr. McDonald: "Where did he keep this rifle?"

Mrs. Porter: "In his closet."

Mr. McDonald: "When you refer to the 'closet,' what apartment are you referring to? At what apartment are we talking about?"

Mrs. Porter: "*I do not recall any apartment, but maybe one in Dallas.*"...

Mrs. Porter: "*Yes, because in New Orleans he had the rifle, the same rifle, and he kept it in the closet there, too. Every apartment has a closet.*" (II HSCA 228—229)

We have mentioned Marina's intellectual agnosia (agnosia is often caused by some kind of a brain injury, but my usage here is more liberal, suggesting not that Marina has literal agnosia, but that she simply forgets a lot of things we would not expect her to overlook). She doesn't seem to remember much at all: She can't distinguish the rifle when testifying before the Warren Commission, but is able to recognize the rifle in New Orleans as being the same one Lee had at the Neely Street address. I have always felt it was her total lack of interest in all-things ballistic or anything to do with firearms, more than anything else that led to her forgetfulness.

If Marina can't remember at which apartment she photographed Lee with the rifle, as far as the exact address is concerned, that would be believable to me. My guess is if she was shown pictures of their apartment on Elsbeth street and their apartment on Neely street, she would pick Neely street. If she was unable to do this, then that would be odd, if for no other reason than these pictures would become some of the most famous in the history of America. Put yourself in her shoes and uproot yourself and move to Krasavino of Veliky Ustyug in the Vologda Oblast in Russia and see how much you can remember as far as particular locales, towns, items, etc in one calendar year. You may be surprised on how little you would recall with accuracy.

I have met people who have such a lack of interest in things like this, that really don't remember, mostly because they don't care.

At least she remembered that Oswald had a rifle in the United States. It is at least something. I know that a lot of people are less sympathetic with Marina than I am. It's not that I don't think she is withholding information that she actually remembers, but I just can't pinpoint the what and the why.

Mr. McDonald: "Did you notice any change in his personality after he obtained this rifle?"

Mrs. Porter: "Well, Lee liked to be alone by himself quite often. That was a part of his personality, so that wasn't really anything new. But his behavior pattern toward me changed. He was very annoyed by me. It seemed like I felt out of place."

Mr. McDonald: "Did you ever see him—you said that you would see him taking it out and cleaning it. Did you ever see him while he was in the apartment pick up the rifle and to aim it like he would be practicing shooting?"

Mrs. Porter: "He would do that in New Orleans in apartment, you know, the screened porch. He would sit there in the dark with it." ...

Mr. McDonald: "Think back, can you recall whether the rifle had a scope on it? It would be attached to the rifle. Can you recall?"

Mrs. Porter: "No, I don't."...

Mr. McDonald: "Did he keep, did Oswald keep, ammunition, cartridges around the apartment?"

Mrs. Porter: "*He kept rifle and I guess ammunition, what you call, all together, and I wasn't fascinated by rifles, so I never took any interest to look at it or see what it looks like, so I just simply ignored it most of the time.*" ...

Mr. McDonald: "Can you recall overhearing the sound of Lee handling the rifle? In other words, do you recall when he would be sitting on the porch, do you recall loud sounds of what would be moving the bolt or the action on the rifle?"

Mrs. Porter: "*I do not recall right now.*" ...

Mr. McDonald: "Did you ever see him move the action on the rifle?"

Mrs. Porter: "I told you I did not pay attention to what he was doing that much, to give you the descriptions, if he changed the positions or was it any sounds, because I wasn't listening for it."

Mr. McDonald: "Do you know, or do you remember, any time when he would handle the rifle when it seemed like he would be shooting at something, an imaginary object?

Mrs. Porter: "No, I cannot." ...

Mr. McDonald: "Pulling the trigger?"

Mrs. Porter: "*No, I cannot tell you that. It seemed to me that most of the time he picked out the time to be with his rifle, when I was busy with something else. At the time I did not pay any attention. Whether it was deliberate or not, I do not know.*"

Mr. McDonald: "Did you ever handle the rifle? Did you ever hold it?"

Mrs. Porter: "I might have touched it sometime to move the place if you clean the closet."

Mr. McDonald: "Did you ask him where he obtained this rifle?"

Mrs. Porter: "No, I didn't."

Mr. McDonald: "Did he ever take it out, outside the apartment, to practice with it, to do anything with it?"

Mrs. Porter: "Yes, he did."

Mr. McDonald: "And what did he do?"

Mrs. Porter: "He will, like before it gets very dark outside, he would leave apartment dressed with the dark raincoat, even though it was a hot summer night, pretty hot weather anyway, and he would be wearing this, and he would be hiding the rifle underneath the raincoat. He said he is going to target practice or something like that."

Mr. McDonald: "This was one occasion you are talking about with the raincoat?"

Mrs. Porter: "It is several occasions, maybe more than once."

Mr. McDonald: "He did the same thing on several occasions, put the raincoat on?"

Mrs. Porter: "Yes."

Mr. McDonald: "And the rifle under the raincoat?"

Mrs. Porter: "Yes."

Mr. McDonald: "And how long would he be gone?"

Mrs. Porter: "A few hours." (II HSCA 229—231)

Let's think for a second about what has been discussed over what would amount to c. 3 pages in the HSCA witness/hearings volumes (which consists of volumes 1-5).

The neighbor of the Oswalds in New Orleans was a man by the name of Eric Rogers. He was home a lot and claimed to have never seen Oswald on the screen porch of their house dry-firing the Carcano. He did say Oswald was on the porch a lot, but that he was always reading, not dry-firing the rifle in question.

Marina comes across to the House Select Committee as completely aloof from his even having a rifle.

> Mr. McDonald: "… Do you know how he got to the area that he was going to practice shooting the rifle?"
>
> Mrs. Porter: "He told me by the bus, so I thought it was kind of a little, would be suspicious for the people in the bus to see him wearing the raincoat, you know, well, but that is what he told me, that he took a bus." (II HSCA 231-232)

Someone would have to produce some kind of a coat that Oswald had owned, but I know of no evidence whatsoever of Oswald owning *that kind* of a coat that could disguise him carrying the rifle in question. He would have to be able to cover up c. 40 inches of metal and wood and how would he do this sitting down on a bus? There are photos of Oswald in Russia next to Marina and a friend wearing a long coat, but these would have looked highly suspicious on a bus in Dallas, Texas, especially in April of 1963, the time of the attempted shooting of General Walker. It also would have been difficult to conceal a lengthy weapon if he was sitting down on a bus. Notice the following pictures of Lee Oswald in Russia:

Mr. McDonald then asks Marina about the Walker shooting of April 10, 1963. Most of us know her story: she was afraid because of the note Oswald had left for her, and when he came back home was apparently panting and winded; but stated that he had shot General Walker. This has always seemed like a resumé builder to me. It never has seemed sincere, at least in the way that Marina tells the story. It's like he is trying to convince her of something that never took place and that he is someone that he is not.

This is puzzling. We know that Oswald did not go to work at Jaggers-Chiles-Stovall on April 10, as he had lost his job there just days before this incident with General Walker took place. So, why was Marina so disturbed that Lee was not home at *the regular time*, as there would be *no regular time*, as he was now unemployed.

> Mr. McDonald: "So we can hear you. Before the siren, you were saying—
> Let me ask you the question so you can repeat the answer.
> What happened when Lee came home on the night of April 10, 1963?"
>
> Mrs. Porter: "He was very pale, as I said, and he was out of breath, and I was asking, I mean asked him to explain about the note that he left for me, and asked him what happened, and he said that he just tried to shoot General Walker. I asked him who General Walker was. I mean how dare you to go and claim somebody's life, and he said, 'Well, what would you say if somebody got rid of Hitler at the right time? So if you don't know about General Walker, how can you speak up on his behalf?' Because he told me that he wasn't— just a minute. He said he was something equal to what he called him a fascist. That was his description." (II HSCA 232—233)

The Walker incident begs to be juxtaposed with an incident that would occur more than seven months later. This is what we are to believe: Oswald shoots one bullet at General Walker, 100-120 feet away according to General Walker, and misses. He then buries the rifle, so he obviously does not bring it home, but when he does arrive many minutes later, he is panting and out of breath, but we do not know if he had been walking or running, though running may have looked suspicious. Fast forward seven months later to November 22, when, I am assuming, he was in no better shape than seven months prior, he allegedly fires his rifle three times in a

261

much more nervous situation, then ran as fast as he could for seventy-five to ninety seconds, was discovered by a police officer and considered not to be out of breath. The two events don't seem to sync very well.

How would Oswald have transported the rifle out of his Neely Street apartment house on the second floor unnoticed on April 10? When did he depart to shoot General Walker? Why didn't Marina protest when he was getting ready to leave? Lots of unanswered questions.

> Mr. McDonald: *"You say he returned late that evening. Do you recall seeing him go out that morning, the morning of April 10?*
>
> Mrs. Porter: **"I don't remember. I probably have."**
>
> Mr. McDonald: *"But it is your testimony he did not come home after work, before going out to try to shoot General Walker?"*
>
> Mrs. Porter: *"I really do not remember now. He might, didn't come from work, or maybe he left and come back later."*
>
> Mr. McDonald: *"Do you recall seeing him leave the apartment with the rifle around April 10?"*
>
> Mrs. Porter: *"I don't remember. I am sorry."*
>
> Mr. McDonald: *"When he returned that evening, about what time did he get back?'*
>
> Mrs. Porter: **"I don't remember the time. Quite late."**
>
> Mr. McDonald: "Pardon me?"
>
> Mrs. Porter: "Pardon me?"
>
> Mr. McDonald: *"Was it early in the evening, late in the evening?"*
>
> Mrs. Porter: *"I assume it is very late in the evening."* (II HSCA 233)

We know that Oswald returned without the rifle. Did he really bury it in the earth? Or, was someone holding it for him? Where is the note? What did it say? What happened to it? Can anything be verified when it comes to the Walker incident? At all? Very frustrating. Marina's answer: "I cannot remember now." You would think she could remember something about the event. Again, anything at all would help. But instead, her most consistent answer: *"I can't remember, or I don't remember."*

What facts do we know for sure: Oswald was unemployed, with a lot of excess time on his hands. The attempted murder of General Walker happened around 9:00 p.m. All seven of the police reports that I read say the bullet that was fired was a steel-jacketed bullet, not a copper-jacketed bullet. Google maps indicated it was c. 6.3 miles from 214 Neely Street to 4011 Turtle Creek Boulevard. It also indicated it would take c. 20 minutes to get there by car, given normal traffic conditions. Taking a bus would have amounted to more time getting there and returning. One theory suggests that Oswald had hidden the rifle a few days before the Walker shooting, but that means he would have to retrieve it before going to Walker's house. And apparently, he hid it again in the earth, and then retrieved it later. This all seems like a long way to nowhere to me. It doesn't seem as if anyone who is asking Marina questions is aware of anything that I have just typed, which is negligence of the first order.

In previous testimonies by Marina, she speaks of Lee having a notebook, photographs of the Walker house, etc, but Marina told Lee to get rid of it and he is supposed to have burned everything in a sink.

Why this wasn't known at the time of the House Select Committee on Assassinations in the late 70's is a mystery.

It continues…

> Mr. McDonald: "Did you contact—Well, what was your reaction when he told you that he had attempted to shoot an individual with his rifle?"
>
> Mrs. Porter: "Well, all of a sudden I realized that it wasn't just a manly hobby of possessing the rifle. He might, he is capable of killing somebody with it. I was very disappointed to discover that trait or characteristic in my husband. I really didn't have much choice. I had no place to go. I wasn't approve of his actions; no." (II HSCA 235)

Marina couldn't be troubled to pay attention in New Orleans to Oswald's rifle exercises on the porch. But now, in revelatory fashion, she understands all things after the Nixon incident, which she claims she stopped Lee from shooting Nixon, because she locked him in the bathroom, *from the outside*. She forgot to pay any consideration when Oswald continued to play with the rifle and went for target practice, not to mention she could not recognize the rifle for the Warren Commission.

> Mr. McDonald: "Mrs. Porter, you moved to Dallas in the fall of 1962 to the Neely Street address?"
>
> Mrs. Porter: "Probably that's correct." (II HSCA 237)

263

The Oswalds relocated to 214 Neely Street in early March 1963, after a succession of violent fights between Marina and Lee caused them to be evicted from their Elsbeth home.

Now the backyard photos rear their head. It was only a matter of time, as they always find time to speak:

> Mr. McDonald: "... Mrs. Porter, do you recognize the photographs placed in front of you?"
>
> Mrs. Porter: "Yes, I do."
>
> Mr. McDonald: "And how do you recognize them?"
>
> Mrs. Porter: "That is the photograph that I made of Lee on his persistent request of taking a picture of him dressed like that with rifle.
>
> Mr. McDonald: "Please tell us what happened. This was at the Neely Street address?"
>
> *What happened on this occasion when Lee asked you to take those photographs?"*
>
> Mrs. Porter: "*Well, first of all, I refused to take picture because I did not know how to operate camera, and he told me, he insist that I will take it, and he said he will show me how, if I just push the button. So I took one picture, I think, and maybe he changed the pose, I don't recall. Maybe I took two pictures, but I was very annoyed by all the incidents.*" (II HSCA 239)

There are five backyard photos that we know about (CE-133-A, CE-133-B, CE-133-C, the "hunter of fascists" copy signed "copyright G. deM.," and one which only shows the backyard at Neely St., with no persons in the photograph). I talked with Marina on the phone three times in the mid to late nineties. She told me that she had taken two pictures. That doesn't exactly clear things up, but if you research this case long enough, you get used to non-answers.

> Mr. McDonald: "Now if you will look at the photographs as are displayed on the exhibit, he is wearing, he is holding a rifle and he has got a handgun in a holster attached to his belt. *Had you seen the handgun before, before you took the photograph?"*
>
> Mrs. Porter: "*I don't think so. Anyway, I do not recall.*"

Mr. McDonald: "Well, do you recall if this was the first time when you were taking the photograph that you had seen him, or that you had known that he owned both the rifle and a handgun?

Mrs. Porter: "It is possible." (II HSCA 239-240)

Marina took the photos of her husband with the rifle and the pistol and she did object, but not enough to make a difference. She went along with his desires, or as she called them, "his little boy games."

Marina seems to say that yes, it is Lee, and I probably took them and seems to indicate that she is annoyed with the questions. The third photo, 133-C, or by HSCA documentation, exhibit F-380. Her response is that they all "look alike and I probably took them". She is then shown the "Hunter of fascists, ha ha ha," photo and things get uncomfortable.

Mr. McDonald: *"Have you had a chance to look at the reverse side? Do you see the phrase that is written in the upper right-hand—"*

Mrs. Porter: *"Can I consult with my attorney [James Hamilton]?"* ...

Mr. McDonald: "In the upper right-hand corner of the photograph on the back, do you recognize the handwriting?"

Mrs. Porter: "No, I don't. That is what I was discussing with my lawyer. We tried to find out if that was written by me. I mean as I told him, that my handwriting does change a few times a day. I do not write same way, you know, in the morning and maybe at night, so it is hard for me to claim even my own handwriting, but you have certain way of writing, habit of writing certain letters, so I know for sure that I could no, I do not write certain letter that way. So, at first, I thought it was maybe my handwriting, but after I examine it, I know it is not." (II HSCA 242)

This is just weird. Period. I have no idea why Marina would consult with her attorney over a handwriting situation. Is "hunter of fascists" a dig at her husband, who she often thought of as a little child in his activities. When we read Marina stating that her handwriting changes throughout any given day, I literally have no comment at all. You cannot help but speculate about what she is afraid of, or why this caused her to consult with her lawyer.

"Hunter of fascists" may be a connection to Walker, because Lee claimed he was a fascist. I have always believed that Marina, not Lee, wrote the "hunter of fascists" caption. I don't think he would ever have written that; and the handwriting doesn't seem to be his. Looking at Oswald's handwriting seems to eliminate him rather quickly.

I believe it is Marina's. She stammers around the issue, admitting it would be something she would say and then backtracks and says it even looks like her handwriting, but at second look, she says she doesn't print like the handwriting on the back of the photograph. If she didn't write, then who did and why? The photo was unearthed by the DeMohrenschildts when they returned from Haiti. The big unanswered question is what would be the motive for either one of the DeMohrenschildts to write anything on the back of the photo, let alone "hunter of fascists." Why choose to write it in the Russian language?

I could see Marina writing on the back of the photo as a way to mock her "little boy" husband, especially after the attempt on General Walker's life. We know that George DeMohrenschildt razzed Lee about missing General Walker in a comment when they discovered that Lee had a rifle in his apartment.

I will continue to believe that it's Marina's handwriting. I have seen samples of Marina's handwriting, in the Cyrillic alphabet, (Marina Nikolayevna Prussakova) and in our traditional English alphabet. I think she wrote it, though I couldn't prove it beyond a reasonable doubt.

Remember, Marina did admit, "…it would sound like me….at first look I thought it was, but then I start to examine it, I don't think it is my handwriting."

> Mr. McDonald: "…*regarding all of the photographs, the different poses that we have seen, the photos you took of Lee, did you ever destroy any photographs of this nature?*"
>
> Mrs. Porter: "*Well, it have been brought to my attention just recently. Apparently I did. I forgot completely about it until somebody spoke about. I think I did.*"
>
> Mr. McDonald: "And how many did you destroy?"
>
> Mrs. Porter: "*I don't remember.*"
>
> Mr. McDonald: "When did you do that?"
>
> Mrs. Porter: "After Lee was arrested."
>
> Mr. McDonald: "Did anyone tell you to do this?"

Mrs. Porter: "*I don't remember*. I think I was just afraid that it will be more evidence Lee and could be against me too.".…

Mr. McDonald: "Was anyone with you when you did it?"

Mrs. Porter: "*I don't remember*." (II HSCA 244)

Mr. McDonald asked Marina about what they would have taken to New Orleans. Lee moved to New Orleans in late April and then two weeks later, Marina moved there, with the help of Ruth Paine. Who packed the rifle, which we assume went with Marina and Ruth Paine, since he apparently dry-fired it while sitting on his porch on 4907 Magazine street in New Orleans?

Congressman Preyer continues to press Marina and she continues to avoid answering directly:

Mr. Preyer: "So that you and Mrs. Paine later brought all of the… remaining luggage?"

Mrs. Porter: "Yes."

Mr. Preyer: "Including the rifle. You mentioned that when he first got the rifle, he thought, as I understood your testimony, that it was the manly thing to do, and I assume that you felt that was natural for him to have a rifle at that time, but that after the Walker incident, you stated that you realized he was capable of killing someone with it.

When he went to New Orleans by himself, and you were left in Dallas with Mrs. Paine, did it occur to you to dispose of the rifle, or the pistol, to get rid of it, so that he could do no harm, further harm with it?"

Mrs. Porter: "Not really, because by that time I was afraid of Lee, and most of the time I did not, I tried not to do something to antagonize him."

Mr. Preyer: "You were physically afraid?"

Mrs. Porter: "Excuse me?"

Mr. Preyer: "Let me ask along that line, just before he went to New Orleans, what was his treatment of you?"

Mrs. Porter: "Well, he was quite brittle, sometime toward me.".…

Mr. Preyer: "What do you think he would have done if you had gotten rid of the rifle?"

Mrs. Porter: "Well, he probably would have got rid of me."

Mr. Preyer: "Pardon me?"

Mrs. Porter: "Well, I cannot answer this question. I don't know what he would have done."...

Mr. Preyer: "We have asked you at various times what he said about President Kennedy or his family and other political figures. At this time in New Orleans did he have anything to say about President Kennedy or his family?"

Mrs. Porter: "During the New Orleans period Mrs. Kennedy was expecting a child and Lee told me about that. He was quite concerned about her health and he informed me that she has a few miscarriages before and he was hoping nothing would happen to this baby. I think he said the baby died." ...

Mr. Preyer: "What were his comments about the Soviet Union?"

Mrs. Porter: "He did not talk about Soviet Union in order to compare America and Soviet Union. When Soviet Union was discussed, it was in the case that he wants me to go back. He doesn't want me around anymore. He thought that I go back or we come back to the Soviet Union."

Mr. Preyer: "He talked about you going back to the Soviet Union?"

Mrs. Porter: "At times it was me and sometimes it was both of us." (II HSCA 250—252)

We know that Oswald got up on the morning of November 22nd and left without Marina's awareness, or Ruth Paine's awareness either.

Oswald seemed to want Marina to return to the Soviet Union, but we don't know exactly why. Did he foreknow something that would suggest it would have been difficult for her to stay in the United States? Alone and barely speaking English would be a difficult hurdle to jump, yet she has seemed to overcome a lot of obstacles and is still living outside Dallas, nearing her 81st birthday as I type these words.

At this time their daughter June was fifteen months old and Rachel would be born in about five months. We can obviously deduce from this that Marina was pregnant. The children are seemingly carried on the waves of their parents' decision, almost like actors in a make-believe drama about to air on CBS.

> Mr. Preyer: "During your stay in the Magazine Street apartment in New Orleans, was Lee ever gone for long periods of time? By that I mean, say, as much as 5 days and night consecutively?"
>
> Mrs. Porter: "No; he spent only one night in jail once and that is the only time that he was not present in the house with me."
>
> Mr. Preyer: "That is the only time he was gone overnight?"
>
> Mrs. Porter: "Yes." (II HSCA 252)

It is hard to say what Marina Oswald Porter is doing at this point. You read and listen to her testimony and it seems like a rabbit hole that you never come back from. She forgets, doesn't remember, gives deceptive testimony; and in the end what is she really saying?

If Lee Oswald is cavorting with people of a shady or surreptitious character, then you have to account for all of the witnesses who have testified that Oswald never went anywhere, and this is both from his landlord and surrounding neighbors.

Is he seen at Lake Pontchartrain Cuban exile camps? Is he seen in Clinton and Jackson, Louisiana with Clay Shaw and David Ferrie in an attempt to get both registered to vote, making it easier to gain employment in a mental institution? The evidence seems pretty convincing that he was, or there was someone who looked an awful lot like Lee Harvey Oswald roaming those parts of the United States.

I give over one hundred pages to Marina Oswald's testimony and at the end it seems more confusing than when I started. It depends which side of the coin you want to look at and where you think the trail leads.

> Mr. Preyer: "Now I would like to ask you about three names at this time and ask you whether you or Lee knew either of these three people. First, is Clay Shaw. Did you remember knowing Clay Shaw?"
>
> Mrs. Porter: "I did not know Clay Shaw ever until I had to testify for Mr. Garrison in New Orleans. That is when I learned about, I mean this name."
>
> Mr. Preyer: "Do you know whether Lee knew Clay Shaw before the time of the Garrison trial?"
>
> Mrs. Porter: "I don't know about that. I had never seen or heard the name."
>
> Mr. Preyer: "Did you know Guy Bannister?' [sic: Banister]

Mrs. Porter: "Who?"

Mr. Preyer: "Guy Bannister."

Mrs. Porter: "No."

Mr. Preyer: "And you don't know whether or not Lee knew Guy Bannister?"

Mrs. Porter: "I don't know, but I never heard that name either."

Mr. Preyer: "Do you recall ever going to Guy Bannister's office in New Orleans with Lee?"

Mrs. Porter: "No; I don't. For what purpose?"

Mr. Preyer: "You had no recollection of going with him?"

Mrs. Porter: "No."

Mr. Preyer: "Do you know David Ferrie? Does that name refresh your recollection at all?"

Mrs. Porter: "Somehow the name sounds familiar right now, but I don't know where I heard it before. I cannot put the face on the name." (II HSCA 252- 253)

Congressman Preyer then brings Carlos Bringuier, an anti-Communist, juxtaposing it with the Fair Play for Cuba leaflet fiasco, suggesting behaviors that seems to play against each other.

Mr. Preyer: "That is the background for why I ask you this question, and that is, was Lee a true Communist?"

Mrs. Porter: "No, he was not."

Mr. Preyer: "Could you explain that a little more? Do you believe he was sincere in his beliefs?"

Mrs. Porter: "No, I don't. Like newspaper reporters call him Marxist or Communist. He was neither of those. He maybe was so called self-proclaimed Marxist because it happened to be maybe he read the book and maybe he agrees with Karl Marx, some of the theories, but as far as belonging to the party or something like that, that is not so."

Mr. Preyer: "You are saying that he was a self-proclaimed Marxist and that, as I understand it, that he had difficulty working with any, within any party?"

Mrs. Porter: "He did not call himself a Marxist or say I believe in that kind of ideas." ...

Mr. Preyer: "Did he continue to take Communist or Socialist newspapers and literature throughout his life in this country?"

Mrs. Porter: "I don't know." (II HSCA 254)

This seems a tad bit odd, because even if for some reason she would not have been aware that Lee was receiving Communist newspapers in the mail, which I find hard to believe, she couldn't possibly have forgotten that she took pictures of him holding them – could she?

Mr. McDonald: "How did you arrive or how did Oswald arrive at a decision to leave New Orleans? You had only moved there a few months prior. What caused him to decide to send you back to Dallas?"

Mrs. Porter: "Well, by this time he came up with ideas of leaving United States. He was planning to go back to the Soviet Union or try to get visa to Cuba."

Mr. McDonald: "Did he want to go to live in Cuba?"

Mrs. Porter: "I assume that he did."

Mr. McDonald: "What specifically did he say?"

Mrs. Porter: "Well, he said that he go over there first and then he will send for me." ...

Mr. McDonald: "Let me backtrack a minute. Did you ever have discussion with Lee Oswald about hijacking an airplane?"

Mrs. Porter: "He approached me with that idea and I thought it was a very ridiculous thing to come up with." ...

Mr. McDonald: "When did you first learn of his planned trip to Mexico City? When did you first know about that?"

Mrs. Porter: "Shortly before I left for Dallas with Ruth Paine."

Mr. McDonald: "How did you learn of this?"

Mrs. Porter: "He told me about his plans to go to Mexico City and visit the Cuban Embassy over there." (II HSCA 256—257)

I have no doubt that whatever Marina was thinking, the one thing on the forepart of her brain was the fear of being deported. She had to be aware of most things connected to her husband and that alone should have caused even more fear, not knowing exactly what he was going to do. The rifle, photographs, Walker, New Orleans, losing his job, Right-wing Reilly Coffee, talk of going back to the Soviet Union or Cuba if at all possible. This did not seem to be a series of events that was going to have a happy ending. Not to mention she can't speak English and would be homeless with a toddler and a new-born baby, if Lee was arrested for whatever kind of subterfuge he was flirting with. I might have taken my chances back in the motherland.

Mr. McDonald: "Where did Lee get the money to travel to Mexico City?"

Mrs. Porter: "Well, he told me that he was saving from his paycheck, putting it aside. We have very moderate spending, only bare necessities."

Mr. McDonald: "Did he show you the money he had saved?"

Mrs. Porter: "No."

Mr. McDonald: "What was your reaction to this whole affair, going to Mexico City, going back to Dallas?"

Mrs. Porter: "I was very upset about it. I did not know if I would see Lee again. I had to be responsible for one child and I had expecting another one. So, anyway, I was quite lost. On top of everything, I could not share that with no one." ...

Mr. McDonald: "When he did return to Dallas, did he tell you about his experience in Mexico City?"

Mrs. Porter: "In very short terms that he was unsuccessful and he talked with some people over there. They denied him a visa and he was very disappointed."

Sylvia Odio now makes an appearance in Marina's testimony (see Appendix #2)

Mr. McDonald: "Do you know if he traveled through Dallas on the way to Mexico City?"

Mrs. Porter: "Excuse me?"

Mr. McDonald: "Do you know if he traveled through Dallas? Did he go to Mexico City from New Orleans by way of Dallas?"

Mrs. Porter: "I don't know that."

Mr. McDonald: "Did he ever mention the name Sylvia Odio?"

Mrs. Porter: "No." (II HSCA 259—261)

Lee Oswald's lack of gregarious behavior with other people, his lack of any friendships, fights with Marina, his use of the alias O.H. Lee are brought up, and also the neighbors helping him to get a job at the Book Depository.

And this is the result:

> Mr. Preyer: "Well, I think all of these questions may perhaps be summarized this way, the questions of whether he was secretive or whether he could work with people. Can you visualize him working with an accomplice?"
>
> Mrs. Porter: "Personally, I can't." (II H 262)

FBI S/A James Hosty is discussed, and Marina comments, or maybe just the opposite. *"Do you know when the last time Lee saw Hosty before November 22, 1963?"*

> Mrs. Porter: *"No, I don't remember the day."* (II HSCA 264)

When November 21, 1963 was brought up, Marina asked what day of the week that was. Are you kidding me? She claims to have no memory of Oswald's appearance at the Paine house on that day, except it was at the end of a workday. She is either the most oblivious person on planet earth; or engages in mendacity like no one we have ever met. Of course, she was brought up in Soviet Russia, where lying was an existential skill.

You would think they may have asked her about seeing a paper bag that Lee may have brought home on that Thursday. Wesley Frazier certainly claims to have never seen it.

Marina Porter did say that Lee arrived relaxed, with an eagerness to listen to her, not normal for Lee:

> Mrs. Porter: "OK, so that was quite interesting news too, and I was asking Lee about the President being in Dallas, and he did not make any comment about it at all. It seemed like he didn't— well, like before I said that he was more listening to me, but now when I recall back, it was quite unusual that he did not want to talk about President Kennedy being in Dallas that particular evening. That was quite peculiar."
>
> Mr. McDonald: "What did he say? What did you say to him about President Kennedy's trip to Dallas?"

Mrs. Porter: "It was quite exciting, you know, for me to talk about, but it seemed like he is changing the subject or just refused to talk about, but it wasn't in any way hostile way or violent form. Just looked like he just ignored a little bit you know to talk about."

Mr. McDonald: *"What did he say? Do you remember?"*

Mrs. Porter: *"No, I don't."*

Mr. McDonald: "How did he dismiss talking about Kennedy? Did he say—"

Mrs. Porter: "Maybe changed subject about talking about a newborn baby or something like that."

Mr. McDonald: *"How many times did you bring up the subject of President Kennedy coming to Dallas?"*

Mrs. Porter: *"I don't remember how many times now."*

Mr. McDonald: "Did it come up more than once?"

Mrs. Porter: "Probably." …

Mr. McDonald: *"Did you ask whether he was going to watch President Kennedy when he came through downtown Dallas?"*

Mrs. Porter: *"I don't remember that."* (II HSCA 268—269)

Marina Porter's recollections of the Paine garage, which Harold Weisberg called a monument to clutter in his book, *Whitewash,* are priceless.

The rifle was supposedly on the floor inside of a blanket among Michael Paine's power tools, in a garage that could only make room for one car.

Mr. McDonald: *"Could you get an automobile in the garage at the same time?"*

Mrs. Porter: *"I don't remember."* (II HSCA 270)

There is more:

Mr. McDonald: "What happened the next morning?"

Mrs. Porter: *"I am sorry, it is very hard for me to remember right now details, so whatever I told Priscilla, that was the truth. My memory was much fresher then, and you can take the statements in the book as a true fact."* (II HSCA 271)

Never mind that Marina makes a common error of redundancy when she refers to something as a true fact, when all facts are true by definition. *Marina and Lee* was based on data in 1964, when Marina's resistance was at its lowest point. It seems a little exploitive, but as we know, things didn't end well for Priscilla McMillan either. She was declared *persona non grata* and thrust out of the Soviet Union.

You have to at least wonder why?

The book's publication no doubt was released to counter the HSCA hearings, knowing that Marina was going to testify. McMillan had intelligence connections (CIA), and was given immunity in order to testify before the HSCA. So, this is the person who is to be the source for Marina Oswald Porter. Odd partners.

Marina was not a U.S. citizen in 1978 and may have had a fear of expulsion from the U.S. at this point. Hard to say.

She was watching television with Ruth Paine and this led to the following exchange:

> Mrs. Porter: "Well, I did not understand English, but I think Mrs. Paine told me that shots came from school-book depository."
>
> Mr. Preyer: "Did you have any intuitive feelings about the shooting at that moment?"
>
> Mrs. Porter: "Well, for instance, my heart kind of stopped or ached. I don't know how to describe the feeling. I felt very uneasy and uncomfortable, and I was afraid that maybe my face will betray me, so I went outside. I didn't want Ruth Paine to see. The blood was rushing to my cheeks."
>
> Mr. Preyer: "You were feeling uneasy and uncomfortable because you thought Lee might be involved?
>
> Mrs. Porter: Well, for an instant, it did cross my mind. I thought to myself I hope it wasn't Lee."
>
> Mr. Preyer: "When did you first learn of Lee's involvement?"
>
> Mrs. Porter: "When policemen came at Ruth Paine's house and told me through her that Lee was arrested." ...
>
> Mr. Preyer: **"But you did see Lee at the police station not long after the assassination, I believe."**
>
> Mrs. Porter: **"I don't remember."** (II HSCA 273)

No one in the history of legal testimony has a more oblivious memory. It is now getting ridiculous, if we're not already there.

> Mr. Preyer: "**While he was in jail, did he ever call you on the telephone?**"
>
> Mrs. Porter: "**I don't remember.**"
>
> Mr. Preyer: "Did he ever at any time give you any hint as to why he did it?"
>
> Mrs. Porter: "No."
>
> Mr. Preyer: "Or anything as to whether he had any accomplices?"
>
> Mrs. Porter: "No." (II HSCA 274)

Marina was asked about some of the disparities in her testimony, and her response was that she was afraid, and wasn't comfortable with how the FBI handled her. And, of course, her go-to claim: *she didn't remember*. I can understand this to a certain extent, as I am sure for someone that young and unable to speak much English at all, it would be very frightening. I am sympathetic to this, but there are some things I just can't fathom she would ever forget.

> Mr. Preyer: "…if you saw the pistol during the Nixon incident [*I have serious doubts about the so-called Nixon incident*], **why did you tell the Secret Service at that time that you had never seen Lee with a pistol?**
>
> Mrs. Porter: "**Well, maybe at the time they questioned me, I could not remember. Maybe I tried to protect myself from something. I do not know.**" (II HSCA 278)

After a list of her inconsistencies are read into the record, she was asked, "Would you like to make a general statement at this time about the earlier inconsistencies in your testimony?" (II HSCA 278)

> Chairman Stokes: "You never heard him [Lee] speak of him [President Kennedy] in a hostile manner?"
>
> Mrs. Porter: "No."
>
> Chairman Stokes: "Then is it consistent, in your opinion, then, that a man who spoke of President Kennedy as he did also was accused of having killed the President?
>
> Mrs. Porter: "That is very hard for me to comprehend."

Chairman Stokes: "Now, have you on occasions indicated that you thought perhaps he was not shooting at President Kennedy but was trying to hit someone else?"

Mrs. Porter: "It was my aloud speculation which doesn't have any foundation for it because it was very hard for me to even think about a person who could, like someone can do such a thing to him. The reason I mentioned Mr. Connally, I mentioned his name only because Lee was corresponding at one time in his life with Governor Connally." ...

Chairman Stokes: "*Were there several occasions in which he expressed himself regarding Governor Connally?*"

Mrs. Porter: "*I don't remember right now.*" (II HSCA 279-280)

The testimony of Mrs. Marina Porter, then resumed after a recess.

Congressman Dodd, in almost frustrating fashion, pushes the envelope about Lee Oswald's guilt and his capability and culpability concerning the assassination of President Kennedy. He alludes to the Walker and Nixon incidents and her response is that, yeah, Lee "was capable of such a crime."

Mr. Dodd: "Do you believe he acted alone?"

Mrs. Porter: "Yes, I do." (II HSCA 286)

Marina Porter, like a lot of people, may have some inkling of an opinion as to whether Lee Oswald could have committed such a crime, but she has no proof at all that he did. A lot of witnesses will argue for or against a conspiracy, just because they were in Dealey Plaza that day, but that does not mean they are correct. In that regard, they are merely accidental tourists.

This seems to be another ridiculous notion by the HSCA, as if Marina had some kind of gnostic insight into the machinations of Oswald's activities on that fateful day.

Her testimony carries little weight in the larger scheme of things.

After Congressman Dodd probed Marina in a way that could possibly have led to some interesting revelations about the Oswalds' journeys, especially after they left the Soviet Union, Congressman Ford put Marina's credibility on the table for all to view:

Mr. Ford: "*Mrs. Porter, you have told so many different versions of this period for various reasons, to protect Lee, to protect yourself, to keep from being sent back to Russia because of fear or strong emotions.*

I want to ask now are you sure that at this point you are really clear on these facts, or have your many stories confused you as well as the American people?"

Mrs. Porter: *"The question is so long it is not easy to answer."*

Mr. Ford: *"Let me repeat it to you in parts then.*

You have told many different versions of this period for various reasons. You have testified that you did this to protect Lee, to protect yourself, to keep from being sent back to Russia, because of fear, or strong emotions. Are you sure that you have not confused yourself; do you know the truth at this point? What are you telling us? At what point are we to believe what you are saying before this committee?"

Mrs. Porter: *"May I consult with my attorney, please?"*

Mr. Ford: *"Yes."*

[Witness consults with counsel.]

Mrs. Porter: "I am sorry. If you are trying, if you are asking me if I do know anything more than I already said, that is what the question was."

Anyway, I am telling absolutely the truth. I do not know anything more [**this is *not* the issue, Marina**]. Of course, it is very confusing when you read so many things in the newspapers, and I am just as anxious to find the answers as everybody else." (II HSCA 290—291)

Is this simply a case of "The mask which an actor wears, may well become his face." Has she lied for so long that she can no longer distinguish the truth?

Now let the reader scan the following passage to determine if Marina was saying she hated the United States or just the opposite, due to her broken English. Remember, earlier she stated she had nothing against the United States:

Mr. Fauntroy: "It does strike at least this member as strange that you could get married in 6 weeks."

Mrs. Porter: "Well, he was appealing to me. I did not marry him because he was American who will bring me back, I mean who

Zapruder Frame #188

Zapruder Frame #223

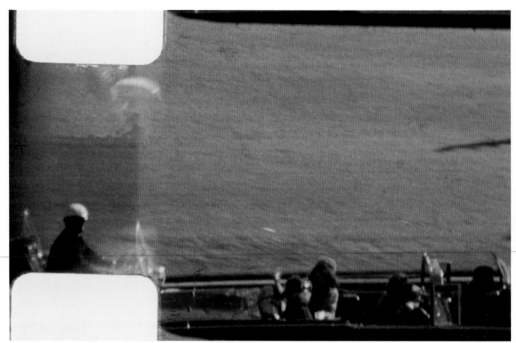

Zapruder Frame #326

Zapruder Frame #327

Zapruder Frame #328

Zapruder Frame #333

Zapruder Frame #335

Zapruder Frame #337

will take me to United States. In fact, if I knew that he will come back, I would not marry him."

Mr. Fauntroy: "So it was not a motivation of your wanting to come to United States?"

Mrs. Porter: "No."

Mr. Fauntroy: "That may have been" –

Mrs. Porter: No.

Mr. Fauntroy: That is not the explanation for the 6 weeks?

Mrs. Porter: No, it is not, because of my hatred of United States. (II HSCA 293)

Mrs. Porter informed Washington D.C. Congressman Fauntroy that it was just a chance occurrence that she married Oswald in six weeks and not because she was wanting a free pass to the United States. She also stated, and this is important, and that she would not have married him if she understood he was going back, "*because of my hatred of United States.*" (II HSCA 293)

Her broken English can be confusing at times. I am not sure why this statement, out of everything Marina said, was not challenged. Odd.

Congressman Fithian used his allotted time to get back to the "Hunter of fascists, ha ha ha" controversy: "I have only had a little bit of study of the Russian language, but even a very cursory, very brief glance at the back of that photograph would indicate that not even a grade school student of Russian writing would have written that." He then proceeds to give a fairly intricate treatise on the quirks and precision of the Russian alphabet and comes across as someone who is more familiar with the Russian language than he has up to this point indicated." (II HSCA 294)

I have always thought this was a blown opportunity. Marina should have been called up to some kind of a board and asked to write the inscription on the back of the photo without aid of observation. But she wasn't and that is too bad.

Chairman Louis Stokes returned to the previous testimony regarding her opinion that Lee had been guilty in the assassination.

Chairman Stokes: "Let me see if I can refresh your recollection to this extent."

Do you recall during the Warren Commission hearings the

late Congressman Boggs saying this to you: Let's get an answer. I think this answer is quite important.

Mrs. Oswald: "On the basis of all the available facts, I have no doubt in my mind that Lee Oswald killed President Kennedy. At the same time I feel in my own mind, as far as I am concerned, I feel that Lee, that my husband, perhaps intended to kill Governor Connally instead of President Kennedy."

Chairman Stokes: *"Do you recall that question being asked by the late Congressman Boggs, and your answer as I read it?"*

Mrs. Porter: *"I do not recall. I never, you know, went back and read my testimony. But if it is printed, that is—since you refresh my memory, that is possible. I am for sure I said that."*

Chairman Stokes: "So that I understand you, my having read this to you, does this now then refresh your recollection of what you said on that occasion?"

Mrs. Porter: "Because I do not remember Senator so and so that you mentioned it, it was so many people around, so many faces, I did not remember, you know, person."

Chairman Stokes: *"I can understand you perhaps do not remember that particular Congressman. What I am saying to you is, with my having read this to you now, does this refresh your recollection of what was asked of you and what you said on that occasion?"*

Mrs. Porter: *"Well, I really do not remember what I said, but if under oath to the Warren Commission I gave that testimony, that is my testimony."*

Chairman Stokes: "Then you do not deny that that was your testimony."

Mrs. Porter: "No." (II HSCA 300—301)

Excerpts from Priscilla McMillan's book, *Marina and Lee* are put into the record. Quoting from the book, Stokes quotes McMillan concerning intent: "In his eyes, his political ideas stood higher even than himself. He would talk about Marxism, Communism, and injustice all over the world." (*Marina and Lee*, p. 434)

Chairman Stokes: Did you tell Miss Johnson that?"

Mrs. Porter: "That was Miss Johnson's conclusion about study-ing Lee as a person. Her findings weren't based only on what I told her. She did great research and met with lots of people who knew Lee. That was her conclusion, and I agree with her."

Chairman Stokes: "Did you tell her that he talked about Marx-ism to you, and about communism to you, and about injustice all over the world to you?"

Mrs. Porter: "Probably."

Believability was a topic that seemed to keep rearing its head a lot, especially near the end of Marina's testimony: Marina did not seem to like the House Select Committee and their constant probing of the is-sues.

Chairman Stokes: "There has been some discussion with you with reference to the fact that you told certain untruths to both the FBI and the Secret Service for the reason that you wanted to protect Lee. At the same time, you were the individual who revealed to the FBI what you knew about the General Walker shooting; is that correct?"

Mrs. Porter: "Yes."

Chairman Stokes: "Can you explain to us why you would attempt to protect him by telling untruths about other things, such as the rifle, the trip to Mexico, things of that nature, and then reveal to them something that no one else in the world knew but you?" (II HSCA 302—303) ...

Chairman Stokes: "*Didn't you tell Miss Johnson about someone that you walked over to, that you recognized in a railroad sta-tion, that you walked over to, a KGB agent?*"

Mrs. Porter: "*I don't remember that right now.*"

Chairman Stokes: "*Do you recall talking with anyone in the or-ganization that you were in, the Komsomol, about the fact that you were being watched?*"

Mrs. Porter: "*I probably have, but I do not recall now.*"

Michigan Congressman Sawyer once again brings up the issue con-cerning the "Hunter of fascists, ha, ha, ha." You get the impression that the HSCA panel, at this point, believe that Marina wrote that message herself.

> Mr. Sawyer: *"When DeMohrenschildt led you to understand, from whatever he said, let you understand he had known about the shooting by Oswald at Walker, what precisely did he say then?"*
>
> Mrs. Porter: *"I do not recall the incident, you know, very clearly."*
>
> Mr. Sawyer: *"Did you ask Lee about how he knew about it?"*
>
> Mrs. Porter: *"If I did, I do not recall right now, or remember."*
>
> Mr. Sawyer: *"Was there anything in what DeMohrenschildt said that may have been given the impression that he may have participated in that shooting?"*
>
> Mrs. Porter: *"It never crossed my mind, sir."* (II HSCA 306)

It may have never crossed her mind, but her ability to make black appear white and make white appear black is disturbing, as to what is going on with Marina. Is she oblivious? Confused? Lying? Hard to say, but at the least she has a very bad memory or feels that if she is honest, she herself may be found culpable. She did not become a citizen of the United States until c. 1989.

Congressman Preyer then pursued a line concerning motive in reference to Oswald's actions. He seemed to probe for the question of motivation. Mrs. Porter seemed to indicate it was personal demons that clouded Lee's judgement and not politics. Of course, if Oswald never pulled the trigger that day, then all of this is moot.

Concerning FBI S/A James Hosty, that she did not "remember Mr. Hosty's face at all, but I remember visit of his before assassination, and I think he came twice, because after the first visit Lee was upset and he told me if this man come back again, to take number of his license, his car's license, and that is what I did, so instead of, you know, answering that he had been there once, logically it is twice before assassination. But I do not remember this man afterwards at all." (II HSCA 310)

I am puzzled as to why Oswald would jot down Hosty's license plate? Hard to say, unless the infantile side of Oswald wanted to do something to his car. God only knows what. Silly, I know.

Ohio Congressman Devine asked Marina about Lee's Russian abilities when they were first introduced:

> Mrs. Porter: "During the few dances with him he spoke with accent, but I did not know he was from America...He spoke with

accent but lots of people in Russia do speak with accent. They don't speak Russian very well; they have different nationalities than Russians."

Mr. Devine: "But his Russian was pretty good at that time?"

Mrs. Porter: "It was pretty good, yes." (II HSCA 311)

What is odd about this is that Lee Oswald is not recorded anywhere that I know of speaking Russian. It seems weird that he never spoke Russian for us to hear. He obviously knew some Russian by all accounts. What is tremendously peculiar is that his printed Russian is near perfect, while his English is an embarrassment to read.

Near the end of Marina's testimony, she was asked whether her husband had mental problems and was somewhat unhinged. "Well, I was only 21 when he died. I was not mature enough to recognize the symptoms, but I don't think anybody in their right mind can commit crimes like that. Right now I do assume the person was ill." (II HSCA 312)

20

JACK D WHITE –
SEPTEMBER 14, 1978

On September 14, 1978, Jack White testified before the HSCA in Washington, D.C.

C hief Counsel G. Robert Blakey goes into his expected recitation prior to introducing a BBC interview of Malcolm Thomson, who "examined copies of two of the backyard photographs. He found that they were fakes."

Testimony was subsequently taken from Jack White, who at the time of his testimony "had been studying them and looking at them, say for 15 years. I did not start these tests and prepare the artwork you see here until anywhere from 3 to 5 years ago." (II HSCA 337)

In his opening remarks, Blakey again seems to understand only the basics when it comes to the issues concerning the assassination. He says that the photos were "of Lee Harvey Oswald with a holstered pistol strapped to his waist, holding a rifle in one hand, and in the other copies of *The Militant* and *The Worker*, both Communist publications." (II HSCA 319)

"If the backyard photographs are valid, they are highly incrimina-
tory of Oswald, and they tend strongly to corroborate the basic
story told by Marina Oswald. If they are invalid, how they were
produced poses far-reaching questions in the area of conspiracy
for they evince a degree of technical sophistication that would almost necessarily raise the possibility that more than private parties conspired not only to kill the President, but to make Oswald
a patsy." (II HSCA 319)

How are they condemning of Lee Harvey Oswald? Taken prior to
April 5, 1963, one being assigned or addressed to George DeMohrenschildt by an unknown party, I am somewhat uncertain as to what they
could have demonstrated in court, in reference to the events of November 22. It doesn't seem to prove much of anything.

Mr. Blakey: "Despite the efforts of the Warren Commission to set-
tle questions about the *two pictures*, Warren Commission critics
have refused to let the matter rest. They have persisted in doubting
their authenticity, charging that they are, in fact, composites." ...

Mr. Blakey: "Marina Oswald, in addition to giving two different
versions of when the backyard pictures were taken, gave different
versions of the number of pictures taken. At first she testified
that she took one picture. She later testified that she took two
pictures.

In addition, Marguerite Oswald, Oswald's mother, testified
that soon after the assassination she and Marina destroyed yet
another picture, in which Oswald was holding the rifle over his
head with both hands. No copy of such a photograph [*or negative*] has ever been uncovered." (II HSCA 321)

An early question put to Jack White, by counsel Genzman, concerned work that he had done.

Mr. Genzman: "Have you analyzed any of these photographs?"

Mr. White: "Yes; *over a period of about five years.*" ...

Mr. Genzman: "What opinions have you formed about the backgrounds of the photographs?"

Mr. White: "I believe the backgrounds in the three photographs
you see here are virtually identical. I think they were all taken
from a single camera viewpoint. The backgrounds would have

had to be either a single photograph originally, or else the camera for all photographs would have had to be on a tripod or some other support for stabilizing the camera in one position."

Mr. Genzman: "What opinions have you formed about the heads in the photographs?"

Mr. White: "The heads in [CE-133] A and B are identical to one another with the exception of the lip area, which shows strong signs of retouching. I was not able to adequately compare the head on C to A and B because I did not have an adequate quality print at the time I made the comparisons."

Mr. Genzman: "Thank you. What opinions have you formed about the heads in relation to the bodies?"

Mr. White: "When you make the heads in A and B an identical size, the bodies are different lengths. In fact, all three bodies are slightly different lengths than each other if you make the heads the same size.

For instance, if you make the heads the same size, you might say that A has a normal length body, B has a longer body, and C has a shorter body."

Mr. Genzman: "Did you determine whether the heads and the bodies are of the same individual?"

Mr. White: "I did not do any extensive analysis of the bodies. Some critics believe these are three different bodies. I have nothing to say about that, but I do believe that the heads on A and B are the person called Lee Harvey Oswald, down to a point right below the lips. In fact, the face is a single photograph. It is not two different photographs of the same individual. It is a single photograph." (II HSCA 323-324) ...

Mr. Genzman: "Based on your findings, what is your conclusion about the backyard photographs?"

Mr. White: "Well, just as Oswald said, I think they are fakes." (II HSCA 324)

Mr. Genzman: "Why do you think these fakes were made? ..."

Mr. White: "It is fairly obvious after the fact that they were made to implicate Oswald in the alleged assassination [there is nothing "alleged" about the assassination—it happened] by tying him to the assassination weapon."

White then concentrated on some mechanical issues, and presented his own self-made graphics, and at one point stressed the body stance.

> Mr. Genzman: "Did you make a determination as to the body stance in 133-A?"
>
> Mr. White: "Yes, I think the body stance is in position out of balance with the background. If you compare the verticals in the background to the balance point of the body, you find that the figure could not be possibly standing in that position because it is out of balance. If you make a parallel line from the center of the chin that is parallel to this post in the background, you find that the point of balance falls approximately 3 to 4 inches outside the weight-bearing foot. You can try this yourself by suspending a plumb bob from your chin and in order to get it to fall at a point 3 or 4 inches outside your weight-bearing foot, you will be off balance and you will fall over." (II HSCA 324—335, *passim*)

The HSCA went to great lengths to dishonor Jack White, though he was permitted to have the original 133-A and 133-B before him as the examination continued. His absence of expert training even though he was in the graphic arts business, proved to be an impediment in the minds of the people asking him questions.

White performed tests that were rigorously controlled to the assassination rifle. White repeated every available photograph of CE-139, made composites, and found that the metal lined up correctly in each; however, the butt ends didn't match at all.

> Mr. Genzman: "Briefly what did you determine from your study?"
>
> Mr. White: "It is my opinion that we have been shown by the authorities more than one gun as being the assassination weapon." (II HSCA 344)

At the end, almost as an 'in your face' moment, of White's testimony, he is excused, but then bracketed, on the grounds that the BBC film which went before his testimony, uncovering the research of Mr. Thomson in Edinburgh, Scotland, was subsequently denounced:

> Mr. Blakey: "After studying the [*HSCA panel's*] reports, Mr. Thomson deferred to the panel's conclusions that the photo-

graphs revealed no evidence of faking, noting the thoroughness of their investigation and emphasized that the opinions he expressed earlier were based on examination of copies of photographs, not the original negatives and first generation prints as had been the case in the photographic panel analysis process.

Mr. Thomson did, however, reserve his opinion on the chin in the backyard pictures which is suspiciously different from the chin he had observed in the Dallas arrest photographs of Oswald. He also remained skeptical as to the ability of a computer to detect a photocopy composite photograph." (II HSCA 347)

Professor Blakey told me when I interviewed him in 1998, that Jack White was a mistake and proved to be an embarrassment to the entire proceedings. It was hard to read and watch without grimacing. He said the two witnesses he regretted not calling were Bill and Gayle Newman.

21

SGT. CECIL W KIRK –
SEPTEMBER 14, 15, 25 1978
(W/CALVIN MCCAMY)

On September 14, 1978, in the p.m. session, also on September 15, and also on the 25th in 1978, Sgt. Cecil W. Kirk testified before the HSCA in Washington, D.C.

C alvin S. McCamy and Sergeant Cecil W. Kirk testified together on September 14 and 15, and then Cecil Kirk testified again on September 25. Kirk was from the identification branch of the D.C. Metropolitan Police Department. Both McCamy and Kirk were members of the House Select Committee's photographic panel, so as the HSCA did with Dr. Wecht, they will now do to Jack White – follow his testimony with a rebuttal from their "scientists."

The first question is an attempt to counter Jack White, as he admitted to not working with the originals pertaining to the backyard photographs, but from those replicated from the original negatives.

> Staff Counsel Goldsmith: "What was the reason for the panel taking this approach [*of using only the originals*]?"

> Sergeant Kirk: "When you move away from first generation material, you lose in tonal quality. You are likely to pick up artifacts in the copying material and lose detail in the highlights and lose detail in the shadows." (II HSCA 351)

Kirk then gave a demonstration about how the photos should have looked and how they should have been processed. Kirk indicated that the proper procedures were not taken in reference to the backyard photos.

Kirk further made a comprehensive assessment of the Imperial Reflex Camera that took the backyard photos, and he would eventually conclude that it was indeed the camera that took the "backyard photos." (II HSCA 361 ff)

Ruth Paine very conveniently supplied the camera to the Dallas Police Department, as she did other items as well, just weeks after the assassination. She was too conveniently helpful at times.

Kirk visited the National Archives and ascertained that other photographs had the same inscriptions on the prints as CE 133-A, et al. Kirk and McCamy's testimony were suspended, so Joseph P. McNally, a handwriting expert, could give testimony. McNally was unavailable the next day for testimony. On September 15, the following day, the testimony of Calvin C. McCamy and Cecil W. Kirk resumed. We will pick up their testimonies, as if there has not been a break, due to the testimony of Dr. McNally.

Sergeant Kirk previously testified that the photographic panel had studied the backyard photos, and there was a suggestion that other photos had been studied as well.

> Mr. Goldsmith: "Mr. McCamy, and Sergeant Kirk, I would like to ask you both, what was the panel's conclusion regarding the backyard pictures showing Lee Harvey Oswald with the rifle and the revolver and the militant newspapers?"
>
> Mr. McCamy: "We found no evidence whatsoever of any kind of faking in these photographs."
>
> Mr. Goldsmith: "Sergeant Kirk?"
>
> Mr. Kirk: "I might add that we also established the camera that the photographs were taken with." (II HSCA 418—419)

Committee chairperson Stokes then had a number of illuminating questions, which led to some fascinating answers.

Mr. Stokes: "Sergeant Kirk and Mr. McCamy, aside from the technical analyses that were applied to these materials, which indicate of course that there is no evidence of fakery in these photographs, are there any practical considerations that suggest these pictures were not faked?"

Mr. Kirk: "Well, sir, it was established by the Warren Commission and the FBI that both the papers and the rifle probably did not arrive in Dallas until around March 27 or 28. Mr. Oswald autographed one of the photographs on April 5. He was dismissed from the company he worked with, where he had darkroom operations open to him the following day.

We established that the film was probably developed by an amateur, and the DeMohrenschildt print was probably at least processed and washed and dried by an amateur. It is the panel's belief that the so-called drugstore prints were made much later. So even if we don't regard the testimony of Marina Oswald, where she says she probably took the photographs on March 31, the narrowing of the time in which fakery could have been done has been narrowed considerably. We are talking about the pictures, even if they were taken on March 28 or 29, processed and autographed by April 5, certainly narrows the parameters of time these photographs could have been faked or altered."

Mr. Stokes: "That, then, brings me to another concern I have, and that is whether the panel's analyses of these photos was limited solely to the allegations that have been made by the Warren Commission critics, or did you take into consideration other analyses?"

Mr. McCamy: "Yes. The analysis went, I think, quite a ways beyond what the critics had brought up…" (II HSCA 419)

Bear in mind the following episodes, commencing not long after April 5, 1963: Oswald lost his job; Walker was shot at; DeMohrenschildt commented about Lee's missing of Walker in an assassination attempt, whether in jest or in earnest; Oswald left for New Orleans; New Orleans entailed a brief work stint, an arrest, radio debates, and finally the return of Marina to Texas and the departure of Oswald to Mexico City.

It is difficult to suggest a particular time that Oswald dropped everything, retrieved negatives that he had awkwardly prepared at Jaggers-Chiles-Stovall prior to being fired, and had them processed.

291

We know that Oswald, at Marina's suggestion, destroyed his notes for the Walker attack, and that burning was done in his sink at 214 W. Neely which may have included photographs.

Or were those prints made much later by someone else? Like the cartridges and the clip, there is no evidence that Lee Oswald or Marina possessed them or had any photos developed.

Critical comments about the research community then appeared:

Mr. Preyer: "I would like to ask each one of you, Mr. Kirk and Mr. McCamy, for your comments on one general question, and, that is, as professionals in this field, what have you learned from this investigation?"

Mr. Kirk: "Well, sir, Confucius was once accused of saying a picture is worth a thousand words, and that is obviously not true because he didn't have photography during his day. He is alleged to have said that one scene is worth a thousand tellings.

It appears that a lot of people who criticized or found fault with these photographs were relying on a lot of tellings, a lot of second and third generation prints, and we all came to one seeing and one telling, in effect. We are saying that we found no indications that these photographs have been faked in any way."

Mr. Preyer: "Mr. McCamy, do you have any general comments concerning professionalism and how these investigations should be conducted?"

Mr. McCamy: "Well, yes, yes I do, Mr. Preyer. The allegations have been based on observations by people least qualified to make the observations. This has resulted in false observation, and, therefore, false premises on which to base theories. The lesson I think is very clearly taught, and I might say taught at extreme expense, and it is the age-old lesson that a little learning is a dangerous thing.

I think that all who watch these proceedings or read this record will benefit from the observation that Mr. Blakey had the wisdom, when questions arose, to refer those questions to people who knew the answers or knew how to find the answers." (II HSCA 422)

Cecil Kirk, "director of the mobile crime lab" of the Metropolitan Police Department in Washington, D.C. resumed his testimony on

September 25 in the Cannon House Office Building, Washington, D.C. (IV HSCA 362ff)

Chief Counsel G. Robert Blakey, in his traditional narration, gave a good abstract of who and what Sergeant Kirk would be about, although it is fair to say that much more has been learned about this subject since 1978.

> Mr. Blakey: "Thank you, Mr. Chairman. Another way the committee has tried to shed light on the so-called two-Oswald mystery is by comparing photographs taken over the years of the man identified as Lee Harvey Oswald, photographs taken when he was in the Marines, after his return from the Soviet Union, and during the period he was detailed at the Dallas police headquarters on November 22 to November 24, 1963.
>
> "To try to determine if the photographs in question show the same person, the committee asked a panel of anthropologists to study them, to see if the shape and structural features of the face match from photo to photo. Mr. Chairman, before proceeding with an analysis of the photographs, it is necessary that we note and take testimony on an issue that has been raised about one of them, the photograph of Oswald when he was in the Marines. In it, the head, appearing before a height chart, appears to be disproportionate in length, leading some critics to claim it had been doctored.
>
> "Sergeant Kirk will also address alleged differences in Oswald's height as he appeared in different photographs." (IV HSCA 362)

It is challenging for a non-photographic expert, to make sense of Sergeant Kirk's testimony. He photographed a 5'9" Washington, D.C. Metropolitan police officer, M.W. Lee, in front of a height stand as suggested in the Oswald 13-inch head photo. But Kirk then had Lee move 7 inches away from the chart, then 14 inches, and somehow, the size of his head in relation to the chart, changed.

> Mr. Kirk: "It was determined that at the time these photographs were taken, an ID camera, much used in the military as well as other types of the Government, was a type of camera that was mounted on a dolly, with the lights and the camera and the numbering chart affixed where it could be pushed out of the way when not in use. So, if Mr. Oswald was brought into the in-

duction center to be photographed and told to stand next to the height chart, it didn't really make any difference to the photographer whether or not Mr. Oswald was standing next to the height chart or not, because he could move the camera up or away from Oswald to get the photograph that he wanted.

"This chart on the right demonstrates the fact that unless Mr. Oswald was standing directly with his back against the wall and the camera was at the correct distance, it would not be an accurate recording of his true height."

Kirk added that such photography in police work had generally gone out of vogue, for the very reasons that he is there to testify—the potential inaccuracies built into the process of taking "height" photos. (IV HSCA 363—364)

Once again, the margin of error gets more extended:

> Mr. Goldsmith: "Let me ask you this, then: Is it unusual for official records to report disparate heights for any particular individual?"
>
> Mr. Kirk: "No; it is not."
>
> Mr. Goldsmith: "Why not?"
>
> Mr. Kirk: "We have found—and the Air Force has conducted studies to bear out the same point—that people are almost an inch taller in the daytime, in the morning, than they are in the afternoon. Also, studies conducted both by the Air Force and by law enforcement people, when they would ask people to describe their height, roughly one-third of those interviewed said they were 2 inches taller than they actually are, and the other two-thirds said that they were at least 1 inch taller than they actually are. In other words, the American male sees himself as being from 1 to 2 inches taller than his actual height if he is asked." (IV HSCA 364)

If people are taller and shorter at different parts of the day, then this scenario likely confuses most people. Oswald then seems locked into the final conclusion that he is the one in the photographs, to the exclusion of all others, without any kind of manipulation having gone on.

The panel members didn't seem to have any questions for Cecil Kirk.

The backyard photos have always been a source of controversy in this case, since one of them graced the cover of *Life* magazine on February 21, 1964 and incriminated Oswald ex post facto. I don't think any of them were faked, for reasons stated earlier. I have somewhat of an aversion to screaming fakery when it comes to the evidence. If everything is fake, then what is there to discuss? There needs to be good reasons with evidence, if we are going to cry fake. The back of JFK's head autopsy photograph, Fox-3, seems awfully suspicious, as do some of the X-rays, at least the lateral one and the AP in respect to the mysterious 6.5 mm object, but other than that, I will assume the evidence is real, allowing us definite points of tangency.

22

JOSEPH MCNALLY –
SEPTEMBER 14, 25 1978

Joseph P. McNally, testified twice, the first being on September 14. He is a handwriting expert and was called to possibly determine the identity of the writer of "Hunter of Fascists, ha ha ha" photographic caption on the back of one of the backyard photographs.

"To this end, 45 samples of Oswald's handwriting were selected and experts in the field of document identification were asked to examine them.

"Today an expert will discuss the three samples. They are a signature from Oswald's fingerprint card when he was arrested in New Orleans in August 1963; his passport application dated June 24, 1963, and a list of handwritten questions found among his possessions." (II HSCA 371)

> Mr. Brady: "What analysis was the panel asked to perform?"
>
> Mr. McNally: We were asked to examine and compare certain writings and signatures and also to determine whether there were any alterations, falsifications, or eradications on these particular documents."
>
> Mr. Brady: "Whose samples of handwriting did the panel examine?"
>
> Mr. McNally: "We examined samples of the handwriting of Lee Harvey Oswald, Jack Ruby, and also of Marina Oswald." (II HSCA 372)

McNally testified that the passport application name of Lee H. Oswald, as well as the signature of Lee Harvey Oswald on the "Hunter of fascists" photo "were written by the same individual." There was a somewhat lengthy discussion which endeavored to describe the process used, by which that conclusion and succeeding conclusions were decided. (II HSCA 376 ff)

The handwriting panel came to a comparable inference with respect to an assessment of the Lee Harvey Oswald on the "Hunter of fascists" photo with Lee Harvey Oswald's arrest card from August 1963 in New Orleans. There was an attempt to harmonize other documents as well.

McNally affirmed that the "Copyright G. deM" on the "Hunter of fascists" photo was evaluated with the George DeMohrenschildt's handwriting and determined not to have been written by DeMohrenschildt.

McNally then gave testimony concerning the phrase "Hunter of fascists, ha ha ha," and handwriting samples from both Marina and Lee Oswald, "They matched *neither* Marina nor Lee Oswald's writings." (II HSCA 386)

McNally contended that "Hunter of fascists, ha ha ha" was a juvenile tracing over what had been an earlier and original impression of that phrase. The original was essentially eradicated by the subsequent tracing, "it has effectively obliterated the original writing that was there and makes this whole particular section unidentifiable." (II HSCA 387)

During the five-minute question round for each congressman, Mr. McNally affirmed to Floyd Fithian, his total lack of ability to identify the "Hunter" writing: "As a matter of fact, the writings as they exist right on that particular document now are quite different from the writings done by both Lee Harvey Oswald and Marina Oswald."

> Mr. Fithian: "So your conclusion is that these may not in fact be the writings of either Lee or Marina?"
>
> Mr. McNally: "What we are seeing there are definitely not done by them." ...
>
> Mr. Fithian: "Let me just ask you whether or not it is your judgment that the same person wrote all three words plus the "ha, ha, ha"?
>
> Mr. McNally: "I believe so." (II HSCA 389)

When Fithian attempts to prove something concerning the Russian language, by comparing letter formations, loops, and other connections, it is not plausible that anyone understands what he is attempting to validate. It was terribly confusing.

McNally reiterated his belief that the inscription was a tracing. "I am of the opinion that the writing to me seems to be done by somebody who is not conversant in Russian and I think were following the forms they say on the page. That occasions the deviations from the original Cyrillic alphabet." (II HSCA 392)

After way too many pages of testimony concerning the "Hunter of fascists, ha ha ha" inscription, what was profited? Nothing, other than he kept repeating that neither Marina nor Lee wrote the inscription.

I'm not sure what anyone was anticipating, except that maybe Lee Oswald wrote the message and then gave the photo to George DeMohrenschildt, signed by Oswald on April 5, 1963, which was 5 days before someone took a shot at General Edwin Walker. Ergo, if you can prove that Oswald wrote "Hunter of fascists, ha ha ha, it might strongly suggest that Lee Oswald had fired the shot at General Walker," and that he had a proclivity for violence.

If Marina or Lee didn't write the inscription, then who did? The key question is: who would have had access to the photograph between when it was taken on Sunday, March 31, 1963, around noon and then the time it was developed, possibly by Oswald at Jaggers-Chiles-Stovall, and April 5, which was a meager five days later? The Oswalds were away from everyone, living in seclusion at 214 W. Neely Street. Their contacts would have been quite minimal.

The picture was snapped on Sunday, March 31, 1963, and then dated to George DeMohrenschildt on Friday, April 5, 1963. The Walker incident took place on Wednesday, April 10, 1963. The following weekend, after the General Walker incident, the DeMohrenschildts gave an Easter bunny to June Oswald. When the rifle was noticed during the DeMohrenschildts visit, he made an observation, insinuating that Oswald had shot at Walker and missed.

This is becoming way too convenient. Why on earth would Oswald give a piece of evidence, which was incomparable for the cover of *Life* magazine, to George DeMohrenschildt, a known oil geologist, stamp collector and spy? It makes zero sense. That DeMohrenschildt would have given someone like Lee Harvey Oswald the time of day is even more remarkable.

Another possibility is that the HSCA, in going through the silliness of the Warren Commission, developed doubts that Oswald fired at Walker. There is a lot of opposing evidence, like witnesses seeing people around the residence just before the shot; people seeing a car departing; a 30.06 *steel jacketed bullet* recovered by police; and General Walker's own testimony that he knew that Oswald had not shot at him and that is a remark that should be taken seriously, especially from someone with a strong right-wing bent. He could have done damage to the "Commie", but chooses not to.

He supposedly left a note. Sylvia Meagher stated that Oswald made several comments not in keeping with an attempted assassination attempt on a distinguished political person.

Oswald told Marina that the Embassy would assist her. I'm not sure that is true. They may have wanted to simply stay away from Marina and not get involved. Hard to say.

Oswald told Marina there was a possibility that he might not come back home and there could be something in the paper about the incident. That wouldn't do Marina any good, since she couldn't read much English at the time. Oswald was an attention whore and wouldn't have let that opportunity slip by to get some kind of notoriety. (see Sylvia Meagher, *Accessories After the Fact: The Warren Commission, the Authorities, and its Report*, pp. 283—286 and *passim*)

On September 25 Joseph McNally, a handwriting expert, testifies for the second time. (IV HSCA 253ff)

In an extensive conspiracy-or-no-conspiracy preface, House Select Committee chief counsel G. Robert Blakey made a number of points and one in particular should resonate with most people who advocate a Warren Commission interpretation of events in Dallas: "To be sure, conspirators seldom shout their intentions from the roof tops or publish their thoughts in the newspaper." (IV HSCA 253)

McNally had studied a large assortment of documents, which are then put into the record of the HSCA, in the middle of volume IV. Mr. Klein than asks Mr. McNally about them.

> Mr. Klein: "Did the entire panel have an opportunity to view these documents?
>
> Mr. McNally: "They did."

Mr. Klein: "Did the panel members after examining those documents come to any conclusions with respect to those documents?"

Mr. McNally: "Yes; they did."

Mr. Klein: "Would you please tell the committee what they concluded?"

Mr. McNally: "The conclusion of the panel was that the writing on all of these original documents was all done by the same individual. That also included a number of photographs and photo reproductions. We also concluded these were done by the same individual. However, a word of caution must be introduced here because there are four or five of these documents which were only photo reproductions or photographs examined and compared with the other writings. These photographs of course cannot be examined with the same detail that the original document can be, and there is always some possibility that there are some alterations or something on these particular photographs which cannot be determined because they are not the original document.

"There is only one document on which we jointly could not arrive at any specific conclusion, and that is the so-called note, JFK exhibit F-506. That particular document is a very fuzzy reproduction and that particular reproduction we could not make any definite determination as to whether or not it was the same writing as all the other writings examined and compared and determined to be from the same individual."

JFK Exhibit F-506 is the "Dear Mr. Hunt" note/letter of November 8, 1963. It will be discussed where it fits in to the related testimony, in due course.

Mr. Klein: "Mr. McNally, is it the conclusion of the panel that, in all cases where original documents were provided, they were written by the same person?"

Mr. McNally: "It is." (IV HSCA 352)

There are certain documents that are referred to and analyzed by Mr. McNally: The foremost document cited was signed when Oswald joined the Marines in 1956; a document from the Soviet Union in 1959; an August 9, 1963 arrest-related document, and a document signed on his return to Dallas in October of 1963. Klein noted they were all signed by Lee Harvey Oswald or Lee H. Oswald, (which was how Lee Oswald usually signed his name) and Mr. McNally authorized that they were all signed by the same person. (IV HSCA 353)

From there, it's a lot of loops and whirls within the Russian alphabet.

> Mr. Klein: "Is there any evidence to indicate any of these documents were forged or altered?"
>
> Mr. McNally: "There is none." (IV HSCA 355)

They also compared some the celebrated Hidell signatures, and they all agree with the handwriting of Lee Oswald. (IV HSCA 356ff)

> Mr. Klein: "... I would direct your attention to the document marked JFK F-506, dated November 8, 1963."
>
> Mr. McNally: "I have it."
>
> Mr. Klein: "Do you recognize that document?"
>
> Mr. McNally: "I do."
>
> Mr. Klein: "For the record, would you read that document, please?"
>
> Mr. McNally: "In the upper right-hand corner is the date November – N-o-v 8, 1963: 'Dear Mr. Hunt: I would like information concerning' –c-o-n-c-e-r-d-i-n-g 'concerning my position. I am asking only for information. I am suggesting that we discuss the matter fully before any steps are taken by me or anyone else. Thank you. Lee Harvey Oswald.'"
>
> Mr. Klein: "Mr. Chairman, I should state for the record that a copy—not the original but a copy—of the document was sent in 1975 to an author of a book on the Kennedy assassination [cited in Henry Hurt, *Reasonable Doubt*, as a "Texas assassination researcher"]. It was sent anonymously and he allowed the panel to see the copy that he had of that document.... Is that a fair and accurate representation of the document that you have before you?"
>
> Mr. McNally: "It is." :
>
> Mr. McNally: "The reason we could not reach any conclusion regarding this particular document is number 1, this is of course a photo reproduction. It is a peculiar type of photo reproduction in the fact that we have a photo reproduction, yet at the same time it has some of the characteristics of being photo reproduced

from a microfilm enlargement which was originally out of focus. So that on this particular document here—and I made the original slide this enlargement was made—the photo reproduction was quite fuzzy. This is an extremely good reproduction of that particular fuzzy original photo reproduction.

In this particular case, it is so fuzzy that an accurate examination could not be made of it. The feature about this document— as it relates to the other documents as written containing the name Lee Harvey Oswald and all the other writing that we have here—is that this document itself, although the writing pattern or the overall letter designs are consistent with those as written on the other documents, this is much more precisely and much more carefully written.

"There is no great deviation from the writing of Oswald insofar as to individual letter design forms are concerned. However, it is the method of writing that is so precise and so careful, it is a little bit out of the ordinary from most of the writing I have seen.

Strangely enough, getting down to the signature of this particular document, a part of the signature agrees with the signature of Oswald or the other writings we have signed 'Lee Harvey Oswald,' and part of it does not agree with his."

Continued...

"Another peculiar feature here also is the fact that though not all of the signatures of Mr. Oswald are signed 'Lee Harvey Oswald,' there are seven or eight where we do have the name 'Lee Harvey Oswald' signed in full and in none of them do we have a misspelling. In this particular signature 'H-a' and we have a little slurring off here and a 'v' and a 'y.' So that part of this signature is missing, and that does not occur in any of the other Oswald signatures.

"Again, in the writing of the latter part of 'Oswald,' very unusual in all of the Oswald signatures that we have seen. In this particular instance the 'd' is smaller and much more precise than the preceding 'l.' This is another characteristic which does not occur consistently in the other Oswald signatures. So, a suspicion is aroused by the fact that this is an extremely precise type of writing even though it does agree basically with the overall writing characteristics of the previous Oswald writings. And a suspicious circumstance in the fact that the middle name 'Lee Harvey' differs significantly in the 'H,' in the misspelling of the word, and a slight aberration in the lower part of the 'y' and in the latter part of the signature 'Oswald." And for these reasons we were unable to come to any firm conclusion regarding this particular document. It is suspicious, although we are not able to accurately determine that it is specifically a forgery and at the same time not able to accurately determine whether or not it corresponds to all of the other writings that we have identified." (IV HSCA 357—359)

The nature of the note is dubious at best. The note was dated November 8, 1963, a Friday, when Oswald was at work at the Texas School Book Depository and then caught a ride home with Buell Wesley Frazier, and continued at the Paine residence until Tuesday morning, because Monday was Veterans' Day (called Armistice Day at this point).

The handwriting is suspicious, to be sure, but what about the document in general. Does it yield any fruit? It looks like Oswald's cursive handwriting, but I can't say for sure, because I'm not a handwriting expert.

Besides the obvious possibilities of H.L. Hunt or E. Howard Hunt, both of whom figure in the JFK story, let me offer another avenue we might walk down. This goes along with the theme of *military intelligence* I have been hinting at throughout the entire book. An unidentified individual whose name was John Hurt/Hurd, who was referenced to Marina Oswald Porter in an HSCA deposition regarding whether or not she had heard the name from Lee Oswald, is a real possibility. The name was an individual, related to *US Army intelligence*, whom Lee Oswald attempted to call on Saturday night, November 23, 1963.

The DPD operator involved did not put the call through, but Oswald was told there was no answer. Some extremely odd events, possibly covert, occur when Lee Oswald is allowed to use the telephone. Oswald went to place the call at the jail telephone booth, lifted the handset and asked to place a long-distance call. The operator who took the call, Mrs. Alveeta A. Treon, who had been told by her supervisor, Mrs. Louise G Swinney, that two unknown men said Lee Harvey Oswald would be placing a call that evening. The Dallas City hall telephone operators were located on the 5th floor of the Dallas Municipal Building. Alveeta A. Treon, [1920-1999] age 43 at the time of the incident, listened in. Mrs. Treon actually took the call and then deferred to her superior,

Mrs. Swinney. Oswald gave Mrs. Swinney two telephone numbers in Raleigh, North Carolina: (919) 834-7430 and (919) 833-1253 to call.

Mrs. Swinney wrote down the numbers, alerted the two unidentified men who were eavesdropping in the next room. Where did Oswald get these phone numbers? There is no indication he asked for a long-distance information operator and appears that he knew these numbers from memory.

Mrs. Treon remembered when Oswald tried to place the call and told the HSCA that she was dumfounded at what happened next. Mrs. Swinney opened the (telephone) key to Oswald and told him, "I'm sorry but the number doesn't answer." She unplugged and disconnected Oswald without ever trying to put the call through. A few moments later Mrs. Swinney tore the page off her notation pad and threw it into the wastebasket. But, Mrs. Treon wrote down everything and at the behest of her daughter, who worked in the same building and told her mother this would be an interesting thing to hold on to, kept the LD (long distance) slip. And that is why we have a copy of that slip until this day. I have included a copy of that slip at the end of this chapter.

It was obvious, according to Mrs. Treon, that Mrs. Swinney was visibly shaken after the non-phone call and after the two unknown men had thanked Mrs. Swinney for her cooperation, they left.

Thank goodness that Mrs. Treon had the mind to write everything down, while Mrs. Swinney was taking down the identical information, because once Mrs. Treon passed the call over to Mrs. Swinney, she stayed on the line, listening to everything Oswald said and wrote it down. This event took place c. 11:15 p.m.

By referencing a 1963 telephone directory, the 834-7430 number was in fact John D. Hurt, who turned out to have been contacted by the HSCA.

He did tell the HSCA that he had worked in Army Counterintelligence during World War II, was disabled and collecting a full military pension. He told the HSCA staff that he had the identical telephone number for the last 20 years

Someone did not want Lee Oswald getting through to North Carolina on the evening of the 23rd. Louise G. Swinney was only doing what she was told and according to Mrs. Treon was highly agitated after the whole process came to an end. She was just following orders.

But whose? You have to go up the ladder to people more powerful than the DPD, but even so, this was an event bigger than the local level.

We just don't know any more than this: Dr. Grover Proctor has done exceptional work on this topic and you should visit his website to get a fuller picture of the events that night.

AC stands for area code
da stands for did not answer
ca stands for cancelled

23

JOHN CLEMENT HART –
SEPTEMBER 15, 1978

On Sept. 15, 1978, John L. Hart gave testimony before the HSCA Washington, D.C.

John C. Hart was asked to narrate and explain the Yuri Nosenko data, based on interviews held on May 19-20, 1978. Nosenko was not allowed to testify, although why is not explained. The Russians certainly knew he was in this country.

House Select Committee Chief Counsel G. Robert Blakey, having introduced the committee's interest about Lee Oswald's activities in Russia, noted the private sessions with Nosenko and then proceeded to narrate the salient points of Nosenko's narrative. The material is from Blakey, unless otherwise indicated. (II HSCA 482ff)

> "By April 1964 Nosenko had been in the United States for near-ly two months. Already top officials of the Soviet Russia and counterintelligence sections of the CIA had nagging doubts as to whether he was a bona fide defector.

Information that Nosenko had given about Oswald, for one thing, aroused suspicions.

The chief of the Soviet Russia section had difficulty accepting the statements about Oswald, characterizing them as seemingly almost to have been tacked on to or have been added, as though it didn't seem to be part of the real body of the other things he had to say, many of which were true.'"

"Nosenko told the FBI about his knowledge of Oswald and the fact that the KGB had no contact with him. The conclusion of the March report by the FBI reads as follows:

'On March 4, 1964, Nosenko stated that he did not want any publicity in connection with this information but stated that he would be willing to testify to this information before the Presidential commission, provided such testimony is given in secret and absolutely no publicity is given, either to his appearance before the commission or to the information itself." (II HSCA 482; quoted material from FBI summary report)

During his period of hostile examination, which began on April 4, 1964, Nosenko was given three polygraph tests. The results of those examinations were given to Mr. Richard Arther, a member of the American Polygraph Association. "As for the two questions about Oswald on the third test, Mr. Arther characterized the first as 'atrocious' and the second as 'very poor' for use in assessing the validity of Nosenko's responses." (II HSCA 484)

"The Warren Commission received FBI and CIA reports on Nosenko and his statements about Oswald but chose in its final report not to refer to them." (II HSCA 485)

With regard to finances, Blakey reported that the CIA had put Nosenko on the role in 1969 at a salary of $16,500.

"As of 1978 he was receiving $35,325 a year."

"In addition to the recorded yearly compensation in 1972, Nosenko was paid for the years 1964 through 1969 in the amount of $25,000 a year less income tax. The total amount paid was $87,052. He also received in varying increments from March 1964 through July 1973 amounts totaling $50,000 to aid in his resettlement to the private economy.

To this day, Nosenko is a consultant to the CIA and the FBI

on Soviet intelligence, and he lectures regularly on counterintelligence." (II HSCA 485)

Nosenko started his part-time job on March 1, 1969, at $16,500. Welcome to American capitalism and the world of the intelligence community.

In 1978, he was pulling down $35,325. As a full-time janitor, I earned $5.05 per hour that same year earning $10,504 annually.

He was paid for *six* years: 1964, 1965, 1966, 1967, 1968, and 1969 @ $25,000 per year; total, $150,000. He took home $87,052, meaning he lost $62,948 in deductions.

Nosenko spoke to the House committee on five occasions. During two of these sessions, staff members took notes. In the third, Nosenko gave a sworn deposition, and on July 19 and 20, 1978, Nosenko testified before the committee in executive session. There was no substantive variation in Nosenko's recounting of the facts. There have been, howev-er, significant inconsistencies over the years in Nosenko's story.

Let me here note one: Nosenko has always insisted that the KGB never had any contact with Oswald. He stated in both 1964 and 1968 that the KGB determined that Oswald was of no interest to them and did not even bother to interview him.

And exactly why didn't KGB officers ever speak to Oswald before they made the decision about whether to let him defect?

"We didn't consider him an interesting target."

When asked if he knew of any other defector who was turned away because he was uninteresting, Nosenko answered, no. Nosenko said the KGB not only did not question Oswald when he asked to defect, it also did not interview him later when it was decided he would be permitted to remain in Russia. At no time, Nosenko told the committee, did the KGB talk to Oswald....

According to Nosenko, the KGB would have been very interested in the fact that Oswald worked at the air base in Japan from which the super-secret U-2 spy planes took off and landed.

And in 1959, would the Soviet Union have been interested in some-one who had served as the radar operator on an air base where U-2's took off and landed?

"Yes, sir. It would be very interesting."

But Nosenko maintained that the KGB never spoke with Oswald, so it didn't know that he had any connection with the U-2 flights. (A brief sample of Yuri Nosenko interrogatories, contained in the narration of House Select Committee Chief Counsel G. Robert Blakey, II HSCA 485-486)

Nosenko makes the claim that the KGB had no awareness of Oswald's military background. This is simply not true. Richard Snyder claimed that Oswald made an offer to supply the Soviets with military data that he had concerning his radar undertakings with the U-2 spy plane when he was based in Atsugi, Japan. The U.S. Embassy in Moscow was meticulously bugged by the Soviets. The Soviets would have known and been all over Oswald, if Snyder was even remotely accurate in his assertions.

Nosenko said there was no curiosity about Oswald, but his request to stay would have been information enough. The KGB would have been able to ensnare Oswald in all kinds of lies, had that been their intention and purpose.

What about Oswald's defection? What effort was made by Oswald to become a Soviet citizen? Did he make a request to the Supreme Soviet for citizenship, and why was he refused? Oswald's defection and supposed request for citizenship would have been looked upon as a coup from a disinformation perspective, when an American chose the workers communist paradise over the greed of capitalism. The fact that Oswald was an American marine made such a pronouncement even more of an upheaval.

Was Oswald really eager to become a Soviet citizen after all. Hard to say, but after all these years, he seems more like a fake defector.

Blakey told the committee the FBI had elected not to send anyone to be examined with regard to their report on Nosenko, but the CIA had sent "John Clement Hart as its official representative to state the agency's position on the committee's Nosenko report." (II HSCA 487)

Blakey forgot to mention that Hart retired from the CIA in 1972. But his narration did include that "He has written two extensive studies on Soviet defectors, one of which, dated 1976, dealt with the handling of Yuri Nosenko by the CIA." (II HSCA 487)

The 1976 study necessitated six months, and comprised full-time efforts of the witness, plus four aides. "We collected from various parts of the agency ten four-drawer safes full of documents, and we had also access to documents which were in repositories in other parts of the Agency, and which we simply didn't have room to collect in our office." (II HSCA 490)

Hart made a succinct statement, implying that he was going to read from some notes and tell the Committee all about Nosenko, at least as much as the CIA knew.

Representative Dodd wanted a recess, remarking that the committee had organized a report on Nosenko and presented it to the CIA, assuring everyone they would respond.

> "Am I to assume that this detailed outline consisting of a single page, listing four subtitles, is the summary of Mr. Hart's presentation?... What I would like to request at this point is that this committee take a 5- or 10-minute recess, and we have the benefit of examining your notes from which you are about to give your testimony, so that we could prepare ourselves for proper questioning of you, Mr. Hart." (II HSCA 488)

Dodd wanted the five or ten minutes to make copies of the notes that Hart was going to work from. Chairperson Stokes suggested that Hart simply go ahead, "and then in the event that you deem it necessary to have additional time to review his notes, or to prepare an examination of him after his testimony, that the Chair would grant you that time at that time."

Dodd said that would be fine.

Hart vowed to speak of "a series of cumulative misunderstandings" in the Nosenko affair, adding,

> "I will endeavor to show that the handling of Nosenko by the Central Intelligence Agency was counterproductive from the time of the first contact with him in Geneva in 1962, and that it continued in a manner which was counterproductive until the jurisdiction over the case was transferred to the CIA Office of Security in late 1967, specifically in August of that year." (II HSCA 489)

Hart talked of his uneasiness at confirming in public, as some of the material was classified. He did acquiesce to a couple of things. Nosenko's IQ, as measured on the Wexler scale, was very low in terms of memory, although the context was June 24, 1964, right after the beginning of his hostile interrogation. [*hostile is by no means a hyperbole*]

Hart further noted that

> "defection is in itself a major life trauma....it has both psychological and physical effects on people, and anybody who has, as I have had to do, had considerable contact over the years with defectors, knows that a defector is usually a rather disturbed person, because he has made a break with his homeland, usually with family, with friends, with his whole way of life, and above all he is very uncertain as to what his future is going to be." (II HSCA 491)

Compare Nosenko and Oswald. Nosenko was eagerly sought by the U.S. intelligence community, and seemed to have the anticipation of a reasonable and adequate life style afterwards.

Nosenko made the choice to leave his Soviet life behind him. We still don't know exactly why Nosenko decided to defect, unless it was to save his own life. Maybe he felt that he had come under some misgivings by the Soviets for his earlier dealings with Americans.

If you are Nosenko, defection would be a massive upgrade, because as shocking as defection may be, it is preferable to standing and facing a firing squad. Nosenko was not traumatized by relocating. He was traumatized by the United States, especially when they found out he could now discuss the Soviet existence of a person by the name of Lee Harvey Oswald.

Although he was interviewed about Oswald years after the fact, the djini had to be kept in the bottle in 1964, because the Oswald script had already been predetermined.

How does this parallel to the Oswald defection?

We are informed time and again that Oswald did not travel to the Soviet Union on an operation for our government, though his mother would disagree with that until her death.

We are informed that he was let into Russia on a six-day visa, and when the visa wasn't prolonged, he failed in a suicide attempt. If Oswald couldn't take his own life from just a few inches away, how could he take the life of JFK from 265 feet? An odd juxtaposition.

Oswald actually did leave everyone behind, which meant his mother, a brother, and a half-brother whom he had shunned for most of his adult life, as short as it was.

Did Oswald leave friends behind? I can't think of one friend he had in the United States, before he left for the Soviet Union. Any classmate he would have was lost immediately upon joining the Marines. The Marines certainly weren't shy to get rid of him.

He doesn't have any known friends. He only left Marguerite and Robert Oswald behind and he wasn't especially chummy with either of them.

Oswald didn't seem to know very much Russian, but Nosenko did know a reasonable amount of English. Nosenko was put inside what amounts to a brick cube at Camp Peary in Williamsburg, Virginia. It would be Nosenko's terror of all terrors.

Hart said that Nosenko, for safety purposes and to make sure no one was following him, often stopped at bars before reaching the local CIA safe house in Geneva. The result, according to Hart, is that Nosenko was often drunk before he arrived in America. Or to quote Nosenko himself, he "was snookered." (II HSCA 491)

Hart specified that Nosenko had a good enough working knowledge of the U.S. Embassy that he was able to list, for removal, "52 microphones which were planted throughout the most sensitive parts of the American Embassy in Moscow." Hart added that some people have stated that Nosenko was given that intelligence to get his foot in the door, but Hart claimed that there had never been a case where a defector would come stocked with that kind of data. (II HSCA 492—493)

Hart said that Nosenko was kept detained for 1,277 days; but was only questioned for 292 of those days.

> "The rest of the time, which is 77 percent of the total time of incarceration, he was left entirely unoccupied and was not being questioned.
> "There was, in other words, no effort being made to get at more information which he might have." (II HSCA 501)

Hart also testified concerning attempts to get intelligence out of Nosenko with the use of sodium amytal, but that was overruled by CIA Director Richard Helms; he was instead polygraphed for ten days.

The following exchange then takes place:

> Mr. Hart: "Since the October 18 [*polygraph*] test was the most significant because it was the one which had to do with the Oswald matters" –

Chairman Stokes: "I wonder if the gentleman would suspend for just a minute. It is about 1:30 now...."

Hart answered that he could conclude his testimony in 15 minutes—perhaps short-circuiting the process as such, so he continued. (II HSCA 502-503)

Nosenko was polygraphed for 28 hours and 29 minutes, rendering anything that he said totally useless. He was left, strapped in the chair during lunch breaks.

"In addition to that, it was later discovered that while he was actually not being interrogated, he was left strapped on the chair where he was sitting so that he could not move. And so, while lunch breaks were being taken, he actually was not being interrogated but he was still strapped to the chair.

"Now these lunch breaks, or whatever they were, perhaps they were also used as time for further preparation of questions. But at any rate, the record shows that they lasted, for example, on October 20, from 12:15 to 3:30, and on October 21, from 12:45 to 4:45. That is 4 hours that the man was left in the chair with no rest." (II HSCA 503)

Mr. Hart: "That is all I have to say in this presentation, Mr. Chairman."

Mr. Stokes: "Thank you, sir.

"I think this is probably an appropriate place for us, then to take a recess.

"The committee will recess until 2:30 this afternoon, at which time we will resume questioning of the witness." (II HSCA 504)

The testimony of John L. Hart, retired CIA agent, resumed. Mr. Dodd begins his questioning:

Mr. Dodd: "Mr. Hart, thank you for your statement this morning. Mr. Hart, let me ask you this question at the very outset. Would it be fair for me to conclude that it was the responsibility of the Central Intelligence Agency to find out, from whatever available sources between late 1963 and 1964, what the activities and actions of Lee Harvey Oswald were during his stay in the Soviet Union?"

Mr. Hart: "Congressman, I want to answer that by telling you that I do not know—"

Mr. Dodd: "Let me say this to you, Mr. Hart. Wouldn't it be a fair assessment that the Central Intelligence Agency had the responsibility during that period of time to examine whatever information could point to or lead to those activities, to provide us with information regarding Lee Harvey Oswald's activities in the Soviet Union? Isn't that a fair enough, simple enough statement?"

Mr. Hart: "Sir, I can't agree to that in an unqualified manner for several reasons. May I give the reasons in sequence?" (II HSCA 505)

Mr. Hart: "In a telephone conversation between the then Director of Central Intelligence, John McCone, and Mr. J. Edgar Hoover, which took place on the 16th of November 1963 at 11:20 a.m., Mr. McCone said: 'I just want to be sure that you were satisfied that this agency is giving you all the help that we possibly can in connection with your investigation of the situation in Dallas. I know the importance the President places on this investigation that you are making. He asked personally whether the CIA was giving you full support. I said they were, but I just wanted to be sure you felt so.' 'Mr. Hoover said, "We have had the very best support that we can possibly expect from you." (II HSCA 505)

Hart then told Dodd that, with respect to Oswald, the CIA, although exceptions had occasionally been made, could not operate within the United States, "and the Central Intelligence Agency had no particular, in fact, did not have any assets capable of making an investigation within the Soviet Union, which were the two places really involved." (II HSCA 506)

Congressman Dodd slowly began to back former CIA-analyst Hart into a corner. Hart resisted, but Dodd was adamant:

Mr. Dodd: "Well, after listening to your statement for 1 hour and 40 minutes this afternoon, do I take it that you would concede the point that, as the CIA's activities pertain to one vitally important source, potential source of information namely, Mr. Nosenko, that in the handling of that potential source of information, as it bore on the assassination of a President of the United States, the Central Intelligence failed in its responsibility miserably?"

Mr. Hart: "Congressman, within the context of the total case, I would go further than that. I would say that the Agency failed miserably in its handling of the entire case and that since the Lee

Harvey Oswald questions was part of that case; yes." (II HSCA 507)

Dodd made an additional point, quoting a statement from the Warren Commission report: "All of the resources of the U.S. Government were brought to bear on the investigation of the assassination of the President, and in light of your last answer, that conclusion was false?
Would you agree with me?"
Hart avoided with non-answers. (II HSCA 507)

> Mr. Dodd: "…why should this committee believe anything that Mr. Nosenko has said when, after your testimony, you state that he was intimidated, not interrogated, for more than 3 years, that he was probably hallucinating during various stages of that interrogation, that he was, according to your testimony, a man of a very short memory; that he was drunk or at least heavily drinking during part of the questioning; that there are no accounts, verbatim accounts, of some of the interrogation but rather notes taken by people who didn't have a very good knowledge of Russian. Why then should we believe any of the statements of Mr. Nosenko, which from point to point contradict each other, in light of the way he was treated by the Central Intelligence Agency from the time he defected in January of 1964 until today?"
>
> Mr. Hart: "I believe there are important reasons you should believe the statements of Mr. Nosenko." Then after admitting to errors regarding Oswald, he rehashed the revelations of the microphones story. But in response to the next Dodd question, Hart responded: "No, sir. I am not asking you to believe anything in connection with his statements about Lee Harvey Oswald." (II HSCA 508)

Nosenko was ultimately changed into a zombie by the U.S. government, but he did tell us some interesting non-Oswald information.

> Mr. Dodd: "I don't recall you once mentioning the name of Lee Harvey Oswald in the hour and 30 minutes that you testified, and I am intrigued as to why you did not do that, why you limited your remarks to the actions of the Central Intelligence agency and their handling of Nosenko, knowing you are in front of a committee that is investigating the death of a President and an essential part of that investigation had to do with the accused as-

sassin in that case; why have you neglected to bring up his name at all in your discussion?"

Mr. Hart: "The answer is a very simple one. I retired some years ago from the Central Intelligence Agency. About 3 weeks ago I received a call from the Central Intelligence Agency asking me to, if I would, consent to be the spokesman before this committee on the subject of the Nosenko case. I said that I will be the spokesman on the subject of the Nosenko case; but I will not be the spokesman on the subject of Nosenko's involvement with Lee Harvey Oswald. That was a condition of my employment. And if they had attempted to change that condition before I came before this body, I would promptly have terminated my relationship because I do not want to speak about a subject concerning which I do not feel competent." ...

Mr. Dodd: "So it would be fair for me to conclude that really what the Central Intelligence Agency wanted to do was to send someone up here who wouldn't talk about Lee Harvey Oswald."

Hart then recommended that further or other questions should be put to the Director of the CIA.

Dodd repeated to Hart that he told them he would not "talk about Lee Harvey Oswald and they said that is OK you can go on up there." (II HSCA 509 and *passim*)

Hart told the committee, based on a series of Dodd's stated inconsistencies by Nosenko, "I would simply disregard it." (II HSCA 511]

The vast majority of the remainder of Hart's testimony is simply CIA-bashing, with Hart consenting that mistakes were made in the earliest handling of Nosenko.

The CIA sent someone to give testimony before the House Select Committee on Assassinations and *stipulated that they would not discuss anything concerning or conjectured about Lee Harvey Oswald.*

It is simply beyond belief that the agency could not only get away with this stipulation, but almost boast in their arrogance.

Congressman Sawyer seemed to have a fascinating confrontation with Nosenko's arrest and subsequent incarceration in the cube at Camp Peary, Virginia, the location being classified at that time. Hart compared the cube to a vault where safe-deposits are kept, with a solidly barred door, 10 feet by 10 feet, with no windows.

For amusements, Nosenko created a chess set out of fibers of his clothing, and a calendar out of the lining from his clothing.

> "He was desperately trying to keep track of the time, so he made himself calendars out of lint. But in the course of his having been compelled to sweep up his room or clean up his room, why these calendars were of course ruined, so he had to start all over again." (II HSCA 518)

> Chairman Stokes: "Let me ask you this. One of the responsibilities of this committee is to assess the performance of the agencies in relation to the job that they did, cooperating with one another and with the Warren Commission in terms of the investigation of the assassination.
>
> "In light of your statements here to other members of the committee with reference to the performance of the agency which you have described as being dismal, et cetera, if I were to ask you to rate the performance of the agency in this matter on a scale of 1 to 10, with 10 representing the highest number, top performance, where would you rate them?"

> Mr. Hart: I would rate it at the lowest possible figure you would give me an opportunity to use. I am perfectly willing to elaborate on that, Mr. Chairman.
>
> "I have never seen a worse handled, in my opinion, worse handled operation in the course of my association with the intelligence business." (II HSCA 522-523)

Hart said that the CIA contemplated either eliminating Nosenko or sending him to an insane asylum. Instead, they put him on a generous income as a consultant, but Hart was not capable of explaining exactly what Nosenko was doing to earn that sizeable salary. (II HSCA 525 and *passim*)

Dodd continued to press as to why Nosenko could state that Oswald was of no interest; and would finally ask if Nosenko expected a harsh period when he defected and came to the United States.

> Mr. Hart: "Congressman, I believe from what I know of Soviet treatment of defectors from the United States, who were valuable defectors, as he [*Nosenko*] was, that they have been treated extremely well, that they have been given much less trouble, they have been welcomed, in fact.
>
> "Everything has been done to encourage that other people

like themselves would come to the Soviet Union. They are usually given a stipend immediately, as Oswald was. They are given decent living quarters, which Oswald was. They are treated extremely well, as Oswald was.

On the basis of what he knew of how the Soviet Union treated defectors, he would have assumed that he could be treated very well." (II HSCA 528)

Near the very end of his testimony (II HSCA 535), Mr. Hart defended Nosenko as a person:

"May I say something more, Mr. Cornwell. He does periodically get very upset. He got very upset, for example, on the subject of the Epstein book. He is a very—he is a normal human being, and when he feels that he is being maligned, he gets just as upset as anybody else around." (II HSCA 535)

Hart is most likely discussing Epstein's *Legend*, which is full of despicable comments about Nosenko, maybe this is because Epstein was repeatedly refused his requests for an interview with Nosenko, a privilege only granted to Gerald Posner. What should that tell us?

24

SR. EUSEBIO AZCUE LOPEZ –
SEPTEMBER 18, 1978

On Sept. 18, 1978, Sr. Eusebio Azcue Lopez testified before the HSCA in Washington, D.C.

ollowing the transcript/tape-based "interview of Sylvia Tirado
Bazan, the former Sylvia Duran, Chief Counsel G. Robert Blakey
provided a narration prior to the testimony of Eusebio Azcue,
who was Sylvia Duran's superior at the Cuban Consulate in September
1963, and to whom Oswald, crying and angry, was referred on his last
visit to the Cuban Consulate on September 27, 1963. (III HSCA 126ff)

Eusebio Azcue was the Cuban consul in Mexico City in September
1963, at the time Lee Harvey Oswald allegedly visited there. When
Oswald, or an impersonator, found out from consulate employee Sylvia Duran, that it would take a week for him to get a visa to travel to
Cuba, Oswald had a temper tantrum until Azcue, the consul himself,
was forced to step in.

Committee Chairman Stokes invoked the "do not stand" rule once
again, and administered the oath to Mr. Anthony J. Hervas, who would

319

serve as the translator for Azcue, then living in retirement in Cuba. Michael Standard, attorney with Rabinowitz, Boudin & Standard of New York, acted as counsel for Azcue. "For the past 17 years the office has represented the legal interests of the Government of Cuba in the United States." (III HSCA 126)

Also present were Sr. Ricardo Escartin, first secretary and consul of the Cuban Interest Section in Washington; and to his left, Capt. Felipe Villa, of the Ministry of the Interior of the Republic of Cuba.

> Mr. Standard: "Mr. Chairman and members of the committee, I appear here today in two capacities. One, to reflect the view of the Cuban government that the assassination of President John F. Kennedy was an act of the vilest kind, an act unacceptable by any standards of human and political behavior.
>
> "Both at the time of the convening of the Warren Commission and today, the Cuban Government has cooperated to the fullest extent in providing what information it has at its disposal to the U.S. authorities investigating the event.
>
> "Second, to accompany two former consuls of the Republic of Cuba who were present in Mexico City in the period September 1963 through August 1964, both of whom appear today of their own volition, and as a result of the Cuban Government's decision to provide the Congress of the United States with the testimony of such witnesses as may aid in the process of gathering evidence regarding the assassination.
>
> "On the day following the assassination, President Castro, in a speech televised to the people of Cuba, and devoted exclusively to the implications for his country, said, and I quote:
>
> 'It is in the interest of the American people and all the people of the world that it be known – that it be demanded what is really behind the Kennedy assassination, that all the facts be revealed.'"
> (III HSCA 126—127)

The interpreter for Eusebio Azcue Lopez was Anthony J. Hervas, and he was sworn in as if he was a witness himself. Mr. Azcue was 67 at the time of his HSCA testimony, meaning he would have been fifty-two at the time of the assassination.

> Mr. Cornwell: "For how long a period of time or until what date did you hold that position?"

Senor Azcue: "Until November 18, 1963, though since the month of September of 1963 I had started to turn over affairs to the new consul who was to replace me, Mr. Alfredo Mirabal." (III HSCA 128)

Mr. Cornwell: "And on November 18, 1963, when you did ultimately turn over that position to Senor Mirabal, where did you go?"

Senor Azcue: "I went directly and definitively to Havana." (III HSCA 128)

With respect to the June 6, 1978 deposition of Sylvia Tirado (Duran), it seems as if she was asked what Azcue thought about the assassination of JFK, the incident with "Oswald" at the Embassy, and the on-air execution of Oswald. Translation is always a matter of both interest and worry, though it appears that Duran was asked over and over what Azcue thought of the three aforementioned occurrences.

Duran intermittently noted, "He was not there," but it is not stated clearly, if my recollection serves, that he had left for Cuba four days prior to the assassination.

Mr. Cornwell: "Senor Azcue, in a previous interview with the staff you stated that the very first occasion to your memory on which you saw this individual was 1 to 2 days before the date on the application. Is that still accurate to the best of your memory?"

Senor Azcue: "It is something that I cannot state categorically. I cannot state whether it was on the very same day, a day before, or several days before, and I am in a position to explain why." (III HSCA 130)

Mr. Cornwell: "Please do."

As far as Oswald being at the Consulate, in addition to September 27th, we know he wasn't there before that particular date, and because the 27th was on a Friday, the Consulate would have been closed on the 28th and the 29th (Oswald visited Richard Snyder in Moscow on October 31, 1959, when that Embassy was supposed to be closed, since it was a Saturday); and Oswald (or whoever was impersonating him) was not in Mexico City very much beyond September 30 to October 1. This is a problem that will impinge on the Sylvia Odio story. (*see Appendix #2 concerning Sylvia Odio*)

Senor Azcue: "He approaches us. The secretary normally takes care of the case. There is no need for me personally to go out to see him unless he specifically requests that I do so, as a special case, that he requests either my presence or the presence of another Cuban consul responsible. He did so. He requested my presence because when he initially formulated the application with the secretary, the secretary explained to him all of the requirements that he would have to fulfill in order to obtain the visa. And as he was carrying along certain documents which he believed would be sufficient for the visa, and the secretary could not resolve the case, he then calls upon me to see whether I, upon examination of those documents, can proceed to issue the visa immediately. I answered negatively.

"The documents that he submits are not enough. He is exhibiting or producing documents such as, one, attesting to his membership in the U.S. Communist Party. Also another indicating that he is a member of the Fair Play for Cuba Committee. Also another document indicating his residence in the Soviet Union, as well as a marriage certificate to a Soviet citizen.

"Upon presentation of these documents, he thinks that I will be able to solve his problem and grant him a visa. I at that time tell him that this is not sufficient; that I must request authorization from the Cuban government. And at that point he agrees to proceed to fill the application out in order to process the visa.

"At that point, he leaves the consulate, conceivably to look for some photographs [*so this is the first visit, when Azcue dealt with Oswald*]. One could think whether he returned on that very same date with the photographs; it is possible that he might have returned on that very same date with the photograph, or that he might have returned the following day. [*not possible: it would be Saturday, but it did work out for him in Moscow in 1959*]

As far as the date that appears herein and **bearing in mind that I received him on three occasions** maybe it would be possible to determine that on this very same date, it is possible, I cannot fully guarantee this, it is possible that on the same day he might have made the first two visits to the consulate; one during the morning very early, and the second one a little later, bring the photographs in order to complete the application. There is a sufficient time for such a thing." (III HSCA 130-131)

Azcue is suggesting that Oswald had proof, "attesting to his membership in the U.S. Communist Party." The FBI could not corroborate the existence of such documentation, which I assure you, they wanted to find such connections. This statement should have set off a Fourth of July fireworks spectacle, because this was one thing that the FBI wanted to nail down, but as I said, they never could.

A number of researchers see Oswald as an FBI informant, which by FBI regulations he was (see Fain memo, June, 1962, who conducted the first known interview of Lee Oswald following his return to the United States; Oswald agreed to contact the *Bureau if* contacted by Soviet intelligence, making him a PCI – potential criminal informant – of the FBI), it would be reasonable for him to be in the Communist Party of the United States (CPUSA), because a good proportion of the affiliation of that organization was made up of FBI agents, finding out what other FBI agents were saying and doing.

Sylvia Duran testified (in a sworn deposition) that Oswald went to the Cuban Consulate, and was told he needed photographs; he left and returned with four photos on his second visit that same day in mid-afternoon.

According to Duran's story, two copies of his application were made, not the six that Azcue made reference to above. The photographs, or some of them, were attached.

Oswald left again but returned in the early evening when the Consulate was closed for that kind of business. Possibly rejected by the Russians, Oswald pleaded with Duran with some anger used for immediacy, to the point that she went and got Azcue to meditate the dispute. There was more shouting, until Azcue told Oswald to get out.

Either Duran or Azcue is incorrect, not that one of them is lying, but one statement is incorrect.

> Mr. Cornwell: "Directing your attention, then, to the second occasion on which, as you have just described, the individual returned with photographs which could be attached to the visa application, what occurred on the second occasion?"
>
> Senor Azcue: "I did not assist. I was not present at the very time when the secretary receives the photograph and fills the documents. That is a function that pertains properly to her. He very probably insisted once again on the need to proceed urgently to Cuba or to transit Cuba.

323

"As the amount of time required to process this document by our own Government was one that I could not predetermine, it could be a matter of 15 days, 20 days, or the response could be negative; during this second visit that he makes to me I bring up or note if he had already had a visa to go to the Soviet Union, I would be in a position to grant him a visa to Cuba without the need to consult my Government, in terms of a transit to the Soviet Union.

"This should have been clearly stated or established during the course of the second visit that he made. Whether it might have been on the same day or 2 days thereafter, I tend to believe that it will have been on the date that appears on the application, that is to say on the 27th." (III HSCA 131)

Earlier Azcue stated "and bearing in mind that I received him on three occasions," but now asserts he did not meet with Oswald on the second visit. This could be innocent. Hard to tell with any kind of certitude.

> Mr. Cornwell: "After that conversation, did you again see the individual, did he return to the consulate?"
>
> Senor Azcue: "Yes, sir. That was the third and last time I saw him. He possibly thinking that his documents had been legalized orally, verbally, that I would consequently change my attitude and in view of the legality of the document would grant him the visa; those were his hopes. And in addition, one noticed that he was very anxious that we grant him the visa, because we never had any individual that was so insistent or persistent, in spite of our refusals which were logical and legal."
>
> Mr. Cornwell: "Did all three of these visits occur during normal working hours at the consulate?"
>
> Senor Azcue: "We never received anybody, any individual, outside these regular office hours." (III HSCA 132)

In sworn deposition, Sylvia Duran insisted that all three visits were on the same day, and that the third and concluding visit was after the close of the business day.

> Mr. Cornwell: "Do those pictures of that individual appear to you to be the same individual who visited the consulate in Mexico City on the occasions you have previously described to us?"

Senor Azcue: "Truly, this photograph is the one I saw for the first time when the honorable U.S. committee members came to Cuba in April of this year, and I was surprised that I believe that it was not the same person. Fifteen years had gone by, so it is very difficult for me to be in a position to guarantee it in a categorical form. But my belief is that this gentleman was not, is not, the person or the individual who went to the consulate."

Mr. Cornwell: "Directing your attention to the period of time immediately after the assassination, the day of the assassination or the day after the assassination, did you during that period of time have an occasion to see pictures of the alleged assassin in the newspapers or to observe on television the man identified at that time as Lee Harvey Oswald?"

Senor Azcue: "Yes, sir, not so close to the date, not in the first few days, not immediately thereafter. Some time I calculate approximately—and I say this because I am not a great movie fan, but it was in mid-December approximately—I saw at that time the film in which Ruby appears assassinating the Oswald who was there, and I was not able to identify him and only two months had gone by since I had seen the Oswald who appeared at the consulate. And I had a clear mental picture because we had had an unpleasant discussion and he had not been very pleasant to me and I did not recognize him when I first saw him. I did not recognize Oswald.

"The man who went to the consulate was a man over 30 years of age and very thin, very thin faced. And the individual I saw in the movie was a young man, considerably younger, and a fuller face."

Mr. Cornwell: "What hair color did the individual have to the best of your memory who visited the consulate?"

Senor Azcue: "He was blond, dark blond."

Mr. Cornwell: "Did the individual you saw in the movie, the person who was killed by Jack Ruby, resemble more closely the individual in these photographs to your memory than the individual who visited the consulate?"

Senor Azcue: "I believe so." (III HSCA 136)

Azcue is unable to identify a face he should by no means ever forget: the person in the photos is not the man who went to the consulate, but the man shot by Ruby has a closer resemblance to the man in the photographs. It suggests that either the Cuban government, or ours, dummied the photographs and inserted Oswald's in their stead, which would be easy to do.

> Mr. Cornwell: "I would like to show you JFK exhibit F-434. Do the representatives from the National Archives have the original or a small photograph of that exhibit?
> .... [*LHO passport, including photo, entered into evidence.*]
>
> Mr. Cornwell: "**Did the individual who visited the consulate look like that individual?**"

Senor Azcue: "**No.**" (III HSCA 136, 138)

Mr. Cornwell: "What differences were there?"

Senor Azcue: "Many differences. The individual who visited the consulate is one whose physiognomy or whose face I recall very clearly. He had a hard face. He had very straight eyebrows, cold, hard, and straight eyes. His cheeks were thin. His nose was very straight and pointed. This gentleman looks like he is somewhat heavier, more filled, his eyes are at an angle with the outside of his eye, at an angle with his face. I would have never identified him or recognized him.

"I believe I can recall with fairly good accuracy the individual in such a way that I could recognize him now in a group of 100, that is better than a photograph of him because obvious during a period of 15 years he might change. I think I could recognize him, and this is not him."

Mr. Cornwell: "We would like to show you what has been previously admitted into evidence in this case as Exhibit 194. As you can see, Senor Azcue, the pictures on the right are simply blowups of the same visa application, but I would like to direct your attention to the two pictures on the left which come from photographs taken by the Dallas Police Department. I ask you if that individual looks like the man who visited the consulate."

Senor Azcue: "I would have never recognized him as I did not recognize him in the movie where he dies, and I can, however, identify him or think of him as the person who was killed or assassinated by Ruby. It is a question of personal evaluation on my part, but it is clearly imprinted." (III HSCA 138-139)

Sylvia Duran's Oswald was quite thin, whereas Azcue's Dallas Oswald is slightly more hefty. The claim on skinny, or just being noticeably smaller than the Dallas Oswald, plainly excludes the Mexican mystery man, who wound up as Commission Exhibit 237 and Bardwell Odum Exhibit #4 and was not the Oswald at the consulate. The man in CE-237e seemed to be heavy-set, although not overweight, just stocky.

So according to Azcue and Duran, as opposed to CIA cameras, the mystery man remains a mystery. He cannot recognize the Dallas Oswald as the man who visited the Consulate. He can recognize the Dallas Oswald as the man killed in Dallas, but nothing more.

He should have been asked for a comprehensive and detailed description, beyond what he gave about facial characteristics, because Cornwell is well aware of Silvia Duran's description of him, specifically that he was 5'3" tall.

This certainly plays into the two Oswalds theory, which has been around since the mid-sixties and the writing of Richard Popkin's, *The Second Oswald.*

> Mr. Cornwell: "The staff of the committee has had an opportunity to speak to Mrs. Sylvia Duran, and during the interview with her she expresses no doubt about the fact that the person who was killed in Dallas by Jack Ruby was the individual who visited the consulate. [*and was 5'3" tall*] Do you have any reason to question her memory or the reason that her memory might differ from yours?"
>
> Senor Azcue: "Categorically, I could not affirm it without any doubt. However, it is possible that she might be more susceptible to impression or more impressionable than I. I remember what I saw on the film and also what I saw on TV later or maybe before. I remember that moment when he was killed; and I remember I did not recognize him. I did not have any prejudices or preconceptions.
>
> "I wanted to recognize, however, only 2 months had gone by. It was between September and November. At that time, I was much younger. That was 15 years ago, and I think that because of my own profession I probably had better eyes. And because of the impression that was made by this person who visited the consulate, for these reasons, maybe my version is correct or more correct." (III HSCA 139)

327

Mr. Cornwell: "Thank you. I have no further questions."

This concludes Azcue's testimony to Gary Cornwell. Other members of the House will then question additionally.

Sylvia Duran was very guarded in her testimony, as the reader can sense her thought processes constantly going to the ultimate question: How much can I tell them before I'm at risk? It is almost pathetic, yet you can't help but feel sorry for her.

Azcue did not have that problem. He saw who he saw and said so. Sylvia Duran's identification put her at risk. You can sense, again, almost a paralytic fear.

> Chairman Stokes: …. The Chair recognizes [*Congressman*] Mr. Preyer."
>
> Mr. Preyer: "Thank you, Mr. Chairman. Senor Azcue, it is good to see you again. As I understand it, at the time Lee Harvey Oswald visited the consul in Mexico there were three people who could have seen him: yourself, Sylvia Duran and Mr. Mirabal. Is that correct?" (III HSCA 139)

Congressman Preyer's first question seems ominous. After listening to several denials that the man killed by Ruby was the same man who visited the consulate, Preyer sadly reverts to the Warren Commission and asks about Lee Harvey Oswald visiting the consulate, despite the repeated denials that the Lee Harvey Oswald killed in the basement of the Dallas City Hall was the man in the consulate.

> Mr. Preyer: "Did your return to Cuba have anything to do with your encounters with Oswald or did it have anything to do with the assassination of President Kennedy?"
>
> Senor Azcue: "It was not related to any of those things. I returned to Cuba because all of my family was already there. As of June of that year I had been awaiting a consul to replace me because I already had a son studying in Havana and a son working there and already in June they had given me permission to return permanently to Cuba.
>
> I was not able to return before because they were not sending me a consul to replace me, and the reason I did not leave immediately upon Mr. Mirabal's arrival was, first, because I had to train him. He did not have any experience in the handling of consular

affairs there, and second, because there was a meeting or congress of consuls being held at that time and I was asked to stay. This was because of my connections developed over the 5 years that I had spent there."

Mr. Preyer: "So that it is fair to sum up your answer by saying that you were not recalled by the Cuban Government; but, you, at your request, returned to Cuba?"

Mr. Hervas: "Excuse me, sir, did you say at your wish?"

Mr. Preyer: "Yes, at his wish."

Senor Azcue: "I cannot say it was at my wish exclusively. I need the permission of the Government of Cuba, but I had requested my return in June, because, as I noted previously, my sons were back in Havana. One was already working. One was studying there. I was then alone in Mexico with my smaller daughter, and I also wanted her to study in Cuba. I wanted to return there." (III HSCA 140)

You get the impression that Mr. Azcue is a loyal son of Cuba, with a serious affinity for his homeland.

While this question seriously disputes the witness, at least it's a direct question about the identity of every individual who ever attended one of her parties.

The witness has already said that Mr. Mirabal had arrived prior *to* September 27th, the *supposed* date of the arrival of Oswald, so it cannot be speculated that Azcue was replaced because of Oswald's angry exchanges.

Mr. Preyer: "After Oswald visited you the first time, that visit ended when you sent him out to have a photograph taken, as I understand it. Was there a place nearby where he could have had the photograph taken?"

Senor Azcue: "Yes, yes, about four or five blocks away in a street known as Calzada de Tacubaya. There are photographic studios. Possibly Sylvia might have pointed out to him where he could obtain the photographs, or maybe he already had the photos."

Mr. Preyer: "Well, in the photographs on the application, and also in the passport, Oswald appears to have on a tie and a sweater. How was he dressed when he came to the Embassy, to the consulate?"

Senor Azcue: "I always imagine him or visualize him as wearing a suit, coat and pants, trousers, with a pattern of crossed lines, not very clear design. Blue, some reddish. I never conceived of him or visualized him wearing a light sweater. When I saw this photograph in April of this year, I also noted that the clothing he was wearing was not the same." (III HSCA 143)

I don't recall any suits being among Oswald's belongings that were dragged into the Dallas Police Headquarters, following searches at both the Paine house and his rooming house at 1026 N. Beckley.

Mr. Preyer: "If analysis of that handwriting, of that signature on the visa application showed it to be Lee Harvey Oswald's signature, would you still believe that the man who visited you in the consulate was not Oswald?"

Senor Azcue: "Under such circumstances I would have to accept that I was being influenced or that I was seeing visions." (III HSCA 145)

This is the scenario where a situation is presented in which a *maybe* answer is prompted; but translated into case closed.

Mr. Preyer: "Thank you, Mr. Chairman. ..."

Mr. Dodd: "Now, did I understand your testimony correctly, that you were not aware of how the photograph on the exhibit, the visa application, you are not aware of how that photo got on that application? In fact, you had not seen the photograph on the application?"

Senor Azcue: "That is the case. Sylvia Duran was handling that area. She typed in the form, affixed the photo, had the applicant sign the forms. In the meantime, there was no reason for us consuls to be present there observing the procedure. We were simply in our private offices. We had a lot of work."

Mr. Dodd: "The reason I asked you that question, is that when several of us had the opportunity to interview you in Cuba a few short months ago, on page 14 of our interview, which I hope you have a copy of, I was questioning you and I asked you:

"Going back to the physical appearance of Lee Harvey Oswald, apart from having a receding hairline, was there any gray in Lee Harvey Oswald's hair? You responded: 'You know he had blond hair. It is all very interesting. You see this picture, I really did not study carefully. The picture was taken by the secretary and she applied it to the application.'

"It would seem from your response to my question then that, one, you did see the picture on the application or that you did not see the picture on the application then, but were merely looking at it when it was in front of you, and that you had very specific knowledge as to how the picture got on the application, that in fact Sylvia Duran stapled it to the application."

Senor Azcue: "Yes; it is a matter of routine. She is the one who handles all of these detailed operations. I could assure that she was the one who did it without having seen her do it. There was no one, no other person there, that would do that work for her, and neither Mirabal nor I did that work." (III HSCA 151-152)

It enriches the conspiracy story to have Consul Eusebio Azcue repeatedly deny that the man who arrived at the Consulate was not the same man killed by Jack Ruby, but that seems to sidestep one vital question that nobody wants to ask.

Here is that question:

"If you, Mr. Azcue, do not see any resemblance between the man in this photograph and the man killed on live TV by Jack Ruby, could you please tell us how Sylvia Duran attached the photos of a man that she also would not have recognized, if you did not recognize him? She was right there, with him. Didn't she take note of the fact that the photos did not match the individual?"

Possible Answers: (1) Sylvia Duran was so frightened by her police interrogation, detention, and threats that she would have agreed to just about anything, including going along with this investigation. (2) She saw a different photo from the individual she dealt with, got scared, and realized that there were forces involved that were playing for keeps. (3) Another option would be that someone substituted for the photograph of the individual who made application at the Consulate. And a fourth consideration would be that Azcue is being misleading – a form of lying with a specific purpose; in this case, the specific purpose is to expose a conspiracy wholly within the powers-that-be in the United States.

His motivation? Re-read the part where he told Mr. Preyer that he didn't really enjoy looking at a book full of pictures taken at Cuban Consulates or Embassies by spy cameras of U.S. pedigree.

> Mr. Thone: "Exactly. Now my question. Did you report this to the Cuban Government and if so to whom and what happened on your report in this regard?"
>
> Senor Azcue: "I reported this to some of my friends in the Ministry of Foreign Affairs. But in fact, in truth I was aware of the fact that it was my testimony of my own, it was of my own imagination. And that the conditions under which I had seen him in the film at the time he was killed, with distorted features as a result of pain, it is conceivable that I might be mistaken.
>
> "I reaffirmed my view when Attorney Garrison of New Orleans stated that the Oswald who visited or was at the consulate was not the one who allegedly killed Kennedy, because of the date he departed New Orleans and the date he had visited the consulate in Cuba. So that confirmed my own view, and at that point I believed that as being the truth. And then I communicated this. And that was probably filed, recorded.
>
> "I did not write a report. I made an oral report. But it would be necessary to investigate whether such a report in writing exists or does not.
>
> "But that was the time when I saw my own views confirmed in my opinion that there were two Oswalds. Garrison shares the same opinion." (III HSCA 154)

Nobody bothered to question Azcue what he did when he left Mexico City and returned to Cuba in November 1963. Seems important. But what?

> Mr. Fithian: "Thank you. Mr. Azcue, Lee Harvey Oswald was a radar operator in the Marines and was familiar with the U.S. spy plane, the U-2. Did Oswald ever mention to you his service in the Marines or in the military in the United States during your conversation with him as he was trying to get a passport to Cuba?"
>
> Senor Azcue: "He did not provide any information on his own background other than the presentation of the documentation that he had brought forth in connection with his application. It was clear, and I was able to check out from the first time, that his only intent was to obtain a visa immediately. Therefore, his

background, especially his non-revolutionary background, was of a nature that he had no interest at all in communicating to us.

"He was interested in telling me that he was a member of the Communist Party, that he was a resident of the Soviet Union. In other words, that which he believed would be sufficient to obtain the visa. And our conversations were always extremely brief, because I used to put an end to these conversations, referring to the instructions I had from my government of a need to obtain their prior authorization before issuing any visa, either the final destination visa to the Soviet Union, so that I may be in a position to provide him, but with the visa of the Soviet Union already affixed to his passport. Everything went around that very issue. He did not speak a single word outside of that issue." (III HSCA 156)

This doesn't seem to be the Oswald that most of us think we know. Lee Oswald liked to leave calling cards and this would have been a prime moment to impress his hearers with some Russian, but he didn't. Oswald almost always knew how to leave his calling cards.

It is painstakingly obvious that the HSCA had no desire to get to the answers we all wanted. Both Duran and Azcue were clear in their answers that Lee Oswald, the man shot by Jack Ruby, was not the man at the Cuban Consulate on September 27 (when Sylvia Duran testified that "Oswald" made three appearances) or sometime after. The issue is avoided with Azcue.

Duran designated "Oswald" as 5'3" tall (*which was Duran's height by the way*) and with blond hair. Azcue was not asked Oswald's height, which is odd. Azcue did agree, however, with the blonde hair, thought the individual was about 35 years old or older, but disagreed with Duran and remained unconvinced that the man shot by Ruby was the man at the Consulate. He also did not assent that the man in the photos and stapled to the visa application was the man he had an argument with.

Oddly, the entire conversations at the Consulate were conducted in English, even though, fifteen years later, Azcue needed a translator in his dealings with the HSCA.

Remember, Senor Azcue was shown a photograph of Oswald and was asked if this was the man who visited him in September 1963. He said, "This gentleman...the man...was over 30 years of age and very, very thin faced...He was...dark blond...He had a hard face. He had very straight eyebrows, cold, hard, and straight eyes. His cheeks were thin. His nose was very straight and pointed." I know of no one who has ever described Oswald as having straight eyes. Azcue was not questioned by the Warren Commission. He did, however, testify before the House Select Committee on Assassinations. The Committee showed Azcue photographs of Oswald, and he said this was not the man at the consulate. (III HSCA 136-138)

There were numerous sound recordings of Oswald. His debate on the radio with some bitter anti-Castro persons, as well as the famous Friday night press conference – there were plenty of opportunities to say to Senor Azcue, "Close your eyes and listen carefully ... Is that the voice of the man you spoke with?" But it didn't happen. Images can be more susceptible to interpretation than voices, particularly when one is vociferously arguing with the other voice. An opportunity, a vital opportunity, was lost, or it was deliberately forfeited.

Gary Cornwell was given the floor to deal with the June 6, 1978 appearance of Mrs. Bazan (Sylvia Duran) before the House Select Committee, and a photo of her was displayed on an easel, "and we also have a transcript of the interview marked for identification as JFK exhibit F-440A, and a tape recording of excerpted portions of that interview..." (III HSCA 4-5) Her entire interview with Mr. Cornwell is found in III HSCA 6-119. She was technically not one of the 52 witnesses who appeared before the entire Committee, therefore is not included directly in this book.

25

SR. ALFREDO MIRABAL DIAZ –
SEPTEMBER 18, 1978

On September 18, 1978, Senor Alfredo Mirabal Diaz testified before the HSCA in Washington, D.C.

T he testimony of Senor Mirabal was also given through a translator, Mr. Hervas (who also translated for Eusebio Azcue, and is noted as an interpreter from the State Department), questioned by House Select Committee staff counsel, Michael Goldsmith.

Alfredo Mirabal was the consul for the Cuban embassy in Mexico City in September of 1963. He succeeded Senor Azcue in his position. He claims to have seen Lee Harvey Oswald on two separate occasions during his service as consulate of the Cuban embassy. Although Mirabal didn't actually take care of Oswald, he was there to hear the confrontation between him and Senor Azcue, who was still there training Mirabal at his job. Mirabal stated that "from the very first moment it appeared to me as if this instance could be the case of provocation. I sensed that there was an intent to create some kind of a scandal, of a disturbance. That was my feeling." (III HSCA 174) He stated that this happened on two occasions and lasted for about 15-20 minutes each time. He said the two visits happened shortly after his arrival to the embassy as an employee.

Mr. Mirabal said he remembered Oswald presenting a card or credentials that indicated he belonged to the Communist Party of the United States. He responded, "I also have been a Communist for a number of years and that generally we do not use credentials or a card to identify ourselves ... we are identified to ourselves as Communists by our own behavior and by our own ideas. I was surprised by his unusual interest in using identification as a Communist." (III HSCA 176)

Mr. Goldsmith continued the questioning of Senor Mirabal:

> Mr. Goldsmith: "Mr. Mirabal, while you were Cuban consul in Mexico City, did you ever see Lee Harvey Oswald?"

The first interesting question is phrased for the benefit of those who endorse the official position of the federal government and believe that Lee Harvey Oswald is guilty. It is baffling as to why Mirabal wasn't asked to describe the individual yelling at Senor Azcue. Also, it would have made sense to show him a picture of Oswald in the custody of the Dallas Police. But this didn't happen.

Continuing, with asking Mirabal about seeing Oswald when he was consul in Mexico City, and whether he ever saw Lee Harvey Oswald while he was consul in Mexico City:

> Senor Mirabal: "Twice, on two occasions, when he was at the consulate processing visa application."
>
> Mr. Goldsmith: "Did anything unusual happen when Oswald was applying for his visa?"
>
> Senor Mirabal: "Yes; since he first came for the visa, I must note that I do not know English, and therefore it was my colleague Azcue who took care of him, though he had in fact concluded his responsibilities in the position. When I arrived, he stayed on to help me out and he, together with my secretary, took care of this visitor.
>
> "From inside my private office I could hear loud voices, and I came out of my office several times to see what was happening in the area where the secretary worked. I asked my colleague, Azcue, who was taking care of the visitor, I did not know who the visitor was. But my colleague Azcue told me that the visitor was in need of an urgent visa, that he was in a great hurry to travel to Cuba. However, as our own procedures dictated, and as our instructions from the Ministry of Foreign Relations provided, we were not authorized to issue a visa, and therefore the visa was not issued. He continued in this discussion."
>
> Mr. Goldsmith: "**Did Mr. Oswald get involved in arguments with Mr. Azcue on both occasions that he, Oswald, visited the consulate?**"

Senor Mirabal: "*Yes; on both occasions there were discussions or arguments to such an extent that from the very first moment it appeared to me as if this instance could be a case of a provocation. I sensed that there was an intent to create some kind of a scandal, of a disturbance. That was my feeling.*"

The second time the same thing happened. There were three visits: a procedure, a return with photos, and a subsequent return, by Oswald with the promise that he had the Russian visa, and the succeeding squabble with Azcue. Now there are only two visits, and an argument each time.

Mr. Goldsmith: "*Mr. Mirabal, please look at the picture that appears in that application. Is the person whose picture appears in this visa application the same Lee Harvey Oswald who visited the Cuban consulate requesting a visa?*"

Senor Mirabal: "*I really did not observe him with any great deal of interest.* He for me was one of many who visited the consulate. The image that I have of him, I believe that the answer is *yes, that he is the same person.*" (III HSCA 173-174) ...

Mr. Goldsmith: "Mr. Mirabal, after the assassination of President Kennedy, was there every any discussion at the Cuban consulate or Embassy [*do they know and understand the difference?*] concerning whether the Oswald arrested in Dallas was actually the same person identified as Oswald who visited your consulate requesting a visa in September 1963?"

Senor Mirabal: "Yes, on the day following the assassination, it is my own secretary that communicates this information to me in the morning when I arrive at the consulate. At that point, she advises me of the fact that the assassination has occurred. Later, and I cannot recall exactly how late or how soon thereafter, she communicates to me the fact that the alleged assassin is the same person that came to the consulate." (III HSCA 174-175)

It is not clarified if the secretary, (though not precisely identified) was Sylvia Duran, and whether she made these allegations before or after she was apprehended and detained by the police, whose presence in this entire episode is never explained.

Mirabal himself was not arrested or warned, but Sylvia Duran was re-arrested and informed of her child's well-being.

Staff counsel Goldsmith then read from the Comer Clark article where it was purported that Castro had confirmed his awareness of Oswald's existence at the *embassy* and that Oswald had made a remark about the prospect of killing Kennedy.

> Mr. Goldsmith: "Mr. Mirabal, do you recall Mr. Oswald making the remarks that are allegedly attributed to him?"
>
> Senor Mirabal: "I feel that what has just been read is totally absurd, it is incredible. In addition, it is totally false, it is a lie, and it is impossible to image that that has been stated." (III HSCA 175)

Representative Sawyer reminded Mirabal that he did not speak English so how could he so plainly accuse Oswald of making an allusion of "killing President Kennedy," especially if he did not comprehend what was said?

Mirabal replied that Azcue and his secretary would have reported any such conversation, "without any doubt, have informed me if he had stated anything of such a nature." (III HSCA 176)

Mirabal added,

> "In fact, I noticed that he presented a card or credentials as belonging to the Communist Party of the United States. I understand, or it is also my understanding, that the Communist Party of the United States stated that he never belonged to the party. I was surprised by the fact that the card seemed to be a new card.
>
> "I must say that I also have been a Communist for a number of years and that generally we do not use credentials or a card to identify ourselves as members of the party. Rather, we are identified to ourselves as Communists by our behavior and by our own ideas. I was surprised by his unusual interest in using identification as a Communist. I think it would be interesting to know how he obtained the card." (III HSCA 176)

Mirabal described Oswald, when asked about his conduct and behavior, but not his appearance

> "As I recall him, he was a rather small man, medium height or somewhat less. I believe he was wearing a coat, short hair. I do not recall him having a moustache. He did have a serious expression on his face. He appeared hard or tough, someone who is upset or unhappy.
>
> That is the image that I retain of him." (III HSCA 177)

26

THOMAS J. KELLEY –
SEPTEMBER 19, 1978

On September 19, 1978, Thomas J. Kelley gave testimony before the HSCA in Washington, D.C.

The testimony of Secret Service Inspector Thomas E. Kelley, Secret Service liaison to the Warren Commission follows next. He was the Assistant Director of Protective Intelligence and Investigations in Washington, D.C., and at the time of his HSCA appearance the Assistant Director of Protective Operations in Washington, D.C.

In the beginning of his narration, House Select Committee G. Robert Blakey noted, "Of all of the Federal agencies that were in any way involved in protecting President Kennedy or investigating his assassination, the Secret Service has come in for the most scathing criticism. Within hours of the tragedy in Dallas, press accounts were pointedly suggesting that the agency had been derelict in its duty to provide Presidential security." III HSCA 320)

By its own charter, the Secret Service did not, in 1963, investigate the crime of presidential assassination. Their job is protection, and since the killing of that particular federal official – the President – was not a federal crime in 1963, they had no jurisdiction and their charter forbade such an inquiry.

They may have done some investigation and may have done so for a couple of reasons: They were so dazed by the events that they forgot their own rules, as they had done in allowing the overly wide 121-degree turn from Houston Street onto Elm Street, just before the assassination.

Secondly, they may have not had a choice, as they would not have wanted the FBI doing all of the investigating and would have looked bad as a result.

Secret Service Chief Rowley was the only Secret Service agency director that ever lost a President. Despite that, the most recently created Secret Service training facility is named for him, which I find an affront to the pride of the Presidency, and also to John F. Kennedy.

The more obvious questions were raised first. Why had the motorcade been routed through Dealey Plaza, an open, park-like area surrounded by tall buildings? Why wasn't there more physical protection for the President? Why, for example, were there no agents in the limousine itself, forming a human shield? Why was the limousine moving at such a slow speed? And why were agents in an open car directly behind the limousine so slow to respond at the sound of the first shot? (III HSCA 320)

The Secret Service cannot be disparaged as far as the investigation of the assassination, as that is not their job. They are to provide protection. Period. Once protection is breached, they can return fire and do anything needed to protect the President, *carte blanche*, and no questions asked. But when the crime against the president has stopped, they do not investigate the crime. It is not within their dominion.

What about Blakey's assertions that Dealey Plaza is surrounded by tall buildings? In my many trips there, it's replete with wide open spaces, as it was in 1963. In terms of pure math, it's **348 feet from the middle of Main Street to the Texas School Book Depository**, and it's **495 feet from the southeast corner of the Texas School Book Depository to the Triple Underpass.** It forms a geographic shape that resists simplistic definition. *If we imagine a rectangle, 348 feet on two sides and 495 on two sides, just how surrounded is it?*

Using the Book Depository/corner of Elm and Houston as the northeast corner of the area, the following geometries apply: There are buildings on the eastern wall which constitutes the eastern side of Houston Street which is 348 feet; there is one building, the Book Depository, between Houston Street and the Triple Underpass, and the Depository is 110 feet square, so that's 110 feet, obviously. There are no tall buildings to the west, only a railing above an underpass, and the railing is at the same level as the sidewalk in front of the Depository. To the south, there were no tall buildings until well south of Commerce street. So out of a possible 1,706 feet, the perimeter of the rectangle, only 458 (348 on Houston, plus 110 on Elm) or 26.84% of the perimeter is surrounded by tall buildings. I am going to assume Chief Counsel Blakey is unaware of this.

Compare that to the few blocks of Main Street just east of Houston, it's a canyon of taller buildings, with no breaks.

The motorcade route from where the vehicles turned right, from Harwood onto Main Street: The entire area there is surrounded by tall buildings, which is a lot more than 458 feet.

It's not a strenuous walk to trek from the corner of Houston and Main to the western end of the Depository Building. A leisurely walk from Harwood and Main to Houston and Main is substantially longer.

There were two agents in the limousine, but they proved to be of diminutive usefulness in the time of tragedy. There was never any hint, that President Kennedy himself felt unprotected. Physical protection for Kennedy seemed to be in place.

The car traveled leisurely because that is the nature of parades. Traveling by crowds of people at high speed will not win anyone any votes, not to mention it could be dangerous if there are a lot of people lining the sidewalks.

The limousine did not go down Main Street at a high rate of speed and then slow down on Elm. The speed on both streets was approximately the same.

Most people thought the first shot was a backfire of a motorcycle or a firecracker, although Governor Connally and motorcycle rider Marrion Baker, immediately thought it was a rifle shot.

341

How much reaction can truly be generated in 5.6 seconds, or 8.3 seconds, or any small number you can cogitate?

The limousine had armor plating underneath, but that is not the issue. The choice of the route, guaranteeing the 121-degree turn, is to be condemned, but also not an issue here. The choice of Roy Kellerman as SAIC for the trip to a place as hostile as Dallas, Texas, was probably a poor choice, but that was not made by Roy Kellerman. His only unfortunate choice was going for the radio and not the President. But that also is not the issue here, as there were no agents in the limousine, says G. Robert Blakely, though incorrectly.

There were fifteen Secret Service agents in close proximity to the limousine at the time that the assassination took place. This is important. Only six of them gave testimony to the Warren Commission, and the testimony of the two in front of the limousine would carry little or no weight.

Only Winston Lawson and Forrest Sorrels (in the lead vehicle), William Greer and Roy Kellerman (in the presidential limousine), Clint Hill (in the follow-up vehicle), and Rufus Youngblood (in LBJ's vehicle) testified.

So only 40% of the agents on the scene ever testified before the Warren Commission. Those who did not testify were: Emory Roberts, Sam Kinney, Glenn Bennett, George Hickey, Jack Ready, Paul Landis, and William McIntyre, all of whom were in the follow-up vehicle and all of whom had the best assessment of what happened in front of them. There were two presidential aids in the vehicle, Ken O'Donnell and Dave Powers. O'Donnell testified, Powers gave an affidavit, but neither is a member of the Secret Service.

In the vehicle behind LBJ's car, T. Lem Johns and "Woody" Taylor were also not called to testify, and Johns actually exited the vehicle and ran alongside the knoll before getting back into a camera car.

Some of their perceptions would have been worth a few questions. They did not call any of the Secret Service agents on the scene. If they had called Clint Hill and asked him to echo his testimony about seeing the rear portion of the President's skull lying on the seat of the limousine, it might have made an indelible impression.

The speed of the limousine was determined by the wide turn that needed to be made by the limousine, which was never previously taken by the driver of the limousine, or by the advance team. There were no dry runs before the motorcade. S/As Winston Lawson, the advance agent for Dallas, and Forrest V. Sorrels, SAIC for the small Dallas office, did ride the motorcade route from Love Field to the southeast corner of Houston and Elm Streets. It was at that point that Jesse Curry pointed and said, and I'm now paraphrasing, "Then it's onto the on ramp of the highway right over there, and a quick run to the Trade Mart."

S/A Bill Greer, the driver of the limo, almost hit the outer curb on the north side of Elm Street. The larger press busses had to reduce speed to make the turn. The motorcycles were hemmed in and also had to slow down.

Beside the slowing down onto Elm street, it was extremely clunky and lacked any kind of grace.

When the limousine came out of the turn, Greer was given another nightmare: a dozen or more people on the overpass 400 feet away and closing fast. They had been allowed there by the police, to the chagrin of the Secret Service.

They had not been removed by the pilot car, which was far enough ahead of the lead car, in front of Jesse Curry's car, that it should have stopped and given orders immediately. But no one did. When you see who is in the pilot car, there may be good reasons as to why they didn't stop and issue any kind of decree to move off the overpass.

Nobody was watching the TSBD because the FBI never told anyone about their worries, even after Oswald sent them a mystery letter, that he delivered personally, days before the assassination. If the letter postulated any threat, then the FBI was derelict to the utmost. And they were.

Nobody cleared the railroad workers from the underpass. They should not have been there and Bill Greer knew it. As he was entertaining thoughts about how to proceed in face of this menacing observation, the most awful nightmare ensued. It could not have gone worse.

Why such an undecided action, if any at all, of the agents in the follow-up car to the opening shot? A compelling question, as their performance is indefensible. There is a difference in their describing what was heard.

Too many people swore to the following,

> "I heard what sounded like a firecracker, and then I heard the second shot…"

My question to every one of those individuals would have been: *What happened to the first shot?*

You cannot have a second shot, unless you have an initial shot. John Connally is in the minority when he said he heard what he recognized to be a rifle shot.

If we work from the standard 5.6 seconds in Dallas, or the recent adjustment of 8.3 seconds based on the acoustical analysis, and after 35 minutes of hanging on to the vehicle at speeds up to 25 miles per hour, the agents in a **fourteen-mile-long motorcade** route did not react immediately, if at all, but neither did anyone else.

Many people are still seen standing motionless after every shot was fired. Altgens 5, (Z-255) showing the limousine in mid-block on Elm street and the President reacting with his hands going up toward his throat, and the Secret Service inactive, shows no crowd recognition of the assassination in progress, even though it was already 2.45 seconds over, out of the total of 5.6 (or the 8.3 adjustment) seconds. If you use frame 210 of the Zapruder clock as the first shot, (though Z-189/190 seems a more precise description for the first shot) and Z-255 (the timing for Altgens 5 synced with the Zapruder film), then that means that 43% of the time of the assassination has passed and the only people producing a reaction are the Secret Service men looking around endeavoring to determine if they should jeopardize their careers by climbing on the President because of a possible firecracker.

Citizens like Bill Newman reacted quickly, and he hadn't been pumping adrenalin for fourteen miles of a presidential motorcade. He heard a shot come humming over his head, which did not come from the Book Depository, as he was west of the Stemmons Freeway sign, and he hit the ground.

Blakey told me in 1998 that it was a mistake not to call Bill and Gayle Newman to testify before the HSCA. He felt they would have been credible witnesses.

The House Select Committee determined to do their own prodding into the evidence: "It has assembled data on threats against President Kennedy from Secret Service files, in an effort to establish a basis for a fair, objective analysis. This has enabled the committee to scrutinize the extent to which Secret Service protective measures reflected the agency's grasp of potential danger to the President during the Kennedy years.

"In other words, was the Secret Service in part to blame for the
assassination because it failed to gather sufficient information on
security problems in Dallas, or because it failed to analyze that
information for its full significance?" (III HSCA 320)

Blakely then gives us a brief history of the Secret Service. The irony
is, the Secret Service was founded by President Lincoln, but only as an
investigative agency to concern itself with counterfeiting, a major problem during the paper money era of the Civil War.

At the turn of the century, the Secret Service was successful in seiz-
ing some Congressmen in western land frauds; to prevent any such
events in the future, the Bureau of Investigation was created (later, it
was called the FBI). "So, the original FBI [*BI, actually*] men were eight
agents transferred from the Secret Service." (III HSCA 321)

The BI/FBI confusion in Blakey's narration is hardly the only fac-
tual error, as he also noted that the Secret Service was only involved in
two presidency-related events, one being in "February 1932," involving
President Franklin Roosevelt, who was fired on, and the 1950 event at
Blair House.

In this statement, Blakey is a year off. Anton Cermak, Mayor of Chi-
cago, was shot on February 15, 1933, in the company of President-elect
Franklin Roosevelt, and Cermak died nineteen days later. Herbert
Hoover was President for all of 1932.

Technically, the Secret Service was not legislated to provide full-
time protection for the President until 1951, under President Harry S
Truman

It is noteworthy that the Secret Service did protect Presidents, although they were not charged with that responsibility, well before 1901.
There were Secret Service agents in proximity to James Garfield when
he was shot on July 2, 1881, and a Secret Service agent stationed near
William McKinley, given his position of proximity to some dignitary,
possibly allowing McKinley to be shot on September 6, 1901. Blakey is
telling half-truths in this portion of his narration. Blakey also compared
JFK's approach to the Presidency with that of other presidents:

"President Kennedy posed a problem for the Secret Service from
the start. As a policymaker, he was liberal and innovative, perhaps startlingly so in comparison with the cautious approach of
President Eisenhower. His personal style was known to cause

agents assigned to him to tear their hair. He traveled more frequently than any of his predecessors, and he relished contact
with crowds of well-wishers. He scoffed at many of the measures
designed to protect him and treated the danger of an assault
philosophically, if someone wanted to kill him, he reasoned, it
would not be very difficult to stop him. On at least one occasion,
President Kennedy was literally 'lost' by the Secret Service detail
guarding his hotel room." (III HSCA 321-322)

Fifteen agents were stated as being in the motorcade, but Forrest
Sorrels was a local, Dallas SAIC, and Glenn Bennett, in the follow-up
car, was borrowed from Protective Research. Clint Hill and Paul
Landis were agents assigned to Mrs. Kennedy. Bill Greer was a driver
agent.

A film clip showed agent Donald Lawton being waved away as the
motorcade is leaving Love Field to begin the 14-mile journey. He was
assigned with Dallas agent Roger Warner, to guard *Air Force One* at Love
Field during the time the procession was away from it. He had already
been given the charge to be at the airport and have everything ready for
the departure, to Austin, Texas.

Both had assignments to guard AF-1 at Love Field, and the Queen
Mary, which was behind the presidential limousine was loaded, so there
would be no reason for Lawton to leave his post and ride in the Queen
Mary, especially since there would not have been room. My suspicion
is that he had some unanswered question from the AIC in the Queen
Mary; but didn't get an answer. However, Clint Hill, when interviewed
on C-Span, November 8, 2010, stated that Lawton was joking with the
agents riding in the motorcade and saying, "All right fellas, I'm going to
lunch. Have a good trip." Secret Service specialist Vince Palamara dis-
agrees with this explanation given by agent Clint Hill.

The motorcade accounts for only fifteen agents. Some were already
at the Trade Mart. In addition, there were agents waiting at the LBJ
Ranch, getting ready for the barbecue that had been planned for the late
afternoon and evening after the Dallas trip.

Protection was spread too thin, but even if there had been 100
agents in the motorcade, would it have made any difference? The agents
weren't acting as human shields. No protection, even of the President of
the United States, is 100% fool-proof. Ever.

On the day of the assassination, Presidential Assistant Kenneth O'Donnell told a Secret Service agent,

> "you are not at fault. You can't mix security and politics. We chose politics." (III HSCA 322)

Kelley testified initially to being in Louisville, Kentucky, at the time of the assassination and arrived in Dallas in the evening. He also attested that he sat in on four interrogation sessions of Lee Oswald and said there were too many people present for any kind of interrogation to be successful. (III HSCA 325)

He indicated he was upstairs at the time of the shooting of Oswald and getting to the basement as the ambulance was backed in, and that he tried to get into the ambulance with Oswald, only to be prevented by Jim Leavelle and L. C. Graves, who got into the ambulance instead.

Kelley was then asked, "During the time between your first conversation with Lee Harvey Oswald and the time the shooting occurred, did you make any attempt to ascertain what his background had been?" (III HSCA 326)

Kelley didn't answer the question, but instead commenced talking about different events after the shooting occurred, and how information was received from Marina Oswald, the FBI, the Dallas police, "and the State Department had some information on him in connection with his trips to Russia. The *military* was supplying information to our headquarters and it was being provided to me in Dallas." (III HSCA 326)

He doesn't seem to understand the question, hence the follow-up: "Did you make any attempts personally to obtain information from the Secret Service files about Lee Harvey Oswald's background in connection with the Cuban organization?"

> Mr. Kelley: "Well, the inquiry we made of the Secret Service files was whether the Secret Service had anything on Oswald prior to the assassination, and we had none." (III HSCA 327)

At the time of the Assassination Records Review Board, it was indicated that Thomas Kelley used to kid about having interviewed Oswald in the Dallas jail, yet he never wrote up a final report on the event. As I have been saying from time to time and will continue to say, *Odd*; which seems to explain everything and at times nothing.

Mr. Matthews: "Mr. Kelley, when you were in Dallas conducting the investigation, were you the person in charge of the assassination investigation on behalf of the Secret Service?"

Mr. Kelley: "Yes; in Dallas."

Mr. Matthews: "Did you request the field offices to conduct investigations of suspects who they thought may have a connection with the assassination?"

Mr. Kelley: "In connection with the assassination? No; I don't know that we sent out any requests, that I sent out any requests like that out." (III HSCA 327)

It gets worse:

Mr. Matthews: "Now, Mr. Kelley, you were aware of an investigation concerning special agents who were alleged to have been drinking the night before and the morning before the assassination?"

Mr. Kelley: "I am aware of that inquiry, yes."

Mr. Matthews: "To your knowledge, were any of those agents found in violation of Secret Service rules?

Mr. Kelley: "I don't think they were found in violation of any Secret Service rules warranting any action. It was an area of poor judgment, I presume, but *there was no specific violation of any rule.*

"Of course, the inquiry indicated that their action the night before had nothing, no bearing, on what happened in Dallas." (III HSCA 327)

Thomas J. Kelley is an Inspector in the Secret Service, which makes him a high ranking official. He seems to be clueless that Secret Service regulations strictly forbid the consumption of alcohol by any agent in any Presidential protective group situation.

An extract from the Warren Commission testimony of Secret Service Chief James J. Rowley may be of some help here: This was a violation of Secret Service rules Chapter 1, Section 10, page 7:

"The use of liquor. Employees are strictly enjoined to refrain from the use of intoxicating liquor during the hours they are officially employed at their post of duty or when they may reasonably expect that they may be called upon to perform an official duty." (5 H 451)

Each agent was mandated to submit a written memorandum to Secret Service Chief James J. Rowley, soon after the assassination, stating the hours they were at entertainment sites, and the amount of alcohol consumed. If there had been only bad judgment, this would not have been necessary.

Kelley reviewed the conduct of the agents in the motorcade and found none to be negligence in their duties. This is beyond preposterous. He reviewed the conduct of the driver of the limousine, but never thought to interview him. Why not?

> Mr. Matthews: "Had the driver of the vehicle received any training in defensive driving or evasive driving?"
>
> Mr. Kelley: "Not in a formal sense. However, Mr. Greer who was driving the President's car at that time and the other agents who were assigned as drivers had long practice and history of driving the Presidential vehicles and the security vehicles." (III HSCA 328)

I would assume that only a seriously trained government agent would know what to do in the event of the Presidential limousine coming under gunfire during the execution of their responsibilities.

> Mr. Matthews: "Mr. Kelley, the special agent in charge of the White House detail testified before this committee that he had been removed from his position, that he had considered his conduct a demotion. Did you have occasion to review his performance?"
>
> Mr. Kelley: "Yes; that man [Gerald Behn], of course, was not at Dallas. I had occasion to review his performance at other times, but he was not present in Dallas." (III HSCA 328)
>
> Mr. Matthews: "Now in the week following the assassination, did you receive any reports from the field offices, reporting results of their investigation or whether there were any subject, or other agents connected with the assassination?"
>
> Mr. Kelley: "Yes; we received several reports. At that time, there were several rumors going around that Oswald had been seen in various places and Oswald had connections in various cities. And these reports were coming to us and being evaluated."
>
> Mr. Matthews: "What was the nature of those reports generally? Did they identify any particular organization?

Mr. Kelley: "They were generally running out *rumors* concerning Oswald being seen with certain people in other cities. There was a report coming to us from New Orleans that Oswald had been seen in New Orleans, had been arrested in New Orleans, and had been participating in some pamphleteering activities in New Orleans." (III HSCA 329)

How did these stories increase?

Mr. Matthews: "Mr. Kelley, I call your attention to a report that was written by a special agent [*Abraham Bolden*] in Chicago, a synopsis of which indicates that an informant advises that he had been in touch with a group of Chicago Cubans who may be involved in the assassination of the late President Kennedy."

Mr. Kelley: "Yes."

Mr. Matthews: "Can you state whether or not you were aware of that investigation while you were in Dallas?"

Mr. Kelley: "Yes; I was."

Mr. Matthews: "Did you file a report in connection with that matter?"

Mr. Kelley: "No; I didn't file any report that I recall. It was information coming to us." (III HSCA 329—330)

Should the people responsible for the condition of the Secret Service agents be held in doubt?

Mr. Matthews: (following up on previous non-answers) : "Mr. Kelley, I refer to JFK F-419, the report that I have discussed with you previously, a synopsis of which indicates that information had been received from an informant indicating that if the assassination of the President involved an international plot or conspiracy and that if there was evidence connecting Fidel Castro, the person who would have been responsible for carrying out any action on the part of Fidel would be Quentin Pina Machado, a Cuban terrorist used by Castro to carry out any Castro action."

Mr. Kelley: "Yes."

Mr. Matthews: "Did you make any determination to investigate the authenticity of that information?"

Mr. Kelley: "We did not make a separate investigation by the Secret Service." (III HSCA 330) ...

"The Secret Service was not in the business of gathering intelligence. We were in the business and are still in the business of evaluating the intelligence we receive. So, we were dependent and depending a great deal on the other intelligence agencies to furnish us information." (III HSCA 331)

They were inept and that is being gracious. Kelley would later testify that there was an awareness of the Cuban concerns, as expressed in letters obtained and seized from Cuba, as well as an awareness of the Joseph Milteer (see chapter 3) threat and the Ku Klux Klan and the white racist component it stood for.

He did not testify to anything being done about any of those points.

> Mr. Matthews: "Was there ever any attempt made to connect this information to the later information you received about Quentin Machado?"
>
> Mr. Kelley: "Not by us, and I am not familiar with what followed in the investigation, mostly because we never made any connection between this investigation and this threat with the Oswald matter [which, of course, was a solo effort...], with the assassination in Dallas." (III HSCA 337)
>
> Congressman Ford, of Tennessee, then began questioning Inspector Kelley insistently:
>
> Mr. Ford: "**Did you evaluate the reaction of agents in Dealey Plaza to the sound of gunfire?**"
>
> Mr. Kelley: "**Yes, I considered it and I thought about it.**"
>
> Mr. Ford: "*You thought about it?*"
>
> Mr. Kelley: "**Yes.**"
>
> Mr. Ford: "Governor Connally testified before this committee that as an experienced hunter, there was no question in his mind that the first sound was rifle fire. The evidence before this committee so far has indicated that in all probability the first shot missed. The medical and autopsy testimony has indicated that the third shot was definitely the fatal blow. We have had experts to establish that the time between the first and third shot was over 7 seconds.
>
> I want to ask you, Mr. Kelley, what consideration did you give to the reaction between the first, second and third shot of the two agents riding in the presidential limousine? And also the agents immediately behind the limousine?"

Mr. Kelley: "It is very difficult to second-guess what a person should have done in a crisis like that [*"try reacting" comes to mind*] or just what he knew had happened. I think from talking to the agents, I don't think any of them knew they were under fire until they saw the President so badly wounded.

"The agents, of course, in the follow-up car were some distance away from the action. Their training and what their responsibility was, of course, was to look at the crowd. They were not looking at the President. Their instructions are that they ought to be looking away from him, to see what was going on.

"The two people in the car, of course, were facing the other way. I don't think any of them realized at the time the first shot went off that they were under fire. We had a parade situation with motorcycles alongside of you, the crowd cheering, people making a great deal of noise, as is usual in a political motorcade of that type, and in summary, I just don't think the agents knew they were under fire until much too late to do anything about it."

Mr. Ford: "Yes, but what training did the agents receive?"

Mr. Kelley: "Well, the training, the agent had extensive training as to how to handle a crowd and how to attempt to keep themselves, between danger and the President's body. They have a great deal more training now than they had then, but even in those days there was specific training procedures that the agents went through, the recognition of gunfire, a very difficult problem for anyone I think in those situations." (III HSCA 337—338)

More questions by Ford; he continued to be answered by Kelley as if he were a shrewd and crafty man, who was not wanting to give away any information.

The drinking and late-night events on Thursday night into Friday seemingly was not hurtful to the protective detail? Seriously?

William Greer was apprehensive about maneuvering the limo, and Kellerman wanted to get the vehicle out of harm's way. But Chairman Stokes gently reminded Kelley, "That is only after the third shot." Ouch.

Mr. Kelley: "Yes."

There are way too many of these simple yes answers to be acceptable, but Kelley did get away with it; he had retired earlier that year, in 1978. So, in a sense, he was an "untouchable". (III HSCA 345)

Stokes reminded Kelley that the President's agents all failed to react,

> "And referring back to the question posed to you by Congressman Ford with reference to reaction time, did you study the [*Zapruder*] film from the viewpoint of whether the reaction time of the agents was in accordance with what you felt would be top performance?" (III HSCA 344)

> Mr. Kelley: "Yes, Mr. Chairman, and it was reviewed, we reviewed it very thoroughly with the agents who were involved. The motorcade was moving. You can recall in the Zapruder film the very great difficulty Clint Hill had in even reaching the car to assist Mrs. Kennedy, and the agents were just not able to get up to that car in time." (III HSCA 344)

Kelley could have given a more comprehensive answer and said,

> "The agents were just not able to get up to that car in time, one, because they never tried, and two, because the one who did leave the running board, S/A Jack Ready, was recalled." But those mitigating factors were overlooked. ...

> Chairman Stokes: "But doesn't your investigation reveal that in the Vice-Presidential car there is a reaction on the part of Agent Youngblood immediately?"

> Mr. Kelley: "When the caravan in the motorcade begins to move out, there, is, when it is apparent that the motorcade has been fired on, and it was apparent that the motorcade had been hit, and the motorcade begins to move out from the area is when there is the reaction." (III HSCA 345)

The only evidence that Rufus Youngblood reacted came from Vice-President Johnson and there is no visual evidence I have seen to support this.

By the time it was recognized that the motorcade had been fired upon, it was all over. Six seconds (or 8.3) is not a lot of time, except in the cases of individuals who are theoretically trained to react in such time frames. Whether it is 6 or 8 seconds, it is over in a flash, so any reaction time has to be awfully fast. For Kelley to sit there and produce such rubbish is to make a liar out of Rufus Youngblood and also make a liar out of himself. When the caravan in the motorcade was fired upon, who reacted immediately?

Only Clint Hill. Period.

Lem Johns bounded out of the vice-presidential follow-up car and headed where the crowd was going up the knoll, but that was after the need for any protection was moot.

Kelley is testifying under the guarantee to a reaction that never occurred, except for Bill Greer belatedly stepping on the gas. The follow-up car lagged quite a distance behind the limousine, as we see in the Nix and Muchmore films, and was still going slowly enough at the time when they reached the Stemmons Freeway ramp that the agents were still on the running boards. There would have been no reason why any of those men would have any need to jump off the running boards at that point. They should have been inside the vehicle and moving a whole lot faster, as the entire event was not yet known, not even until this day. The follow-up car does not catch up until quite a way down the Stemmons Freeway, when S/A Hickey is visible with the AR-15. That particular photo helped maintain the fiction that the follow-up car was, in fact, following up. At the point that photo was taken, the follow-up was within a few feet of the limousine, and traveling at a high rate of speed. But in Dealey Plaza, the limousine was on its own.

Kelley could not remember details about what happened at the after-hours event the night before the assassination, except the reason for it: "It was a long time ago. This was an after-hours club where they had apparently, where drinks could be served. It was also a place, the only place open at the time in the area where the agents could go and have something to eat, and they went to this place for that purpose."

He could not recall the place even being discussed.

> Chairman Stokes: "**How late were these agents about, that night?**"
>
> Mr. Kelley: "**I am sorry, Mr. Congressman, I don't recall. It was late in the morning. It was after midnight.**"
>
> Chairman Stokes: "**Can you tell us how later after midnight?**
>
> Mr. Kelley: "**No, I am sorry, I can't. I don't recall the details of that investigation.**" (III HSCA 345)

The part about the Secret Service agents going out to eat (in some cases until 5:00 A.M.) comes under the general heading of poppycock. They were protecting the President in what would fall under the category of a ritzy hotel. As the providers of presidential protection, they could have snapped their fingers and been served meals, so any other excuse is pure nonsense, which is being kind and generous. The committee members knew more about the late-night, after-hours occurrence than the Secret Service Inspector called to testify about it, which is sad.

In terms of sanctions for better protection, Kelley verbally threw his hands up and said: "The people who have assassinated Presidents of the United States have a characteristic running through them. They are all these loners, these people who have a grudge, with a mental history. Oswald fit that category exactly. The closest thing we had to a political assassination was, of course, the attack on Blair House, but there, again, the people that attacked it had mental problems." (III HSCA 349)

The Lincoln assassination, for which John Wilkes Booth was eventually shot dead, four conspirators were hanged, and four others sent to the equivalent of Devil's Island, was a political event and a conspiracy.

It can be argued that all murderers have mental problems. But this is just as absurd as the rest of Kelley's testimony. And yet, he got away with it. He wasn't the only one who did. Very little came his direction in way of a challenge.

When Oswald's interrogation not being tape recorded arose, Kelley specified that the Dallas police did not have a tape recorder, and he did not feel he had the right to demand that one be produced. Really? The event wasn't significant enough? I keep waiting for the punch line that never comes.

> "On hindsight, I should have wired myself before I went in there. But it was just my own position that I did not think I should insist on a recording of it." (III HSCA 351)

"Wire myself?" This means someone else is recording, at an alternative location. Huh?

The questioning continues.

> Representative Edgar: "In your conversation with Lee Harvey Oswald, what did he say to you?"
>
> Mr. Kelley: "He indicated to me that he was a Communist but not a Marxist." (III HSCA 352)

The question of reaction time was again raised by Congressman Sawyer:

> Mr. Sawyer: "Also, along the line of the questioning of Chairman Stokes, I, too, was impressed in watching the Zapruder film at how rapidly Governor Connally reacted to that first shot and all through the series of three shots there was no visible reaction by any of the agents that were in the pictures. **Do they receive any training in recognizing by sounds the sound of rifle shots or pistol shots?**"
>
> Mr. Kelley: "*They do now*. They receive formal training in it. In those days, the young agents that were on the detail, the trained agents that were on it, *all had a great deal of physical attributes. There was no formal training in the recognition of shots before that.*"
>
> Mr. Sawyer: "There is now?"
>
> Mr. Kelley: "Agents are always qualified with pistols. They were qualified with their firearms and the use of shoulder arms, but there was no specific training on the recognition of pistol shots or rifle shots."
>
> Mr. Sawyer: "What also surprised me about the reaction by Governor Connally and the nonreaction by the agents through that time frame of say 7 or 8 seconds is that the agents, I would think, would be alert for exactly that kind of thing, be concentrating on it much as a sprinter might concentrate on listening to the starting gun, whereas Governor Connally would have had other things on his mind.

And yet their reaction, for being there for that real purpose, is surprising, their total lack of reaction to it for such a long time-frame."

> Mr. Kelley: "Mr. Congressman, you know, Governor Connally was hit with a bullet." [*The Congressman probably does know that.*]
>
> Mr. Sawyer: "Not at the first shot. He turned to see where the shot came from and testified here – and it is perfectly obvious in the picture that he recognized the rifle shot and spotted pretty much where it came from and he was hit by the next shot.
>
> "Well, anyway, aside from that, one other thing that impressed me when I was in Dallas and looking at this was the so-called grassy knoll location, that we were told no one had either

checked out or even stationed as much as a Dallas policeman there.

"If you are familiar with the situation, the fence runs along the top of the grassy knoll, a solid fence with trees overhanging, and there is nothing behind it at all but a big, unoccupied gravel parking lot and railroad tracks and a perfect escape situation.

"Apparently, it was somewhat of a hangout for bums since there are wine bottles and everything else laying around back there.

"I am just amazed that the Secret Service would not have been alert to that kind of a situation because you could have killed the President from there with a handgun." (III HSCA 354—355)

For all the talk of what the Secret Service should have done and where they should have been, they were only in three places: The motorcade, Love Field to stand guard at *Air Force One*, and at the Trade Mart; that is it. There were only sixteen Secret Service agents in the motorcade on the fourteen-mile route, which would have meant one agent for every c. 1,500 yards. That is not a lot.

A contradiction then ensues:

Representative Devine: "Do you feel that the Secret Service and/or the FBI failed in its pre-assassination investigation?"

Mr. Kelley: "No, Mr. Devine. When you look at the background of Lee Harvey Oswald, a number of government agencies had information on him. No one government agency had it all and the Secret Service had none.

"However, if we had, if we knew the totality of his background and if we knew that he was working in the bookstore at that time, I feel that the Secret Service would have done something [not stated] to ensure that we knew what Lee Harvey Oswald was doing at the time of the parade. We would have seen that he was at work or we would have seen what he was doing in the bookstore if we knew the totality of it.

"He turned out to be the kind, as I say, of the typical [*Allen Dulles*] assassin, the typical assassin of Presidents, a loner, a man with a history of mental problems, a bitter man, a man who felt himself a failure." (III HSCA 355)

The sworn testimony of Secret Service inspector Thomas J. Kelley was an absolute shambles.

There is one final point to make and that is a memorandum dated February 14, 1964, released by the Assassination Records and Review Board. In it, Chief Inspector Kelley is bemoaning the legislation of the assassination of a president being a federal crime. He was hoping it would remain a state crime at the time, though now it is a federal crime. He said it would give *another* opportunity for a *"Seven Days in May"* situation. He was suspicious of the FBI being in charge of a federal assassination, lest it potentially get them off the hook, if they were behind it. It's an interesting document, mainly because of the word *another*. The movie, *Seven Days in May,* is a political thriller about an attempted coup of the President of the United States by the military. Does Kelley believe, by the use of the word *another*, that there had already been a coup by the *military* to overthrow the president. You decide.

27

James J. Rowley –
September 19, 1978

On September 19, 1978, James J. Rowley testified before the HSCA in Washington, D.C.

Rowley was the "Director of the Secret Service from 1961 until his retirement in 1972." (III HSCA 356)

Rowley's testimony was not much different from that of Thomas Kelley, unfortunately:

> House Select Counsel Matthews begins: "**Did you receive any report about the agents' performance in Dallas?**"
>
> Mr. Rowley: "*We did receive reports from time to time* **on Dallas, but what specific report are you referring to?**"
>
> Mr. Matthews: "**Well, did you receive a report indicating how the agents had performed at the time that the shooting episode occurred in Dealey Plaza?**"
>
> Mr. Rowley: "**The report indicated** *that they performed adequately under the circumstances.* **The action of Agent Clint**

Hill, that he was attempting to take some action, is indicative of the agents' response."

We know that he did not hear any radio broadcast at 12:30 p.m., because that was only 11:30 p.m. in Texas, and President Kennedy was still in the air, about to arrive at Love Field.

> Mr. Matthews: "Did you play any role in supervising the investigation itself?"
>
> Mr. Rowley: "No, sir." (III HSCA 357-358) ...
>
> Mr. Matthews: "At the time of the assassination, had the Secret Service established any procedures for the handling of physical evidence?"
>
> Mr. Rowley: "I think basically they handled the physical evidence as they would any other evidence, particularly evidence in the criminal field." (III HSCA 358)

More slippery answers from the Secret Service.

Mark North's *Act of Treason: The Role of J. Edgar Hoover in the Assassination of President Kennedy*, insists that J. Edgar Hoover personally suppressed recurring cautions of threats against President Kennedy not shared with the Secret Service, Rowley testified otherwise: "...we already had their [*FBI*] cooperation to the extent that they were able to provide us with intelligence information prior to that time." (III HSCA 390)

In reference to the sending of Inspector Kelley to Dallas:

> HSCA Representative Ford: "Was he there to investigate who may have been involved in the assassination or to review the performance of the Secret Service in connection with the assassination?"
>
> Mr. Rowley: "He was there to become involved in the investigation to determine the facts surrounding the investigation."

Ford then quotes precisely from Rowley's June 18, 1964 Warren Commission testimony in which he stated that he had no information or facts about anything beyond Lee Harvey Oswald. Ford continued,

> "We have heard testimony from Mr. Kelley indicating that there were assassination plots investigated by the Secret Service in ear-

ly 1963. Were you aware of those investigations at the time of your testimony before the Warren Commission?"

Mr. Rowley: "I would have to look at the reports themselves, Mr. Congressman, to see whether my initials were on them. In that report that you speak of, it was established that there was not any activity directed against – or of interest to us as it affected the President of the United States."

Why would such documents exist? A report regarding no threat to the President, makes no sense. Doesn't sound logical, but instead suspicious...

Mr. Ford: "Going back to the first question, you said, 'I have no such facts sir.' The second question you also said, 'I have no such information.' I am asking you now, were you aware of the investigations at the time you appeared before the Warren Commission?"

Mr. Rowley: "Well, if I made that statement, then I was not aware of those facts." (III HSCA 390—391)

That answer is miles from the question asked, and the chasm between the question and the answer takes that answer beyond ludicrous. Rowley's answer is to limit the possibilities to one, and then abolish that possibility.

He's commenting on reports he didn't read, which is embarrassing. He's worse than Kelley, because he was at the top ring of the pyramid. Ford pushes harder, putting the actual documents in Rowley's hand, and then Rowley sees his initials and remembered, and adds

"This was a year before the assassination. We are talking about 1962." (III HSCA 391)

Rowley will later testify that Kelley would not have had time, in all the confusion, to rent a tape recorder. Is he serious? Rent one, for goodness sakes go buy one, you are the Federal Bureau of Investigation and you can't spring for a tape recorder? Now he's just being annoyingly stupid.

"...no one had an opportunity to ask questions because in addition to the people that he described there, there were also the press right beyond the perimeter trying to ask questions." (III HSCA 393)

Congressman Sawyer returned to the line of questioning he had previously put to Inspector Kelley: the inept response time of the agents. Rowley, who is completely out of the loop in regard to Secret Service procedures, answered,

> "Well, I think there is an exhibit from the Warren Commission that shows that one of the cars had the door swung open apparently after the first shot which two agents are attempting to get out at about that time which may not have been in the Zapruder film." (III HSCA 395)

Rowley is suggesting the Mercury sedan (not a convertible) that was the follow-up vehicle for the vice-president's convertible. Rowley gave this testimony almost fifteen years after the assassination, in total unfamiliarity with the fact that the Secret Service vehicle in question rode with its doors open.

There are no visual suggestions at all that two agents were attempting to leave the vehicle, and beyond that, only one, T. Lem Johns, did exit the vehicle for a very brief amount of time.

Rowley also displays an inadequate knowledge of the Zapruder film, which I have no idea how many times, or if he ever actually saw the film.

Chief Counsel Blakey was equally out of the loop on the issue of the Mercury sedan. "This exhibit [*Altgens 6*], Mr. Chairman, has already been entered in the record. It is a photograph taken, according to the best evidence in the record, at approximately the time, according to the acoustics, of the second shot which would be approximately 1.6 seconds after the first shot.

I wonder if the clerk would use the pointer [*regarding the Altgens photo on an easel*]. You can see the Secret Service agents in the follow-up car have turned their heads [*at least three, Roberts, Kinney, and Hill, are still observing Kennedy*]. You can see four Secret Service agents [*seven are visible – the only one not visible is George Hickey*]. Two of them have turned their heads and are beginning to look back at the depository.

If you look back at the third car, the white car behind the President's limousine, the doors are opening [*they were open the whole time*]. The evidence in the record would indicate that it is from that car that Secret Service agents [*"agent," singular: Lem Johns*] came in an effort to protect Lyndon Johnson, the Vice President, who was following the President's car." (III HSCA 396—397)

A final thought about Rowley's testimony. The most egregious of sins is having one witness testify while the person who can confirm or refute your testimony is sitting close enough to hear you, absorbing his answers so he/she doesn't make the first witness look deceitful.

The Warren Commission lived and breathed this process. All three autopsy doctors were in the same room, and Humes did the talking. Then Finck and Boswell, also present, were asked if they agreed. No one is going to disagree at that point.

Kelley had a sizable number of distortions in his testimony. It was up to the House Select Committee to call a separate witness and ask the very same questions. The witness in this case was Rowley, who already had heard the questions put to Kelley and his answers. Rowley had no motivation at all to rectify the assertions made by Kelley.

It's the reason that witnesses to a crime are questioned separately. The heart of the case will be where their accounts form a division in the evidence, not what they say in harmony. That opportunity was totally lost here.

This finished the Secret Service testimony and their leading officials. Their answers were both imprecise and inadequate.

Congressman Ford of Tennessee asked some tough questions, but when they had to persistently engage in a line of interrogation that the witness did not have a mind to deal with, they halted and never pursued it any further.

You are already aware of that, if you have read this far.

28

JAMES R. MALLEY –
SEPTEMBER 20, 1978

On September 20, 1978, James R. Malley testified before the HSCA in Washington, D.C.

Malley was the FBI liaison to the Secret Service when the JFK assassination was under investigation. He played a major role in the four volume FBI report, (known as the Gemberling Report) handed over to President Johnson in December of 1963. (III HSCA 457ff)

In his narration, Chief Counsel G. Robert Blakey addresses the misunderstanding pertaining to jurisdiction that brought the FBI into the investigation of the shooting of the President. Texas didn't seem to understand either, as they did not word the indictment against Oswald properly. It was all about confusion, and the record is incomplete because of the folly and mystification.

The FBI was busy in the heart of the turmoil, having kidnapped the chain of possession, the whole of the evidence and putting it on a plane back to Washington D.C. ***"The problem became moot, however, when***

President Johnson ordered the FBI to enter the case in the interest of national security." (III HSCA 456)

How is national security (a phrase that is repeated so often as to become nauseating) a concern when the sum of the FBI's energies was simply to denounce and revile Lee Harvey Oswald? Evidence initially pointed to him on a cursory level, to be sure, but only on a cursory level. Proverbs 18:17 says, "The one who states his case first *seems right*, **until** the other comes and examines him."

Blakey then read a several-page synopsis of the evolution of the Bureau of Investigation (what it was initially called) to the *Federal* Bureau of Investigation, to the complete purview of J. Edgar Hoover for smashing communists and generating advantageous crime statistics.

In respect to the Warren Commission, Blakey adds, that there were 80 agents on the crime scene within hours, and most completed their work within a month. This group came in and was told to avoid Gordon Shanklin's 75-man office, but instead report directly to Hoover. And they did.

Hoover comes in for condemnation, as Blakey repeats Arthur M. Schlesinger's charge that "Hoover had the racist instincts of a white man who had grown up in Washington when it was still a southern city." (III HSCA 457-460)

The FBI had, prior to the assassination, considered Jack Ruby sufficiently knowledgeable about 'criminal elements in Dallas' to contact him as a potential informant on "nine separate occasions…" (III HSCA 461)

This would make Ruby a legitimate FBI informant, not a potential informant, since he was contacted on nine separate occasions. Blakey's narrations are getting more dramatic, always concluding with a more grandiose and dramatic reason to convict Lee Harvey Oswald.

As stated earlier, Malley, an inspector in the General Investigative Division and principal assistant to Director Alex Rosen, was credited with having "played an important role in putting together the Bureau's *four-volume report* on the assassination given to the President in December 1963." (III HSCA 462)

The cited four-volume report was published in five volumes, giving it a certain literary pedigree rare to such publications. It also doesn't help to believe in the veracity of James Malley, if he can't seem to remember how many volumes a report is that he helped to write.

365

When Malley "was called," he asked Chairman Stokes, "Where do you want me to sit?"

Chairman Stokes replied, "At the witness table right in front of me." (III HSCA 462)

Malley would testify in preliminaries that he heard about the assassination when he was sitting in Alex Rosen's office, on the radio, "to catch, I believe it was the 12:30 news. That was the first time I learned anything about it."

If in Washington, D.C. at the time of the assassination, the first broadcast they could have heard would have transpired at 1:37 p.m. Eastern time. Malley added that he couldn't do anything, but was then in touch with Alan Belmont, and that they both knew the FBI had no jurisdiction. "He [*Belmont*] did indicate to me that he had been in touch with Mr. Shanklin, who was the Special Agent in charge of Dallas...." (III HSCA 463)

Malley later gave testimony that "close to 3:00" (*Eastern time, 2:00 in Dallas*) the General Investigative Division took over, but nothing was done in the way of marching orders: "I don't recall that I received any instructions on that particular afternoon. In reading this statement, Mr. Blakey has mentioned that there was a lot of confusion. There was. Because up until around 7 o'clock, if my memory is correct, there was a definite uncertainty as to what jurisdiction the Bureau had.

> "As I understand it, Belmont had instructed the Dallas office to be certain that they stayed in a position where they would know exactly what was going on and what the Dallas police were doing so that possibly nothing would be interfered with in the way of evidence and nothing lost." (III HSCA 463-464)

Following the shooting of Oswald by Ruby, Assistant Director Courtney Evans (Special Investigative Division) sent Malley to Dallas.

> HSCA Counsel McDonald: "Were you given any instructions on going to Dallas?"
>
> Mr. Malley: "There was no time for instructions. I was told to get the first plane that I could and Evans commented that undoubtedly by the time you arrive in Dallas, Belmont will have a number of instructions for you and he probably will be on the phone waiting for you to arrive."

Mr. McDonald: *"Did you receive any instructions when you got to Dallas?"*

Mr. Malley: *"I did. As I recall, I arrived in the Dallas office somewhere near 8 o'clock, possibly a little later, and was immediately told to get in touch with Mr. Belmont, which I did. Mr. Belmont informed me that the Director had been in touch with President Johnson, that the President was very upset about the number of comments being made by certain individuals in Dallas, mainly the district attorney, the chief of police, and the sheriff's office. He requested that I contact each one of them and see if I couldn't put a stop to the miscellaneous statements they were making relating to the assassination and what investigation was going on."* (III HSCA 464)

Two days after the assassination, the FBI silenced all three of the local authorities, the Dallas police, the Sheriff's office, and the office of the district attorney; all of whom had jurisdiction over the FBI.

Malley added that Police Chief Jesse Curry and Sheriff Bill Decker were both very agreeable and cooperated.

"In speaking with Henry Wade it was a little bit different story. He informed me that he had been a former FBI agent, *which I was well aware of*, that he had been district attorney for a number of years, that he felt that he was qualified to decide what statements he could make and what ones he should not make." (III HSCA 466)

Malley was then read Hoover's "convince the public that Oswald is the real assassin" memo and solicited to remark.

Mr. Malley: *"Not having talked to Mr. Hoover, I certainly am not in a position to say what was going on in his mind. I can give you my interpretation of what he would have meant by it. That would simply mean that because of such a crime of that magnitude, he was talking to either the President or Jenkins, whichever it was, saying that the public needs to be settled down.*

"As far as saying that Oswald is the man and nobody else, I don't think you can take that interpretation from such a one-sentence remark as that." (III HSCA 466)

More discriminatory memory registers with another high-ranking, but retired, Federal agent:

Mr. McDonald: "When you were in Dallas, Mr. Malley, was active consideration being given to investigating the possibility of a conspiracy?"

Mr. Malley: "That existed from the minute it happened. I can't say that I saw a memorandum to this effect or a memorandum to that effect or a telephone call, but I do know it was on everybody's mind, was there somebody else involved. It was an essential part of the investigation to find out.

Mr. McDonald: "These discussions of conspiracy, were they active in the Dallas field office?"

Mr. Malley: "You are asking me a question that dates back 15 years ago and I am not in a position to truthfully answer you and say this happened or that happened in the way of some conversation I had." (III HSCA 477)

No FBI agent was attempting to seek out a conspiracy. Instead, every single agent was afraid that some kind of conspiracy information would be supplied, and it would have opposed the decrees from the headquarters of government.

Rowley said he tried to have the Mexican border closed. How about Texas airports, bus stations, train stations, or roadblocks on the highways? Nothing like this was done that weekend.

The same applies to a number of doctors, both pre- and post-mortem or any medical personal that was either at Parkland, in an attempt to save the President's life, or at Bethesda for the autopsy: had they recalled the truth exactly as it happened, they would have been damaged financially. As far as the people who handled the so-called pristine bullet and couldn't recall it, or put pieces of skull back in place on the President's head; but didn't know where, exactly, on the cranium. That kind of deficiency in memory is complete and utter nonsense.

It was convenient not to remember, so they didn't. You could make an excuse for Mrs. Kennedy, however, that does not explain what [*references to wounds deleted*] occurred more than six months after the assassination, during her June 5, 1964 Warren Commission testimony.

Maybe Clint Hill was extremely traumatized, both in his perception that he got to JFK's limo too late and what he saw, or didn't see, in the back of JFK's head when he did arrive, and then the four horrifying minutes that he hung on for dear life, at high speeds headed toward Parkland hospital.

As for the rest of them, they saw things, they heard things, and they knew things, yet they denied it.

After Malley stated that as soon as he learned of the appointment of the Warren Commission [*November 29, 1963*], he got a ticket for the first plane he could catch to leave Dallas for Washington D.C., so he could have an informal chat with J. Lee Rankin. He was questioned about the believable urgency of the release of the Gemberling Report:

HSCA Counsel McDonald: "Well, the report came out in early [*December*], 1963, prior to the 12th, and the report said in essence that Lee Harvey Oswald killed the President alone.

Do you know why this report was put out so rapidly?

> Mr. Malley: "I can only tell you that based on what I was told in Dallas, they wanted to put it out much faster than it was put out."
>
> Mr. McDonald: "They wanted to."
>
> Mr. Malley: "It was strictly on the basis of letting the President, the Attorney General and a few others [*know*] that they felt needed to know immediately what the facts were as of that time. It was my understanding that information was going to be disseminated long before it was."...
>
> Mr. McDonald: "*Prior to your return to Washington, when you learned you were going to be liaison with the Warren Commission, you must have been aware that they were discussing the formation of such a commission.*"
>
> Mr. Malley: "*I don't remember whether I ever heard that there was a possibility of the Warren Commission being formed or not. I have no way of thinking back and recalling whether I did or didn't.*" (III HSCA 481)...
>
> Mr. McDonald: "With that in mind, could you explain to us how the General Investigative division would have been handling any organized crime aspects, the possibilities, if there were some, to the assassination?"
>
> Mr. Malley: "As briefly as I can, if any name showed up either in the investigation of the assassination of President Kennedy or in the investigation being conducted by the civil rights section of the shooting of Oswald, there is no question in my mind, and you would have to double-check with the supervisors, but if a criminal figure of any known standing had been mentioned or

any criminal figure that had a lot of information in the files on him, I don't have any doubt they would have discussed it with the individual supervisors down in the organized crime unit." (III HSCA 485)

Several organized-crime-linked names came up in the FBI's investigation. There is not proof of any illegal behavior wherein there is an association with the Kennedy assassination and the Mafia, though it also doesn't represent a comprehensive clearing or discharge of culpability.

For Malley to say that no organized crime names surfaced is either untruthful or confirmation that the FBI had a tiny arena they were observing.

Mr. McDonald: "Were you aware of the fact that Mr. Hoover was involved in the, I guess we could say, the blocking of the first choice for the Warren Commission general counsel, a man by the name of Warren Olney. *Were you aware of that situation?*"

Mr. Malley: "*I don't recall that I was ever told.*"

Mr. McDonald: "*Did you learn of it subsequently?*"

Mr. Malley: "*I don't remember it. If I did know, I don't remember it now.*"

Mr. McDonald: "*One of the other items that has come up over the years regarding the Warren Commission and Mr. Hoover was that it has been reported that Mr. Hoover had dossiers or files, on members of the Warren Commission and staffs. Were you aware of this, and I am not referring to security-check files, but just things that we would call a dossier. Are you familiar with that?*"

Mr. Malley: "*I don't recall if I was ever told. It seems to me it would be a normal procedure if you were dealing with a large number of staff members and committee members, that it would be well to know exactly what was transpiring on each one [technical name: spying], from your standpoint of your dealings with him.*

"If one of them said this on a certain date, contradicted himself on another date, certainly, it would be well to have had a record of what was going on. So, when you refer to a file, a dossier on each one, I can well understand why they might have had such a thing."

Mr. McDonald: "Mr. Malley, I just have one further question. And that is with the benefit of hindsight of 15 years and looking back on what went on, in your opinion, was the overall investigation of both the assassination of the President and the murder of Lee Harvey Oswald handled properly?"

Mr. Malley: "Well, I might turn that around just a little bit and say you have had the benefit of the Church Committee investigations, you have had the benefit of the Warren Commission *[if that's a benefit, sign me up for the detriment]* and you had the benefit of all our files. Maybe you could tell me what you feel we did wrong and I will be glad to answer what you think we did wrong."

Mr. McDonald: "Well, we appreciate you trying to turn the table on us—but we are here to ask the questions."

Mr. Malley: "No, I am not trying to turn the tables. I am just asking you what you feel we did wrong and if I am not entitled to that, well, that's that." (III HSCA 486-487)

Representative Dodd seized the moment on Malley's "I don't recalls;" and his remarks that the Bureau's investigation only did the bidding of the Warren Commission when so asked. Malley claimed that all Bureau files were given to the Warren Commission.

Dodd then questioned Mr. Malley about the "Hosty letter," which was not widely known about until the mid-1970s.

Mr. Dodd: "So using that example, there was not a full sense of cooperation in terms of making the information available?"

Mr. Malley: "Well, I would have to say, is there a man in this room who never made a mistake in judgment?"

Mr. Dodd: "I am not suggesting that there is a mistake in judgment. You are talking about a letter, written in the hand of the man who has been accused of assassinating the President, to an FBI agent in Dallas. That is not a mistake in judgment, that is a decision on the part of someone not to turn over a very valid and important piece of evidence."

Mr. Malley: "I can't answer your question any more than saying what I have already." (III HSCA 492)

The double-talk that tracked Kelley and Rowley is a disgusting exhibition of power mongering and it would only get worse when Richard Helms testified.

29

JAMES H. GALE –
SEPTEMBER 20, 1978

On September 20, 1978, James H. Gale testified before the HSCA in Washington, D.C.

Professor Blakey opened with, "The FBI security case on Lee Harvey Oswald was opened on October 31, 1959, after it was learned that he had defected to the Soviet Union and had informed officials at the American Embassy in Moscow that he intended to provide radar secrets to the Russians." (III HSCA 512)

The United States seemingly became aware of Oswald's defection, because he walked into the American Embassy on that date and generated an outburst in the presence of Richard Snyder and John McVickar. Would the United States have discovered about Oswald's defection if he had not gone to the Embassy to put on this demonstration? Didn't the U.S. have assets at places of embarking to Russia, such as Helsinki, Finland?

If Oswald had gone to the American Embassy and claimed he was going to give radar secrets to the Russians, then the obvious question needs to be asked: "Why was he brought back to this country?" And why wasn't he arrested inside the embassy, since he was technically on U.S. soil? More explanation is needed.

If any American had taken a U.S. Marine Corps discharge, (the discharge was given to Oswald way too quickly) because of his mother's supposed grief and misery and then skipped to Russia, it would at best seem odd or suspicious. That raises the ugly thought: If there was no imaginable reason, there had to be a very powerful reason to get him back, and it was not to learn the machinations of a Russian radio factory. It had to be larger than that. Oswald got the military discharge and eventual return to this country, with his Russian wife, way too easily.

After these introductory remarks, the next witness, "Mr. Chairman, is a retired official of the FBI, James H. Gale. Immediately after the assassination of President Kennedy, Director Hoover assigned Mr. Gale to conduct an inspection of the Bureau's performance in the Oswald security case prior to the assassination. Mr. Gale's reports resulted in the censuring of a number of FBI employees." (III HSCA 512)

Gale later concluded that, "Oswald should have been on the security index. His wife should have been interviewed before the assassination and investigation intensified, not held in abeyance, after Oswald contacted Soviet Embassy in Mexico."

> Mr. Genzman: "Did J. Edgar Hoover agree with your conclusions?"
>
> Mr. Gale: "Yes, he did."
>
> Mr. Genzman: "Directing your attention to page 3, can you find any indications there that Mr. Hoover agreed with you?"
>
> Mr. Gale: "He made several observations concerning excuses made by Dallas personnel that they had not interviewed Mrs. Lee Harvey Oswald. Oswald had been drinking to excess and beat up his wife on several occasions. The agent indicated there should be a 60-day cooling-off period and Mr. Hoover said that this was certainly an asinine excuse."

It seems odd to me that you would move or silence 17 agents or superiors, including Assistant Director William C. Sullivan, because they overlooked to talk with the suspect's wife. The document noted that the future suspect was executing violent aggression upon his wife. Lee Oswald should have been talked to right away upon discovering this data, and then on a regular basis subsequently.

> "And also, after Oswald returned from Dallas, [*returned where from Dallas?*] no interview was conducted of Mr. Oswald because they said that they were trying to avoid giving the impression that she was being harassed or hounded because of her immigrant status." (III HSCA 527)

Oswald should have been on the security index because "Field and seat of government employees [*a phrase that quickly becomes sickening*] who handle instant case maintain subject did not come within the security index criteria. Inspector [*Gale himself*] does not agree claiming that Oswald came within the following category. *Investigation has developed information* that individual, though not a member of or participant in the activities of subversive organizations, has anarchist or revolutionary beliefs and is likely to seize upon the opportunity presented by a national emergency to endanger the public safety as shown by overt acts or statements within the last 3 years established through reliable sources, informants, or individuals." [*definition of the security index*]

> Mr. Genzman: "Why did you think that Oswald came within this category?"
>
> Mr. Gale: "I felt that Oswald came within this category because of his contact with the Fair Play for Cuba Committee. He passed out pamphlets [*where did he obtain the "pamphlets"?*]; had a placard around his neck reading "Hands off, viva Fidel.' He had also engaged in certain other activities which I felt came within the purview of the security index. He defected to Russia. He stated he would never return to the United States for any reason. [*So why was he allowed back?*] He stated that he was a Marxist and had advised the Department of State that he would furnish the Soviets any information he had acquired as a Marine aviation electronics expert.
>
> "He also affirmed in writing allegiance to the Soviet Union and said the service in the Marine Corps gave him a chance to observe American imperialism. According to the State Department, he displayed the air of a new 'sophomore' party liner at the time.
>
> "Upon returning to the United States, he displayed a cold, ar-

rogant and generally uncooperative attitude and refused to take the Bureau polygraph tests to determine if he had cooperated with the Soviets or had a current intelligence assignment.

"And he also subscribed to the *Worker*, east coast Communist newspaper, and he had also written a letter to the *Worker* asking for literature saying that he was forming a Fair Play for Cuba Committee in New Orleans and he sent honorary membership to those fighters for peace, Mr. Gus Hall and Mr. Ben Davis, and he was arrested August 9, 1963 [*in New Orleans*], for passing out Fair Play for Cuba pamphlets on the street, and shortly thereafter, he was interviewed on radio and said Russia had gone soft on Communism and that Cuba was the only revolutionary country in the world today.

"So, for those reasons, I felt he should be on the security index."

Mr. Genzman: "Thank you. Did J. Edgar Hoover agree with you that Oswald met the criteria of the security index?"

Mr. Gale: "Yes, he did." (III HSCA 528)

It is seemingly obvious that the FBI does not want to see what and who they were fully aware of: Guy Banister, David Ferrie, and Clay Shaw, suggesting that Oswald was not some Marxist revolutionary, but one of Banister's *agents provocateur*.

Oswald was arrested for "disseminating leaflets", which Inspector James H. Gale knew was not the case. Oswald was arrested because he was assaulted. Period. He was never arrested for passing out the leaflets. Carlos Bringuier and Celso Hernandez, who attacked Oswald, got a free walk, when they should have been charged with loitering, at the least. Lee Oswald did not slip through the FBI cracks. The truth comes out and makes the behavior of Hoover, Gale, et al, obvious for what it was: Nothing.

HSCA Counsel Genzman: "What would have been the result if Oswald had been on the security index?"

Mr. Gale: "I don't think it would have had any result insofar as the assassination was concerned. I don't think it would have prevented the assassination. I don't think it would have had any material effect insofar as the assassination was concerned at all. It was an internal error. They did not have him on there, and I felt

375

he definitely met that criteria and that he should have been on there." (III HSCA 529)

Behind all of Gale's investigation, all of his inferences, and all of his testifying before the House Select Committee, was ultimately a complete and utter charade. "Gale finished his report in about two weeks, without ever leaving Washington or personally interviewing a single agent, supervisor, or headquarters official." (Gerald D. McKnight, *Breach of Trust: How the Warren Commission Failed the Nation and Why*, p. 269)

The dishonor then converts to a cover-up:

> Mr. Genzman: *"Can you explain how they [17 agents and supervisory personnel] were disciplined in general terms?"*
>
> Mr. Gale: *"Some were censured and some were censured and put on probation."*
>
> Mr. Genzman: *"Were any employees suspended or transferred at this time?"*
>
> Mr. Gale: *"Not to my recollection."* (III HSCA 529)

The agents were censured, but their ineptitude had no effect whatsoever. That is the entirety and essence of what this total word-game testimony was about.

Gale then came out with the most obvious statement of the gag rule that could be envisaged from a federal official:

> Mr. Genzman: *"What conclusion did you reach concerning the testimony of FBI witnesses before the Warren Commission?"*
>
> Mr. Gale: *"The conclusion reached by me was that some of this testimony was not adequately handled. We felt that they were testifying in too flamboyant a fashion and were not confining themselves to the facts and testifying the way they were supposed to as FBI personnel."* (III HSCA 541)

The colorful portrayal was stated in later testimony, by S/A Hosty's representation of the Dallas Police station as "Grand Central Station."

The lawbreaker is FBI policy, not the agents, yet it was the agents who garnered the punishment, while FBI policy was still considered holy.

With the KGB, there is no doubt what they would have done. Further escape doors became needed:

> Mr. Genzman: "Would you re-read the last sentence of that paragraph?"
>
> Mr. Gale [*reading*]: "However, it is felt that with Oswald's background we should have had a stop on his passport, *particularly since we did not know definitely whether or not he had any intelligence assignments at that time.*"

For years, a lot of us have felt that Marina Oswald was coerced into saying things or giving ambiguous evidence out of fear that she would be deported to Russia.

It was not an honest concern, as the United States could not deport people to the Soviet Union at that time.

That was part of the wait in the Oswalds' trip to America in 1962, a journey begun in 1961, but delayed because Marina Oswald, the wife of an American citizen, could not be conferred a travel visa from the Soviet Union to the United States.

The reason is that the U.S. State Department has a policy [*243 (g)*] which states that no visas shall be issued to individuals from nations to which the United States could not deport them. Initially, Marina was told to get a visa to a moderately harmless site, like Belgium, and then get the visa to the U.S. from there. Eventually, to speed up the Oswalds' trip back to the U.S., the State Department waived regulation 243 (g).

It is believed by most researchers that Oswald had intelligence assignments, but not known if any of them were active at the time he went pursuing a passport. Gale is obliged to deny it:

> Mr. Genzman: "Mr. Gale, according to some individuals, this sentence implies that the FBI did at some point determine that Oswald had connections with some U.S. intelligence agency."
>
> Mr. Gale: "That is not what I meant. What I meant in writing that sentence was that we did not know definitely whether he had any intelligence assignments at the time, but I felt in my mind that he possibly could have had intelligence assignments based on his Russian background, his defection to Russia, and the fact that he would not take the polygraph examination, and also because of his activities with the Fair Play for Cuba Committee. However, I

had no concrete information to establish any of those possibilities." (III HSCA 542)

In one breath Gale says, "That is not what I meant," but then affirms
it was precisely what he meant, and then he defaults with the usual defector resumé entries. The FBI had more to gain when Ruby shot Oswald than anyone else.

> Mr. Genzman: "Mr. Gale, was there ever any internal inspection
> of the Bureau's investigation of the assassination of President
> Kennedy?"

> Mr. Gale: No; I was never called upon to make any investigation
> of the Bureau's investigation of President Kennedy. All of my in-
> vestigation here was confined to the pre-security investigation of
> Mr. Oswald and I conducted no investigation of anything that
> was done insofar as the investigation of the assassination." (III
> HSCA 542)

The deception has been passed to a new generation.

It was later discovered, after the publication of the Warren Report,
that the majority of agents and supervisors concerned, which ranges
well beyond the 17 who were disciplined, did not believe that Oswald
belonged on the security index,

> "and Mr. Belmont took the position that rather than saying all of
> these employees were mistaken in their judgment, the criteria
> should be changed. Mr. Hoover took the position that they were
> more than mistaken." (III HSCA 547)

Gale didn't know what other agents did with it, because he didn't
work for other agencies.

Beyond that, there was "I don't recall," or "I can't remember back
that far." When he couldn't say that he didn't remember, he was pre-
dictably unclear, or denied the question being asked by using the exact
wording of the question being asked. To quote Socrates concerning the
Sophists of his day, "They made the worse appear the better reason."

30

PRESIDENT GERALD R FORD –
SEPTEMBER 21, 1978

On Sept.21, 1978, former President Gerald R. Ford testified before the HSCA Washington, D.C.

F ormer President Gerald R. Ford requested he be allowed to make an opening statement:

> "I trust the committee understands my particular situation. I am most willing to respond to any and all questions relating to my service on the Warren Commission and related matters, but I must respectfully refuse to answer questions on the principle of Executive Privilege that relate to the period from August 9, 1974 to January 20, 1977, the time that I served as President of the United States." (HSCA III 562)

This superficial refusal anticipates that Ford has already ruled out answering specific questions. Once again, the fix seems to be in. If Ford isn't going to be able to answer certain questions, then why have him testify? What concerning the Warren Commission and Lee Oswald

379

would he not be able to answer? After all, the Commission that he sat on said Oswald performed the crime by himself and had no confederates at large, so what is there to hide?

> "The **conclusions** and recommendations of the Commission **were unanimous**. (1) We believe the Commission report, despite questions that have been raised over the past 14 years, was an authoritative document covering one of the most tragic episodes in the history of the United States. (2) *In my own case, the staff of the committee has submitted a set of questions and requested responses in specific areas of inquiry. I will be glad to respond to the questions as propounded by Mr. Cornwell or members of the committee and I thank you for the opportunity to make my opening statement.*" (III HSCA 562)

Was it pondered by the Commission and was there unanimous support of the *alteration made by Ford in the President's wounds*; admitted to, and published, on July 3, 1997, under the headline, 'Ford Altered JFK Report on Bullet.'

The approval of the conclusions of the Warren Report were not undisputed. Some members opposed, while one refused to sign the report until language was changed that was agreeable, especially concerning the single bullet theory. The original findings simply were not unanimous.

What was the bigger sin, the killing of the President or the disgrace that passed for an exploration into that killing? And how many other witnesses were given the questions in advance and then allowed to read from planned, scripted answers? You might be surprised.

Ford passionately defends every conceivable action of the Warren Commission, though the Church Committee had given warnings that some agencies were not supportive – and others were, at times, virtually combative. Non-answers, or reaffirmations of the Warren Report, are the standard responses by Ford.

> Gerald D. McKnight's book, *Breach of Trust: How the Warren Commission Failed the Nation and Why* is an excellent and accurate, not to mention documented account of the Warren Commission because it does not rely on the faith people have in the Warren Report's kind of "scholarship," that Ford depended upon during the course of his prepared – oh, let's just say it –*scripted* testimony.

Ex-president Ford stated: "I do not believe that if there was any association between some CIA officers and members of the underworld that that would have changed the conclusion of the Warren Commission.

However, had the Warren Commission known of any assassination plots directed against Castro, this might have affected the extent of the Commission inquiry. In other words, if we had known of any assassination plans or attempts by an agency of the Federal Government, it certainly would have required that the Commission extend its inquiry into those kinds of operations by an agency of the Federal Government.

But from what I have known of those plots, what I have read or heard, I don't think they, in and of themselves, would have changed the conclusions of the Commission." (III HSCA 570)

With respect to assassination plots against Fidel Castro and other foreign leaders, there was a gentleman sitting in the room during Ford's time on the Warren Commission, who was involved in creating and developing those proposals. That would be Allen Dulles, former head of the CIA.

Congressman Devine did bring up a thought-provoking point, saying,

"if such a thing would occur they would go through the same autopsy procedures as they did back in 1963; whoever is President would be taken to Bethesda Hospital, and he would be looked at probably by clinical pathologists rather than forensic pathologists. It is my understanding also, Mr. President, that the Metropolitan Police Department here has anticipated that type of need for any so-called VIP procedure where they have everything available, they have videotapes available, they have forensic pathologists available. That leads up to this question, Mr. President, do you in your capacity as former President, as a former Member of the Congress that has been deeply involved in the Warren Commission and the assassination problems, do you have any recommendations that you would like to make to this committee either legislatively or procedurally as it may relate to an assassination like this occurring in the future?"

Former President Ford: "Well, No. 1, I am glad that some plans have been laid to maybe make the procedure in this case of another tragedy in better, more professional hands. I am talking about the autopsy. From what I read, this committee has determined that the autopsy procedure in Bethesda was not conducted by the experts or professionals in that area. That was of course unfortunate, and I trust that what is now laid out would eliminate whatever the difficulties were at the time of President Kennedy's assassination." (III HSCA 580)

If Gerald Ford is now coming upon the insight that Kennedy's autopsy was the most bungled forensic procedure in the history of the United States government, how can he sit there and explain each and every decision reached by the Warren Commission?

Congressman Dodd of Connecticut read a memo into the record from Cartha "Deke" DeLoach, an Assistant Director of the FBI in 1963. The memo was dated December 12, 1963:

"I had a long talk this morning with Congressman Gerald R. 'Jerry' Ford R. Michigan in his office. He asked that I come up to see him. Upon arriving, he told me he wanted to talk in the strictest of confidence. This was agreed to.

Ford indicated that he would keep me thoroughly advised as to the activities of the Commission. He stated this would have to be done on a confidential basis, however, he thought it should be done. He also asked if he could call me from time to time and straighten out questions in his mind concerning our investigation. I told him by all means he should do this. He reiterated that our relationship would, of course, remain confidential."

Ford indicated that the information was accurate, "and yet you said that you had terminated your relationship with Mr. DeLoach in terms of these kinds of meetings after this December 17 meeting you had with him?" (III HSCA 585)

I highly doubt the relationship ever ended. If so, there certainly would have been a passionate memo to Hoover, and an even more ferocious reply from Hoover, that some dirt would be found with regard to Ford.

The House Select Committee brought in the three existing Warren Commission members, Ford, McCloy, and Cooper, so they could share their observations.

Ford was probed about supposed meetings with Cartha DeLoach during his Warren Commission tenure, and he committed congressional perjury when he stated he and DeLoach had only met once, before the Commission started, and it was only a social call. The record does not support this. The HSCA did not push him on his response; and let him exit in majestic fashion.

The data that Hoover had in regard to Ford, Boggs, and Warren may well support their selections to Johnson's Commission. It is an easy picture to envision where Johnson and Hoover had a private meeting and looked through a list of contenders whose resumés had been compromised by Hoover.

Ford's abilities to control the FBI, though a different Bureau after the death of Hoover, had shown his inclination to be a team player by his book of the assassination that used *classified materials* to remind the American public of Oswald's guilt.

He forever fraternalized himself by pardoning Nixon, which doomed any possibility of his actually winning an election in 1976, before any charges were brought against Nixon.

Those acts must be calculated against the eulogy provided for Ford by George H.W. Bush, who said that Gerald Ford's signature on the Warren Report was the everlasting proof of the document's honesty. Sure.

31

JOHN SHERMAN COOPER –
(W/JOHN J. MCCLOY)
SEPTEMBER 21, 1978

On September 21, 1978, John Sherman Cooper and John J. McCloy, gave testimony before the HSCA in Washington, D.C.,

There was a bit of unfinished business remaining from the testimony of former President Gerald Ford:

Chairman Stokes: "Would you have identified for the record, counsel, the gentleman who has so ably assisted President Ford and who will be assisting these gentlemen?"

Mr. Cornwell: "It is Mr. Dave Belin. He was a member of the Warren Commission staff and he has been here as counsel for the President."

Mr. McCloy: "He is not acting as counsel for me. I know him and have great respect for him; but he is not here as my counsel." (III HSCA 599)

House Select Counsel Cornwell indicated he had only one question for Senator Cooper, and that it was based on a recent television broadcast in which Cooper stated that there had been dissents among Warren Commission members regarding the so-called "magic bullet."

Prior to Cooper's response, he read a prepared statement, finding harmony on certain details mentioned in the testimony of former President Ford. Of course.

Once again, present in the hearing room were numerous people who all had access to similar data, just like during the Warren Commission hearings.

It was not unusual, in Warren Commission hearings, for several witnesses to be present at once, even though only one was being questioned. Case in point: The pathologists, Humes, Finck, and Boswell. Humes was asked the majority of the questions, and then Finck was asked a few questions, and Boswell was asked eleven questions, and they all revolved around, "And you agree, then, with Commander Humes' statement?" This should raise serious questions about propriety.

Nothing is learned this way. If there were three people who had been in the autopsy room, you have three sets of perceptions. But when you put them together in the room, you are lessened by two and reduced to one, as it was Humes' testimony and the tacit agreement of the other two that was put in the record.

It wasn't done correctly in 1964 and it is not happening in 1978. Cooper and McCloy were present for Ford's testimony, and no doubt had the occasion to read his written answers, so there was a limited if not a zero possibility that either of them was going to testify to something contrary.

This is the same strategy used by the Commission these two men served on. Get the witnesses in the room together. If they testified separately, without knowing what each other said, there just might be contradictions, and that would not be good.

For all of the talk about the HSCA being a huge upgrading over the Warren Commission, there were times in which it fell back to basic Warren Commission procedure, and most likely for the same point: Keep the conspiracy genie in the bottle.

In a court of law, a witness cannot be in the courtroom when other witnesses are testifying. Marguerite Oswald, always an annoyance, was in the courtroom during the Ruby trial. Although she was not asked to testify, her mere existence could have created an empathy vote, so the defense attorneys subpoenaed her, hence dismissing her from the courtroom.

Neither the Warren Commission nor the House Select Committee on Assassinations was a legally constituted court of law.

Cooper eventually answered:

> "We did have disagreements at times in the commission, and, as I have noted, I think the chief debate grew out of the question as to whether there were two shots or three shots and whether the same shot that entered President Kennedy's **neck** [*still not getting it right, 15 years later*] penetrated the body of Governor Connally." ...

> "This question troubled me greatly. If not the first witness, one of the first witnesses was Governor Connally of Texas." Cooper indicated that he recalled Connally's testimony "very clearly," and he repeated the familiar Connally invocation, including an observation worth repeating, "***that the rifle was a perfect rifle for that kind of firing...***"

> "I must say, to be very honest about it, that I held in my mind during the life of the Commission, as I have since, that there were three shots and that a separate shot struck Governor Connally. It was determined, as shown in the report of the Commission, which I can read to you, but I know you are familiar with the report. It states there was disagreement on this issue, particularly as the subject was debated, that there were differences of opinion about it.

> The **majority** [but not all] believed that the same shot struck both President Kennedy and Governor Connally..." (III HSCA 600)

He has just made a perjurer out of former President Gerald R. Ford, who stated,

> "The conclusions and recommendations of the Commission were unanimous." (III HSCA 562)

Cooper is quoting Connally reasonably well. However, the logic destroys all conceivable ideas of the single bullet theory. Cooper has Connally saying that he wanted to look at the President over his left shoulder.

The bullet that was fired from the sixth floor of the Texas School Book Depository was going from right to left, at approximately a 12-degree angle. If the President was to Connally's left, looking at them from the rear, (where he would have to be for Connally to look at him over his left shoulder) a bullet going right to left through Kennedy could not possibly have then moved in such a way that it hit Connally in his right shoulder area. It's the 90-degree turn problem, only this time, the bullet had to make two such turns.

From this point forward, anything that Senator Cooper would add would be at the least *misinformed*. His prefatory statement regarding Connally: "*If not the first witness, one of the first witnesses, was Governor Connally of Texas.*"

Actually, the first witness called to testify was Marina Oswald, on February 3, 1964. Governor Connally became the fifty-second witness, when he and Mrs. Connally testified together. Not even close. I may be nitpicking, but I lean toward accuracy.

I honestly wouldn't expect Senator Cooper to recall this, though he was on the Commission. I can see how he could forget the order of witnesses. This is either bad memory or simply not being attentive, but I wouldn't put it in the category of sinister.

Nevertheless, Connally didn't show up until 78 days after the first witness. Cooper was accurate, as he was listed as present for Connally's testimony.

Cooper did not testify to any great extent. Counsel Gary Cornwell essentially put the same form of "what were your concerns" immediately to McCloy:

> Mr. Cornwell: "...but I would like to ask you about one subject matter. In an interview with our staff previously, and I hope I am quoting you substantially accurately, you expressed the view that the Commission did have enough time to reach its conclusions, but that you were greatly disturbed by the rushed composition and writing of the report. I wonder if you would explain that to us and comment upon it, if you would.

> Mr. McCloy: "I will be very glad to. I would like to read a very brief statement from some notes about my general attitude toward this examination and the conclusions which we arrived at 14 years ago.

> With respect to this particular question that you put to me, there
> was a book called I think, *Rush to Judgment,* or some title, and
> I had that in mind when I received this inquiry. There was no
> 'rush to judgment.' We came to a judgment in due course. There
> were some questions of style in regard to the preparation of the
> report where I would like to have had sort of a lawyer-like chance
> to make it a little more clear, from my point of view, as to what
> our conclusions were; but I had no question whatever about the
> substance of the report.
>
> As I say, it had only been a matter of style and I had a feeling at
> the end we were rushing a little bit the last few days to get to print
> rather than to arrive at any conclusions. We had already arrived
> at our conclusions. It was just a matter of putting them into good
> form. (III HSCA 601)

McCloy added to the irrelevant by proclaiming the dedication to the
truth of everyone who came near the inquiry. He handed out compli-
ments to everyone who participated, from the maligned Dallas police
force, to the FBI sleuths and those of the CIA who were called to assist,
and the Secret Service and a number of other agencies.

> "And, lastly, I would like to do justice to the Commission itself
> and its staff in arriving at these conclusions. These factors have
> not been sufficiently stressed either here, so far as I know, and
> indeed, in any of the commentaries I have seen over the years."
> (III HSCA 602)

When McCloy ceased patting himself on the back, Cooper took
over, and made a few positive comments, not as praising as McCloy,
but positive. He suggested that the CIA was not as forthcoming as it
perhaps could have been. This is true.

McCloy said about Allen Dulles:

> "You know the experience of Allen Dulles. He gave permission,
> to assassinate foreign leaders. He also had knowledge, while on
> the Warren Commission of plans to assassinate Fidel Castro of
> Cuba."

It would have also been worthy of a sentence or two to mention
that Dulles was separated from the Directorship of the CIA by the man
whose death he was investigating, and by coincidence, he was appoint-

ed on November 29, 1963 to the Warren Commission, two years to the day after he had been fired by JFK.

Both McCloy and Cooper were asked if they made private advances to the FBI regarding the assassination, and both denied that any such movement had been considered or even contemplated.

> McCloy concluded: "I do make this final statement. I don't think many people have ever read the *Report*. Who has read the 26 volumes of this case? How many even read the summary? If you read the summary, it takes a long time. (III HSCA 609-610)

It is the very reading of the 26 volumes that is the most convincing case for conspiracy. I read as much of them as I could after they were published, though not for a few years, since I was still quite young at the time. When I finally got to High School, as I began reading them, I possessed neither my own set nor spare money to purchase one of the sets at the time. I took several fourteen-mile rides to the Niles Library, which not only had the volumes, but a very good section of JFK assassination literature. I read the volumes, before I actually moved to Niles in the mid-eighties. I also read every conspiracy and non-conspiracy book that I could get my hands on. Since then, I have obtained a set of the volumes, as have a lot of researchers. I've gone through them in their entirety at least 3 times over the years, with some sections gone over many times. I have done the same with the HSCA volumes as well.

John Sherman Cooper, the closest thing to a friend that Jack Kennedy had on the Warren Commission, is wrong when he says no one reads the volumes. Allen Dulles made similar statements. Several people have read the volumes.

McCloy furnished a personal awareness referencing a bullet wounding event that he saw, and how his perceptions of that occurrence permitted him to invest undying faith in the single-bullet theory and not have any struggle with the films that showed the President's head move violently backward when, supposedly, hit by a shot from behind. Okay.

I would remind Mr. McCloy that John Kennedy was only hit in the soft tissues, with no bone being struck by a missile (at least no bone in the first wound), while Connally had a rib shattered, a large wrist bone shattered, and a bullet fragment lodge in his femur.

Connally was shot in the wrist, not the hand, demonstrating McCloy's misunderstanding of the events. It is true that Connally didn't know that he had been shot in the wrist, and the reason for this lack of knowledge, is that he was already going into shock from his first wound when he was later hit with a separate bullet and shot through the wrist.

Watch the Zapruder film and only look at Connally. He is hit c. Z-235 and then again just after Z-313, which is the fatal head shot to President Kennedy, c. 327/328,

McCloy will be very disappointed with the HSCA's conclusions, even though he was sent there, to quickly try and hold together the crumbling official verdict. It would soon change drastically.

McCloy gave the pre-packaged, neatly scripted answers, which included the head-scratching curiosity that over 80% of Americans held the findings of the Warren Commission to be somewhere between undependable and disproven.

I did detect words of truth in McCloy's statement; that the FBI did a lousy job, and that you don't always know when you've been shot. True, but Governor Connally certainly would have known, according to his doctors.

When Mr. Sawyer from Michigan was hailing his conversion to the single-bullet theory, he commented about a picture [film] taken on the opposite side of the street where "Mr. Magruder" [he meant Mr. Zapruder, I assume] was standing.

While Sawyer was convinced that the single-bullet theory was a reality, he might have had trouble blending that data with the HSCA's medical panel, which determined that the bullet that entered the President's back, not his neck, traveled in an upward direction of 11 degrees.

If that was correct, then the bullet did not hit Governor Connally. The bullet most likely exited the vehicle over the windshield.

The autopsy pictures are important to the case, obviously, and should have been entered into evidence, though they were not by the Warren Commission or the House Select Committee on Assassinations.

Perhaps unknown to both Sawyer and McCloy was that Earl Warren's own father was bludgeoned to death in 1938, so his feelings about horrible photographic portrayals might have been somewhat heightened and possibly influenced his decision not to put the autopsy pictures in the record.

Justice demanded that he put a 1938 murder behind him and study the medical evidence. Many would claim the autopsy photos should have been published, and to this date, almost 60 years after the fact, the U.S. Government has never published any of them.

By contrast, the X-rays are not in any manner gruesome, or the kinds of things that would give one nightmares.

McCloy speaks as if he is an authority on the autopsy photographs, though it was stated that only Earl Warren saw any photographic work taken from the autopsy, and then it was only one photograph (which one, we don't know). The photograph allegedly gave Warren night-mares for some time, perhaps because of how it indirectly related to what happened to his father.

Sawyer never asked a question. He simply re-stated his own beliefs in order to re-invigorate the single-bullet theory, and congratulated McCloy for knowing the difficulty inherent in proving a negative to a certainty.

This is the old boys' network at its foulest.

The Warren Commission also had the right to require testimony; but chose not to exercise that right. Robert Surrey, who did publishing work for right-wing organizations and printed the "Wanted for Treason" cir-culars, stated on 32 occasions that he refused to answer the question posed on the grounds that the answer might tend to incriminate him. He got away with it. He was even told he didn't have to respond to any of the questions if he didn't want to.

If there are two certainties in the Kennedy assassination, it is that JFK was killed and the second one is that there would be no smoking gun in any agency's file that Lee Oswald was on their payroll as an in-formant.

Cooper's point about not many people reading the 26 volumes is well-taken, but it is also self-defeating. There were 26 volumes to dis-courage people from ever imagining the depths of the Commission's work.

Ruby's mother's dental plates?

Oswald's pubic hairs?

Really?

Sixty-six pages of unintelligible tracings from Jack Ruby's polygraph examination which, might just as well have been an examination of any-one.

Of course nobody read that garbage, because you couldn't. I have read those volumes three times and still refer to them when the need arises, including research for this book.

The reason I have read them was simply that I thought if I gave them enough attention, I might find something worthwhile. Not very often. Though I am reminded of something Mortimer Adler once said about the "Great Books." There is more error in them than truth, but that is important, because you don't understand truth unless you see the error that it corrects.

The Commissioners did not attend the vast majority of the Hearings themselves, and that makes me question any statements they made concerning investigation.

Their appointments were broadcast, on November 29th of 1963. They heard the first testimony sixty-six days later, a rather long interruption and time for a trail to go cold.

They did not visit the crime scene until late May, more than six months after the crime, and although the entire Commission did not go to Dallas, it's outrageous that none of them got there until they were writing the chapters of the report.

Ford was hailed by the House, where he had served a mere five years earlier, with Chairman Stokes noting, at the end of his testimony, "As one of your former colleagues here in the House, it has been an honor to have had you here."

This, of course, was before Ford's 1997 revelation that he moved President Kennedy's wounds in order to more neatly accord and yield clarification with the Warren Commission's findings. Shameful.

32

J. Lee Rankin –
September 21, 1978

On September 21, 1978, J. Lee Rankin testified before the HSCA in Washington, D.C. He was the former general counsel of the Warren Commission.

Mr. Klein began the questioning:

HSCA Counsel Klein: *"Was there any discussion at that time about the goals of the Commission?"*

Mr. Rankin: *"The only discussion* was that we were to try to *find* out who *the assassin* was and whether there was anyone else involved in it beyond the person whom we found to be the one who committed the act."* (III HSCA 613)

Rankin couldn't remember the five different categories, so he asked Mr. Klein to list them for him:

"Well, I wouldn't wish to miss any of them. If you have them, if you will just recite them, I can tell you whether they are correct or not."

Mr. Klein: "The facts of the assassination, the identity of *the assassin, the background of Lee Harvey Oswald*, conspiracy, and the death of *Lee Harvey Oswald*. Are those the five areas?"

Mr. Rankin: "That is correct." (III HSCA 613)

If your aim is to find *the* assassin, and two of the areas are directly related to Lee Harvey Oswald, it is easy to see what their conclusion will be.

There were groupings of the staff to explore different aspects of the case; "facts of the assassination," "Lee Harvey Oswald," and the "death of Lee Harvey Oswald," but a possible conspiracy was not even considered. They avoided conspiracy and never seemed to entertain that as a likelihood. It doesn't appear that they even considered looking into anyone except Lee Harvey Oswald.

Mr. Klein: "In 1964, at the conclusion of the investigation, what was your opinion of the performance of the Federal Bureau of Investigation?"

Mr. Rankin: "Well, as to their cooperation with us, I thought it was good. We were critical about some of the things that happened about alerting the Secret Service, about information that they knew about and we learned they had not informed the Secret Service about. That was all in the report.

But as far as not being frank and open with us and reveal what information they had, we assumed that they did that. I did, at least, and I think the Commission did."

Mr. Klein: "You have partially anticipated my next question, which is, today, 1978, with what you learned over the course of the years, what is your opinion with respect to the performance of the Federal Bureau of Investigation?"

Mr. Rankin: "Well, I have been very much disappointed with some of the things that have been revealed and I have, of course, no personal knowledge about those matters. I have just read them in the press from the reports of investigations by the Senate committee and others...

"It seemed to me from my experiences that they were more professional than to say anything of that character. When I learned that they were supposed to have known about plans for an assassination that were underway in the CIA, according to the investigation of the Senate committee, and did not report it to us and that we didn't receive any such information from the CIA, it was quite disheartening to me to know that that kind of conduct was a part of the action of our intelligence agencies at that high level."

Mr. Klein: "I only asked the question as applying to the FBI, but your answer applies to the CIA and the FBI; is that correct?"

Mr. Rankin: "I think it was our experience as it is revealed by investigation on the Senate committee. With the CIA it is worse than with the FBI because the FBI apparently did not originate the assassination plans [*against Castro*...] and apparently the CIA did. So, the FBI only happened on to them or were informed about such plans and then did not convey them to us.

But the CIA, they were apparently involved in them and did not alert us to the situation at all, give us any opportunity to take the action that we should have had the chance to, or investigating that type of information."

Mr. Klein: "As General Counsel of the Warren Commission, you had no knowledge whatsoever of the assassination plots against Fidel Castro?"

Mr. Rankin: "That is true, I did not." (III HSCA 614—615)

It is curious that the General Counsel, the ambassador of the event, seemed to indicate that it wasn't as clear as the former President of the United States or the other Warren Commission emissaries

How about the Hosty note? That wasn't withheld, as FBI secured it and took it directly to the toilet. Literally.

What seems to tell us everything we need to know about Lee Harvey Oswald is the commercial from Klein's Sporting Goods containing the declaration for the $12.95 Mannlicher-Carcano, as well as descriptions for trailers for numerous other, higher-quality rifles that had very positive portrayals scripted about them, but the Mannlicher-Carcano did not.

It would never be the weapon of choice for someone who is going to shoot anybody, least of all the President of the United States.

Mr. Klein: "Were there any pressures exerted not to find a *foreign* conspiracy because of the dire consequences that such a conspiracy might have for war or peace?"

Mr. Rankin: "None at all. There was a conscientious effort throughout to try to discover anything that would reveal that there was a conspiratorial action about the assassination of the President. ... I think that they did an adequate job in what happened in the Soviet Union and whether there was any involvement there was necessarily a very difficult matter because of the closed nature of their society. Our opportunity, even with the best penetration that we were able to learn of by our own intelligence people, to reach within that society and discover material that could be relied on, was quite sparse to say the least." (III HSCA 615-616)

Rankin's statement, that there wasn't any pressure to not find a foreign conspiracy, seems to be at odds with the traditional story of this scenario. It was stated that Earl Warren left the White House with tears in his eyes, knowing that there was a possibility of a nuclear war that could kill 39 – 40 million Americans, if he didn't accept the position to lead the commission and convince the general public of no such situation.

Congressman Sawyer: "Did you make any effort either as a staff, or, to your knowledge, as a Commission, to determine just where Oswald was going at the time he was intercepted by Officer Tippit?"

Mr. Rankin: "We speculated on it but speculations aren't worth much."

Mr. Sawyer: "Did you come to any reasonable hypothesis as to where he was going?"

Mr. Rankin: "We all agreed that he was on his way to try to escape, but where we didn't know, and everything from that point on was just one person's guess against another's."

Mr. Sawyer: "Of course, I presume you were aware that the direction in which he was heading at the time he was confronted by Tippit kind of led to nowhere with respect to either escape routes or anything, just out in the neighborhood?"

Mr. Rankin: "We didn't think that was really the complete answer because at that point he was very hard pressed and we thought he was more in the posture of just running."

Mr. Sawyer: "We..., did you find out that Jack Ruby's apartment was about two or three blocks up the street, also on the direct route he was going?"

Mr. Rankin: "Yes."

Mr. Sawyer: "Did you also find out that in the Dallas newspaper announcement of the President's visit, that on the same page was the identity of an informant who had substantially destroyed the Communist Party in Texas by informing to the FBI and he was identified as living just about two blocks up the street, also on the direct route he was going?"

Mr. Rankin: "I don't recall that I was aware of that." (III HSCA 617-618)

Rankin is stating that when Oswald happened on to Tippit, that he killed him because he was on his way to escape.

Logic please? Oswald could have used the bus stop in front of his rooming house at 1026 North Beckley? Why didn't he? Oswald's encounter was only nine-tenths of a mile away on foot. This is far from an ideal getaway plan. Was he on his way to meet someone? We will never know, but something is a little muddled here.

The question to Rankin about where Oswald was going was ridiculous to begin with. They didn't find any maps on him and we aren't even sure how well he knew the area. He had become proficient with the Elsbeth Street and nearby W. Neely Street neighborhoods quite well, but that was not going to help him here.

Mr. Sawyer: "*Based on the testimony of those doctors and the evidence developed, they were, for example, like 4 inches off on the point of entry of the head wound, which, of course, projected, would be a horrendous error.*"

Mr. Rankin: "*I don't know that. I have heard that your staff discovered that and that Dr. Humes has admitted he was that much off. At the time it was, and since, until I heard that, it was difficult to imagine that a man conducting an autopsy could make that kind of a mistake when he was observing the body that he was examining, and so forth.*" (III HSCA 619)

No comment necessary.

Mr. Sawyer: "Did you ever receive any advice from the FBI about the 17 agents that were subjected to administrative discipline because of their mishandling of the pre-assassination information about Ruby—not Ruby, Oswald?"

Mr. Rankin: "I think that is very shocking too. I think we were entitled to that information and a frank disclosure by Mr. Hoover that he felt they should be disciplined and why, and that we should have been able to go into that and try to discover whether it had any effect on our work." (III HSCA 620)

Rankin added,

"My relations with Mr. Hoover deteriorated a great deal after the report came out, and I was quite surprised to learn that he took this position with the agents in light of his severe criticism of me and the report, but it appeared to me that this action was quite confirmatory of some of the criticism that the Commission had made in the report about some of the failures of the FBI in its liaison with the Secret Service." (III HSCA 626 - 627)

When he was asked about Yuri Nosenko, Rankin suggested that the CIA claimed Nosenko was a plant and would only be out to deceive the commission:

"I had nobody on the staff and I had no Commissioner with such expertise. I do not think Allen Dulles could have done it." (III HSCA 621)

With regard to the Warren Commission holding open hearings [*they did hold one, at Mark Lane's request, as he was the witness*], Congressman Sawyer commented, "As some people who watched it said that Mr. Lane had done for the legal profession what the Boston Strangler did for the door-to-door salesman." (III HSCA 621)

I have no idea what he means here. It doesn't seem to make any sense at all; but here we also see the infamous "some people said" canard.

Congressman Edgar: "Did he [*Hoover*] resent the fact that you were double checking the FBI's investigation?"

Mr. Rankin: "Every agent that I had anything to do with when I did that resented it. But I just had to do it anyway and I kept on doing it. Of course, that didn't help with any of them. They soon could find that out."

Rankin indicated that what he anticipated and thought the FBI would do was not what they actually did. In the process, he controverted a good number of federal witnesses and three former Warren Commission members. (III HSCA 640 and *passim*)

Rankin is saying that the Warren Commission started out with an objective outlook for truth, and not with faith in the FBI's conclusions, as described in the Gemberling Report of December 9, 1963, which stated that Oswald was the lone assassin and there was no conspiracy.

After using the FBI as their chief investigators, however, the Commission determined the same, in September 1964, as the FBI had on December 9, 1963.

Seems like a convenient coincidence.

The firing time is unstated in the recreation tests concerning the alleged assassin's ability to make the shots on November 22, 1963. The FBI tests are subject to the same human fragilities that all manner of tests are; as they only measured the amount of time necessary to work the bolt on the Mannlicher-Carcano rifle and re-chamber a round in order to fire it, in 2.3 seconds.

The FBI avoided any tests of the time interlude between the firing of a shot, the 2.3 seconds of working the bolt, plus the time necessary to re-acquire the moving target, either with the use of the iron sights or, with the telescopic sight. You will never see those statistics.

The shooter had the gun outside the window, according to one or more witnesses. Once a shot is fired through the small opening, the gun had to be moved to work the bolt, and then the moving target has to be re-acquired. That process is not the FBI time of 2.3 seconds. Josiah Thompson, in *Six Seconds in Dallas*, re-published that chart to show its absurdity.

Rankin spoke like there never was a variance with the staff. *If everyone agrees, someone is lying.*

The foolish answers emerged throughout Rankin's testimony, even in respect to the autopsy photos and X-rays.

Rankin said the Kennedy family did not want the photos and X-rays published. Soon after the calamity, it was something worth giving thought to.

The autopsy medical evidence was deceitful, despite Rankin's assertions. There were five doctors involved (including Dr. Karnei and Dr. Ebersole), plus technicians, plus Sibert and O'Neill, yet only one doctor testified, and that was Commander James J. Humes. He was subsequently revised by the Clark Panel, the HSCA, and Gerald Ford. Drs. Finck and Boswell were simply asked to confirm Humes' testimony.

Boswell was asked a total of eleven questions.

The rest were never heard from.

X-rays are harmless items. The whole argument against making the X-rays public is silly.

Mr. Rankin should have been asked what Chief Justice Warren meant when he told reporters that there were things that would not be revealed in your lifetime. And, secondly, if full disclosure is your promise, then can you explain why the Commission placed 357 cubic feet of materials in the National Archives, not to be viewed until 2039, *seventy-five years* after they were placed there.

If Oswald was seeking attention, then why depart the TSBD, when he could have just sat down on the boxes and waited for someone to find and arrest him. He could have been led outside and shouted his guilt to the rooftops.

This did not happen. Instead, Oswald was almost instantly opposed by a police officer, who attested to his calm state, even with a gun pointed at him. The attention-seeking assassin would have gladly conceded. But he did not. An innocent person would have responded to the manifestation of a gun.

But Oswald did nothing at all.

But something has gone very wrong. A taxi-cab ride, and home to get a weapon for self-defense. It had to be for self-defense, because it was not on him when he committed the murder.

Then when cornered by police, something was again extremely wrong, with the attention-seeking killer doubling down by killing a police officer.

In a number of brief exchanges, the attention-seeking assassin denied all guilt. He simply said, "I'm just a patsy."

Oswald was then put before television cameras for everyone to see, and he once again rejected all charges, stating he had not even heard about shooting a policeman.

The voice of Jesse Curry in the background corrected him: "Yes, you have."

Oswald seemed to grow pale in gloomy fear. But no admission of guilt and he was pulled away.

Thirty-six hours after his brief press conference, Oswald was again displayed in front of live television cameras and in a matter of seconds he would be dead. Where was this desire for notoriety and fame? It was nowhere.

He would never see his two children again.

To claim Oswald was seeking attention or smirking is simply a fantasy world that the Warren Commission knew all too well.

33

NICHOLAS KATZENBACH –
SEPTEMBER 21, 1978

On Sepy. 21, 1978, Nicholas Katzenbach gave testimony before the HSCA in Washington, D.C.

Nicholas Katzenbach filled in for Robert Kennedy during his absence from the Justice Department, after the death of President Kennedy.

Congressman McKinney turned to the subject of the famous memorandum sent by Katzenbach to Johnson's aid Bill Moyers on November 25, 1963.

"I would like to start out by asking the question as to your exerting tremendous pressure right after the assassination to get the FBI report out and to get a report in front of the American people. This is somewhat evidenced by your memorandum to Mr. Moyers of November 25. *What was your basic motivation in looking for such speed?*"

Mr. Katzenbach: "*I think my basic motivation was the amount of speculation both here and abroad as to what was going on, whether there was a conspiracy of the right or a conspiracy of the left or a lone assassin or even in its wildest stages, a conspiracy by the then Vice President to achieve the Presidency, the sort of thing you have speculation about in some countries abroad where that kind of condition is normal.*

"It seemed to me that the quicker some information could be made available that went beyond what the press was able to uncover and what the press was able to speculate about was desirable in that state of affairs." (III HSCA 643)

I assume that Katzenbach's uneasiness was because of what the press was able to unearth. The press suggestion sounds credible. I'm not sure if this was to engage in suppression, but the quick response makes it sound like it.

Mr. McKinney: "In your deposition to the committee on page 8, you suggested that one of your interests was that the facts, all of them, had to be made public and it had to be done in a way that would give the public, both in this country and abroad, the confidence that no facts were being withheld at all.

Do you think that pushing for this type of speed might have hurt the accuracy of the report or brought about the fact that some people would question the speed of its issuance, its thoroughness, its completeness?"

Mr. Katzenbach: "I do not think the two notions are connected, Congressman. I think the motivations for getting some kind of report out, some facts out early were the ones that I have stated." (III HSCA 643)

If you can hearken back to September 11, 2001, the strikes against certain symbolic edifices made the immediately passed Patriot Act seem like the right thing to a lot of people.

Mr. McKinney: "In other words, it is safe to say that with the mere mention of another investigation or another investigation or an investigative commission, Mr. Hoover would have considered it as somewhat of an insult to the FBI in its activities in this area." (III HSCA 644)

J. Edgar Hoover tried his very best to discourage Lyndon Johnson from assigning such a commission. He was vehemently opposed to the Warren Commission.

McKinney read from Church Committee testimony in respect to FBI cooperation:

> "Isn't this really sort of a stone wall attitude toward the Commission, toward the Attorney General, the Assistant Attorney General, and almost everybody else involved?"
>
> Mr. Katzenbach: "Yes, it can be viewed that way. The Bureau, during the time that I was in the Department of Justice, had a very strong view that they were going to do investigations. ... What they resented was our talking with an agent in the field about an investigation he was doing, or about something he was familiar with rather than get that report coming back through the FBI bureaucracy and coming out with Mr. Hoover's signature... That is not all bad. They simply did not want to be pinned with the views expressed by some agent in the field. If they did not acquiesce in those views or if they had other information available to them which cast some doubt upon those views, and I can understand that, as frustrating as it often was." (III HSCA 649)

Congressman Dodd went back to the Katzenbach-Moyers memo of November 25th, "1. "The public must be satisfied that Oswald was the assassin; that he did not have confederates who are still at large; and that the evidence was such that he would have been convicted at trial. This was November 25, 1963, three days after the assassination."

> Mr. Dodd: "Why was it so important that the public be satisfied that Oswald was the assassin? ... Why was it so important to prove that 3 days after the assassination?"

Katzenbach did not do very well in a rather belabored answer; and tried to say that if the situation were different, and since it was not otherwise, the agenda stated in the memorandum should be precisely announced. He concluded,

> "I don't think this is artistically phrased. Perhaps you have never written anything that you would like to write better afterwards, Congressman, but I have."
>
> Mr. Dodd: "You won't get me to say that." (III HSCA 653)

This next exchange had substance. Dodd got aggressive and Katzenbach responded with a *mea culpa, mea culpa, mea maxima culpa,* and Dodd was not about to concede anything.

Dodd soon asked Katzenbach a question based on a statement he had made when interrogated by Gary Cornwell, with regard to CIA assassination plots.

Katzenbach stated,

> "No. In fact, I never believed there were such plots. I testified to this before but I remember at one time they were in the White House at the time of the Dominican upheaval [*spring, 1965*] and I remember Lyndon Johnson asking a direct question to Dick Helms about assassination and got a flat denial from Mr. Helms that the CIA had anybody involved. It was a short conversation and you can qualify it any way you want to, but I went home pretty confident."

Dodd then asked,

> "Did you prepare any memorandum at that time, after that conversation, or do you remember that conversation so clearly that you have no doubt in your own mind that Mr. Helms told the President of the United States in 1965 that there were no assassination plots?"

> Mr. Katzenbach: "I remember the conversation. It is hard to remember verbatim word for word. The question may well have been 'Have we ever been involved in any assassination of anybody,' and the answer to that may well have been the flat 'no.'

> "I don't know, I don't remember exactly how the question was phrased, but it obviously had to do at that time with Vietnam, and I was satisfied from that that we didn't engage in that kind of activity in this country, and I suppose I was satisfied in part, Congressman, because it was so incredible to me that we should have." (III HSCA 654)

This seems a little disingenuous for someone as high as Katzenbach was in the Justice Department hierarchy to suggest, "In fact, I never believed there were such plots." No wonder these plots go undetected all over the globe

With regard to Helms, Congressman Sawyer addressed a question to Katzenbach:

"I just have a single question. Mr. Hart, who was a spokesman for CIA here in connection with their having taken into custody for some 3 years Yuri Nosenko, the Russian defector, said that their authority for putting this man in a specially built isolation cell for 3 years, was you, that Helms had gone to you and gotten an OK for this. Is that true?"

Mr. Katzenbach: *"I have no recollection of any conversation involving Mr. Nosenko with Mr. Helms. There may have been such a conversation. I don't think that I authorized putting anybody in jail for 3 years. ... I think if somebody said we have a defector, we don't know whether he is a true defector or not, we have got him under some questioning, I wouldn't have—I don't suppose that would have bothered me very much. But when you talk about incarceration for 3 years, and so forth,* that seems to me a different proposition." (III HSCA 655)

Katzenbach always rejected any awareness of Yuri Nosenko, but was asked by Chairman Stokes, "How did you learn of it?"

Mr. Katzenbach: "I learned of it when the gentleman [*Edward J. Epstein*] writing a book called me up about 3 or 4 months ago or 6 months ago; and asked me about it. And I said, 'Who is Nosenko'?"

Katzenbach further said that the only occasions when the CIA approached him "fell into two categories: One was when they wanted to wiretap or some electronic device to be put within this country, they came to me; and the only other thing is whenever they wanted a book suppressed they came to me and I told them not to do it." (III HSCA 663)

Chairman Stokes: "Mr. Katzenbach, as a witness before our committee, you are entitled at the conclusion of your testimony to have 5 minutes in which to make any comment that you so desire relating to testimony before this committee, and I extend to you at this time 5 minutes for that purpose, if you so desire."

Mr. Katzenbach: "I will be very, very brief, Mr. Chairman.

"I regret that the Warren Commission report was inadequate, if it was inadequate in many respects, and that as a consequence this committee has felt, the Congress has felt through this committee the necessity to reexamine the assassination.

"I am sure that you, sir, and all the members regret that equally.

"I have confidence that what this committee is doing and will do in its report, will reflect the wisdom and integrity of its members."

Chairman Stokes: "Thank you very much, and on behalf of the committee, we certainly thank you for your appearance here and for the cooperation you have given this committee and the time you have expended in giving us the benefit of your testimony. Thank you very much."

Mr. Katzenbach: "Thank you."

Chairman Stokes: "You are excused." (III HSCA 679)

34

RICHARD HELMS –
SEPTEMBER 22, 1978

On September 22, Richard Helms testified before the HSCA in Washington, D.C.

House Select Chief Counsel G. Robert Blakey, in his usual narration, underlined the arrival of former CIA Director Helms by stating, "Over the years, the Central Intelligence Agency has conducted a massive investigation of Lee Harvey Oswald, the proof of which is a 142-volume file at the Agency headquarters in Langley, Va."

Several principal questions remain:

Was the CIA's post-assassination investigation of Lee Harvey Oswald thorough and reliable, and did the Agency share with others the relevant information it had or later learned?

Was there a pre-assassination relationship between the CIA and Oswald? If so, could that relationship have extended to complicity in the assassination, or short of that, might it have led the Agency to seek to hide the relationship out of fear of being accused of complicity.

Much of the mystery is, of course, the result of the secretive nature of the CIA and its understandable unwillingness to reveal operational information. (IV HSCA 1)

The witness before Helms, Nicholas deB. Katzenbach affirmed, that Helms had lied to President Johnson about assassination plots, and also felt that Helms' account that Katzenbach had given authorization to quarantine Yuri Nosenko was an innovation on Helms' part.

Blakey concluded by stating,

> "Mr. Chairman, it is appropriate to note that the committee's questioning of Mr. Helms today will be based on documents that have been released by the CIA in accordance with the Freedom of Information Act. The select committee has also, in the past week, reached agreement with the CIA for the declassification and release of certain documents not previously available to the public. These newly released documents will also be referred to in today's hearing." (IV HSCA 5)

Helms was represented by counsel Gregory B. Craig, of Williams & Connally.

> HSCA Counsel Goldsmith: *"Mr. Helms, what role, if any, did the Agency have in the investigation of the assassination of President Kennedy?"*
>
> Mr. Helms: *"At the time that the Warren Commission was formed, the Agency did everything in its power to cooperate with the Warren commission and with the FBI, the FBI having the lead in the investigation. As best as I can recollect, it was the Agency's feeling that since this tragic event had taken place in the United States, that the FBI and the Department of Justice would obviously have the leading edge in conducting the investigation, and that the Agency would cooperate with them in every way it was possible, and the same applied to the Warren Commission."* (IV HSCA 9)
>
> Mr. Goldsmith: "Did this particular desk officer ever complain to you about interference with Mr. Angleton, who was then chief of the CIA staff?"
>
> Mr. Helms: "I do not recall any complaint, Mr. Goldsmith." ...

Mr. Goldsmith: "Has Mr. McCone ever indicated to you that he was not satisfied with the flow of information from below upstream to him?"

Mr. Helms: "In connection with this investigation?"

Mr. Goldsmith: "Yes, sir."

Mr. Helms: "Not that I am aware of, Mr. Goldsmith. I think, if knowing Mr. McCone, if he had been dissatisfied, he would have made his dissatisfaction clear and I wouldn't have forgotten it." (IV HSCA 10—11)

Mr. Helms was questioned if Allen Dulles had any kind of cooperative role between the Warren Commission and the CIA.

Mr. Goldsmith: "To what extent did he attempt to represent the interests of the CIA while serving as a member of the Warren Commission?"

Mr. Helms: "I have no idea, Mr. Goldsmith."

Goldsmith asked for JFK F-529 to be shown to Helms. It was a Memorandum for said Subject: "Deputy Director for Plans [Helms] Discussion with Mr. Dulles re: the Nosenko Information on Oswald." It is clear that Dulles was acting way beyond his role as a member of the Warren Commission, and was endeavoring to divert the Nosenko data, and that he and Helms were in one accord on that point.

Paragraph 3 was significant: "It was agreed that an effort might be made to find such language if Mr. Dulles is again unsuccessful in persuading his colleagues to eliminate any reference to the Nosenko information from the report. To attempt this, however, we would have to know precisely in what context the Commission intended to make use of the Nosenko information. This, Mr. Dulles will have to determine from Mr. Rankin. He will do this as soon as possible. He knows that I am leaving this week and therefore, will contact you as soon as he has the information he needs from Mr. Rankin."

Mr. Goldsmith: "Does this exhibit, Mr. Helms, refresh your memory on the extent to which Mr. Dulles may have represented CIA interests while serving 'as a member of the Warren Commission'?"

410

Mr. Helms: "I don't read that memorandum that way Mr. Gold-smith." (IV HSCA 13—19, *passim*).

It is obvious that any question asked of Mr. Helms is irrelevant because they will be responded to untruthfully or deceitfully.

Here is an example:

Mr. Helms: "I was rather puzzled by some of Mr. Hart's testimony the other day before this committee. He seemed to go into lurid detail about Nosenko's treatment, but when it came time to make his contribution to the purposes of the committee hearing, in other words, what Nosenko knew about Oswald, he had no clarification to make and nothing to contribute.

"Yet he was here as the official representative of the Director of Central Intelligence, as I understand it. It was almost as though his purpose was to use his testimony before this committee to excoriate some of his former colleagues for the handling of the Nosenko case." (IV HSCA 28)

The Director worked hard to look bad, and did so by sending some lackey, who was a retired agent. If Helms was so upset, then why didn't he approach the HSCA and testify himself about Nosenko?

As to Mr. Hart's testimony regarding the CIA's consideration for the discarding (*meaning liquidation, i.e., death*) of defector Yuri Nosenko, as well as the polygraphs mentioned by Hart, Mr. Helms admitted an inch but nothing close to a mile:

"I think the first one [*the first polygraph*], it has been admitted, was for the purpose of bringing pressure to bear on him.

"As to those lurid comments about the disposal, I have already addressed myself to those. I knew nothing about these comments; I knew nothing about a written confession; I knew nothing about anything of those things at the time. They may have been written down by Deputy Chief of Soviet Bloc Division, but I have not seen his notes. All I know is that I was never aware of this, and therefore there was never any indication on the part of anybody in a position of responsibility in the management of the Agency to do anything with Mr. Nosenko except to try to establish his bona fides somehow." (IV HSCA 100)

Helms acted as if Nosenko had to run extra laps at track practice and nothing worse. The truth was harsher than that.

Helms attempted to avoid an issue about lost Oswald documents, and he toned down the impact of them, but HSCA counsel Goldsmith was not having it at all, asking that if they didn't mean a hill of beans, why were they labeled "secret" or "eyes only"? We know so much more today about the role of the CIA, thanks to the works of Jefferson Morley, John Newman, and Malcolm Blunt, to name a few. The CIA had been monitoring Oswald for over four years at the time of the assassination. Why, if he was some kind of nobody? This is a question that Warren Commission fanatics have to address.

> Mr. Helms: "I don't know. Maybe it was overclassified. A lot of documents in the agency were. (IV HSCA 211).

Congressman Sawyer was not going to be silenced:

> Mr. Sawyer: "*You have testified about your considering assassinating people along with the Mafia. It is nothing new to you people apparently to assassinate somebody?*"

> Mr. Helms: "*That is your statement, Mr. Sawyer.*"

> Mr. Sawyer: "Well, I thought that was what you have been testifying to here about willingly becoming a party to an assassination either by syringe, by gun, or by poison pills of Castro. So, once we get in the acceptance of that line, it doesn't seem to me so out of line that would be one of the things you would consider [*referring to Nosenko*], and apparently your deputy division chief did consider it.
>
> "It seems to me the only other option would be to pay him off and handsomely enough so he would keep quiet about all this when you let him go. You obviously couldn't deport him very well at this point in time, and it just appears to me as I look at that it is perfectly plain that you exercised the option of paying him off.
>
> "Do you dispute that?"

> Mr. Helms: "Yes, I dispute it."

> Mr. Sawyer: "You said you paid over a period of time some half a million dollars, is about what it amounts to as both in lump-sum payments and in monthly stipends to a guy that the Agency never decided wasn't, in fact, there to mislead it and give it false

RICHARD HELMS – SEPTEMBER 22, 1978

information. *You paid that as a consultant; and you say the motivation was not at all to pay him off. Is that your position?"*

Mr. Helms: *No sir. I am counting to 10. That is what my mother taught me to do under these circumstances."*

Mr. Sawyer: *"You are doing what?"*

Mr. Helms: *"I am counting to 10."*

Mr. Sawyer: *"Well, I will be patient if it takes that long."*

Mr. Helms: "The effort in Mr. Nosenko's case and the only option that we had available to us in my opinion was to resettle him and give him a new identity and handle him in such a way he would have a chance to make a life for himself on the American scene.

"It has been 5 years since I had anything to do with his case. I don't know what has been done to him since."

Mr. Sawyer: "You said you could not just put him out on welfare. What do we do with most immigrants that come in either from Indochina that are refugees or regularly admitted immigrants? We may provide them some educational help in the language, and that sort of thing, but we don't pay them off. Here you are talking about sums of money that wouldn't be mentionable in the same breath as welfare, and I just say as I look at this thing, taking all these facts you have testified into account, it would just seem to me on the face of it that it was a payoff. I am surprised to hear you deny it."

Mr. Helms: *"I believe that under the Constitution you are entitled to your viewpoint and I am entitled to mine."*

Mr. Sawyer: "Well, you did, in fact, plead guilty to having withheld information from the Senate committee, didn't you?"

Mr. Helms: "No, sir, I did not."

Mr. Sawyer: "I thought you had."

Mr. Helms: "I did not. I pleaded nolo contendere."

Returning to Nosenko, and Mr. Helms' ways of mendacity:

Mr. Sawyer: "But you invested in building a whole separate vault and building around it, and so forth, for the purpose of accommodating Nosenko; did you not?"

Mr. Helms: "I asked this morning if anybody from the commit-tee had looked at the building. It was no vault, as I recollect it. I don't think it was a very expansive building at all."

Mr. Sawyer: *"Where was it located?"*

Mr. Helms: *"It was located in Virginia."* (IV HSCA 244—245)

Camp Peary is in Virginia and was an army installation that covered for the CIA's nonsense. That military base was made up of 60 military police and cadets in training.

Helms added,

"I think this *inquisition* has been admirably handled." (IV HSCA 247)

How did they so repeatedly get away with such non-answers? Easy. No one had the courage to really challenge them. Why? Money. If any-one on the HSCA had tried the 'damn liar' routine with Helms, the CIA would have put a lot of cash into some other candidate's mailbox, so that the offending HSCA congressperson would never be heard from or seen again.

That is how the assassination operated, and that is how the cover-up has been sustained.

35

DR. CLYDE COLLINS SNOW –
SEPTEMBER 25, 1978

On Sept. 25, 1978, Dr. Clyde Collins Snow gave testimony before the HSCA in Washington, D.C.

The House Select Committee anthropology panel was comprised of Ellis Kerley, Steven Rosen, and Clyde Collins Snow. Dr. Collins spoke on behalf of the panel.

In the expected narration of House Select Committee Chief Counsel G. Robert Blakey, it was indicated that the panel would compare photographs of quite a few individuals, to include the question of who was in the doorway, Billy Lovelady or Lee Harvey Oswald? Another question will involve the tramp photographs and different allegations. A third accusation will involve the examination of the Joseph Milteer photo taken by AP photographer James "Ike" Altgens. This seems a little repetitive in reference to the tramps and Milteer, but let's see where it takes us.

"The implications of these questions is enormous, about a Watergate burglar and a former long-time CIA officer to direct the 1972 break-in might have been involved in the assassination or that a militant conservative who had talked of killing President Kennedy was standing along the motorcade route. These implications, are of course, of a conspiracy. The committee therefore asked its panel of anthropologists to compare the photos in question with known photos of the men they allege to show." (IV HSCA 366)

You can't help but think, as you read the narration of Blakey, that the panel is going to come up with reports that it was Lovelady, the three men were actual tramps, and that Milteer really wasn't there. It seems to be a *fait accompli*.

Before any definitive dialogue, HSCA Counsel Genzman asked the kind of measurable question that was absent in the days of the Warren Commission:

Mr. Genzman: "How exact is this [*forensic anthropology*] approach?"

Dr. Snow: "It can vary largely. The exactness of the approach depends to a large extent on the quality of materials that we are given. If the photographs are of poor quality or if there is variation in the subject's pose or the apparent age and features of that sort, we are apt to be less firm in our conclusions than we are if we are given good quality photographs of the individual and uniform poses."

Mr. Genzman: "How certain can you be of your findings?"

Dr. Snow: "Again, it varies with the kind of materials we are given. In some cases, for example, if we are given photographs of individuals to compare with very little variation in the position of the subject's head in the photograph and of good quality, we can, in some cases, come up with a positive identification, or positively exclude the individual beyond reasonable doubt. In other cases we have to qualify our opinions, using such language as 'probable' or 'possible.'" [Single quotation marks added for emphasis.]

Mr. Genzman: "For example, what if you were given photographs of identical twins; could you differentiate between them?"

416

Dr. Snow: "I doubt very seriously whether we could. There are undoubtedly differences, even in identical twins, but whether our measuring techniques are refined enough to discern such differences, I would doubt." (IV HSCA 368)

In regard to the doorway photograph, Altgens 6:

Mr. Genzman: "What was the issue before the panel of anthropologists?"

Dr. Snow: *"The issue was to analyze the photographs to determine whether or not the figure in the door was indeed Lee Harvey Oswald or Mr. Lovelady."*

Mr. Genzman: *"What is the panel's conclusion?"*

Dr. Snow: *"Our conclusions were that it is highly improbable that this figure in the doorway was indeed Lee Harvey Oswald. It is considerably more probable that it is Mr. Lovelady."* (IV HSCA 372)

I've always believed it was Billy Lovelady in the doorway, largely based on the hairline alone and that people both inside (like Buell Wesley Frazier) and outside of the building at the time, who knew Lovelady, said it was him standing there. As previously stated, the photographic evidence has swayed me as well.

"Another feature we noticed was that in the photographs of Mr. Oswald taken about the time of his arrest, he had begun a little incipient pattern of baldness, but in Mr. Lovelady this same type of baldness was more extensively developed at that time. And judging from the hairline in the photograph, the general pattern resembles that seen in Mr. Lovelady more than it does in Mr. Oswald.

"Another feature we noted was that Mr. Lovelady has a widow's peak, an extension of the hair beyond the main hairline here, and it is sort of eccentrically located, shifted to the right. And we also get a suggestion of that, this widow's peak displaced to the right in the figure in the doorway." (IV HSCA 373)

One tirade embarked upon by a JFK researcher said that photo was faked, just like for some people, everything is fake. This has bothered me over the years about as much as saying it was Lovelady in the doorway. As I stated earlier, if everything is fake, then there is not much to discuss. Some things have been faked, but I tend to side on the less as opposed to the more.

With respect to the tramp photos:

> Mr. Genzman: "What were the issues before the panel of anthropologists?"
>
> Dr. Snow: "We were asked, again, using the best available information and the best available materials, to metrically and morphologically compare these photographs with those of the tramps to see whether or not any of these individuals could be identified as one or more of the tramps."
>
> Mr. Genzman: "What are the panel's conclusions?"
>
> Dr. Snow: Our conclusions were that none of the individuals who have been alleged to have been tramp A are indeed tramp A; that the individual alleged to have been tramp B is not that tramp; and of the two individuals alleged to be tramp C, this one, Mr. Hunt, is not the tramp, but this one, Mr. Chrisman, his measurements are consistent with the face of tramp C."
>
> Mr. Genzman: "Are you able to make a positive determination as to whether Mr. Chrisman is tramp C?"
>
> Dr. Snow: "We cannot positively identify him as tramp C." (IV HSCA 377)

With respect to the Milteer photo:

> Mr. Genzman: "What has the panel of anthropologists concluded?"
>
> Dr. Snow: "We concluded that the individual in question is not Mr. Joseph Milteer."
>
> Mr. Genzman: "What was the basis of this conclusion?"
>
> Dr. Snow: "The basis of our was conclusion was that, first, although you can see this is very little material to work with, we found one feature of interest, in that there is a suggestion here that this individual had rather full lips, whereas in this photograph and others of Mr. Milteer we found that he is relatively thin-lipped. We also found a series of photographs of Mr. Milteer [*how did they authenticate that the photos were, in fact, of Milteer?*], some taken before the assassination, this one I believe in 1957, others several years later, that show that he, at least in 1957, was

abundantly endowed with hair and as late as the early 1970s he also has hair, where in the photograph of the spectator [*Altgens photo of Houston Street*] we see an indication of extensive balding with an almost full exposed crown here. So, unless it could be demonstrated, I believe, that Mr. Milteer habitually wore hair pieces, I think we could rule him out on that basis." (IV HSCA 379-380)

Dr. Snow and his panel of experts also performed calculated measurements to establish that the individual in the Altgens photograph stood 5'10" tall, plus or minus one inch. "We were able to compare that estimate with an estimate furnished us by the committee from an FBI investigative report of Mr. Milteer which indicated that he was rather short. It gives his stature as 5 foot 5 inches. So, there is a *six-inch* discrepancy here."

Snow went on to depict the sidewalk throng, using average adult heights, and Milteer, cited as a "5-foot 4-inch man" is compared to 16 females and 7 males that were selected.

"Of the adult females he is clearly taller than all 16 of them and he is clearly taller than at least 4 of the 7 males. And using the population of the statural statistics that we have available, and assuming that this is sort of a random collection of Dallas spectators, we concluded that the probabilities of this man being 5 foot 4 inches tall—the odds against it are several thousand to one." (IV HSCA 380-381)

36

DR. BOB R. HUNT
SEPTEMBER 25, 1978

On September 25, Dr. Bob R. Hunt testified before the HSCA in Washington, D.C.

In his typical narration, House Select Committee Chief Counsel Blakey specified that Dr. Hunt would be discussing photos that the critics had insinuated display "shapes or blurred images that critics have contended are gunmen. Most of these gunmen are in the vicinity of the grassy knoll." (IV HSCA 386)

> HSCA Counsel Goldsmith: "Dr. Hunt, what was the photographic evidence panel asked to do with the various pictures and films that have been alleged to show gunmen in Dealey Plaza?"
>
> Dr. Hunt: "We were given two tasks. The first task was to apply modern technology in the enhancement of imagery. The second task, of course, was to interpret the results of that processing and to bring results of our interpretations and conclusions to the select committee." (IV HSCA 389)

Ultimately the dialogue moved to the images in the upper floor windows of the Texas School Book Depository, as demonstrated in the Hughes Film, the Dillard photo, and the Powell [*Army intelligence*] photo. We previously talked about these issues to some extent in chapter three.

> Mr. Goldsmith: "What issues were raised by these photographic materials?"
>
> Dr. Hunt: "The issues principally concern themselves with what is visible within the sixth floor School Book Depository window. I am pointing to the window on the sixth floor and there is evi-

dent there is a rectangular shape. If you view this [*Hughes*] motion picture, the Hughes film, for example, as I am pointing to now, if you view this in a motion picture sequence, one notices several things.

"First of all, the image formed at this window positions itself near the top left edge of the frame and then, as the camera pans, following the Presidential car, that image begins to drift and move in toward the center. As you watch it do that, you get the distinct impression there is some sort of motion or a change of the object within the window. So, the issue, of course, is exactly what are we looking at there? Is that the potential assassin? That is the issue presented by the Hughes film."

Mr. Goldsmith: "Dr. Hunt, before you proceed to the Dillard photograph, was any other issue presented by the Hughes film aside from the motion in the alleged assassin window?"

Dr. Hunt: "Yes. There is another set of widows over here immediately to the left and off of this particular print, which was made which shows another set of windows in the School Book Depository and there have been assertions or allegations that something can be seen with respect to a person or persons in that window looking out."

No inference at all is invited with respect to these statements.

Mr. Goldsmith: "Please proceed now to the Dillard exhibit."

Dr. Hunt: "OK. The Dillard exhibit, since it has been taken presumably just a few seconds after the last shot was fired, if we look at an enlargement of that image, the question we concern ourselves with is the following: There are some objects very definitely visible in front of that window. There is a box, what we interpret to be a box, another box sitting over there. But behind the window there is a great deep shadow. The question is, within that deep shadow is it possible to see things by contrast enhancement techniques of the kind that I described earlier?"

Mr. Goldsmith: "That is essentially the same issue that exists for the Powell photograph?"

Dr. Hunt: "That is correct, essentially the same issue, namely, to look inside, what is the deep shadow in that window." (IV HSCA 401-402)

Dr. Hunt would affirm that what he saw in the Hughes film was not the movement of any human entity. Will the empty Powell photograph become some kind of a cutout or prototype for the Hughes and Dillard photos? Let's wait and see.

> Mr. Goldsmith: "In that case, to what was the motion attributed?"
>
> Dr. Hunt: "The panel's conclusion was that the motion which is perceived if you view the movie is attributable to photographic artifacts, namely the change in contrast from frame to frame, the change in focus as the image of the window moves around in the frame of the film."
>
> Mr. Goldsmith: "Is it possible there was a human object in that window, but it simply was not perceptible on film?"
>
> Dr. Hunt: "It is very possible that there was a human object there, but it would be beyond the perceptibility of the imagery as recorded on film is the panel's conclusion." (IV HSCA 404)

Many scientific or mechanical reasons are cited, but at the end of the day it is simply professional v. professional, or as is usually spoken in legal circles, expert v. expert. People will have faith in the expert they choose to accept, for a variety of reasons. Other analyses have been performed on the film, principally that of ITEK Corporation, are presented, but Dr. Hunt asserted that,

> "Itek Corp. did not carry out any of the elaborate procedure for controlling the contrast that we did, which means they were much more subject to a false perception of motion as a result of contrast failures. By that I mean the following: What you see as an object, if it is both shadow and light, is strictly dependent upon the photographic processes resulting in the contrast of that object being recorded on film. If there were changes in contrast, there would be a much greater probability of motion being perceived. We, of course, tried to hold the contrast constant by our processing."
>
> Mr. Goldsmith: "Are you saying then that such motion would be characterized as caused by photographic artifact?"
>
> Dr. Hunt: "Photographic artifact, photographic anomaly." (IV HSCA 405)

With respect to the Dillard photo, it was subjected to some form of unique radiation and X-ray image enhancement.

> Mr. Goldsmith: "Was the panel able to make a finding as to the presence of someone at the sixth-floor window?"
>
> Dr. Hunt: "Yes. The enhancement of the sixth-floor window shows there was no one at the window." (IV HSCA 406)

With regard to the Powell color slide; "Again, looking within that window, you see no details of a human form or face." (IV HSCA 406)

The conclusion is that there were no people in any of the three findings, and no questions asked, as to what was present in those windows, because there does seem to be something in both the Hughes and Dillard photographs.

The testimony then proceeds to the Willis slide (the Z-202 image, similar to a Hugh Betzner image), the Moorman photograph, and F-161, which

> "shows a segment, one print if you wish, from 8 mm film made by a gentleman named Nix. You are showing an enlarged piece of that film cropped out from the original 8-millimeter film in the lower half, and in the upper half an even greater enlargement centering on the region that you are seeing here on the left."
>
> Mr. Goldsmith: "What issues did these photographic items raise with the panel?"
>
> Dr. Hunt: "Using the label, 'the retaining wall,' we are looking at the Dealey – of the retaining wall there is a dark object, which I am pointing to right here. It has been alleged or asserted the dark object represents a gunman standing at or behind the retaining wall [*"black dog man"*]. That is the main issue which is being addressed in all these, because each of these images shows the retaining wall at some point in time."
>
> Mr. Goldsmith: "Is this retaining wall in the grassy knoll area of Dealey Plaza?"
>
> Dr. Hunt: "Yes. This is usually referred to as the grassy knoll. You can see the rise of the slope of land coming up where the retaining wall sits." (IV HSCA 407-408)

The evidence here is that the original Nix film is the best possible technique to use. But what happened to the Nix film? As far as I have been able to establish, Orville Nix's granddaughter, who is attempting to recover the original film, has not yet seen it and has been told that they never will. (*See chapter three for more on the history of the Nix film*) Like so much else, it has gone missing.

Dr. Hunt explained that one of the procedures used was using the flesh-tone measurements of Marilyn Sitzman, as she was standing next to amateur photographer Abraham Zapruder. Other expert measures were also used.

Mr. Goldsmith: "*What was the panel's conclusion?*"

Dr. Hunt: "*Based upon the flesh-tone measurements which we took off of the object at the wall and comparing those to similar measurements on the flesh tones on Zapruder's secretary, we concluded this was a person standing at the wall.*"

Mr. Goldsmith: "Did the panel make any effort to determine whether that person was holding a rifle?"

Dr. Hunt: "Yes. We tried to examine the nature of this linear feature which you see right here [*not sure what photo is referred to, but if a guess is allowed, I suspect it would be the badgeman photo*]. If you look at this object you perceive something like a head or face with flesh tones, shoulders and arms, with flesh tones in the region I am pointing to here, and then you perceive this linear object which runs out of the hands roughly at a 45-degree angle. We would have liked to deblur the image. Since we couldn't, the only thing we could do was to ask ourselves: what is the probability of this being a rifle? We could not make a conclusion on that because there is another evident blur at the 45-degree line throughout this image. This linear object we perceive runs at the same direction as the blur which is apparent in the image. It is equally likely, therefore, that this is either a real object of some kind, or simply a small dark object in the image which was stretched out in the motion blur of the camera during the period in which the picture was taken."

Mr. Goldsmith: "Dr. Hunt, I would ask you to refer now to JFK F-129 which was the Moorman enlargement at the far left. I would ask what type of enhancement method was applied to this photograph."

Dr. Hunt briefly explained the difficulty in accomplishing technical augmentation on a Polaroid photo, such as the Moorman picture. Watch the film, *Blow Up*, by Michelangelo Antonioni, and one of the points of the film, though not the only one, is that blowing up the picture only makes it more grainy and less clear to see what is in the frame. The movie is more about the uncertainty of life, but I will let the viewer enjoy that experience for themselves. Great film.

> Mr. Goldsmith: "What conclusion, if any, did the panel reach concerning this photograph?"
>
> Dr. Hunt: "We found no evidence of the person that is visible in the Willis photograph in the Moorman photograph." (IV HSCA 410)

The attempted Nix film enhancement is then explicated succinctly, with the concession that there is a slight blur, which the photographic panel tried to delete.

> Mr. Goldsmith: "Was the panel able to reach any conclusion as to the presence of a gunman by the retaining wall?"
>
> Dr. Hunt: "Over here at the retaining wall area we see some pattern of light and dark, shaped roughly like a triangle. You see that better in the enlargement, which we have shown here. The panel could not conclude this was a person. We see no flesh tones associated with that region of the sort we find over here on Zapruder and his secretary." ...
>
> Mr. Goldsmith: "Was the panel able to discern any sign of a flash or puff of smoke?"
>
> Dr. Hunt: "No. They found no flash or puff of smoke in that retaining wall area of this film." (IV HSCA 411)

Dr. Hunt thought the blurring seen on the Nix film could explain what some people say is a puff of smoke that is perceptible.

Zapruder frame 413 is then addressed, which claims to show the back of a gunman's head and a rifle extending in front, as if endeavoring to shoot. A series of intricate tests were run which supplied computations and results which eradicated the potential of the image being an assassin in the bushes. "The bush actually exists in this region about 10 or 15 feet from Zapruder, right near the point of the retaining wall.

Consequently, we conclude that this was not a head in the bush. This was literally a man standing out near this area of the sidewalk in the plaza." (IV HSCA 416)

Congressman Floyd Fithian questioned Dr. Hunt about a comparison of the boxes in the sniper's window as seen in the Dillard photo, taken just seconds after the last shot, and the photo [*by Army Intelligence agent James Powell*] taken several seconds after that.

> Dr. Hunt answered Fithian: "You are correct in perceiving that there is something which we could ascribe to a change in the configuration of the boxes." As far as how it happened, Hunt continued a moment later: "There are two possible explanations, I guess, for that, that the panel considered. One is that we are seeing boxes which are in the room, but because of perspective, our line of sight, is different; we are seeing different boxes than were visible in the other picture.
>
> "The second explanation is that there has been physically a movement of the boxes in the room during the time which elapsed between the taking of those pictures." Hunt goes on to discuss that because the boxes in the bright, high-noon sun, it tends to rule out the "perspective issue." ...
>
> Mr. Fithian: "Well, if it generally tends to rule that out, then it seems this committee would be left with only one conclusion, and that is, that a box was actually moved."
>
> Dr. Hunt: "That would be my only personal conclusion, that somebody or something moved boxes around in that room during the time of taking of those two pictures." (IV HSCA 423)

As soon as the shooter left, if he was ever in that window, he was gone and not seen again. For the boxes to be repositioned, it would have mandated human involvement, and that makes it absolutely necessary for a person other than Lee Oswald fleeing downstairs for the soda machine. In spite of eyewitness testimony that almost immediately proposed the far right window on the next-to-the-top floor, it took until 1:12, which is *forty-two minutes later,* for the police to appear in the sniper's nest and discover two (*maybe three*) spent cartridges.

When Hunt spoke of somebody or something in the Hughes or Dillard photos, it would have been rational to ask what the *something* could have been. There have been scientific and non-scientific answers offered for many of the controversies that researchers have proposed, and re-gardless of my proposition, that Blakey's *science* was taking the fun out of proposed research, it was encouraging for Dr. Hunt to submit two likelihoods, and then theorize which is the more trustworthy of the two probabilities that could be ruled out, and then what appeared to have taken place was the more ominous possibility. It was likewise as refresh-ing that Congressman Fithian permitted this line of interrogation to be taken to a conclusion.

Maybe the boxes were moved? There seem to have been three differ-ent configurations. Arnold Rowland saw someone with a gun at 12:15, long before the tragedy in relative terms, and the FBI combed the world to find people to make him out to be untruthful. And onward it goes...

37

LOUIS STEVEN WITT –
SEPTEMBER 25, 1978

On September 25, Louis Steven Witt testified before the HSCA in Washington, D.C.

Blakey begins his introduction of Louis Steven Witt with the following: "When the Zapruder film of the Kennedy Assassination was made public, critics and people in general were fascinated by the sight of a man with a black umbrella standing just a few feet from the Presidential limousine. It was a sunshiny day so what purpose could anyone have for an umbrella?

The theories about the umbrella man, for the most part, attributed to him some sinister intent. At the very least, he was a signal man for the actual gunmen, although one critic proposed the idea that a firing device concealed in the umbrella was the weapon used to assassinate the President." (IV HSCA 428ff)

> Representative Genzman begins: "Why were you carrying the umbrella that day?"

Mr. Witt: "Actually, I was going to use this umbrella to heckle the President's motorcade."

Mr. Genzman: "How had you gotten this idea?"

Mr. Witt: "In a coffee break conversation someone had mentioned that the umbrella was a sore spot with the Kennedy family. Being a conservative-type fellow, I sort of placed him in the liberal camp and I was just going to kind of do a little heckling."

Mr. Genzman: "Are you saying you were going to use the umbrella as a symbol for the purpose of heckling?"

Mr. Witt: "I think that would cover it."

Mr. Genzman: "On November 22, 1963, were you aware of the motorcade route?"

Mr. Witt: "No. Not really. ..." (IV HSCA 431)

Witt was not aware of the motorcade route, but just happened to be in the absolute perfect spot in Dealey Plaza, that anyone could be in, at the time of the shooting.

Witt stated that he was sitting on what would be called the grassy knoll, awaiting the motorcade, but was surprised when it started down Elm street. He then said that he walked toward the street, while fidgeting with the umbrella:

"As I moved toward the street, still walking on the grass, I heard the shots that I eventually learned were shots. At the time somehow it didn't register as shots because they were so close together, and it was like hearing a string of firecrackers, or something like that. It didn't at that moment register on me as being shots."

Mr. Genzman: "Did you react in any way?"

Mr. Witt: "No. I continued to move forward and finally got this umbrella up in the air. I think by the time I got the thing up in the air I was over and possibly standing on the retaining wall."

He was at the curb line of Elm Street, not near any retaining wall. Maybe he designated things differently and called them by the wrong names, but his diction and terminology are at best odd.

Mr. Genzman: "Did President Kennedy see your umbrella?"

Mr. Witt: "I have no way of knowing. I really don't."

Mr. Genzman: "What do you next recall happening?"

Mr. Witt: "Let me go back a minute. As I was moving forward I apparently had this umbrella in front of me for some few steps. Whereas other people I understand saw the President shot and his movements; I did not see this because of this thing in front of me. The next thing I saw after I saw the car coming down the street, down the hill to my left, the car was just about at a position like this at this angle here." [which means that Witt, since the car was still to his left, since he was positioned at the Stemmons Freeway sign, would have viewed the wounding inside the limo from close up]. (IV HSCA 433)

As Witt indicated, the follow-up car "ran up on the President's car and a man jumped…" In Altgens #6, the follow-up vehicle is on the bumper of the Presidential vehicle. By Altgens #7, it is no longer even visible, and it fades equally from the Muchmore and Nix films.

Witt was then asked if the umbrella fired any kind of projectiles and he rejected all such questions.

Witt was probed by Congressman Fauntroy to display "the way in which you held the umbrella on that specific date, but he was informed by counsel for the committee you had made a specific request that you not be asked to make such a demonstration; is that correct?"

Mr. Witt: "That is correct."

Chairman Stokes. "OK. And is that still your request to this committee?"

Mr. Witt: "Yes, sir. I—my line of thinking is that since we are not in the same area, we couldn't exactly duplicate what I did there. The only thing my doing that, it would just be more fodder for an overeager press back in Dallas to show this off and continue to embarrass me and my family, more so than we have already been embarrassed."

Chairman Stokes: "Certainly."

Mr. Witt: "We – I would add at this point that we have been through quite a bit. I brought it on myself, but nevertheless, we have been through quite a bit already." (IV HSCA 443)

demonstrate by rapping your knuckle on the table about the time interval you feel you remember the shots were fired."

Mr. Witt: "I don't know if I could really give you a good example, but it was just [*the witness wraps three times rapidly on table*]." (IV HSCA 445)

Witt was asked about people hurrying about, after the shots:

Mr. Devine: "***I am talking primarily about spectators. Was there any movement among the spectators that you noticed?***"

Mr. Witt: "***Not as I recall spectators. There were people who seemed to run up from the street to the grassy knoll, but somewhere along the way I heard these were Secret Servicemen or plainclothesmen.***" (IV HSCA 445)

Mr. Edgar: "*Were you frightened about the fact that you had deliberately set out to cause a scene or an embarrassment to the President?*"

Mr. Witt: "***Not frightened as such, but at that time there was a great deal of what I would have to describe as hysteria in the Dallas area about the President being killed. It could have been extremely unwise for me to have volunteered and become known at that time. It could have been dangerous to me or my family.***" (IV HSCA 450)

This sounds almost exactly like Howard Brennan's reasoning (see Appendix #1). Eventually, however, the examination returns to the dark-complected man that was standing next to Witt during the shooting sequence, and afterward sat down next to him after the shooting ended.

"I have one more question for Mr. Witt: You have indicated that you have learned over these years now that the umbrella man was considered a factor; that even someone has suggested that

431

the umbrella was a gun and that it may have been a signal. You may want also to know, and, therefore, to help us, that the person sitting beside you has been alleged to have been a Cuban and that other pictures taken in the plaza suggested that he may have been talking on a two-way radio while he was sitting beside you. It would have been of great interest to us to identify who that person sitting beside you was. For that reason I simply ask, is there anything that you can recall about the person that would enable us to find him, even as we found you, because your story sounds plausible?" (IV HSCA 451)

Witt stated that if there had been a two-way radio dialogue, he feels he would have been mindful of it.

Witt also mentioned how he had been treated considerately, and added,

> "The only other thing I would care to say is that I think if the Guinness Book of World Records had a category for people who were at the wrong place at the wrong time, doing the wrong thing, I would be No. 1 in that position, without even a close runner-up." (IV HSCA 453)

This would get my vote for the most accurate statement that Witt made during his entire testimony.

Just before I started to write the final version of this book, I reread Witt's testimony and it gave me pause to reflect about umbrella man, Witt, and a You Tube video I watched a few years ago. It was a video of Josiah "Tink" Thompson talking about umbrella man with Errol Morris, a tremendous documentary film maker. I watched this very brief analysis of umbrella man by an elder statesman of the critical research community, a first-generation investigator. Thompson, as I mentioned, was engaging without ever being sensational. But what really captured my attention was his description of the two layers of history, quoting from an essay that John Updike wrote about umbrella man. On the macro level, Updike says there is that dimension where everything goes well and natural laws are obeyed. On the micro-level, however, there is a dimension that is similar to the quantum dimension that attempts to describe physical reality where incredibly weird and indescribable things take place.

All of this is set up to suggest that "umbrella man" fits into that weird, indescribable world where the bizarre and "Occam's razor" clash as we attempt to find which is the best explanation of the events surrounding Louis Steven Witt. I normally yield to Occam's razor (the simplest explanation is usually the most accurate), but disagree with that implication, implying there is an accurate, though admittedly, more convoluted way to explain what happened in regard to Louis Steven Witt, a.k.a., "umbrella man."

Blakey makes the statement that the committee located Mr. Louis Steven Witt. This just simply is not true, at least not exactly.

A *Life* photographer by the name of Arthur Rickerby took a picture, that through photographic enhancement techniques, the committee was able to obtain a blow-up of the photo where the umbrella man appears clearly enough to be identified (IV, HSCA 429 ff). The photograph was then released to the press, which according to Witt's own testimony, though the individual is never identified, was apparently one of Witt's good friends who had been the genesis of the revelation (IV HSCA 444).

This "good friend" was later revealed to be researcher Penn Jones Jr., who contacted the local press. They converged according to Witt himself, "and started barraging him with questions" (IV HSCA 444). Witt was no longer working for the Rio Grande Insurance Company, which had merged with another insurance company in 1968, but was now a warehouse manager. Jones claimed that Witt would not answer any questions, but quickly said he was willing to appear before the HSCA in Washington, if needed. That seems to be a very odd response to Jones' questions.

He doesn't seem to be exactly sure of the reason for going downtown to view the motorcade, except some extraneous reasoning about the umbrella being a sign to heckle President Kennedy in reference to his father's stance on Nazism during World War II. He said he wasn't the type of person who liked to bring notice to himself, but on this day, he decided to break the mold and harass the President of the United States. It seems odd that on November 22, 1963, Witt decided to arise from his dogmatic slumbers, and emerge out of his cave of shadows into the sunlight of public protest. In fact, of the 1,037 days that President Kennedy was in office, this is the only time anyone ever opened an umbrella in any motorcade he was in and it just happened to occur when the limousine was exactly parallel to the man holding it, with shots coming into the car at that precise moment.

When he was asked what he did when he reached the grassy knoll, Witt stated "I think I went sort of maybe halfway up the grassy area... [*and*] sat down" (IV HSCA 432). As we shall see, there isn't any evidence in all the extant films or photographs that verifies the testimony of Louis Steven Witt. He goes on to say the "motorcade had already made the turn and was coming down Elm Street... before I became aware it was there" (IV HSCA 432).

With the two lead cars, sirens, motorcycles, people cheering and, as stated earlier, Mr. Witt doesn't realize the President is about to go by, even as late as the actual turn onto Elm Street. I realize perceptions can be deceiving, but isn't this stretching credulity to the breaking point?

Though I commented earlier that Witt had remarked about fiddling with his umbrella and trying to get it open as he was walking toward Elm Street, the Zapruder film seems to indicate someone who is firmly established on the curb of Elm Street, and serious about their intentions. The Nix and Muchmore films also don't indicate this kind of almost erratic behavior.

Witt also claims to have heard shots while walking towards JFK (though the Zapruder, Nix, and Muchmore films has Witt firmly entrenched and in place) as the limousine approached. He says they didn't register as shots, because they were so close together, like a string of firecrackers going off. Shots being heard close together should be something that would be followed up with some kind of clarification, but of course, it wasn't. He admits that his entire testimony was rehearsed the night before. It is like reading the sanitized Warren volumes of testimony, where there is rarely any clarification of questions or repeated inquiry. It is way too clean and pristine. The HSCA has more clarification moments, but everything is so rehearsed that when a point of interest emerges, there is never any follow up to probe deeper or more penetratingly. He says he heard "the jamming on of brakes, motorcycle policeman right there beside one of the cars" (IV HSCA 433). It is odd that this same commotion didn't alert others, but we don't know that for sure.

Witt seems unaware that the President was so close by, yet the extra jamming of the brake serves as some kind of epiphany. When he arrived at his final positioning, he says he was at the retaining wall. What? If he was half-way up the grassy knoll and moving forward, and ends up at the retaining wall, then he was either walking backwards or walking northward with his back to Elm Street. Both scenarios are preposterous. Witt either doesn't understand the geography of Dealey Plaza, doesn't know the difference between a curb and a retaining wall, or should have rehearsed his story a little better before walking out on stage.

Witt claims he didn't see the President shot because he was fiddling with his umbrella and it was in front of his face. The Zapruder film shows the umbrella man looking directly at the Presidential limousine as it passes by, with his umbrella held high into the air. He then says that after this he saw the limousine coming toward him down Elm street. He says the car was "stopping, the screeching of tires, the jamming on of brakes..." (IV HSCA 433). He gets even more confusing. He says he had been standing on the retaining wall and just sat down. Once again, either Witt thinks the curb is the retaining wall, doesn't have his story straight, or is lying. If I sound somewhat repetitious, it is because Witt is so repetitious that my analysis becomes that way as well.

Now he is back on the retaining wall sitting down. He claims to have been unaware that JFK had been shot until he got back to the insurance office; but was seemingly polarized by the events of the moment, for something he isn't aware of until later on that day. He seems terribly confused.

He was interviewed the evening before his HSCA testimony by Mr. Genzman, which of course suggests coaching, which happened a lot with both the Warren Commission and with the HSCA. Genzman must have been horrified, however, at how Witt answered the questions on this day. Mr. Fauntroy asked Witt where he worked, indicating he was either not paying attention or wasn't present during this question. Hard to tell.

Fauntroy then asked Witt about where he kept his umbrella. Witt said that he kept them in the car, at work, in the closet, and even stumbled over one in the garage one day. This guy had more umbrellas than the Penguin! He then goes on to describe, at the request of Mr. Ford, the many uses of an umbrella. Obviously, the conversation has sunk to all-time lows here. He stated the real reason he went to view the President was to heckle him based on conversations he had during coffee breaks at work. As Richard Trask says, "He had been told that the open umbrella "was sort of a sore spot with the Kennedys," since it symbolized Prime Minister Neville Chamberlain's (*who often carried a black umbrella*) and United States Ambassador to Great Britain Joseph P. Kennedy's apparent appeasement of the Nazis prior to World War II.

And to repeat, Witt says as he was moving forward and opening his umbrella he heard shots and, by the time he brought his umbrella over his head, "I was at the retaining wall and standing on it" (IV HSCA 440). Doesn't Fauntroy, or anyone else for that matter, think it is odd that Witt makes this statement? He, I think, obviously means the curb, but keeps calling it the retaining wall. You would think at the very least that clarification would be in order. He couldn't possibly have been standing where he said he was. He does recall seeing a couple covering their children, which was probably a reference to the Newmans, who were west of Witt, indicating he has looked at photographs indicating as much. He says he never looked directly at the dark-complexioned man sitting next to him, and that there was never any dialogue, other than the man saying, "they done shot them folks."

When it came time for Stokes to open the umbrella, so as to lay to rest any speculations about there being a dart gun or some kind of flechette device in it, the scene becomes a comic relief skit. Cynthia Cooper was asked to open the umbrella, but not toward Mr. Stokes, to be sure. He suggested she point it toward the press and cameras, which of course, induced laughter throughout the Committee room. I tried to count the spokes in the umbrella at Z-228, which is probably the best photo of the opened umbrella, and while the view may not be the best, there seems to be 12 spokes. I could count them after Ms. Cooper opened the umbrella when Witt was giving testimony, and it looks like there are also 12 spokes. I am assuming this is the number of spokes in a standard umbrella. There is another picture of it as well, F-405, but it is just too crumpled to count anything with precision, though again, there seems to be 12 spokes. But even if 12 spokes are seen in Z-228 and when the umbrella is opened during Witt's testimony, it doesn't prove they are the same umbrella, only that each has 12 spokes.

Witt stated to Mr. Devine that he heard three or more shots in very rapid succession. Again, Witt went on to say he wasn't aware of the person next to him, sitting or standing. How could Witt not notice him, especially when, it appears, they both stood and sat at the same time? He claimed earlier something the dark-complected man said, but now has amnesia and doesn't even recall his presence, or at the very least the exact time the gentleman to his right appeared, possibly at the time of the assassination or sometime later. They sat close to each other in an all-too casual manner. Witt refers to the people running up the grassy knoll, and indicates he thought they were all "Secret Servicemen or plainclothesmen" (IV HSCA 445). I don't want to nit-pick at his words, but it seems to me the Committee should have sought clarification on more than one occasion.

Saying that he didn't know that the president had been shot, especially where he is standing, is just nonsensical to me. He said he went back to his place of employment, and only then did he realize the president had been shot. Knowing where he was standing, according to the film footage and still photographs taken that day, he couldn't possibly have been unaware of the President being shot. He was also ignorant about which direction the shots came from or the number of shots, only that they had been in rapid succession. That is at least somewhat understandable. When pressed he said the total number of shots were three or more.

Mr. McKinney asked him if he noticed anything or anyone by the picket fence or the retaining wall. He said he hadn't, "because at no point was I ever facing that direction," even though he had earlier stated that he "was at the retaining wall and standing on it" (IV HSCA 449, 440). Witt then stated he didn't even know where the picket fence is. Even after 15 years and all of the attention paid to the picket fence on the grassy knoll?

Mr. McKinney then attempted to summarize Mr. Witt's thoughts. He admits it is difficult to do, in view of Witt's trouble in doing so with his own thoughts. This seems grossly understated, given Witt's testimony. To be fair, Witt may just be a simple man who isn't articulate and recollecting very well, or he was mostly brought out to dance for the HSCA.

Mr. Edgar then asked Witt why he didn't come forward and tell what he knew to the police. He said he wouldn't have come forward due to the danger involved. For someone who is oblivious to so many things happening that day, yet is afraid to come forward with any information, because of the danger involved, seems highly fictional. Hard to believe he would have been aware of some kind of conspiratorial plot that day, when he can't distinguish between a curb and a retaining wall. A lot of witnesses were seemingly afraid that day, Brennan, Benavides, etc. Witt simply says that he can't recall what he was thinking that day.

Witt can give no details, except one utterance made by the dark-complexioned man, when asked about the gentleman sitting to his right, and about the possibility he was using or holding a two-way walkie-talkie. He had said earlier, that if the person to his right would "have been carrying something, it would not have registered on me at this particular time" (IV HSCA 436). He concludes by promising to never demonstrate again. The world can now rest.

Louis Steven Witt is not the only individual to have been named the "umbrella man." Gordon Novel, who bears a striking resemblance to umbrella man in Bothun #4 (see photo below) has also been designated with this title.

You will have to decide for yourself if Louis Steven Witt is telling the truth. He is either telling the truth, but terribly confused about the geography of Dealey Plaza or simply making this all up. Is our good friend "Tink" Thompson correct? Is this a matter of reading something into a situation that simply isn't true, or is the simplest, yet obviously more bizarre explanation the right one after all? At the end of the day, some claim you can count the spokes of the umbrella just to the right of the Stemmons Freeway sign that fateful day and then count the spokes in the umbrella that Witt brings to the Committee and they just don't match...but even if that is true, and I was unable to do it with precise accuracy, though I think I counted twelve spokes. It may just mean Witt grabbed the wrong umbrella. After all, he did have a lot of umbrellas and apparently still does.

Whoever the man was with the umbrella that day, his behavior and that of the man next to him is at best odd and at worst sinister, but this case has always seemed to incite the bizarre and the fantastic. Are we on the quantum level historically here or do we see this for what it really is, another stooge on the government stage wearing a mask? If the government was probing for truth, why didn't they ask Witt for a picture of himself c.1963 and compare it to the Rickerby photo? Most of us know the answer. The HSCA and other so-called investigations weren't really investigations at all. And now, almost 60 years after that terrible day, many of us are still very, very frustrated.

38

JACQUELINE HESS
SEPTEMBER 25, 1978

On September 25, 1978, Jacqueline Hess gave testimony before the HSCA in Washington, D.C.

H ess, was "in charge of the mysterious deaths project." (IV HSCA 454ff) Hess began her testimony by being shown the list of names at the conclusion of Donald Freed's and Mark Lane's *Executive Action*, and the statement by an actuary employed by the *London Sunday Times* stating very high odds against so many significant individuals dying in such a short time. Initially, the actuary is quoted as citing odds of "1 in 10 to the 29th power, or 100,000 trillion to 1." (IV HSCA 462)

The House Select Committee sent a letter to the *London Sunday Times* and received a response that the data represented a "careless journalistic mistake and should not have been published. ... There was no question of our actuary having got his answer wrong: It was simply that we asked him the wrong question." (IV HSCA 464)

The Committee engaged an actuarial firm, and it was demonstrated "the impossibility of attempting to establish through the application of actuarial principles, any meaningful implications about the existence or absence of conspiracy." (IV HSCA 465)

> Hess continued: "Despite the fact that an inference of conspiracy, as here postulated by the critics, did not exist, we nevertheless decided not to dismiss the cited deaths out of hand, but rather, to look more closely at the nature of certain specific deaths to determine whether or not they could individually be considered

mysterious or in some other manner a reflection of some sort of conspiracy." (IV HSCA 465-466)

The significance of some witnesses is rejected, so they could lessen the conspiratorial claims of some, while others, notably heart attack victims such as Earlene Roberts and Dr. Nicholas Chetta, are simply ruled out as heart attack victims. When in doubt, dodge. "Our final conclusion on the issue is that the available evidence does not establish anything about the nature of these deaths which would indicate that the deaths were in some manner, either direct or peripheral, caused by the assassination of President Kennedy or by any aspect of the subsequent investigation." (IV HSCA 467)

With that simple discharge, this part of the case was locked and sealed. The names of those inspected were read into the record, though the list is not inclusive and covers the known oddities among the research community.

I'm not generally a subscriber to some massive mystery death theory, but it is my suspicion that a few people simply knew more than they should have; and their deaths involved some manner of foul play.

When Congressman Edgar asked why "Mr. DeMohrenschildt's" name was not included, Hess answered, somewhat obliquely, "His was one of those which deemed further investigation and became part of a great investigative effort." (IV HSCA 467-468)

In other words, no answer. I have no idea what that is insinuating.

39

Earl Ruby –
September 26, 1978

On September 26, 1978, Earl Ruby testified before the HSCA in Washington, D.C.

E arl Ruby stated that he loaned his brother Jack $15,000, with an additional explanation that the money was never paid back and "he had other investors from what I understand in opening of the Carousel." (IV HSCA 502)

His brother Earl also said that in 1959, apparently the year Jack lost the last $6,000 he was loaned, that he made a trip to Cuba to see Lewis McWillie, as the trip was paid for by McWillie. "He thought very highly of McWillie and it was more or less of a friendship visit." (IV HSCA 504)

Ruby's testimony suggested that Jack Ruby had sent Lewis McWillie a gun; but said that McWillie was afraid to pick it up at the post office.

Earl Ruby is also questioned about a telegram transmitted from his place of business, Cabo Cleaners, in 1962 to Cuba, and it is stated that in a prior deposition, Ruby had no awareness of the telegram. Later, in a letter to the Committee, August 17, 1978, Ruby said that there are six states in the United States which contain a Cuba (Alabama, Illinois, Kansas, New Mexico, New York, and Ohio), and as a result, he could now plainly assert that no telegram had been sent to Havana, Cuba.

Mr. McDonald then read from an IRS document designating the telegram was sent, April 1, 1962, to Havana, Cuba. Several pages of dialogue follow, which contain many breaks by Adelson interrupting the attorney for Ruby. The issue was terminated and unsolved. (IV HSCA 507-510)

Ruby expounded that his brother explained to him in person, what his reasons were for shooting Lee Oswald: "When I saw him personally in Dallas, I did ask him and he said when Oswald walked out of that doorway, he had a silly smirk on his face as though it seemed to Jack that he really felt good about it, and that is when Jack lost control of himself and shot him."

> HSCA Counsel McDonald: "Did you ask Jack what he was doing in the basement that morning of the Dallas Police Department?"
>
> Mr. Ruby: "We talked about it and he said he had gone to send a telegram and he saw the commotion in front of the police station and went over to see what was doing and went down in there, that is how it happened."
>
> Mr. McDonald: "Did you believe what he was telling you?"
>
> Mr. Ruby: "I had no reason not to believe him."
>
> Mr. McDonald: "Did you ever ask him if he was involved with anyone else?"...
>
> Mr. Ruby: "At one time when he was in the hospital, because it was much easier to talk to him there, we weren't talking through the cell, and I asked him point blank if he had ever known or met Oswald before, and his words were absolutely not, 'are you nuts.'? Those were his words to me."...
>
> Mr. McDonald: "Did you ask him anything further, did you probe on it?"
>
> Mr. Ruby: "No; not that I can think of right now. We talked at length many times but so many conversations about the trial and the attorneys and many times he was worried about my family and myself as to our well-being and, in fact, one time he was sur-

prised I even answered the phone. He thought I had been killed, for some reason or another." ...

Mr. McDonald: "Did he ever give you any hint that he was involved with someone else in the killing of Oswald?"

Mr. Ruby: "Absolutely not." (House Select Committee testimony of Earl Ruby, 4H 511-513)

Earl Ruby was adamant that Jack was not good at keeping secrets, and seemed genuinely contrite at the end, and that the family had paid out large sums of money to get his brother Jack a new trial, but then he was diagnosed with terminal cancer. If there is ever a time for truth, that is ordinarily it.

Attorney Adelson specified that Ruby's mental state did not involve some kind of psychomotor epilepsy as his attorney, Melvin Belli, had contended, but that he was in a serious state of paranoia. He was only one floor from the mental ward, where screeches showered at all hours, day and night, and he was also familiar with Leon Uris' book *Exodus* and consequently, thought about all kinds of horrendous circumstances about the Jewish population, not just in Dallas, but all over the United States.

Adelson was permitted to speak, though never sworn in; and was unrelenting that it was Jack Ruby's mental persecution that he was living with day and night and was the cause for his repeated wishes to be taken to Washington after he had given testimony from his Dallas jail cell to Earl Warren, Gerald Ford, and Arlen Specter.

Adelson was questioned more than Earl Ruby was, by the different congressmen in the aftermath of his candid testimony before Counsel McDonald.

Earl Ruby seems to be an example of who you call to testify, when you don't want to entertain unpleasant data. Between 1947, when Jack Ruby moved to Dallas to join their sister, Eva Grant, and November 24, 1963, when the Warren Commission was created, the two brothers were together three or four times, in a sixteen-year period.

The only thing we learned from Earl Ruby's testimony was that his brother, Jack, told him he did not know Lee Oswald and that he had shot him because of a smirkish grin. Okay.

Another Warren Commission disaster was divulged, by House Select Committee General Counsel Blakey, when he requested the introduction of Exhibits JFK F-591, F-592, and 593:

"In a lengthy memorandum, Hubert and Griffin recommended that the FBI be instructed to secure the records, and that Commission Chairman Earl Warren address a letter to telephone companies to secure preservation of existing records.

"Some records that were specified in the Griffin-Hubert request were obtained, but the extensive preservation they had envisioned was not carried out, an investigative step that Hubert and Griffin ultimately agreed to.

Griffin has said that Commission General Counsel J. Lee Rankin vetoed the recommendation on grounds that it was too far reaching and would create too great a burden on private companies." ...

"In another memorandum dated April 4, Griffin and Hubert said they needed additional assistance in evaluating the phone records that were available. *Though it was suggested by Rankin that Chief Justice Warren's security guard might be able to devote some time to the project, the project envisioned by Griffin and Hubert was never conducted.* In a subsequent memorandum dated May 14, the adequacy of the Ruby investigation was discussed, but ultimately compromises were worked out and the Commission's work was completed." (IV HSCA 545, 548)

Blakey noted that,

"Between Jue and August of 1963, Jack Ruby placed seven long-distance calls to one Lewis J. McWillie. McWillie was a close Ruby associated, as Ruby told the Warren Commission. In 1959, Ruby had visited Lewis McWillie in Havana, where McWillie was working in an organized crime-connected casino."

There is also notice taken of a twelve-minute phone call between Ruby and Irwin S. Weiner, a mob mouthpiece. "In the immediate days following President Kennedy's murder, the FBI sought to question Weiner about the call he had received from Ruby on October 26. According to an FBI teletype of November 28, 1963, Weiner refused to respond to questioning by FBI agents in Chicago with regard to his contact with Ruby, and he declined to assist the investigation in any way." ...

Though the Warren Commission was aware of Ruby's phone call to Weiner, the Commission never sought to have him questioned under oath. Additionally, neither Ruby nor his brother, Earl, were ever asked by the Commission about their relationship with Weiner." (IV HSCA 563 - 564)

How appropriate is this? "I'm not talking to the FBI," Weiner said, and that was that? Are you kidding me? If you or I tried that, we would be put in a holding cell, until we found a willingness to get talkative with FBI agents. Different rules.

So, Weiner was asked to give witness in executive session before the HSCA:

> "Weiner declared the purpose of Ruby's call was to seek assistance in the labor dispute he was having with his Dallas nightclub competitors. Ruby asked for aid in putting up a bond related to his attempt to file for an injunction against his competitors. Weiner testified that he declined to assist Ruby; and had no further contact with him." (IV HSCA 564)

Why didn't he offer this plain and nontoxic rationalization to the FBI in 1963?

> "...the committee has not found another reference to an effort by Ruby to put up a bond in connection with seeking an injunction against his competitors. In his appearance before the committee, Weiner further testified that he had lied to a reporter when he said in a taped interview that Ruby's phone call to him on October 26, 1963, had nothing to do with labor problems.
>
> Weiner testified he had refused to submit to FBI questioning about Ruby in the weeks following the assassination because he believed Bureau agents had harassed his daughter by implying that he might be connected to the assassination. **Weiner stated he could not specifically recall where he was on the day of the assassination or on the day Ruby shot Oswald, though he believed he was on a visit to Miami.**" (IV HSCA 564- 565)
>
> "Two, a call made on September 24, 1963, by an investigator for New Orleans Mafia leader Carlos Marcello to a woman in Chicago who was present with Ruby on the night before the assassination."

The committee found that **David W. Ferrie** had called the number of **Jean West** and had spoken for at least 15 minutes. On November 21, 1963, Miss West visited Ruby in Dallas, accompanied by a mutual friend, **Lawrence Meyers**. Miss West and Meyers had drinks with Ruby shortly before midnight on November 21 at the Cabana Motel." (IV HSCA 567)

Recall that when Meyers' deposition was taken by the Warren Commission, the evidence acquired was that he was from Chicago and blissfully married. There was no mention of *Jean West*, but other testimony has put her at the scene with Meyers, though she is usually cited as *Jean Aase*. **These names should be committed to memory, because of a hinted-at theme throughout the book:** <u>**military intelligence**</u>.

Blakey is structuring towards the book he will eventually write, [G. Robert Blakey and Richard N. Billings, *The Plot to Kill the President: Organized Crime Assassinated JFK; the Definitive Story*], where he makes David W. Ferrie out to be an organized-crime-connected person, not the right-wing fanatic and anti-Castro character that he was.

40

CAPT. JACK REVILL
SEPTEMBER 26, 1978

On Sept. 26, 1978, Capt. Jack Revill testified before the HSCA in Washington, D.C.

Following the listing of phone call data, Blakey called the subsequent witness, Lt. Jack Revill of the Criminal Identification Department (CID) of the Dallas Police Department.

House Select Counsel Andrew Purdy: "In your work with the intelligence division, did you gain access to information concerning all types of criminal activity or just specific types?"

Lt. Revill: "All types of criminal activity."

Mr. Purdy: "Do you have any knowledge of specific criminal activities by Jack Ruby?

Lt. Revill: "Nothing specific. I knew Jack Ruby by reputation."
(IV HSCA 569)

One important issue in the trial of Jack Ruby, is when officers were asked how they knew the suspect was Jack Ruby. In a few situations, the answer was "Because I had previously arrested him."

The point is: Lt. Revill should have known more than "nothing specific" about Jack Ruby.

Revill talked about prostitution, narcotics, illegal gambling, and organized crime elements in Dallas, in the 1950's and 1960's, but in each particular example about the involvement of Jack Ruby, Revill had no data to share with the HSCA.

Mr. Purdy: "Did you have any knowledge of Jack Ruby's associations with any gamblers or anyone else involved with illegal activity?"

Lt. Revill: "Jack Ruby was the type of person who would have been acquainted with persons involved in gambling activities and other criminal activities, but as far as Jack Ruby being actively engaged or a member of any groups, no, nothing to indicate this." ...

Mr. Purdy: "What was your general impression of Jack Ruby?"

Lt. Revill: "Jack Ruby was a buffoon. He liked the limelight. He was highly volatile. He liked to be recognized with people, and I would say this to the committee: if Jack Ruby was a member of organized crime, then the personnel director of organized crime should be replaced."

Mr. Purdy: "Did Jack Ruby receive any benefits or favors from members of the police department in their treatment of him?"

Lt, Revill: "I sincerely hope not." ...

Mr. Purdy: "Did the FBI provide the Dallas Police Department with the identities of or information concerning the FBI informants in the 1950's and 1960's?"

Lt. Revill: "No, sir, they did not."

Mr. Purdy: "Were you aware that the FBI had contact with Jack Ruby in 1959 to try to develop an informant relationship with him?"

Lt. Revill: "No, sir." ...

Mr. Purdy: "As I am sure you know, Jack Ruby was present in the police headquarters on a number of occasions during the weekend following the assassination of President Kennedy. To your knowledge, was his presence ever challenged by any member of the Dallas Police Department?

Lt. Revill: "Not to my knowledge."

Mr. Purdy: "Why do you think this was the case? Do you think it was because he was known to so many officers?"

Lt. Revill: "I have no way of knowing why he was not challenged except that the police and courts building was not secured during the day of the assassination of Mr. Kennedy. The following day, which was Saturday, November 23, it was not secured, and on the date of Ruby's assassination of Lee Harvey Oswald, the only area that I have knowledge of that was supposed to be secured was the basement area where the transfer of Mr. Oswald was to take place."

Mr. Purdy: "Was anyone punished for the lax security present in the police department headquarters during that weekend?"

Lt. Revill: "Not to my knowledge. One man who currently serves as my administrative sergeant feels that he was maligned due to his activities. This is Sgt. Roy Gene Vaughn, who at that time was a uniform patrolman who was assigned to the ramp on Main Street leading into the basement of the city hall, and Sergeant Vaughn has told me that he feels that he was punished in that his efficiency, his personal evaluation, numerical score, was cut a couple of points, and that is the only thing that I have ever heard." (IV HSCA 570-572)

Lt. Revill was asked about Ruby getting admittance to the basement on the morning of November 24th, and though he doesn't protect Roy Vaughn, it is obvious he has a soft spot for Vaughn. He stated that from unbiased and independent statements from Sergeant Don Flusche it was obvious that Jack Ruby, whom Flusche actually knew, did not enter down the Main Street Ramp.

Lt. Revill stated that he personally measured the distance from the Western Union counter to where Jack Ruby shot Oswald, and it was c. 454 feet. He then performed tests that were timed, which persuaded him that the distance could be covered in 1:30 or 1:35, so time was not an issue.

"There are also two other alternatives, and it is a possibility. After determining that information from Sergeant Flusche, Mr.

Moriarity and I personally walked to the basement of city hall, and I found some more steps. I have been there in that building off and on almost 28 years, and I didn't know the steps were there; never paid any attention to them. There is another set of steps here that lead into the basement of city hall." (IV HSCA 588) ...

Congressman Sawyer: "Did you ever ask Jack Ruby following this how he got into the basement?"

Lt. Revill: "Yes, sir; I did. On December 1, Lieutenant Cornwall and I went to the Dallas County jail and interviewed Jack Ruby.

"Jack refused to discuss with us his entrance or access into the basement. He told us this would be a part of his defense tactics. Again, on December 3, I interviewed Jack Ruby and he repeated the same thing. He refused to discuss how he gained entry into the basement." (IV HSCA 589)

Did Ruby think that his means of gaining entry would soften the character of his televised crime? If so, this is a mystery to me, but then so was Jack Ruby. This goes beyond momentary lunacy.

Mr. Sawyer: "Was there every any kind of finding as to negligence or otherwise on the protection of this area made by your unit?"

Lt. Revill: "I think it is a foregone conclusion that there was negligence; we let the man get killed. But as far as being able to identify any one individual as being responsible or negligent, no, sir." (IV HSCA 591)

Lt. Revill was asked by Congressman Dodd about the supposed 3:00 p.m., CST run-in with FBI S/A James Hosty, and Revill narrated the affair just as he had before the Warren Commission: "He [Hosty] just happened to be coming into the building. We both parked our cars. He approached me, and again from memory, he commented to the effect that Lee Harvey Oswald, a Communist, had killed President Kennedy." (IV HSCA 604)

In his HSCA description, Revill set the time as possibly 2:30, but "It was at a time after Oswald had been taken into custody at the Texas Theater but before his arrival at the Police and Courts Building [which would make it *well before 2:30 or 3:00*]. Furthermore, Revill was not, at the time of Hosty's statement, mindful that Lee Oswald had been arrested. Revill added that he wrote a memo regarding the event: the famous "Gannaway memo" that appeared on April 22 and caused spasms in the Warren Commission because it suggested negligence on the part of the FBI to contact the Secret Service; but also stated he trusted that the memo would never appear.

> Mr. Dodd: "Would you tell this committee why you hoped it would never come up?"
>
> Lt. Revill: "Because Jim Hosty was a friend of mine and I knew that Hoover would crucify him." [*Someone is now speaking ill of Mr. Hoover... rare.*]
>
> Mr. Dodd: "Crucify him for what?"
>
> Lt. Revill: "For making that statement. ... I relayed the information to my captain at that time, Pat Gannaway, shortly after our conversation, and he instructed me to reduce it to writing.
>
> At that time I told him, 'If I do, Jim Hosty will be crucified or penalized by the Bureau,' and to that he said, 'I don't care, you put it on paper.' I put it on paper." (IV HSCA 606)

41

LEWIS MCWILLIE –
SEPTEMBER 27, 1978

On September 27, Lewis McWillie testified before the HSCA in Washington, D.C.

The material that is discussed on September 27th is completely redundant and superfluous. There are names of certain mob figures that are exposed and put into the arena, and Lewis McWillie is aware of some of those, but unable to precisely say if Jack Ruby knew them as well.

This seems like more of an annoyance to simply go through a series of names and determine which Castro jail they were incarcerated in and though it may point to motive, it certainly misses the overall aim and only serves as a disruption and interference, as we wait for something to happen.

Lewis McWillie used rule 6 for his testimony, indicating he was not to be televised or recorded during his testimony, not to mention the taking of photographs would be forbidden. He was able to garner some laughter from the audience, stating he couldn't tolerate Jack Ruby for any sustained period of time.

Howard Shapiro, a House Select Committee staffer, walked to the easels, as we have seen many do already, to display documents that suggested Ruby had been to Cuba twice.

> "As I said, these exhibits are blowups of materials which the committee received from the Cuban Government earlier this year. We have two cards – and we have a blowup of the front side and the back side of each card.
>
> "What these cards indicate are two visits to Cuba by Jack Ruby, and further they indicate the dates of those visits. The first card indicates that Jack Ruby entered Cuba on August 8, 1959, the date of entry being written in on the back of the card. The front of the card indicating that Jack Ruby left the United States from New Orleans.
>
> "The back of the card also indicates that Jack Ruby left Cuba on this visit on September 11, 1959; therefore, the card indicating that Jack Ruby was in Cuba from August 8 to September 11, 1959.
>
> "The second card indicates that Jack Ruby entered Cuba on September 12, 1959, and left on the 13th of September 1959, and the front side of the card would indicate that his entry from the United States was from Miami, Fla. Thank you, Mr. Chairman." (V HSCA 197-198)

Chairman Stokes: "Now, does that information help refresh your recollection, first, as to whether Jack Ruby came in August and left in September, and also whether he remained there over a period of 6 days?"

Mr. McWillie: "Sir, he stayed there 6 days, as far as I can remember...."

Chairman Stokes: "August 8 was his entrance date, a departure date of the 11th—September 11.

Mr. McWillie: "Oh, no, no, he wasn't there that long."

Chairman Stokes: "He wasn't there that long?"

Mr. McWillie: "No, sir."

Chairman Stokes: "During the period of time that he was there, did he leave the country and come back again during that 6-day period?"

Mr. McWillie: "No, sir." (V HSCA 198)

After the entrance of a few exhibits, House Select Committee Chairman Stokes throws some disorientation into the present account by submitting "into the record an FBI report dated November 29, 1969 [*most likely a misstatement or a misprint, as the FBI was not doing any investigating in 1969.*], concerning the records of the Merchant State Bank in Dallas as they pertain to Jack Ruby. [JFK exhibit F-585] …. That exhibit will reflect information concerning Jack Ruby's use of safety deposit box No. 448. Among other dates listed, that exhibit will indicate that Jack Ruby was admitted to the safety deposit box on August 20, 1959, and September 4, 1959. [*Recall that Ruby was purportedly in Cuba on August 20, 1959; he may have left for the mentioned McWillie vacation on or after visiting the box on September 4, 1959.*]

> "Mr. Chairman, I would also like to enter into the record at this point the *FBI report by Agent Charles Flynn, which is the FBI's record of the status of Jack Ruby as a potential criminal informant.*" (V HSCA 201—205, including the cited exhibits)
>
> "In summary, what these records will tend to indicate is that Jack Ruby was in Dallas, Tex. On August 6, August 21, August 31, and September 4, 1959. Therefore, *if the Cuban records are correct*, Jack Ruby was in Havana, Cuba, on August 8, 1959; he must have left Cuba and returned to Dallas and traveled to Cuba again prior to the September 11 departure date that has been mentioned earlier.
>
> "Now, Mr. McWillie, if Mr. Ruby made a 1-day trip in and out of the country, would you be able to tell us what that trip was about?"
>
> Mr. McWillie: "If he did make a trip, I would not know about it, sir; and I would think I would know it, and I didn't see Jack Ruby after he left that one time." (V HSCA 221)

The testimony then repeats what McWillie had already said about Ruby attending the casino at night when McWillie was running things, and then the added list of questions about what Ruby was doing that McWillie apparently didn't know anything about.

McWillie denied any knowledge of Ruby as some kind of negotiator or representative for Cuba and America,

> "Because I know for a fact, he wasn't there over 6 days when he visited me."

455

Chairman Stokes: "We will have the—"

Mr. McWillie: "I couldn't have stood it that long." ...

Mr. Shapiro: "These cards here indicate a trip on Jack Ruby entering Cuba on August 8, 1959, and leaving on September 11. Therefore, the card indicates that Jack Ruby was there for a period of 1 month and 3 days."

Mr. McWillie: "No way, he wasn't there not over 6 days. I took him to the airport."

Chairman Stokes: "Mr. McWillie, does that clear it up?"

Mr. McWillie: "That is clear all right, but that is not right, because when he came to visit me he stayed 6 days at the most; he stayed 6 days and there is some foul up with that ticket or something. If he had stayed there a month, I would say a month, I wouldn't be ashamed to say it. Jack Ruby was the kind of fellow that 6 days would be long enough to be around him. I am sure he wasn't there a month. [*Laughter.*]"

Chairman Stokes: "You are pretty sure then?"

Mr. McWillie: "I am not trying to be smart, sir."

Chairman Stokes: "I understand."

Mr. McWillie: "I am telling it like it is."

Chairman Stokes: "Did you ever ask Mr. Ruby to get you four guns from Ray Brentley's [*Brantley*] gun store and send them to you in Cuba?"

Mr. McWillie: "No, sir; I have been asked that a dozen times and I didn't do that. In the first place, Jack Ruby couldn't have sent any guns to Cuba and I couldn't have gotten them in Cuba. If I had, I hate to think what would have happened to me.".…

Chairman Stokes: "Here is Jack Ruby's testimony to the Warren Commission, volume 5, page 201, says that you had called Jack Ruby from Cuba, asking him to pick up four Cobra pistols at Ray Brentley's hardware store and send to you.

"According to Jack Ruby, you were concerned about the new regime coming in, you wanted some protection. Your testimony is that this never happened?"

Mr. McWillie: "This never happened, sir, and there is no way I could call Jack Ruby and ask him to send guns over there because every call was monitored in Havana, every call, and I would hate to get caught with a gun in Cuba when I was there." (V HSCA 234—235)

The Jack Ruby testimony, taken from 5 H 201 in the Warren volumes is contextually from an exceedingly discursive conversation, not untypical for Jack Ruby during that particular testimony, but he disavowed that someone had verified with Ray Brantley, who ran a hardware store and sold guns, that Ruby had never made such a call about "four little cobras." (5 H 201)

Congressman Floyd Fithian brought up the "Fair Play for Cuba" reference cited in the April 4, 1978 House Select Committee deposition, and it was quickly modified to state that McWillie had committed an assault against an individual at the Miami Airport and that it was that fellow who was involved with the "Fair Play for Cuba," and not McWillie. (V HSCA 238)

The testimony of Lewis McWillie came to a close; however, McWillie asked, "Congressman, am I free to go home?" to which he responded that he was "free to go."

42

JOSE ALEMAN –
SEPTEMBER 27, 1978

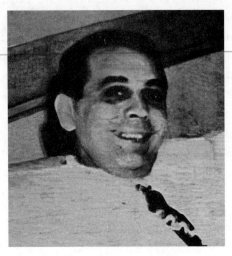

On September 27, 1978, Jose Aleman testified before the HSCA in Washington, D.C.

Jose Aleman, who was the son of the one-time minister of education in Cuba, c. 1947, quickly transported Jimmy Hoffa into the picture:

> House Select Counsel Cornwell: "And during this period of time [*a hotel meeting, c. June or July, 1963, Miami*] tell us specifically what was discussed, what was said by Mr. Trafficante, and what, if anything, you said in reply with respect to Hoffa and the political scene?
>
> Mr. Aleman: "Well, he [*Trafficante*] was very much upset. He said that the way the President was getting into Hoffa, a man of the workers, blue collar, and a man that was a very hard-working individual, and that at the same time he was very much upset. I mean, he thought for a long period of time."

Mr. Cornwell: "Very much upset what Kennedy had been doing to Hoffa, and he felt sympathetic toward Hoffa describing him as a man—

Mr. Cornwell: [*continuing*] "Of the workers?"

Mr. Aleman: "Very much."

Mr. Cornwell: "Go ahead. What did the conversation lead to next?"

Mr. Aleman: "At one point he said, 'You see this man, he is not going to be re-elected, there is no doubt about it, he has been the man that has been giving everybody a lot of troubles and he is not going to be re-elected' and I don't know why he said that to me or anything. Then he said—"

Mr. Cornwell: "Did you make a reply to that?"

Mr. Aleman: "Yes; I said he has a lot of Democrats backing him and so far it looks very well. I don't see anything that he is not going to be re-elected or anything."

Mr. Cornwell: "And what, if anything, did he reply?"

Mr. Aleman: "Well, he said he is not going to be re-elected, you don't understand me, he is going to be hit." (V HSCA 305)

Jose Aleman said that he didn't have any knowledge of what the phrase "going to be hit" meant, and also said that Trafficante continued to talk and Aleman didn't attempt to interject anything into the conversation.

It seems slightly ridiculous that someone who had confessed to being part of the coup against Batista, and also attempted take part in the overthrow of Castro, not to mention owned a hotel in Miami Beach, would claim to be oblivious concerning the phrase "going to be hit"? Someone sounds nervous and scared.

The first interview with Jose Aleman, which was conducted by Gaeton Fonzi, gives suggestion he knew precisely what was meant, and a comparable response came through intensely in a Washington Post article penned by George Crile.

Mr. Cornwell: "Mr. Aleman, that [*JFK Exhibit F-601*] in an excerpt from a report of an investigator of ours, Gaeton Fonzi, dated March 12, 1977, and I would like to specifically direct your attention to the first paragraph which reads as follows: 'Aleman said in more than one way that Trafficante did specifically tell him that Kennedy is "going to get hit." He also specifically confirmed the quote that Crile printed in the *Washington Post* on this point: "Aleman says that he argued that Kennedy would get re-elected and Trafficante replied, 'No, Jose, he is going to get hit.'"

"Let me ask you, did you meet with Mr. Fonzi on that occasion?"

Aleman responded with a lengthy answer, and when that got nowhere, he resorted to the "I was trying to recollect things from a long period of time" excuse. (V HSCA 314—315)

Most people understand very well the story that implicates Trafficante in the quote about Kennedy and how he "is going to get hit," yet the person who heard the threat against the President of the United States had trouble recalling it.

As Aleman tried to avoid and get around the fact that he comprehended Trafficante's meaning, he regretted the lack of safety when he was flown to Washington and met by House Select Committee staffers. He suggested that Trafficante knows of Aleman's accusations, and he feared for his safety

> "There is some connection between Santo Trafficante and the Cuban Government. There's no doubt about that. I came very brave here to this committee to talk that I had been concerned with this and you should pay attention, as patiently as I have been with you people, and react." (V HSCA 323)

> Mr. Cornwell: "Thank you. I have no further questions."

In later clarification, it was suggested that Aleman's testimony was based chiefly on fear of Trafficante (the next witness to testify), rather than a straightforward description of events.

43

SANTOS TRAFFICANTE –
SEPTEMBER 28, 1978

On Sept. 28, Santos Trafficante gave testimony before the HSCA in Washington, D.C.

G eneral Counsel Blakey: "Mr. Chairman, I understand Mr. Trafficante has requested that there be no radio, TV, photographs,
or recordings made of him at any time during his testimony.
Consequently, it would be appropriately consistent with the rules of the
committee and the House to enter an order to that effect."

The opening question was Trafficante's full name, and the next was
his address, so it is difficult to understand why he requested the black-
out. Then, when Chairman Stokes got as profound as,

"Will you tell us when and where you were born?":

Mr. Trafficante: "At this time I want to exercise my privilege and
my constitutional right to take the Fifth amendment."

> Chairman Stokes: "Mr. Chairman, I request that you have the clerk show the witness JFK exhibit No. F-141, an order of Judge Gasch conferring immunity upon the witness and compelling his testimony." (V HSCA 346)

Trafficante was having some health problems and asked that to be taken into consideration during the course of the questioning. Seven prescriptions he was taking was then read into the record. "In essence, Mr. Trafficante is an ill man and has significant cardiovascular disease, making him at great risk for a recurrence of myocardial infarction. His angina is brought on by stressful events, either physical or emotional."

Once the immunity dispute was taken care of, Trafficante publicly revealed that he was born on November 15, 1914. Not exactly earth shattering.

Trafficante was questioned about being detained, which is the word he used in response to this line of inquiry, by Cuban officials and was then asked when it happened.

> Trafficante: "I cannot tell you the exact date, but the thing was that *I was detained*, I was being—how would you call it [*conferred with counsel*]—I got news that Cuban officials were looking for to put me in jail because one of the things was that I was a Batista collaborator. They raided my apartment, they were looking for money, they tore up all the furniture, they used to come and get me at nighttime, take me out in the woods, trying to tell where I had my money, this and that, until I finally went into hiding. And they kept on and nobody knew what was going on.
>
> I mean, these were a bunch of – most of them were 15, 16, 17 years old. They had weapons; it was a bad time to be around there."

> Chairman Stokes: "Now, do the dates June 8 to August 18, 1959, sound about the time you were imprisoned?"

> Trafficante: "Well, no. I was imprisoned on June 21ˢᵗ. I was there because one of my daughters got married on that day, and I had been in jail before. I had been in jail, I would say, at least a month or two. They let me out that day to go to the wedding because the thing was that these people thought—when they finally arrested me, they thought that I was being, that I was wanted in the United States for all kinds of charges—narcotics...."

Stokes: "So it wasn't actually like a prison, was it?" [*Trafficante referred to it as "Trescornia, which was an immigration center."*]

Trafficante: "No; it was not. We had it pretty good. ... We had our own food coming in and everything. It was like a big camp, like a big concentration camp. We had our own room, it wasn't too bad." (V HSCA 353)

In spite of what the reader may think of Trafficante, the reader has to at least ponder, if some goons came in and ruined your way of income, tossed you in a holding camp, and devastated your living quarters, would that establish a good enough cause for retribution?

Subsequent to the entries from unspecified dates in late 1960 and into 1961, where Trafficante was enlisted to serve as an interpreter for various people, including John Roselli, Sam Giancana, and Robert Maheu, to assassinate Castro, added facts are now sought:

Chairman Stokes: "Mr. Trafficante, did you ever handle or carry poison pills to be used in the assassination of Castro?"

Mr. Trafficante: "No, sir, absolutely not."

Chairman Stokes: "Did Roselli ever give you the poison pills?"

Mr. Trafficante: "No, sir."

Stokes read from the 1967 CIA Inspector General's report in reference to the CIA's belief that Trafficante's involvement was more than what he was acknowledging, with immunity, but when the question is issued, Trafficante doesn't change anything in his responses:

Chairman Stokes: "Having heard what the Inspector General has said about this operation, would you in any way change your testimony?"

Mr. Trafficante: "No, sir." (V HSCA 363)

Chairman Stokes: "Mr. Trafficante, did you at any time receive any money for your participation in this situation?"

Mr. Trafficante: "How was that, sir?"

Chairman Stokes: "Did you at any time receive any money from anyone for your participation in the assassination—"

Mr. Trafficante: "Not a penny, no way, shape, or form."

Chairman Stokes: "Tell us what your reason was for agreeing to act as interpreter in this situation."

Mr. Trafficante: "Well, I thought I was helping the U.S. Government. That's what my reason was. And as far as the gambling and monopolies on this and that and all that trash about dope and prostitution, that's not true. If things were straightened out in Cuba, I would have liked to have gone back there. If I could gamble, I would gamble; if I couldn't gamble, I wouldn't gamble. But the reason was that I thought that it was not right for the Communists to have a base 90 miles from the United States. The same reason when the First and the Second World War, they call you to go to the draft board and sign up. I went and signed up. That's the reason. And we all like to make money."

Chairman Stokes: "I don't quite understand."

Mr. Trafficante: "I mean, we all like to make money in case there was a thing I was doing it for money, for this and for that, about going back to Cuba and gamble and have casinos or cabarets, stuff like that." (V HSCA 363 - 364)

I assume it was very annoying and unsatisfying for a lot of people and certainly the representatives of the House Select Committee, that Trafficante constantly referred to the U.S. Government in reference to the assassination of Fidel Castro. That couldn't possibly sound sweet to the ears, especially for members of Congress, who were, or at least represented, the United States government

The subject then moved forward from the Castro plots to the likelihood that CIA-Mafia plots against Castro went in reverse and became schemes against President Kennedy.

Chairman Stokes: [*reading from JFK Exhibit F-409, a Jack Anderson column*] "Before he died, Roselli hinted to associates that he knew who had arranged President Kennedy's murder. It was the same conspirators, he suggested, whom he had recruited earlier to kill Cuban Premier Fidel Castro.

By Roselli's cryptic account, Castro learned the identity of the underworld contacts in Havana who had been trying to knock him off. He believed, not altogether without basis, that President Kennedy was behind the plot.

Then over in another section, it says:

According to Roselli, Castro enlisted the same underworld elements whom he had caught plotting against him. They supposedly were Cubans from the old Trafficante organization. Working with Cuban intelligence, they allegedly lined up an ex-Marine sharpshooter, Lee Harvey Oswald, who had been active in the pro-Castro movement.

According to Roselli's version, Oswald may have shot Kennedy or may have acted as a decoy while others ambushed him from closer range. When Oswald was picked up, Roselli suggested the underworld conspirators feared he would crack and disclose information that might lead to them. This almost certainly would have brought a massive U.S. crackdown on the Mafia.

So, Jack Ruby was ordered to eliminate Oswald, making it appear as an act of reprisal against the President's killer. At least this is how Roselli explained the tragedy in Dallas.

> Chairman Stokes: Mr. Trafficante, do you have any knowledge of that?"
>
> Mr. Trafficante: "No knowledge whatsoever."
>
> Chairman Stokes: "Do you have any knowledge concerning any retaliatory action by Mr. Castro?"
>
> Mr. Trafficante: "No, sir." (V HSCA 365—366)

This is nonsense. Let's say Oswald *was* proficient with a rifle, but that doesn't explain his ability to use a piece of war surplus junk, the famed Mannlicher-Carcano, with any kind of precision, that he supposedly put together, with only God knows what, in the Texas School Book Depository.

One prerequisite for attempting to assassinate and murder the President of the United States is that you cannot fail. Lee Oswald's only connection is that he admitted to being a patsy. I can't think of anyone, who if they wanted to execute the President of the United States, would have depended on the achievements of Lee Harvey Oswald using a Mannlicher-Carcano, war surplus rifle.

Beyond ridiculous.

Lee Oswald was seemingly energetic in pro-Castro movements, but his leaflet crusade at its best, distributing 1,000 handbills, especially if he is to be looked upon as a Cuban activist and leader, is destined for failure. The leaflet campaign seems to have been staged entirely for the cameras. Nobody who is that much of a loser would be thought about for the job of killing a President.

Mr. Stokes: "Mr. Trafficante, do you know the person AMLASH, a Cuban official involved in the CIA operation also called AM-LASH, which was designed to kill Castro?"

Mr. Trafficante: "Yes." ...

Chairman Stokes: "And after you met him, was a relationship established between the two of you?"

Mr. Trafficante: "No, just a hello and goodbye, and that's it." ...

Chairman Stokes: "Mr. Trafficante, after January 1, 1962, and prior to November 22, 1963 did you have contacts with any Cuban official concerning business dealings?"

Mr. Trafficante: "Not that I remember. Cuban officials in Cuba, you mean?"

Chairman Stokes: "Right, with Cuban officials in Cuba."

Mr. Trafficante: "No, sir."

Chairman Stokes: "The answer is no, sir, right? Mr. Trafficante, Mr. Aleman stated that you paid Castro's G-2 agents in the Miami area. Have you ever given any aid or assistance to individuals you know or suspected were working for Fidel Castro after January 1, 1962, and prior to November 22, 1963?"

Mr. Trafficante: "Absolutely not; never."

Chairman Stokes: "Mr. Aleman also stated to this committee [*the previous day*] that he has 'no doubt' that there is affiliation between the Castro government and yourself."

Mr. Trafficante: "There's no affiliation whatsoever between Castro government and myself. There never has been." (V HSCA 368-369)

Chairman Stokes: "Do you know a Lewis McWillie?"

Mr. Trafficante: "Yes, sir. I seen him around Havana a lot."

Chairman Stokes: "During the period that you were detained at Trescornia, do you recall seeing Lewis McWillie visiting out there?"

Mr. Trafficante: "I don't recall it, be he might have come. He might have." ...

Chairman Stokes: "Mr. Trafficante, did you ever know a Jack Ruby?"

Mr. Trafficante: "No, sir, I never remember meeting Jack Ruby."

Chairman Stokes: "Never remember meeting him?"

Mr. Trafficante: "No."

Chairman Stokes: "Are you aware that it has been alleged that Jack Ruby visited with you while you were at Trescornia; have you heard that?"

Mr. Trafficante: "There was no reason for this man to visit me. I have never seen this man before. I have never been to Dallas; I never had no contact with him. I don't see why he was going to come and visit me."

Chairman Stokes: "Were you aware of any of the activities of a Jack Ruby?"

Mr. Trafficante: "No, sir." ...

Chairman Stokes: "Mr. Trafficante, I want to ask you a question that is very important to this committee, and that is, did you have any foreknowledge of the assassination of President Kennedy?"

Mr. Trafficante: "Absolutely not; no way."

Chairman Stokes: "Had you ever known, or had you ever heard the name Lee Harvey Oswald prior to the day President Kennedy was assassinated?"

Mr. Trafficante: "Never had in my life." (V HSCA 370-371)

Chairman Stokes: "Are you aware of any threats made by Mr. Marcello against either President Kennedy or Attorney General Kennedy?"

Mr. Trafficante: "How was that, Mr. Stokes?"

Chairman Stokes: "As a result of these conversations you had with Mr. Marcello, the fact that he was upset."

Mr. Trafficante: "Right."

Chairman Stokes: "You were upset about it. Are you aware of any threats made by Mr. Marcello against either President Kennedy or Attorney General Kennedy?"

Trafficante: "No, sir; no, no chance, no way." (V HSCA 373)

Chairman Stokes: "Was there anything else you discussed [*with José Aleman*] at that time?"

Mr. Trafficante: "As far as the Kennedy situation, I want to tell you something now, Mr. Stokes. I am sure as I am sitting here that all the discussion I had with Mr. Aleman, that I never made the statement that Kennedy was going to get hit, because all the discussion I made with Mr. Aleman, as sure as I am sitting here, I spoke to him in Spanish. No reason for me to talk to him in English language because I can speak Spanish fluently and he speaks Spanish, that is his language. There was no reason for me to tell him in English that Kennedy is going to get hit. I deny that I made that statement."

Chairman Stokes: "When did you first become aware that he had made the statement?"

Mr. Trafficante: "When it was first published in some newspaper, the *Post* or the *Times*, 2 or 3 years ago."

Chairman Stokes: "Were you aware of the fact that he had also told the FBI about it much earlier than that?"

Mr. Trafficante: "I read it in the same article, I think, that he was an FBI informant at that time."

Chairman Stokes: "Are you aware of the fact that he said that he had had a very involved discussion with you about politics? Did you ever discuss politics?"

Mr. Trafficante: "I don't remember having that discussion with him by himself, like he claims, like I read it in the paper."

Chairman Stokes: "When we take the statement that he attributed to you, when he says that you said he is not going to be re-elected, and then when he says you said, 'No, Jose, he is going to be hit'. How could he in any way misstate a statement like that from anything else you have said to him?"

Mr. Trafficante: "Because, first of all, like I told you, I was speaking to him in Spanish, and in Spanish there was no way I could say Kennedy is going to get hit. [*Really?*] I didn't say that. I might have told him he wasn't going to get re-elected."

Chairman Stokes: "What were you basing that on?"

Mr. Trafficante: "I could have told him that he was not going to get re-elected, not that Kennedy was going to get hit."

Chairman Stokes: "How did you know Kennedy was not going to get re-elected?

Mr. Trafficante: "I thought he wouldn't." (V HSCA 375-376)

There is further discussion concerning Mafia matters, but nothing is ever gained by it. Trafficante reiterates that Aleman spoke on his best day, broken English, so the conversation was in Spanish. Stokes completed the questioning and no one asked, or raised any more questions for Mr. Trafficante, which does strike me as unusual.

In the following commentary by Counsel Blakey, he noted that Trafficante's appearance before the committee ended the information put forth that organized crime, or the Mafia, generated the assassination. "Obviously, the possibility cannot be dismissed, although it can hardly be said to have been established. At this point, it is, in your words, Mr. Chairman, perhaps only a little more than a "suspicious suspected," not a "fact found." (V HSCA 378)

44

RALPH SALERNO –
SEPTEMBER 28, 1978

On September 28, 1978, Ralph Salerno testified before the HSCA in Washington, D.C

S alerno begins his questioning with a presentation that suggests that he is familiar with quite a few organized crime members at the famous Appalachian, New York gathering that dates to November 14, 1957, which was the day before Santos Trafficante's birthday. One of the individuals who was there identified himself as Louis Santos and gave as his address, a hotel in Havana. He was, by the way, also known as Santos Trafficante.

Salerno named some of Santos Trafficante's associates from the Appalachian meeting. A few of these individuals were serving time in prison or had passed away while in prison. "Mr. Trafficante here, in his testimony, acknowledges a long-time friendship over a period of years, one in which the people involved could have great confidence in themselves with Sam Giancana. Mr. Sam Giancana has been the victim of a homicide and has been killed. Mr. Trafficante indicated in his testimony here this morning that he knew John Roselli, that he had dinner with that gentleman 3 weeks before he was killed, his body dismembered and stuffed into an oil drum and thrown into the sea only to come up in Biscayne Bay.

> "My unit in New York City Police Department on September 22, 1966, interrupted a luncheon in a restaurant know as Stella in Queens County, N.Y. Mr. Marcello was present at that luncheon. Mr. Trafficante was present at that luncheon." (V HSCA 382-383)

These statements came immediately after the 20-year-old Appalachian facts and does suggest guilt by association, but ultimately proves nothing because it was by now known that these people were connected with each another.

> Mr. Cornwell: "Which of the types of organized crime that you just described is it that Santos Trafficante and Carlos Marcello are associated with?"
>
> Mr. Salerno: "They are leaders of an organized crime syndicate, each of them, in their home areas." (V HSCA 386)

The guilt by association theme continued with references to Eliot Ness and Al Capone. Eliot Ness, After his Untouchables role, Eliot Ness was appointed U.S. Commissioner for Venereal Disease after World War II.

Salerno continued his critique on organized crime until the lunch adjournment. (V HSCA 434)

In the afternoon session, limited wiretap discussions point to Robert Kennedy clamping down on particular associations: two Mafia gentlemen, Pat Marcy and John D'Arco, along with Congressman Roland Libonati.

Libonati on Robert F. Kennedy:

"I killed six of his bills. That wiretapping bill, the intimidating informers bill ...."

Libonati thinks that John Kennedy was a sweetheart, but "Robert F. Kennedy is cruel." (V HSCA 446)

> Mr. Cornwell: "Apart from, I take it, the fear that the organized crime element in this country had that the Kennedy administra-

tion was destroying them, as demonstrated by this surveillance, was there any realistic expectation if they had done something so drastic as to kill the President, and there I take it, by doing so remove his brother from the position of Attorney General, and take the two of them out together, would that have in any way helped them? What realistic expectation was there that the pressure to prosecute the Cosa Nostra would have diminished by such an act?"

Mr. Salerno: "Two things which we learned toward the answer. Number 1, was their expectation; they from time to time advised that, but I think more to the point is the actual record of what transpired in this effort following the assassinations. We will add some data to the existing charts and you will be able to see exactly what did happen following the assassination of President Kennedy." ...

Mr. Cornwell: "If then there were facts which could have created a motive, if there were means in the control of organized crime, can you tell us was the electronic surveillance of the FBI, which you received, adequate to give some answers to the question of whether or not La Cosa Nostra as an institution, in other words, La Cosa Nostra at the commission level, at the governing body level, could have considered or sanctioned the assassination of the President or of Lee Harvey Oswald?"

Mr. Salerno: "My professional opinion, based on the electronic surveillances and other evidence available, is that it is more than sufficient to give a reasonable answer to that question. The question is that all of that evidence gives no indication at all that the national commission of La Cosa Nostra directed, approved, or in any way was concerned with the assassination of President Kennedy."

Mr. Cornwell: "Would it be possible that some member, some leader, may have undertaken such a thing without the Commission's approval?"

Mr. Salerno: "Yes; it is very possible, and as a matter of fact, at that particular moment, in November of 1963, there was a great example of it."

Mr. Cornwell: "Very briefly, if you are able to, will you tell us how it is that in the early 1960s an organization which, according to your testimony, is characterized by discipline, strict control, rules, and regulations, and has at its disposal violence, could have been in such a condition that one of its members could be un-controllable or could do things which were not sanctioned by the commission?"

Mr. Salerno: "I believe that the conditions that existed in 1963 were reflective of the effectiveness of the Federal drive during 1961, 1962, and for most of 1963. The normal smooth opera-tion, which had existed for more than 30 years, were interrupt-ed. The cracks were beginning to show in many, many ways." (V HSCA 454—455)

It is ridiculous to rely on the FBI, with regard to organized crime, since they (Hoover) had declared that it did not exist.

Bureau headquarters was complete pandemonium on November 22, 1963, when they recognized that one of their informants had been accused with the shooting of the President. The FBI's rush to judgment was to declare Oswald immediately guilty, based on his known resumé at the time, so no later investigation could discover his other resumé, as it were.

If the FBI's ELSUR (electronic surveillance) program picked up data (which it did) relating the assassination to figures beyond their grasp or who were working within the Central Intelligence Agency on black-ops and were untouchable, then it is easy to see why they would not make that information public.

If Lee Oswald caused difficulties for the Bureau, then what kind of obstruction would Marcello, Trafficante, or Giancana have posed for them?

Mr. Salerno seemed to be saying that Attorney General Bobby Ken-nedy did such a noteworthy job in regard to organized crime, that the fundamental infrastructure was so marred that it permitted someone within that organization to go rogue in Dallas, Texas, in November, 1963.

Trafficante's testimony was then tested:

Chairman Stokes: "Mr. Salerno, you were here this morning and heard Mr. Trafficante testify that his role in the assassination plot upon Fidel Castro was that of being an interpreter. Would you tell us please, whether a man who holds the position you have described here so eloquently and articulately would perform the role of an interpreter in that type of assassination plot?"

Mr. Salerno: "No, sir; he would not."

Chairman Stokes: "What then would his role be in such a plot?"

Mr. Salerno: "Sir, based on my knowledge of the three individuals who were working with the CIA, I believe that the first approach was in fact made to Mr. Roselli. Mr. Roselli could not and would not have entertained agreeing to work for the CIA or taking any action with the CIA without the permission of Giancana.

I believe Giancana's real role was, No. 1: to approve Roselli's working with the CIA, No. 2, to approach his peer, Mr. Trafficante, and asked for his cooperation." (V HSCA 456)

Salerno would appraise the information and submit someone is lying: Johnny Roselli, José Aleman, or Sam Giancana, or Santos Trafficante. "So, I think you have to evaluate his testimony in view of all of the other evidence, and I think it would be at least naïve to accept it at face value." (V HSCA 457)

Afterwards:

Congressman Edgar: "Let me ask a couple of questions about Mr. Oswald. In your opinion, is it enough for Oswald to have had an uncle by the name of Charles Moret [*Murrett*], who is a bookie, to in any way link Oswald to organized crime?

Mr. Salerno: "I think it is a single fact on which you cannot base any serious premise. If it can be joined with other facts in a preponderance of evidence, then you might be able to come up with a reasonable conclusion."

Mr. Edgar: "Well, then, let me raise the second possible connection, and that is with David Ferrie, who worked in the same building that Oswald was in for a time, or at least it is alleged that that occurred. Would that have been enough of a connection?"

Mr. Salerno: "By itself no, but again, in concert with many, many other facts it might."

Mr. Edgar: "Moving to the question again about Mr. Ruby, it is interesting for us to examine the relationship, if any, between a Mr. Trafficante and a Jack Ruby. Would it have been the custom for somebody like Trafficante, who is at one level, to have any association with somebody like Ruby? Would that be a custom or a norm?"

Mr. Salerno: "Without any intermediary who might have known them both and introduced one to the other, it would be very, very unlikely." (V HSCA 464)

I have never felt that Jack Ruby could be regarded as an organized crime figure. He was simply not to be confused with anyone in the Cosa Nostra. He was more of a stooge.

This ended the testimony of Mr. Salerno, the HSCA authority on organized crime, who did established proficiency, but ultimately shed no light whatsoever on the serious issues in the case.

45

JUDGE BURT W. GRIFFIN –
SEPTEMBER 28, 1978

On Sept. 28, 1978, Judge Burt Griffin gave testimony before the HSCA in Washington, D.C

I n his narration, Chief Counsel Blakey had a lot to say about the organized crime capacity following the testimony of Earl Ruby, Lewis McWillie, José Aleman, Santos Trafficante, and Ralph Salerno,
which didn't actually plumb the depths, but Blakey had his logic:

> "Nevertheless, it is fair to say the committee's investigation into
> the possible involvement into organized crime has been more
> complete than that of the FBI or the Warren Commission in
> 1963 and 1964. It is also fair to comment that had this sort of
> investigation taken place at that time when the evidence was
> fresh, it is possible, though hardly a sure thing, that a lot more
> information might have been forthcoming. But the committee
> must face this fact. The question of organized crime involvement
> is still an open one. Nothing that has been uncovered excludes it

and much that is new points toward it. Yet frustration may be the result of this committee's efforts too.

"To address the issues raised by this frank recognition of the possibility of ultimate frustration and comment on the investigation of the Warren Commission and this committee, as well as the future, the committee has invited the Hon. Burt W. Griffin to appear here today." (V HSCA 470-471)

Griffin, oddly, then became his own witness:

"Let me say in seriousness, that the purpose of my remarks is to discuss with the committee the question of what is the proper process for investigating political murders that have national implications. That is what I would like to reflect upon in these minutes with the committee.

"I propose to begin that inquiry with a brief discussion of what I perceive to have been the goals of the Warren Commission and the Warren Commission's successes and failures. And I would like to end with some suggestions for dealing with future political murders." (V HSCA 472)

The Warren Commission was designed primarily to achieve four goals. First, to establish the true facts surrounding the assassination of President Kennedy and the murder of Lee Harvey Oswald. Second, to accomplish that mission in a manner that would satisfy the broadest segment of influential people and the American public in general. Third, to do it in a manner that would not unnecessarily disrupt the stability of the national government and its conduct of international affairs or jeopardize the national security. And fourth, to conduct this inquiry in a manner that would avoid damaging the reputations or employment of individuals against whom there did not exist convincing evidence of criminal conduct." (V HSCA 472)

According to Judge Griffin, conspiracy rumors ran wild, but he also commented on the McCarthy era and the witch-hunt that it underwent and connected that to the era of yellow journalism that led to the Spanish-American War.

"So that the fears about the inability to find the truth and to document it in a persuasive manner were not inconsiderable or insubstantial ones, as far as the members of the Warren Commission were concerned.

"And it was important that a reliable body be established to investigate and report honestly the facts that surround the murder of Lee Harvey Oswald and of President Kennedy in order to minimize the possibility of such disastrous consequences.

"At the outset of the Warren Commission's activities, speed seemed to be an important element in the Commission's operations. [*Then why wait 66 days before calling their first witness?*]

"Initially, the White House informed the Commission that it should complete its work and make its report prior to the national political conventions that were scheduled for the summer of 1964." (V HSCA 473)

Judge Griffin added:

"At no time prior to the report's issuance did any Member of Congress attempt to use the uncertainties of the assassination to oppose Johnson administration policies. So long as the Commission was operating, the White House, in fact, achieved its goal of preventing the uncertainties that surrounded the assassination from interfering with its own conduct of public policy." (V HSCA 474)

"As a practical matter, the Commission leadership decided not to pursue further the various speculative theories on conspiracy unless two things could be found. First, unless they could find substantial evidence that a specific suspected conspirator had had personal contact with Lee Oswald or Jack Ruby during the period when that person could have counseled or assisted Oswald or Ruby in the events of November 21-23, 1963."

"And second, and the two would have to go together, unless there was some evidence that such suspected conspirator desired to kill President Kennedy or was involved in a common political activity with Lee Harvey Oswald. ...

"The overriding short-term political objective of President Johnson in establishing the Warren Commission was achieved. That is, the determination of public policy was not substantially affected by the uncertainties of the assassination and no member of Congress or political opponent of President Johnson was able to mobilize public sentiment through manipulation of fears that grew out of these uncertainties.

"Almost no probative evidence bearing upon the identity of participants in the murders has been uncovered by the legions of Warren Commission critics. No witness, unknown at the time of the original investigation, has come forward with information showing that any specific person assisted or encouraged either Oswald or Ruby in their murders. The most significant newly discovered information has been that evidence in the possession of governmental agencies was deliberately withheld from the Warren Commission. If that evidence had been provided to the Commission, I personally have no doubt that our investigation, that is the investigation of the Warren Commission, would have been extended substantially." (V HSCA 474—475)

To say "no witness unknown at the time of the investigation" is to use ugly words. It is to admit that we knew about Ferrie, Banister, and Shaw, et al, but did not follow any of those leads at all. Griffin addressed that reflection in a rather odd way: "However, it must be recognized that a decision to terminate government investigation also unleashed a private witch hunt, and the committee must evaluate that byproduct.

"Let me turn next to what I believe were the failures of the Warren Commission. It is clear that the Warren Commission failed to prevent the assassination from becoming a long-term political issue." (V HSCA 475)

"A second failure, and a glaring failure, was its inability, the Commission's inability, to gain full cooperation from the investigative agencies.

The Committee, I know, has carefully examined the areas in which the CIA, the FBI, and the Dallas Police Department failed to provide candid and, I might say, loyal assistance to the Warren Commission, and I will not attempt to go into those."

"I think there was also a failure by the Warren Commission of investigative tactics. The style of the Commission's own staff was in retrospect not fully one of criminal investigators." (V HSCA 476)

Judge Griffin speaks about losses by not going off the record, but they did go off the record, it did happen hundreds of times, and many more times that do not materialize in what Judge Griffin refers to as a complete record. Arlen Specter interviewed the autopsy doctors between eight and ten times before they gave their testimony, which amounted to a carefully manipulated script. The American public should be out-raged that this was done. Why such a careful acting session? What were they afraid of that the doctors might say?

The real panic was that the constant conspiracy was going to get you in due course.

> "You must remember, Mr. Chairman, that in those days we trust-ed the various agencies of Government with whom we dealt, much more than we trust them now." (V HSCA 477)
>
> "To my knowledge, in that period, the FBI never established a list of possible conspirators with either Jack Ruby or Lee Os-wald, and if it had such a list, it never placed them under surrep-titious investigation; or if it did so, the existence and nature of such investigations was certainly never revealed to me, and I had responsibility for investigating Jack Ruby.
>
> "Nor was there any indication that the FBI in that period used its own agents in an undercover capacity under any circum-stances, or pursued the practice in that period of our history of infiltrating suspect groups, except through paid informants." (V HSCA 477)

Why is it that being trusting and naive go so well with patriotism, or is it nationalism and jingoism? Burt Griffin must be joking or is incred-ibly naïve, when he states that the FBI did not gain access to mistrusted or suspecting groups. The FBI made up the majority of the membership of the Communist Party of the United States of America (CPUSA).

He is also ignoring that both Oswald and Ruby were FBI informants.

> "The FBI fully used its standard investigatory techniques for ap-proximately 2 months before any member of the Warren Com-mission was able to initiate his own investigation [*which did not happen, as the FBI made up the witness lists, not the Warren Com-mission*]. That 2-months delay substantially undermined the abil-ity of the Commission to investigate a conspiracy.
>
> "First, obviously, all tracks were cold and any conspirator had 2 months to flee or hide.
>
> "Second, all possible suspects and conspirators had ample time to learn what direction the Government's investigation was taking.
>
> "Third, after 2 months the investigatory agents of the FBI were frankly impatient, since they were convinced that they had

done a thorough job and that a staff of Commission amateurs could do no better." (V HSCA 477—478)

Griffin stated repeatedly concerning the lack of investigators on the Commission and that no one on the Commission had any background in Cuban/Soviet affairs:

"The Commission itself employed only two persons with any substantial background in any of those areas ("pro- and anti-Castro groups in the United States and Mexico, Cuban counterintelligence and espionage, Soviet counterintelligence and espionage, the possible involvement of organized crime figures with such foreign groups, and the linkages of all those groups to the FBI, CIA, and the Dallas Police force.

"The Commission itself employed only two persons with any substantial background in any of those areas, and that was only in the area of organized crime.

"We did have two individuals who had been members of organized crime staff in the U.S. Department of Justice.") (V HSCA 478)

It is utterly absurd to claim that the Commission lacked expertise in these matters with the former head of the CIA, Allen Dulles, sitting on the panel. Dulles could have called in experts with a snap of his finger.

The reason for Dulles being there was obfuscation. If something came across the desk that was risky, Dulles was not going to explore it, but he was on hand to conceal it.

As researcher Walt Brown points out in his excellent book, *The Warren Omission: A Micro-Study of the Methods and Failures of the Warren Commission*, Dulles was present in the hearing room for more testimony than any of the other six Commissioners; and asked the most questions (2,154) of any of the seven commissioners. By comparison, Ford asked 1,772, Cooper asked 926, McCloy, 795, Warren, 608, Boggs, 460, and Richard Russell, 249. By comparison, Griffin by himself asked more questions, as he and Leon Hubert, of all of the 'pairs' of counsel, asked far and away the most questions, with Hubert outpolling Griffin even though both were cast out as outsiders for doing just that, going outside the chain of command.

Earl Warren's 608 questions only amount to 28% of the questions posed by Dulles, and the lion's share of Warren's questions were introductory in nature: "Did you have a good trip?" "please state your name," blah blah, and were not substantive. His answers, on the other hand, ("No," "No," and many other "No's" each time Jack Ruby asked to come to Washington) are more significant.

Griffin continued:

> "Certain basic records, such as telephone call records, hotel registrations, transportation manifests, immigration records, photographs of the murder scene (singular, my emphasis), and audio recordings would have had to have been comprehensively acquired for possible future use and analysis whether or not they had any immediate evidentiary value. This approach would have required a different staff and a different relationship to the President and to the Attorney General." (V HSCA 478)

Also,

> "The problems of proof of a conspiracy are probably too great or else the suspicions with which this committee is dealing are in fact not well-founded. The select committee, I would suggest in those regards, should consider the possible reality that under the American system of civil liberties and the requirement of proof beyond a reasonable doubt, that it is virtually impossible to prosecute or uncover a well-conceived and well-executed conspiracy." (V HSCA 480)

Because of a prior commitment, Chairman Stokes had to depart the hearing room. While Griffin was testifying, Stokes interjected to say he had to leave, but that he had a couple of things to say before permitting other members to ask questions.

Griffin responded,

> "I yield 3 minutes to the chairman." (V HSCA 486)

Stokes then states:

> "Human testimony is sharply qualified by human perception and memory, to say nothing of bias, motive to lie, or fear of retaliation. It is, therefore, less reliable than scientific analysis or documents written, not for litigation, but as an accurate record of actual events. In this context particularly, we must, as I have said, always distinguish between a suspected and a fact found.

"Another point must be repeated for emphasis. These proceedings have not been a criminal trial. There was no indictment, there was no defendant, there was no prosecutor, there was no defense counsel. The normal rules of evidence found in criminal proceedings have not, therefore been applicable here." (V HSCA 487)

Stokes then gave a statistical itemization, noting 59 [*actually 52*] witnesses appearing before the HSCA in public testimony in 17 days, stating that the witnesses varied from "noted political figures and ordinary citizens, a former President of the United States, a current president of a foreign country and an individual who carried an umbrella on one sunny day in Dallas.

"In all, there were 385 trips to 564 points for a total of over 1,870 days in the field, and the work continues and has continued during the course of these very hearings that we have held in this room.

Witness interviews, for instance, have totaled over 1,548. Seventy-five witnesses were questioned in executive session, 41 of whom were immunized. Over 500 files from the CIA, the FBI, the Secret Service, the Departments of State and Defense, as well as other agencies, have been reviewed. Files that range from a few pages to thousands. The FBI file on Lee Harvey Oswald alone consists of 238 volumes containing 5,754 serials.

"Now, let me also point up some of the statistics related to some of the scientific projects which were made a major part of these hearings. First the contractors. The photo analysis enhancement: 470 man-days were consumed at a total cost to the committee of $9,500. For acoustical analysis, for radio transmissions in Dallas on November 22, 1963, 160 man-days at a cost of $72,000. For simulated gun tests in Dealey Plaza in conjunction with the acoustical test, 38 man-days at a cost of $3,850. The total, 668 man-days, $167,350.

"As for consultants, for photoanalysis enhancement, 270 man-days at a cost of $50,000. Pathology, 101 man-days at $29,000. Ballistics 110 man-days at $12,000. Medical illustrations, 78 man-days $10,000. Handwriting analysis, 35 man-days at $6,000. Methodology 20 man-days at $3,200. Polygraph analysis, 16 man-days at $2,500. Dentistry examination, 8 man-days at $1,500. Neutron activation analysis, 23 man-days at $1,500. Fingerprint analysis, 3 man-days at $600. The totals, 828 man-days, $146,200.

"As all can clearly see, these hearings, while illustrative of our work, have reflected only part of that work. This then would conclude my comments on the work of the committee and our public hearings." (V HSCA 488-489)

Congressman Floyd Fithian brilliantly cut to the crux of the matter and said "we couldn't ask for something we didn't know existed. It reminds me ever so much of the chicken and egg dilemma that we get into sometimes in life." (V HSCA 491)

Fithian's logic is not irrational. But it did beg the question somewhat. The Warren Commission as an investigatory team had a mandate to complete, involving three murders in a span of 46 hours and 51 minutes. Their budgetary constraint was a clock.

In Stokes' statistical summary 41 witnesses were given immunity. That is 41 more than were given immunity by the Warren Commission. Why?

On September 28, 1978, at 4:56 p.m., EDT, The House Select Committee on Assassinations, adjourned, *sine die*. (V HSCA 498)

A *sine die* adjournment means it is the final adjournment of the final meeting of that stated group. Local municipalities regularly hold a *sine die* meeting when new town councils or new board of education representatives are elected. The old group adjourns, *sine die*, and the new group begins their deliberations; but, the House Select Committee was not finished. They would meet one more time on December 29, 1978, at which time the acoustics evidence of the fourth shot from the grassy knoll would be established.

And the planet would never be the same, even though, that shot missed.

46

PROFESSOR MARK WEISS –
DECEMBER 29, 1978
W/ MR. E ASHKENAZY

On December 29, 1978, Mr. Mark Weiss and Mr. Ernest Aschkenasy testified before the HSCA in Washington, D.C.

C hairman Louis Stokes gives the initial narration, following in the footsteps of G. Robert Blakey.

"The Chair at this time wishes to make some opening remarks. Today, the Select Committee on Assassinations will hold 1 day of public hearings into the assassination of President John F. Kennedy. As those of you who followed our Kennedy hearings may recall, I observed at their conclusion (September 27, 1978, late afternoon, but prior to the *sine die* adjournment at 4:56 p.m., EDT) that there might be a need for 1 or more additional days of public presentation of evidence. What I had in mind was the prospect of more hearings for our acoustics project, which is an analysis of an audio tape recorded at the scene of the assassination. The results of the project were first presented in a public hearing on September 11. Today we will hear an independent review of those results." ...

"The committee is also now prepared to reach its final conclusions and to make its final recommendations on all of the questions before it in both the assassination of President Kennedy and Dr. Martin Luther King, Jr., which, indeed, it will do tonight after this public session has adjourned. Nevertheless, because of the significance of the new acoustics analysis, the committee thought it would be appropriate to examine it and explore its implications in public hearing before the formal vote by the committee." (V HSCA 499)

It is doubtful, at this late hour of the committee, that the HSCA would have brought back an acoustics expert who would give overwhelming evidence of a fourth shot, and then vote that only three shots were fired and all of them by Lee Harvey Oswald. There seems to be a predestined attitude that the HSCA was putting these guys on the stand to make their case, and not to simply re-emphasize old Warren Commission dogma.

Blakey's narration points to what had been learned from Dr. James E. Barger, that there was a 95-percent chance of two shots on the acoustic tape, a 60- to 70-percent chance of a third shot, and finally, "there were indications of a fourth shot from the grassy knoll, but at the time he was to testify in a public hearing of the committee in September 1978, Dr. Barger was only willing to call it a 50-50 probability.

The committee then asked two independent experts who had been recommended to the committee by the Acoustical Society of America to review the work of Dr. Barger and determine if they might be able to refine it. Prof. Mark Weiss and his assistant, Mr. Ernest Aschkenasy agreed to try to refine Dr. Barger's work. At the committee's request, they focused on the third shot, the one that Dr. Barger thought might have come from the grassy knoll." (V HSCA 554)

Following the resumés of Mr. Weiss and Mr. Aschkenasy, Deputy Counsel Gary Cornwell got to the task at hand:

Mr. Cornwell: "Based upon the work, were you able to reach a conclusion with any greater degree of certainty as to whether or not that shot [shot #3, grassy knoll] did or did not occur?"

Mr. Weiss: "Yes, sir, we did."

Mr. Cornwell: "And what was your conclusion?"

Mr. Weiss: "It is our conclusion that as a result of very careful analysis, it appears that with a probability of 95 per cent or better, there was indeed a shot fired from the grassy knoll." (V HSCA 556)

Numerous questions arose, as the thought of a fourth shot and a conspiracy would not be allowed to rear its head with that much simplicity. Regarding the truth of the echo patterns:

Mr. Weiss: "... In fact, if you had to listen, as in the specific case of Dealey Plaza, if you had a listener standing someplace in the Plaza, say on the sidewalk near the depository building, and he stood still and a rifle was exactly held in another place, as the rifle fired, he would hear a succession of echoes. If it was fired again, he would hear identically the same succession of echoes if nobody moved. If he came back 15 years later and the buildings were the same, as they are in this case, and he stood in the same spot and a rifle was fired from exactly the same spot and the temperature of the air was the same he would, in fact, even then hear exactly the same sequence of echoes. ..."

Mr. Cornwell: "Were there other, more complex or more sophisticated principles that you were required to use in your analysis which were not so well established, which were never or less well established?"

Mr. Weiss: "No, sir. We only needed to apply these basic well-tested, well-established principles; nothing more." (V HSCA 557-558)

The testimony of the two scientists was highly technical, or it may be that questions did not take into consideration the high degree of acoustic expertise that was at stake. There was a lot of repetition.

The location of the motorcycle is discussed in some detail. Weiss suggested that one of two things would transpire: either the assessments and tests would locate the motorcycle, or they would prove that the motorcycle was not nearby and nullify the proceedings. They were able to locate the motorcycle.

Regardless of all the technical material, once you get to page 566 of volume V, the data seems to be relatively easy to understand. It's really all about time and distance of similar echoes.

In expounding on the search for connecting echo patterns (knoll to microphone, plus some math), Weiss came across a problem:

> Mr. Weiss: "Now, after a while we got some very good agreements with this set of data here that was not as good for the echoes that were at a distance there. All right, so we started adjusting again; in fact, we got excellent agreement for here. Only what happened now was, we didn't get such good agreement as we had before for the early echoes.
>
> And after doing this enough times, the light finally dawned, and it occurred to us that the concept wasn't complete. We weren't dealing with a shooter here and a microphone here [*he is illustrating on the easels during this testimony*]. We were dealing with a shooter here all right, but with a microphone that wasn't just here; it was in motion; it was going down the street. If it was a motorcycle in the motorcade, it had to have been in motion; it couldn't just be standing there in the middle of the street; and, in fact, if it was going down the street it was probably going at about the speed of the motorcade, which was supposed to be about 11 miles an hour.
>
> So, we started moving the microphone down the street at 11 miles an hour, and for this set of moved positions—now predicting what the echo pattern would be at every position as it comes on down—let's say, at what time it would receive each of these echoes.
>
> This is a somewhat more complicated process. It is the same process; it just takes a lot longer because you have to do a lot more calculations.
>
> As soon as we started doing that, it became immediately obvious we could quite easily find positions for the rifle and for the motorcycle, such that the match at both the early and the late echoes was getting increasingly close; and, in fact, once we were there, we were practically in the ballpark. It was a little more work, and we closed on a set of echoes that we could predict that matched the observed impulses on the pattern with an accuracy of approximately one-thousandth of a second."

Mr. Cornwell: "So you found that by moving the microphone at approximately 11 miles an hour, the peaks that you have predicted the wave form would look like were correct all the way through from the beginning to the end of particular parts of a tape?"

Mr. Weiss: "That's correct. That's correct."

Mr. Cornwell: "And each of those peaks fell exactly where you would expect them to fall within one-thousandth of a second?"

Mr. Weiss: "That is correct. In fact, I have on here numbered some 22 peaks for which I can predict an echo path that will match it to within one-thousandth of a second."

Mr. Cornwell: "Are you able to quantify in some fashion the probability that results from the ability to identify a large number of peaks, as you did, to that degree of precision?

Mr. Weiss: "Yes, if you have a fit of some 22 points, you have a terrific fit to begin with. It really is hard to imagine this could be an accident, but you can't express it in those terms. You have to reduce it to some formal number that you can actually show is reasonable." ...

Mr. Cornwell: "From that, I take it that you have established to a very high confidence level that it is a shot from some sort of firearm.

Let me ask you if you were able to tell from the wave forms what kind of firearm it was, whether it was supersonic or subsonic, or a rifle or a pistol?"

Mr. Weiss: "Right. Of course, we have been dealing, up until now, with the question of the sounds of the muzzle blast, which this is identified as, and of all the different echoes that come in later on.

"Now if—if this was a rifle firing a supersonic bullet, then we would expect that immediately preceding the sound of the muzzle blast we would find the sound of the shockwave generated by the blast while it is in flight that always precedes the muzzle blast; and, of course, it precedes it because the bullet is flying at a speed much greater than the speed of sound.

And if we look in the data, we, in fact, do find a very strong impulse preceding the muzzle blast by a reasonable distance that is not so close so that it could not possibly be it, nor is it too far away. It is pretty much in the right position to be considered to be a probable shockwave sound, recorded just before the recording of the direct muzzle blast sound..."

489

Mr. Cornwell: "So are you telling us that the indications are that it was a supersonic bullet and, therefore, probably a rifle?"

Mr. Weiss: "That is correct." ...

Mr. Cornwell: "And if that's the direction it was aimed, can you tell us how far out the bullet went before it terminated?"

Mr. Weiss: "No, I cannot, because in order to know that you have to know both precisely where the rifle was fired—and, as I indicated, you cannot know that really—and you must know exactly what the muzzle velocity of the bullet was, and there is no way of determining that from these data." ...

Mr. Cornwell: "And if you were to vary the velocity of the rifle bullet from, say, what you might expect to be a normal rifle velocity, somewhere in the 2,000-foot-per-second range up to something considerably higher, up to the upper 2,000 or perhaps 4,000-foot-per-second range, I take it that every time you would vary any assumption like that you would also conclude that there would be a different assumption about where the bullet struck?"

Mr. Weiss: "That is correct. Even if one makes the assumption that it was aimed directly at the head of the President, you could for a range of such velocities, assume that it falls short of the target, that it fell at the target, that it went well beyond the target. There is simply no way of knowing." (V HSCA 568—572)

Later, Weiss would distinguish between the sound recordings by the professional hi-fidelity (hi-fi was stylish and sophisticated back then) microphones that were spaced eighteen feet apart in Dealey Plaza for the acoustic re-enactment, and the less-sophisticated type of microphone accessible at the time on a1963-1964 Dallas Police motorcycle.

"Well, the effect of that can be predicted. But to confirm our understanding of this, we arranged with the New York City Police Department to perform some experiments at their shooting range in the Bronx. We went out there, and they trotted out an old Harley-Davidson motorcycle and put a transmitter on it, vintage 1963 or 1964, and an old microphone pretty much the same kind as was used by the Dallas Police Department, and we performed some experiments with people firing rifles at various locations sometimes with the motorcycle facing the shooter, sometimes with the motorcycle crosswise to the shooter. At the same time, we made sound recordings using high fidelity equipment of the sounds of the shots." (V HSCA 581—582)

Ultimately, the tests showed that the patterns they were basing their data on were reasonably and rationally similar, and the only disruptive variable would have been if the motorcycle windshield was obstructing the sound from successfully reaching the motorcycle's microphone.

Cornwell specified that he had no more questions.

Chairman Stokes continued the examination:

> "Professor Weiss, I guess I am sort of reminded this morning how, some months ago, when several members of this committee and I appeared before the House Administration Committee, which is the committee of the Congress that recommends funding for all of the committees in Congress, and one of the distinguished members of the committee posed the question to me, he said, 'Stokes, has your investigation revealed anything that would change the course of history?' And I said to that Member of Congress that nothing that we had uncovered thus far would, in my opinion, change the course of history.
>
> I am sure that as a scientist that you are aware of the enormous impact that your testimony has here today because if the committee accepts your testimony, the committee then, in effect, accepts the fact that on that particular day in 1963 when the President was assassinated, there were two shooters in Dealey Plaza.
>
> From that premise, one can further assume association, and then from association there can be the further legal assumption, the possibility of a conspiracy. So, I am sure that you are aware of the enormous impact of your testimony here today in terms of history."

Mr. Weiss: "I am, sir, yes, sir." (V HSCA 582)

Chairman Stokes asked Weiss to present a possible push-back, which he did, but he repeated his argument that every computation was checked, re-checked, and checked again.

> Chairman Stokes: "Then as a scientist, you are comfortable with the statement to this committee that beyond a reasonable doubt, and to a degree of 95 percent or better, there were four shots in Dealey Plaza?"

Mr. Weiss: "Well, I would agree with that, with the somewhat clarification, that since our work concentrated primarily on the third shot, the one from the grassy knoll area, I would imply for the moment, limit the statement to that, with a, again, a confidence level of 95 percent or higher, which I guess if I were a lawyer, I might well express as beyond a reasonable doubt, that the shot took place. And then relying upon the corresponding confidence expressed by Dr. Barger about the other shots, I would agree with the statement that there is an overall probability of 95 percent or better that there were four shots fired in Dealey Plaza." (V HSCA 583—584)

Weiss was then questioned by Congressman Preyer, "*For example, what is the possibility of the backfire on a motorcycle making this sort of waves and spikes?*"

Mr. Weiss: "*Well, the answer to that question is, first, I haven't had the opportunity to examine the waveshape of a backfire of a motorcycle, so I cannot say absolutely that this might not resemble it in some way, but if there was a motorcycle backfiring in this instance, that motorcycle was up there behind the stockade fence in Dealey Plaza.*" (V HSCA 585 - 586)

Mr. Devine then asked, "Do you consider Dr. James Barger an expert?"

Mr. Weiss: "Yes, Sir, I do."

Mr. Devine: "And do you respect his opinion very much?"

Mr. Weiss: "I do."

Mr. Devine: "Do you think he made an incomplete study, inasmuch as, his conclusions, when he testified here, I think on September 11, suggested that there was about a 50-50 chance that a shot was fired from the grassy knoll?"

Mr. Weiss: "No, sir. That study, as it was being performed, was moving exactly along the path that any study of this sort ought to move."

Mr. Devine: "Yet you saw fit to supplement his study by a number of things—and I have outlined them here—by seeking to determine where the source of the sounds were, where reflection surfaces were, where the motorcycle was—you assumed it was in the neighborhood of the strongest impulses from the grassy knoll—the velocity of sound at the temperature given on November 22, 1963, as well as the time intervals of the echoes.

"Now did Dr. Barger fail to take these important things into consideration in his study, or are these things that you found necessary in order to arrive at a different conclusion?"

Mr. Weiss: "No; as a matter of fact, Dr. Barger actually intrinsically used all of his information in his study and, in fact, it really was as a result of his study that we were able in the first place to say that the motorcycle was there in Dealey Plaza. It was because of his study that we were able to say that at the time of shot No. 3 it was, in fact, in the vicinity of the microphone No. 4 position in the array when the experiment was performed in Dealey Plaza.

All of the things that Dr. Barger did were natural steps along this kind of investigation. I am sure that had it been continued or, had there been more time available to Dr. Barger, this further result would have been the natural evolution of that process."

Mr. Devine: "Thank you." (V HSCA 586-587)

This question is nothing short of accusatory. Mr. Weiss should have answered: "I have explained exactly why Dr. Barger found a 50% chance of a knoll shot, and what factors I used, which Barger was about to use but was called to testify before his study was fully done, that strongly suggest a 95% chance of a knoll shot."

Mr. Devine has impugned Weiss as some kind of arcane science charlatan, but I'm curious what he would have said about neutron activation analysis in 1964 and then today with the work of Eric Randich?

Weiss will not, however, let this insult pass him by.

When Congressman Edgar was given his time to question the witnesses, mainly Professor Weiss, he specified he had brought along individuals "who have come and attempted to help me with this." (Dr. Arthur Lord, professor at Drexel University; Dr. Francis Davis, dean of science at Drexel University, and Dr. Marvin Wolfgang, a criminologist and professor at the University of Pennsylvania.) (V HSCA 595)

This was an effort to refute the conspiracy findings implied in Weiss's testimony.

Weiss and Aschkenasy repudiated the offensive with some science of their own, and parts of the scientific answers are unfathomable, not on the basis of the science, but on the basis that the coverage was horrendous. Was the shoddy reporting unintended or calculated?

Many questions were an attempt to deflate the conclusions, but Weiss fielded them extraordinarily well.

Congressman Floyd Fithian then took a different approach:

> Mr. Fithian: "Dr. Weiss, when you performed the test on the Harley Davidson with the New York Police Department, did you discover any characteristics that might help us understand why the officer inadvertently had the microphone on?"
>
> Mr. Weiss: "Yes. I think Mr. Aschkenasy can answer."

> Mr. Aschkenasy: "I am certainly glad you asked that question. At the time we conducted those tests, there was an officer who had been a member of the motorcycle police force in New York City for quite a while. Once he saw we were playing around with the microphone and radio, and he was assisting in turning on the motorcycle and turning it off at our directions, he let on as to how many times that stupid microphone would go on every time he pulled the brake cable, because the brake cable passed within a half inch of the microphone button that activates the microphone, enabling it to transmit. That was a totally voluntary comment on his part which indicated to us that indeed it is possible inadvertently for a microphone to transmit without the rider being aware of it." (V HSCA 608)

Questions were raised as to why tests were not done to figure if the data involving the knoll shot could have been created by a pistol or a rifle, and after General Counsel Blakey addressed it, Gary Cornwell added:

> "I might not just for the committee's interest that marksmen with the Dallas Police Department that fired the pistol hit in an area after several shots, I did not check it all the way to the end, but after several shots you could cover all of their pistol shots with a quarter, so even though they were obviously excellent shots, the distances involved are not lengthy, so that, roughly speaking, the ability to hit a target at those distances would be somewhat comparable whether you used a pistol or a rifle." (V HSCA 614)

This is the final day of the Committee's work, and a number of important depositions have been put into the record (among other reasons, because the HSCA volumes are so difficult to obtain), it seems awfully odd that two members have been virtually silent, and no indication that they were ever even present: Yvonne Braithwaite Burke, of California, and Charles Thone, of Nebraska, are for all intents as much absentees as was Richard Russell of the Warren Commission.

The ultimate irony is they spend a fortune to hire acoustics experts, and when they testify before the U.S. House of Representatives, the microphone doesn't pick up their voices. Only in America, my friend.

The scientists were only pursuing shots that emanated from the Book Depository and the grassy knoll

This stuff gets complex, and I don't claim the proficiency to make an accurate resolve. Who am I to tell these experts that they are wrong?

If you posit two shooters in Dealey Plaza, you have a conspiracy, unless you conclude that two lone nuts, each without conspiratorial motive, within the millions of square miles in the United States, were brought together purely by chance in an area of 3.07 acres.

To even imagine that seems ridiculous, but I suspect that even though Stokes knew what was coming, as Cornwell manifestly led the witness through testimony, the impact of the science totally anesthetized him.

47

H. B. McLain –
December 29, 1978

On December 29, 1978, H. B. McClain testified before the HSCA Washington, D.C.

G eneral Counsel G. Robert Blakey provided distorted data in his preface to the testimony of H. B. McLain.

"FBI expert testimony to the Warren Commission indicated that Oswald's rifle could not be aimed and fired in less than 2.25 to 2.3 seconds. ... As you will also recall, Mr. Chairman, I reported to the committee on September 11 the results of preliminary tests conducted by the staff at the Metropolitan Police Department firing range in Lorton, Va., under the general supervision of Sgt. Cecil Kirk. Those tests established that a Mannlicher-Carcano could be operated accurately in considerably less time than had been indicated by the FBI. ... The difference between the two sets of tests may be accounted for by the simple fact that a telescopic sight was used by the FBI while the open iron sights of the Mannlicher-Carcano were used by committee staff marks-men." (V HSCA 615- 616)

It is a misconstruction by HSCA Chief Counsel Blakey to make the statement as cited. The time of 2.25-2.3 seconds was the FBI's timing to work the bolt of the rifle, which was most likely wrong. The error in Blakey's statement is, to reacquire a moving target through a telescopic lens, available to make the weapon more sniper-appearing, takes considerable time, because the following sequence must occur:

Shot fired. Gun moved slightly to work the bolt-action. Gun returned to shoulder rest position. Eye replaced next to telescope. Rifle moved to reacquire and track the moving target.

Those activities in the hands of John Q. Citizen (presuming he's using the arcane, obsolete Mannlicher-Carcano rifle) cannot be done in 2.3 seconds. Never.

Overlooked by the HSCA is the way the sight was affixed on the Oswald rifle. A shooter would have to hold the rifle in an obdurate configuration, because the telescopic sight, displayed off to the left, would be of little value because a shooter holding the weapon would look through the telescopic sight and see his own left arm, which would not be much help.

I am always amazed on how many so-called government officials got a look at Oswald's rifle and yet rarely said it was nothing but junk. FBI fingerprint expert Sebastian Latona did attest to that effect, but authorities were brought in, to state that the Carcano was as good as anything in use by the United States Armed Forces, c. 1964, which they knew better. Proof: why wasn't our military using this excellent rifle if it was so accurate?

A Mannlicher-Carcano, not the gun found in the Texas School Book Depository, was used for the re-creation tests. Why wasn't the "assassination rifle" used? Any answers would be embarrassing to our government.

The acoustics tests specified a gap of 1.59 seconds between the first and second shots, or .71 seconds less than the FBI testified to. In order for all the injury and destruction to have been done in such a brief amount of time, the weapon had to be operated with unprecedented swiftness, accuracy, and rapidity.

Nowhere to be found in the FBI expert testimony is there any mention of aiming or re-aiming the weapon. The 2.3 data was the operational time to pull the trigger and work the bolt, bringing the next bullet up into the chamber. Period.

The time required for the eye to reacquire the target, a brief but still even a long time using the iron sights, and even a longer time period using the off-centered telescopic sight, which was not integrated in the 2.3 second testimony by the FBI.

For the House Committee to insinuate that .71 seconds, or a full 30% of the time cited by the FBI could be smoothed off, is far too much, notwithstanding who is cited as the competent shooter. There is no idea of any wild or ridiculous shots, but only expert accuracy, and Lee Oswald was barely a marksman, if that.

> Mr. Cornwell: "Officer McLain, the exhibit [*JFK exhibit F-679*] which we just marked for identification and which I showed you last night reflects that there were five motorcycles assigned to ride as the lead in the motorcade in front of Chief Curry's car, and then there were four motorcycles initially contemplated on November 21, the day before the motorcade, to escort the President's car on the left rear side, and another four motorcycles on the right rear side.
>
> Would it be consistent with your memory that those initial plans were altered somewhat on the actual day of the motorcade, and that in fact only two motorcycles flanked the President's car on the left and right in close proximity to it?"
>
> Mr. McLain: "Yes; sir; that's the way it was."
>
> Mr. Cornwell: " … We have reviewed film coverage of the motorcade, and I would ask you if it would be consistent with your memory that you rode several car lengths back, but still on the left side of the motorcade from the President's car?"
>
> Mr. McLain: "Yes, sir; I rode in the general vicinity of Vice President Johnson's car."
>
> Mr. Cornwell: "Do you happen to recall who would have been riding to your rear on the same side of the motorcade?"
>
> Mr. McLain: "I believe that was [J.W.] Courson."

Cornwell asked if the position differed, in terms of distance from the Vice President's car.

Mr. McLain: "Yes, it would vary from, say, the Vice President's car back to the bus, some four or five car-lengths, I would say." (V HSCA 625)

The distance from the Vice-President's car to the bus was closer to 24 car lengths, than McLain's guess of four or five. There were several VIP and camera vehicles (in addition to security) between Johnson's car and the first bus, and the cars were not in the least approaching the position of bumper-to-bumper.

That alignment was only true of the Presidential limousine and the follow-up car. The purpose of a motorcade is to generate a parade-like impression, so each car was set far enough apart from the previous and the following vehicles, so its occupants had a chance to respond to the crowd and wave and be applauded by the crowd. That can't be achieved by cars being too close together.

McLain being alongside or in the general vicinity of Vice President Johnson's car is at variance with the photographs that show him a number of car lengths behind that vehicle.

The statement that there were four or five car lengths, in McLain's estimation, between where he might have been when he was next the Vice President's car to the occasion(s) when he dropped back to the bus, (of which there were two) is misleading.

There were ten cars between the Vice President's car and the first of two busses: the Vice-Presidential follow-up car, the Mayor's car, the National Press Pool car, camera cars numbers 1-3, Congressmen's cars numbers 1-3, and a VIP car, then the first bus.

That's ten cars, but because it is a parade, the cars are not driven as they would be in customary traffic. They are spaced well apart, so the crowd can cheer at each passing group.

That means that for each vehicle, there was an additional one car length, putting McLain twenty car lengths behind Johnson's car, when he was alongside the first press bus.

From that estimate, we are forced and with shame, to measure all of McLain's perceptions based on that accuracy. Unfortunately.

Mr. Cornwell: "Do you have a memory of hearing any shots while you were in Dealey Plaza?"

Mr. McLain: "I only remember hearing one."

Mr. Cornwell: "And approximately where were you when you heard that shot?"

Mr. McLain: "I was approximately halfway between Main and Elm Streets on Houston." (V HSCA 629)

The photo clearly is not Houston Street, so Officer McLain, who will become an expert on his motorcycle skills, has to be instructed as to what street he was on. Sad.

The distance from the center stripe of Main Street to the north curb of Elm Street is 348 feet. According to cited testimony, McLain was half-way, or 174 feet, when he heard the only shot he remembered, and we can only assume it was the last shot, as that one would have been directly toward him. Our arithmetic must contain another 60-90 feet for the turn from being completely on Main Street to Houston Street, so McLain would have to travel approximately 238 feet between the third shot, and the HSCA's fourth shot, which occurred less than one second later.

Let's work in the opposite direction, at the estimated speed of 11 miles per hour (probably an *overestimate*), because the vehicles in the front had to slow down severely to make the Houston-Elm Street turn.

But let's give McLain his 11 miles per hour. In that hour, he would travel 58,080 feet. In one minute of that hour, he would travel 968 feet, and in the one second in which he heard, presumably, the last shot, he would have traveled 16 feet, 1.5 inches. This is not half-way between Main and Elm streets, and not by a long shot, which was also something not happening at the same time. The shot McLain heard was a short one.

His perceptions are very poor, so when he claims, as he has frequently at JFK conferences, that his microphone was not open, and that it wasn't him, just bear in mind his documentation to this point. He isn't the most accurate witness.

Beyond that, Officer McLain (still an officer after 26 years on the police force at the time of his testimony before the HSCA) was unable to testify as to which channel (1 or 2) his motorcycle radio was set on. It should have been Channel 1 as a matter of routine. Channel 2 was to be used for specific, presidential communication. A photograph of a motorcycle from Parkland, suggested, but not proved to be H. B. McLain's, showed the transmit button to the left, indicating Channel 1. (V HSCA 635-636)

Mr. Cornwell: "... Did you, to your memory, have a stuck microphone that day?"

Mr. McLain: "Not that I know of."

Mr. Cornwell: *"Do you know whether or not it would have been possible for your microphone to have been stuck in the open position without your knowledge?"*

Mr. McLain: *"Yes, sir; it has been before."*

Mr. Cornwell: *"Under how many different circumstances in your particular case?"*

Mr. McLain: *"I'm scared to say."* (V HSCA 637)

He will deny the charge vehemently, although he had no way of knowing whether his radio was on or not. It's not something that blinks or gives off a sound signature, like the panic button on modern automobile keypads. Having your microphone stuck in the open position is impossible to detect.

The members of the committee tried to make rational sense how McLain could recognize himself in the photos, and there does seem to be some attempt to understand the machinations of a stuck microphone, but nothing is confirmed or invalidated.

McLain said he saw: "a bunch of pigeons flew [*fly*] out from behind the book depository."

Such a flight of birds was captured in one of the three photos taken by Mal McIntyre at roughly the Stemmons on-ramp, west of the Triple Underpass. His pigeons seemed to be flying up and away from the Trinity River bottom, and while such birds will depart at the sound of any gunshot, if Hollis B. McLain's birds flew off the TSBD because of Oswald, those pigeons could have been reacting to a knoll shot, which could have been what McLain heard, since it was the only sound of a shot coming toward him, which is a point not to be overlooked.

But McLain's denial of using the radio tends to aid in the confirmation that his mike was open, rather than denying it. The explanation provided by Weiss and Aschkenasy, referring to their experience with the New York City Police motorcycle riders, suggests that a microphone does not get stuck in the *on* position as much from use as it does from proximity to other parts and cables on the cycle.

HIDDEN IN PLAIN SIGHT

When you actually use the radio, you depress a button, say your piece, and then release the button, and a current of static will usually confirm that you are no longer communicating.

McLain would have no opportunity after the first shot, to even be aware of that small, ending rush of static through his microphone.

McLain was well behind the lead cars. He could have heard Curry's signal on either a different channel that was stuck or he could have accelerated slightly, or braked, and cleared the channel.

As for speed, regardless of what you think of limousine driver Greer's actions, the President's vehicle was accelerating before McLain's motorcycle was increasing speed.

Once the Lincoln limousine got moving, it was doing close to seventy miles an hour, and for an officer on a motorcycle to catch it within the four miles to Parkland, would mean he was traveling reaching speeds of 85-90 miles per hour, at least for cycles that were starting well back, like McLain. It is remarkable that he was able to catch the cars at all.

After almost seventy pages of science, the testimony of H. B. McLain is somewhat refreshing, as it frequently takes on the common, John Q. Citizen tone.

As the two men traveling with the motorcade, McLain and Courson are a moderate distance apart, with McLain in the far left portion of the left of three lanes, and Courson in the middle of the far right lane.

But the reader should recall at times during McLain's testimony, he is there to swear that his microphone was not stuck in the 'on' position; therefore, there was no shot from the grassy knoll.

He is attempting save the day between the testimony of Weiss and Aschkenasy in the morning session, and Dr. Barger following him.

It's the last day of testimony and closing statements, and the Deputy Counsel does not know if Dallas Police records exist.

That is simply embarrassing.

McLain said he was on the (his) motorcycle, and he should not have to defend himself. His previous testimony established he was in that place. This witness was present in the hearing room when testimony from Weiss and Aschkenasy was being taken.

As we have stated earlier, that is simply horrible procedure.

48

DR. JAMES E BARGER (REDUX) –
DECEMBER 29, 1978

Dr. Barger was called back and resumed his testimony from September 11, 1978, on December 29, 1978 before the HSCA in Washington D.C.

D r. Barger was re-called because in his earlier testimony, he suggested only a 50% trustworthiness element regarding the alleged grassy knoll shot. More proficiency and expertise were sought from Dr. Weiss and Aschkenasy, and they gave the grassy knoll shot a very high rating, and gave examples of what that high reliability factor deciphered into, that Barger was re-called to agree or disagree with the acoustic findings of Weiss and Aschkenasy. *This is monumentally important*. This was the conclusion of the House Select Committee on Assassinations testimony, and it would be this authentication that would either cause the House Select Committee to simply restate the Warren Commission's decision of three shots; or break new soil with a fourth shot.

Mr. Wolf begins early on with the following question:

Mr. Wolf: "During that test firing, what were the two locations used to fire weapons from?"

Dr. Barger: "Weapons were fired from the sixth floor, corner window, southeast corner of the Texas School Book Depository and from behind the fence on the knoll at this point." (V HSCA 647)

It is not clear what this point is, if you are only reading Barger's testimony. Thankfully, I have all of the audio testimony of the 52 witnesses, not to mention about one-third of this on video. I put in my video of Dr. Barger and he points at the very corner of the stockade fence, before it juts back toward the railyard at the eastern end. Having both audio and video has made this journey both easier and fun. Barger should have been asked to describe what I just said, but he wasn't.

There were several instances in the depositions taken by the Assassination Records Review Board, primarily by Jeremy Gunn acting as lead counsel, and in virtually every instance, Gunn was asked for a verbal re-stating of the question and he gave an answer that was clearer for the witness to understand.

Mr. Wolf: "Were weapons fired from each location at each of the targets?"

Dr. Barger: "That is correct. Rifles from the Texas School Book Depository were fired at each of the four targets. A rifle from the knoll was fired at each of the four targets. I am sorry; at targets 2, 3, and 5 [?]. We did not fire at target one for safety reasons. In addition, a pistol was fired from the knoll position here at target location No. 3." (V HSCA 647)

Target one that was not fired at for safety reasons. It was fixed close to the range of Z-165—Z-175. It depicts the position of the Willis girl before she started to run along with the limousine.

Mr. Wolf: "Does this exhibit represent those recordings made during the re-enactment which matched the original Dallas Police dispatch tape with a correlation coefficient of at least .5?"

Dr. Barger: "Yes, they do. I wish at this time I could say a few words about the stark simplicity of the matching procedure that was used."

Mr. Wolf: "Surely."

Dr. Barger: "If I may briefly, to clarify this exhibit, since it came after three hours of explanation the last time, there were obtained at each of these microphones the series of echoes that were received by them when each of these rifles was fired, and it was suggested the last time that I spoke that these might be likened to fingerprints. That is not just a bad idea.

"There is a pattern of sounds that emanate from each microphone when each rifle is fired that is unique and that pattern is as much a fingerprint that identifies two things uniquely, the location of the rifle and the location of the receiver. Now obtained on the Dallas Police recording that we discussed this morning were the sounds of impulses, segments of impulses that look like fingerprints, too. They were badly smudged by the presence of noise. We sought to match the fingerprints we measured in the reconstruction with the fingerprints that had been recorded, perhaps by Officer McLain in 1963. We did that matching. We did it in a numerical way. The numerical procedure allowed us to score each match.

"Now we had 432 different combinations of rifle shots and microphones, so we had 432 fingerprints, as from 432 individuals, and we wished to see if any one of those individuals were on the tape recording as recorded by Officer McLain, perhaps. So, we matched each of the 432 fingerprints with each of the microphones, that is, to see if any of them matched at all. We had a scoring procedure. Every time the match was so good that the score was higher than .5, we said that is a very likely match. That individual may exist at that place on the tape. Now, I can explain what this is." (V HSCA 648-649)

With passion to demonstrate his method, Dr. Barger misspoke. McLain did not record anything; his microphone transferred it to the Dallas Police communications center, where it was recorded onto a Dictabelt. It is an apparent misspeak that Barger, if asked to clarify, would have recognized.

Mr. Wolf: "When was that matching process completed?"

Dr. Barger: "It turned out there were 2,592 matches to achieve, and each one was somewhat difficult because of the smudging of the fingerprints, and since the fingerprints were only obtained on the 20th of August, it was not until the 6th of September that each of the 2,592 comparisons had been made.

"Now that was four days before the hearing, given that it takes 1 day to prepare for 1 day's testimony; we had 3 days to wrestle with the fact that there were, in fact, four possible matches of fingerprints identified in the Dallas tape. And at the time that I spoke on the 20th of August I indicated that of the six segments on the Dallas police recording that contained any impulse patterns at all, in other words, potential fingerprints, the first one began at this time. We found no scores matching with any of these test shots higher than .5. However, a short time later, about a second and a half later, there was a series of sound impulses on the Dallas tape which, in fact, scored above my threshold of .5 to be considered as a potential fingerprint. We found when the rifle was located in the Texas School Book Depository, which is here and, fired at the target 1, which is here, we passed our threshold, and we got a score, a matching fingerprint score that was higher than .5 for the microphone located in the second array, microphone 5, that one right there." (V HSCA 649)

This could be slightly puzzling. The test firings were conducted on August 20th. Barger stated his discoveries and connections were completed on September 6th; and then his testimony was on September 11th, 1978.

Mr. Wolf: "Does your prediction of the locations of the motorcycle correspond to the testimony given by Officer McLain this morning?"

Dr. Barger: "Yes. In my judgment it certainly does. The officer was able to remember—I was very pleased to hear—that when he was around the corner from Main onto Houston, he could see the Presidential limousine disappearing around the corner here from Houston onto Elm. That distance would be on the order of 180 feet. So, he would then be somewhere around 180 feet, perhaps a little less, from the Presidential limousine at that time. Now, the distance from where we think that he was at the time of the first shot, which is here, to the distance where the Presidential limousine was at the time of the first shot is about somewhere between 120 and 138 feet. Again, there is an 18-foot uncertainty. I just said that we have located with our acoustic analysis the result that the motorcycle was 210 to 138 feet behind the limousine at the time of the first shot, which is right about here. Officer McLain remembers having been about 160 to 180 behind at this time. He would have, therefore, had to close a little gap, had to gain a bit on the Presidential limousine as he came down Houston." (V HSCA 650)

From the northwest corner of Main and to the southwest corner of Elm and Houston is more than 180 feet.

Mr. Wolf: "Thank you. You may return to the witness table, Dr. Barger.

"At this point, Mr. Chairman, I would ask that we mark as JFK exhibit F-680 a report that has been submitted to the committee by Mr. Anthony Pellicano. Mr. Pellicano is an independent investigator who submitted a report to the committee after Dr. Barger's testimony in September. *Mr. Pellicano has never worked for the committee or been affiliated with the committee in any capacity.*" (V HSCA 651)

[*JFK exhibit F-680 was marked for identification and follows:*]

The exhibit is an 18-page private analysis of the tape, based on a copy supplied to Mr. Pellicano by Mary Ferrell. Pellicano finds fault in several areas with the initial, September 11th "Barger" conclusions, as the report was submitted on December 13, 1978, prior to the additional public testimony of Professor Weiss and Mr. Aschkenasy.

Pellicano, a name unknown to researchers c. 1978, presented himself as the President of Voice Interpretation & Analysis, Ltd., of Westchester, Illinois, and provided a listening of hi-tech equipment he used for his study "which would probably have been required for such a determination." (V HSCA 655)

Those remarks were prefaced by referring to shots fired, "...I had never been completely satisfied with the Warren Commission Report in this regard." (V HSCA 655)

As it happened, *the Warren Commission did no acoustic work* (*so what is he not satisfied with?*) and Pellicano would dissent from the Barger/Weiss /Aschkenasy findings.

The report is detailed and ends with a two-part conclusion.

CONCLUSION

A. It is concluded that the noise impulses detected during the period immediately preceding the sound of the bell were not shots.

B. It is concluded that the motorcycle with the open microphone on Channel #1 was not a part of the motorcade, but was in fact, located along the route of the motorcade from Dealey Plaza to Parkland Hospital. (V HSCA 670)

> Mr. Wolf: "Dr. Barger, have you had an opportunity to review the report submitted by Mr. Pellicano?"
>
> Dr. Barger: "I have read it."
>
> Mr. Wolf: "I would like to read parts of this report to you and ask you to comment on it. Mr. Pellicano characterizes his work as a deduction from your testimony, in addition to some independent investigation of his own. The first portion I would like to read is on page 4. I will read the paragraph and ask you to comment. It says:
>
> "The first significant finding involved the sound of the motorcade sirens on the channel 1 tape. If the motorcycle with the open microphone had been with the motorcade, it would be expected that the sirens' sound would have started at full volume, and, if the motorcycle had continued with the motorcade, would have continued for the trip to Parkland Hospital. On the other hand, if the motorcycle had remained at Dealey Plaza, the sounds would have started at full volume and the volume would have decreased as the motorcade pulled away. The sounds of the siren on the tape, however, seem to increase, peak, and decrease, as if they were approaching, passing, and leaving the open microphone position.
>
> While this observation is admittedly somewhat subjective, if true it could indicate that the motorcycle was not with the motorcade; but was at some point along or near the route taken by the motorcade on its way to the Parkland Hospital. Can you comment on that, please?" (V HSCA 671)

Submitting this material at this time in the proceedings is tremendously abnormal. How many other individuals provided reports, completely independent of the House Select Committee, in anticipation of having them recognized by the committee?

So why was this particular one accepted?

Why was it supposed that sirens heard in the vicinity of 12:55, i.e., 2 or 5 minutes after the presumed time of the shots, when we know the shots were fired at either 12:29 or 12:30 p.m.?

HSCA Counsel Wolf would use this unofficial and unconfirmed report as the basis for his questions to Dr. Barger, an exceedingly unacceptable procedure, to say the least.

This entire portion of the resumed testimony of Dr. Barger is dubious, if for no other reason than a total stranger, expressing himself as an acoustic expert *ipse dixit*, mails in data and as a result, challenges the committee's chosen scientists.

> Dr. Barger: "I can't remember all that, but while I was still focusing on what you were saying, the statement was made that it would be expected that the motorcycle radio that we have placed in the motorcade would pick up the sounds of the siren on the chief's car that would presumably have been turned on just after the shooting. I think I heard that. Is that it?"
>
> Mr. Wolf: "That is correct." (V HSCA 671)

The two Secret Service vehicles, the Presidential limousine and the follow-up car, occupied by eight Secret Service agents, all hit their sirens before Jesse Curry hit his siren, because he was less aware of events than the occupants in both Secret Service vehicles, due to the fact that he was past Dealey Plaza at this point, as the aforementioned cars were not. This is yet another perfectly good reason of why non-investigators should not be put in charge of investigations, such as the broad-daylight murder of the President of the United States.

> Dr. Barger: "The chief's car was in front of the Presidential limousine and would have been at this time at the underpass, or just beyond, a distance of at least 300 feet from the position of the motorcycle as we have placed it. Now the sound of a siren 300 feet away from a running motorcycle with as much background noise as there was in the Plaza at that time would not have been audible. In other words, I would disagree with the assumption that it could be heard. A little simple arithmetic indicates since the source level of sirens is around 120 decibels and the transmission loss from that particular chief of police car to the motorcycle would have to be at least 40 decibels, the sound pressure level of the siren at the position of the motorcycle could not have exceeded about 80 decibels, but we have seen that insensitive direction of the motorcycle microphone, it being a directional microphone and not sensitive to sounds from the front, was

pointed at the chief's car. So that the ambient noise level in the microphone at that time, which was 90 decibels, and also would have been coming in on the insensitive access of the microphone. So, I don't believe that that assumption that you would hear this siren is true. That was not a very short answer."

Mr. Wolf: "So, therefore, you would also disagree with Mr. Pellicano's deduction that since the sound of the sirens occurred somewhere in the vicinity of 12:33, 2 or 3 minutes after the presumed shots, the motorcycle could not have been in Dealey Plaza?"

Dr. Barger: "Yes."

Mr. Wolf: "I would now like to read from page 14 of the submission to the committee and ask you to comment upon this statement. It concerns a question I believe Congressman Dodd in part addressed this morning about the ringing of a bell that appears on the tape. The report states:

"The sound of the bell on the channel 1 tape requires that a bell be located within an acoustical range of the open microphone. There was no such bell in or near Dealey Plaza. While it has not been identified as the same bell, there was a bell in the tower of the Lucas Baptist Church, 4435 Rosewood (near the intersection of Luck and Rosewood), Dallas, Tex., located 0.6 miles from the position of the designation of a three-wheel motorcycle on traffic control duty on the Stemmons overpass over Industrial Boulevard. Can you comment on that passage?"

Dr. Barger: "The sound of the bell occurred a few seconds after the time of the fourth shot. I don't remember exactly when. It indicates that there was a transmitter on a motorcycle or perhaps in a squad car of possibly also a walkie-talkie, but a transmitter that was transmitting a little after the fourth shot that was within sound range, audible range of a bell. I agree completely with Office McLain's statement that more than one transmitter can share a receiver at one time. This is true whenever the strength of the carriers of all the radios in question are within the capture ratio of the receiver in their intensity." (V HSCA 671-672)

The Pellicano conjecture and wrap-up is that siren volume increases and decreases. Barger's answer is McLain would not have heard Curry, which does not precisely address the matter, and that McLain's microphone was not responsive to noises in front of it.

But McLain was looking at the Book Depository at the time of the first shot. Based on the photograph that he recognized of himself and J. W. Courson, racing down Elm Street at a time when photographers from the previous cars were already on foot and filming makes it apparent that they were literally left behind.

McLain began to slow as he reached Houston Street, as he testified to being close to the press bus, and that would have necessitated dropping back from the photos in which he acknowledged himself. He would have been facing the TSBD during the entire shot sequence, be it three or four shots.

It is known that there were multiple sirens at work, but what is not known is how many. Lost in Barger's arithmetic is that a siren is not just loud, as that is its purpose. Sirens produce piercing sounds, which is their intent. The sounds of the siren would increase and decrease in intensity. Curry and the Secret Service vehicles were already at Stemmons Freeway, when McLain and Courson were still on Elm Street, so that would lessen the incoming volume. The siren was not activated in the vehicle carrying the president and the governor.

Wolf is apparently unaware of the time of the assassination. The Hertz sign in the photos taken by Mal McIntyre, attached with entries in the Dallas Police Department logs (whose clock was certified by the Warren Commission to be kept in sync with the atomic clock, located at the U.S. Naval Observatory, the official residence of the Vice President), indicates clearly that the shots were either fired in the last few seconds of 12:29, or at 12:30.

Barger gave satisfactory answers, and they seem perfectly logical.

> Mr. Wolf: "Thank you, Dr. Barger. I would now like to address the testimony Professors Weiss and Aschkenasy gave this morning. Have you had an opportunity to review the work of Professors Weiss and Aschkenasy?"

> Dr. Barger: "Yes, I have."

> Mr. Wolf: "What did you do to review independently their work that was done for this committee?"

> Dr. Barger: "In the first place, shortly after my testimony at the previous hearing, I met with Professor Weiss and Mr. Aschke-

nasy and members of the committee staff, to discuss how best we might reduce the uncertainty in the results that we had obtained at that time, in particular relating to the possibility of a third shot... We contributed in that discussion to the concept of an analytical extension of our work, which is, in fact, the analytical extension that they carried out. So, we were familiar with the parameters that they would need to know and also with the procedures they intended to follow. I asked them what parameters they were using and found in each case that I agreed with them. In other words, we checked their procedures and the parameters that they used.

"In addition, and perhaps most importantly, at the stage where they had finished with all their strings—as they were illustrating this morning—and had identified the echo-producing objects in the plaza that caused the echoes at positions near microphone 4 there, where we found the shot may have occurred and where it may have been received, we looked at those echo-producing objects for that location that they found with their very accurate and diligent procedure and made a judgment about each one as to whether it would be able to produce an echo of sufficient strength to be heard in the motorcycle microphone, considering the direction from which it had to arrive at the motorcycle microphone, considering what we now know the direction the microphone is pointing at that time."

Mr. Wolf: "In your testimony on September 11, addressing particularly the third impulse in the Dallas Police dispatch tape, you stated that the probability of this being a shot from the grassy knoll was 50-50. Professor Weiss and Mr. Aschkenasy, today, whose testimony you heard, stated that the probability of this being a shot from the grassy knoll was *95 percent or better*. You have reviewed the work of Professor Weiss and Mr. Aschkenasy. Do you agree with their assessment?"

Dr. Barger: "Yes; once we checked their procedures, their parameters, and their echo-producing objects, we received from them the results of their match...."

Mr. Wolf: "Your ability to state with 95-percent certainty, now, what was only a 50-50 percent probability in September was, in essence due to the narrowing of the match time from six one-thousands of a second to one-one thousandth of a second. Is that, in essence, correct?"

Dr. Barger: "Yes sir. ... That is why we stated independently, although their number was quite similar to ours, that we felt that the likelihood of there having been a gunshot from the knoll and received at that point now to be about 95 percent or possibly better." (V HSCA 672—674)

Counsel Wolf concluded his examination following that response.

Mr. Devine: "In another vein, Dr. Barger, I think the testimony originally was that Officer McLain was putting along at 11 or 12 miles per hour in the motorcade. After the shot was fired, they took off for Parkland Hospital when it was necessary for them to rev up and had trouble catching the limousine. Did I understand you to say that even with the open mike that there was no measurable difference in motorcycle noise, that the decibels were such that it wouldn't make any difference if we are talking about that motorcycle having the open mike on it? It would seem to me as a layman that there would be considerably more motorcycle noise when he took off for Parkland Hospital."

Dr. Barger: "Well, there definitely was. I believe in my previous testimony I did not focus on what the motorcycle may or may not have done after the shooting on the basis of the sound that it made. On the other hand, you have just focused me on that.

"The noise level of the motorcycle as perceived through the radio was rather high up until about 2, about 3 seconds before the first shot was fired. In other words, the motorcycles have greatly reduced speed 3 seconds before the first shot was fired, which was a very fortunate thing in the sense that it made it easier to see these smudged fingerprints of gunfire, because otherwise they would have been merely obscured by the noise.

"Now, that motorcycle noise stayed down in this reduced level, it did not go off, it stayed down at this reduced level, and it was reduced by about 10 decibels, which we measured—the noise level was reduced by 10—decibels, and it stayed that way for about 30 seconds, 30 or 40 seconds, and then it rose again to as loud a level as it had previously been and even greater, and stayed that way for several minutes. In other words, the motorcycle stayed at a low speed for less than a minute, certainly, about half a minute, after the shots, and then it speeded up again and it went even faster than it had before, and it continued to do that for at least 2 minutes." (V HSCA 678)

Once McLain navigated the turn from Main onto Houston, he dropped back slightly, which was similar to having his engine idling, at least at the moment when he entered upon Houston Street, and for c. five seconds thereafter, when the first shot would have been fired.

This motorcycle sound analysis can provide a transition from an acoustic awareness of events to the physical cognizance of the same events.

It is paramount that McLain is on Houston Street, while the complete shooting sequence takes place on Elm Street. This data would confirm that, but also that he was well back on Houston.

McLain testified he only heard one shot. Inasmuch as he is on Houston Street, and his windshield is pointing directly north at the Book Depository, it's reasonable to suggest that the one shot he heard was the one shot not discharged from the Book Depository.

He wasn't asked where he was when the shot he heard was fired. As far as I can figure, he would have been close to midpoint of Houston Street, halfway between Main and Elm Streets.

The photo submitted during McLain's questioning, showing motorcade photographers on the ground and filming, with McLain and J. W. Courson in the backdrop (the only vehicles shown), trying to catch the motorcade, is in harmony with the data Dr. Barger has supplied. The two motorcycles are quite a way behind the Presidential limousine at this point.

Why was McLain inactive for so long, after hearing the one shot? It seems clear from McLain's testimony, that confusion among eyewitnesses and perceptions regarding the number and location of shots could be a role of their positioning in reference to shots and echoes.

The issue of the temperature comes up during the questioning:

Congressman Dodd: "There has not been any significant improvement in the science that would have prohibited them [*the Warren Commission*] from utilizing this kind of testing?"

Dr. Barger: "No." (V HSCA 681)

Mr. Dodd: "Could you now go back for us, if you would, and give us your assessment on all four of these impulses, with the degree of probably again, now including the assessments or reassessments of Dr. Weiss and associate."

Dr. Barger: "Yes; the first point is that their refinement of our technique that they applied to the third shot, which has indicated that in all likelihood was a shot, does not affect materially my estimates of the likelihood on the other three.

"Now, in case that answer boggles your mind—if it does not, I will not elaborate."

Mr. Dodd: "Oh, elaborate. If it does not mine, I am sure it does somebody's."

Dr. Barger: "OK. My reasoning had gone this way: I had achieved 15 correlations over my threshold level of .5, each of which was a potential shot. I do not mean to say that. Each one was a potential match with a test shot, and if several came at one incident time, as they did, they all together were just indicating the same shot.

"Since I had used the plus or minus 6 millisecond time window—which might also be called, inelegantly I would say, a fudge factor—it allows the test patterns from two adjacent microphones to resemble one another, and, in fact, you do see that when we get more than one correlation coefficient passing my threshold, that they do tend to be from adjacent microphones.

In any case, 15 times our test for matches of fingerprints with or smudge fingerprints were successful.

"Now I went through an argument then with red X's that indicated that 6 of those 15 were certainly false alarms, the word that I used to describe a situation when my matching process indicated a match when, in fact, it should not have, and I was using independent evidence from pure acoustical evidence in order to make the judgment that those 6 were false alarms, as in fact, you may recall that if one of them had not been a false alarm and in fact had been true, the motorcycle would have had to go 55 miles an hour to get from one place to another in the time that was available, and it clearly did not do that.

"So, using that kind of reasoning, I found that 15 of those, 6 of those 15, were obviously disjoint and, therefore, clearly false alarms.

"OK. I had 15, and 6 were obviously false. Therefore, I knew that my system, which was designed to catch motorcycles, had a propensity for false alarms. And what was that propensity, I had to make a judgment. I said of that remaining nine that were not of the six that I was sure were false alarms, some of those, too, must be false. I judged that probably about 3 or 4, which would give me, or 2 or 3, which would have given me 8 or 10 false alarms, and 6 or 7 correct detections. That was a judgment, and so I said it is close enough to be 50-50 that I will judge that the false alarm rate in this experiment is 50 percent.

"Now, when I had a shot indicated by one single match of my fingerprint with a smudge print on the Dallas tape, the only one I could put a 50-percent probability on was that one. On the other hand, the first shot had three that were not judged to be false alarms."

Mr. Dodd: "So what percentage would you give to that?"

Chairman Stokes: "Time of the gentleman has again expired. I will permit the answer."

Dr. Barger: "He will probably ask for more."

Mr. Dodd: "What percentage, I am just trying to get back, does this change all the percentages you gave us?"

Dr. Barger: "This is a long-winded answer, because as indicated it would be, but the answer is no, it does not change it and here is why. I had made the judgment, if my false alarm rate was 50 percent the first time because I had six that I knew were false, and I suspected there were a couple of others in there, and that made it half false, half true, 50 percent.

"Now, all Professor Weiss and Mr. Aschkenasy have done is prove that one of those is not false. That does not materially change that situation, so I still think the false alarm rate is about 50 percent.

"Now, when, if I make an assumption that each of the 15 events that we see on that board are independent, then I or any-one else can calculate the probabilities that each of those shots did occur. In the case of the first one, where there were three in-dications of .5 each, that works out 87 ½ percent likely, and one-eighth unlikely. In the case of the second shot there were likewise three that were not, three correlations that passed the test that were not impeached as obvious false alarms and, therefore, the operative or probability on that one is also 87 percent. In the case of the last one there were two that were unimpeached, so the probability works out to 75 percent, and in the case of the third one there was only one, so that was 50, it was 50 percent. And did I make a mistake on the second one? OK."

Chairman Stokes: "Time of the gentleman has again expired."

Mr. Dodd: "I am not going to ask for any more time." (V HSCA 682-684)

I am not sure what Dr. Barger was referencing when he gave this account, and considering that he ambled off from his science often, a proclivity not shared by Weiss and Aschkenasy, he comes across as verbose about certain things.

Dodd seems annoyed by the entire give-and-take.

Further approval of the answer was sought:

Congressman Fithian: "We are sure, you are confident that the sounds, the shapes of the sounds that you measured are gunshots, in plain language, that is what you are telling us?"

Dr. Barger: "Quite confident, yes."

Mr. Fithian: "And that is to the exclusion of any other sounds short of a bunch of cherry bombs that would have set up that kind of impulse, but would still have been missing for shots 3 and 4 the shock wave, is that correct?"

Dr. Barger: "That is correct." (V HSCA 684) ...

Mr. Fithian: "Finally, this committee will soon have to decide what we are going to do with this rather startling evidence, and I am sure, given the nature of the world, that we will soon have our critics, within weeks, if not days, and certainly within months and years. Where will those critics be attacking this particular part of whatever they may be as a result of this testimony?"

Dr. Barger: "Well, that is a very good question. I sure would not want to give anybody any ideas."

Mr. Fithian: "Well, if I may interject, I am just sure that the startling nature of this information will prompt the most careful scrutiny that has yet been applied to the Kennedy assassination."

Dr. Barger: "Of course it will, and it should. It will take me a little while to answer this question because I want to, you know, to try to think of the most important items.

"The reason I have to think is because—this long—is because until recently I felt that the major shortcoming of our work, and when I say 'our,' I mean Bolt, Beranek and Newman's and Queens College and the committee staff's in particular, was that there was no evidence that there was a motor vehicle where we had found it to be. And I must say that would have been I thought a very obvious place from which to attack the analysis. I feel now that that particular issue is no longer at the top of my list.

"I think the most serious problem, the most serious problem we have as analysts is determining these probabilities.

"There are two kinds of assumptions you can make when you compute the probabilities that we have computed. One is that each event that occurs is statistically independent of all of the others, and the other assumption is quite the opposite, that they are not independent events, but they are all related. And if you make either of these two assumptions, you can get an answer and it is not always the same answer. And determining whether these spikes on the Dallas tape, in determining whether these are statically dependent, in other words, do they resemble each other here and here and here or do they just come at random, is a question that can be answered mathematically only if you have enough of the data, and we do not have enough.

"So, the hardest thing for us to do is to give accurate calculations—well, we can give accurate calculations, but we have to make assumptions, and the assumption of statistical independence, randomness in the noise, is an assumption that I have made when I analyzed my own results, and also those of Professor Weiss and Mr. Aschkenasy. People have been complaining that we did this. I do not think they can improve on it, because there is not enough data to answer the question. But literally, it is a problem." (V HSCA 685-686)

In Conclusion: Recent research by Don Thomas, in concert with the acoustics evidence by Richard Mullen and James Barger, relatively speaking, puts the acoustical shot fingerprint at frames 175, 204, 224, 313 and 326, with the time intervals placed at 1.65, 1.1, 4.8, and 0.7 (the last being the time interval between frame 313 and 327, obviously). The final tally for the entire interval seems to be c. 8.3 seconds from the first until the last shot, not the popular 5.6 seconds that ruled the research community for years.

Appendix I

The Curious Case of Howard Brennan

Howard Brennan is addressed, because the HSCA never called him, though he was the Warren Commission's star witness and poster boy. To understand Brennan is to understand the Warren Commission.

Howard Leslie Brennan was born on March 20, 1919, in Oklahoma. One does not have to travel very far through the assassination literature to discover him. He appeared in front of the Warren Commission 3 times, all on the same day. There are also 2 affidavits connected to him as well. It is our job to sort through all of this and see if we can make any sense of his testimony. He was the poster boy, who supposedly identified Oswald in the sixth-floor window. So, in that sense, he is vitally important. His testimony, like so many others, is a metaphor on how the Warren Commission treated their witnesses: steered them in a particular direction when they didn't say what the Commission wanted to hear, ignored and moved on when they were obviously lying, ignored them when they said things that were at variance with what the Commission wanted to hear, or created hypotheticals that had nothing to do with the case and end up being red herrings diverting away from the real evidence at hand. Read through the testimonies of the medical personnel and see how many times Arlen Specter guides the witnesses down a path that leads nowhere, or better yet, creates hypotheticals in an attempt to get them to say something they really didn't. Brennan will be no different. Again, keep in mind, he is their Golden Ticket, because his description eventually leads to the identification and arrest of Lee Harvey Oswald. Let's see how this worked itself out that weekend and beyond.

Brennan testified, on March 24, 1964, at around 9:00 a.m. in Washington, D.C. His testimony resumed twice that day in the presence of other witnesses who gave testimony on that day. This was common, as all three autopsy doctors were in the same room during each of their testimonies. It was common for the Commission, but ridiculous and should not happen in a murder investigation. Warren Commission members present for Brennan were Earl Warren, Representative Gerald Ford, John McCloy, and Allen Dulles; also present were chief counsel J. Lee Rankin, senior counsel Norman Redlich, and junior counsels David Belin and Joseph A. Ball, and finally Charles Murray, "observer." It is interesting to note who was not there, namely Richard Russell, Hale Boggs and John Sherman Cooper. As some critics have pointed out, these three had their differences with the majority. And, in fact, Russell filed a dissenting report at the final Commission executive session meeting. Were these differences manifest in their lack of attendance?

As noted above, also present in the hearing room were Bonnie Ray Williams, Harold Norman, James Jarman, Jr., and Roy Truly. Notice has been taken of the absurdity of such a process, as Williams, Norman, and Jarman, who were friends, were not about to criticize each other. It just was not going to happen.

Brennan remarked that upon his arrival into Dealey Plaza, "there was a man having an epileptic fit, a possibility of 20 yards east—south of this corner. And they were being attended by some civilians and officers and I believe an ambulance picked him up." (3H 141-142) We know that the person in question is Jerry Belknap, who did have an "apparent" seizure, but upon arriving at Parkland hospital decided to not stay but instead left. He did pay the medical expenses for his short trip to the hospital, but it remains somewhat of a mystery as to what was happening. So much so, that someone should have interviewed him and attempted to find out what was really going on with Belknap that day, if anything. It just seems odd.

Brennan then told David Belin, who was the main interlocutor for questioning him, that he "jumped up on the top ledge." (3H 142) The witness was referring to the retaining wall around the reflecting pool opposite the Book Depository. But it's an odd statement, because his inarticulateness makes it sound like he literally jumped on the top ledge and was standing, which he wasn't and that there is more than one ledge, which there isn't. He simply sat down, which I will assume is what he meant in all of his unletteredness.

The interview takes a turn and with a quick sleight of hand a moment of monumental proportion is lost. Belin shows Brennan CE-479 and notices that Brennan's legs are not dangling on the front side, which they would be if he was sitting and facing north toward the Texas School Book Depository. Listen to the exchange:

> Mr. Belin: All right. I hand you now what the reporter has marked as Commission Exhibit 478. (The document referred to was marked Commission Exhibit No. 478 for identification.)
>
> Mr. Belin: I ask you to state, if you know, what this is.
>
> Mr. Brennan: Yes. That is the retaining wall and myself sitting on it at Houston and Elm.
>
> Mr. Belin: You remember that the photographer was standing on the front steps of the Texas School Book Depository when that picture was taken on the 20th of March?
>
> Mr. Brennan: Yes; I do.
>
> Mr. Belin: And the camera is pointed in what direction?
>
> Mr. Brennan: South.
>
> Representative Ford: Are those the positions where you were sitting on November 22?
>
> Mr. Brennan: Yes, sir.

Warren Commission Hearings Volume XVII p. 197 (CE-477 and CE-478)

Warren Commission Hearings Volume XVII p. 198 (CE-479)

Howard Brennan facing east looking over his left shoulder (color slide of Z-188)

As we shall see, this is not true, but Belin clearly let it slide, because Brennan was one of their stars. This pre-empted them from questioning Brennan about the real facts underlying his testimony. That function was left to researchers and they revealed the shenanigans of the witnesses and far worse, the Warren Commission itself. His testimony was not only believed that day; but was blessed with the imprimatur of the Warren Commission. Belin, had to know this was not accurate, because he noted that Brennan's legs were "not dangling on the front side there, is that correct?" Brennan replied they were not. But Belin did not press the matter. He quickly moved on to ask Brennan what he was wearing on that fateful day. This is your next question after wondering why Brennan's legs aren't seen, as they should have been, had he been where he said he was sitting.

Belin had showed him one negative, (couldn't the FBI provide photos or at least a decent diagram for Brennan to respond to regarding his location?) or one frame from the Zapruder film—seems to be Z-188—which absolutely shows him looking east toward the jail and not north, where he is positioned during the reenactment photo shoot. Belin handed him a magnifying glass. The negative had been enlarged. (Not by much if a magnifying glass is needed, although Brennan by this time had suffered diminished eyesight due to an accident.) Listen to how Warren Commission Counsel David Belin broaches the topic:

> "This appears to be a negative from a moving picture film [Z-188, approximately—and keep in mind, the negative of which he was handed had already been published in *Life* magazine as a color photo]. *And I will hand you a magnifying glass*—the negative has been enlarged. This negative appears to be a picture of the Presidential motorcade on the afternoon of November 22nd. I ask you to state if you can find yourself in the crowd in the background in that picture."

From his previously noted reply, Brennan also knew that exhibits CE-477 and CE-478—which were recreations shot in March—were inconsistent with what he was swearing to. The actual photo, CE-479, shows Brennan sitting on the ledge of the reflecting pool, facing east towards Houston Street, not north toward the Texas Schoolbook Depository. Yet, note what author Richard Trask writes: "Brennan had been sitting on the concrete retaining wall by the north reflecting pool and was facing the Book Depository." (Richard Trask, *Pictures of the Pain: Photography and the Assassination of President Kennedy*, p. 493) That is rubbish and Trask must know it. He has a keen eye for detail and often brings out matters that the casual reader would not necessarily notice. It is clear from a collection of Zapruder frames that Brennan was, in fact, facing *east* and had to lean his left arm well back to look over his shoulder to see Kennedy's car *when it was in front of the Depository*. Brennan would pose, on March 20 (Brennan's birthday), sitting right in the middle of the concrete wall looking into the Depository, and again, David Belin caught him lying. Yet when the Warren Commission *staffers* placed Brennan for purposes of understanding his visual abilities on November 22nd, they went along with this deception. They moved him a full 90 degrees and approximately 25 feet, around the concrete wall at the north end of the reflecting pond, so that Brennan, for "witness credibility" was sitting directly in front of the door of the Texas School Book Depository, facing north.

At least one early critic seems to have noted this departure from the record. Josiah Thompson included a photo to verify that fact on page 185 of *Six Seconds in Dallas*. The photos on that page show the Presidential limousine passing between the center of the concrete wall and the front door of the Book Depository—and nobody is sitting there.

Researcher Dale Myers once told me that if I only understood the geography of Dealey Plaza, then and only then, would I truly understand the testimony of Howard Brennan. In his book, *With Malice*, he says concerning Brennan's placement in the Plaza as "perched atop a cement wall directly across from the Book Depository." It gives the impression—and I know this because Myers clarified this for me in an email—that Brennan was directly across from the Depository as in CE-478. Dale Meyers is wedded as much as Belin to Brennan, let us call them the B&B's.

Reading Belin and Brennan is what leaves informed people aghast when they comprehend Commission assertions, and someone who did as much research as Myers should be cautious not to repeat things which have caused a large segment of the public to lose confidence in the Warren Report. Brennan's "directly across" from the Depository statement before the Warren Commission is undermined, because the Zapruder frames in 18H always show Brennan facing east. (see 3H 142 and 18H 1-20) And he is looking toward Houston Street, with his back to the camera, and not, as he posed for the Commission, facing north, into the front door of the Texas School Book Depository. Brennan diving behind the wall as the report rang out, would be senseless if he was where the Commission said he was. He wasn't.

Brennan marked the inaccurate photo that he posed for to show where he "dived" "as the gunfire rang out." It is not "behind the wall," where Brennan portrayed himself. It's behind the wall from where he actually was, and by diving, he could not have seen anything in the sixth-floor window, hence, another problem. If he had dived like he said he did, the distance would have been somewhere around 30 to 35 feet! When the dust settles, and it does quickly for Howard Brennan, and you make him your star witness like the Warren Commission did, all bets are off.

His falsehoods began on the afternoon of the assassination to Sheriff Decker's office, stating the same nonsense he blathered on about before the Commission. In Decker Exhibit 5323 (19H 454-543, passim), Brennan stated the following:

> "I proceeded to watch the President's car as it turned left at the corner where I was and about 50 yards from the intersection of Elm and Houston and to a point I would say the President's back was in line with the last window I have previously described [when] I heard what I thought was a back fire."

To allude that he was tracing the path of the motorcade and saw how the President could be Oswald's target is absurd based on CE-479, where we can see exactly which direction he is facing and he is not, I repeat, he is not following the movement of the limousine as it turned from Houston onto Elm and proceeded in a westward direction.

Howard Brennan is positioned by William Manchester "directly across from Roy Truly's group at the warehouse entrance." There may be some Euclidean truth to that, in that a straight line could be drawn between Truly, et al, and Brennan, but their lines of vision would most assuredly *not* intersect. As Brennan perjured himself in front of the Warren Commission repeatedly and was caught by Warren counsel David Belin, so Manchester accepts this falsity at face value. One rule of research: check the sources, especially original sources. A lot of embarrassment can be averted if this was done on a more regular basis. Truly, et al, were looking *south*. Brennan was facing *east,* as shown in the approximate range of Z-200—the sequence where Phil Willis is shown stepping briefly off the curb. Brennan is facing the jail and has his left arm well behind him, in order to look over his left shoulder—had he desired to see Truly and company. There is no evidence he ever did see him during the 26.55 second run of the Zapruder film.

Belin asks him what happened after he first sat down. He goes on to explain he was people and window watching, which is okay, but when the President approached and passes by him, you would expect him, or anyone for that matter to focus on the President and the rest of the motorcade. He is asked to identify the window where he claims to have seen someone and then after some odd remarks by Brennan, he finally circles the window and places the letter A next to it. He says he saw a man in the 6th floor window and then is asked to describe what he saw. Grab your socks and hold on, you can't make this stuff up. He says, referring to the shooter in the 6th floor window:

> He was standing up and resting against the left window-sill, with gun shouldered to his right shoulder, holding the gun with his left hand and taking positive aim and fired his last shot. As I calculate a couple of seconds. He drew the gun back from the window as though he was drawing it back to his side and maybe paused for another second as though to assure himself that he hit his mark, and then he disappeared. (3H 144)

At this point, I can assure you there is something Brennan did not know. The window is thirteen inches from the floor at its bottom and twenty-six inches from the floor at the top of its opening. Our possibilities are somewhat finite, either the shooter was kneeling down and then stood up or he shot through the glass, which is beyond ridiculous. He saw the man in the window from the waist up, even though the window opening was below the knees of a man between 5'9" and 5'11", Oswald's changing heights.

Yet, according to Brennan, he was able to describe the shooter with precise accuracy and what he was thinking as well. Not sure how Brennan could possibly know the what and the why of the shooter he described. He also did not observe a scope. I'm not sure why; he described everything else with almost divine-like accuracy. But then again, he said the colored men he saw on the 5th floor "were standing with their elbows on the window-sill leaning out." (3H 144) One other thing before we leave the B&B show is that he claimed to be able to see the shooter from the hips up. This is now getting beyond ridiculous. Howard Brennan did not identify Lee Oswald and he could only have seen the window in peripheral vision from how he was positioned.

By the time of his Warren Commission testimony, his vision was quite poor, mainly because of an accident involving steam after the assassination. On January 31, 1964, he was sandblasted, causing extreme damage to his vision. He was treated for something like 6 hours by a Dr. Black, who said Brennan's eyesight was not good. He would have had trouble seeing the Book Depository, but I'm not sure his eyes were so badly damaged that he would have forgotten, by a distance of twenty to twenty-five feet where he had been sitting. (3H 147) As a side note, speaking of the Depository, there were several questions asked of Brennan regarding "the Texas School Book Depository," but Brennan continued to testify regarding the "Texas Book Store." His grammar and syntax are among the worst of any witness in terms of command of the English language. Similar disregard for linguistic niceties would be present in the testimony of the limo driver, William Greer, and Mary Bledsoe. With 488 witnesses who appeared before the Warren Commission, this was probably to be expected.

Brennan, at times, seems to be carefully placed that day and when he isn't, just change the direction and he will be placed where you want him. One photo is taken from the door, straight on, to Brennan. The other is taken from behind, and he hasn't moved. In a subsequent exhibit, he will mark the spot—behind the entirety of the cinderblock wall at the corner of Houston and Elm—where he "dove" for cover while he was admittedly watching the assassin take aim for his last shot and then depart the window. Once the assassin left, according to Brennan, he dove for cover—a dive that amounted to approximately 25 feet. The reality of where Brennan was, when coupled with the other fairy tales he told about meeting and greeting all seven commissioners present (there were four), knowing "Governor Warren" well, and the invite to meet Mrs. Kennedy, disqualify him from any pretense to credibility. It is almost as if a "mystery weekend" was going to be staged, so that it could not be overlooked in the scenario that day, to make him fit into the Commission's preconceived evidence trail. Again, taken with all his qualifications, Brennan is a metaphor, like so many others.

Let's briefly mention some of the medical witnesses that fit into the metaphor scenario I have been mentioning, so you can see what I mean. When Specter is questioning Dr. Humes, the lead autopsy doctor, he was talking about the fragments in JFK's skull and asks a question with a predetermined end. Specter asks, "Were these all fragments that were injected into the skull by *the* bullet?" (2H 353) It was Specter's very slick and skillful way of limiting the inquiry to one bullet, hence we see the magic bullet in gestation. Even Humes didn't say this, but Specter sure did. Specter engaged in his "let's assume for a moment," just so there is something in the record that at least makes it look like the witness said something they really didn't. At times, Humes seemed befuddled.

When questioning Dr. Charles Carrico, the good doctor is telling of a 5mm by 8mm wound in the front of the neck. Commissioner Dulles asked, "Where did it enter?" Carrico: It entered—at that time we didn't know—..." Dulles (interrupting): "I see." (3H 361-362)

There are times when questioning the medical witnesses Arlen Specter will engage in his 'Let's assume for a moment," in which he asked Carrico, and not just him but successive medical witnesses, to make a variety of postulations. They were all the same: if the President had been shot from behind, in the rear neck, would the wound in the front be an entrance or an exit. Of course, only one answer applies in that case and it matched with what the Commission wanted to hear. (3H 362)

When Specter was interrogating Dr. Kemp Clark, the resident neurosurgeon at Parkland Hospital, he testified to "a large, gaping wound in the right posterior part, with cerebral and cerebellar tissue being damaged and exposed. (6H 20) Clark would later comment that he thought this was an exit wound. (6H 21) A few pages later, Specter asked, "Now, you described the massive wound at the **top** of the President's head, with brain protruding..." (6H 25) This all has to be seen for exactly what it is. It isn't just Howard Brennan committing perjury and it being ignored, because it happened all through the Warren volumes. Just see how Specter directs the choir to get just the right note from each individual, so as to get the same refrain every time: *all shots came from behind and the magic bullet is the only reality that explains what happened with those seven wounds to those two men.*

529

Before Dr. Clark is finished, Arlen Specter asks, what has to be, one of the most asinine questions out of the 109,930 that were asked to the 488 witnesses. Specter asks, "Dr. Clark, in the line of your specialty, could you comment as to the status of the President with respect to competency, had he been able to survive the head injuries which you have described and the total wound which he had?" (6H 26) Clark says the wound was massive and in the back of the head. Specter never buckles and his pressure causes Dr. Clark to realize what is happening and he actually answers this silly question, when everyone and his mother know there was no way JFK could have survived those wounds.

The testimony of another witness, Dr. Charles R. Baxter was engaging and tended to slap back at Specter. His observations were quite telling. At one point he said, "…literally the right side of his head had been blown off. With this and the observation that the cerebellum was present—a large quantity of brain was present on the cart" (6H 41). Baxter continued to describe the right side of the head and what he saw. Specter then asks, "Did you notice any bullet hole below the large opening at the **top** of the head?" (6H 42) There it is again, Specter was constantly referring to the top of the head when talking with the doctors, yet I don't recall Baxter ever mentioning the top of the head. A massive wound or hole in the back of the head will not work for the Commission and Specter was not about to let that happen.

I will mention one more example of Specter's shenanigans. When he was questioning Dr. Ronald Jones, he continued with his back-of-the-head reference by the doctor and then his mentioning the top of the head. Jones simply testified to the destruction to the back of JFK's head, with brain matter hanging out. (6H 63-4, 56)

The point of these examples is that it doesn't matter if it was a Parkland doctor or Howard Brennan. Brennan is simply one example—but a good example, because he was their poster boy as to what was seen in the sixth-floor window and the eventual arrest of Lee Harvey Oswald—of how the Warren Commission and their disciples guided witness after witness. It was virtually always down the same path of substituting top for back, not believing the testimony or description of a witness, not recognizing perjury or doing anything about it when they did. They attempted to drive witnesses down a particular narrative road and all in the name of sustaining their lone-nut scenario and single bullet silliness. It's easy to locate when it is happening, whether it be led by Belin or Specter or Dulles. But its retroactively reprehensible that it was foisted on the American public to conceal the fact of the perpetrators that constructed a coup in 1963.

Lest you think it can't get any more bizarre, let's hearken back to Brennan and watch the metaphor continue to blossom. Brennan claimed, after Belin asked him what direction the gun was pointing, that it was 30 degrees downward and west by south. Are you serious? He doesn't seem to be able to distinguish east from north or standing from sitting, but then we are asked to believe this man, with obviously limited intelligence, can say what direction and the degree of angularity the gun was pointed? Maybe later he would express it in terms of algebraic geometry. Yet recall, he did not observe a scope! Even though he said he saw up to 85% of the rifle. (Vol. III, p. 144)

When Belin asked him how many shots he heard, he remarked that, "positively two. I do not recall a second shot." (3H 144) I don't mean to nitpick, but really, I heard *positively* two, but then says he *doesn't recall a second shot*! Apparently, the word positively needs to be redefined. Belin tried to bail out his friend, he replies to this contradiction by saying, "You mean a middle shot between when you heard the first noise and the last noise?" How can there be a middle shot between two shots? He then adds he thought the first shot was a backfire. And he then says "… subconsciously I must have heard a second shot, but I do not recall it." (ibid) Wisely, Belin dropped the subject and asks him for a description of the shooter.

He describes the man he saw in the window as 5 foot 10 inches, 160-170 pounds and white. After the shots were fired, Belin asked him what he did next. Brennan said he asked a police officer, within just a few minutes of the assassination, to get him someone in charge, "a Secret Service man or an FBI." (3H 145) The policeman took him to a Mr. Sorrels, who was sitting in an automobile in front of the TSBD. This is likely another Brennan shenanigan. Secret Service agent Forrest Sorrels went to Parkland hospital with the motorcade and didn't return to the corner of Houston and Elm for about 25 minutes. Sorrels would subsequently testify that he did not return to Dealey Plaza until 12:55. This means that Brennan's quite brief interval could have been no less than twenty-five minutes. Brennan would tell Sorrels, "I could see the man taking deliberate aim and saw him fire the third shot," and said, "then he just pulled the rifle back in and moved back from the window, just as unconcerned as you could be." (Deposition of Forrest V. Sorrels, 7H 348-349)

This raises a couple of issues. First, on the 12/3/63 Dallas police log of radio transmission, at 12:44 PM, there is a description of the suspect as being 5' 10", white, male about 30, weighing 165, carrying what looked like a 30-30 or some type of Winchester. As we have seen from the time factor involved, it is highly unlikely that Brennan was the source of the "description of the alleged assassin." But then who was? The sinister quality of this is what is really unsettling. The Dallas police were also horrifying in the area of records-keeping that afternoon.

Yet Inspector Harold Sawyer got a description broadcast at 12:44, and it is usually credited to Howard Brennan's keen observations, although we know he couldn't have been the origin of such a description, because he was looking in a different direction and diving at the same time. And Sawyer said he did not recall who his witness was. (Michael Benson, *Who's Who in the JFK Assassination*, p. 408)

By Brennan's account, he stated clearly that he had seen an individual with a rifle aim for a shot. Yet Sawyer's broadcast, as it appears on the Dallas police radio logs, stated to the dispatcher, "It's unknown whether he is still in the building or not known if he was there in the first place." (CE-1974) How could this be Brennan?

So, it can be stated that Brennan spoke to Sorrels, but clearly not at the time implied by the Warren Commission. And not before 12:55—*after* the "description of the suspect" was broadcast—if, in fact, there had been a suspect in the Texas School Book Depository Building.

Brennan was not the source. And, in fact, after a thorough inquiry, J. Edgar Hoover declined Brennan as the source for Sawyer. (FBI memo from Rogge to Rankin 11/12/64)

Somebody had to be given credit, so the Warren Report placed Brennan "on Elm Street directly opposite and facing the building." (p. 5) And now the Warren Report stated that the broadcast description was "based primarily on Brennan's observations" and that Brennan's visual accuracy most probably led to the radio alert at 12:45 p.m. (Warren Report, pp. 5, 144, 649)

Primarily? But if it wasn't Brennan, then who was it? And why don't we know "who was it"? As I have argued, Howard Brennan's credibility has to be questioned. He would state that he only saw the assassin from the chest and upward, but that is clearly an invention by Brennan, predicated on the fact that he assumed the windows in the Texas School Book Depository were at the normal height where windows would be installed. However, to repeat, the sixth floor Depository windows were thirteen inches above the ground, which means that when "Brennan's assassin" fired and then stood up, Brennan would have had to strain to identify the man's knees. considering that the window he allegedly fired from began at a height of only thirteen inches above the floor, how could anyone reasonably approximate his height at slightly below six feet? You simply couldn't.

There is simply too much falsity in his subsequent testimony to the Warren Commission—and they caught him at it, but since his "*seeing the assassin*" was critical, this was overlooked. Again, Brennan, like so many others is a metaphor on how to invent, ignore and guide all of us through the labyrinth of deceit that is the Warren Report.

Please keep in mind that Brennan later wrote a book that was posthumously published. The title of the book was *Eyewitness to History*, which, as seen above, is almost risible. As I mentioned earlier, he stated that he was good friends with "Governor Warren," personally gave testimony to all seven members of the Warren Commission, which he did not. Only four were present during his testimony. And he claimed he was guarded by an FBI agent who was a JFK look-alike and doubled for JFK often. And he was asked by Chief Justice Warren if he would like to meet Mrs. Kennedy. This is a widow who was so full of grief that she wouldn't give her only testimony to the Commission for another four months, but, of course, she would just love to have tea and crumpets with Howard.

Nothing should surprise us about Brennan's book or testimony. But just keep in mind: this was the Commission's star witness. When I interviewed Professor Robert Blakey in 1998, who was the Chief Counsel for the HSCA, I asked him why they never called Brennan. He commented that he would have done more harm than good. Yet in Volume 2 of the HSCA volumes on page 3, even they cannot get away from Brennan, when the same Blakey says that Howard Brennan saw a man fire one shot from the depository.

The police lineups rear their heads eventually. Oswald, as everyone should recall, protested these assemblies vociferously, because—due to his dress and age—he stuck out like a sore thumb. Brennan admitted to seeing Oswald on TV multiple times when he got home, at somewhere between 2:45 – 3:00 p.m., CST. Yet he then told the police at the lineup (Brennan was escorted to the Dallas Police Station c. 6:00 p.m.) that he couldn't positively identify anyone. (3H 148) He then revised his story and said he didn't identify Oswald, because he thought the assassination might have been part of a Communist plot and so he feared for the safety of his family. Brennan would later state that he feared he would be a target of an international conspiracy if he identified Oswald (Deposition of Forrest V. Sorrels, 7H 354-355). Yet, if he was the courageous patriot the Warren Commission made him out to be, then we would expect him to stand his ground and take his chances. He didn't. Accordingly, the FBI had to supply him with the "communist plot" excuse, which he then adapted. (Mark Lane, *Rush to Judgment*, p. 91). Yet, there is further evidence of just how suspect these lineups were. Consider the following:

> Mr. Belin: "Do you remember how many people were in the lineup?"
>
> Mr. Brennan: "No; I don't. A possibility *seven more or less one.*"
>
> Mr. Belin: "All right."

No, it's not even close to being all right. Brennan has just indicated the lineup was somewhere between six and eight individuals. There never was any such thing. We know there were four people in the lineup. It was only four people for each of the lineups in which Lee Harvey Oswald was a participant.

> Mr. Belin: "Did you see anyone in the lineup you recognized?"
>
> Mr. Brennan: "Yes."
>
> Mr. Belin: "And what did you say?"
>
> Mr. Brennan: "I told Mr. Sorrels and Captain Fritz at that time that Oswald—or the man in the lineup that I identified looking

more like a closest resemblance to the man in the window *than anyone else in the lineup… "*

Mr. Belin: "Were the other people in the lineup, do you remember—were they all white, or were there some Negroes in there, or what?"

Mr. Brennan: "I do not remember."

This is Texas in 1963, three months after the March on Washington. Brennan gave a description of a man as 5'10", 160-170 pounds, fair complexion, and slender build. Nobody reminded him that the identification was based on an individual kneeling down, allegedly firing out of a window that was *thirteen inches* above the level of the floor. Brennan then viewed a skewed lineup, with three better-dressed individuals *and did not provide a positive identification of Oswald.*

Belin, and this is only my suspicion, actually was fed up with Brennan, with his comments about and his inaccuracy as to his own placement, which Belin challenged without calling him out on it. Belin had to be disappointed, in addition, to Brennan's "7 person," plus or minus, lineup, which is an illusion. So, he asked, if by chance it had been a bi-racial lineup, which is about as unlikely of an occurrence as Howard Brennan telling the truth.

This needs a context. As Mark Lane noted in *Rush to Judgment*, although the Warren Report states that Brennan picked Oswald out of a lineup, and as noted above, Brennan told Belin the same, this is not backed up in the actual record, that is in the exhibits in the 26 volumes. (Lane, pgs. 11, 91) It would seem to me that if someone thought he had seen the assassin of the President of the United States—before seeing him on TV and in the newspapers prior to the lineup—wouldn't he be so charged up that he would recall every imaginable detail. Maybe not of everything, but certainly of the lineup. Well, Brennan got the number of stand-ins in the lineup wrong and he could not recall if there were people of color in it. (Ian Griggs, *No Case to Answer*, p. 91) There is no mention in the official police record of the lineups that Brennan was present at any of them. (Commission Exhibit 2003, p. 293) Captain Will Fritz, who said he supervised all the lineups, could not recall Brennan being at one. (Volume 4, p. 237) One has to wonder, how long would Brennan have lasted under a real cross examination before the prosecution decided to withdraw him?

In fact, prominent California attorney and junior counsel for the Warren Commission, Joseph Ball, did not believe Brennan. According to Edward Epstein, Ball based his doubt on the failure of Brennan to identify Oswald at a lineup and his similar failure to do so during an FBI interview. He then reversed himself before the Commission. (Epstein, *The Assassination Chronicles*, p. 143) Ball also was dubious about Brennan's failure to describe the alleged assassin's clothing and the fact that Brennan seemed to say the shooter was standing, when the Commission concluded he was kneeling at the window.

Notwithstanding Joseph Ball, Howard Brennan got his "fifteen minutes." Norman Redlich, a very important fixture on the Commission, overrode Ball's reservations at the insistence of the Commission. (ibid, p. 144)

Brennan said that, after Oswald had been killed, he felt at peace to come forward and identify him as the killer he saw in the 6th floor window. We have already dealt with the ridiculousness of him being able to identify the person he claimed to see, based on the height of the window, how the person would have had to position himself to fire a rifle and being able to see anything clearly on that day. I've sat where Brennan actually was on November 22, 1983, and I couldn't see a damn thing in that window. Sure, it was open to a height of 13 inches, but as we have demonstrated, that would not have helped him see what he claims he saw. Apparently, Brennan was told by a Mr. Lish that film footage of him talking with the Secret Service were cut, seemingly at Brennan's request, so the Commies wouldn't track him down and rub out him and his family. Again, I'm speechless.

Belin asked Brennan a series of directional and geography questions and trust me, Brennan is no Rand McNally. Near the end, McCloy asked him if he were a Bible reader and Brennan humbly says that he didn't read it as much as he should, but that he had to wear glasses when he did. I would certainly agree that Brennan does not suffer from an overdose of Holy Writ.

The curious case of Brennan is a little like Benjamin Button: he gets more childish and infantile as time goes by. It is often like reading the words of a child. He simply makes things up including where he was sitting, to jumping off the ledge about 30 feet, to what he actually saw in the window, to his circus antics when he went to DC to meet with the

Commission. If this is their star witness bolstering their case, then they didn't have a case, my friend.

At the end of the day, he had to be a disappointment, even to the Commission. Brennan has now become a symbol, like so many others that were interviewed by the Commission; a symbol for everything that was wrong with the Warren Report. A report based on knowing liars, suborned perjury, bizarre flights of fantasy, all incorporated into a shabby and shoddy investigation. Both Brennan and the Commission are tarred by the same brush. They simply are not kosher. Howard Brennan passed away on December 22, 1983. Like Joseph Ball, I don't take Brennan seriously. Unlike Ball, I don't take the Warren Report seriously, either.

APPENDIX 2

SYLVIA ODIO, OR, WHO'S THAT KNOCKING ON MY DOOR?

Sylvia Odio

That is the question. Who were the three mysterious male figures who knocked on Sylvia Odio's door, late in the closing week of September 1963? I am going to try and sort through the evidence, beginning with her testimony before the Warren Commission and then move on to others, who claim to have knowledge of that ominous night. The starting point of any inquiry is piercing into original sources, whether they be documents, films, photographs or eye-witnesses. As an early disclaimer, I will not give the La Fontaines the time of day. There book is a textbook example of innuendo, unsupported claims and just making things up as they go. Let's see, however, where the evidence does lead and if we can draw some kind of conclusion on this matter.

Sylvia Odio was born in 1937 in Havana, Cuba to very wealthy parents, who had helped Castro, until her father felt betrayed. She had been in Dallas since March of 1963. She had been in the United States from 1951-1954, when she went to a Catholic high school in Philadel-

phia. She went back to Cuba and eventually studied law for three years, until it was interrupted by Castro. She then settled in Dallas in March of 1963. There was a large anti-Castro Cuban community that was living in Dallas at the time.

Sylvia claims she was visited during late September, in the evening, by three anti-Castro men, two of them identified themselves as members of JURE, using their war names, Leopoldo and Angelo. They first asked for her sister Sarita, asking if she was the oldest, which Sylvia corrected them and said *she* was in fact the oldest. Sylvia said her sister Annie had initially answered the door. She had come over to babysit and was not living with her, as some have mistakenly said. She was helping with Sylvia's children and also with the packing, since Sylvia had to be out of her apartment by the first of the month. The men were identified as Cubans and as Sylvia remarked, low Cubans, not educated. There were two Cubans and one American, who was introduced to her as "Leon" Oswald. The conversation proceeded with it mostly being in Spanish, though Sylvia remarked that the American said a few words in Spanish, like he was trying to be cute, such as Hola.

Sylvia mentioned at one point that 'Leon' spoke up and asked if her father was still in the Isle of Pines, where he was being held in Cuba.

She said they knew an enormous amount of detail about her father and said that they were very good friends of his. Her father, Amador, was in prison, along with her mother, Sarah, for anti-Castro positions. They told her they had arrived from New Orleans, which, if not with "Leon" Oswald, then how did he get there, because their dialogue with Sylvia certainly indicates they were all together and had come together. They seemed to be in a hurry, as they told her two or three times they were going on a trip; but didn't say where. They also mentioned "Leon Oswald" was thinking about joining the resistance group in Cuba. Lee Harvey Oswald, as we know, had been living in New Orleans in the summer of 1963. He was about to travel to Mexico City, where he was trying to get a visa to go to Cuba, or so the story goes.

There has been much speculation about who two of the men were. What do we know? Several researchers claim that Angel Murgado, who used the war name Angelo, fought at the Bay of Pigs and was one of Bobby Kennedy's Cubans and Bernardo de Torres, who used the name Leopoldo, were the two mystery men. Apparently, Leopoldo was the one who made the oft-quoted statements about "Leon Oswald," along with the follow-up telephone call a day or two later. A Florida newspaper identified the two Cubans years ago and actually interviewed Murgado. Murgado said they arrived at Odio's apartment shortly after Oswald, which seems odd to me. I cannot imagine that Oswald arrived first and just hung out in the Odio's living room, waiting for his compatriots. Neither Sylvia or Annie ever mention this – and they were there. To me this is a huge red flag on the veracity of Murgado's story. The story always was they drove together in a red car, or at least left in one, since according to this tale, Oswald was not in the car with them upon their arrival. The theory is that Leopoldo said things to Odio out of earshot from Angelo, because of Angelo's undying loyalty to the Kennedys.

When Joan Mellen interviewed Angel, he told her he vomited the weekend of the assassination after he heard the news. Mellen goes on to suggest that Bobby Kennedy knew about Angel/Angelo before the assassination and that he was working for the FBI, and because of this knowledge concerning Oswald, Bobby was silenced forever and could never mention this to anyone. Sorry, I just don't buy it. Murgado suggesting that Oswald arrived before anyone else, which is at complete variance with what either of the Odio sisters ever said, makes his account suspect at best. My reason is that whatever you might think of Sylvia Odio, I cannot think of one thing she ever said that was proven wrong or fallacious. I suggest if you are going to make such audacious claims, it would be nice to have more than a conversation with someone to justify those advances.

The next day, one of the men, most likely Leopoldo, since Sylvia stated that he did most of the talking, called back to Sylvia's house and went into great detail to describe "Leon Oswald." He said he was a former Marine, a crack marksman and someone who believed that President Kennedy should have been assassinated for a failed Cuba invasion at the Bay of Pigs. He also described Leon as kind of loco, or nuts. When Sylvia saw the initial television coverage of the assassination, without hesitation she recognized Oswald as the American visitor who had been at her home.

The question that is the motif of this essay is, Who is this for? Sylvia? There doesn't seem to be an easy recipient for what is being said. How would anyone know that this visit would ever get back to anyone? The way the FBI got into the mix seems to be by complete happenstance. In volume 10 of the HSCA Report and page 28, we have a fairly clear description of how this came about:

(95) According to Sylvia Odio's close friend [much more about that later], Lucille Connell, she received a call from Sylvia's sister Sarita who told her that Sylvia had fainted and was in the hospital. (117) Sarita also told her why Sylvia had fainted and the fact that Sylvia had met Oswald and that he had come to her apartment. (118) Connell could not recall exactly when Sarita called; she said it was either the day of the assassination or the day after. (119) Connell said that Sunday, however, she was speaking on the telephone to a friend of hers, Mrs. Sanford Pick, then working as a receptionist in a Dallas law firm office, when they both saw Ruby shoot Oswald on their television sets. (120) Connell recalled: "And she said to me, 'Oh my goodness, Ruby was in our office last week and had power of attorney drawn for his sister.'" (121)

(96) Connell said that later that same day she happened to be speaking with another friend, Marcella Insua, the daughter of the head of the Dallas Cuban Relief Committee. Connell mentioned to Insua what her other friend had said about Ruby being in her law office. (122) Insua, Connell said, happened to have American children to whom she was teaching Spanish. (123)

In that class, she got into a discussion of the Kennedy assassination and mentioned that she knew someone who knew someone who had some dealings with Ruby. (124) It also happened that there was a son of a local FBI agent in Insua's class. (125) That was how the FBI subsequently came to contact Connell and learn about the Odio incident.

The reason I include this lengthy quotation from the HSCA volumes is because the narrative is so circuitous that it requires this to explain to the reader how the FBI came to invade the situation. The reader may or may not know that Sylvia was dating a Catholic priest at the time by the name of Father MacChann. Lucille Connell (pronounced Kinnell) also had a close relationship with the Father. It is pretty easy to connect those dots that led to a rivalry between the two women, who previously had been very close. Ultimately Sylvia believed and stated that Connell's betrayal of her was because of her jealousy and rivalry with the Catholic priest.

Sylvia's story appears by all accounts to be reliable. Her sister Annie saw all three men and independently identified Oswald when she saw him on television after the assassination. Before the assassination took place, Sylvia had written about what happened that September evening in a letter to her father. He wrote back to his daughter and referred to her letter, which she wrote before the assassination, and to an unknown person, most likely the character of Leopoldo, who claimed to be his friend. Sylvia was having adjustment difficulties, mostly due to her husband who had abandoned her and that she was raising her four children by herself. As a result, she was seeing a psychiatrist, Dr. Burton Einspruch, who testified that she was a reliable witness to the House Select Committee on Assassinations. Both Sylvia and Annie were somewhat reluctant to tell their stories, because of the possible backlash against the Cuban community. As was explained earlier in the article, it was by chance that the episode ever became known to the FBI.

According to Odio, the meeting with the three men could have possibly occurred on Wednesday, September 25, but more than likely took place on Thursday, September 26, possibly even Friday, September 27. No matter what date you pick of these three, all of them seem to coincide with Oswald's Mexico City trip. Oswald is said to have been in New Orleans on the morning of 25 September, when a check in his name was cashed. He is presumed to have arrived in Mexico City early on

27 September, when he registered at a hotel and made his first visits to the Soviet and Cuban diplomatic compounds. Guillermo Garcia Luna, the owner of the Hotel del Comercio, claimed that Oswald checked in sometime between 10:00 am and 11:00 am on Friday, September 27, 1963. Oswald does not seem to have been able to drive and had a minimum amount of money. The bus was the most likely way for Oswald to have traveled to Mexico City, assuming he didn't have any associates. With associates, then a car may have been the mode of transportation. The itinerary the Warren Commission used is as follows. It involves three distinct bus trips:

1. leaving New Orleans shortly after midday on the 25th, and arriving in Houston, 350 miles away, very late the same day;

2. leaving Houston early on the morning of the 26th, and arriving in Nuevo Laredo on the Mexican border that afternoon;

3. leaving Nuevo Laredo an hour or so later; and arriving in Mexico City shortly before 10am on the 27th.

If all or even some of this is true, then some things become quite disconcerting. (a) Either the real Oswald was on a bus hundreds of miles away when Sylvia Odio was introduced to 'Leon Oswald' in Dallas; or (b) Oswald met Odio in Dallas and then travelled to Mexico City by some other means, which must have involved assistance from at least one accomplice; or (c) Oswald did not visit Mexico City at all. The episode also poses a similar problem to having an impostor in Mexico City. Either Oswald had associates, or he was impersonated in Dallas as well as Mexico City. As you can see, there is no easy or comfortable solution to the Odio incident.

Apart from the question as to whether Lee Harvey Oswald was impersonated, a more sinister issue is the telephone call which planted information linking Oswald to the assassination and strongly suggests he was being set up to take the blame.

Sylvia Odio was set to testify in public session before the House Select Committee on Assassinations, though reluctantly, until Chief Counsel Blakey cancelled her testimony, along with Antonio Veciana, so he could give more time to the theme of organized crime. Ms. Odio had something to say and it was damning to the official version.

APPENDIX 3

R.I.P.: THE BLACK DOG MAN BY MARTIN SHACKLEFORD

O ne of the more persistent myths in Kennedy assassination research is the idea that someone was perched with a gun behind the concrete retaining wall on the grassy knoll in Dealey Plaza. This individual has long been dubbed "The Black Dog Man." It is a misnomer, as we shall see.

Like many myths, this one has been exposed in whole or part by a variety of independent researchers. The author owes a debt of gratitude for the work of Robert Cutler, Richard Trask, Bill O'Neil and Matthew Smith, who provided some of the elements which eventually came together to create this article. A little after noon on November 22, 1963, secretary Marilyn Sitzman went down into Dealey Plaza with her boss, Abraham Zapruder. As they prepared for the filming of the President's motorcade, Ms. Sitzman saw a young black couple eating their lunch on a bench in front of and below the pedestal on which she and Mr. Zapruder were standing. The location of the bench is indicated in a detail from a chart which appears in Richard Trask's comprehensive study of the photographic evidence. The bench appears in a film frame and in a photo which also shows the paper lunch bags from which the couple had been eating. One was drinking an orange pop, and one a red pop. When the shots began, the young woman was standing up, looking toward Elm Street. She appears, as the image long identified as "The Black Dog Man," in the Hugh Betzner and Phil Willis photos. An enlargement from the Betzner photo, published by Matthew Smith, definitely looks like a woman

The House Select Committee on Assassinations photo panel found flesh tones in the image; and it is clear from good color copies of the 5th Willis photo that the flesh tones of the image are darker than those of most of the other people in the picture, including Zapruder and Sitzman, approximately the same distance from the photographer.

When she stood up, she apparently set her orange pop bottle on the concrete wall, where it appears, orange tone visible in a good enlargement, in the third photograph by Jim Towner. Sitzman later recalled seeing the bottle. Barbara Rowland mentioned police inspecting a pop bottle there. After the last shot was fired, Sitzman heard the crash of breaking glass, which was "much louder than the shots were and the young couple ran up the steps, last seen heading for the pergola area behind her. The breaking glass was apparently the red pop bottle, which left a pool of red pop, later mistaken by some spectators for a red snow cone or a pool of blood.

An image often mistakenly cited to bolster the theory of an assassin in this location is frame 413 of the Zapruder film, which shows the back of a man's head and a straight image, which somewhat resembles a rifle. Also in the image is a bush located just in front of Zapruder. The image of the "rifle" passes between Zapruder and the leaves of the bush indicating it (probably a branch) was closer to Zapruder than the leaves (similar images, though not as long, appear elsewhere in the frame, also crossing leaves). On the other hand, leaves appear between Zapruder and the man's head, indicating the man was beyond the bush. Robert Cutler has established that the man is probably one of the three men standing on the knoll steps, visible in the Moorman photograph and Muchmore film, among others. The preponderance of the witness and photographic evidence, then, indicates that the figure long referred to as "The Black Dog Man" was in fact a young black woman, part of the couple having lunch on the knoll that day. Logic, too, tells us that an assassin is unlikely to have positioned himself in plain view of Zapruder and Sitzman. In addition, Sitzman clearly stated that no shots were fired from any location that close to her. "Black Dog Man," rest in peace.

NOTES

1. She reported this to Josiah Thompson, in an 11/29/66 interview; the transcript is cited by Richard Trask, Pictures of the Pain: Photography and the Assassination of President Kennedy (1994, Yeoman Press, Danvers, MA), p. 73 (hereafter cited as Trask); full citation is in footnote 4, p. 148.

2. Trask, p. 56.

3. Trask, p. 76; on p. 74, he identifies the photo as having been taken by Johnny Flynn of the Dallas Morglin News.

4. Trask, p. 75.

5. Phone conversation 10/16/94 with Bill O'Neil, regarding his 10/25/92 conversation with Marilyn Sitzman in Dealey Plaza during the A.S.K. Conference (hereafter O'Neil phone).

6. Matthew Smith, JFK: The Second Plot (1992, Mainstream Publishing Company, Edinburgh).

7. HSCA v. 4, p. 410.

8. See, for example, p. 24 of Robert J. Groden, The Killing of a President (1993, Viking Studio, New York) (hereafter Groden).

9. An excellent enlargement appears on p. 194 of Groden.

10. 10/24/94 letter from Bill O'Neil, summarizing his 10/25/ 92 conversation with Sitzman (hereafter O'Neil letter).

11. Warren Commission v. 6, p. 184, cited by Trask, p. 74.

12. Trask, pp. 73-74; O'Neil phone; O'Neil letter.

13. O'Neil letter.

14. This was photographer Malcolm Couch's assumption in his Warren Commission testimony; it is also featured prominently in a chapter in Unsolved Texas Mysteries by Wallace O. Chariton, Charlie Eckhardt and Kevin R. Young (1991, Wordware Publishing, Texas).

15. For a high-resolution color copy, see Groden, p. 195.

16. O'Neil letter: referring to the Badgeman location, about the same distance, Sitzman stated "the blast of a high-powered rifle would have blown me off that wall." She did allow, however, that a shot

could have been fired from "farther down, closer to the overpass... or maybe they were using silencers."

The following illustrations provided by Martin Shackleford may help illustrate his aforementioned thesis:

1) Jerry Organ's excellent 2002 blowups of BDM from the Betzner and Willis photos.

2) Blowup from a film frame showing a person turning away from the BDM location. It looks like a frame from the Wiegman film.

3) The bench and the young black couple in the Darnell film.

4) A portion of one of Don Roberdeau's charts showing the area with locations of Sitzman and the bench, as well as the pool of red pop.

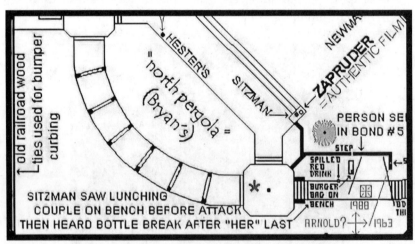

5) Darnell frame showing a little boy stepping around the pool of red pop.

6) Sheriff's deputies examining the lunch bag on the bench.

7) Jim Towner photo blowup showing the other pop bottle sitting on the wall.

8) The man in frame Z413 with a chart showing he was one of the men on the steps.

APPENDIX 4

LIFE'S THREE VERSIONS

The following article is used by permission from John Kelin:

Told by One
of Its Members

OCTOBER 2 · 1964 · 25¢

The October 2, 1964 issue of *LIFE* magazine has a singularly notorious place in the JFK assassination saga.

For reasons never really accounted for, there were at least three versions of that issue. Its cover story was about the just-published Warren Report.

"I am at a loss to explain the discrepancies between the three versions of LIFE," one of its editors conceded privately.

The article appeared under the byline of Gerald R. Ford. Conflicts of interest don't get much more blatant. But that is not our concern here.

The article featured eight Zapruder frames, numbered (by *LIFE*) 1 through 8.

Note how each of the two frames at right are labeled #6. At the top is Z-323. The lower frame, of course, is the infamous Z-313.

According to Jerry Policoff, Z-323 was the original frame used as illustration #6 in this article. The caption corresponding to it is at the top of the next page of this web site.

Two subsequent versions of the 10/2/64 *LIFE* appeared. Both used Z-313 as its #6 frame. But one of them has the caption beginning "The direction from which shots came," while the other uses the caption beginning "The assassin's shot struck" as its description of #6.

In all three versions, *LIFE* printed the Z-frames as an overleaf – that is, you had to turn the page between the captions and the pictures.

See pictures below.

These are the two versions of caption #6.
Neither one accurately describes the pictures.
Both suggest a single gunman.

6. The assassin's shot struck the right rear portion of the President's skull, causing a massive wound and snapping his head to one side.

6. The direction from which shots came was established by this picture taken at instant bullet struck the rear of the President's head and, passing through, caused the front part of his skull to explode forward.

Here are the complete sets of captions.

Note that there is also a difference in caption #3. (*See the two pictures below*)

The reason for changing #3 seems plain enough. The top version says "Some members of the commission believe..." suggesting a lack of unanimity on the single bullet theory. (*#3 also has Connally doing different things, twisting in pain and twisting around*)

It seems odd to me they hadn't yet got their story straight. After all, it had been nearly a year since the assassination. (By "they," I mean whatever set of *LIFE* and government agents colluded on this article.)

There is a slight difference in the wording to caption #5, too, but I don't see how it changes the meaning.

Caption #8 is also different. The lower version at right had less space available due to the altered caption #6. But it also eliminates specific reference to Jackie Kennedy's undignified crawl "on her hands and knees."

By the way, that line above the captions says, "*Color sequence* shows how the President was killed." I cropped it to save space.

nmis-
a for-
Rep.)

of Michigan; Rep. Hale Boggs (Dem.) of Louisiana; Sen. Richard Russell (Dem.) of Georgia;
Chairman Earl Warren, Chief Justice of the United

States; Sen. John Sherman Cooper (Rep.) of Kentucky; John J. McCloy, and Allen Dulles. J. Lee
Rankin, at right, is chief counsel to the commission.

uence shows how the President was killed

1. A moment before the first bullet was fired, the President and Mrs. Kennedy, Governor and Mrs. Connally, smiling and waving, were passing in front of the brick building where the assassin was taking aim.

2. President Kennedy clutched his hands to his throat. The commission determined that a bullet had entered the back of his neck and ripped through the lower front portion of his throat. They believe the wound would not necessarily have been lethal.

3. As Mrs. Kennedy reached to help her husband, Connally twisted in pain. Some members of the commis-

sion believe the governor was struck by the same bullet that had emerged from the President's throat, and that Oswald's second bullet missed. Connally, however, believes he was hit by the second bullet. He told the commission he heard a shot and turned to his right to see if Kennedy was all right.

4. Both Kennedy and Connally began to slump. A Secret Service agent sitting beside the driver turned to look back while onlookers, unaware that anything was amiss, applauded.

5. The President's head fell forward into Mrs. Kennedy's arms just be-

fore the assassin fired another bullet.

6. The assassin's shot struck the right rear portion of the President's skull, causing a massive wound and snapping his head to one side.

7. As the President lay dying beside her, Mrs. Kennedy pulled herself out of the seat.

8. Crawling on her hands and knees across the rear deck of the limousine, Mrs. Kennedy reached out to Secret Service man Clinton Hill, who leaped aboard. He pushed Mrs. Kennedy back into the car and the driver raced to the hospital, 3.4 miles away.

mmis-   of Michigan; Rep. Hale Boggs (Dem.) of Louisi-   States; Sen. John Sherman Cooper (Rep.) of Ken-
: a for-   ana; Sen. Richard Russell (Dem.) of Georgia;   tucky; John J. McCloy, and Allen Dulles. J. Lee
(Rep.)   Chairman Earl Warren, Chief Justice of the United   Rankin, at right, is chief counsel to the commission.

uence shows how the President was killed

1. A moment before the first bullet was fired, the President and Mrs. Kennedy, Governor and Mrs. Connally, smiling and waving, were passing in front of the brick building where the assassin was taking aim.

2. President Kennedy clutched his hands to his throat. The commission determined that a bullet had entered the back of his neck and ripped through the lower front portion of his throat. They believe the wound would not necessarily have been lethal.

3. As Mrs. Kennedy reached to help her husband, Connally twisted around. He told the commission he

heard a shot and turned to see if Kennedy was all right. It is still not absolutely clear which bullet hit the governor. Though he believes it was another bullet—the second fired by Oswald—the commission concluded that it probably was this same one that had passed through the President's throat.

4. Both Kennedy and Connally began to slump. A Secret Service agent sitting beside the driver turned to look back while onlookers, unaware that anything was amiss, applauded.

5. The President's head fell forward into Mrs. Kennedy's arms

just before the assassin fired again.

6. The direction from which shots came was established by this picture taken at instant bullet struck the rear of the President's head and, passing through, caused the front part of his skull to explode forward.

7. As the President lay dying beside her, Mrs. Kennedy pulled herself out of the seat.

8. Crawling across the rear deck of the limousine, Mrs. Kennedy reached out to Secret Service man Clinton Hill.

In 1966 Vince Salandria, who first identified the different issues, wrote to *LIFE* editor Ed Kern. Kern's reply has been quoted by Salandria, Policoff and others, especially the first few sentences. I include the letter here in its entirety.

The "Thompson" Kern refers to is Josiah, aka Tink. The "recent story" is "A Matter of Reasonable Doubt" in the November 25, 1966 *LIFE,* which called for a re-opening of the assassination investigation.

The balance of the letter, I think, lays the groundwork for the ongoing pseudo-debate over the details of the assassination, and the promotion of confusion and mystery.

"To me," Salandria observed many years later, "the three versions of *LIFE* and *LIFE's* lies about what the Zapruder film revealed, showed in microcosm, an elegant example of how the U.S. media criminally joined with U.S. governmental civilian personages, and with the national security state apparatus to employ deceit in seeking to prop up the Warren Report."

LIFE

TIME & LIFE BUILDING
ROCKEFELLER CENTER
NEW YORK 10020

EXECUTIVE OFFICES
JUDSON 6-1212

11/28/66

Mr. Vincent Salandria
2226 Delancey Place
Philadelphia 3, Pa.

Dear Mr. Salandria:

I am at a loss to explain the discrepancies
between the three versions of LIFE which you cite.
I've heard of breaking a plate to correct an error. I've never heard of doing it twice for a
single issue, much less a single story. Nobody
here seems to remember who worked on the early
Kennedy story; it was one of those team efforts
with several researchers, and the researchers
who worked on it have either left or been shifted
to jobs in bureaus or overseas. I was not involved
in the Warren Report story at all until just
recently.

I'm glad you have written me, even though
I'm not able to be much help to you regarding the
1964 LIFE story. I've heard a great deal about you
from Thompson and others; and I hope in due course
that we will be able to meet. For me, the recent
story in LIFE is only the first effort in what I
hope will turn into a long-range, small-scale investigation of the more conspicuous and interesting
unsolved mysteries of the Kennedy slaying. In doing
this I realize that I'm merely treading a path
already well trodden out by many abler people before
me, and it would be presumptuous to expect to uncover anything new at this point. But at least, if
nothing else, there is a job of public education to
be done--or continued--and this is what I depend
on to justify my effort.

Tink and I have recently been talking a lot
about the head shot; and I gather from him that
this is also a special interest of yours. Last week
we reached the following tentative conclusions
after studying the Zapruder film:

1. one shot to K's head came from behind,
because: a) Humes and Fink testified to an entrance
hole in the rear of the skull, which had the
characteristics of an entrance hole; b) K's head

snapped forward at least three inches between
312 and 313; c) the bullet fragment marks on
the windshield trim and the small hole in the
windshield itself can only have been associated
with K's head shot and must have been caused by
a shot coming from the rear.

 2. a second shot may have struck K in the
head from about 2 o'clock with reference to the
axis of the car. But, if so, it must have struck
at 313, since in no frame subsequently can one
see any fresh shower of brain tissue such as would
have been occasioned by a second hit to the head.

 3. The first shot to the head from behind may
have snapped K's head forward slightly. Because 314
is blurred, the position of K's head cannot be
accurately measured from any fixed point on the car.
In 315, as nearly as I can make out, K's head is
almost exactly in the same position as it was in 313
but his right shoulder has come up and a little
forward, and he has begun the twist to the left
and his head has started to snap back toward the
back of the seat. These movements, as I see it,
would accord with a simultaneous shot from 2 o'clock.
His head seems to reach the back of the seat at
about 321, or perhaps a frame or two earlier (these
are also blurred).

 4. If I am right in thinking that the forward
snap occures before the sideways snap, then the
shot from the rear would have struck K a tiny
interval before the shot from the side.

 5. The chief problem I see with the shot-
from-the-side theory is the presumed career of
the bullet after it entered K's head/ If it entered through the right temporal region--which
at that instant may have already become a region
of exposed brain tissue caused by the earlier shot--
the bullet ordinarily would have traversed the interior of the skull diagonally and exited from
the left side of the head. One would expect
a massive wound on the left side of the head.
Yet I have found nothing in the autopsy report
or in the testimony of doctors at Parkland and
Bethesda to suggest this. Neither does the Zapruder
film show it--although the left side of K's head
is to be sure turned away from the camera. There
is only an ambiguous sketch in Exhibit 397 which
shows certain markings on the left side of the head
where I would look for an exit wound.

HIDDEN IN PLAIN SIGHT

6. Could a bullet from 2 o'clock have exploded
in K's head or have been deflected? If K's skull
was still intact when this bullet reached it, I
supposed it might have exploded. X-rays evidently
reveal many fragments of bullet in K s brain. But
are there enough fragments to account for two bullets?
If K's skull was no longer intact when the 2 o'clock
bullet struck it, one would hardly expect the
bullet to exploded on striking soft exposed brain
tissue. If the bullet, on the other hand, had been
deflected, one would expect to see evidence of this
either in tangential damage or by an exit hole at
an angle to the bullet s path. Is there evidence
of this?

7. Thompson assures me that neurologists
deny that K's head movement to the left-rear could
be examaxixy a neural reaction to nerve tissue
damage in the brain, likex nervous naxfxxxt reflex
for instance. He tells me that it happens too
quixkly. But this possibility is so crucial that
I think it needs thorough and paixstaking investigation before it is jettisoned altogether.

Best wishes

Edward Kern

Edward Kern

559

This "three versions" matter is not the magazine's only sin, as we know. *LIFE* also mis-represented the Zapruder film in its December 6, 1963 issue.

At the time, few had seen the Zapruder film. Funny how those who did — *LIFE,* Dan Rather — consistently described something other than what's really there.

The "three versions" is but a single chapter in the sordid story of media complicity. *LIFE* be not proud.

> Since by this time the limousine was 50 yards past Oswald and the President's back was turned almost directly to the sniper, it has been hard to understand how the bullet could enter the front of his throat. Hence the recurring guess that there was a second sniper somewhere else. But the 8mm film shows the President turning his body far around to the right as he waves to someone in the crowd. His throat is exposed—toward the sniper's nest—just before he clutches it.

I put this site together after flipping through some assassination literature and coming across published remarks by Richard Stolley.

Stolley is the *LIFE* editor who brokered the deal between the magazine and Abraham Zapruder in 1963. "There have been charges that *LIFE* tampered with the film, removed or reversed frames, diddled with it to confound the truth," he wrote in 1992. "Nothing like that ever happened."

Semantics. Methinks he doth protest too much.

•••

It's quite possible that a lot of people have heard about *LIFE's* three versions; but have never actually seen them. Hence this site.

Ideally, interested readers would have a copy of each version in hand. That's the best way to get the full impact.

LIFE has a version of its October 2, 1964 issue online. But – *surprise!* The WR article is incomplete. Frame #6 is omitted. A few other things are out of whack, too, but I shan't detail them here.

Presenting this stuff on a web site has posed several problems. In its heyday, *LIFE* was an oversized publication, and I have a rather ordinary-sized flatbed scanner. I've done the best I could. I don't have a large, clean copy of the issue's cover. You can see the thumbnail in the upper-right portion of this page. What I show on this site's home page is not the actual cover.

Jerry Policoff's article, "The Second Dallas Casualty: The Media and the Assassination of Truth," describes *LIFE's* three versions. It can be found in the anthology *Government by Gunplay*. The topic is also detailed in an article Policoff co-wrote with Robert Hennelly, first published in *The Village Voice* and included in *JFK: The Book Of The Film; The Documented Screenplay* (see pp. 489-90).

Vince Salandria discussed it in "A Philadelphia Lawyer Analyzes the Shots, Trajectories, and Wounds," published in *Liberation* magazine in January 1965, and reprinted in *History Will Not Absolve Us*, by E. Martin Schotz. It's also in *False Mystery*, a collection of Salandria's assassination writings.

Salandria described the matter in his 1998 COPA speech. (Search the keywords Life magazine.)

Finally, I describe it in *Praise from a Future Generation*, pp. 396-8.

[See John Kelin, "Conspiracy Theory? Why No One Believes the Warren Report," *Kennedys and King* and Hardback —editor]

ACKNOWLEDGMENTS

There are so many people to thank that it is scary to write this page, lest you forget someone and offend those in that oversight.

Researchers abound on this page. I consulted so many works, that without, it would have been an insurmountable task to begin. Most of my internal documentation in the book is from either from the Warren Commission tomes or the HSCA volumes. Where other works were consulted, I hope I gave proper credit to those fine researchers. Over the years, I have learned so much from so many people, from the early days of Vincent Salandria to the present day and Jim DiEugenio. As far as the publication of this book is concerned, there are some that clearly stand out. Without the kind words and suggestions of Jim DiEugenio, I wouldn't be typing this manuscript. Jim has helped in posting essays of mine on his wonderful website, Kennedys and King and at some point has emerged as the leading spokesperson for the Kennedy assassination. He is a wealth of not just knowledge, but the accompanying insights that go with his understanding of the case.

Len Osanic, of Black Op Radio, has been kind enough to interview me on several occasions and make contacts on my behalf that have proven to be quite fruitful. His show is simply the best in the field of assassination research. There are other good ones as well, to be sure, but Len's quantity and quality of the years has become legendary.

Martin Shackleford, who I have been corresponding with since the late 1990's has been a steady flow of information that has always made me think and sometimes obliged my mind to reevaluate the data. All of these people have been more than kind in their giving of time and answering my inquiries. There are many others I have had contact with, but without the aforementioned researchers, this book would have proven more than difficult to write.

And then there are my friends, whom I spend time with throughout any calendar year, that either kindly listen to my diatribes or push back and force me to logically accept or ultimately reject my notions about the case. Steve Russell, who often discusses the case with me during a rousing game of Strat-o-Matic baseball on Saturday mornings. George and Liam, along with Chuck and Jess Nelson, who have attended a plethora of my talks I have given over the years and always ask intelligent questions. They make my talks fun because of their questions. Dr. Jeff Dennis, who will often push back at my leanings and force me to either come up with better explanations or jettison them altogether. His friendship and pushback is invaluable. Della Bundle, who has attended many of my JFK talks and is always both an encouragement to my research and a friend of over forty years. I can't remember a time when we weren't friends. Ricky Evans, who centers me spiritually and helps me keep focus on the things that really matter, not to mention his expertise in the medical field of cardiovascular technology, a field he worked in for over 25 years.

Jason DeVoir, who has discussed a lot of different scenarios with me over the years, and like many others, will not hesitate to challenge my interpretations and force me to give better answers. Father Bob Creagan, who through his kindness invites me to the glorious city of Kalamazoo, Michigan every year to give a JFK talk to the local citizenry. To my friend Dino, who owns a lovely Pancake House within the city limits of St. Joseph, Michigan, and his son Demo. I wrote a lot of my book in his restaurant, while eating bacon and eggs. Their friendship mean a lot to me. To my students at Lake Michigan College, who have heard me cover the evidence in the JFK case, ad infinitum, ad nausea, and have kindly attended my lectures at the local libraries (for extra credit, of course) but often ask very good questions.

Walt Brown, who I have been talking with since the mid-nineties, has been an encouragement and a source of information that has made understanding the Kennedy case a whole lot easier. His contribution to the case, especially The Warren Omission, has been invaluable. Thanks for all of your help and suggestions over the years.

To my right arm, Brooke Timm, who for years has been running the power points when I give presentations throughout the Southwestern Michigan area, without which my talks would have been less than impressive. Her dedication, professionalism, and reliability has made my talks more enjoyable than had she not been there. A million thanks!

To the Bible Study group in Sawyer, Michigan. So many of them attended my talks over the years and have always been supportive of my books. They are a source of joy every week when we meet!

To my dog, who has recently passed on, Chi. He was a constant companion for sixteen years. He spent many a night at my feet as I typed out the contents of this book. He heard me laugh, cry, scream in frustration, and sigh in comfort, as the end was nearing for both him and this book. He is missed every day: requiescat in pace.

To Archie, our new pug, who has more energy than ten people, listens to me frustrations as Chi did earlier. He has brought happiness to our home.

To Kris Millegan and Trine Day Publishing, who believed in this book and me and decided to publish it for the fall of 2023 on the 60th anniversary of the Kennedy Assassination. Your confidence and easiness to work with made the publishing process as smooth as a summer breeze. Thank you.

And finally to my wife, Beth. She is more than just supportive of my endeavors and more than just a listener of my ideas surrounding the case. She truly supports my goals and proudly offers to voice them to her friends about my progress. She has also listened to my theories and my analysis of the evidence in the case-non-stop. As I said when we got married, it is never us against each other, but her and me against the world. I love her and am happy to have her with me on our path as we trek through the vicissitudes of what life has left to offer us. Soli Deo Gloria!